THE Hundred-Year STRUGGLE FOR Israel AND Palestine

An Analytic History and Reader

Revised Edition

Victor Lieberman

University of Michigan

Bassim Hamadeh, CEO and Publisher
Christopher Foster, General Vice President
Michael Simpson, Vice President of Acquisitions
Jessica Knott, Managing Editor
Stephen Milano, Creative Director
Kevin Fahey, Cognella Marketing Manager
Al Grisanti, Acquisitions Editor
Jamie Giganti, Project Editor
Brian Fahey and Luiz Ferreira, Licensing Associates

First published in the United States of America in 2012 by University Readers, Inc.

Trademark Notice: Product or corporate names may be trademarks or registered trademarks, and are used only for identification and explanation without intent to infringe.

16 15 14 13 12   1 2 3 4 5

Printed in the United States of America

ISBN: 978-1-62131-128-7

Cover photo credit: Burned-out Egyptian tank in Sinai 1973; Israeli civilian vehicles destroyed in a bulldozer rampage in 2008; Arab irregulars near Jerusalem 1948. The latter is from the Middle East Archive, St. Anthony's College, Oxford, Desmond Morton Collection.

www.cognella.com 800.200.3908

My thanks to Todd Endelman, Alan Strathern, and the students who have taken History 244, the History of the Arab–Zionist Conflict, for their contributions, direct or indirect, to the current volume.

Note to Readers

The two parts of this book are coordinated insofar as "Part One: Overview" and "Part Two: Readings" are divided into the same five subsections. The overview can be read profitably in its entirety before proceeding to the readings. But insofar as the readings amplify and document the overview, some may find it useful to consult the readings for each subsection before resuming this historical overview.

Maps

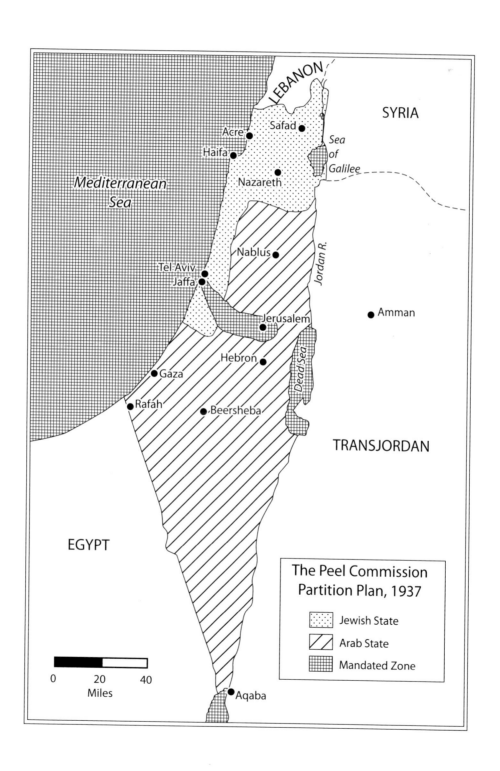

The Peel Commission
Partition Plan, 1937

Jewish State

Arab State

Mandated Zone

LEBANON

SYRIA

Safad

Acre

Haifa

Sea
of
Galilee

Mediterranean
Sea

Nazareth

Nablus

Jordan R.

Tel Aviv

Jaffa

Jerusalem

Amman

Hebron

Dead Sea

Gaza

Rafah

Beersheba

TRANSJORDAN

EGYPT

0   20   40
Miles

Aqaba

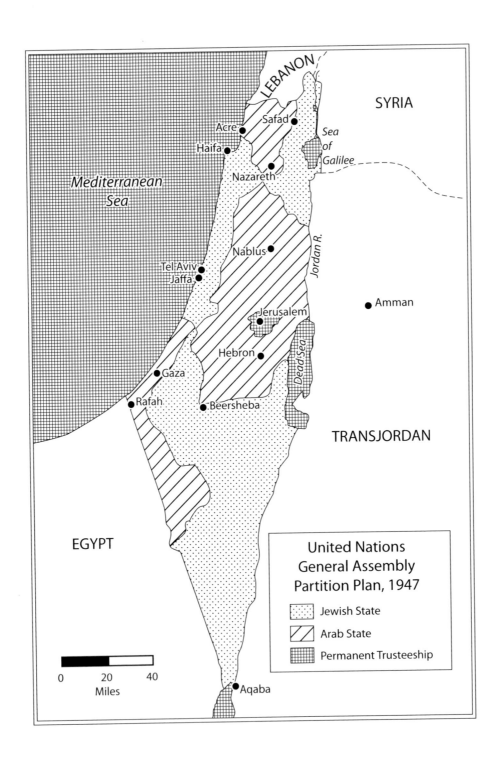

United Nations General Assembly Partition Plan, 1947

- Jewish State
- Arab State
- Permanent Trusteeship

LEBANON

SYRIA

Acre • • Safad •
Haifa • *Sea of Galilee*
Nazareth •

Mediterranean Sea

Nablus •

Tel Aviv •
Jaffa •

Jordan R.

• Amman

Jerusalem •

Hebron •

Dead Sea

• Gaza

Rafah • • Beersheba

TRANSJORDAN

EGYPT

0   20   40
Miles

• Aqaba

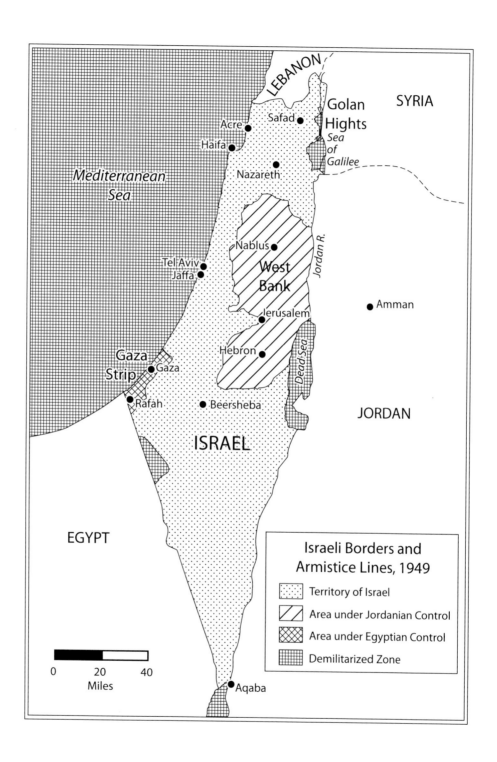

LEBANON

SYRIA

Golan
Hights

Acre •
Safad •

Haifa •

*Sea
of
Galilee*

*Mediterranean
Sea*

Nazareth •

Nablus •

West
Bank

Tel Aviv •
Jaffa •

Jordan R.

Jerusalem •

• Amman

Hebron •

Gaza
Strip

• Gaza

Dead Sea

• Rafah
• Beersheba

JORDAN

ISRAEL

EGYPT

Israeli Borders and
Armistice Lines, 1949

Territory of Israel

Area under Jordanian Control

Area under Egyptian Control

Demilitarized Zone

0   20   40
Miles

• Aqaba

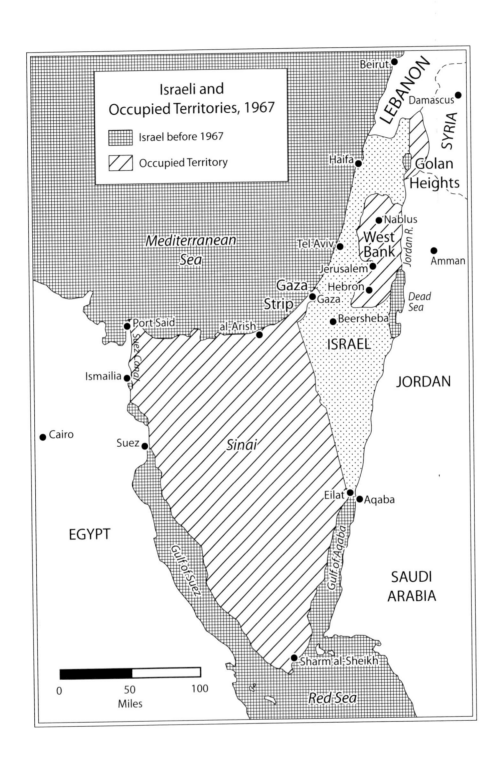

Israeli and
Occupied Territories, 1967

Israel before 1967

Occupied Territory

Beirut

LEBANON

Damascus

SYRIA

Haifa

Golan
Heights

Mediterranean
Sea

Nablus

West
Bank

Tel Aviv

Jordan R.

Jerusalem

Amman

Gaza
Strip

Hebron

Gaza

Dead
Sea

Beersheba

Port Said

al-Arish

ISRAEL

Ismailia

Suez Canal

JORDAN

Cairo

Suez

Sinai

Eilat

Aqaba

EGYPT

Gulf of Suez

Gulf of Aqaba

SAUDI
ARABIA

Sharm al-Sheikh

0   50   100
Miles

Red Sea

Maps based on Mark Tessler, *A History of the Israeli-Palestinian Conflict* (Second Edition, Bloomington, IN; Indiana University Press, 2009), pp. 243, 262, 265, 400.

PART ONE
Overview: The Hundred Years War

By Victor Lieberman

Introduction

By global standards, the conflict between Zionists and Arabs for control of Palestine/Israel has not been particularly bloody. From 1936 to the present, the number of deaths—probably fewer than 80,000 Jews and Arabs altogether—is far less than ten percent of those deaths inflicted by the war in Afghanistan, or by the Iran–Iraq war, or by the Vietnam War.

But in duration, in continuous world attention, and—if such a thing can be measured—in sustained passion, the Zionist–Arab struggle has few 20th-century equals. Although the origins of the conflict can be traced to the late 19th century, for argument's sake, let's date its onset to riots in Jerusalem in 1920. By this reckoning, it is well on its way to becoming another Hundred Years War.[1] Israelis have now fought numerous low-level conflicts with Arab guerrilla organizations, the last one pitting Israel against Hamas from late 2008 to early 2009, and five wars against Arab states (in 1948–1949, 1956, 1967, 1973, and 1982). Across the globe, the century-long conflict between Jews and Arabs has inspired more websites, books, films, articles, and essays—much of it polemical—and more demonstrations, boycotts, and calls for solidarity with one side or another than any regional conflict in history, including the Vietnam War. The UN General Assembly, the UN Security Council, and other UN agencies have devoted more energy

to Israeli-Arab affairs than to any single world problem. Repeatedly, this issue has generated great power tensions, even raising the possibility of a U.S.–Soviet military confrontation in 1967. To this day the conflict remains the focus of intensive mediation efforts by the United States, Russia, and the European Union—efforts that Iran and its regional allies, Hamas and Hezbollah, oppose bitterly. Even if current attempts were to produce an agreement, who can say how long it would hold before Israelis and anti-Zionists were once again at each other's throats?

A Palestinian Narrative

So how did we arrive at this dreadful impasse? Why has it persisted so long? Why have all efforts at resolution failed? Which side is chiefly at fault? Let's begin by considering in turn anti-Zionist and Zionist versions of history. We do so not because one or the other is necessarily "correct," but because these rival narratives are commonly heard, because they capture the passions involved—and because they tell us at the outset that if we are to master intellectually this complex conflict, we must consider very different perspectives.

The anti-Zionist interpretation of Mideast history places primary responsibility on what it sees as the alien, aggressive nature of Jewish activity. In 1881, when the modern Zionist movement began, Jews constituted less than six percent of the population of the lands now known as Israel, Gaza, and the West Bank. Thereafter, successive waves

---

1   The thrones of France and England fought the original Hundred Years War, 1337–1453, for control of what is now western and northern France.

of Jewish immigrants from Europe poured into these territories until by 1947, Jews, numbering about 650,000, comprised some 33 percent of the total population. This influx proceeded in flagrant disregard of the wishes of the local residents, precisely because the latter had no political control over their own affairs. Until the British captured the area in 1917–1918 during World War One, it was part of the Ottoman Empire, whose Turkish rulers, although Muslims, permitted small-scale Jewish immigration.[2] From 1918 to 1948, the British controlled what are now Israel, Gaza, and the West Bank—known collectively as Palestine— at first by right of conquest, and after 1922, under a mandate granted by the League of Nations. For most of this period, the British permitted—indeed, encouraged—Jewish immigration on a large scale. Palestinians, that is to say, the non-Jewish Arab inhabitants of the mandate, protested to the British passionately and repeatedly against what they saw as nothing less than an invasion of their land by unwanted strangers, but because by its nature, colonial rule had no use for popular sovereignty or democracy, such remonstrances had little effect. Zionism was thus part of an imperialist project to transform Palestine (and indeed much of the Arab world) to fit European and Jewish, but not local, aspirations.

After World War Two, anti-Zionists claim, the injustice of British policy was enormously compounded by the decision of the United Nations, dominated by European powers and the United States, to divide British Palestine into Jewish and Arab states—again, without ever bothering to gain the consent of the people of Palestine themselves. The Holocaust created insufficient Western sympathy for the Jews to allow large-scale Jewish immigration to Great Britain or the United States—but sufficient sympathy to insist that Jewish refugees be admitted wholesale to Palestine. Once again, Europeans and Jews decided to promote their needs at the expense of the Palestinians. The latter bore no responsibility for the Holocaust, but now they, not the Europeans, who were responsible, had to pay the price.[3] In 1947 the UN voted to give the Jews, who were only 33 percent of the population of Palestine, 55 percent of the land for an independent state, while the Arabs, some 67 percent of the populace, got the rest. Naturally, Palestinians and the neighboring Arab states resisted this unjust decision. Yet despite their efforts, in the ensuing war, the Jews not only grabbed another 23 percent of historic Palestine, but used the fighting as a pretext to execute a program of systematic ethnic cleansing that had always been central to Zionist ambition. Carried out under cover of war, the forcible expulsion from their homes of over 750,000 Palestinians created the refugee problem that remains at the heart of the Mideast impasse.[4]

Thereafter, according to this narrative, Zionist policies of territorial expansion and racial/ethnic purification continued. Not content with 78 percent of historic Palestine, Israel in 1967 launched a war in which it seized most of the rest of Palestine from Jordan, along with the Golan Heights from Syria, and the Sinai peninsula and Gaza from Egypt. To fulfill its long-standing goal of settling Jews throughout Palestine, which the Jews regarded as their God-given patrimony, Israel proceeded—in blatant disregard for international law

2 Founded in 1299, the Ottoman Empire lasted officially until 1923, and at its peak exercised varying degree of authority over the eastern and southern shores of the Mediterranean, the Balkans, Asia Minor, the Fertile Crescent, and the Hejaz.

3 Or, as Yezid Sayigh argues in *Armed Struggle and the Search for a State: The Palestinian National Movement, 1949–1993* (Oxford: Clarendon Press, 1997), 4, the salvation of the Jews was to come at the expense of another people who had done them no harm.

4 *Cf.* Rosemarie Esber, *Under the Cover of War* (Alexandria, VA: Arabicus Books, 2009). Estimates of Palestinians displaced in 1947–1949 vary considerably. Arab estimates ranged from 750,000 to 1,000,000. The Israelis proposed 520,00, and the British claimed between 600,000 and 760,000. Baruch Kimmerling and Joel Migdal, *The Palestinian People: A History* (Cambridge, MA: Harvard University Press, 2003), 156. Benny Morris, *The Birth of the Palestinian Refugee Problem Revisited* (2nd ed., Cambridge: Cambridge University Press, 2004), 1 also estimates between 600,000 and 760,000.

and world opinion—to plant settlements in newly occupied territories until today over 550,000 Jews live in what had been parts of Jordan, namely, East Jerusalem and the West Bank. Arab communities in the West Bank are increasingly fragmented by settlements, bypass roads, and security barriers. They are deprived of water rights and land, routinely humiliated by Israeli army personnel, and subjected to vigilante violence by Jewish settlers in a system of racial oppression that President Jimmy Carter has likened to South African apartheid.

Within Israel proper—as opposed to the occupied West Bank—Israel also follows a policy of racial discrimination. Because Israel is defined as a Jewish state, Israeli Arabs, although citizens, face legal restrictions and pervasive social and economic discrimination. Most outrageous of all, Palestinian refugees cannot return to their homes in Israel. But anyone of Jewish ancestry or any convert to Judaism anywhere in the world—even if she or he has never set eyes on Israel—has a right to "return" to that country.

In short, Zionism, in this interpretation, is an alien, deeply unwelcome intrusion into the Mideast and a permanent source of regional tension. In the words of the 1968 Palestinian National Charter, Zionism "is a colonialist movement in its inception, aggressive and expansionist in its goals, racist and segregationist in its configurations and fascist in its means and aims."[5]

An Israeli Narrative

This, then, is not an uncommon anti-Zionist critique. Obviously, Israel's supporters see things very differently.

To begin, they deny that Israel is in any sense alien or illegitimate. Historically, they point out, Jews have maintained intimate religious and physical ties to the Land of Israel for at least 3000 years. Legally, moreover, a Jewish homeland in Palestine enjoys unquestionable validity. Not only does Israel today enjoy diplomatic relations with

154 countries around the globe, but the 1947 vote by the UN General Assembly to create a Jewish state—a decision that expressed the opinion of mankind enshrined in international law—won overwhelming support and has never been revoked or seriously challenged. That historic decision, in turn, embodied a moral imperative. Given the horror of 20th-century anti-Semitism and the impossibility that Jewish survivors in 1945 would return to the lands of their people's near extinction, for hundreds of thousands of Jews, there was no refuge anywhere in the world other than Palestine. The 1947 plan to divide Palestine into Jewish and Arab states was not inequitable, because most of the 55 percent of Palestine awarded the Jews was barren desert. What is more, Palestinian claims that they bore no responsibility for the Holocaust ignore the fact that the leader of Palestinian nationalism in the 1930s and 1940s, Hajj Amin al-Husayni, fled with his proteges to Berlin during the war, broadcast regularly over Nazi radio, and supported Nazi efforts to exterminate world Jewry.

Impugning Zionism's authenticity by portraying it as a creation of British colonialism also is fundamentally flawed, because Zionism was a movement of national salvation whose dynamics derived not from British society, but from central and eastern European Jewry. Unlike European settlers in America or Australia, Jewish immigrants to Palestine had a deep historical and emotional connection to the land they entered. Unlike colonialists, they did not seize local property, but paid handsomely for it. And they regarded the British colonial relation as no more than a convenient tactical alliance, whose collapse led to Jewish–British violence from 1944 to 1947.

Moreover, to follow the Zionist narrative, Palestinian displacement after 1947 and failure to create an independent state reflected not Jewish aggression, but Palestinian intransigence and chronically inadequate leadership. Palestinians love to see themselves as victims, when, in fact, by repeatedly choosing violence over negotiations and maximalism over reasonable compromise, time and again they proved to be their own worst enemies. Had they accepted in 1937 or 1947 partition plans that would have met the legitimate needs

---

5 Quoted in Kimmerling and Migdal, *Palestinian People*, 249.

of both communities, not only would a Palestinian state have arisen decades ago—something that has yet to happen—but there never would have been a Palestinian refugee problem. In 1947–1948—as in 1920–1921, 1929, and 1936–1939—Arabs, not Jews, initiated violence. It was the Arabs' decision in 1947–1948 to reject the UN partition plan, to launch an unprovoked war against the Jews, and to attempt to annihilate the Jewish community that led directly to the Palestinian exodus.

Today, Palestinians complain bitterly about Israel's occupation of the West Bank. Again, however, the occupation grew directly from the Arabs' 1967 military effort, warmly supported by Palestinians, to destroy Israel. Without that assault, Israel never would have seized the West Bank from Jordan. Nor, Zionists claim, was that the last instance of self-destructive Arab/Palestinian behavior. After lengthy Israeli–Palestinian peace negotiations, in 2000 President Bill Clinton proposed a compromise that would have returned 97 percent of the occupied territories to an independent Palestinian state. Prince Bandar of Saudi Arabia, a lifelong supporter of the Palestinians, warned the Palestinian leader Yasser Arafat, "Since 1948, every time we've had something on the table we say no. Then we say yes. When we say yes, it's not on the table any more … Isn't it about time we say yes? … I hope you remember, sir, what I told you. If we lose this opportunity, it's not going to be a tragedy, it's going to be a crime."[6] Yet Arafat not only rejected Clinton's proposal, he sanctioned a terrorist campaign that poisoned the atmosphere and destroyed any prospect of successful negotiations for years to come. Likewise, in 2005 Israel unilaterally left Gaza in the hope of reducing tensions—only to have Hamas use that territory to launch thousands of missiles on Israeli civilians.

Finally, Zionists argue, charges of racism are pure propaganda. Embodying distinct physical types from Europe, Asia, and Africa, including over 120,000 black Africans, Israeli Jews are one of the most racially diverse populations on earth.

6   Alan Dershowitz, *The Case for Israel* (Hoboken, NJ: John Wiley and Sons, 2003), 118–19, citing *The New Yorker,* March 24, 2003.

What they share is not race, but a state-sanctioned religion—a religion whose official status is similar to that of Islam in at least 30 Muslim countries. Although as non-Jews, Israeli Arabs do face discrimination, as participants in the only established democracy in the Mideast, their lot is far better than that of minorities in the vast majority of Arab and Muslim countries.

The core of the problem has never been any particular Israeli policy. Rather, it has always been the insult to Arab pride embodied in a Mideast state led by Jews, a traditionally inferior group. Because the very idea of a Jewish state is anathema, the most Israel's foes have ever been willing to offer Israel is suicide on the installment plan.

A Preliminary Synthesis

Here, then, are two radically different views of responsibility for the Zionist–Arab conflict. Which interpretation is right?

Both narratives are valid in the sense that both, so far as they go, are more or less factually correct. But both also are flawed, because they suffer from three grave deficiencies. First, they tend to cherry-pick evidence that suits their biases and to exclude material that is inconvenient. Both interpretations are "true," but only partially so. Second, both posit a static, essentialist image of the other community. They assume that certain traits—aggressiveness in the case of Zionists, irrational intransigence in the case of Palestinians—are inherent and immutable. Thus, they ignore ways that these communities influenced one another and changed through the process of interaction. Third, both narratives are deficient insofar as neither shows much sympathy for the fears and vulnerabilities of the other community. Without such sympathy, no genuine historical understanding—much less reconciliation—is possible.

This book seeks to synthesize—and at the same time, transcend—these two narratives to create a more complete, less partisan, more intellectualized perspective. This does not mean that we split the difference in every instance, that truth always lies in the middle, or that the behavior of both sides always was equally edifying. It does mean that we are not going to find cardboard heroes and villains. And it requires that each student of the subject make an honest effort to confront the prejudices with which he or she may have entered the discussion.

With these guidelines in mind, what might a reconstruction of the Hundred Years War for Palestine/Israel look like? Here I suggest four general propositions, which the rest of Part One will flesh out and which the readings in Part Two will substantiate in detail.

First, as Jews point out, Zionism built on very longstanding Jewish attachments to the Land of Israel. But Zionism itself was an entirely novel response to conditions specific to 19th- and early 20th-century Europe. In objective terms—if not in the self-image of Zionist pioneers—the entry of hundreds of thousands of European Jews into Palestine between 1880 and 1940 was indeed a fundamentally alien intrusion generated outside the region. In this sense, the Palestinian narrative is correct.

Second, again, as Palestinians allege, Zionism relied on British patronage, and ultimately on British bayonets, to establish a beachhead in Palestine. Yet Zionism was anything but a typical colonial project reliant on inspiration and direction from the mother country. Its dynamism grew not from Britain, about which the vast majority of Zionist settlers knew little or nothing, but from the dire political and economic situation of Jews in eastern Europe. As such, Zionism's self-characterization as a national liberation movement distinct from developments in the colonial metropole is justified.

Third, Zionist success in settling Palestine in the first half of the 20th century and in defending Israel after 1948 reflected the fact that Jewish leaders, reared in a European milieu, had access to Western organizational and political techniques, and European and American capital and economic skills, that put them two to three generations ahead of the Palestinians. British policy aside, this made it extremely difficult, if not impossible, for Palestinians to contain their foes' ever-growing power.

Fourth, from the 1920s to the present, the nightmare of annihilation has haunted both communities. Endemic anti-Semitism, culminating in the Holocaust, convinced the Jews that if they did not secure Palestine, the Jewish people might disappear. Repeated threats by Arab leaders to obliterate the Jewish state and to expel the Jewish population—and now Iranian President Mahmoud Ahmadinejad's pursuit of nuclear weapons along with his fervently expressed hope that Israel be wiped off the face of the earth—gave the existential fears that Jews brought with them from Europe a new, understandable Mideastern lease on life. But in turn, from the 1920s and 1930s Zionism's gathering success aroused deep-rooted fears among the Arabs of Palestine that their most basic rights were being trampled, that they were being marginalized in their own land, that they too might disappear, if not physically, then culturally and politically. Unwilling to accept the legitimacy of the other's national movement—because to do so seemed tantamount to committing national suicide—both sides frequently adopted a zero-sum view of politics. However, since the Jews grew stronger while the Palestinians grew weaker, each political compromise the Palestinians were offered—in 1937, 1947, 1967, and 2000—presented them with considerably worse terms than the previous offer. This long-term deterioration in their position merely deepened Palestinian humiliation and bitterness, rendering acceptance of an expressly Jewish state impossible for most, if not all, Palestinian leaders.

Mutual bitterness is now so deeply ingrained that compromise will be exceedingly difficult without sustained outside mediation and pressure. As 2011 opens, the Arab world is in turmoil, and the prospects for a stable peace agreement are not particularly promising. And yet if Zionist–Arab relations are a story of continuous conflict, they are also a story of repeated efforts at resolution. Some trends are favorable, including the legacy of earlier negotiations, a sense of mutual exhaustion, and the Palestinian Authority's growing security and economic expertise. It is by no means impossible that such factors will combine with increased external mediation finally to end the Arab–Jewish conflict short of its centenary anniversary.

 # Origins of the Conflict to 1947

The Arab–Israeli dispute has never been a simple two-party contest. At various times, it has involved conflict between Arabs and the British and Jews and the British, between Palestinians and Arab governments, between different Arab states, between the Soviet Union and the United States, and between Iran and the United States. At its heart, however, it has remained a struggle for the same small land between two political movements: Zionism and Palestinian nationalism. Both borrowed heavily from European nationalism, and both made notable advances under the British, who, as noted, controlled Palestine from 1918 to 1948. But by virtue of its European origins and close ties to Western culture, Zionism arose earlier and proved more powerful . We thus begin our narrative by considering the birth, first of Zionism, and then of Palestinian nationalism, and the interactions between these movements during the period of British control.

Zionism to c. 1940

Jewish ties to the Land of Israel are ancient. Jews claim descent from Abraham, to whose offspring in Genesis 15:18 God promised what is now Israel and its surrounding territories. For much of the period from c. 1100 B.C.E. to 400 C.E, Israelites or Jews were the chief ethnic group, and a major political force in Israel/Palestine. Even after the Roman defeat of Jewish rebellions in 70 and 135 C.E. forced large numbers into exile, significant Jewish communities remained

in Palestine and continued to reside there into modern times. What is more, for centuries Jews around the world prayed daily that they might return to Zion, a term that most often refers to Jerusalem, and by extension, the biblical Land of Israel. Jerusalem, toward which all synagogues face, remained the spiritual heart of Judaism. This shared sense of history, ritual, and cosmic destiny provided Jews in five continents with a powerful communal identity that was, in some ways, a precursor to Zionist nationalism.

These traditions, however, also differed from modern Zionism in basic respects. For one, although Jews prayed fervently for a return to the Land of Israel, as a practical matter before the advent of political Zionism in the late 19th century, very few moved there. In 1880 only 24,000 Jews lived in what would become Palestine/Israel, which was six percent of the local population, and less than half of one percent of world Jewry. In part, this immobility reflected a belief that the return to Israel had to await the Messiah, when life on earth would be utterly transformed. By contrast, modern Zionists, whose outlook was essentially secular, focused on the world at hand. They wanted Jews to return to Israel not at the end of days, but in their own lifetime. They were convinced that salvation depended less on divine intervention than on political mobilization, land acquisition in Palestine, and patronage by the great powers. And their claim to lead the Jewish people derived not from their knowledge of religious tradition, but from their understanding of contemporary European politics and culture.

Given these novel features, how did Zionism arise? It was, I already noted, a response to changing conditions in mid- and late 19th-century Europe, in particular, the rise of exclusive national ideologies at the expense of more tolerant and inclusive imperial traditions, and the erosion of relatively stable social systems in favor of more fluid, often psychologically disorienting, market-based systems. As urbanization, commerce, and enhanced social and geographic mobility robbed many Europeans of their sense of rootedness and dignity, nationalist ideologies encouraged members of newly imagined national communities to rebuild their self-esteem by stigmatizing peoples who were not part of the nation. Jews provided a particularly attractive target, both because churches had long defamed them as Christ killers, outcasts, the antithesis of honest Christians, and because the success of individual Jewish businessmen and professionals seemed to symbolize all that was unfamiliar, immoral, and unnatural in the new world of capitalism. In fact, in the late 1800s, the vast bulk of Jews in eastern Europe—where world Jewry was concentrated—were wretchedly poor, and getting poorer. Nonetheless, they became the focus of violent antimodernist, anticapitalist resentments.

Ambitious, upwardly mobile Jews had long assumed that if they followed Gentile standards of education and deportment with sufficient diligence, and if they abandoned claims to a separate communal identity, eventually they would be accepted by their hosts. That is to say, they would be viewed as good Frenchmen, good Germans, good Hungarians, and so forth, of the Hebrew faith. But ever more virulent anti-Semitic movements began to blight such hopes. This was true even in France, home of Jewish emancipation, where the infamous Dreyfus Affair of 1894 to 1906 (in which anti-Semites framed a Jewish army officer on charges of treason) convinced many that no matter how educated, how cultured, how patriotic they became, they would never be accepted as members of the nation by their non-Jewish neighbors. That anti-Semitic movements in Germany, Austria, and other lands in the late 1800s began to adopt openly racial—as opposed

to more traditional religious—definitions of Jewishness only deepened that pessimism.

In response to these conditions, in the late 19th century, a number of east European Jewish thinkers and organizations began urging Jews to return to the Land of Israel. But it was Theodor Herzl, the Austro–Hungarian father of modern political Zionism, who pushed this growing sense of alienation to its logical conclusion. After setting forth his ideas in a book *The Jewish State* in 1896, the following year he convened in Basel, Switzerland the first congress of what became the World Zionist Organization. If Jews were ever to achieve dignity and security, Herzl and his followers argued, they must cease being a minority among Gentiles. They must create a sovereign national state of their own.

Borrowing from contemporary European discourse the concepts of national territory, national language, popular sovereignty, and citizenship, Zionism was, in fact, one among many late 19th-century European movements of "national revival." But Zionism was also unique in that the intended national language, Hebrew, was no one's primary tongue, and the territory which it claimed as its patrimony, the biblical Land of Israel, was far removed from the places where most would-be members of the nation actually lived. Zionism's primary appeal lay not with the tiny Jewish population of Ottoman Palestine, nor, for that matter, with the Jews of western Europe, most of whom, Herzl's message notwithstanding, retained their assimilationist hopes. Rather, Zionism, as it cohered into an organized movement, appealed most strongly to the impoverished Jewish masses of Russia, Austria–Hungary, and Romania, who had never identified in any basic sense with their host cultures—who, in fact, cherished ethnic difference. Among these groups, Zionism fused with a new secular, socialist ethos to inspire what eventually would become large-scale movements of emigration and colonization in Palestine. Bolstered by two such waves—each wave of emigration being termed an *aliyah* ("ascent")—from 1881 to 1914 Jews grew to about 14 percent of the population of Palestine.

World War One (1914–1918) dramatically bolstered Zionist prospects in two ways. On the one hand, following the wartime collapse of the Russian and Austro–Hungarian Empires, political instability in eastern Europe generated a series of horrific pogroms that claimed 60,000 Jewish lives and intensified the Jews' desperation to escape. The United States was the preferred destination for most, but with stringent postwar American prohibitions on further immigration, Palestine loomed ever more attractive. On the other hand, after 1918 control of Palestine passed from the defeated and disintegrating Ottoman Turkish Empire—which had been at best begrudgingly tolerant of Jewish immigration—to Britain, which in the Balfour Declaration of 1917 formally committed itself to create in Palestine a Jewish "national home." Indeed, in entrusting Britain with the mandate for Palestine, the League of Nations in 1922 expressly enjoined Britain to do so.

Accordingly, Britain, upon taking control of the mandate, opened the country to large-scale Jewish immigration and land purchases. From 1919 to 1939, three more *aliyot* boosted the Jewish population to about 445,000, or nearly 30 percent of Palestine's inhabitants. The fifth *aliyah* of 1932–1939 produced by far the largest spurt in immigration, fueled both by eastern Europe's dire poverty and anti-Semitism, and by the rise of Nazism in Germany. Now, for the first time, large numbers of German Jews, many of them well educated and comparatively prosperous, went into exile. In 1934 over 45,000 Jews, and in 1935 over 66,000, entered the territory of the mandate. Suddenly, a Jewish majority in Palestine began to seem feasible.

While three out of four immigrants settled in urban areas, including Haifa, Jerusalem, and the new Jewish coastal city of Tel Aviv, a critical minority helped to expand rural cultivation. Although Jews usually paid high prices to acquire land from Arab owners and although much of this land was originally swampland or empty waste, from those areas that were cultivated the new owners often evicted the Arab tenants with little or no compensation. Many of the latter had farmed the properties for generations. Not surprisingly, even though the number relative to the general Palestinian population was modest, such displacements intensified the Arabs' bitter resentment of Zionism.[1] Yet in the opinion of Zionist leaders, for both Jews and Arabs a policy of cultivating Jewish-owned land with all-Jewish labor was preferable to a system of European overseers and indigenous underlings, such as in white-ruled South Africa. In ideological terms, self–sufficient Jewish rural labor represented the triumph of the "new Jew," strong of body and bold in spirit, at one with his "native" soil, over the stereotypically weak, cringing urban "ghetto Jew" of old.

To appreciate more fully the world from which Zionism sought to rescue its adherents, note that in the 1930s central and eastern Europe were swept by waves of ever more intense, irrational anti-Semitism. If Nazi Germany went furthest in removing Jews from national life, Romania and the new postwar states of Poland, Austria, and Hungary also sought in varying degrees to restrict Jewish occupations, to boycott Jewish businesses, to eliminate or curb Jewish influence in the arts and culture, to segregate Jews socially, and to humiliate and isolate them. Drawing on centuries of clerical Judeophobia, nationalist parties appealed to the lower middle classes, the peasantry, the declining aristocracy, and the lower clergy. Large sectors of the population thus absorbed these teachings in graphic form: The Jew is a swindler, the Jew is the enemy of all decent people, the Jew is Satan, the Jew is filthy, the Jew is vermin, the Jew

---

1   On Jewish land purchases, and on varying estimates of the number of tenants displaced as a result, see Kenneth Stein, *The Land Question in Palestine, 1917–1939* (Chapel Hill: University of North Carolina Press, 1984), 52–59, 108–111, 128–29 and *passim*; Kimmerling and Migdal, *Palestinian People*, 36–37; Rashid Khalidi, *Palestinian Identity* (New York: Columbia University Press, 1997), 98–101; Mark Tessler, *A History of the Israeli–Palestinian Conflict* (2nd ed., Bloomington, IN: Indiana University Press, 2009), 177–78; Benny Morris, *Righteous Victims* (New York: Vintage Books, 2001), 110, 123; James Gelvin, *The Israel–Palestine Conflict* (2nd ed., Cambridge: Cambridge University Press), 106.

is a cancer in the bloodstream of humanity—and in the logic of Nazi pseudoscience, for the benefit of mankind, the Jew must be removed as an act of public sanitation.[2]

Anti-Semitism propelled Mideast history. It was the shrieking, winged beast that scattered the Jews before it. And as they fled pell-mell to Palestine, the Jews in turn, as we shall see, filled the Palestinians with existential dread.

Benefiting from ever greater numbers of skilled educated German and Polish immigrants, and from infusions of European and American Jewish capital, the Jewish community of Palestine, known as the Yishuv, was transformed. From 1922 to 1947 the Yishuv's largely self-sufficient economy grew at an annual rate of 13.2 percent, one of the highest rates in the world. Citrus cultivation expanded rapidly, and industry became ever more diverse and technologically advanced.[3] At the same time, the Yishuv developed a modern European-style state in embryo. Under the aegis of the Jewish Agency, whose establishment was authorized by the League of Nations mandate, Jews built their own systems of finance, internal administration and defense. The Jewish Agency, for example, created specialized departments for political affairs, economics, land settlement, and immigrant absorption. An Elected Assembly, or parliament of the Yishuv, was chosen by secret ballot, with executive authority vested in a National Council. In a carryover from the Ottoman period, the Yishuv also ran its own taxation and school systems. In 1920 a rudimentary guard force, the Haganah (Defense), was created, as was the General Confederation of Labor. In addition to protecting worker rights, the latter body operated an array of agricultural, commercial, and industrial enterprises. The efficiency and comprehensiveness of these interlocked institutions gave Jews a critical organizational advantage over their Arab foes during the fighting of 1936–1939 and 1947–1949, and later allowed Israel to advance far more rapidly than other newly independent states.

How did Zionist leaders justify their growing presence in what was, and had been for many centuries, an overwhelmingly Arab country? How did they view the people of Palestine? What political goals did they espouse? Until the late 1930s, the Socialist leadership of the Yishuv, under David Ben-Gurion and the Labor Party,[4] championed a pacific, gradualist, conciliatory ethos. Proudly and unapologetically, they justified Jewish immigration by citing historic ties to the land, legal sanction from the League of Nations—and the brutal fact that for ever growing numbers of European Jews, Palestine offered the only possible refuge. In part because many Palestinian Arabs had only begun to think of themselves as a nation distinct within the wider Arab world (see below), and in part because Jewish leaders did not want to admit they faced a national rival comparable to themselves, they insisted on seeing local Arabs as part of a far larger Arab community with little attachment to Palestine per se. Yet they also insisted that Jewish and Arab interests under the mandate were in no way opposed to one another. Palestine, they maintained, had plenty of room for everyone. What is more, Arabs could only benefit economically from Jewish capital and markets—in fact, the eviction of tenants notwithstanding, there was some evidence to support this claim[5]—and from

2 Robert Wistrich, *A Lethal Obsession* (New York: Random House, 2010), chs. 1, 2.

3 Rashid Khalidi, *The Iron Cage* (Boston: Beacon Press, 2007), 13–14; Samih Farsoun and Naseer Aruri, *Palestine and the Palestinians* (2nd ed., Boulder, CO: Westview Press, 2006), 65–76.

4 The term "Labor Party" is here used loosely. In 1930 three labor factions, including the Unity of Labor Party that Ben-Gurion had helped found in 1919, joined to form Mapai —the Israel Workers' Party—which in 1968 merged with two other groups to form the Israel Labor Party.

5 On Arab economic fortunes under the mandate, see Khalidi, *Iron Cage*, 86–87, 91–92; Kimmerling and Migdal, *Palestinian People*, 60–64; Efraim Karsh, *Palestine Betrayed* (New Haven: Yale University Press, 2010), 12–16; Tessler, *History of the Israeli–Palestinian Conflict*, 177–80, 210–18; Morris, *Righteous Victims*, 110–12; Khalidi, *Iron Cage*, 86–87, 91–92; Farsoun and Aruri, *Palestine and the Palestinians*, 77–89.

European notions of personal freedom, progress, and gender equality. Denying any long-term conflict between Jewish and Arab welfare, they thus sought to maintain their Socialist aversion to militarism and war. This pacifist orientation distinguished Zionism from most other European nationalist movements in their formative phase. But at the same time self-congratulatory Zionist assumptions about the inherent superiority of Western civilization were entirely typical of European thought in this period.

In public, Zionist leaders downplayed talk about a Jewish state. Certainly they opposed anything smacking of majority rule so long as Jews remained in the minority. For the indefinite future, they said, all energies must focus not on politics, but the practical tasks of immigration, settlement, and economic development. In private, however, most Zionist leaders assumed that if the Jews ever gained numerical superiority or parity with the Arabs, they indeed would create a Jewish-led polity in all, or part, of Palestine. In 1929 Ben-Gurion, for one, thought in terms of a federation between Jewish and Arab cantons, analogous to Switzerland. So long as Arabs' individual rights were protected and their living standards rose, Zionists told themselves that Arabs would acquiesce in, even welcome, such a development. Most Zionists failed to see that Palestinians had begun to define themselves as a political community with their own non-negotiable aspirations, and that they emphatically rejected material uplift as compensation for political and cultural marginalization. But because mainstream Zionist leaders sought to continue building the Yishuv unhindered—and because they wanted to maintain Zionism's benevolent self-image—they prohibited expressions of hatred against Arabs, and denied that intercommunal violence was likely, much less inevitable.[6]

The right wing of the Zionist movement, the so-called Revisionists led by Vladimir Ze'ev Jabotinksy, ridiculed this position as hopelessly naive and self-deluding. In Jabotinsky's view, Zionist and Arab national interests by the 1920s already were profoundly incompatible, as anti-Jewish riots in 1920–1921 and 1929 testified, and were growing ever more so. That Arabs would resent an alien intrusion in their midst was only natural; in a sense, Jabotinsky sympathized with them. Yet he was convinced that Zionism's moral obligation to save European Jewry greatly outweighed the moral claim of the Arabs—comparing the two was like comparing starvation to appetite, he wrote—and for the Zionist mission to survive, the Yishuv would have to resort to military force. It must surround itself, in his words, with an "iron wall." Only when Arabs realized that they could not destroy Zionism would change occur within Palestinian society, and moderates come to the fore. Then, and only then, could serious political negotiation and compromise begin.[7]

Although Jabotinsky remained outside the Zionist mainstream, in the late 1930s a combination of events pushed Ben-Gurion and the Labor Party toward a more aggressive, urgent (some would say, realistic) policy reminiscent of Jabotinsky. From 1936 to 1939 the Arab Revolt, directed against Jews and British alike, showed that sustained, large-scale Arab violence was not merely possible, but a looming reality (see below). In response to that uprising, a British body of official inquiry, the Peel Commission of 1937, recommended partitioning Palestine into Jewish and Arab states, on the assumption that communal cooperation had become impossible. At the same time, Polish, Hungarian, Romanian, and German anti-Semitism—reinforced by the global Depression of the 1930s—lent Zionist efforts to provide a refuge for European Jews a new sense of urgency that contrasted with early

6   Anita Shapira, *Land and Power: The Zionist Resort to Force, 1881–1967* (Stanford: Stanford University Press, 1992), pts. 1, 2; *idem, Berl: The Biography of A Socialist Zionist* (Cambridge: Cambridge University Press, 1984), chs. 10–13.

7   Avi Shlaim, *The Iron Wall* (New York: W. W. Norton, 2001), 11–16; Shapira, *Land and Power*, 154–63. On the pre–1940 evolution of the Zionist right led by Jabotinsky, see Colin Shindler, *The Triumph of Military Zionism* (London, 2010).

assumptions that the Jews still had plenty of time to rescue their brethren. Yet even as they reacted to the Arab Revolt by endorsing Peel Commission proposals for separation and by strengthening the Haganah defense force, many Yishuv leaders continued, albeit with ever less conviction and plausibility, to preach the ultimate compatibility of Jewish and Arab interests.

Palestinian Political Movements to c. 1940

Like Zionism, Palestinian nationalism steeped itself in European notions of national territory, national rights, and self-determination. Much as Zionism fed on the disintegration of the multi-ethnic Austro–Hungarian and Russian Empires, Palestinian nationalism arose from the collapse of the Ottoman Empire.

Yet compared to its Jewish/Zionist counterpart, a Palestinian political identity developed quite late. Under the Ottomans, who ruled the area from 1516 to 1917, although Jerusalem and its surrounding region were revered as a Muslim holy land, no single administrative or political unit corresponded to modern Palestine/Israel. Nor did the people of that area exercise independent political authority. Residents of what would become mandatory Palestine normally identified themselves, depending on context, as Arabs, as South Syrians, as Christians or Muslims, as members of a particular village or clan—but not as Palestinians. In other words, there was as yet no conception of a specifically Palestinian nation or political community. As was true throughout the Arab world, local notables cooperated willingly with the Turkish-led Ottoman administration, because it afforded them prestige and income, and because they regarded that empire as Islam's best defense against Western threats. Shortly before World War One, notions of a more specifically Palestinian identity began to circulate among the educated urban elite, including journalists, officials, and landowners. But as yet, this had no popular resonance, and even within educated circles, it competed with and overlapped with Ottoman loyalties and with emergent notions of pan-Arab unity.

When at the end of World War One the Ottoman Empire disintegrated and British troops occupied Palestine, the local elite's first response was to replace Ottomanism with support for a unified pan-Arab state. The goal was to incorporate all Arab areas stretching from modern Saudi Arabia and Israel to Iraq in a single Syrian-centered kingdom under Prince Faisal, whose influential family ruled the Muslim holy city of Mecca. To win Arab support against the Ottomans during the war, the British themselves initially supported Faisal's project. Had a unified Arab kingdom/ nation materialized, Palestinian Arabs might have felt less vulnerable to Jewish pressure than they became once the British mandate isolated Palestine from the rest of the Arab world. In such circumstances, it is conceivable that the bitter Arab–Zionist split of later years might have been avoided. Indeed, Faisal and Zionist leaders briefly explored an arrangement by which Zionism could have developed under an Arab, rather than a British, political umbrella. But this was not to be. In the face of faltering British resolve and resolute opposition by the French—who wanted Syria for themselves—and with only intermittent enthusiasm among regional Arab leaders, Faisal's pan-Arab dream collapsed in 1920.[8] Two years later the League of Nations formally divided Faisal's would-be domain between the two leading European powers, with Britain receiving one mandate for the future Iraq and a second for Palestine, and with France awarded a mandate for what would become Syria and Lebanon.

Seeing that Palestine for the foreseeable future would remain under British control, and building on tentative prewar notions of Palestine as a more or less distinct region, local Arab elites now began to promote an explicitly Palestinian political persona focused on the modest territory of British-controlled Palestine separate from other Arab lands. "Southern Syria no longer exists," an

---

8   After the French forced Faisal to leave Syria, the British compensated him with the crown of the newly created state of Iraq.

Arab Congress in Haifa declared in 1920, some two years before the League of Nations formally ratified the British mandate. Thus they abandoned the "Southern Syria" designation that Palestine would have assumed had Faisal's Syrian-centered regime survived. "We must defend Palestine," they concluded.[9] (In much the same way, after the British in 1921–1923 closed the area east of the Jordan River to Jewish settlement and established an autonomous Arab government in Transjordan, Zionism was forced to compress its once expansive territorial visions to the far more modest confines of the mandate west of the Jordan.)

In the 1920s and 1930s a network of associations, congresses, religious bodies, political parties, and publications arose within Palestine to advance Arab interests, and, in varying degrees, to promote the nascent Palestinian national ideal. These included Muslim–Christian Associations, the Arab Congress and the Arab Executive, the British-created Supreme Muslim Council, the Youth Congress, and the Palestine Arab Party, most of which sought to unite Palestinians in opposition to Zionism. Hajj Amin al-Husayni, the scion of a famous Jerusalem clan, derived substantial prestige and patronage from his leadership of the Supreme Muslim Council, whose British subvention made it the most financially secure of these various organizations. These advantages and his passionate anti-Zionism soon made him the acknowledged leader of prewar Palestinian nationalism. Until 1948 political authority remained in the hands of wealthy notable families like the Husaynis and Nashashibis. But as private and government education, urbanization, white-collar employment, Arab-language publications, and literacy expanded, the circle of politically active people began to widen. Political involvement spread both geographically, to include small towns and interior districts, and socially, to embrace mid-level government employees,

merchants, teachers, journalists, and eventually urban laborers and some peasants.

What message did these organizations promote? Palestinians, they proclaimed, were a national community distinct from the Jews and the British within Palestine and (although this was maintained less consistently) from Arabs without. Palestinians were deeply attached to lands their families had occupied for generations and would not accept displacement by uninvited colonists. (The fact that Jews had a lower social status than Muslims made what many Palestinians regarded as Jewish pretensions all the more insufferable.) As early as 1913 the newspaper *Filastin* (*Palestine*) ran a poem entitled "The Zionist Peril" and asked in its editorial, "Do you accept to see our country stolen?"[10] Replying to Ben-Gurion's claim that Jewish immigration was a blessing because it raised Arab living standards, Musa Alami, a Palestinian nationalist who was a Cambridge University law graduate, avowed that he would prefer to see his country remain barren for a hundred years until Arabs could develop it themselves than to have Jews do it for them.[11] Declared another Palestinian witness in 1937 before a British commission of inquiry, "You say we are better off, you say that my house has been enriched by the strangers who have entered it. But it is *my* house, and I did not invite the strangers in, or ask them to enrich it, and I do not care how poor or bare it is, if only I am master in it."[12] Nationalists argued that basic notions of popular sovereignty, national self-determination, and democracy propounded by Europeans themselves demanded that the long-established people of Palestine, not the Jews, be allowed to determine the country's future. In 1937 al-Husayni promised that under a future Palestinian state, no Jew who had entered after 1917 would be allowed to stay.

---

9   Kimmerling and Migdal, *Palestinian People*, 85, citing Yehoshua Porath, *The Emergence of the Palestinian-Arab National Movement, 1919–1929* (London: Frank Cass, 1973), 107.

10   Khalidi, *Palestinian Identity*, 58.

11   Shabtai Teveth, *Ben-Gurion and the Palestinian Arabs* (Oxford: Oxford University Press, 1985), 129, 132.

12   Calvin Goldscheider, *Cultures in Conflict: The Arab-Israeli Conflict* (Westport, CT: Greenwood Press, 1963), 63.

This is not to say that without the threat of Zionism, Palestinian nationalism never would have arisen. The florescence during the interwar period of Egyptian, Iraqi, and Syrian nationalism shows that in the absence of Jewish settlement, European colonial rule itself was sufficient to provoke popular demands for independence, even as European political norms provided an organizational and thematic vehicle to express such demands. Yet within the Arab world, Palestinian nationalism was unique in that, at least until 1936, it tended to identify Zionists, rather than the colonial power, as its primary opponent. Much as resistance to anti-Semitism became the defining characteristic of Zionism, resistance to Zionism became a linchpin of Palestinian identity. In their rivalry for the same small territory, these two forms of nationalism—Zionism and Palestinian nationalism—imported a similar conceptual armature from Europe and began to deploy comparable techniques of popular mobilization, including a loose array of political parties, nationalist newspapers, popular militias, youth groups, women's associations, sports clubs, and so forth.[13]

Despite these parallels, however, from 1920 to 1940 the Yishuv grew ever stronger, while Palestinian political organizations became more fragmented and ineffectual. These trends presaged the final victory of Zionism in 1947–1948. Why, then, this growing discrepancy between the two national movements?

Most obviously perhaps, the Palestinian cause suffered because, as just indicated, the national persona it sought to promote had shallow historical and cultural roots. Zionism grafted itself to a Jewish communal consciousness that was ancient, widely shared, and emotionally intense. By contrast, a Palestinian—as opposed to an Arab or Muslim—identity cohered only in the 1920s and long remained superficial, socially uneven, and in tension with other affiliations. Depending on context, in the 1930s the same person still might define himself as a Palestinian, a South Syrian, or as a member of the "Arab nation." This fluidity and indeterminacy of identities made it difficult to form focused, stable, and genuinely popular political organizations. As late as 1938, the principal leader of the Arab Revolt in Palestine against Britain and the Jews eschewed a specifically Palestinian label, instead declaring himself commander of "The General Arab Revolt in Southern Syria"—a term that recalled Prince Faisal's Syrian–based pan–Arab project.[14]

Reinforcing these cultural legacies was a variety of critical differences resulting from the Jews' earlier exposure to European norms. As I already noted, the early appearance of Zionism itself, and its precocious ideological and organizational expression, were entirely a function of the fact that Zionists, coming from Europe, became familiar with modern nationalism perhaps two generations before their Palestinian counterparts.

Likewise, because Jewish immigrants arrived with European technological and commercial skills, and because they had access to large flows of European and American capital, the Yishuv developed a uniquely dynamic economic base. It is true that between 1922 and 1947 the Palestinian Arab economy grew briskly, at over six percent per year. But the Jewish economy, recall, grew over twice as fast. In 1936 per capita Jewish income already was 2.6 times greater than per capita Arab income—an advantage that had obvious political and military implications.[15]

Furthermore, European background meant that Jews—despite the Zionist ideal of rural labor—remained far more urban than Arabs: 81 percent versus 30 percent in 1939. This afforded them more efficient systems of communication and political organization than were available to

---

13   On the development of Palestinian national consciousness, Kimmerling and Migdal, *Palestinian People*, pt. 1; Muhammad Muslih, *The Origins of Palestinian Nationalism* (New York: Columbia University Press, 1988); Khalidi, *Palestinian Identity*.

14   This was Fawzi al–Qawuqji. Kimmerling and Migdal, *Palestinian People*, 116–17. Also Sayigh, *Armed Struggle*, 9–10.

15   Khalidi, *Iron Cage*, 13–14; Tessler, *History of the Israeli–Palestinian Conflict*, 188–90; Farsoun and Aruri, *Palestine and the Palestinians*, ch. 3.

a dispersed peasantry. Cinema, and to a lesser extent, radio were preeminently urban. An urban base also gave Jews more direct control over nodes of transport and communication, which helped them suppress Arab resistance, most notably in 1947–1948.

Not surprisingly, a far higher proportion of Jews also attended primary and secondary school, reinforcing their openness to nationalist communication. In 1931, 22 percent of Arabs could read, compared to 86 percent of Jews. Thirteen years later, the percentage of Jewish children age 5 to 14 enrolled in school (97 percent) was still three times greater than that among Palestinian Arab children. At advanced levels, the gap was yet greater.[16] Politically charged newspapers, magazines, and books circulated widely among Jews, whereas in Palestinian villages, where illiteracy typically approached 90 percent, the population tended to be isolated, apathetic, and only dimly aware of Palestinian nationalist agendas. Often national, or even regional, politics interested only one or two people in a village. At the same time, by instilling and upgrading technical skills, widespread literacy spurred Jewish economic growth.

The immigration experience itself contributed to higher levels of solidarity in the Yishuv than in Palestinian society. Leaving one's home and settling in a strange land, where Hebrew, not a European language, was the preferred tongue, automatically tended to weaken earlier attachments. Although probably only a minority of the Yishuv were ideologically committed Zionists, and far fewer concerned themselves with notoriously fractious Zionist politics, all those joining the Yishuv, by definition, saw themselves as members of a Jewish community. At the same time, the Yishuv's Socialist economic policies minimized gaps between rich and poor. But Palestinian society was deeply fragmented by village localism; by tensions between Christian (some 12 percent) and Muslim Arabs; and by a politically paralyzing social distance between educated, wealthy, largely landowning elites and the masses of peasants and urban laborers. Such distinctions in education, speech, deportment, and economic interest made cross-class communication, not to mention popular mobilization, extremely difficult. The elite itself, morever, was riven by endemic family and clan rivalries at both the national and local levels. Competition between the Husayni and Nashashibi families, each of which had numerous clients and partisans throughout Palestine, was particularly venomous.

Finally, compounding and reflecting these social and material weaknesses were questionable Palestinian political strategies. Because they were loath to recognize Jewish political claims, Palestinian leaders rejected British proposals in the 1920s to create joint Arab–Jewish legislative and advisory bodies, even through those reforms probably would have enshrined Arab superiority. Likewise, they turned down the territorial proposals of the Peel Commission in 1937; and more surprisingly, insofar as it was markedly favorable to Palestinian Arab interests, Palestinian leaders rejected the British White Paper of 1939. (A White Paper is an authoritative policy statement.) In effect, as we shall see, Palestinian leaders tended to combine rhetorical maximalism with programmatic minimalism.

Sensing their own weakness, realizing that their best efforts to halt immigration had failed and that if current trends continued they would become a minority in their own land, the Arabs of Palestine grew ever more bitter—and frightened of the future. In 1936 Moshe Sharett (born Moshe Shertok), one of the Yishuv's Arab experts and a Labor Party leader, warned, "Fear is the main factor in Arab politics. … There is not a single Arab who has not been hurt by the entry of Jews into Palestine; there is not a single Arab who does not see himself as part of the Arab race. … Previously [Palestine] had an Arab face, and now it is changing."[17]

The most ominous sign of this distress was escalating violence. In 1920–1921 and in 1929, Arabs attacked the Jewish quarters in Jerusalem, Tel Aviv, Jaffa, Safed, and other locales. Shouting

---

16 Khalidi, *Iron Cage*, 14–15; Farsoun and Aruri, *Palestine and the Palestinians*, 75–76.

17 Shapira, *Land and Power*, 227.

"Palestine is our land and the Jews are our dogs," mobs in 1929 murdered some 60 members of the 3,000-year-old Jewish community of Hebron, women and children included, and expelled the rest.

Finally, in 1936, with the fifth *aliyah* assuming ever more threatening demographic dimensions, Arabs declared a general strike and launched an armed uprising, the aforementioned Arab Revolt, which continued intermittently to 1939. Having started in the coastal cities, the revolt then spread to the interior hill country, where it drew strength from a peasantry hostile, in varying degrees, to the Jews, the British, and wealthy Palestinian elites based along the coast. Totaling perhaps 15,000 at their peak, guerrillas launched hit-and-run attacks on police stations and military installations, and sabotaged oil pipelines, railroads, roads, and bridges. Inland traffic was soon paralyzed. Indeed, between mid-1937 and late 1938 the British lost control over much of rural Palestine, as the green, red, and black Palestinian flag waved over countless villages. But with war in Europe a growing danger and Palestine guarding the eastern flank of the strategically critical Suez Canal, not for a moment could Britain consider permanently abandoning Palestine. Accordingly, Britain deployed over 20,000 troops and units of the Royal Air Force to restore order, a task that was facilitated in the end by poor coordination and bitter internecine feuds among the highly localized guerrilla bands. In the course of the anti-insurgency campaign, over 5,000 Palestinians, including many of their best fighters, died and 50,000 were detained, of whom 146 were hanged.[18]

By the time the revolt was suppressed, it had profoundly shaken all parties. Seeing Arab violence through a European prism—not as a predictable response to Zionist settlement, but as manifestations of anti-Semitism to which they would no longer submit meekly—the Zionist leadership became more determined and militant. It was only in response to the revolt that the Haganah became a serious military force. For their part, the British, we shall see, effectively abandoned their commitment to Zionism as a result of the uprising. Among Arabs, the revolt popularized new heroes and symbols and helped to disseminate a Palestinian national identity. But at the same time the revolt killed off much of the most promising Palestinian leadership, exhausted the population, and weakened popular ties to traditional elites. It also provoked severe conflict between the Husaynis and Nashashibis, effectively destroyed whatever Palestinian national organizations had existed, and led the British henceforth to seek advice not from Palestinians, but from neighboring Arab states. Thus, the revolt not only advertised, but accentuated Palestinian weakness, and foreshadowed the complete collapse of Palestinian society in 1948.

Would a more accommodating, pragmatic strategy have served Palestinian interests more effectively? One could argue that the Jews' situation in Europe was so catastrophic that nothing would have stopped the Zionist drive for a refuge in Palestine. Of necessity, Jews would have pocketed any concessions and used them as a basis for their next set of demands. Indeed, this was the reasoning of al-Husayni at the time, and some statements by Ben-Gurion can be seen as lending support to this view. At the time of the Peel Commission in 1937, for example, Ben-Gurion wrote of his hope that the borders of a Jewish mini-state would prove temporary, and that a combination of massive immigration and economic and military might would allow such a state to expand across most or all of Palestine—ideally by agreement with the Arabs, but if necessary by more unilateral means.[19]

But another interpretation, consonant with that of the noted Arab-American scholar Rashid

18 Sayigh, *Armed Struggle*, 2; Kimmerling and Migdal, *Palestinian People*, ch. 4; Farsoun and Aruri, *Palestine and the Palestinians*, 89–93.

19 See, for example, Michael Neumann, *The Case Against Israel* (Petrolia, CA: Counterpunch, 2005), 59; Howard Sachar, *A History of Israel from the Rise of Zionism to Our Time* (3rd ed., New York: Alfred Knopf, 2007), 207–208; Morris, *Righteous Victims*, 138–39.

Khalidi,[20] argues that Palestinians were at one and the same time insufficiently and excessively militant. Events in 1929 and 1936–1939 showed that in most circumstances the British would respond to force with concessions. If Palestinians had organized limited violence along with strikes and popular actions in the 1920s before the flood of Jewish arrivals, perhaps they could have induced the British to limit immigration much earlier than they did. But to capitalize on such concessions, Palestinian leaders would have had to show far greater tactical flexibility. In particular, their interests probably would have been better served if they had accepted British reform proposals in the 1920s and the opportunity to create an independent Arab state offered by the Peel Commission in 1937, or by the White Paper of 1939. In so doing, Palestinians might have cemented Arab ascendancy and placed publicly agreed, permanent limits on Jewish expansion. Their decision to reject all such initiatives meant that Arab attacks on Jews proved emotionally cathartic, but politically barren. In 1947 Palestinian leaders would replay this combination of political inflexibility and tactically ill-considered violence, with yet more disastrous results.

The Twice–Promised Land: Shifting British Policies, 1917–1940

As these two national movements cohered and clashed, the British tried to navigate between them, all the while subordinating both parties to British imperial interests. Although some leading British statesmen (Winston Churchill among them) were lifelong Zionists, and although the mandate allowed the Yishuv to grow from a struggling collection of settlements into a state-in-embryo, by and large the British government maintained an instrumental, rather than emotional, view of Zionism. From 1917 to 1948, Britain's only consistent objective was the welfare not of the Jews, but of the British Empire. Palestine, as noted, protected the eastern approaches to the Suez Canal,

which, in turn, was Britain's lifeline to India, the Far East, and Australia. Not only was Britain's early Zionist sympathy largely pragmatic, but as Arab opposition intensified, Britain backpedaled, until by 1939, it had turned almost 180 degrees from a pro-Zionist to a substantially pro-Arab position. Ultimately, however, the British failed to satisfy either community—or indeed, to preserve their empire.

The Balfour Declaration was a letter issued in November 1917 by the British Foreign Secretary Arthur James Balfour to the head of Britain's Zionist Federation. In this letter, the government expressed itself in favor of "the establishment in Palestine of a national home for the Jewish people," and promised to use its "best endeavours" to achieve that objective. In issuing this commitment, Britain sought not only to foster what was widely viewed as a noble humanitarian enterprise, but to win international Jewish support for its war effort; to provide a moral rationale for its expected takeover of Palestine that could blunt German, French, and American criticism; and to implant in Palestine a population that would counter indigenous opposition but which, by virtue of its weakness, would be dependent on the British. Pursuant to its obligations in the Balfour Declaration and the mandate, Britain not only opened Palestine to markedly increased Jewish immigration and land purchase, but provided much needed public works employment for immigrants.

Yet even at this early date, the British sought to address Arab concerns. In 1922, after the first serious Arab riots, the government issued the first of three major White Papers on Palestine. Each document marked a further weakening of Britain's Zionist commitment. The 1922 White Paper explicitly denied that the Jews would be allowed to set up a state of their own or to dominate Arabs, and to the outrage of Jabotinsky, closed off the entire area east of the Jordan—some 80 percent of the territory of the original Palestine mandate—to Jewish settlement. Thus, as we saw, Transjordan arose.

A year after the yet more serious Arab riots of 1929, a second White Paper called for the

20   Khalidi, *Iron Cage*, chs. 1–3.

first time for sharp curbs on Jewish immigration and land purchase. Although Zionist lobbying in London prevented these recommendations from being implemented, political and economic pressures continued to erode British support. The Depression obliged Britain to reduce overseas military expenditure. More ominously, Mussolini's and Hitler's opposition to both Zionism and British imperialism won an increasingly sympathetic, if opportunistic, hearing in some Arab circles, not least with Hajj Amin al-Husayni, still the acknowledged leader of the Palestinian cause, who as early as 1933 expressed to the German consul in Jerusalem his "hope for the extension of the fascist anti-democratic, governmental system to other countries."[21] (This, despite the fact that Hitler, with his usual subtlety, once described Arabs as "half-apes."[22]) In 1936 the Arab Revolt convinced British leaders that they would have to move yet more decisively to placate Palestinian opinion. The aforementioned Peel Commission of 1937 sought to cut the Gordian knot by separating the two parties, with a Jewish state on about 18 percent of mandate territory, an Arab state in some 75 percent, a small British-controlled corridor from Jerusalem to the coast, and 225,000 Arabs transferred out of the Jewish sector (see Maps). Outraged, Palestinian leaders rejected out of hand this effort to give Jews any part of a country they regarded as sacred Muslim soil and rightfully theirs. The revolt intensified.

Two years later, with the revolt not yet completely vanquished, with war looming in Europe, and with Mideast oil and Mideast transport routes occupying a vital position in British strategic calculations, the British finally moved to sever completely their ties to the Zionist project they themselves had helped to initiate. The White Paper of 1939 called for: a) a ceiling of 75,000 Jewish immigrants during the next five years, and after that time, an end to all Jewish immigration without Arab consent; b) severe immediate restrictions on further Jewish land purchases; and c) the creation within ten years of an independent Palestine under majority—that is to say, Arab—control, Arab–Jewish relations permitting. "If we must offend one side, let us offend the Jews rather than the Arabs," Prime Minister Neville Chamberlain announced with cold logic.[23] Now it was the turn of the Jews to denounce "perfidious Albion" and to challenge Britain. The reversal of British policy that began in 1922 was essentially complete.

The Impact of World War Two

The 1939 White Paper sought to mollify Arab anger, but to achieve a permanent settlement in Palestine, two conditions would be necessary—neither of which was realized.

First, the Palestinian leadership would have had to accept the White Paper and work with British authorities to implement it. The governments of Egypt, Iraq, and Transjordan urged al-Husayni to do precisely that, but in the end he declined, because the British would not agree to halt all immigration immediately, and because the promise of independence struck him as suspiciously conditional. He remained attuned to the hard-line sentiment of the Arab Revolt, whose slogan was "The British to the sea, and the Jews to their graves." In retrospect, to recall Khalidi's argument, this was a historic blunder, for it threw away by far the best offer Palestinians would ever receive and surrendered the political initiative to Zionists, the British, and Arab governments. Thereafter, as noted, Britain looked for Arab advice on Palestine policy not to Palestinian leaders, but to those Arab governments.[24] Al-Husayni's suspicions notwithstanding, the 1939 White Paper held out a credible promise that Arabs would gain political control over 100 percent of mandatory Palestine within ten years. By contrast, the Peel Commission had offered them about 75 percent, the UN partition plan of 1947 offered 45 percent, the armistice of 1949 left Arabs with only 22

21 Morris, *Righteous Victims*, 124–25.
22 *Ibid.*, 165, citing Philip Mattar.
23 *Ibid.*, 158.
24 See esp. Khalidi, *Iron Cage*, 114–18.

percent, and the 1967 armistice—still nominally in effect—left Palestinians with nothing at all.

But the second crucial condition for the 1939 White Paper to have succeeded was for Jews to have stopped immigration and land purchases. However, with the Nazi onslaught, Jews not only sought frantically to circumvent the British blockade of the coast, but they did so with a growing measure of world sympathy, as hundreds of Jews perished at sea in forlorn efforts to reach Palestine. Together, Arab fears and Jewish desperation tore the 1939 White Paper to shreds.

The neutering of the White Paper was only one aspect of a far more sweeping transformation in Palestine that issued from World War Two. The first world war, we saw, gave Zionism a great power patron (fickle though that patronage proved) and greatly enhanced opportunities for Jewish settlement. Far more dramatically, World War Two led directly to the creation of the state of Israel in 1948. Why this decisive transformation? Although its effects could be contradictory, on balance World War Two changed the strategic equation in Palestine and the Mideast in favor of the Jews. It did so, first, by weakening Palestinian Arabs and their new patron, Britain, and second, by strengthening the Zionists, as well as the United States and the Soviet Union, which now became Zionism's great power backers.

Consider first the Arabs and Britain. True, during and after the war, extensive oil reserves allowed Saudi Arabia and Iraq to exert influence on British, and to some extent American, policy on behalf of the Palestinians. But pro-Nazi sympathy by prominent Iraqi, Syrian, and Palestinian figures—al-Husayni among them—did little to endear them to the victorious allies. Al-Husayni, in particular, spent the war broadcasting on Nazi radio and organizing Arab and Muslim support for the Axis.[25] In combination with internecine feuds dating from the Arab Revolt, al-Husayni's wartime activities and his imperious style left the Palestinian movement in considerable disarray after 1945.

If the war thus undermined the Palestinian cause, it took a heavier toll on the British, who emerged nearly bankrupt, stripped of foreign reserves, and heavily dependent on the United States for loans and economic support. One result of economic dependence was the surrender to the United States of British political and military hegemony in the eastern Mediterranean. Insofar as the American electorate in general, and President Harry Truman in particular, were increasingly pro-Zionist, this had major implications for Palestine. In 1947, when the UN considered the proposal to partition Palestine into Jewish and Arab states, Britain wanted to vote against it, as its Arab allies requested—but decided to abstain, for fear of offending its American creditor and patron.

At the same time as it weakened the Palestinians, the war dramatically improved Zionist prospects. In moral and physical terms, of course, the war was an unspeakable obscenity. By virtually exterminating European Jewry, the Nazis not only inflicted the greatest calamity in Jewish history, but deprived the Zionist movement of a vast reservoir of potential settlers and soldiers.[26] One can speculate that if the Nazis had persecuted, but not annihilated, the Jews, and if the Jews then had been able to open the gates of Palestine, Zionism after 1945 would have been incomparably more formidable than it became. And yet it is also clear that the Holocaust instilled in world Jewry an unprecedented desperation, unity, and militancy. "What could show more poignantly," Jews asked, "that if we are ever to be safe, we need a state and an army of our own?" In North America, home to the largest Jewish population, many of whom before the war had little use for Zionism, political and financial support for Zionist organizations now rose exponentially. In 1947 alone, American Jews raised $100 million to help Jewish refugees, most of them

25   Jeffrey Herf, *Nazi Propaganda for the Arab World* (New Haven: Yale University Press, 2009); Gilbert Achcar, *The Arabs and the Holocaust* (New York: Metropolitan Books, 2009).

26   On Zionism, the Yishuv, and the Holocaust, see Dina Porat, *The Blue and Yellow Stars of David* (Cambridge, MA.: Harvard University Press, 1990).

bound for Palestine, and the Yishuv. In Palestine itself—where Britain's post–1939 refusal to let in refugees effectively had condemned hundreds of thousands to Hitler's gas chambers—embittered Jewish fighters, including at first both the mainline Haganah defense force and more marginal terrorist groups, launched widespread attacks on British installations and personnel in 1945 and 1946. Their goal was to break the blockade and force the British to quit Palestine so it could be opened to immigration. Thus, six years after suppressing the Arab revolt, the British faced surging militancy and a frontal challenge from its allies in that earlier struggle.

As the enormity of the Holocaust became known, Zionist demands that Palestine admit Jewish survivors gained powerful international support—which was deeply ironic, considering that the Jews came away from the war convinced they could rely on no one but themselves. In fact, Gentile sympathy for Zionism, and the Jews' sense of isolation, were complementary insofar as many Europeans felt guilty they had done nothing while the Jews were being systematically slaughtered.

It was in the Soviet Union that pro-Zionist European sentiment became most significant shortly after the war, because the USSR emerged as—by far—the continent's strongest power. Until 1945 the Soviets had been hostile to Jewish nationalism, but now Soviet hopes that a left-wing Jewish state would provide the USSR with a toehold in the Mideast at the expense of Britain and the United States produced an about–face that was as influential as it was dramatic. Had the USSR's Joseph Stalin, who controlled at least 11 votes in the UN out of 57, opposed Israel's creation, it never would have arisen.

Given emerging Cold War tensions, perhaps the most remarkable thing about Soviet support for Zionism was that it coincided with vigorous American advocacy. Backed by Christian Zionists, left-wing unionists, some African-American leaders, and of course Jews, Truman was instrumental in getting the UN to vote for Israel's creation. He also made certain that the United States was first to recognize the new state. If the Soviet Union after 1945 bestrode central and eastern Europe, the United States exercised unmatched economic and political influence on a global scale. Thus, World War Two made Zionism a client of the world's only two postwar superpowers.

Zionists promptly used that support to hammer the British. Deferring to Arab sensibilities, Britain in 1945 was still trying to prevent Jews from entering Palestine, but a series of well-publicized incidents involving desperate refugees elicited widespread condemnation in Europe and America of British "inhumanity." Brought to their knees by such criticism, by continuing Jewish terrorist attacks, by the rising cost of mandatory defense in a period of economic stringency, and by Truman's carping opposition, in February 1947 the British finally threw in the towel and returned the mandate to the United Nations so that the world body could attempt to resolve the mandate's future.

Following majority and minority reports by a UN special committee of inquiry on Palestine, on November 29, 1947, the UN General Assembly voted to approve the majority report as embodied in General Assembly Resolution 181. This divided Palestine into a Jewish state, with 55 percent of the territory containing some 540,000 Jews and 400,000 Arabs, and an Arab state in the other 45 percent, with 800,000 Arabs and 10,000 Jews. Another 100,000 Jews and 75,000 Arabs lived in Jerusalem and Bethlehem, which was to be an international zone (see Maps).[27] Thus, Herzl's dream of an independent state (as opposed to Balfour's more vague concept of a "national home") finally received international sanction.

The passage of this resolution by a vote of 33 to 13 and ten abstentions, with the voting broadcast live on radio around the world, reflected a constellation of forces. As noted, Western pangs of conscience over the Holocaust were surely a key element. In addition, Europeans and Americans identified more readily with Jews, who were familiar, and with the modernity of the Zionist project, than they did with Arab culture, of which

---

27 The 55 and 45 percent figures refer to mandate lands exclusive of this small international zone proposed for Jerusalem and Bethlehem.

they knew very little. African and Asian states might have been expected to support Arabs over European Jews, but in the Philippines, Liberia, China, and other countries, the U.S. government and/or Jewish businesses applied pressure. By contrast, the Arab states failed to mount an effective lobby. Finally, many countries—including most Latin American states, who were some 40 percent of UN members—decided that the choice was not between right and wrong, but between greater and lesser evils—and that harm to the Palestinians was more tolerable than further harm to the Jews.

Was this decision morally or politically valid? Given that both Jews and Palestinians had legitimate historical and moral claims, Zionists argue that partition was the only logical solution. Although the Jews received 55 percent, Palestinians got by far the better deal, because most of the 55 percent was relatively worthless real estate in the Negev desert in the south. Moreover, as a practical matter, there was simply no place for Jewish survivors to go to other than Palestine. They could not be expected to return to ferociously anti-Semitic Germany and eastern Europe—in fact, postwar riots against Jews in Poland, Hungary, and elsewhere killed hundreds of would–be returnees—while the United States, for all its goodwill, refused to take in significant numbers. If Palestinians were not chiefly responsible for Jewish suffering, neither were they blameless, given their leader's Nazi embrace and their refusal to let refugees from Hitler's "final solution" gain asylum. Like others on the losing side in 1945, it was fitting that they suffer some penalty. Finally, Zionists argue, the creation of a Jewish state was not only morally just, but legally unassailable. As successor to the League of Nations, the UN was fully empowered to rule on the mandate. Supported not only by the United States and Europe, but by the great bulk of Asian, African, and Latin American states, the 1947 vote to partition Palestine was not even close. Despite the UN's subsequent expansion to include all of Africa and Asia, that body has never sought to revoke its original decision.

To these arguments, of course, anti-Zionists offer a variety of rejoinders. They deny that the Jews had a legitimate claim to Palestine. Every country has been occupied by a succession of peoples. Because the Romans ruled England 1,700 years ago, are Italians now entitled to part of England? That the Jews in the 1930s and 1940s had no place to go but Palestine was sad, but hardly the Palestinians' fault. Palestinians as a whole never expressed any great enthusiasm for Hitler, and in any case al-Husayni's role in the Holocaust was marginal. The real reason Palestinians, and not Europeans, had to pay the price for anti-Semitism both before and after World War Two was that the Palestinians were weak. Jewish immigration could be forced on them by British and then Jewish guns—but America and England were strong, so no one could force them to accept refugees they did not want. Finally, anti-Zionists question whether the League of Nations or the United Nations truly represented "world opinion." Both bodies were created by Western nations to serve their own interests, and if Muslim and non-Muslim lands that were still colonies in 1947 had been allowed to vote, the outcome well might have been different.

These, then, were arguments that were, and still are, made on the question of partition. But by the close of 1947, whatever the moral and legal arguments, it was clear that Palestine's future would be resolved not by words, but by force of arms.

If we stand back and take a long–term perspective, we may summarize historic developments to 1947 in the following way. The chances that Zionist settlement in Palestine could have a peaceable resolution were never good. At the outset, this prospect was reduced by the failure to incorporate Palestine within a pan-Arab state, such as Prince Faisal envisioned. Had it arisen after World War One, such a state might have reduced Palestinian fears of being swamped. But standing on their own, cut off from wider Arab support, Palestinians became hostage to precisely such anxieties. Thus they grew ever more determined to deny that Jews were a political, as opposed to a religious, community, and to refuse any Zionist connection to the land. Invariably it was Palestinians who initiated large-scale violence. Such attacks only reinforced deep-seated Jewish insecurities and stoked hitherto subdued demands for an independent Jewish state. But in reciprocal fashion, the Zionists' essential indifference to Palestinian feelings and aspirations, their dismissive attitude toward Palestinian nationality, and their determination to maximize Jewish immigration at all costs fed the Arabs' worst fears and strengthened their determination to defend their patrimony.

In sum, both communities were haunted by the specter of extinction, whether physical in the case of the Jews, or cultural and political in the case of the Palestinians. The same elixir—immigration to Palestine—that was life for the Yishuv was poison to the Arabs. Ultimately, what drove the entire process forward was something beyond the control of either people—namely, ever more vicious European anti-Semitism and the Jews' ever more panicked search for a haven. Jews could not halt anti-Semitism, and Palestinian Arabs could not stop the Jews. Like a couple trapped in a disastrously unhappy marriage, both sides fed hostility to the point of homicidal rupture.

Expanding the Conflict, 1947–1967

The Catastrophe/The War of Independence, 1947–1949

The decades from 1947 to 1967 were marked at either end by transformative wars. The first war, from 1947 to 1949, established Israel in the face of Palestinian and Arab opposition, and radically altered regional demography by precipitating the massive expulsion and flight of Arabs out of Israel, and of Jews from Arab lands into Israel. The second war, in June 1967, not only confirmed Israel's existence, but saw the Jewish state occupy the remaining lands of the old mandate, along with strategically important territories in Egypt and Syria. During these 20 years, in a development that started as early as 1939, the Palestinian national movement was substantially eclipsed not only by the Jews, but by Arab state actors.

The first war grew directly from the UN partition resolution of November 29, 1947. In Tel Aviv that night, Jewish crowds danced in the streets to celebrate the impending appearance of what was expected to be the first independent Jewish state in 2,000 years. But Palestinians reacted with anger and dismay to what they considered the theft of over half of their country. From Cairo, al-Husayni, still widely recognized as leader of the national movement, declared the partition resolution null and void. In the days immediately following the passage of the resolution, Arabs began attacking Jews in cities and settlements across Palestine, sparking a confrontation that would lead to full-scale war. Although no doubt many Palestinians opposed such attacks, and although radical Jewish groups—namely the Irgun and the Stern Gang—promptly retaliated with terrorist outrages[1] of their own, historians of different political persuasions—Zionist,[2] anti-Zionist,[3] neutral[4]—concur that Palestinians started the fighting in 1947.

As in the late 1930s, al-Husayni and his allies justified rejectionism by arguing that Jews had no moral claim to Arab lands, that Zionists would never be satisfied, and that they would merely use any concessions as a springboard to more annexations. But whatever the validity of such long-term speculation, in 1947 there is no evidence that Jews were planning to seize areas outside those allocated by the UN. For four months after the war started, the principal Jewish military force, the Haganah, maintained an essentially defensive posture. A partitionist mentality had come to

---

1 "Terrorism" is here defined as violence targeted against civilians, rather than military personnel, in order to achieve a political objective.

2 Karsh, *Palestine Betrayed*, ch. 5; Allis Radosh and Ronald Radosh, *A Safe Haven* (New York: Harper Perennial, 2009), 279-80.

3 Esber, *Under the Cover of War*, 140–47; Shlaim, *Iron Wall*, 30.

4 Kimmerling and Migdal, *Palestinian People*, 148–51; Tessler, *History of the Israeli–Palestinian Conflict*, 261, 263; Benny Morris, *1948* (New Haven: Yale University Press, 2008), ch. 3; Morris, *Righteous Victims*, 189–91.

dominate mainstream Zionist leaders. Their overriding goal in 1947 was to provide a safe haven for refugees within the territory that the world body had awarded them, and on November 29, they expected, and were content, to remain indefinitely within those borders.

What the Palestinian attacks of 1947 and the full-scale invasion by Arab states in 1948 did accomplish, however, was to provide Jews with an opportunity they otherwise would have lacked to seize additional lands. If Arabs were going to destroy UN-designated boundaries by force, Jews eventually decided that they too had no obligation to respect those boundaries. However justified their fears and resentments may have been, in 1947 (as in 1936) the Palestinians seriously misjudged their own and their foes' respective strength. This miscalculation led to a destruction of Palestinian society so complete that, while the 1947–1948 conflict is known to Israelis as the War of Independence, among Palestinians it is simply the Catastrophe, *al-Nakba*.

In fact, the fighting that lasted from November 30, 1947, to March 1949 fell into two phases.[5] The first phase, to mid-May 1948, was a civil war within the mandate between Jews and Palestinians. For the first four months, Palestinians clearly had the upper hand, and Jews generally remained on the defensive. As in 1936–1939, their rural bases and guerrilla strategy let Palestinians cut communications and supplies between Jewish urban centers on the coast and interior Jewish communities; while guns supplied by Arab states or turned over by the British now gave them a modest early advantage in weaponry. Seeing the Haganah's ineffectual response, in December 1947 the British Foreign Secretary Ernest Bevin confidently predicted that the Jews would get their "throats cut."[6] By March of 1948, Arabs had succeeded in isolating much of the eastern Galilee and the Negev. Most ominously, Jewish West Jerusalem, subject to an Arab blockade, seemed about to fall. Arabists in the U.S. State Department now persuaded the Truman administration to consider withdrawing support for partition in favor of a UN trusteeship.

And yet the underlying balance of forces favored the Zionists. The Palestinians' 2:1 demographic superiority rarely translated into comparable battlefield superiority, both because Jewish mobilization was more efficient, and because Jews alone enlisted women. By incorporating Irgun and Stern Gang irregulars into the Haganah and integrating local militias, the Jews developed a centralized military command that was backed by the Yishuv's impressive civilian apparatus. By contrast, never having recovered from the 1936–1939 revolt and lacking a comparably strong national consciousness or grass-roots organization, the Palestinians had great difficulty coordinating strategy and supply.

Sensing that these structural factors favored them in the long term, but at the same time recognizing that if they did not quickly relieve Jerusalem and turn around the battlefield situation, their entire enterprise would be lost, the Haganah decided to shift gears. By early April 1948, the nucleus of a unified command was in place. Modern arms from Communist Czechoslovakia, financed by Jewish communities overseas, began to reach forward units. Accordingly, in April the Haganah opened its first major offensive. This quickly broke the siege of Jerusalem and overran most towns, villages, and all mixed cities within the territory the UN had allocated to the Jewish state. In the opening phase of guerrilla warfare, Palestinian decentralization had been an advantage. But once the Haganah—soon to be renamed the Israel Defense Force or IDF—counterattacked, that same localism and Jewish control of urban transport hubs precluded a coordinated response. As the Jews picked off Arab villages and districts one at a time, the Palestinian position collapsed with astonishing suddenness. Of critical importance, Jewish success also reflected a new policy, embodied in the so-called Plan D (to which we

---

5   For descriptions and analyses of the fighting from 1947 to 1949, see Morris, *1948*; Eugene Rogan and Avi Shlaim, eds. *The War for Palestine* (2nd ed., Cambridge: Cambridge University Press, 2007); Karsh, *Palestine Betrayed*.

6   Sachar, *History of Israel*, 297.

shall turn shortly), to expel Arab inhabitants from villages and towns behind Jewish lines.

The second phase of the war began with British withdrawal from Palestine and Israel's declaration of independence on May 14, 1948, which immediately precipitated an invasion by the armies of Egypt, Syria, Transjordan, and Iraq.[7] Jewish actions against the Palestinians had evoked deep anger across the Arab world. Responding to that sentiment, the Arabs states' announced goal was to restore the rights of the people of Palestine (although in practice, as we shall see shortly, that objective was often subordinated to the interests of various Arab governments themselves). Until late June 1948, the Arab state armies had more combat and support troops, as well as weaponry that was superior in quality and quantity to Zionist arms. Arab armies could choose the time and place of attack, while their control of the high ground in the West Bank promised a strategic advantage over the Jewish–dominated coast. In Transjordan's British-trained and British-officered Arab Legion, the Jews faced an experienced, first-rate army. Even Haganah commanders on the eve of the Arab invasion rated the chances of Israel's survival at only at 50:50, while many knowledgeable external observers were yet less sanguine about Jewish prospects. Undeterred by the inaccuracy of Bevin's 1947 prediction, the British Foreign Office asserted confidently, "In the long run the Jews [will] not be able to cope … and [will] be thrown out of Palestine unless they come to terms with the Arabs."

On the other hand, during this second phase, Israel again enjoyed key advantages, both material and political. Jews had shorter lines of supply and communication, and their rank and file usually were more disciplined and technologically adept. Whereas a UN arms embargo from May 1948 began to deprive Arab armies of weapons and critical spare parts, Israel flouted such restrictions through its access to Czech armaments, including aircraft, and through private arms dealers, who snapped up World War Two surplus wherever they could. Israeli troops not only boasted higher levels of literacy and technical skill, but were far more motivated. Whereas Arab soldiers fought far from their homes for a somewhat abstract cause, Jews, with the Holocaust a searing memory—and with Arab vows to exterminate the Yishuv ringing in their ears—were convinced that their only choice was between victory and annihilation.

What is more, despite Arab strength on paper, in practice, interstate rivalries crippled Arab cooperation. Transjordan's King Abdullah sought, above all, to secure the West Bank and Jerusalem, and so long as that ambition was satisfied, did not object in principle to Israel's existence. Although imprecise demarcation of their respective spheres eventually led to bitter fighting along their interface, Israel and Transjordan maintained an informal understanding to split between them the lands that the UN had set aside for a Palestinian state. Iraq, whose Hashemite ruling house was related to that of Transjordan, supported the latter. But Egypt, viewing Transjordan as a rival for leadership in the Arab world, and Syria, fearing Transjordan's designs on its own territory, both opposed Hashemite ambition.[8] In short, although Israel faced war on three fronts, in the north, the center, and the south, it faced three separate foes and was able to defeat, or check, each one in turn.

In the north, Israeli forces blocked a Syrian invasion and went on to seize all of the Galilee, even entering briefly into Lebanon. In the center, they annexed extensive areas that had been allocated to the Palestinian state north and southwest of what is now the West Bank, and secured the vital link to western Jerusalem. In the south in a series of campaigns lasting until March 1949, the IDF blocked an Egyptian push along the coast toward Tel Aviv, then destroyed Egyptian forward positions, and finally broke into the Negev, seizing

---

7 Lebanese military involvement was nominal. Other Arab states also sent token military or financial assistance. See Rogan and Shlaim, *War for Palestine*, esp. essays by Shlaim, Matthew Hughes, Rashid Khalidi, and Madawi Al-Rasheed.

8 The ruling house of Saudi Arabia also sought to frustrate its traditional rival, the Hashemites, at every turn. See Al-Rasheed in Rogan and Shlaim, *War for Palestine*, 228–47.

that entire desert, including the port of Eilat on the Gulf of Aqaba. An Egyptian captain recalled bitterly at one point, "The Jews were attacking us from the flank that the Iraqis were supposed to be protecting. We discovered that the Iraqi army had withdrawn, without even telling us. … It was the turning point in the war."[9]

To be sure, the fighting was not entirely one sided. After its agreement with Transjordan unraveled, the IDF had a very difficult time against the Arab Legion, which retained East Jerusalem, including the holiest site in Judaism, the Western Wall of the Second Temple. Israel also met some reverses against Syria, leading to the creation of three small demilitarized zones west of the international border. Overall, Israel took heavy casualties, with fatalities about one percent of the total population. And yet there was no mistaking Israel's historic achievement. By July 1949, when the final armistice agreements were signed, not only had the Jews defeated four invading armies, not only had they secured their first independent state since the Romans, but they had annexed an additional 23 percent of mandatory Palestine (see Maps). Despite repeated Arab vows to sweep Zionists into the sea, a Jewish state had taken root in the heart of the Muslim world. This dramatic triumph nurtured an Israeli national consciousness among disparate Jewish immigrants. But in the Arab world, a sense of failure would dominate political discourse for decades.

Refugees: Palestinian

If the Arab world at large had reason to regret this outcome, the suffering of Palestinians was particularly acute. Probably between 600,000 and 850,000 Palestinian Arabs, over half those in the mandate and some 65–85 percent of those within Israel's 1949 borders, were expelled or fled from their homes.[10] Religious and educational institutions, economic enterprises, family networks all were shattered, and Palestinians were scattered across the Arab lands. Refugees seethed with anger against the Zionists and against the wider world that allowed such a monumental crime to occur. Palestinian art and literature, not to mention politics, proclaimed—and continue to express—an all-encompassing sense of anguish, loss, and injustice.

The exodus is of far more than historical or humanitarian interest, for it raises political questions that remain at the heart of the Mideast conflict: Who was responsible? What should happen to the refugees? What would constitute a just settlement of the refugee issue?

In the Arab narrative, the Jews expelled the Palestinians with predetermination and without justification. The war of 1947–1948 provided no more than a welcome excuse to implement a program of systematic ethnic cleansing that Zionists had long intended. This interpretation indicts Israel as a state, born in sin, that is fundamentally illegitimate, while preserving the Palestinians' self-image as blameless victims.[11]

The Israeli narrative argues that there was no preconceived plan, that many Arabs fled voluntarily or in response to their leaders' requests, and that any Jewish expulsion of Arabs that did occur responded to wartime necessity. Had Palestinians not initiated hostilities, there would have been no exodus. This view preserves Israel's claim to be more moral than its violent neighbors, and thus more entitled to Western support.[12]

---

9   Ahron Bregman, *Israel's Wars* (2nd ed., London: Routledge, 2000), 27. See Avi Shlaim, *Collusion Across the Jordan* (New York: Columbia University Press, 1988).

10   See p. 8 n. 4 *supra,* plus Gelvin, *Israel–Palestine Conflict,* 135.

11   For partisan statements of this view, see Esber, *Under the Cover of War*; Ilan Pappe, *The Ethnic Cleansing of Palestine* (Oxford: One World, 2006); Nur Masalha, *Expulsion of the Palestinians* (Washington, DC: Institute for Palestine Studies, 1992).

12   For a partisan statement of the Zionist position, see Karsh, *Palestine Betrayed*; idem, *The Arab–Israeli Conflict: The Palestine War 1948* (Oxford: Osprey Publishing, 2002).

Again, each statement captures only part of a complex dynamic. As with any major event, it is useful to distinguish between long-term causes and short–term precipitants. One long-term factor was the close interpenetration of Jewish and Arab settlement, which prevented either defeated party from finding easy local refuge, and made flight the logical option. Given this residential pattern, along with the rejection by both sides of a binational solution and the depth of Arab fears, large-scale flight was virtually inevitable once the battle began to turn against the Palestinians.

At the same time, Palestinian society in 1947 was particularly predisposed to fragment because of weak cross-class and supra-local linkages, to which we have referred. By extension, the inadequacy of Arab institutions for education, transport, health care, and governance obliged Arabs to rely far more heavily on British services than did the Jews. But in late 1947, when the exodus began, the British were about to leave. Limited Palestinian cohesion and an associated dependence on the departing British thus constituted a second precondition for the exodus.

A third was the growing inclination among Yishuv leaders to regard population transfer as a legitimate and attractive option. To be sure, this never became official policy, which to 1948 and beyond insisted that Palestine had ample room for both peoples. Zionist leaders dared not speak openly about the possibility of transfer, for fear of antagonizing both Arabs and Israel's Western supporters. Israel's Declaration of Independence promised "full and equal citizenship" to Arabs and Jews. Nor was this merely for external consumption: in March 1948 Haganah orders issued in Hebrew in secret (not in English for propaganda), told all officers to secure "the full rights, needs, and freedom of the Arabs in the Hebrew state without discrimination" and to strive for "co-existence with freedom and respect."[13] And yet as a practical matter, between 1937 and 1947 more and more Zionist leaders (and indeed, many non-Jewish statesmen in England, America, and Arab capitals) assumed that partition would be accompanied by an Arab exodus, whether forcible or voluntary, from Jewish areas. Transfer, one could say, was in the air. Once Arab forces sought to destroy the Jewish community, once Jews felt they had to choose between national survival and moral purity, this legacy conditioned Jews to regard transfer not only as natural, but as highly desirable.[14]

A final background factor was fear engendered by reciprocal stereotyping. Believing that they faced extermination by an inhuman foe, both communities were primed for flight. But the fact that Jews really had no place to go, whereas Palestinians could enter neighboring Arab lands, undermined Palestinian steadfastness and left them more mobile.

In response to such factors, the exodus unfolded in a series of stages that have been charted by Benny Morris, the most widely respected authority on this matter.[15] From December 1947 until March 1948, while the Yishuv was yet on the defensive, the general deterioration in security, the decline of British services on which Arabs relied, Stern Gang terrorism, and intra-Arab disorders precipitated the flight of many middle and upper-class Palestinians. These were the Arabs who could best afford to move, perhaps 75,000 total. A similar elite displacement had occurred during the early stages of the Arab Revolt of 1936–1939.

From April to July 1948, the flight of the upper classes, an ensuing rise in unemployment, and British withdrawal further sapped Arab morale. Yet in March 1948, it was the Jewish decision to switch from defense to offense—prompted by fears that if they did not change strategy, Jerusalem would fall, America would withdraw support, and

---

13   Benny Morris, "And Now for Some Facts," *The New Republic*, May 8, 2006, 28.

14   Morris, *Righteous Victims*, 252–58; Morris, *Birth of the Palestinian Refugee Problem*, ch. 2.

15   See Morris, *Birth of the Palestinian Refugee Problem*; *idem, 1948*. My analysis of both background factors and stages of the exodus relies substantially on Morris. Good overviews may also be found at Tessler, *History of the Israeli–Palestinian Conflict*, 291–307; Sachar, *History of Israel*, 330–36; Kimmerling and Migdal, *Palestinian People*, ch. 5.

the entire Zionist project would collapse—that proved most critical. After March, mass Arab flight almost always came in anticipation, or in the aftermath, of Jewish military assaults. Lacking sufficient troops to garrison hostile communities, Jewish leaders saw no alternative to emptying strategic districts behind their front lines so as to link up major concentrations of Jewish population and secure their borders before Arab state armies invaded. In this period, the Haganah's Plan D, which specifically authorized Jewish commanders to evict or garrison hostile populations, provided sanction for almost any action that local officers chose to take, in effect opening the door to large-scale expulsions. Thus, extensive districts in the Galilee, the coastal plain, and the northern Negev that had been Arab for many centuries suddenly lost the vast bulk of their Arab inhabitants. These months also saw Jews conduct a number of brutal massacres of prisoners and civilians, the most infamous of which was the killing of at least 93 Arabs by the Irgun and the Stern Gang in the village of Deir Yassin, near the road to Jerusalem. The vast majority of victims in Deir Yassin were unarmed civilians, including women and children, many of whom were murdered as they emerged from their homes to surrender.

Admittedly, local Jewish actions varied quite considerably, with the Jewish mayor of Haifa imploring Arabs not to leave and with Arab villages in much of the Galilee remaining unharmed. There was never any master plan of expulsion, as confirmed by the fact that at the end of the war 150,000 to 160,000 Arabs remained within Israel. However, it is clear that in the spring of 1948, with Jews feeling that their backs were against the sea, and with the impending pan-Arab invasion hardening IDF hearts, Zionist actions—and the fear of such actions—turned a limited Arab exodus into a panicked flight of perhaps 300,000 additional refugees.

Finally, from July to November 1948, as IDF victories multiplied, many Jewish commanders became yet more enthusiastic about the benefits of Arab departures, and forced or encouraged the departure of another 300,000 to 350,000 demoralized Palestinians. At this point, when Jews clearly

had the upper hand, strategic considerations became less important than the simple desire to reduce a disloyal or suspect population and to seize their property. Contrary to some Zionist accounts, at no stage is there evidence that vast numbers of Palestinians moved in response to requests from Arab leaders abroad. Moreover, once Arabs fled an area, even after hostilities ended, the IDF quickly adopted a policy of forcibly preventing their return. Indeed, the Israeli government deliberately destroyed most of the roughly 350 abandoned Arab villages and towns.[16]

As part of a proposed peace agreement, in December 1948 UN General Assembly Resolution 194 said that those "refugees wishing to return to their homes and live at peace with their neighbors should be permitted to do so at the earliest practicable date." This resolution would provide the basis for Palestinian insistence, not much less vigorous in 2011 than in 1949, that refugees and their descendants have an inalienable "right of return" to Israel. The Truman administration, Israel's ally, agreed that Israel had a humanitarian responsibility to take back a substantial number, perhaps 200,000 or 300,000, and expressed strong disapproval when Israel demurred. In response to American and European pressure, in mid–1949 Israel offered limited repatriation as part of an overall peace settlement. It agreed *either* to take back 100,000 refugees *or* to annex Gaza, which held some 200,000 refugees. But both offers stipulated that Arab countries first accept Resolution 181 and recognize the Jewish state. Arab leaders found these proposals completely inadequate, and no progress was made on the refugee issue.

Refugees: Jewish

The expulsion and flight of Arabs from Israel was the best known, but by no means the only, massive population displacement growing from the events of 1947–1949, for it paralleled the reverse expulsion/flight of Jews from Arab lands to Israel. In essence, these twinned movements

---

16   Kimmerling and Migdal, *Palestinian People*, 165.

reflected the postwar transformation of multi-ethnic empires, Ottoman and then British, into more exclusive national units. As such, they mirrored the exchange at the end of World War One or World War Two of Greeks and Turks within what was once the Ottoman Empire; of German and Slavic populations within the old Austro-Hungarian, Prussian, and Russian empires; and of Hindus and Muslims within the former British Empire. Empires, operating in autocratic fashion above society, had easily accommodated ethnic and religious minorities. But nationalist movements, each speaking from below in the name of a unified "people," were inherently far more intolerant.

In thrall to such exclusionary logic, Arabs, as well as Zionists, embraced ideas of population transfer and expulsion. In effect, Jewish nationalism and various Arab nationalisms became co-heirs to the Ottoman and British imperial legacies. The story of 1947–1949, therefore, is by no means simply a story of Jews displacing Arabs—rather, it is a tale of mutual large-scale exclusion.

Indeed, in Arab circles the idea of physical expulsion was expressed more openly, with less self-censorship and embarrassment, than among Jews. In part this was because the Jews' alien origins and small numbers made expelling them more "natural" and feasible than expelling Arabs, who had been in continuous occupation of Palestine for centuries, and who, until 1948, remained a large majority. Moreover, Zionists had absorbed European liberal assumptions that a modern state could be true to a national ideal and still grant equal rights to religious and ethnic minorities.[17]   Arab thinkers had less exposure to—and less sympathy for—Western liberalism. Not only did prominent Arabs call unapologetically for the Jews' physical annihilation, and not only did Jordan later forbid citizenship to Jews, but Palestinian and Arab forces from 1947 to 1949 expelled from their homes virtually every Jew they encountered. In the Haifa oil refinery, in the Etzion Bloc south of Jerusalem, and en route

---

17   *Cf.* Bernard Reich, *A Brief History of Israel* (New York: Checkmark Books, 2008), 47.

to the Hadassah Hospital in Jerusalem, they also massacred fighters who had surrendered and unarmed Jewish civilians, including doctors and nurses, with brutality and on a scale comparable to Deir Yassin.

Arab military weakness ensured that the number of Jews displaced within the territory of the old mandate remained small, probably fewer than 10,000. Starting in 1948, however, somewhere between 550,000 and 800,000 Jews also fled or were expelled from countries around the Arab world. These displacements too reflected the growth of exclusionary nationalisms, in both its pan-Arab and local variants, in lands that had been part of the Ottoman Empire and/or had been occupied by Europeans.

Serious anti-Jewish, anti-Zionist agitation began in Iraq, Syria, Lebanon, and Egypt in the 1930s, but it was the fighting in Palestine in 1947 that, as noted, sparked Arab outrage and demands for retaliation against local Jewish communities. From 1947 to 1955, anti-Jewish legislation, economic boycotts, and lethal mob attacks helped to persuade the bulk of Syrian Jews, and virtually the entire Jewish populations of Libya, Yemen, and Iraq, to flee, with the great majority moving to Israel. From 1955 to 1967, notwithstanding well-intentioned official efforts to halt the exodus from Morocco and Tunisia, once those countries and Algeria gained their independence from France, a similar wave of pan-Arab, anti-Jewish agitation contributed to a mass exodus of North African Jews. Apart from those in Algeria, again most left for Israel. In Egypt, too, after the 1956 war with Israel, anti-Jewish agitation, dismissal of Jewish employees, and well-advertised arrests of prominent Jews quickly eviscerated the community. All told, whereas 65–85 percent of Palestinian Arabs fled Israel, by 1967 some 95 percent of Jews had abandoned their homes in Arab lands, where Hebrew communities had flourished since antiquity.

This Jewish exodus differed from the Palestinian exodus in at least three respects. First, Palestinian displacement came first and was more concentrated, while Arab displacement of Jews was in some sense retaliatory, and extended over a longer period. Thus, whereas *al-Nakba,* the Catastrophe, was restricted to 1947 to 1949,[18] the chronology of Jewish flight stretched from 1948 to 1967 and beyond. Second, Palestinian motivation was invariably negative—before the fighting, no Palestinians wanted to leave their homes— whereas many Jews were attracted to Israel by Zionist and/or messianic sentiment, or by hopes of improved livelihood. Religious inspiration, for example, was important among Yemeni Jews, while economic aspirations influenced many in Tunisia and Morocco. By the same token, whereas Arab leaders rarely urged Palestinians to leave their homes, Zionist organizations devoted considerable resources to encouraging Jewish departures from Iraq, Yemen, and elsewhere. Third, by starting the fighting in 1947, Palestinians bore a not inconsiderable degree of responsibility for their own fate, but the cowed Jewish minorities of Arab lands never offered any provocation. That is to say, there was a plausible security rationale for Palestinian expulsion, but none for Jewish expulsion.

The two refugee movements resembled one another in that both were triggered by hostilities in Palestine starting in late 1947 and were similar in size. Both destroyed long-established communities, inflicting enormous psychological pain and material loss. More basic, both expressed in graphic form the host population's yearning for national homogeneity. In effect, Jewish and Arab nationalists produced a double displacement all across the Mideast, where multiethnic, pre–national empires once held sway. On both sides a desire to confiscate refugee property whetted the appetite for expulsion. One credible estimate puts the value of Jewish assets seized in Arab lands at $6 billion,[19] while in Israel, one in three Jews

soon lived on property seized from Arab refugees. Finally, much as Palestinian refugees became implacably hostile to Israel, embittered Jewish refugees from Arab lands became one of the most consistently anti-Arab political constituencies within the new Jewish state.

Why did Israel not seek political advantage by emphasizing the plight of Jewish refugees the way Arab states drew attention to the suffering of Palestinians? Why is the Jewish expulsion relatively unknown? Both movements benefited Israel directly, the one by reducing an unwelcome minority, the other by expanding Israel's Jewish base. The last thing Israel's leaders wanted to hear in 1949 (or indeed in 2011) was an Arab offer to repatriate Jewish refugees in return for the repatriation of Palestinian refugees. Political self–interest therefore told Israel to say as little as possible about the entire issue of refugee displacement. However, a similar logic impelled Arabs to highlight at least the Palestinian half of the equation, in the hope of reversing a development that had gravely weakened them.

But if Arab leaders wanted to destroy Israel, why did they consent in the first place to the large-scale strengthening of Israel's population? Often officials were enticed by bribes, or more critically, by the prospect of seizing Jewish wealth. In some cases, they assumed that the large-scale entry of diseased, malnourished, and aged refugees actually would overwhelm Israel's fragile economy. In other instances, they complied with international requests to release local Jews on humanitarian grounds.

Israeli and Palestinian Societies, 1949 to 1967

Between 1949 and 1967 both Jews and Palestinians grappled with the legacies of the War of Independence/the Catastrophe. Jews, of course,

---

18   Note, however, that the 1967 war prompted a further displacement from the West Bank to Jordan of perhaps 230,000 Palestinians, some 60,000 of whom later returned. Tessler, *History of the Israeli–Palestinian Conflict,* 402–403.

19   In contemporary values. "Jews Displaced from Arabs Lands Finally Recognized," *Ha'aretz,* March 12, 2010. This was probably larger than Arab properties,

but how much larger is unclear. See too Malka Hillel Shulewitz, ed., *The Forgotten Millions* (London: Continuum, 1999).

exulted in their hard-won independence.[20] Yet at the same time, they faced intimidating demands: to withstand continuing Arab state hostility, to create a viable political system, settle a flood of Jewish immigrants, develop the economy, and pacify Israel's Arab minority. In addressing these problems, Israel could call on the legacy of the Yishuv, the technical skills of European Jews, and high levels of external support.

At its birth, Israel already had a political system inherited from the Yishuv that allowed it to avoid the extremes of dictatorship and ungovernability experienced by many newly independent states. The prewar Elected Assembly was now reborn as the Knesset, which chose the Prime Minister, while prewar administrative departments under the Jewish Agency quickly morphed into governmental ministries. Like its predecessor, the Knesset was chosen by proportional representation,[21] which in turn made necessary coalition governments involving multiple—often fractious—parties. Although prone to patronage and instability, this setup accommodated diverse interests and allowed Israel, under the leadership of Ben–Gurion and his Israel Workers Party (Mapai),[22] to address successfully the central domestic challenges of immigrant absorption and economic growth.

In Israel's first eight years, the population tripled (to roughly two million) through the large-scale arrival, first of European Jews—Ashkenazi Jews—and then of Jews from Muslim lands. By 1955 the latter, known as Mizrahi Jews,

accounted for 92 percent of all newcomers.[23] All too frequently diseased and illiterate, many Mizrahi Jews found Ashkenazi norms and prejudices intimidating. Recognizing the danger of national fragmentation, which was all the greater in that both Ashkenazim and Mizrahim were internally divided by their communities of origin, the government instituted compensatory school programs for disadvantaged Mizrahi youth. Additionally, the government abandoned its initial insistence on rapid assimilation in favor of cultural pluralism, and stressed the unifying value of a common language (Hebrew), of war commemorations, and especially, of universal military service. Indeed, as an instrument—along with the public school system—of Hebrew–language education and of national integration, the IDF arguably became Israel's premier institution. By the late 1960s, the Ashkenazi–Mizrahi educational and income gap was eroding, and almost 20 percent of all marriages were between European and Afro-Asian Jews—a proportion that would rise steadily thereafter.

In Israel's first years, wartime damage, the burdens of massive immigrant absorption, and socialist inefficiencies severely overstrained the economy. From the mid-1950s, however, immigration and reconstruction demands began to ease, while socialist policies were supplemented by more effective market mechanisms. More critical, Israel began to receive modest U.S. aid, substantial West German reparations for the Holocaust, and extremely generous support from world Jewry. Along with improved economic management, sustained but controlled immigration, and an increasingly productive workforce, such capital inflows let Israel settle broad interior regions and diversify industrial production. In the 1960s economic growth accelerated through massive infrastructural projects, including a national water system that sent water from the Sea of Galilee to the coast and to the arid northern Negev, and new

---

20　On Israeli political, economic, and social history to 1967, Sachar, *History of Israel*, chs. 14–20.

21　That is to say, voters chose parties on a national basis, and each party got seats in the Knesset based on the percentage of the national vote it obtained. This contrasts with the American system of constituencies, wherein voters choose a congressman for their local district.

22　Ben–Gurion was Prime Minister from 1948 to 1963, except for a brief interlude from late 1953 to 1955. Mapai remained in power until 1968, when it merged with two other groups to form the Israel Labor Party, which in turn held power to 1977. *Cf.* p. 16, n. 4 *supra*.

23　Mizrahim ("those from the East") often are also called Sephardim, although the latter term, referring specifically to Jews whose ancestors left Spain, generally is less accurate.

port facilities at Ashdod on the Mediterranean and Eilat on the Gulf of Aqaba. The latter became Israel's gateway to Asia and East Africa. In all, from 1952 to 1965, Israel's GNP grew by 250 percent, industrial output quadrupled, with growth particularly marked in machinery, electronics, and chemicals; and the population became more evenly distributed around the country.

Meanwhile how did Israel's non-Jewish Arab minority, some 15 percent in early 1949, fare? The answer depends on one's yardstick. Given that Israeli Arabs were citizens of the Mideast's only functional democracy, they enjoyed political rights—including the right to vote in free multiparty elections and to organize their own political parties—unknown to the vast bulk of Arabs outside Israel. In 1951 Israeli Arab women became the first in the Arab world to gain legal equality. In terms of physical welfare too, Israeli Arabs did well by regional standards. Improved infant health care made possible one of the world's highest population growth rates, Arab agrarian productivity rose sharply, and levels of Arab school enrollment were rarely matched elsewhere in the Mideast.[24] Compared to ravaged Jewish communities, and indeed many non-Jewish minorities, in Arab countries, none of which faced a security threat comparable to that facing Israel, their situation was also attractive.

The picture looks quite different, however, if one compares Israeli Arabs, not to people outside Israel, but to their Jewish fellow citizens—a comparison they themselves made most easily. Arab cultural legacies, discrimination at the hands of Jews, educational facilities generally inferior to those of Jews, and IDF restrictions on Arab labor mobility all ensured that Arabs usually held the least-skilled, poorest-paying jobs. In border areas until 1966, martial law, sometimes brutally applied, curtailed not only Arab movement, but freedom of expression and organization. Laws designed to prevent Arabs from reclaiming property lost in 1948 produced a bitterly resented confiscation of up to 40 percent of Arab lands in Israel, for which compensation was often

inadequate. Above all, Israeli Arabs suffered from a sense of marginality and isolation. Distrusted as a potential fifth column, they lived in a country whose flag, anthem, army, and national holidays were for Jews only, and reminded them of their own dispossession. At the same time, until 1967, they were generally cut off from the wider Arab world.[25]

Palestinians outside Israel experienced much the same loss of autonomy as their brothers and sisters within Israel, but in this case the agents of Palestinian dependence were neighboring Arab states. Transjordan and Israel, we saw, agreed to divide between themselves the lands that the UN had allocated to a Palestinian Arab state. In 1950 Transjordan officially annexed those lands west of the Jordan River, currently known as the West Bank—thus, Transjordan was renamed Jordan— and extended citizenship to its Palestinian residents. Given that two-thirds of his subjects were now Palestinians (indeed two out of three of all Palestinians lived in Jordan), the Hashemite monarch Abdullah naturally sought to present himself as sympathetic to Palestinian aspirations. But in practice, what he and his successor, King Hussein (r. 1952–1999), sought, above all, was Jordanian national cohesion and stability, which meant suppressing not only Palestinian irredentism directed against Israel, but expressions of a separate Palestinian identity. Post-1949 tensions between Israel and Jordan notwithstanding, they therefore were united in their hostility to Palestinian nationalism. In Jordan, the word "Palestine" in official documents was outlawed,[26] along with commemorations of the Catastrophe and all political parties. To ensure that Palestinians did not capture the state apparatus, the monarchy entrusted the army and security services to

---

24 Sachar, *History of Israel*, 532–38.

25 The Arab Druze community developed a much closer relation with the Jewish state than did other Arabs, often serving in the IDF, and benefited accordingly. On Arabs in Israel, Kimmerling and Migdal, *Palestinian People*, ch. 6; Farsoun and Aruri, *Palestine and the Palestinians*, ch. 5.

26 David Lesch, *The Arab–Israeli Conflict* (New York: Oxford University Press, 2008), 163.

loyal Bedouins in the eastern part of the kingdom. These policies enjoyed some success insofar as many wealthier, better-educated Palestinians moved to the East Bank, integrated themselves into local economic and political structures, and internalized a Jordanian persona.

However, the great bulk of Palestinians, especially those in refugee camps and those on the West Bank, resisted any resettlement plans that implied abandoning their claims to return to their homes in what had become Israel. Until that hope was realized, most preferred to remain in the camps supported by the United Nations Relief and Works Agency (UNRWA), which provided basic food, shelter, and education. In the 1950s and 1960s, three themes suffused Palestinian fiction, poetry, and art, not to mention political expression: the bitterness of exile, which was likened to the separation of a child from its mother or a lover from his beloved; the idealization of a lost past in Arab Palestine; and the yearning for return and redemption.[27]

If anything, refugee conditions in other Arab states often were worse than in Jordan. In the tiny Gaza Strip, for example, which came under Egyptian control, population densities were higher, the economy weaker, and refugees more isolated than in the West Bank. Not only did the Sinai desert interpose between Gaza and Egypt proper, and not only did the refugees reject plans to help them resettle in Sinai, but the Egyptian government, unlike Jordan, refused to grant Palestinians citizenship—which merely heightened their sense of marginality. Like Jordan, Egypt claimed to champion Palestinian interests, but kept refugees from forming independent political organizations. In Lebanon, Syria, and Iraq, smaller refugee populations also faced a variety of restrictions imposed variously to prevent economic competition with local people, to forestall instability, and to preserve the refugees as a political tool against Israel.

Thus, in Arab states as well as in Israel, Palestinians tended to become an underclass substantially isolated from the host population without an authentic national voice. Whereas Jews from diverse locales gathered in Israel and developed an increasingly cohesive national identity, Palestinians were scattered in several countries, none particularly supportive of Palestinian aspirations. Faced with an unfamiliar, often hostile environment, refugees, particularly in the camps, tended to retain—indeed, reinforce—the institutions of family, clan, and village that had sustained them before their dispersal.

And yet the late 1950s and 1960s also saw impressive elements of dynamism that pointed Palestinian society in new and more promising directions. Partly through UNRWA and partly through advanced schooling in Arab, European, and American institutions, many Palestinians became increasingly well educated and economically competitive. This led to employment opportunities in Europe, North America, and especially the Gulf states and Saudi Arabia, opportunities that in turn fostered a Palestinian global diaspora reminiscent, ironically, of the Jewish diaspora in its concern with education and self–improvement.[28] Members of this diasporic community, who maintained close ties to those still in the refugee camps but who at the same time represented a new social element, shared an emphasis on uplift and social mobility, a determination to retain and nurture a distinctive Palestinian identity—as well as a visceral hatred of Israel. As we shall see, it was from the ranks of this emergent elite, many of relatively humble origins, that fresh political organizations would emerge, among which Fatah would become preeminent.

Israel and the Arab States, 1949 to 1967

Independent Palestinian political groups, however, would not come into their own until the late 1960s. For almost two decades after 1949, the very name "Palestinian" (which even before 1949

27 Kimmerling and Migdal, *Palestinian People*, ch. 7. On the Palestinian diaspora, see too Farsoun and Aruri, *Palestine and the Palestinians*, ch. 4.

28 *Cf.* Sayigh, *Armed Struggle*, 88.

had limited currency) tended to fall into disuse, while the collapse of Palestinian social and political institutions removed Palestinians as players in Mideast politics. Israeli relations with the Arab world until 1967 thus focused almost entirely on Arab governments, who spoke in the name of the refugees, but who often remained more concerned with their own national interests.

For some years after the armistice agreements of 1949, many observers held out hope that Israel and the Arab states would resolve their differences. Israel wanted to guarantee its borders and reduce its heavy military burden. Israel's neighbors also wanted to stabilize frontiers, to relieve Palestinian distress, and in the case of Jordan to obtain a Mediterranean trade outlet. Flickering optimism persisted as late as 1955, when Israel, Jordan, and Syria seemed ready to accept a U.S. plan to share the waters of the Jordan under an arrangement modeled on the Tennessee Valley Authority.

In the end, such hopes were blighted by intransigence on both sides. Israel continued to refuse what Arabs considered minimal concessions on the refugee issue. Israel justified its position by arguing, first, that Arabs had rejected the UN partition and had initiated the violence that led to the displacement; second, that no other major group of postwar refugees had ever returned; third, that if Israel could absorb Jews expelled from Arab lands, Arab countries could do the same with Palestinians; and fourth and most basically, that hundreds of thousands of bitter returnees would threaten Israel's very survival. Although rarely acknowledged, powerful economic considerations also barred the way: By 1954, as noted, one-third of Israeli Jews lived on absentee property, and some 60 percent of Israel's land consisted of tracts once owned by Arabs. In essence, Israel had the land and demography it wanted—and was loath to give up those hard assets for what it feared would be empty gestures of peace. Israel maintained this stance despite considerable U.S. pressure, with Ben-Gurion declaring at one point,

"The United States is a powerful country. Israel is a small and weak one. We can be crushed, but we will not commit suicide."[29]

The ascendancy within the Israeli government of security-first pragmatists, led by Ben-Gurion and the IDF Chief of Staff General Moshe Dayan, over more dovish elements eager to explore the possibilities of reconciliation led to a series of provocative Israeli actions that helped to polarize Arab–Israeli opinion. In 1954, for example, fearful that a scheduled British military pullout from the Suez Canal Zone might encourage Egypt to threaten Israel, an IDF intelligence unit organized a bombing campaign against Western targets in Egypt in the hope that Britain would blame Egyptians and halt their withdrawal. In fact, this crude plot was soon uncovered, and served only to poison Israeli–Egyptian relations at a time when, some argue, Egypt's new leader, Gamal Abdel Nasser, might have been receptive to détente. Israel's vigorous, deliberately disproportionate military response to cross-border guerrilla raids from Egypt and Jordan had a similar chilling impact on Israeli–Arab relations.[30]

If Jews could summon little sympathy for the plight of the Palestinians or for the concerns of Arab governments, Arab leaders had no more interest in the fears of the Jews. As the Palestinian–American scholar Edward Said argued, 1948 traumatized Arab societies, promoting an abiding sense of humiliation, a distrust of Western values, and a yearning for strong military leaders who could redeem Arab honor.[31] What was seen as the Palestinians' totally unjust expulsion at the hands of Jews, a historically inferior group, became emblematic of Arab self-doubt and resentment. Under the press of such attitudes, not only were a string of leaders sympathetic to compromise— including Jordan's King Abdullah—assassinated by hard-line opponents, but Arab states moved to isolate and weaken the new Jewish state. Thus,

29 Sachar, *History of Israel*, 439–40. Land and property statistics at *ibid.*, 437–38.

30 Shlaim, *Iron Wall,* chs. 2–4.

31 Edward Said, "Afterword: The Consequences of 1948," in Rogan and Shlaim, *War for Palestine*, 248–61.

Jordan and Syria finally rejected the American plan, accepted by Israel, to share the waters of the Jordan. The Arab League and its member states also imposed a diplomatic and economic boycott on Israel; turned a blind eye to, if they did not actively encourage, raids by Palestinian guerrillas into Israel; and backed Egypt's decision to close both the Suez Canal and the Gulf of Aqaba to ships going to or from Israel. In 1955 Nasser, Egypt's charismatic strongman who sought to lead the Arab world, signed a major arms deal with the Soviet Union. Although its main goal was to counter Western—or, as Nasser termed it, "neo-colonial"—influence in the Mideast, Egypt's arms acquisition had obvious implications for the strategic balance with Israel.

In fact, in the early and mid-1950s, most newly independent Arab regimes were too preoccupied with internal problems to risk a second war with Israel.[32] Anti-Israel measures often were designed more for internal consumption, to demonstrate firmness and to uphold honor, than as an indication of practical military action. Not surprisingly, however, Israel, having just survived an invasion by four Arab armies, was inclined to take Arab statements and demonstrations of continued belligerency at face value.

But Israel faced a strategic dilemma: With a tiny population and territory, how could the country meet more or less continuous threats without permanently mobilizing a large military force, and thus crippling its economy? Israel's solution, developed in the course of the 1950s, was twofold. First, on the Swiss model, Israel combined a small, full-time professional force with a large reserve army of civilians, male and female, who could be mobilized in emergencies. Second, to prevent its enemies from overwhelming the professional nucleus before reserves could be called up, in times of danger Israel committed itself to strike the first blow on Arab, not Israeli, soil.[33] This, in turn, required a rapid mobile army,

with large tank units and an extraordinarily high proportion of combat soldiers.

In 1956 Israel experimented with this strategy in a war fought in alliance with Britain and France against Egypt, a war that Arabs—with apt justification—referred to as the Tripartite Aggression. This was the result of a curious diplomatic realignment. From 1949 to 1955, Israel had sought in vain for a great power ally. President Dwight Eisenhower did not share Truman's pro-Israel sympathy, arguing that aid to Israel was pointless since Israel could never survive in the long term. Realizing that ties to American Jewry precluded Israel's supporting the Communist bloc, in the early 1950s the Soviet Union, one of Israel's early patrons, switched to an emphatically pro-Arab, anti-Israel policy. But in late 1955 and 1956, Israel found allies in France, which deeply resented Nasser's pan-Arab support for rebels in French Algeria, and—most surprisingly—in Britain. Despite its Arab sympathies and bitter memories of Jewish attacks, London decided that Nasser's decision in July 1956 to nationalize the Suez Canal, the vital link to Asia, posed an intolerable threat to Britain's global economic and strategic interests. For its part, Israel wanted to reduce or eliminate the danger posed by Nasser's pan-Arab appeals, his acquisition of Soviet arms, and his ever bolder sponsorship of guerrilla raids from Gaza. Israel also sought to open the Gulf of Aqaba, and perhaps even the Suez Canal, to Jewish shipping. In late October and early November 1956, Israel and its new European friends, therefore, joined in an attack on Egypt designed to restrain, and ideally to overthrow, Nasser.

For Britain and France, it was an undisguised fiasco. Unexpectedly strong American as well as Soviet opposition forced them to pull their forces from Egypt with Nasser not only remaining in power, but with his international reputation as defender of the Arabs against neocolonial aggression vastly enhanced. Israeli airborne and armored units quickly captured all of Egypt's Sinai peninsula, but under intense American

---

32 Sayigh, *Armed Struggle*, 12–13.

33 Although the doctrine of preemptive strike was fully articulated only after 1956, in the early 1950s its

advantages were already becoming recognized. Bregman, *Israel's Wars*, 47.

and international pressure, Israel too was obliged to withdraw to prewar positions. No less than its European allies, Israel had reason to regret Nasser's heightened political stature and the withering criticism that the international community, African and Asian countries in particular, directed against Israel's blatant disregard for Egyptian sovereignty.

But at the same time, the Sinai campaign of 1956 had three beneficial results for Israel: 1) Reserve mobilization and the first–strike doctrine worked perfectly. Sinai thus confirmed the lesson of 1948–1949, that the IDF could overcome numerical weakness with organizational and technical superiority. By crushing Egypt's army in a matter of days, the IDF began to win recognition as the strongest army in the Mideast. No longer did Eisenhower, for example, suggest that to satisfy the Arabs, Israel should give up the Negev. 2) To secure Israeli withdrawal, Nasser had to open the Gulf of Aqaba (though not the Suez Canal) to Israeli shipping, halt guerrilla raids from Gaza, limit his forces in Sinai, and let UN forces in Sinai supervise these undertakings. Although some of these concessions were tacit rather than formal (and Nasser would later retract most of them), from 1956 to 1967 Sinai provided Israel with an effective territorial buffer against Egypt. Moreover, opening the Gulf of Aqaba spurred Israeli trade with Asia and Africa, which, in turn, aided development in the Negev. 3) The year 1956 sealed the alliance with France, which had already sold to Israel advanced aircraft and weaponry. France not only stepped up those supplies, but began providing nuclear expertise that contributed to Israel's development of nuclear weapons.

Its self-confidence thus enhanced, in the decade after Sinai, Israel expanded its external ties. While nurturing the French alliance, it developed a close relation to West Germany—whose leaders, in return for substantial economic aid to Israel, sought moral absolution from Nazism's chief victims. In the 1960s, once the Democrats regained the White House, and especially after the 1967 war, American–Israeli relations improved. To circumvent the Arab diplomatic and economic boycott, and to counter its association with

European neocolonialism, Israel also reached out to countries in Southeast Asia, and more especially in sub-Saharan Africa, where in the 1960s it developed extensive missions of economic and technical assistance.

The Six Day War of 1967

If Israel's battlefield success in 1956 was impressive, the Six Day War of June 5 to 10, 1967, proved far more transformative in both an immediate and long-term sense. First, the Six Day War showed even more convincingly than the 1956 conflict that Israel had become the dominant regional military power. This was Israel's most decisive—also its last unequivocal—victory over an Arab state army. Second, its 1967 triumph provided Israel for the first time with strategic depth. No longer did Israel's heartland lie in easy reach of Arab planes or artillery. Third, conquest of Jerusalem and the West Bank, the heart of the biblical Land of Israel, breathed life into Jewish religious nationalism and began to encourage a movement of colonization reminiscent of the early Yishuv. Finally—and perhaps of greatest long–term significance—the Six Day War gave Israel control over 1,100,000 additional Palestinians, residents of the West Bank and Gaza. By abrading Palestinian ties to Jordan, Israel's victory effectively killed the 17-year-old project to assimilate West Bank Palestinians to a Jordanian identity, and thus—quite unwittingly—resurrected the question of the Palestinians' political future. After 1967 Palestinians began to reclaim the political stage from which they had been ejected by the events of 1936 to 1949. In all these ways, although its full implications would not be apparent for decades, the Six Day War was a watershed, second only to the War of Independence/the Catastrophe.

The Six Day War arose not merely from hostility between Israel and the Arab states, although this was obviously the chief source of tension, but also from rivalries between Arab states and between the United States and the Soviet Union. Chastened by the military campaigns of 1956 and burdened with domestic problems, Nasser, for one, could be quite circumspect in dealing with the Jewish state. Yet despite his cautious instincts, he and other Arab leaders found themselves compelled to adopt ever more aggressive rhetorical and eventually practical positions. The novelty of most Arab nation–states, and the fact that they had not yet developed stable political institutions—from 1949 to 1966, Syria alone experienced nine changes of government by military coup—left many Arab leaders highly vulnerable to domestic challenge. Given deep popular anger against Israel, one of the surest ways to gain support was to take strong public stands against the Jewish state, and when possible, to match rhetoric with military action.

This dynamic was reinforced by two sets of intra-Arab rivalries: first, between the so-called radical states (led by Egypt, Syria, and Iraq) and the so-called moderate or pro-Western states (led by Jordan and Saudi Arabia); and second, between Egypt and Syria, both of whom sought leadership of the radical bloc. Each regime tried to bolster its anti-Zionist credentials by accusing its rivals of cowardice and/or by calling ever more loudly for Israel's destruction. The Ba'athist military government of Syria, whose domination by a minority Muslim sect (Alawites) left it particularly insecure, repeatedly went beyond words by sponsoring Palestinian guerrilla attacks into Israel. Syria also sought to divert the headwaters of the Jordan River to reduce Israel's water supplies, and shelled Israeli outposts and cultivators in the demilitarized zones between the two countries. Israel's aggressive response to guerrilla raids, its recurrent threats to punish Damascus, and Israel's own frequent violations of demilitarized zones, both on land and in the Sea of Galilee, merely increased Syrian resentment and resolve. Indeed, General Moshe Dayan once admitted that Israel—not Syria—was responsible for at least 80 percent of the clashes in the demilitarized zones between the two countries from 1949 to 1967.[34]

The result was an escalating series of artillery duels and aerial dogfights along the Israeli–Syrian frontier in late 1966 and early 1967.

What finally pushed the Mideast over the cliff, however, was neither intra-Arab rivalries nor Israeli and Arab aggressiveness alone, but those elements in combination with Soviet provocation. The Soviets and the United States by this time had become locked in a complex contest for influence across the Arab world. In a general sense, by stoking Mideast tensions, the Soviets may have hoped to increase difficulties for the United States, which was already bogged down in Vietnam. More specifically, the Soviets sought to spur Nasser into action so as to relieve Israeli pressure on Syria, Russia's closest Arab ally, whose survival was critical to long-term Soviet strategy. In mid-May of 1967, Russian officials, therefore, gave out deliberately false reports that the IDF was massing troops to invade Syria. Nasser apparently knew that these claims were untrue. But having been pilloried by his enemies for "hiding behind the skirts" of the UN in Sinai, he felt that, if he were to preserve his claims to leadership of the Arab world, he now had no choice but to move against Israel. Accordingly, Nasser reintroduced seven military divisions into Sinai, demanded the departure of UN peacekeepers from Sinai, and closed the Gulf of Aqaba to Israeli shipping. With one stroke, he thus canceled all three of Israel's principal gains from the 1956 war.

If all these steps were provocative, closing the Gulf, which maritime nations in 1957 had declared an international waterway, provided Israel with a legal casus belli. According to Egypt's then Vice President Anwar Sadat, Nasser, recognizing the gravity of his actions, warned his colleagues at the time, "Now, with the concentration of our forces in Sinai the chances of war are fifty–fifty but if we close the Straits, war will be 100 percent

---

34   Bregman, *Israel's Wars*, 66. On the lead up to war in 1967, see too Michael Oren, *Six Days of War* (New York: Ballantine Books, 2003), 23; Sachar, *History of Israel*, 617–20; Tessler, *History of the Israeli–Palestinian*

Conflict, 377–87; Benny Morris, "Provocations," *The New Republic*, July 23, 2007, 47–52. Cf. Isabella Ginor and Gideon Remez, *Foxbats over Dimona* (New Haven: Yale University Press, 2007), which focuses on Soviet involvement.

certain."[35] So too Salah al-Hadidi, the Egyptian chief justice who presided over trials of officers responsible for the 1967 defeat, wrote, "I can state that Egypt's political leadership called Israel to war. It clearly provoked Israel and forced it into a confrontation."[36] As hostilities loomed, Nasser told his parliament on May 25 that the challenge facing the Arabs was "how totally to exterminate the state of Israel for all time."[37]

Yet despite his own belligerence, Nasser waited. In part, probably, he still hoped to score a propaganda victory without actually committing to battle. The Soviets, hopeful that any Israeli initiation of hostilities would provide them with a justification to intervene militarily on Egypt's behalf, urged caution. But most basically perhaps, Nasser held off because his battle plan sought to lure Israel into attacking the supposedly impregnable fortress of Abu Agheila in northeastern Sinai. There, Egypt expected to hammer to death the IDF before launching a giant tank-borne pincers operation that would trap the attackers and then push east into the Negev. The strategic depth of Sinai, which stood between Israel and Egypt's main population centers, and Egypt's large standing army meant that Nasser could afford to be patient.

But Israel, which was only nine miles wide at its narrowest point and whose army could not remain mobilized indefinitely without ruining the economy, had no such luxury. In late May and early June, Israel was not a confident society, eager for war, bent on expansion. On the contrary, it was a society in near panic, convinced that its very existence was threatened, gripped by what one observer called a "collective psychosis."[38] Holocaust survivors rushed to buy poison tablets lest they fall into the hands of the enemy. Crash programs sought to build coffins and turn public parks into cemeteries. And the Israeli Chief of Staff Yitzhak Rabin had a nervous collapse.

After last-minute U.S. diplomatic efforts to resolve the mounting crisis foundered, Israel's leaders decided to implement their first–strike doctrine. On the morning of June 5, Israeli aircraft launched a surprise attack on Egyptian airfields, flying not from the east, as might have been expected, but arcing wide across the Mediterranean and striking the Egyptian heartland from the west. In three hours, they turned 300 out of 340 combat planes into flaming wrecks, virtually destroying the Egyptian air force. Land units then opened a successful night attack on Abu Agheila, whose secrets they had discovered through intensive aerial reconnaissance and spies. Indeed, the IDF had built an exact replica of Abu Agheila in the Negev, where they practiced assaults until, as one historian noted, they could have found their way through the fortress blindfolded.[39] The fall of that mighty bastion blew open the gates to all of Sinai. With air superiority ensured, and with Egyptian escape routes in the west sealed off by Jewish mechanized units and air power, the IDF quickly surrounded Egyptian forces, seizing the entire peninsula and inflicting losses far more devastating than in 1956.

As soon as the fighting with Egypt started, Israel told King Hussein, "If you stay out we will not touch you."[40] But given the taunts of the radicals and the fervor of his Palestinian subjects, Hussein reasoned that remaining outside the war might be more politically dangerous than entering. What is more, he took at face value early Egyptian propaganda broadcasts and Nasser's personal assurance that Egyptian forces had achieved marvelous victories. Jordanian forces thus began shelling Israel's main airport, the outskirts of Tel Aviv, and Jewish West Jerusalem. Israel promptly retaliated with bombing runs, crippling Jordan's small air force, before moving ground troops in to seize the entire West Bank—the most valuable part of Hussein's patrimony, including East Jerusalem and all its holy sites—in two days of

---

35 Bregman, *Israel's Wars*, 72; Sachar, *History of Israel*, 626. Likewise, Nasser told Arab trade unionists at the time, "We knew that closing the Gulf of Aqaba meant war with Israel." Oren, *Six Days of War*, 93.

36 Oren, *Six Days of War*, 310–11.

37 Sachar, *History of Israel*, 633.

38 Shlaim, *Iron Wall*, 238.

39 Sachar, *History of Israel*, 636.

40 Bregman, *Israel's Wars*, 86.

heavy fighting. King Hussein later recalled seeing his troops in retreat: "I saw all the years that I had spent since 1953 trying to build up the country and army, all the pride, all the hopes, destroyed. … I have never received a more crushing blow than that."[41]

Frightened by the fate of Egypt and Jordan, Syria suddenly chose prudence and declined to commit troops to battle. But the IDF and, more particularly, northern residents who for years had lived within range of Syrian gunners, were determined to wreak vengeance on the regime that, in their view, had done more than any other to precipitate war. What is more, with Egypt and Jordan crippled, the IDF could concentrate all its might on Syria. Thus, in two days of bitter, often hand-to-hand combat, Israel seized the Golan Heights, from which Syrian artillery had commanded Israel's Huleh Valley.

When the guns fell silent on June 10, 1967, the Mideast had been transformed. Six days earlier, Israeli cities had been within four minutes' flying time from Arab air bases. Now the situation was reversed: Israeli planes were in easy striking distance of Damascus, Amman, and Cairo. Israel's prewar fears yielded to giddy exaltation. And Israel now controlled the Sinai peninsula, Gaza, the Golan Heights, the West Bank—and, as noted, over a million additional Palestinians (see Maps).

---

41 Bregman, *Israel's Wars*, 87–88.

Sparring for Advantage, 1967–1992

The Six Day war was the third of three major interstate conflicts. The first (1948–1949) had established the state of Israel. The second (1956) was essentially a dry run for the third war (1967), which confirmed the verdict of 1949, tested the first-strike doctrine, and established a new Israeli defensive perimeter. Although until 1977 Jabotinsky's followers remained on the margin of Israeli politics, by 1967 Israel had essentially chosen to follow—or had been forced to follow—Jabotinsky's political prescription. The founder of Revisionist Zionism, you will recall, had argued that Arabs would accept the Yishuv's existence, and negotiations would become possible, only when they realized that they could not physically destroy the Zionist project. With Jabotinsky's "iron wall" an established fact by 1967, the time had come to see if some sort of political accommodation was, in fact, possible. As Jabotinsky had prophesied, this would require basic shifts in Palestinian and Arab attitudes. But as he failed to appreciate, it would require wrenching changes in Israeli mentalities as well.

Because 1967 eventually nurtured on the Israeli side implausible hopes of permanent expansion, and because Palestinians and some Arab states still dreamed of negating 1948, the first two and a half decades after the Six Day War were not very encouraging for those seeking signs of a historic compromise. Although the Palestinians, given the poor hand they had to play, proved most resourceful and imaginative, both sides experimented with new tactics and strategies. Both Arabs and Israelis tested the limits of what

was possible in the world that 1967 had created. Twenty-five years later, mutual exhaustion had given both sides a more realistic understanding of what those limits were, and what changes in self-image and ambition would be needed, if stability ever were to be achieved. Thus by the early 1990s, Palestinians, supported by key Arab states, and Israelis were willing to attempt—unsuccessfully, as it turned out—a negotiated settlement. This section will consider the strategies and frustrations on both sides between 1967 and 1992 that prepared the way for those negotiations.

Labor's Plans for a Temporary Empire

What was to be done with the lands and people conquered during the Six Day War? The Israeli right wing, led by Menachem Begin, wanted to keep all newly acquired areas (with the possible exception of Sinai), and to promote large-scale Jewish settlement in East Jerusalem and the West Bank, or as the right preferred to call the latter, Samaria and Judea. These territories were the historic core of biblical Israel. On coming into power in 1977, the right followed precisely this program.

But from 1967 to 1977, the center–left Labor Party determined policy. Apart from East Jerusalem and a north–south security corridor in the Jordan Valley and the Judean Desert, Labor was willing to trade all the captured territories in return for peace with the Arab states. Labor's reasoning was twofold. First, Labor was convinced that trying to hold on to its 1967 gains would stoke Arab resentment, and thus increase—not decrease—the likelihood of future wars, whose outcome could not be predicted. Second, Labor realized that if it annexed the great Palestinian population blocs of the West Bank and Gaza, Israel could not maintain both its Jewish and democratic character. If all Palestinians were made citizens, they, together with Israeli Arabs, would at once constitute almost 40 percent of the electorate, and with higher Arab birthrates, that proportion would only rise. Because Arabs could be expected to oppose adequate IDF funding and to demand major concessions on security issues, this was a recipe for the collapse of the Jewish state. But to maintain indefinite control over another people without giving them citizenship or voting rights on the South African model was anathema to Israel's democratic norms—and was certain to alienate Israel's supporters in Europe and America. In short, in Labor's view, Israel had no choice but to relinquish most of the territories. This view accorded with United Nations Security Council Resolution 242, adopted in November 1967, which called for peace between Israel and its neighbors, and for withdrawal from most, though perhaps not all, territories occupied in the recent conflict.[1]

The question was: Could partners for peace be found? Although the Arab states, not unlike the Israeli body politic, remained split between hard-liners and moderates, in the Sudanese capital of Khartoum in August 1967 Arab heads of state issued a unanimous declaration with three famous "nos": no peace with Israel, no recognition of Israel, no negotiations with Israel. In the Arabs' view, by attacking Egypt, Israel had again shown itself to be an expansionist power whose actions were no more defensible than Japan's dastardly deed at Pearl Harbor. Israel therefore would have to surrender completely its stolen fruits before negotiations—much less peace—would be possible. While some observers tried to portray the Khartoum declaration as a partial victory for the moderates insofar as it did not call openly for Israel's destruction, Israel's Labor government assumed that Arab leaders meant precisely what they had said, and that, for the time being at least, negotiations were impossible.

Bereft of what it considered a suitable partner, rejecting unilateral withdrawal, but unwilling to retain all the territories indefinitely, Labor decided to hold most of them "in escrow," as it were, until the Arab states were ready to make peace. Convinced that this was only a matter of time, Labor sought to maintain the postwar status quo, in effect to preserve Israel's new territorial cards, until negotiations became feasible. In other words, after 1967 Labor envisioned a strictly temporary dominion.

In the Golan Heights, where most of the population had fled and the cease-fire generally held, Israel achieved a low-cost occupation. In northern Israel and the West Bank, Palestinian guerrilla raids out of Lebanon and Jordan became a serious annoyance starting in 1968, but after King Hussein evicted the Palestine Liberation Organization (PLO) from Jordan in 1970 (see below), the problem eased. In Egypt, Israeli forces were strung along a 90-mile defensive front from Port Said to Suez. Chastened, but not destroyed in 1967 and soon resupplied with Soviet weapons, the Egyptian army used its superiority in artillery and manpower to try to wear down its foe in what became known as the War of Attrition. By August 1970, however, Israeli air reprisals, a new Israeli defensive line, and American mediation had produced a cease-fire that held for three years. Israel's goal was to freeze the Suez front until Egypt agreed to exchange land for peace.

Likewise, "escrow" control of the West Bank meant avoiding disruptive changes until Jordan reclaimed control. The chief exception to this policy was East Jerusalem, which almost immediately after the Six Day War was united to West Jerusalem and declared Israel's "eternal capital."[2]

---

1 With deliberately ambiguity, the English text (though not the French text) of 242 called for "withdrawal from territories," not "the territories," occupied in 1967. On the diplomacy of this period, Shlaim, *Iron Wall*, chs. 6, 7; Tessler, *History of the Israeli–Palestinian Conflict*, ch. 7.

---

2 Insofar as Israel did not want to expand its enfranchised minority, and the vast majority of Arab East

Elsewhere, Israel combined sticks—the IDF ruthlessly repressed guerrillas in Gaza—with carrots designed to win tacit Palestinian acceptance of temporary Israeli rule. On the assumption that before long most of the West Bank would revert to Jordan, Israel kept open the Jordan bridges, applied Jordanian, rather than Israel law, arranged for local civil servants to receive Jordanian salaries, and worked with established pro-Hashemite notables. In the same spirit, Labor rejected right-wing demands to permit Jewish settlement across the West Bank. Although critics complained that the economic relation was "semi-colonial," Israeli markets and infrastructure produced rapid per capita increases in income in Gaza and the West Bank. The victory in 1972 West Bank municipal elections of conservative candidates willing to work with Israel joined encouraging diplomatic overtures from King Hussein, to convince Labor that its policy of temporary empire was indeed realistic, that Palestinians were reasonably content—and that sooner rather than later, in return for the territories, Jordan and other Arab states would agree to make peace.

In the abstract and over the long term, there was much to be said for that approach. But in the mid-1970s Labor's plans were upended by two totally unanticipated developments: The Palestine Liberation Organization—the PLO—of young committed anti-Zionist nationalists displaced the older generation of conservative notables inclined to cooperate with Israel, and in 1973 Egypt and Syria nearly overwhelmed the IDF. Although Israel eventually turned developments on the Egyptian front to its advantage, the military shock of 1973 joined with the PLO challenge and domestic social changes to oust Labor in 1977, in favor of the right-of-center Likud Party, whose territorial and foreign policy, as noted, differed

fundamentally from that of Labor. Any possibility of accommodation was now pushed back by another 15 years. Let's consider, then, the rise of the PLO, the October War of 1973, and the impact of those developments on Israeli policy.

The PLO and the Rise of Palestinian Resistance to c. 1975

Until 1948 the world had seen the Palestine conflict primarily as a struggle between Zionists and the Arabs of Palestine. But with successive Palestinian defeats, the intercommunal contest metamorphosed into an interstate contest. As we have seen, Arab governments—chiefly Egypt, Jordan, and Syria—spoke and fought in the name of the Palestinians, but the latter were consigned to an ever more marginal role. Symptomatic of that marginality, the PLO remained a toothless client of Egypt from its creation by the Arab League in 1964 until 1967.

With the Six Day War, however, the conflict changed shape once again. Now it was Arab governments who were impotent, humiliated, confused. Both Nasser and "Nasserism"—which said that Arab unity had to precede Palestine's liberation and that Palestinian organizations must remain subordinate to the Arab states— were discredited. If they were to redeem their homeland, Palestinians now decided, they would have to do so themselves. Preeminent among a host of Palestinian organizations energized by this new climate of uncertainty, experiment, and hope was Fatah. Having coalesced some five years earlier under Yasser Arafat, Fatah in 1967 moved quickly to develop an independent financial base in the Palestinian diaspora, a political network in the refugee camps, and a guerrilla wing centered in Jordan. By 1970 not only had Fatah wrested control of the PLO from Egypt and completely revitalized the PLO structure with Arafat as chairman, but it had persuaded a mélange of fractious guerrilla and political organizations, representing the totality of Palestinian political society, to shelter under the PLO umbrella. Arafat also forged a nominally unified military command. Stunning in

Jerusalemites preferred Jordanian to Israeli citizenship, the latter were declared "permanent residents" of Israel, entitled to vote in municipal, but not Knesset, elections. Idiosyncratic juridical anomalies also characterized the West Bank, whose residents retained Jordanian citizenship; Gaza, whose people had never enjoyed Egyptian citizenship; and the Golan and Sinai.

scope and rapidity, these achievements presaged a degree of Palestinian unity far more impressive than anything Hajj Amin al-Husayni or any of his successors had achieved.[3]

Organizational innovations were linked to ideological departures. Palestinians, the PLO proclaimed proudly and defiantly, were neither charity cases nor wards of the Arab states. Rather, they were a nation of people who had been unjustly driven out of their homeland, and who now demanded the same rights of self-determination and statehood as any other nation. Through armed struggle, they were determined to regain Palestine in its entirety, and to dismantle the Zionist system in favor of a genuinely democratic state that treated all citizens equally. Much influenced by the Syrian intellectual Sadeq al-Azm, the PLO championed secularism as a way to break the fatalism of Islamic tradition, to tap the power of science, technology, and socialism—and at the same time, to undercut Zionism. As a "theocratic" ideology, Zionism was said to be an anachronism that ignored the lessons of vibrant multiethnic, multireligious democracy in advanced countries like the United States. In offering a non-sectarian state in which Jews, Muslims, and Christians could live in equality and harmony, the PLO promised to bring Jews themselves into the 20th century.

Needless to say, Israeli Jews were unimpressed. Promises of equal treatment, they argued, flatly contradicted the claim in the Palestine National Charter of 1968 that the only Jews who could remain as citizens of the new state were those whose families had lived in Palestine before the "Zionist invasion," that is, before 1917 or even 1881.[4] To Jews this seemed to be a summons not to intercommunal harmony, but to the elimination of 90 percent of their members, in the best tradition of Hajj Amin al-Husayni.

Despite—or because of—intense Jewish hostility, Fatah and the PLO inspired a new dignity and optimism among Palestinian youth. This was symbolized in the image of the *feday* ("one who sacrifices himself"), whose rifle and checkered *kafiya* headscarf recalled the "self-sacrificers" during the Arab Revolt of 1936–1939. In practical terms, Fatah now began to displace the old class of pro-Jordanian notables on the West Bank, those amenable to Israel who had won the elections of 1972. Insurgent elites were younger, better educated, and far more committed to a specifically Palestinian identity. They drew strength from rising impatience with the status quo, from the development of political organizations outside notable control, and—ironically for Israelis—from jobs in Israel that also lay outside traditional elite patronage. To Israel's shock, in the 1976 municipal elections on the West Bank, the new generation of pro-PLO candidates swept the board. They promptly voiced passionate opposition to continued Israeli control and open support for the PLO.

As the PLO expanded its influence in the occupied territories, it also strove to build external bases from which to launch military attacks on Israel. Jordan was the preferred site, not only because its long border with Israel was best suited for such operations, but also because Jordan's population was majority Palestinian and thus inherently sympathetic to the PLO—and in many cases, estranged from Jordan's Hashemite establishment. Operating under the PLO umbrella, Palestinian groups in Jordan created a virtual state-within-a-state that challenged the monarchy and, in fact, attempted to assassinate King

---

3 *Fatah*, which means "opening" or "victory" in Arabic, is a reverse acronym derived from the full name of the movement in Arabic, which translates as the Palestinian National Liberation Movement. On Palestinian nationalist organizations to the late 1970s, see Sayigh, *Armed Struggle*, pts. 1–3; Kimmerling and Migdal, *Palestinian People*, chs. 8, 9; Tessler, *History of the Israeli–Palestinian Conflict*, chs. 7, 8; Farsoun and Aruri, *Palestine and the Palestinians*, ch. 6.

---

4 Tessler, *History of the Israeli–Palestinian Conflict*, 440–41; Benny Morris, *One State, Two States* (New Haven: Yale University Press, 2009), 112–13, 167–68; Sayigh, *Armed Struggle*, 88. On PLO ideology generally, see *ibid.*, ch. 3.

Hussein. In September 1970—which became known to Palestinians as Black September—the kingdom's armed forces struck back, killing anywhere from 1,500 to 30,000 Palestinians.[5] By mid-1971, although most Palestinians in Jordan retained strong PLO sympathies, Hussein had succeeded in completely ejecting Fatah and allied guerrilla groups from his kingdom.

The PLO, however, promptly shifted its main force to Lebanon, which also bordered Israel, but whose central government was too fragmented along religious lines, hence too ineffectual, to threaten Palestinians in Jordanian fashion. (Indeed, by aggravating sectarian tensions, the PLO would help to precipitate the Lebanese civil war in 1975.) With financial support from the diaspora and Gulf state patrons and with military and political help from Syria, the PLO consolidated control in parts of south Lebanon and in the Palestinian refugee camps around Beirut and other Lebanese cities. Thus arose another PLO state-within-a-state, with its own armed forces, judicial system, taxation, schools, radio station, and health care network. Known as "Fatahland," south Lebanon now became the chief staging area for PLO rocket attacks and terrorist operations directed principally against Israeli civilians. Despite punishing Israeli reprisals, such operations continued until Israel's 1982 invasion of Lebanon.[6]

In brief, starting from nowhere, with the frightfully bad hand that history had dealt it, the PLO by the mid-1970s had succeeded in transforming itself into a very credible political, if not military, actor with extensive influence in the occupied territories, fervent support in the Palestinian diaspora, and a strong military/political base in Lebanon.

Finally—and most astoundingly—the PLO forced Israel onto the defensive in the international arena. Step by step, moving methodically from the Arab League to the Islamic Conference to the Non-Aligned Conference and finally to the

UN, Arafat won ringing denunciations of Israeli policy and unqualified recognition of the PLO—not Hashemite Jordan—as the sole representative of the Palestinians. Most dramatically, in 1975 the UN General Assembly, by a vote of 72 to 35, with 32 abstentions, condemned Zionism as "a form of racism." At the same time the General Assembly created a permanent committee on the "inalienable rights of the Palestinian people."[7]

How can we explain this remarkable about-face in the very body that in 1947 had voted to create the Jewish state? At least four factors were at work: 1) Israel's 1967 victory undermined its earlier image as little David fighting mighty Goliath. On the assumption that weakness equates to virtue, considerable world sympathy now shifted from the Jews to their alleged victims, the Palestinians. Much as had been true of Jewish refugees in the 1940s, the Palestinians' weakness—their dispersal and misery—now became their greatest asset. 2) Connected to the previous point, in the 1970s the Vietnam War, African decolonization, and revolutionary movements in Latin America combined to make romanticized dichotomies between "oppressed peoples" and "Western imperialism" ever more popular in Third World countries and among Western leftists. As a tiny state allied to the United States that was at the same time infinitely more vulnerable than the United States, Israel became a favorite target for "anti-imperialists." 3) After the 1973 war (see below), Arab oil producers embargoed America, the Netherlands, and other countries sympathetic to Israel. Remarkable profits from the resultant spike in oil prices allowed Arabs to buy the support of many sub-Saharan states that once had close relations with Israel, but that now broke ties and began voting against Israel in the UN. 4) Arafat was an immensely talented leader with a genius for dramatic gesture and tactical maneuver.

The main point is that by depriving Israel of a negotiating partner, rising PLO influence undermined the entire rationale for Labor's peace

5   Tessler, *History of the Israeli–Palestinian Conflict,* 462–63.

6   On the term "terrorism," see p. 29, n. 1..

7   Tessler, *History of the Israeli–Palestinian Conflict,* 485; Reich, *Brief History of Israel,* 104.

policy. Some in Labor claimed that King Hussein of Jordan remained a viable potential partner, and that his suppression of the PLO during Black September showed he could be trusted to keep Palestinian militants under control. But few Israelis were willing to stake their country's future on the efficiency of Jordanian security services. In any case, Hussein's options were increasingly constrained by the PLO and by wider Arab opinion, which, with the notable exception of Egypt, remained resolutely hostile to Israel and opposed to peace negotiations.

As for the PLO itself, no Israeli government would dream of returning land to an organization pledged to its destruction. In 1967 Labor had assumed that inertia favored accommodation, that time was on Israel's side. But now history seemed to have something very different in store. Israelis were stunned and embittered by PLO successes and by their own growing isolation. As they saw things, they had not sought war in 1967 and promptly had offered to return most of the newly acquired territories for nothing more than recognition and peace. Their reward was international ostracism.

War—and Peace—with Egypt

Israel's growing insecurity was powerfully reinforced by the October 1973 war with Egypt and Syria. From 1968 until mid-1970, recall, Egypt and Israel had fought a War of Attrition along the Suez Canal. Egypt exploited its artillery advantage and its ability to dictate the time and place of attack to subject Israeli forces to punishing bombardment, punctuated by cross-canal commando raids. The idea was to inflict continuous casualties and necessitate open-ended mobilization, which Israel could ill afford. Although Israeli air raids deep into Egypt eventually forced Nasser to agree to a halt, Israel had been bloodied. Even after calm returned, the strain of holding onto Sinai helped to raise the proportion of Israel's GNP devoted to the military from some 10 percent in 1966 to over

26 percent in 1971.[8] Whereas Israeli criticism of military policy had once been unknown, 1971 saw public protests against what seemed to be an expensive and interminable stalemate.

Weighing his foe's vulnerabilities and sensing that the political and military momentum had begun to shift, Anwar Sadat, who succeeded Nasser as President of Egypt upon the latter's death in 1970, decided in late 1972 on a daring gamble: he would attempt a major military thrust into Israeli-held territory. If Egyptian forces could grab and retain the east bank of the Suez Canal, Sadat hoped it would deepen Israeli war weariness, and at the same time invite renewed American involvement. Only America, he realized, had enough leverage with Israel to bring it to the negotiating table. Abandoning Nasser's dream of destroying the Jewish state, Sadat sought merely to break the military/political impasse and open the way to negotiations through which, hopefully, he could regain the rest of Sinai without further fighting.

Clearly, however, political success presupposed military victory, at least on the local level. To avoid the poor coordination that had doomed Arab armies in 1948 and 1967, Sadat persuaded President Hafez al-Assad of Syria to strike in the Golan at the same moment as the Egyptians crossed the canal.

The initial Arab attacks achieved almost complete surprise. On October 6, 1973—which happened to be Yom Kippur, the Jewish Day of Atonement—meticulous planning and poor Israeli intelligence allowed well-trained, highly motivated Egyptian infantry, preceded by massive artillery barrages, to storm across the canal, destroy Israel's defense line, and consolidate positions all along the east bank. In the Golan Heights as well, the Syrians, deploying huge quantities of armor and men in well-planned operations, broke through Israeli lines and seemed poised to descend into the Galilee, into Israel's heartland. Classic IDF strategy had presupposed that Israel would mount the first strike only after its reserves had been fully mobilized. But now the Arabs had

8   Bregman, *Israel's Wars*, 101.

seized the initiative while Israel's reserves, for the most part, were still in civilian mode. So shaken was Defense Minister Moshe Dayan that he warned the head of the Israeli Air Force that the "Third Temple," Israel itself, might well fall.

In the event, the IDF's vastly outnumbered troops, especially in the Golan, exhibited a tenacity born of sheer desperation. Once the reserves began to arrive in force, superior training, gunnery, and tanks allowed Israel to blunt, and then to reverse, the initial Arab advances. Israel derived critical benefit as well from an emergency airlift of American weapons designed to counter Soviet shipments to its Arab clients.

Given the Golan's proximity to Israel's population centers, the IDF counterattack naturally gave that territory priority. Once Syria ran out of Soviet surface-to-air missiles, the IDF recaptured the entire plateau and pushed well beyond the 1967 armistice lines, exposing Damascus itself to attack. Switching planes and troops from the Golan to the Sinai, the IDF then routed overextended Egyptian columns in swirling tank battles in the open desert east of the Suez Canal. Having regained the initiative, the IDF promptly crossed that waterway so as to surround Egypt's Third Army, shattered and stranded on the east bank, and to threaten the Second Army with a similar fate.

Despite this rapid recovery, Israel had been very badly shaken. Because of her questionable performance in the opening stages of the conflict, the Labor Prime Minister Golda Meir resigned in early 1974. The October 1973 trauma, painful memories of the War of Attrition. the PLO's rising diplomatic fortunes, the unraveling of Labor's plans to return the West Bank to Jordan, growing international isolation symbolized by the "Zionism is racism" resolution—all of these factors joined to deepen Israel's gloom, which contrasted sharply with the euphoria of 1967. As national elections loomed in 1977, many Israelis feared that Labor had no viable policy, and could no longer be trusted with the nation's security. Adding to Labor's woes, many Mizrahi Jews began to turn against the Ashkenazi Labor establishment in favor of the recently formed

Likud ("Unity") Party, both because they resented what they saw as Labor's patronizing attitudes to Mizrahi culture, and because Likud's hawkish views on Arabs corresponded more closely to their own.[9]

The result was what has been termed the "earthquake election" of May 1977, which ousted the Labor alignment that had dominated Yishuv/Israeli politics since the early 20th century, in favor of a center–right coalition led by Likud. The new Prime Minister was none other than Likud founder Menachem Begin, Jabotinksy's spiritual heir, former leader of the radical Irgun underground, and the first non-Socialist Prime Minister in Israeli history.

If as a matter of principle Likud tended to oppose territorial concessions, in practice it adopted very different policies toward the Sinai peninsula, on the one hand, and Gaza, the West Bank, and the Golan, on the other. The latter three areas, Likud believed, were critical to Israeli security. Moreover, Samaria and Judea—the West Bank—were biblical lands and together with Gaza, were part of the British mandate, which in effect constituted Begin's map of the Jewish patrimony. But Sinai had weak historical associations and lay outside the mandate. Events between 1967 and 1973 had made it brutally clear even to Likud that Israel lacked the strength to hold Sinai indefinitely. What is more, in return for the restoration of Egyptian sovereignty, Sadat was perfectly willing to demilitarize Sinai. Begin, and indeed Labor before him, quickly realized that Sadat was offering Israel a golden opportunity to neutralize its most formidable opponent and so escape the recurrent threat, nearly fatal in October 1973, of an Arab pincers attack. In a word, Likud and Israel chose to turn military necessity into strategic virtue.

After October, Egypt also was in the mood to compromise, because its early victory had redeemed the nation's honor, while its later reverses had confirmed the folly of continued warfare. Economically, Sadat could afford open-ended

---

9 On Israeli politics, see Colin Shindler, *A History of Modern Israel* (Cambridge: Cambridge University Press, 2008), chs. 6, 7.

mobilization no more easily—indeed perhaps less easily—than Israel. His ultimate goal apparently was to redirect resources from military to civilian purposes, and thus renew Egypt's inefficient economy by developing close ties to the same benefactor as had befriended Israel, namely, the United States. The Soviet Union could provide arms, but not economic modernization, much less sway Israeli policy. In other words, mutual exhaustion forced both Israel and Egypt to adopt more narrow, realistic definitions of national interest under an American umbrella.

For its part, the United States, stung by the Arab oil embargo that had been imposed in retaliation for its support of Israel, was only too eager to court Arab opinion with well-publicized peace initiatives. At the same time the United States saw clearly Egypt's price for switching from the Soviet to the Western camp: America would have to use its influence with Israel to leverage a compromise.

From this tripartite confluence of interests emerged a series of staged Israeli withdrawals from Sinai, brokered by U.S. Secretary of State Henry Kissinger, and then by President Jimmy Carter.[10] In return for peace, the promise of full bilateral relations, strict limits to Egyptian forces in Sinai, and unhindered shipping through the Suez Canal and the Gulf of Aqaba, Israel agreed to remove all soldiers and civilians from the desert peninsula. Negotiations started under Labor, but it was Begin (despite poor personal chemistry with Sadat) who saw them to completion, signing the Camp David Accord with Sadat and Carter in 1978, followed by an Egypt–Israel peace treaty in March 1979. Undoubtedly, by reducing Israel's sense of siege, Sadat's dramatic visit to Jerusalem and his address before the Knesset in November 1977 provided a psychological watershed. For the first time, an Arab leader said publicly that he did not want to destroy Israel, that the Jewish state had a right to exist, and that land could be exchanged for peace. The ensuing agreements of 1978 and

---

10   On U.S. diplomacy and the Arab–Israeli conflict in this period, see William Quandt, *Peace Process* (Washington, DC: Brookings Institution Press, 2005), chs. 3–7.

1979 were the most dramatic breakthrough to that date in the history of Arab–Zionist relations.

Likud's Policy in the North: War in Lebanon

In his speech to the Knesset, Sadat explained that he did not seek peace at the expense of the Palestinians. At his insistence, the Camp David agreement obliged Israel to enter into discussions on the future of the West Bank and Gaza, and during an interim period of no more than five years, to grant the residents of those territories "full autonomy."

"Full autonomy," however, was never defined, and nothing ever came of the discussions. The reason was obvious: Begin never had any intention of relinquishing the eastern territories or allowing a second state to rise between the Jordan and the Mediterranean. After freeing the IDF in the southwest, Begin's goal was to concentrate his strength in the east so as to realize his historic vision of Greater Israel. Nor, despite his heartfelt words on behalf of the Palestinians, was Sadat willing to let the Palestinian issue jeopardize what he viewed as Egypt's overriding national interest in regaining Sinai and shifting Cold War alliances.

In one obvious sense, the PLO and Sadat differed. Notwithstanding some talk after 1974 about reclaiming Palestine in stages rather than all at once, the PLO remained viscerally hostile to the Jewish state, while Sadat made his peace with Israel. But in two other ways, the PLO and Sadat resembled one another. First, more or less unintentionally, both strengthened Likud, with its hard-line policy, at the expense of the Labor Party. The PLO did so by undermining the Jordanian option and stoking Israeli insecurity, while Sadat did so with his October 1973 surprise attack. Second, both helped, temporarily at least, to convert (or reconvert) the Mideast contest from a struggle between Arab states and Israel into a primary struggle between Palestinian nationalism and Zionism. The PLO raised dramatically the Palestinian profile even as Sadat downgraded Egypt's involvement.

Sadat paid a heavy price for what many regarded as this betrayal of the Arab cause: his country was suspended from the Arab League, and in 1981 Sadat himself was assassinated by Muslim fundamentalists in the Egyptian army. Initial enthusiasm among Egyptians for the peace with Israel cooled as the promised economic benefits by and large failed to materialize. Popular sentiment, ostracism by other Arab states, and what Egypt saw as Begin's totally uncooperative policies toward the Palestinians ensured that under Sadat's successor as President, Hosni Mubarak, Egyptian–Israeli relations remained cool.

Begin, however, had what he wanted, namely. security on his Egyptian flank. No longer obliged to worry about a two-front war, Begin and Likud were now free to pursue their ambitions to the north and east. In essence, they sought to assert Israeli dominance in Lebanon, to humble Syria, and to "Judaize" the West Bank and Gaza through large–scale settlement.

Consider first Lebanon and Syria. After being ejected from Jordan in 1970, the PLO, as we saw, developed a new base in south Lebanon, while Beirut became the PLO's new command headquarters. With some 10,000 fighters organized along increasingly conventional military lines, PLO forces in "Fatahland" launched raids and artillery barrages against Israeli towns. Begin responded in 1978 with a major ground incursion. But neither that action, nor preemptive air sorties, nor the stationing of United Nations troops to serve as a buffer prevented new PLO attacks. In 1982, a year after Likud won a second electoral victory, Begin and his new Defense Minister, Ariel Sharon, a war hero in 1967 and 1973, decided on a far more ambitious strategy: a full-scale invasion of Lebanon. With no fewer than 57,000 troops and 1,000 tanks, this operation, dubbed Operation Peace for Galilee, had four intertwined objectives: 1) To protect northern Israel from further attacks. 2) To destroy PLO credibility by forcing it out of Lebanon, which in turn was seen as a precondition for reducing PLO influence in the West Bank and Gaza. 3) To crush Syrian forces in Lebanon, which the Syrians had entered in 1976, ostensibly to end Lebanon's civil war. 4) To install a government in Lebanon led by Maronite Christians, whose hostility to the PLO and Syria rendered them, in the eyes of Begin and Sharon, Israel's natural allies.

Initially, the 1982 invasion went entirely according to plan. But then disaster struck. Negative publicity attending Israel's brutal siege of Beirut joined the assassination of Israel's chief Maronite ally, and the massacre of 700 (the Israeli tally) to 2750 (the Red Cross tally) unarmed Palestinians in the Beirut refugee camps of Sabra and Shatila, to turn a triumph into a nightmare. Although Christian militias carried out the Sabra and Shatila massacres, the IDF turned a blind eye, and was at least indirectly complicit, prompting international outrage. What is more, Israel's military situation began to unravel in 1983, as Syrian forces beefed up their defenses and sponsored increasingly effective guerrilla resistance to the IDF and its Christian allies in central and south Lebanon. In 1983 both Sharon and Begin in effect were forced from office, largely as a result of the Lebanon fiasco. Two years later, a dogged campaign in south Lebanon by the newly formed pro-Syrian Shi'ite militia, Hezbollah, forced Israel to pull out of Lebanon entirely, except for a narrow security zone along the Israeli–Lebanese border.[11]

Israel's Lebanon venture did accomplish one objective. The PLO was forced to withdraw to Tunis—a humiliating departure—which eliminated the threat of PLO attacks on northern Israel. Yet over the long term, this actually strengthened the PLO, because, as we shall see, it led that organization to downplay military in favor of diplomatic

---

11 See Thomas Friedman, *From Beirut to Jerusalem* (New York: Farrar, Straus Giroux, 1989), chs. 1–10. The Christian massacre of Palestinian civilians in Sabra and Shatila refugee camps, for which the IDF shared blame, were on the same scale as the far less well-publicized execution of Christian civilians by Syrian-backed Druze militias in the Shouf mountains of Lebanon in 1983. Yet more ferocious, but hidden from world attention, was the slaughter by Syrian security forces of 10,000–25,000 civilians in the Syrian city of Hama in 1982. Morris, *Righteous Victims*, 550–51; Friedman, *From Beirut to Jerusalem*, ch. 4.

strategies. Thereby, the PLO made itself eligible to participate in peace talks in the 1990s, a development that substantially enhanced the possibility of a Palestinian state. Begin had vowed that no second state would ever arise between the Jordan and the sea. In Lebanon itself, Israel succeeded in alienating all the main communities—Maronite Christians included—and in creating a guerrilla foe in Hezbollah that eventually proved far more formidable than the PLO. The big winner was Syria, which filled the vacuum created by Israel's departure, and proceeded to convert Lebanon into a client state of its own.

Ironically, Lebanon affected Israel in much the same way as it transformed the PLO: defeat obliged both to adopt more moderate, realistic positions. Israel had entered Lebanon expecting to dictate a regional settlement that not only would neutralize Lebanon, but with the PLO vanquished, would allow it to absorb de jure or de facto the West Bank and Gaza. Israel's frustration in Lebanon, however, began to produce a new balance of forces, a new political deadlock. The situation to Israel's north and east during the late 1980s started to recall that on its southwestern flank a decade earlier, when Egypt and Israel, neither able to impose its will, had decided that a negotiated settlement was the only way forward.

Likud's Policy in the Occupied Territories

But before deadlock in the east was complete, before negotiations could become feasible, Israel's plans for the West Bank and Gaza also had to meet increased resistance.

Although from 1984 to 1990 Likud shared power with Labor, Likud's continued electoral strength and the rise of parties to the right of Likud meant that for most of the period from 1977 to 1992, Likud was able to pursue its vision of what is often termed Greater Israel. In effect, this meant erasing the so-called Green Line that had separated pre-1967 Israel from the West Bank and Gaza, so as to include all three units in a single, Jewish-dominated polity.

Likud's motives were both ideological and strategic. Heir to Jabotinsky, the party believed that the Jewish national home included the entire territory of the mandate, and that Jews had a right to settle anywhere in that region, not least in Samaria and Judea. While Arabs in the occupied territories deserved humane treatment and autonomy, they were, in the words of official policy, entitled to "neither sovereignty nor self-determination."[12] Intertwined with ideological perspectives, of course, were military considerations. Israel's pre-1967 borders, only nine miles wide at the narrow waist, were highly vulnerable. Strategic settlement sought both to thicken the country's eastern defenses, and to neutralize large Arab population blocs in Gaza and the West Bank, which prior to 1967 had provided a base for guerrilla activity.

In devising policies for the new territories, Likud leaders made four assumptions: 1) In the east, there was no partner for peace. Unlike Egypt, Syria and the PLO still were committed to Israel's destruction. 2) Economic integration would improve Arab living standards, which in turn would win Palestinian acceptance, if not support, of Israeli occupation. 3) Because Palestinian opposition would be minimal, the occupation would be low cost—that is, Israel would not have to pay a high political or military price to retain the territories. 4) This was a unique, "God-given" (even Likud secularists were tempted to say) historic opportunity to align Israeli geography with the original Zionist vision. By "creating facts on the ground," by planting settlements across the West Bank and Gaza, Likud sought to ensure that no future government could ever withdraw. Of these four assumptions, the first and the fourth had considerable validity, but the second and third proved fatuous.

---

12   Tessler, *History of the Israeli–Palestinian Conflict*, 546. Although Likud intended to hold the Golan indefinitely for security purposes, that region did not figure prominently in Likud's program for the occupied territories, both because most of the Golan's population fled in 1967, and because the Golan, as noted, lay outside the mandate and historic Israel.

Whereas Labor had permitted only small Jewish settlements and had largely confined them to the underpopulated Jordan valley, Likud sought to colonize extensively the densely settled, strategically critical West Bank highlands, particularly east of Israel's narrow coastal waist and around Jerusalem. Colonization drew emotional energy from a stream of religious Zionism which held that Israel's 1967 victories heralded the age of redemption and that settling the territories would hasten the coming of the Messiah. Spearheaded by religious Jews, the Gush Emunim, or Bloc of the Faithful, provided a remarkably effective settler lobby.[13] Realizing, however, that appeals to national security and messianism were inadequate to get large numbers of Israelis to move east of the Green Line, Likud also created economic incentives. Thanks to heavy government subsidies, one could soon buy a spacious West Bank house and property, in easy commuting distance of Tel Aviv or Jerusalem, for less than a tiny apartment would cost in crowded Tel Aviv. Whereas in 1977 under Labor there were only 4,000 settlers in the West Bank (excluding East Jerusalem), by 1993, largely because of economic incentives, there were about 110,000. In 1982 the government announced that it hoped to plant a million settlers within 30 years.[14] Virtually all nations condemned these settlements as a critical impediment to peace talks, and in the view of most states, as a violation of the Fourth Geneva Convention prohibiting population changes in occupied territories. But Israel disputed that legal interpretation. and continued more or less undaunted.

To divert attention from the settlement issue and to conciliate Palestinian opinion, Likud sought to enhance Arab welfare by opening pre-1967 Israel to Palestinian labor, by enfolding pre-1967 Israel and the territories in a free-trade zone, and by investing in infrastructure, education, and

health care in Gaza and the West Bank. By 1987, with jobs in Israel supporting 40 percent or more of the labor force in the territories, unemployment had virtually disappeared. Large-scale remittances by Palestinians working in the Gulf States supplemented income from Israel. In 1967 per capita income in Gaza was $80, but 20 years later, it had reached $1,700. The 18 percent of Gaza households with electricity in 1967 had grown to 89 percent in 1981. Israel created the first seven Palestinian universities. As had earlier been true in Israel itself, improved maternal and infant health care in the occupied territories dramatically raised the rate of Arab population growth—much to Israel's eventual dismay.[15]

By and large, however, Palestinians gave Israel little credit for these changes, because economic improvement accompanied a growing sense of economic and political dependency. Palestinians complained that Israel had locked the territories into a relationship of permanent inferiority, as a source of cheap unskilled labor and a market for Israeli manufactures. Inadequate technical training and limited industrial investment outside pre-1967 Israel meant that Palestinians generally held jobs at the fourth tier of the economic ladder: beneath Israeli Arabs, Mizrahi Jews, and Ashkenazi Jews. Palestinians commuting to Israel could be subject to humiliating, arbitrary treatment by employers and Israeli security forces alike. Meanwhile, back home, everywhere they looked, Palestinians saw Jewish settlements inserting themselves into the familiar Arab landscape, eating up land and water resources, eroding the territories' Arab cultural character

At the same time, Likud's restrictions on Palestinian political activity seemed ever more galling. Until 1977, on the assumption that its control of Gaza and most of the West Bank was temporary, Labor had accorded Arab municipalities wide autonomy and had paid relatively

13 On the early settler movement, see Gershom Gorenberg, *The Accidental Empire* (New York: Times Books, 2006).

14 Tessler, *History of the Israeli–Palestinian Conflict*, 520, 548, 605, 671, 772; Reich, *Brief History of Israel*, 114–15.

15 The first three universities, Bir Zeit, Al-Najah, and Gaza Islamic, were founded or planned under Labor. Data derive from Kimmerling and Migdal, *Palestinian People*, 276, 285, 293; Tessler, *History of the Israeli–Palestinian Conflict*, 524–26; Bregman, *Israel's Wars*, 185.

little attention to political expression. But Likud, intending to retain these areas indefinitely, sought to supplement or bypass municipal councils, which since 1976 had been led by a new generation of pro-PLO activists, with docile, appointed bodies known as Village Leagues. Just how successful this political experiment was may be judged from a 1982 poll commissioned by *Time* magazine, which showed that 98 percent of West Bank and Gaza residents favored an independent Palestinian state, 86 percent said it should be solely under the PLO, while .2 percent supported the Village Leagues.[16] The dissemination in the 1980s of patriotic songs and literature, the display of Palestinian flags in defiance of Israeli bans, and a series of protests and closures—many led, ironically, by students from the new Israel–funded universities—testified to this surging nationalism.

The First Intifada

This, then, was the emotional and political background to the first *intifada* ("shaking off" in Arabic), which from 1987 to 1991/1992 sought to end the Israeli occupation by massive popular protests. The general timing of the *intifada* was governed by the fact that an Arab summit meeting in 1987 seemed indifferent to the Palestinians' plight, by an economic downturn from the mid-1980s, and perhaps most critically, by accelerating Israeli settlement—all of which filled residents of the West Bank and Gaza with a sense of isolation and despair, a feeling that anything was preferable to the status quo.

The immediate trigger in December 1987 was a traffic accident in Gaza involving an Israeli vehicle and a car in which four Arabs were killed. Spreading quickly from Gaza to the West Bank and led by young militants, the uprising came to embrace an imaginative, ever fluid variety of tactics—street protests and demonstrations (in which children often played a prominent role), tax strikes, shop closures, large-scale resignations by municipal workers, fire bombing Israeli property, stone throwing, boycotts of Israeli goods, and the dissemination of underground literature. Caught completely off guard, the normally supple Israeli security apparatus at first had great difficulty responding. Although Hamas, the Islamist radical group, tried to move beyond mere protests to armed attacks, for the most part, these actions remained nonlethal so as to deny the IDF an excuse to crack down with massive force. In 1989 and 1990 the IDF, using curfews, house demolitions, deportations, plastic bullets, and beatings, began to regain the initiative and protests started to die down. But in its early stages, the *intifada* drew vitality from a combination of popular rage and resilient, decentralized organization. The latter involved both PLO representatives and local ad hoc bodies known as Popular Committees, which sprang up in virtually every Arab village and urban district. All told, it is estimated that 45,000 local committees of various kinds operated in the territories during the first *intifada*.[17] Like the revolt of 1936–1939, as a statement of defiance and an affirmation of identity, the *intifada* generated enormous sympathy across the Arab world, now obviously intensified by the rapidity and ubiquity of electronic media.

The first *intifada*, again like the Arab Revolt, also had a major political impact. In fact, the uprising spoke to three audiences. To Israelis, the *intifada* said: "If you think that we will accept occupation forever, if you believe that occupation can be cost free, you are very wrong." No less than Israel's actions in Lebanon, recurrent images on television and in the newspapers of IDF troops beating Palestinians and shooting plastic bullets into crowds cost Israel dearly in world opinion. "Benign occupation" began to sound like an oxymoron. For the first time, many Israelis began to see clearly the Palestinians' deep pain and frustration. High-ranking Israeli generals and think

16   Tessler, *History of the Israeli–Palestinian Conflict*, 567.

17   Bregman, *Israel's Wars*, 192. For views of early Hamas activity in the *intifada,* see p. 73, n. 21 *infra*. On the first *intifada*, Farsoun and Aruri, *Palestine and the Palestinians*, ch. 7; Kimmerling and Migdal, *Palestinian People*, 296–311.

tanks now decided that in an age of missiles and aerial warfare, the territories had become more of a political liability than a strategic asset. Suddenly, therefore, the Green Line rematerialized in Israel's imagination, and even many conservative Israelis began to think that Israel would have to pull back. But at the same time, the PLO's unyielding opposition to Israel left Jews in a quandary: As a practical matter, how could they ever meet Palestinian aspirations without endangering the Jewish state?

To Americans, the uprising declared, "You'll never reach a Mideast settlement over the heads of us, the Palestinians, the people most affected by Israeli policy. Our interests, our organization, and above all, our suffering, must be taken into account." Pictures of IDF repression shocked many Americans as well as Europeans.

And to the Arab states, the *intifada* issued a veiled warning: "If you continue to ignore our plight, your regimes may well face the same popular fury as Israel." Largely in response to the *intifada*, King Hussein in 1988 announced that Jordan was surrendering all claims to the West Bank, which, he declared, should become the nucleus of an independent Palestinian state.

In part, the Mideast conflict has always been a struggle to control the narrative and the pictorial image. Whichever side appears more brutal forfeits world sympathy. Whichever appears more vulnerable often captures that sympathy. As we have seen, such sympathy was among the Jews' greatest assets from 1939 to 1967. So long as Arab states refused compromise and advocated Israel's destruction, they reinforced a view of Israel as the valiant little fighter against overwhelming odds. But after 1967 for many observers, especially on the political left, as Arab states stepped back and Palestinians took central stage, the image began to flip in favor of the Palestinians. The *intifada* now gave an enormous boost to the story of Palestinian victimization and Israeli brutality. Both by sowing Israeli self-doubt and by weakening Israel's international position, the *intifada* thus joined Israel's frustration in Lebanon to help set the stage for serious negotiations.

Hope and Failure, 1993–2010

Pressures for Negotiations

If we stand back to examine the large canvas of Mideast history, the significance of 1967 becomes ever more clear. From 1948 to 1967, Israel was militarily and politically ascendant. Not only did it defeat successive Arab attempts to destroy it, but in response to those threats, it conquered territory in all directions. In 1948 Israel seized another 23 percent of Palestine; in 1956 it temporarily captured Sinai, while in 1967 it took the rest of Palestine, Sinai, and the Golan. But in 1967 this wave, which depended on battlefield success, crested. Unable to retain the Sinai in the face of Egyptian and American pressure, in the 1970s Israel withdrew in return for diplomatic recognition and demilitarization. From 1982 to 1992, as Likud's plan to dominate Lebanon collapsed and Likud's policies in the territories grew increasingly untenable, Israeli frustration along its northern and eastern borders began to recall that with Egypt a decade earlier. Once again, stalemate encouraged Israel to consider trading territory for recognition and peace. In short, in the early 1990s, a second wave, a second move to stabilization, began to engulf the east much as it had transformed the Egyptian frontier some 15 years earlier—although in the east, this movement has yet to climax (and indeed, may never reach fruition).

Perhaps if the PLO had grown stronger as Israel faltered, the PLO would have continued to reject negotiations, in the expectation that its long–term goal of undermining Israel was finally becoming feasible. The truth is, however, that the PLO faced a variety of setbacks at least as formidable as those plaguing Israel. Its goal of taking over all of mandatory Palestine probably had always been a chimera. But in the late 1980s and early 1990s, at least six factors made Palestinian leaders sense that in some respects, history still favored Israel, and a more accommodating stance was therefore necessary.

First, as noted, in an immediate sense, Lebanon weakened the PLO as well as Israel. Exiled in Tunis, far from their home base and no longer able to confront Israel militarily, PLO leaders after 1982 were forced both to downplay heroic talk of armed struggle and to surrender day-to-day authority to local leaders in the West Bank and Gaza. Face to face with the IDF, a new generation of activists saw only too clearly that, for the time being at least, dreams of destroying Israel were absurd, that an independent state in Gaza and the West Bank was the most they could hope for, and that the latter could be achieved only through negotiations. Tunis, if it were to remain relevant, had to listen to these new voices.

Second, from 1990 to 1992 Likud accelerated West Bank settlement construction, especially along the Green Line. By creating ever more numerous "facts on the ground," settlements joined with suppression of the *intifada* to make Palestinian leaders, both in Tunis and in the territories, ever more aware of the enormous power imbalance between the two sides. If the *intifada* had garnered advantageous publicity, it had done nothing practical to halt the settler juggernaut—indeed, it may have intensified Likud's commitment to settlements. Only an agreed solution, many Palestinians began to realize, could stop colonization.

Third, although movement from the Soviet Union to Israel began to increase in the mid-1980s, the collapse of the Soviet Union in 1989 suddenly released a vast wave of talented, well-educated Russian Jewish immigrants. From 1989 to 1991 alone, 340,000 Russians arrived in Israel. This latest, in some ways most impressive *aliyah*—42 percent of the newcomers had scientific and academic professional educations, a figure four times the Israeli average—eventually totaled a million persons. The Russian influx boosted Israel's confidence in its demographic and economic future, and provided yet more potential settlers for the territories.[1]

Fourth, besides supplying Israel with fresh immigrants, the Soviet collapse deprived the PLO of political and diplomatic support from its only big power patron, and denied Syria, the PLO's chief regional supporter, fresh supplies of modern weaponry. Any lingering credibility that the PLO–Syrian military option may have had now evaporated completely.

Fifth, the First Gulf War of 1990–1991 further weakened the PLO. With many Palestinians hailing the Iraqi leader Saddam Hussein as a savior, Arafat endorsed Iraq's 1990 invasion of Kuwait. But most Arab states, Syria included, criticized that attack, and supported the U.S.-led invasion to eject Iraqi troops from Kuwait. Insofar as a vengeful Kuwait expelled Palestinians and, with Saudi Arabia, cut funding to the PLO, the war hurt Palestinians economically as well as diplomatically. Thus Arafat forfeited much of the goodwill the *intifada* had earned. To ingratiate himself with the United States and the Gulf states, a chastened Arafat was obliged to adopt a more conciliatory tone. Unlike Soviet emigration and the end to Soviet support, this PLO setback was

entirely self-inflicted. But in a sense, it too was an artifact of Soviet collapse, insofar as both Saddam Hussein and the PLO had looked to the Soviet Union to balance U.S. power. In the early 1990s, the world suddenly became unipolar.

A sixth factor telling in favor of negotiations was the growing popularity and prominence during the *intifada* of Islamic fundamentalist groups, Islamic Jihad, and more especially, Hamas. Suffice it for now to say that these groups argued that PLO "moderation" never had achieved anything substantial. Arafat, therefore, needed some tangible success to prove that his strategy was not bankrupt. For their part, the Israelis, after flirting with a divide-and-rule strategy, decided that the PLO was a far more attractive potential partner than Hamas. In this way, Islamists helped drive the PLO and Israel together.

What finally provided the critical opening for negotiations, however, was Labor's dramatic victory in the 1992 Israeli Knesset election, ending 15 years of Likud dominance. The election was fought chiefly over relations with the PLO, with whom Israel, under heavy U.S. and international pressure, had entered into tentative discussions, starting with a well-publicized international conference in Madrid in October 1991. Capitalizing on its enhanced influence after the First Gulf War, the United States organized the Madrid conference in an effort to open direct negotiations between Israel, the Palestinians, and major Arab countries. Should Israel drag its feet in the hope that these discussions would fail? This, in so many words, was Likud's policy. Or should Israel negotiate seriously in order to reach a comprehensive agreement? This was the position of Labor now led by the decorated general Yitzhak Rabin, in whose view the *intifada* showed that Israel could never subdue the Palestinians by force alone.

The Oslo Process to 1999

In Madrid, Israel met publicly with a mixed Jordanian–Palestinian delegation, as well as with

---

1 Reich, *Brief History of Israel*, 166–67, 170–72; Shindler, *History of Modern Israel*, 219, 228–29. In 1990 Israel's total Jewish population was only about four million.

delegates from Lebanon and Syria.[2] Although Madrid yielded little of substance, that conference and follow-up gatherings broke the psychological and procedural barrier to direct bilateral negotiations between Israel and its immediate neighbors, most particularly, between Israel and the Palestinians.

Building on that experience, after Rabin became Prime Minister following the 1992 election, he sent representatives to secret meetings with the PLO in Oslo, Norway. These culminated in a televised ceremony on the White House lawn in September 1993, at which time, with President Clinton the smiling matchmaker, Rabin and Arafat shook hands—however stiffly and awkwardly—and signed a Declaration of Principles. Five years earlier, the PLO had agreed to UN Resolution 242, thus implicitly and tentatively accepting the Jewish state. Now the PLO explicitly recognized Israel's right to exist, while Israel recognized the PLO as sole representative of the Palestinian people. Known as the Oslo Accords, these understandings appeared to change the nature of the Mideast, for they formalized the notion that Israeli and Palestinian national claims lay at the heart of the Jewish–Arab conflict, and they announced that a mutually satisfactory resolution of those claims was, in principle, possible. Thereafter, key leaders on both sides would abandon fantasies of controlling the entire territory of the old mandate in favor of two states, Israel and Palestine, living side by side.[3]

While deferring to the future such critical and contentious issues as borders, refugees, and settlements, the Accords set up interim arrangements and a five-year negotiating timetable to produce a final agreement. A Palestinian state-in-embryo, known as the Palestinian Authority (PA), with its own security forces, now arose to administer Palestinian areas, starting with Gaza and Jericho, from which the IDF withdrew in early 1994. Before returning to a rapturous welcome in Gaza, Arafat, who would be elected President of the PA, declared with great emotion, "Now I am returning to the first free Palestinian lands. You have to imagine how it is moving my heart, my feelings."[4] In 1994 Arafat, Rabin, and Israel's Foreign Minister Shimon Peres shared the Nobel Peace Prize. That same year, Jordan became the second Arab land, after Egypt, to recognize the Jewish state and sign a formal peace. Israeli relations with the Hashemite monarchy soon became appreciably more robust than with Egypt. Israel also opened low-level commercial and diplomatic relations with other Arab states.

In September 1995 a second set of agreements known as Oslo II spelled out further IDF redeployments, and gave the PA administrative control over 97 percent of Palestinians living in the territories outside East Jerusalem. To advance reconciliation, the next year the PLO voted to strike from its National Charter calls for Israel's destruction.[5] Early opinion polls showed 2:1 support for a negotiated settlement among both Palestinians and Israelis. Foreign funds now began flooding Israel and PA areas, so that for many the peace process and economic improvement became mutually supportive. In a word, the White House lawn ceremony inaugurated an era of unprecedented optimism, even euphoria. The hundred years war, many dared to believe, was finally coming to an end.

And yet grounds for grave concern remained, because each side retained a vision of a just settlement that was basically unacceptable to the other. Palestinians, for example, assumed that peace meant all Palestinians could return to their family homes in Israel, and that Israel would surrender all lands seized in 1967. Most Israelis rejected both assumptions out of hand. So long as nothing

---

2 On negotiations from 1991 to 1999, see Quandt, *Peace Process*, Part Five; Charles Enderlin, *Shattered Dreams* (New York: Other Press, 2002), chs. 1–2; Dennis Ross, *The Missing Peace* (New York: Farrar, Straus and Giroux, 2004), chs. 1–19.

3 Reich, *Brief History of Israel*, 155, 174; Tessler, *History of the Israeli–Palestinian Conflict*, ch. 12.

4 Tessler, *History of the Israeli–Palestinian Conflict*, 763–64.

5 Ominously to Israeli eyes, however, the PLO failed to draft a new charter without those articles. Morris, *One State, Two States*, 130–32.

had been spelled out, so long as peace remained an abstraction, both peoples could embrace it wholeheartedly, but once hard compromises were needed, enthusiasm was bound to erode. Neither side, but especially the PA, which unlike the Israeli government monopolized the dissemination of information, prepared its people for compromise.

What is more, both communities contained hard-line elements determined to undermine any moves toward reconciliation. On the Israeli side, Rabin's narrow Knesset majority made it difficult for him to resist right-wing groups in the Knesset, both secular and religious, who were hostile to the peace process in principle, and who insisted that Israel continue expanding, if not the number of West Bank and Gaza settlements, then certainly the population of those settlements. Rabin capitulated repeatedly to such demands. Along with Rabin's forceful insistence that Jerusalem remain Israel's undivided capital, this deeply antagonized Palestinians, who argued, with perfect logic, that unilateral actions destroyed the concept of reciprocity that should be central to any negotiations. Yet more corrosive was settler vigilantism, of which the most dreadful example was the massacre of 29 Muslim worshippers by an ultra-Orthodox Jewish terrorist in Hebron in 1994.

Naturally, such actions strengthened Muslim radical groups, most notably Hamas and Islamic Jihad, who used PA territory to stage their own outrages, chiefly suicide bombings against Jewish buses, shopping centers, and other civilian targets. Arafat's response was ambivalent.[6] On the one hand, he still believed that negotiations would yield major benefits and sought to maintain a degree of Israeli goodwill. On the other hand, Arafat saw terrorist attacks as a way to win concessions from Israel, and he feared antagonizing the many Palestinians opposed to peace by clamping down hard on the Islamists. As a result, he tended to equivocate, arresting Hamas small fry, but releasing them once the pressure was off, and leaving Hamas leaders untouched. Whether as a concession to that camp or as an expression of sincere

conviction, Arafat also explained to sympathetic audiences—usually in Arabic, beyond the hearing of most Western journalists—that he saw peace with Israel not as an end in itself, but rather as a stage leading to Israel's ultimate destruction.

These actions naturally infuriated Israelis, by no means all right-wingers, who argued that the only thing Rabin's peace process had achieved was a dramatic increase in terrorist sanctuaries and the death of Jewish civilians. Likud attack ads now set photos of Rabin shaking hands with Arafat against images of Jews blown to pieces by Hamas bombs. In a basic sense, then—although Rabin, unlike Arafat, unequivocally rejected terrorism—both he and Arafat were caught between a commitment to negotiations and the political necessity of collaborating with elements opposed to a settlement. Zealots in both camps worked feverishly to destroy the middle, illustrating Thomas Friedman's famous quip: In the Mideast extremists go all the way, while moderates usually just go away.

Despite these ominous trends, if Rabin had lived, the momentum for peace still might have carried the process to completion. Tragically—and this may be one of those few historical moments when personality was truly decisive—in November 1995 Rabin was murdered by an ultra-Orthodox Jewish nationalist. Lacking Rabin's security credentials to reassure an electorate spooked by fresh Hamas and Hezbollah terrorist attacks that deliberately sought to weaken the pro-peace Labor Party, Rabin's successor as head of Labor, Shimon Peres, lost the 1996 election for Prime Minister to the head of Likud, Benjamin Netanyahu. Although under American pressure, Netanyahu (who came from a distinguished family of Jabotinsky Zionists) agreed to further IDF withdrawals, his obvious lack of enthusiasm for the larger Oslo process helped to stymie negotiations for most of the three years he held office. This deadlock only boosted Hamas at the expense of Fatah, whose popularity, in any case, was being tarnished by PA favoritism toward PLO veterans from Tunis at the expense of local activists, and by ever more credible reports of massive financial corruption within the PA. In short, by early 1999

---

6   *Cf.* Khalidi's analysis in *Iron Cage*, 172–81, referring on 178 to the PLO leadership's "strategic incoherence."

some observers felt that the peace process was heading off a cliff.

Descent to Chaos

Like the initial euphoria after 1993, these fears proved exaggerated, at least in the short term.[7] Sensing perhaps that continued violence would destroy his ultimate objective of obtaining an independent state, and profiting from his security forces' increased experience, Arafat began to crack down on Hamas. What is more, in fresh elections in May 1999, Israelis ousted Netanyahu, whose constant vacillation had pleased few and offended many, in favor of the pro-peace Labor Party leader, Ehud Barak. Whereas Netanyahu, by word and deed, had made clear his distaste for Oslo, Barak, whose reputation as the most decorated soldier in Israeli history gave him great authority on security issues, said that in his view, a Palestinian state, so long as it did not threaten Israel, was perfectly acceptable. Thus, Oslo, written off by some, still seemed very much alive.

Building on progress under Rabin and Peres, Barak first sought a breakthrough with Syria on the future of the Golan Heights. But although tantalizingly close to success, those negotiations foundered over control of the Sea of Galilee's northeast shore. Determined to achieve some sort of rapid change in the status quo, Barak in May 2000 switched his attention from Syria to Lebanon, where he suddenly and unilaterally pulled out of Israel's self-declared security zone in the south. There, Hezbollah had trapped IDF forces in an increasingly difficult 15-year guerrilla war sometimes dubbed "Israel's Vietnam." But while praised at home as a prudent recalibration and as a way to reduce regional tensions, this dramatic retreat let Hezbollah boast, with

justice, that it was the first Arab movement to defeat Israel on the battlefield. As we shall see, the Hezbollah model—if anti-Zionist forces are sufficiently persistent, Israel will grow weary and retreat—probably influenced Arafat to support the second *intifada*.

Barak's main peace effort, however, focused neither on Syria nor Lebanon, but on the West Bank and Gaza. With further IDF withdrawals on the West Bank proceeding as planned, but with intermediate-level negotiations on final status issues dragging on interminably, Barak decided the time finally had come for Arafat and himself to reach a comprehensive settlement, a breakthrough, in direct face-to-face talks. In this daring proposal, he was supported by President Clinton, who hoped that Mideast peace would be his chief international legacy and whose term was drawing to a close. Arafat had no enthusiasm for a summit meeting, arguing, correctly as it turned out, that preparations had been inadequate. But he found it impossible to decline an invitation from the President of the United States, and so from July 11 to 25, 2000, the three leaders convened at Camp David, Maryland, to try to hammer out a final deal.

They considered three principal issues: the borders of a Palestinian state, the status of Jerusalem, and the future of Palestinian refugees. On borders, Barak opened by proposing that Israel relinquish Gaza in its entirety but retain permanently or temporarily 24 percent of the West Bank, which he claimed was necessary to protect Israel's narrow waist, Jerusalem, and the Jordan valley. Objecting strongly to the fragmentation of Palestinian areas into South African–style "Bantustans," and pointing out that Palestinians had already lost the great bulk of mandatory Palestine in 1948, Arafat said that any further territorial concessions were totally unreasonable. He sought the entire West Bank, in effect restoring the boundaries of pre-June 1967, as if the Six Day War had never occurred. Clinton offered a compromise, whereby Israel would keep nine percent of the West Bank, surrender Israeli territory equivalent to one percent, and ensure the contiguity of Palestinian areas. Israel accepted

---

7   On negotiations under Barak, see Quandt, *Peace Process*, 358–81; Ross, *Missing Peace*, chs. 20–26; Enderlin, *Shattered Dreams*, chs. 3–6; Shimon Shamir and Bruce Maddy–Weitzman, eds., *The Camp David Summit—What Went Wrong?* (Brighton: Sussex Academic Press, 2005).

this proposal and Arafat indicated flexibility, so, although the issue was not resolved, progress was marked.

Jerusalem was devilishly difficult, because Jewish and Arab neighborhoods were intermixed, and because Jerusalem's core, including the site known to Muslims as the Noble Sanctuary and to Jews as the Temple Mount, was sacred to both faiths. Barak wanted an undivided city under Israeli sovereignty, but with Muslim control over Muslim holy sites. Arafat wanted the city divided in two as before 1967, but with Jews having guaranteed access to their religious sites. Clinton suggested a Swiss-cheese formula, with Arab and Jewish neighborhoods under Palestinian and Israeli sovereignty, respectively, with national capitals for both states, and with Muslim "custodial sovereignty" over the surface, but not the subsurface, of the Noble Sanctuary. Arafat, however, continued to insist on unqualified sovereignty over the entire sanctuary.

As for refugees, some progress had been made before Camp David through Swedish intermediaries. But in July, Arafat reverted to an earlier position: Israel had to take full responsibility for the displacement of 1947–1948 and accept the right of return of every refugee—and that refugee's descendants—who chose to exercise it. Repeating Israeli arguments that Palestinians, by starting the fighting in 1947, bore chief blame for the refugee problem, that Resolution 194 said nothing about the descendants of refugees, and that to take back millions of Arabs would destroy the Jewish state, Barak rejected these ideas out of hand. On this score, Clinton offered no bridging proposals, and no progress was made.

Camp David was not immediately regarded as a failure. The gaps between the two sides had narrowed, and many observers remained modestly hopeful. What finally destroyed those hopes was the intrusion (or perhaps one should say, the further intrusion) of popular passions into the negotiating arena. On September 28, 2000, the new head of Likud, Ariel Sharon—whom Palestinians detested as an architect of Israel's settlement policy, and as a man who bore at least indirect responsibility for Sabra and Shatila—made a

brief, well publicized visit to the Noble Sanctuary/Temple Mount. Sharon's primary objective probably was to score points in Israeli domestic politics, but Palestinians regarded his visit to Muslim holy sites as a provocation directed at them, and shortly after he left, they began pelting Israeli police with stones. The next day, Friday, as tens of thousands of Palestinians left the Noble Sanctuary compound after prayers, demonstrators and police again confronted one another, with Palestinians throwing stones at police and at Jewish worshippers near the Western Wall. What Palestinians saw as heavy-handed Israeli efforts to contain the outbreaks that day and the next—efforts that produced at least four Palestinian deaths and over 200 injuries—merely fanned Arab resentment. Ignoring calls to restrain the rioting, PA radio and television stations and PA leaders began exhorting listeners to launch a holy war and to "march on Jerusalem." Violence against Jewish settlers and security personnel now raced across the territories. The second *intifada* had begun.

In a determined bid to stem the disorders and to salvage negotiations, in late December 2000, Clinton summoned representatives of the PA and the Israeli government to Washington, where he laid down terms for a settlement that both sides were asked to accept or reject in toto. These terms, most of which represented movement away from the Camp David proposals in favor of the Palestinians, included a three percent net Israeli annexation of West Bank territory (down from eight percent at Camp David), full Palestinian sovereignty over the Noble Sanctuary/Temple Mount, and the right of refugees to receive compensation or to return to a Palestinian state, but not to Israel itself. Barak and his cabinet accepted the proposals, but the United States interpreted Arafat's reply as rejection. With last-ditch talks at the Egyptian town of Taba in late January 2001 doomed by continuing violence and by Sharon's impending landslide victory over Barak in a new election for Prime Minister, the Oslo peace process finally had come to an end.

The second *intifada*,[8] which would last until mid-2002, rapidly intensified. Whereas the first *intifada* from 1987 to 1992 had been an essentially nonlethal protest, this uprising used rifles, hand grenades, and mortars—Israel, ironically, had given most of these arms to PA forces under Oslo—and sent suicide bombers against Israeli civilian targets. Accordingly, the second *intifada* prompted a far more lethal, muscular IDF response. The first *intifada* had been restricted to the territories, but now riots spread to Israel's million-strong Arab minority, who resented their ongoing marginalization and Barak's apparent indifference to their concerns. But the principal difference between the first and second uprisings was this: Whereas the first had increased Israeli sympathy for the Palestinians and had helped usher in seven years of peacemaking, the second had precisely the opposite effect, utterly destroying Israeli goodwill, breeding deep bitterness on both sides, and postponing meaningful negotiations for at least another decade.

Who was to blame for this debacle, for the collapse of Oslo? Incompatible though they may seem at first glance, three interpretations—a determinist, a Palestinian, and an Israeli narrative—all have merit, and in fact can be synthesized in diverse combinations. But none of these three views can be ignored.

In the **determinist narrative**, negotiations failed, not because of mistakes in timing or tactics by one side or the other, but because the basic emotional orientations of the two sides remained irreconcilable.

The trauma of the Holocaust, the memory of endless Arab vows to destroy Israel (and repeated military attempts to make good on those promises), Hamas' implacable hatred, continuous terrorist outrages, Arafat's alleged duplicity—all of these factors made physical security the most basic goal for Israelis. If settlements embodied an ideological drive to settle the biblical Land of Israel, they responded more directly to the need to protect Jerusalem and Israel's narrow waist.[9] Israel's bottom line in negotiations was defensible borders and an end to demands for the right of return, which, Jews feared, would convert Israel overnight into a majority Arab land and open the door to wholesale terrorism.

But if Israelis wanted what they considered essential security, Palestinians sought what they deemed basic justice. Having already yielded 78 percent of Palestine, as a matter of principle they would not surrender any of what remained. Nor would they abandon refugee claims embodied in UN Resolution 194. Nor could any self-respecting leader relinquish control of Muslim holy sites in Jerusalem. As a people who had been made to pay the price for the Holocaust, for which they had no responsibility, and as objects of daily humiliation under Israeli occupation, Palestinians entered negotiations—or in the case of Hamas, bitterly opposed negotiations—not to suffer further humiliation, but to assert their dignity.

In short, emotions pushed in completely opposite directions. The more Israel demanded concessions in the name of security, the more humiliated and resistant Palestinians became, which merely increased Israeli anxieties. Each side's most basic needs remained largely invisible to the other. In this view, a deal was virtually impossible to reach—and even if it had been reached, it would never have held.

Such an interpretation may be too pessimistic. In retrospect, many who actually participated in the talks from 1993 to 2001 felt that Israeli and Palestinian leaders could have acted far more wisely and adroitly than they did. If leaders were constrained by popular emotions, they also enjoyed a certain autonomy, and the particular choices they made were by no means inevitable. However, in identifying political failures, as usual, there are two stories.

---

8   Also known as the Al-Aqsa *Intifada*, with reference to the mosque which Sharon's visit to the Noble Sanctuary implicated, and from which Palestinian protestors exited, on September 29, 2000.

9   One Likud leader admitted that if they could be certain that evacuating all settlements would ensure Israel's physical security, even nine out of ten Likud voters would do so in a heartbeat.

In the **Palestinian narrative**, the chief mistake was the failure of Likud, but more especially of Labor under Rabin and Barak, to halt Jewish expansion in the occupied territories in general, and to stand up to the settler lobby in particular. From 1993 to 2000, even as negotiations proceeded, West Bank settlers (not even including those in East Jerusalem) increased from about 100,000 to 190,000.[10] The settlers consumed scarce resources that Palestinians intended for their own state, fragmented areas of Arab habitation, and engaged in vigilante violence. To protect the settlers against retaliation, Israel built ever more bypass roads, often on land confiscated from Arabs, and imposed more controls. Labor as well as Likud also sought to transform Arab East Jerusalem by building thousands of new Jewish housing units in and around the city. By substituting unilateral actions of this sort for bilateral negotiation, by imposing a solution rather than striving for mutual agreement, such policies destroyed the spirit of Oslo and soured Palestinians on the whole peace process. To be sure, the settlers' appeal to Zionist tradition and the nature of Israeli coalition politics let them wield a political influence far greater than their numbers. But the fact remains that settlers constituted a very small proportion of the Israeli population.[11] If Rabin and Barak had been been more courageous in opposing the extravagant demands of this influential minority, if they had argued more forcefully that the country's long-term need for peace outweighed any short-term advantage in settler expansion, they could have maintained Palestinian goodwill. In combination, settler pressure and Labor equivocation put the entire peace process at risk.

In addition, according to the Palestinian narrative, Barak made four specific blunders: 1) Driven both by Israeli party politics and by personal arrogance, he pushed ahead with final talks at Camp David, even though Arafat warned him that not enough preliminary work had been done, and that the talks were bound to fail. 2) Despite a lot of hoopla, in truth, the concessions on territories and Jerusalem that Barak offered at Camp David were inadequate to meet basic Palestinian requirements. In the words of one knowledgeable American participant at Camp David, the terms Barak offered were nothing Arafat "or any other Palestinian in his right mind could have accepted."[12] 3) Barak, ignoring advice from both Palestinian and Israeli experts, made a fatal error in allowing Sharon's disastrously ill–timed visit to the Temple Mount/Noble Sanctuary. 4) He then compounded that error by allowing security forces to overreact to Palestinian protests. It was Israeli security forces who inflicted the first fatalities, all on unarmed rioters. Without these critical mistakes by Barak, the second *intifada* never would have begun.

The **Israeli narrative** argues that, despite the Palestinians' cherished self-image as helpless victims, settlements responded directly to decisions made by Palestinians and their allies—namely, the decision to attack Israel in 1967, and then to spurn Labor's offer to return most of the recently acquired lands. Do Palestinians think, contrary to all human history, that they can advocate war and pay no penalty when the war fails? Strategically concentrated along the Green Line, settlements explicitly sought to prevent a repeat of the military threat of 1967.

Moreover, to argue that settlements justified rejecting Barak's territorial concessions in 2000 is completely and totally illogical. If continuing settlements were so insufferable, why didn't the PA accept his offer to quit 100 percent of Gaza

---

10   Lesch, *The Arab–Israeli Conflict*, 375; Tessler, *History of the Israeli–Palestinian Conflict*, 772, 820. Jews in East Jerusalem numbered 172,000 in early 2001.

11   About four percent in 2000, excluding those in East Jerusalem.

---

12   Robert Malley, "American Mistakes and Israeli Misconceptions," in Shamir and Maddy–Weitzman, *The Camp David Summit*, 111: "One should not excuse the Palestinians' passivity or unhelpful posture at Camp David. But the simple and inescapable truth is that there was no deal at Camp David that Arafat, Abu Mazen, Dahlan, or any other Palestinian in his right mind could have accepted. That has become far clearer in hindsight. What was put on the table was not a detailed agreement but vague proposals …"

and 97 percent of the West Bank? Palestine would have become independent, not a single additional Jewish building would have been built on Palestinian land, and the settler problem would have disappeared immediately.

Beyond this, Arafat's claim that he lacked time to get ready for Camp David ignores the seven long years he had to prepare his positions. The basic problem was that he had no interest in serious compromise, because (as he candidly admitted to Arab-speaking audiences) his long-term goal remained an arrangement that, sooner or later, would destroy Israel as a Jewish state. Arafat's style, on display both at Camp David and in late 2000, was not to engage in give-and-take, but to restate ad infinitum his initial position. A figure entirely sympathetic to the Palestinians, Prince Bandar of Saudi Arabia angrily warned Arafat that his intransigence was the key obstacle to peace.[13] Clinton, who saw himself as an honest broker, also warned Arafat at Camp David, "You are leading your people and the region to a catastrophe," and afterward directly blamed Arafat— not Barak—for the collapse of negotiations.[14]

Nor, in this interpretation, should Sharon's peaceful visit to the Temple Mount/Noble Sanctuary have inspired a violent response. No one made Palestinians attack Israeli policemen and hurl paving stones on Jewish worshippers. Nor did Israeli security forces overreact. The truth is that Palestinians seized on Sharon's visit as a welcome pretext for wholesale violence; and Arafat, swayed by popular passion and the Hezbollah model, deliberately fanned the flames, hoping to force Israel into more concessions. In effect, he declared war on his peace partners. All Arafat accomplished, however, was to transform a rational deliberative process into armed confrontation, to poison the atmosphere for any further discussions—and thus to kill the best chance for peace in 80 years. In choosing violence over negotiations and compromise, Arafat repeated the same choice Palestinian leaders had made in 1937, 1939, 1947, and 1967.

Israel Returns to Unilateralism, 2001–2006

Whichever pieces of these competing narratives one chooses to accept and assemble into a coherent explanation, the fact remains that 2000–2001 was a watershed, at least in the medium term. Shocked not merely by the collapse of Oslo, which they had assumed would lead to a permanent peace, but more especially by what they saw as the utter viciousness of the second *intifada*, Israelis became convinced that they had no partner for peace, and that any improvement in security would have to come entirely from their own actions. In 2001 Israel, therefore, resumed the sort of unilateral initiatives, unaccompanied by a search for Israeli–Palestinian cooperation, that had had preceded Oslo.

The second *intifada*, which began in late 2000, did not crest for another 18 months. Moving beyond settler targets in the West Bank into Israel proper, Palestinian suicide bombers in 2001 and early 2002 struck public buses, markets, restaurants, night clubs, and hotels, using high explosives packed with nails so as to maximize civilian casualties—which surely fits the classic definition of terrorism.[15] Israelis became frightened to use public facilities, and polls showed that large

---

13 See p. 10, n. 6 *supra*.

14 Benny Morris, "Camp David and After," *The New York Review of Books* 49 (June 13, 2002); Bregman, *Israel's Wars*, 209; Bill Clinton, *My Life: Bill Clinton* (New York: Alfred A. Knopf, 2004), 943–45: "Arafat's rejection of my proposal after Barak accepted it was an error of historic proportions."

15 See p. 29, n. 1 *supra*. From October 2000 to December 2001, 685 Israelis were killed and 4,500 injured. These were overwhelmingly civilians hit by terrorist attacks. Palestinian casualties are estimated at 1,300 killed and 9,700 wounded, most of whom were hit in firefights with the IDF. Sachar, *History of Israel*, 1050; Tessler, *History of the Israeli–Palestinian Conflict*, 777–81. See too Human Rights Watch, *Erased in a Moment: Suicide Bombing Attacks Against Israeli Civilians* (New York, 2002); Mohammed Hafez, *Manufacturing Human Bombs: The Making of Palestinian Suicide Bombers* (Washington, D.C., 2006).

majorities feared that members of their families would be killed or maimed. Suicide bombers came primarily from Hamas and Islamic Jihad, but also from militias responsible to Arafat, who worried that he would lose ground to the Islamists unless he too responded to the deep, popular yearning to punish Israeli "arrogance" and "brutality" by inflicting on the Jews massive, visible pain. With their pictures plastered on the walls of buildings and featured on trading cards for children, suicide bombers were lionized as martyrs who had sacrificed themselves to liberate Muslim Palestine from Jewish occupation.

Deeply shaken, Israeli voters now swung far to the right, replacing Barak with Sharon as Prime Minister in 2001 by the largest electoral margin in Israeli history, and decimating Labor in the 2003 Knesset elections. Israel's new mood matched that of the United States following the historic al-Qaeda attacks in New York City and Washington, D.C., on September 11, 2001. In Israel and the United States, whatever lingering sympathy the first *intifada* had won for Palestinians tended to fade: despite their different origins and programs, to many Western observers, al-Qaeda and Hamas suddenly seemed to be of a piece. With belated support from President George W. Bush, Sharon in March 2002 moved to crush the new *intifada* with Operation Defensive Shield. The IDF reoccupied all West Bank population centers, sealed off the territories from Israel proper, isolated Arafat in his Ramallah compound, imposed curfews and mass arrests, demolished the houses of suicide bombers, confiscated materials that could be used for such operations, and systematically assassinated militant leaders. Suicide bombings in Israel began to fall sharply, virtually ending in 2004. Meanwhile, many Palestinians, badly hurt by Israel's security clampdown and economic closure, began to turn on Arafat and his PA, accusing them of incompetence and corruption, and lamenting the second *intifada* as a frightful blunder.

Yet this was, at best, a tactical victory for Sharon. The question remained: What should be Israel's long-term strategy for the territories? Labor's vision of exchanging land for peace had

been put to the test with Oslo, and in the opinion of most Israelis, had proved a colossal failure.

But Likud's vision of Greater Israel seemed no more practical. With an effective end by 2000 of immigration from the former Soviet Union, which was the last large reservoir of potential Jewish immigrants, and with population growth among Palestinians exceeding that among Jews, "Judaizing" the West Bank grew ever more chimerical. Whereas in 1967, Arabs (including those in Israel) were only 36 percent of those residing between the Jordan and the Mediterranean, by 2003—as a result of high Arab natality, declining Jewish natality, and improved Arab health care —Arabs probably were approaching 45 percent. This was despite the massive influx of Russian Jews after 1989. Even if most Arabs had wanted to become Israeli citizens—which they assuredly did not—Israel could not possibly grant all of them citizenship and survive as a Jewish state. Yet, as Labor had realized years earlier, it was also inconceivable that Israel would retain Arab lands indefinitely without granting local people citizenship and voting rights. Quite apart from the insult to Israel's cherished self-image as a democratic country, permanently disenfranchising millions of subject Arabs would be completely unacceptable to Europe and the United States, not to mention Afro–Asian countries. In an unacknowledged bow to earlier Labor strategizing, Sharon and many Likud leaders concluded that in the long run, Israel had no choice but to withdraw from the great bulk of the territories. By implication, a Palestinian state seemed inevitable.

But since Oslo's failure showed there was no one to whom Israel could safely entrust the territories, Sharon hit on two unilateral expedients. First, he began building an elaborate security barrier, which roughly followed the Green Line of 1967, but which extended east to incorporate the chief Jewish settlements in the West Bank. As the name implied, this sought to prevent suicide bombers from penetrating Israel, and, in fact, it largely explains the dramatic decline in attacks after 2002. At the same time, the barrier demarcated what Israel believed would eventually comprise an independent Palestinian state. Originally eating up some 15 percent of the West Bank, the fence later contracted to include between seven and nine percent,[16] which approximated Clinton's compromise formula at Camp David. East of the barrier, the IDF retained overall security control. But simultaneously, Sharon sought to work with Mahmoud Abbas, Arafat's long-time aide, who was elected PA President in January 2005 after Arafat's sudden death, and who remained responsible for civil administration in Palestinian population centers. Having fallen afoul of Arafat and Hamas, Abbas was regarded by Israel and the United States as a pragmatist who, they hoped, would be able to counter the radicals and eventually negotiate the final status agreement that had eluded Barak and Arafat.

The second element of Sharon's unilateral strategy was to withdraw all Jewish soldiers and settlers from Gaza, while retaining control over the chief entry points to that territory. This evacuation was severely criticized by the Israeli left—who argued, correctly, that Sharon sought to relieve pressure for a more complete and immediate withdrawal from the West Bank—and from the right, who contended, with equal prescience, that it would allow Hamas to follow the Hezbollah model and convert Gaza into a base from which to attack southern Israel. Despite these criticisms and resistance from settlers within Gaza, the withdrawal was completed in August of 2005.

In essence, Sharon had staked out a centrist position, seeing military reoccupation of the West Bank as a temporary necessity, but abandoning long-term dreams of Greater Israel. Unable to quell the conservative critics of his Gaza withdrawal within Likud, in late 2005 Sharon shocked the country by abandoning Likud to form a new centrist party, Kadima ("Forward"), with the help of defectors from both Likud and Labor. Although a massive stroke soon removed Sharon

from the scene, in March of 2006 Kadima, now led by Ehud Olmert, won a convincing electoral victory on Sharon's platform of unilateral withdrawal—and, assuming that a negotiating partner could one day be found, of renewed negotiations. Sharon and Olmert, the former Likud mayor of Jerusalem, had both evolved from advocates of Greater Israel to pragmatic centrists. They would not be the last Israeli politicians to traverse that same route.

Anti-Zionists Turn to Unilateralism: The Expanding Role of Hezbollah and Hamas

Oslo's failure encouraged a turn to unilateralism not only by Israel, but also by its enemies, who pursued a variety of political and military initiatives. As before 1993, the most energetic anti-Israeli actors were nonstate organizations—the cost of conventional war against Israel was simply too high for the Syrian government to pay—and their preferred mode remained guerrilla and terrorist operations.

Yet anti-Zionists actors after 2000 also differed from their pre-Oslo counterparts in crucial ways. First, until the late 1980s Israel's chief nonstate (or substate) opponent had been the Fatah-led PLO, but after 2000 that role was assumed by Hezbollah and Hamas.

Second, while Hamas, like the PLO, was a Palestinian organization, Hezbollah was Lebanese. As such, Hezbollah became the first non-Palestinian nonstate actor to play a significant military role against Israel.[17]

Third, by providing Hezbollah and Hamas with ideological inspiration, diplomatic support, and weapons, a non-Arab state, namely Iran, also became closely involved for the first time in the anti-Israel struggle. Thus, the Mideast conflict leapfrogged beyond the ring of Arab states who had led the struggle since 1948.[18]

---

16   The discrepancy reflects different Israeli and Palestinian calculations. Alan Dowty, *Israel/Palestine* (2nd ed., Cambridge: Polity Press, 2008), 172. On this period generally, see *ibid.*, chs. 8–9; Sachar, *History of Israel*, chs. 37–41; Tessler, *History of the Israeli–Palestinian Conflict*, 819–47.

---

17   Being Shi'ite, it was also the first non-Sunni Arab organization to play a major role.

18   This allowed Persia/Iran to become, in effect, a Mediterranean power for the first time since the Persian

Fourth, whereas the PLO, Egypt, Ba'athist Syria, and Jordan all followed essentially secular ideologies, Hezbollah, Hamas, and Iran were resolutely and avowedly anti-secular. That is to say, whereas leaders in the former group, in keeping with Western Enlightenment tradition, tend to accept that political authority derives from human convention, the leaders of Hezbollah, Hamas, and Iran claim that their authority derives directly from God—whose will, of course, they understand better than any other humans. (This growth of Islamic fundamentalism thus parallels the rise of the religious right in Israel. In both cases, the appeal to "traditional" certainties plays best with the poorest, most culturally encapsulated, least Western-educated sector of the population.)

Fifth, after 2006 the rise of Hamas, which was based in Gaza, produced a split with Fatah and the PLO, based in the West Bank. In formal duration and Palestinian blood—not to mention in its territorial dimension—this split exceeded anything in Palestinian history, including the rivalry between Husaynis and Nashashibis before World War Two.

In an immediate sense, as we saw, Hezbollah ("The Party of God") arose in Lebanon in the mid-1980s in response to Israel's 1982 invasion.[19] More basically perhaps, Hezbollah's waxing fortunes reflected a multigenerational rise in the birthrate among Lebanese Shi'ites, together with the deep resentments that this underprivileged population had long nurtured against Lebanon's dominant Sunni and Christian elites. Fellow Shi'ite Iran, which had been transformed by the revolution of 1979, inspired Hezbollah with its message of redemption for the poor and downtrodden, religious sanctification of daily life, anti-Westernism, defense of Muslim honor, and implacable hatred of the Jewish state, whose domination over Muslims the Shi'ites found

abhorrent. The traditional marginalization of Shi'ite Iran within the larger Sunni-dominated Muslim world mirrored the marginalization of Shiites within Lebanese society. For both Iran and Hezbollah (as indeed for their ally Syria, which was led by the minority religious community known as Alawites) implacable hostility to Israel therefore offered a way to escape sectarian isolation to claim the leadership of a pan-Muslim coalition. For both Hezbollah and Iran, fervent anti-Israel sentiment quickly morphed into the sort of open, unapologetic anti-Semitism not seen on the world stage since the 1940s. Aided by Iran and Syria,[20] Hezbollah built a network of schools and charitable foundations, as well as a formidable guerrilla organization, whose grim persistence and tactical brilliance culminated in Israel's 2000 retreat from its self-declared security zone in south Lebanon.

With this historic victory over the Zionists, Hezbollah's reputation in Lebanon and throughout the Arab world soared. Yet insofar as Hezbollah defined itself as a resistance movement against a foe that no longer occupied Lebanese soil, that triumph also raised embarrassing questions. Lebanese Sunnis and Christians now began to ask insistently: Given that Israel has gone, and given that other Lebanese militias involved in the civil war of 1975–1990 have now disarmed, why should Hezbollah alone retain a private army? Hezbollah's enemies claim that it responded to these pressures by assassinating, or conspiring with Syria to assassinate, Lebanon's principal Sunni leader, Rafiq Hariri, in early 2005. Hezbollah's involvement in Hariri's death, however, has yet to be proven. More certainly, Hezbollah sought to parry criticism by demonstrating its continued value as Lebanon's military shield against Israel. To the unanticipated results of the latter strategy we shall turn shortly.

Hamas, Israel's second principal nonstate enemy in the early 2000s, differed from Hezbollah in that it was Sunni and Palestinian, rather than

---

Achaemenid Empire was defeated by Alexander the Great in 330 BCE.

19   On Hezbollah, see Augustus Richard Norton, *Hezbollah* (Princeton: Princeton University Press, 2007); Judith Palmer Harik, *Hezbollah* (London: I.B. Taurus, 2007).

20   Ba'ath Syria's secular orientation notwithstanding, Syria began to ally itself with revolutionary Shi'ite Iran in the 1980s.

Shi'ite and Lebanese. Moreover, Israel's occupation of the West Bank and Gaza ensured that until 2007, Hamas, unlike Hezbollah, had little military credibility.[21] Indeed, until 2007 it was not a military force per se, but a political, social, and terrorist organization. On the other hand, Hamas resembled Hezbollah insofar as both cohered in the mid- or late 1980s, both were fervently Islamist and hostile to Western secularism, both were unabashedly anti-Semitic,[22] both were sworn to Israel's destruction, and both looked to Iran and Syria for support. In the 1990s, even as Oslo unfolded, Hamas (the name is an acronym for Islamic Resistance Movement, but also means "zeal" in Arabic) built a following, especially in the refugee camps, through its unequivocal anti-Zionism, its extensive welfare and educational programs, its invocation of an authentically Arab, non-Western cultural idiom, and its reputation for honesty, which contrasted with Fatah's increasingly kleptocratic tendencies. More basically perhaps, like Hezbollah, Hamas offered religious "truths" and social support to address the psychological stress associated with rapid population growth.

Hamas attacks on Israelis in the Oslo years deliberately sought to destroy any chance for reconciliation—or as Hamas saw it, for the surrender of Palestinian rights. These attacks cleverly exploited Arafat's dilemma: if he acted as Israel's policeman, he alienated many Palestinians; but if he tolerated the attacks, he antagonized his would-be partner,

Israel. Hence, in practice, Arafat vacillated. Once Oslo collapsed, Hamas argued in self-fulfilling fashion that this confirmed what it had said all along, namely, that negotiations were a waste of time. By spearheading the second *intifada*, Hamas continued to steal the initiative from Fatah, which suffered from the basic incoherence of its message, from the impoverishment accompanying the second *intifada* (when Palestinian GDP fell 40 percent), and from deep popular resentment that corrupt PA officials were driving Mercedes cars and building grand villas, while the people were scrounging for basic necessities.

In what turned out to be a colossal miscalculation, Arafat's successor, Mahmoud Abbas, sought to strengthen himself by calling legislative elections for early 2006. Hamas ran a disciplined campaign, while an overconfident Fatah not only exerted limited effort, but in many districts allowed multiple candidates to split the pro-Fatah vote. Although more impressive in the number of seats than in percentage of the vote, Hamas's victory shocked not only Abbas, Israel, and foreign observers, but Hamas leaders themselves. Desperate to salvage the possibility of renewed negotiations, the United States and the European Union offered to continue aid to a Hamas-led PA, provided that Hamas renounced violence, recognized Israel, and agreed to abide by earlier agreements between Israel and the PA. Hamas refused all three demands. Encouraged by Western countries and Israel, Abbas, through a variety of constitutional maneuvers, some of dubious legality, attempted to prevent Hamas from exercising the power over PA security forces and other institutions to which its electoral victory entitled it. Hamas responded by forming independent militias. As relations between Fatah and Hamas deteriorated, open fighting broke out, culminating in Hamas' rout of Fatah forces in Gaza and its seizure of that territory in June 2007. Hamas promptly destroyed local Fatah institutions, arresting and executing leading Fatah loyalists.

The United States, Israel, Egypt, and the European Union rushed financial and military help to shore up Abbas, still in control of the West Bank, and moved to isolate Gaza. Hamas

---

21　On Hamas, see Matthew Levitt, *Hamas* (New Haven: Yale University Press, 2006); Beverly Milton-Edwards and Stephen Farrell, *Hamas* (Cambridge: Polity, 2010); Loren Lybarger, *Identity and Religion in Palestine* (Princeton, Princeton University Press, 2007); Jonathan Schanzer, *Hamas vs. Fatah* (New York: Palgrave Macmillan, 2008); Azzam Tamimi, *Hamas: A History from Within* (Northampton, MA: Olive Branch Press, 2007).

22　The Hamas founding charter, still in force in early 2011, cites approvingly the Protocols of the Elders of Zion, an absurd anti-Semitic document exposed decades ago as a Czarist forgery, which attributes most upheavals in modern history to a Jewish conspiracy.

nonetheless received clandestine aid from Syria, Hezbollah, and Iran, and the enthusiastic support of most Gazans and, indeed, many in the West Bank (although pro-Hamas organizations in the latter area were repressed under emergency regulations). Thus, by late 2007 the would-be Palestinian state had split, with Hamas establishing an effective dictatorship in Gaza (population 1.5 million) and with Fatah doing the same in the West Bank (population variously estimated at 1.5 to 2.6 million).

The 2006 Lebanon War and the 2008–2009 Gaza War

Israel's unilateral withdrawal from south Lebanon in 2000 and Gaza in 2005 had sought to prevent military overextension and to reduce regional tensions. But because Hezbollah and Hamas filled the territorial vacuum, Israel's retreat had an effect opposite to what was intended. It produced two short, particularly vicious wars, in south Lebanon in July and August of 2006, and in Gaza from December 2008 to January 2009.

Following those of 1948–1949, 1956, 1967, 1973, 1982–1985, 1985–2000, and 2000–2002, these were the eighth and ninth major conflicts between Israel and its Arab neighbors.[23] If we view this 60-year period in its entirety, we find that Israel's principal opponents changed from conventional state armies to nonstate actors, and that the nature of warfare shifted from symmetric to asymmetric. The first four conflicts, through 1973, pitted the IDF against armies whose size, internal organization, strategies, and weaponry resembled—were symmetric with—those of the IDF. Israel's 1982–1985 Lebanon invasion was transitional, because the IDF fought the Syrian army, but also engaged Palestinian and Lebanese

militias. Thereafter, from 1985 to 2009, all of Israel's battlefield opponents—Hezbollah, Hamas, and other Islamist and PLO-linked militias—were nonstate actors. Although these groups receive arms from Syria and Iran, they lack the distinct territorial character, extensive size, organization, and heavy weapons of conventional armies. Unable to stand toe to toe with the IDF, in classic guerrilla fashion they opposed Israel with ambushes, terrorist raids, and mobile rocket attacks. Such contests, by definition, were asymmetric.

Nonstate actors' obvious weaknesses are, first, their inability to change the strategic equation, that is, to inflict serious material and territorial, as opposed to psychological, damage; and second, their inability to defend local infrastructures and populations against air and artillery attack. Sometimes extensive damage erodes popular sympathy for nonstate actors. But this is a double-edged sword, because civilian casualties can strengthen guerrilla support while sparking international condemnation of the conventional actor. Integration into the host population also renders nonstate fighters far more difficult to isolate and defeat than a regular army. In short, asymmetric warfare, more often than conventional warfare, tends to produce messy, ambiguous outcomes. This explains why, in place of Israeli triumphs from 1948 to 1967, no war after 1967 ended in indisputable Israeli victory; and why, as noted, Syria chose to forsake direct contests with the IDF in favor of proxy confrontations via Hezbollah and Hamas. A similar trajectory, by the way, has affected the United States Army, whose last conventional war was in Korea, and whose last indisputable victory, one could argue, came in 1945.[24]

Hezbollah's ultimate goal, reminiscent of that of the PLO and of Arab states in an earlier generation, has been stated unequivocally on numerous

---

23   The full list: The wars of 1948–1949 (Independence); 1956 (Sinai); 1967 (Six Day War); 1973 (Egypt–Israel War); 1982–1985 (Israel's Lebanon invasion); 1985–2000 (the struggle between Hezbollah and Israel in south Lebanon); 2000–2002 (the second *intifada*); 2006 (Lebanon); and 2008–2009 (Gaza).

24   While ejecting Iraqi forces from Kuwait, the Gulf war of 1991 failed to destroy Saddam Hussein, whose continued defiance prompted the second war against Iraq in 2003. Whether that invasion's tactical success will translate into long–term strategic victory remains unclear.

occasions. "Our struggle will end only when this entity [Israel] is obliterated," declared Hezbollah's founding document. "We recognize no treaty with it, no ceasefire, and no peace agreements."[25] So, too, Hezbollah's Secretary–General Hassan Nasrallah has explained, "I am against any reconciliation with Israel. I do not even recognize the presence of a state that is called 'Israel.'"[26]

The war that broke out in mid-July 2006 grew out of a cross-border raid by Hezbollah. Although that operation killed ten Israeli soldiers, Hezbollah's original goal seems to have been to capture alive IDF personnel whom it could exchange for Hezbollah prisoners in Israeli jails. More broadly, the raid probably sought to remind Hezbollah's Lebanese critics that the militia remained central to national defense. Almost certainly Hezbollah did not want a general conflagration, but when Israel responded by pounding targets across Lebanon, it became obvious that Hezbollah's leaders had miscalculated.[27]

At first, Israel was convinced that air power alone could stop Hezbollah rocket fire into Israel and smash its command systems. Israeli planes soon pulverized Lebanon's infrastructure. Yet Katyusha rockets still rained down on civilians in northern Israel. Eager to buttress his weak security credentials, Israel's new Prime Minister Ehud Olmert belatedly sent in ground forces—again with mixed results. Not only did Hezbollah rocket fire continue up to the moment a UN cease-fire came into effect in mid-August, not only was Hezbollah's resistance lionized across the Arab world, but Israel incurred heavy international criticism for causing civilian casualties and damage that were said to be hugely disproportionate

to Hezbollah's initial offense. Israel replied, first, that such losses were the unintended, but inevitable result of Hezbollah's decision to embed itself in civilian neighborhoods, and second, that Hezbollah, unlike the IDF, deliberately targeted civilians.

Despite Hezbollah's public relations success, within Lebanon the staggering human and economic cost of the 2006 war prompted bitter recriminations. The 34-day conflict cost Lebanon some $6 to $10 billion in direct damage and billions more in lost revenue, substantially negating 15 years of post-civil war reconstruction. Nasrallah himself admitted the cross-border raid had been a terrible mistake. In June 2009 an anti-Hezbollah coalition won national elections, in large part because many Sunnis and Christians resented Hezbollah's adventurism and its continuing autonomy.[28] Although less than two years later the anti-Hezbollah coalition lost power, from August 2006 to early 2011, the Lebanese–Israeli border has remained quieter than for any comparable period since 1975. Thus—at least in the short term—Israel's invasion achieved a significant level of deterrence. Although Israel never admitted it, the "hugely disproportionate" nature of its attacks on Lebanon's economic infrastructure probably was central to that success.

The Gaza war of 2008–2009 exhibited a similar dynamic and outcome. If Israel thought that its 2005 military withdrawal would pacify Gaza, Hamas and allied groups saw things very differently. For 38 years, Gazans had suffered under occupation. Now, inspired by Hezbollah, Hamas was determined to redress the emotional and political balance. More specifically, Hamas sought to force Israel to relinquish control over Gaza's air, sea, and land exits, which would facilitate commercial traffic into Gaza, while at the same time

---

25 Anthony Cordesman, *Lessons of the 2006 Israeli–Hezbollah War* (Washington, DC: Center for Strategic and International Studies, 2007), 33. On the 2006 conflict, see too Cathy Sultan, *Tragedy in South Lebanon* (Minneapolis: Scarletta Press, 2008); Norton, *Hezbollah*, ch. 6.

26 Cordesman, *Lessons of the 2006 Israeli–Hezbollah War*, 33.

27 My analysis follows primarily Norton, *Hezbollah*, ch. 6.

---

28 After Rafiq Hariri's assassination in 2005, anti-Hezbollah and anti-Syrian sentiment gave birth to the so-called Cedar Revolution, which forced the withdrawal of Syrian troops from Lebanon, and which went on to win 2005 legislative elections. It was essentially this same coalition that beat out a pro-Hezbollah coalition in the 2009 elections.

easing the flow of arms. After Hamas' 2007 coup, American diplomatic and financial pressure and Israel's blockade served only to increase Islamist defiance. In the first six months of 2008 alone, Gaza militants fired some 2,000 mortars and homemade rockets against nearby Israeli communities. An Egyptian-mediated truce having broken down, in late December 2008, in what became known as Operation Cast Lead, Olmert ordered massive air attacks and a major ground assault against Gaza designed to halt missile fire—and ideally, to overthrow Hamas.

Although Israel went to greater lengths than in 2006 to reduce civilian casualties, it met with even heavier international criticism, culminating in a commission of inquiry authorized by the UN Human Rights Council, to which we shall return. Contrary to Israeli expectations, its invasion and the subsequent tightening of its blockade probably reinforced, rather than weakened, the Gazans' support for Hamas. Once again, asymmetric war offered political advantages to the nonstate actor.

No less familiar, however, was the practical benefit that Israel derived from degrading its opponents' military capacity and civilian infrastructure. Some 14 percent of Gaza's buildings were partially or completely destroyed, including every known Hamas facility, together with Gaza's electrical and water systems. In the aftermath of Operation Cast Lead, from 2009 to May 2011 (the time of writing), rocket attacks on Israel largely stopped, and the border grew quieter than at any time since 2005. Indeed, because Hamas was relatively weak to start with, because tiny Gaza was far more vulnerable to interdiction than Lebanon, and because Egypt until early 2011 was more or less willing to join Israel in imposing an arms embargo, Hamas had difficulty replenishing its arsenal, far more difficulty certainly than Hezbollah, which had an open conduit to Syria.

In a psychological sense, one could argue that the wars of 2006 to 2009 turned the Hezbollah model on its head. Precisely because Israel feared that militants once again would use vacated territory for missile attacks, Hezbollah and Hamas attacks made the Jewish state less—not more—willing to leave the West Bank, which directly abuts Israel's heartland. Indeed, according to a recent interview with Mahmoud Abbas, he and Olmert were on the verge of a peace agreement in late 2008, but Hamas rocket fire and Operation Cast Lead destroyed those secret negotiations. When in early 2009, at the end of the Gaza campaign, a new Likud government under Benjamin Netanyahu took office, it demanded additional security guarantees that Abbas refused. Since then, negotiations have been stalemated or in abeyance.[29]

---

29 *New York Times*, May 5, 2011.

Current Perspectives

Having taken the chronological narrative to early 2011, we turn finally to consider four overarching interpretive themes. These are both retrospective, in the sense that they analyze past events from a particular angle, and anticipatory, insofar as all have something to say about the future of the Arab–Israeli conflict—or perhaps about its resolution. We ask four sets of questions:

1. What has been the historic relation between the United States and Israel, and how does that relation influence current events?

2. How do Palestinians and Israelis perceive themselves, and how do those self-images impact political behavior? In particular, why does victimization play a central role in both national narratives?

3. What territorial and political solutions to the conflict seem feasible? What is likely to emerge from peace talks, should serious negotiations resume?

4. In the long term, which side in the conflict do demographic, economic, and political trends favor? On whom will the Angel of History confer her blessing?

The U.S.–Israel Relation

It cannot have escaped the reader's notice that for the better part of 60 years, the United States has provided Israel with remarkably high levels of support. In 1947–1948, recall, the Truman administration played a pivotal role in creating Israel. In the 1950s the United States sought to steer a more neutral course, but in 1967 President Lyndon Johnson, and in 1973 President Richard Nixon, gave Israel critical diplomatic and military help against the Soviet Union's Arab clients. During the Oslo process, President Bill Clinton strongly endorsed Israel's strategy vis-à-vis the Palestinians, while President George W. Bush (2001–2009) has been described as the most pro-Israel President in history. Since 1982 the United States has vetoed 32 UN Security Council resolutions critical of Israel—more than the total number of vetoes cast by all other Security Council members combined. Every year in the mid-2000s, Israel, a country of only seven million, received over six percent of the U.S. foreign aid budget. Likewise, the IDF has long enjoyed privileged access to the most advanced U.S. weaponry and intelligence.[1]

How can we explain such lavish American support? A 2007 book *The Israel Lobby*, by John Mearsheimer and Stephen Walt, remains by far

---

1 Data principally from John Mearsheimer and Stephen Walt, "The Israel Lobby," *London Review of Books*, March 23, 2006, pp. 3–12. For more extended treatment by those same authors, see *The Israel Lobby* (New York: Farrar, Straus and Giroux, 2007).

the best known analysis of this issue, both because it is cogently argued. and because—unintentionally, perhaps—it fits popular stereotypes about hidden Jewish power.[2] Those scholars begin by dismissing the usual arguments for America's embrace of the Jewish state. Israel, they argue, is not a strategic asset to the United States; indeed, resentment of U.S. support for Israel is a key ingredient in Muslim hostility toward America. Nor is Israel, the strongest military power in the Mideast, deserving of support because it is weak and vulnerable. Nor does Israel's treatment of the Palestinians accord with U.S. moral values; quite the contrary. Rather, in the view of Mearsheimer and Walt, American support reflects a single factor: the extraordinary power of "the Israel lobby," which they define as a loose coalition of individuals and organizations actively working to steer U.S. policy in a pro-Israel direction. Although not exclusively Jewish, the lobby is overwhelmingly led by Jewish individuals and organizations, so in effect, "the Israel lobby," as Mearsheimer and Walt use the term, is shorthand for "the Jewish lobby."

In methods and operation, that lobby is no different from innumerable other political interest groups, like the AARP, the AFL–CIO, the NAACP, the NRA, and the Armenian lobby. But the Israel lobby is exceptionally good at what it does—that is to say, influencing Congress and the executive branch, and helping to mold public opinion. Its influence on Congress and the White House derives from campaign contributions, which go chiefly to Democratic presidential candidates; from Jewish voting blocs in key states, from the circulation of persuasive position papers, and from the appointment of sympathetic personnel, both Jews and non–Jews, to serve as Congressional staffers and executive branch policy makers. Jewish influence on electronic and print media derives to some extent from ownership, but more particularly from sympathetic editors and journalists, letter-writing campaigns, and a commanding presence in respected research institutions.

Without doubt, this theory captures an important dimension of the U.S.–Israel relationship.

Surely, it is not coincidental that the Western country with the largest, wealthiest, most influential Jewish community is also the one with the most consistently pro-Israel foreign policy. But as a total explanation of U.S. behavior, the Mearsheimer–Walt thesis is deficient for two reasons. First, it emphasizes domestic influences on policy to the virtual exclusion of strategic global considerations.[3] Second, in explaining domestic influences, it focuses on Jewish activities, while ignoring or minimizing American support for Israel outside the Jewish community. Consider each element in turn.

If the alliance with Israel offered the United States no strategic benefits, one would be justified in focusing entirely on domestic politics. But that is hardly the case. Since 1945, America's goals in the Mideast have been to prevent any other power from dominating the region, and to minimize upheavals that could threaten the flow of oil. Now it is true that until the 1960s, Israel was not particularly useful in either regard, and after 1948 neither Republican nor Democratic Presidents showed much interest in the Jewish state. But from the 1960s the growth of Soviet influence in general, and the Six Day War in particular, enhanced Israel's appeal. As the region's incontestably dominant power, Israel showed that it could crush Soviet clients like Syria, protect American clients like Jordan, encourage states like Egypt to shift to an American embrace, and provide valuable intelligence on Soviet capabilities. Thus, from 1967 to 1990 both Democratic and Republican Presidents promoted close ties to Israel. This is not to deny that domestic politics often pushed in the same direction, merely to argue that domestic concerns intersected with—and in some contexts remained subordinate to—strategic calculations. The year 1967 was a watershed because the Mideast military balance, not American domestic politics, saw a sea change.

After the Soviet collapse left the United States as the only superpower, global strategy continued to tell in favor of a strong relation to Israel. A

2   See previous note.

3   See Mearsheimer and Walt, *Israel Lobby*, ch. 2 for their dismal view of Israel's strategic value.

stable Pax Americana in the Mideast, with five U.S. client states—Israel, Palestine, Jordan, Egypt, and Saudi Arabia—at the core, now seemed a tantalizing possibility. But the prerequisite for a Pax Americana that the United States could sell to the Arabs was an Israeli–Palestinian deal. In turn, for Israel to feel secure enough to accept a Palestinian state, American support remained critical. Such calculations explain strong backing for the peace process by both the first Bush and Clinton administrations. In the first decade of the 21st century, such views only gained strength from the threat of Islamic radicalism and Iran.

If the Israel lobby truly dictated American Mideast policy, that policy would defer reflexively and instinctively to Israeli positions. In practice, however, when differences arise, American interests commonly trump those of Israel. From 1977 to date, for example, the Zionist lobby and Israel have assiduously sought U.S. approval for West Bank settlements, and have repeatedly asked the United States to move its embassy from Tel Aviv to Jerusalem—without success on either score. In 1992 and 1999, America helped to bring down two Likud governments, not because the Israeli lobby pressured it to do so—on the contrary, the chief U.S. Zionist groups were pro-Likud—but because the United States decided that Likud had become an obstacle to peace.[4] In 2006 America ignored Israeli pleas not to support Palestinian legislative elections. Viewing Iran's nuclear ambitions as a supreme threat, Israel has sought American permission, and ideally, cooperation, for a military strike on Iran—again to no avail.

The second intellectual danger inherent in a single-minded focus on Jewish domestic influence is that it ignores pro-Israel sentiment in the general population. Jewish influence alone cannot explain the pro-Israel sympathies of either Republican Presidents or the U.S. Congress. Some 80 percent of Jewish votes, and a comparable proportion of campaign gifts, go to Democratic presidential candidates. But George W. Bush, as noted, may have been the strongest supporter of Israel ever to occupy the White House, while Democratic President Barack Obama is seen by many American Jews and most Israelis as one of the weakest. Republican presidential aspirants Sarah Palin and Mike Huckabee could not be more pro-Israel, but neither has significant Jewish money or support. Zionist funding of Congressional races is negligible, and what money there is goes heavily to Democrats. Yet, judged by votes and speeches, Republican Congressmen are at least as supportive of Israel as their Democratic counterparts, and quite possibly, more so. Indeed, in fall 2010 the Israeli leadership looked to the expanded cohort of Congressional Republicans— only one of whose 290 members was Jewish—to provide it with the sort of protection against White House pressure that Democrats had been unable or unwilling to provide.[5]

A variety of historical factors have generated this widespread, if low-level, empathy for Israel. Steeped in biblical stories of the Promised Land and the Exodus, for generations many Protestants have seen Palestine as the land that God bestowed on the Jews. Such sentiments were only reinforced by American unease over Christian anti-Semitism. As early as 1891, long before American Jews wielded political influence, 400 of America's

4   The United States undermined Likud through public diplomacy and through direct and indirect intervention in Israeli domestic politics. On the theoretical determinants and practical instruments of U.S. policy toward the Mideast and Israel, see Quandt, *Peace Process*; David Lesch, ed., *The Middle East and the United States* (Boulder, CO: Westview Press, 2007); Michael Oren, *Power, Faith, and Fantasy* (New York: W. W. Norton, 2007), pt. 7; Henry Kissinger, *Does America Need a Foreign Policy?* (New York: Simon & Schuster, 2002), ch. 5; Michelle Mart, *Eye on Israel* (Albany: State University of New York Press, 2006).

5   In one 2010 Florida race for the U.S. House of Representatives, the winner, a non-Jewish African–American Republican, charged that the party of his opponent, a Jewish Democrat who was well known as a champion of Israel, was *insufficiently* supportive of the Jewish state. *Forward*, November 19, 2010, p. 5. Note too that long before he became active in national politics, Lyndon Baines Johnson, like family members before him, was something of a philo-Semite.

leading politicians, churchmen, editors, and businessmen signed a petition to the White House urging that the Ottoman Empire return Palestine to the Jews. In 1922 the U.S. Congress unanimously approved a joint resolution supporting the Balfour Declaration.[6] In recent decades, self–styled Christian Zionists, who constitute perhaps ten percent of Americans and many of whom believe that the birth of Israel and attendant wars in the Mideast conform to biblical prophecy, have become among Israel's most ardent and active supporters.

More general than religiously derived sympathy, however, is the popular identification with Israel as a fellow democracy, whose relatively secular, tolerant values are more attractive than what many see (no doubt with considerable stereotyping) as the more obscurantist practices of Muslim societies. Sympathy for Israel tends to correlate with political conservatism, as suggested by a 2010 poll showing that, while 63 percent of Americans identified more with Israel than the Palestinians (compared to 15 percent who identified more with Palestinians),[7] the pro-Israel proportion among Republicans was 85 percent, among independents 60 percent, and among Democrats 48 percent. Hence, many of the most pro-Israel voices in American politics come from politically conservative areas in the South, the West, and the Midwest with virtually no Jewish voters. Indeed, geographic and party support for Israel tends to correlate inversely with Jewish population. To be sure, Jews tend to feel far more strongly about the Mideast than the general

population; they provide leadership and finance for pro-Israel lobbies. Yet without this generalized goodwill toward Israel, Jews—only 1.8 percent of Americans—would find themselves isolated.

What is more, polls show that from 2001 to 2010, identification with Israel among most segments of the American population rose notably,[8] almost certainly in response to a perception that Israel and America were allies in a "war on terror." Although in some degree these sentiments remain hostage to current events, they also build upon cultural foundations that are unlikely to shift decisively in the short term, and that therefore point to continuing high levels of U.S. support for Israel.

Victimization and Demonization

A second recurrent theme that helps both to explain recent Mideast history and to define future options is the deeply rooted sense of victimization felt, ironically, by both Palestinians and Israelis. Together with their quest for the same small territory and their imprisonment in a cycle of recrimination and violence, this trait, in a sense, unites the two peoples. Indeed, along with Armenians, Jews and Palestinians may be the most justifiably aggrieved peoples in the world. Among wide sectors of both populations a psychology of isolation, vulnerability, and bitterness inhibits the sort of concessions needed for fruitful negotiations.

In general terms, Palestinian grievances are already familiar, but here follows a more focused presentation. Most Palestinians see themselves as victims of what Arafat repeatedly termed "a grave historic injustice." The Arabs of Palestine bore responsibility neither for Jewish suffering that engendered Zionism, nor for the Holocaust that helped give birth to Israel. But in each case, they were made to pay the price for European transgressions. From 1920 to 1948, Palestinians protested against Zionist settlement every way they could. They organized petitions, demonstrations,

---

6   Walter Russell Mead, "The New Israel and the Old," *Foreign Affairs* 87 (July/August, 2008): 32 and 28–46; Reich, *Brief History of Israel*, 19. That to some degree support for Jewish immigration to Palestine reflected opposition to large-scale Jewish immigration to the U.S. does not diminish this historic American identification of Palestine/Israel as the land of the Jews.

7   Some 22 percent favored both sides or had no opinion. Data from http://dailyalert.org/, 2/24/2010. Clearly, Christian Zionists were a significant fraction of pro-Israel supporters, but by no means sufficiently numerous by themselves, to explain these figures.

8   Previous note.

and strikes. They rioted, and from 1936 to 1939 launched an armed revolt. But nothing worked, because they lacked the physical power to stop what was, in effect, a Jewish invasion of their country. At bottom, in this interpretation, Palestine's history from 1920 to 1949 was a story of violence: the violence of colonial imposition, the violence with which resistance was crushed, the violence by which Jews seized Palestinian lands and dispossessed the inhabitants.

Many Palestinians would admit that their leaders made mistakes. But political miscalculation, in this view, was hardly the same as moral culpability. That they made poor decisions in no way weakens the justice of their claims. The Palestinians' only real "crime" was to live in a land that others coveted—and to resist dispossession. By any standard of fairness, Palestinians argue, they were entitled to retain the lands their families had inhabited for generations. But by 1948, Jewish intruders had seized 78 percent of mandatory Palestine.

As if these crimes were insufficient, after 1967 Jews began to encroach on the remaining 22 percent—and continue to do so at an accelerating pace. The confiscation of Palestinian land, the expulsion of Palestinians from their fields, and the suppression of virtually all forms of protest, including peaceful protest, continue to this day.[9] In 1930 Jewish lands were tiny islands in a Palestinian sea. Today, Palestinian lands are islands in an Israeli sea. Even Israel's faithful ally, the United States, criticizes Israeli settlement policy—but refuses to translate abstract opposition into effective pressure. Thus, Israel has been able to blockade, isolate, coerce, and humiliate an entire people with impunity. And despite repeated UN inquires and resolutions, that body has failed to force Israel to retreat, or even to modify its behavior in any substantial way. Precisely because the world community, including most Arab states, has tolerated what Palestinians see as monumental

injustice, they feel abandoned. The popularity among Palestinians of the PLO and Saddam Hussein in the past, and of Iran, Hezbollah, and Hamas in the present, derives from each of these actor's insistence that Palestinian honor and suffering be redeemed.

By extension, outrage and victimization help to explain two central features of Palestinian political culture: the recurrent resort to violence and an insistence on the right of return. To focus on violence is not to claim that Palestinians were the only advocates of force. On the contrary, as just noted, they see their entire history as one long story of brutality directed *against* them. Indeed, after 1936 at virtually every stage of the conflict, Palestinian casualties exceeded those sustained by the Jews. Repeatedly, however, Palestinians were the first to resort to arms, both because they saw themselves as targets of Jewish pressure, and because they felt they had no alternative. Thus, Palestinians initiated violence in 1920, 1921, 1929, 1936–1939, and 1947. In 1967 they supported the drive to war by Egypt, Jordan, and Syria. In 2000–2001 Palestinians launched the second *intifada*, and Hamas rocket fire led to the Gaza War of 2008–2009. A psychology of victimization also helps to explain why during the second *intifada* Palestinians mythologized that most awesome form of self–sacrifice, the suicide bombing mission. Although politically counterproductive—such acts only strengthened Sharon and sparked Operation Defensive Shield—suicide bombings inflicted pain and fear on Israelis comparable to the pain and fear Palestinians felt. Thus "martyrdom operations," as they were called, sought to even the score emotionally.[10] An emphasis on the redemptive value and practical necessity of violence remains central to Hamas.

Likewise, feelings of intolerable injustice explain the Palestinians' talismanic insistence on the right of refugees—as well as their children, grandchildren, and great-grandchildren—to return to their original homes in accord with UN General Assembly Resolution 194. In fact, 194 said nothing about descendants inheriting a right

---

9   For views highly critical of the occupation, by both Palestinians and Israelis, see David Shulman, "Israel and Palestine: Breaking the Silence," *The New York Review of Books* 58 (Feb. 24, 2011) and sources therein.

10   See Hafez, *Manufacturing Human Bombs.*

of return from their ancestors. But it underscored the illegitimacy of displacement and the necessity of redress. At no time during the Oslo process did any Palestinian leader, least of all Arafat, even hint he might abandon the "right of return." At the height of the second *intifada*, over 96 percent of refugees polled in the West Bank and Gaza said that, given the chance, they would go back to their original homes.[11] Return would mean that Palestinian steadfastness and courage had been rewarded, and the shame of defeat erased. In practical terms, of course, the return of four to ten million Arabs (estimates obviously vary) also would mean the end of Israel as a Jewish state. On some level, those interested in negotiations realize the impracticality of such a demand. But so powerful is the constituency for repatriation, so seductive the appeal of Fatah's rival, Hamas, that—in public, at least—even the "moderate" Mahmoud Abbas has refused so far to reconsider traditional claims.[12]

The Jewish sense of victimization differs from that of the Palestinians insofar as its origins lie not in Palestine, but in Europe, in centuries of clerical and secular anti-Semitism culminating in the Holocaust. An explicit determination to prevent a second Holocaust underlies the determination of Benjamin Netanyahu (who, recall, became Prime Minister again in early 2009) not to let Iran acquire nuclear weapons. Insofar as it continues to instill a deep sense of foreboding and vulnerability, the Holocaust, like *al-Nakba*, remains very much alive.

But in another sense, of course, it is ancient history, because unlike the Catastrophe, which Palestinians seek to redress through the right of return, nothing practical can be done to make good the murder of six million Jews. What most frightens Zionists today is what they see as the extreme hostility that the UN, various NGOs, and Western leftists routinely display toward the Jewish state. In the Zionist view, most of this criticism is wildly disproportionate, fundamentally irrational, and, therefore, impossible to assuage, short of national suicide.

Israel is the only country whose religious definition of national community the UN has ever condemned,[13] even though Israel's definition is similar to that of at least 30 Muslim states in the UN. The UN Human Rights Commission denied membership to only one country out of 192—Israel—and subjected only one country—Israel, yet again—to an agenda item every year. The UN Human Rights Council, successor to the Commission, in its first year (2006–2007) passed nine resolutions condemning Israel, but none against such notorious human rights abusers as China, Myanmar, North Korea, Belarus, or Zimbabwe. To 2009 over 80 percent of Council resolutions focused on Israel. Zionists also reject excessive criticism of Israel by such NGOs as Amnesty International and Human Rights Watch. Indeed, in 2009 the founder of Human Rights Watch publicly disassociated himself from his own organization because of what he deemed its obsessive hostility toward Israel.[14]

How do Israel's defenders explain this demonization? For Muslim countries, most of which

---

11 Dowty, *Israel/Palestine*, 210; Kimmerling and Migdal, *Palestinian People,* 406–407. Dowty presents 2003 polling data that complicate the issue by distinguishing more clearly between the refugees' theoretical insistence on the right of return, and a practical disinclination to do so. But in a 2010 poll, two–thirds of Palestinians agreed that "over time Palestinians must work to get back all the land [of Israel] for a Palestinian state."

12 Internal PA documents leaked to *Al Jazeera* and publicized in January 2011 claimed that in secret negotiations with the government of Ehud Olmert in 2008, the PA agreed to an essentially symbolic return of 10,000 refugees a year over 10 years. (Israel countered with an offer of 1,000 a year over five years). But once the reports were broadcast, Abbas and his aides, fearing a popular Palestinian backlash, denied *Al Jazeera's* claims. *New York Times*, January 24–25, January 28, 2011.

13 In the 1975 General Assembly resolution that equated Zionism with racism. However, in 1991, the General Assembly repealed that resolution.

14 Robert Bernstein, "Rights Watchdog, Lost in the Mideast," *New York Times*, Op–Ed page, October 19, 2009.

lack elementary civil liberties, criticizing Israel's human rights record is seen as no more than a convenient weapon. For many self-styled anti-imperialists in the West as well as in the developing world, Israel is an attractive target because it is a Western country that is exceptionally vulnerable. In the words of one anti-Israel boycotter, "Why single out Israel when the US [and] Britain do the same things in Iraq and Afghanistan? [Because] in a country so small and trade-dependent, it could actually work."[15] In Spain, Italy, and Greece, which combine high levels of aversion toward Jews (as measured by opinion polls) with strong left-wing traditions, Zionists see precious little difference between anti-Zionism and old-style anti-Semitism. The latter may be defined as an assumption that the same actions acceptable in other people are objectionable when committed by Jews.[16]

Israel's supporters see hypocrisy in three specific spheres. First, they argue, criticism of Israel's internal policies by comparison to most Afro–Asian countries is absurd. Despite security threats far graver than those faced by any other state, Israel is the only country in the Mideast, and one of the few in Asia, with a tradition of open multiparty elections, an independent judiciary, and a free press. Israeli Arabs vote, serve in the Knesset, run their own political parties, and freely criticize the government. Despite social discrimination, their position is better than that of minorities in Bahrain, Turkey, Pakistan, Iran, Malaysia, China, or some 80 other countries that condemn Israel in the UN—often by invoking analogies to apartheid. If there is any system that resembles apartheid, Israel's defenders claim, it is gender discrimination in Muslim lands like Saudi Arabia, where women are genetic inferiors with a legal status like that of children. But for obvious reasons, the UN has yet to condemn Muslim apartheid.

Second, Zionists adamantly deny that Jewish aggression or expansion is the root of regional tension. The 1947–1949 war grew directly from Arab efforts to destroy a state created and legalized by the United Nations. From 1949 to 1967, there was no occupation of the West Bank or Gaza, but Israel's foes still sought its destruction—which is precisely what led to the occupation of 1967. For the next ten years, Labor earnestly sought to trade the newly acquired territories for peace—only to be scorned by every Arab state but Egypt. In 2000 Israel again offered to return 98 percent of the territories—and was greeted with suicide bombings. In 2000 Israel left Lebanon, and in 2005 Gaza, both of which became bases to launch thousands of rockets against Israeli civilians. In this view, the central problem for anti-Zionists has never been Israeli expansion; rather, it is the mere existence of a Jewish state.

Third, Israel's defenders deny that the IDF acts with undue brutality. No army engaged in asymmetric warfare has avoided heavy civilian casualties. In 1982 Syrian troops slaughtered up to 25,000 of their own people in the rebel city of Hama.[17] From 1994 to 2003, Russian troops killed from 50,000 to 250,000 Chechen civilians.[18] From 2003 to 2009. U.S. intervention produced at least 95,000 Iraqi deaths.[19] In 2009, the Sri Lankan army killed up to 40,000 Tamil civilians;[20] while in Kashmir Indian intervention produced over 47,000 primarily civilian deaths.[21] None of these actions prompted a UN commission of inquiry. But in 2008–2009, when the IDF killed 400 to 700 Gazan civilians, Israel became the chief target

15   Robin Shepherd, *A State Beyond the Pale* (London: Weidenfeld and Nicolson, 2009), 235.

16   Wistrich, *Lethal Obsession*, 442–61, 509–10; "Spanish Soccer Fans Shout Anti-Semitic Slogans ..." *Ha'aretz*, December 16, 2009.

17   Friedman, *From Beirut to Jerusalem*, 76–77.

18   http://en.wikipedia.org/wiki/ Casualties_of_the_Second_Chechen_War

19   http://en.wikipedia.org/wiki/Casualties_of_the_ Iraq_War#Iraq_Body_Count_2. Most such deaths, however, were the result of Iraqi–Iraqi, rather than U.S.–Iraqi, fighting.

20   http://en.wikipedia.org/wiki/Sri_Lankan_Civil_ War#Casualties; *RTT News*, April 25, 2011; *Hindustan Times*, May 2, 1011.

21   http://en.wikipedia.org/wiki/ Insurgency_in_Jammu_and_Kashmir

of precisely such an inquiry.[22] This, despite the observation by Col. Richard Kemp, the British commander in Afghanistan, that the IDF in Gaza "did more to safeguard the rights of civilians in a combat zone than any other army in the history of warfare."[23] All of which convinces Zionists that human rights criticisms have little to do with human rights, and everything to do with tying Israel's hands in future wars and delegitimizing the Jewish state.

Obviously, partisans on both sides have strong evidence to support their worldview. No less obviously, among both Palestinians and Israelis, feelings of victimization make it difficult to admit that the other side's narrative has any validity—while nurturing defiance of a world seen as inherently unsympathetic. "Why pay attention to those who abandon us, who condemn us, no matter what we do? Ultimately, we can rely on no one but ourselves."

Not surprisingly, among both Palestinians and Israelis, such attitudes are most pronounced in the least Western educated, most culturally encapsulated sectors, which often are also the poorest. That is to say, although Hamas attracts educated professionals, its primary base of support has been refugee families, especially in Gaza, and religiously devout families least attuned to Western notions of cultural relativism. Among Israelis, although Likud leaders themselves are secular Ashkenazim, the right draws disproportionately from religious Ashkenazim and poor Mizrahim, while prosperous Tel Aviv is home to Israel's liberal cosmopolitan tradition. Politically conservative, but secular Russian immigrants conform to this model insofar as their Soviet experience inculcated a strong ethno–national identity and

a deep suspicion of cosmopolitan, liberal ideas.[24] Thus on both sides, culturally self-sufficient communities nurturing narratives of victimhood and exclusive virtue instinctively oppose compromise.

Solutions? What Chance for Peace?

Given this history, given these biases, will Israelis and Palestinians ever be able to reach an accommodation? What, if any, formulas for peace seem feasible?

At first glance, the future of the Golan is the easiest part of the puzzle to solve, because the Golan is relatively empty; traditionally, the Syrian government, unlike the PA, has been strong enough to make any agreement stick; and neither Israel nor the Palestinians have historic claims on the Golan. Syria seeks the return of its national territory. Israel wants guarantees of the Golan's demilitarization, diplomatic ties, and a reduction in Syrian support for Hamas and Hezbollah. In 1994 and 1999, the two sides were close to an agreement. Ostensibly, it foundered over the issue of borders near the Sea of Galilee. But more basically perhaps, Syria fears that if it reduces ties to Hamas, Hezbollah, and Iran, its regional influence will suffer, while Israel fears it will trade real territory for a piece of paper. Thus, although both sides talked about a "peace of the brave," in the end neither has put words into action. The current (May 2011) political upheavals in Syria make rapprochement between Jerusalem and Damascus even less likely.

However difficult peace on the Golan is, it is far less challenging than the central conflict between Israel and the Palestinians. Indeed, as the issue of Syrian ties to Hamas suggests, the Israeli–Palestinian issue bleeds easily into the Golan.

In weighing the future of the territory between the Jordan and the Mediterranean, political leaders have considered five scenarios: 1) the one–state solution; 2) the two-state solution, which formed the basis for Oslo, as well as for current efforts; 3)

---

22   This was the so-called Goldstone Commission created in 2009 by the UN Human Rights Council and headed by the noted South African jurist Richard Goldstone. In the case of Sri Lanka, UN Secretary General Ban Ki-moon, acting independently of the Human Rights Council, appointed a three-member investigative panel, but this body lacked the authority of the Goldstone Commission.

23   Bernstein, "Rights Watchdog."

24   *Cf.* Gershon Shafir and Yoav Peled, *Being Israeli* (Cambridge: Cambridge University Press, 2002), ch. 12.

a three-state solution; 4) what might be termed a no-solution solution; and 5) UN recognition of Palestine as an independent state within the 1967 borders. Let's look at each in turn.

The **one-state solution** says that everyone—Jews and Palestinians—between the river and sea should belong to a single political unit. In other words, the old British mandate should be reborn as a sovereign state, in which Jews and non-Jews live together. Yet the one-state solution itself comes in three flavors.

First, the Greater Israel version argues that because the Jews' historic and religious rights to the land trump all other claims, everyone in pre-1967 Israel and the West Bank (Gaza is now usually excluded) should dwell under Jewish control. Arabs would have legal protection and local autonomy, but no citizenship rights, and in some blueprints, would be encouraged to emigrate. Greater Israel was the ideology of Likud when it was in power from 1977 to 1992, and retains the loyalty of perhaps 20 percent of Jewish Israelis, including the right wing of Likud and those to Likud's right. A second version of the one-state solution is that of Hamas.[25] This is virtually identical to Greater Israel, except that Gaza is included, and Jews and Arabs switch places. In this scenario, all of Palestine was given by God as a sacred trust not to Jews, but to Muslims. Some Jewish families of ancient local lineage could remain as a protected minority, but they could never have rights equal to those of Muslims. Moreover, most of those whose families came after 1948 would have to leave. If Greater Israel enjoys 20 percent support among Jews, Palestinian backing for Hamas fluctuates between 20 and 45 percent, to judge from polls and election results.

Because both would inspire violent opposition from their intended victims, the Greater Israel

and Hamas projects would require prolonged and sustained force. Such a situation would remain unstable until the dominant group compelled substantial minority emigration (something Israel has so far refused to consider). Thus, for the foreseeable future, both plans would prolong intercommunal hostility. What is more, both projects directly contradict international norms that require citizenship for all residents of a national territory, and as such would be certain to spark intense international opposition that would probably prove fatal.

A third version of the one-state solution, the binational version, seeks an end to conflict by replacing ethnic supremacy with equality within a single polity. In this scenario, Jews and Arabs would have the same civic and legal rights, government would be chosen through universal suffrage, and the state—Israel/Palestine, Palisrael, Israelstine, or whatever—would belong to no particular ethnicity. This solution obviously appeals to the ideals of equality and reconciliation.

Binationalism in opinion polls receives support from 20 to 25 percent of Palestinians.[26] It is especially popular among Israeli Arabs, for whom it would offer an immediate exit from marginality. Yet because it opposes the idea of distinct Palestinian nationhood, no major Palestinian political organization endorses the idea.

Among Israeli Jews, not even one percent accepts binationalism for four reasons: 1) Demographic trends may condemn Jews to become an ever shrinking minority within the old mandate (see below). 2) Palestinian political culture, Jews fear, is inherently undemocratic, as shown by the dreary dictatorships, complete with the routine jailing and torture of political opponents, that both Fatah and Hamas erected in 2007. "If Palestinians can't even treat one another decently, how will they treat us?," Jews ask. 3) Even if both Jews and Palestinians behaved at first with civility, they probably would be unable to reconcile on such basic issues as the right of return. Deadlock would open the door to violence.

---

25 In early May 2011, as part of its projected reconciliation with Fatah, Hamas announced its willingness in principle to accept a "two-state solution," but since it refused to see such an arrangement as anything more than a temporary way-station en route to Israel's final elimination, the change in its position would seem to be merely semantic.

---

26 In the mid- and late 2000s. Dowty, *Israel/Palestine*, 195, 223.

4) Although South Africa and Belgium offer some hope, the record of far more states with a history of ethnic conflict—Yugoslavia, Czechoslovakia, the Soviet Union, Cyprus, Lebanon, Iraq, Sri Lanka, British India, Rwanda, Sudan, and many other African states—supports a pessimistic prognosis.[27]

If the one-state solution has limited prospects, **the two-state solution**, at first sight, is more promising. In principle, such a formula (whose practical antecedents can be traced to the Peel Commission of 1937) accords with the demand for self–determination that has been central to both national movements from their inception. As noted, such a vision lay at the heart of the Oslo process. It was the basis for the so-called Road Map to peace endorsed by the United States, Russia, the European Union, and the UN in 2003, and it is the explicit goal of President Obama's diplomatic efforts. The Arab League, the Palestinian Authority, and Likud, Kadima, and Labor Prime Ministers alike have endorsed a two-state solution, as have majorities of Israelis and Palestinians in repeated opinion polls.[28]

Given this wide range of support, a two-state solution remains something of a Rorschach test: different parties see in it what they want. But if we consider elements shared by the final Oslo offers, Arab League proposals in 2002 and 2007, and proposals that Ehud Olmert and Mahmoud Abbas discussed in 2008,[29] a viable two-state solution probably would entail the following features.

Israel would relinquish all of Gaza, and some 95 to 97 percent of the West Bank. The three to five percent retained would include settlements closest to the Green Line on the western edge of what Israelis term central Samaria, as well as

settlements north, east, and south of Jerusalem. These would include about 70 percent of all Israeli settlers. Retaining outposts like Ariel and Kiryat Arba, which are a considerable distance from the Green Line, and connecting them via corridors to pre-1967 Israel, would be far more problematic, because such arrangements would impair the Palestinian state's territorial contiguity. In exchange for annexed territories, Israel would surrender pre-1967 lands, fully equivalent in size and value. In effect, therefore, Israel would yield all of its 1967 acquisitions, thereby improving significantly on Barak's offer during Oslo. (The Israeli right wants the surrendered pre-1967 lands to include areas of substantial Israeli Arab habitation, so as to reduce Israel's non-Jewish population. However, precisely because Palestinians want to weaken Israel, Palestinians are unlikely to agree to such a proposal.)

To provide a Palestinian state with the attributes of sovereignty and to afford some protection against Israeli pressures, Palestine would be entitled to its own armed forces. But to ensure that Palestine did not invite Iranian troops or introduce offensive rockets, foreign military personnel would be forbidden, Palestinian armaments would be limited, and American–led and/or Israeli forces would be stationed in the Jordan valley as a trip wire.

In Jerusalem, a version of Clinton's Swiss-cheese formula would be resurrected, with Arab and Jewish neighborhoods under Palestinian and Israeli sovereignty, respectively; with both nations having their capital in the city; and with the holy sites either split between Israel and Palestine, or placed under some sort of international consortium. Israelis would thus abandon their long-held claim to exclusive control over the City of David.

Regarding the refugee issue, which did as much as anything to destroy Oslo, Arab League statements in favor of a "just solution" acceptable to all parties seem to imply something far short of the traditional "right of return." A workable deal might include an Israeli statement of regret for Palestinian suffering (along with a statement of Arab regret for Jewish suffering?), the return to Israel of perhaps 50,000 Palestinians in the name

---

27 On the history of one-statism in the Yishuv period and on one-statism's contemporary hurdles, see Morris, *One State, Two States.*

28 Dowty, *Israel/Palestine*, 189, 191; www.bicom.org. uk/context/opinion–polls. On the position of Hamas, see p. 85, n. 25 *supra.*

29 See the discussions between Olmert and Abbas in Olmert's memoirs, as analyzed in the *New York Times*, January 28, 2011.

of family reunification, unlimited entry to the new Palestinian state, and generous international support for those Palestinians who remained in their current residence. Palestinians would thus abandon their cherished goal of massive repatriation.

When in September 2010 President Obama announced that Israel and the Palestinians would resume negotiations, he expressed hope for a two-state agreement within a year. How likely is success anytime in the near future? At the time of writing, conditions are so turbulent in the Arab world as to belie any prognosis within days of its being issued. One can, however, identify large background forces that are likely to impinge on the outcome.

In some ways, conditions are more promising than during the last push for negotiations, in the 1990s. Assuming—a large assumption—that serious talks resume, this time, in contrast to the 1990s, America and other third parties would seek to break any impasse with their own bridging proposals. All difficult issues would be incorporated into a package deal, which, in theory, should oblige both sides to engage in trade-offs more readily than if, as in the past, each emotion-laden issue were addressed individually. Although Obama's one-year deadline will not be met, a short time line, in principle, should concentrate minds more than the eight-year Oslo process. In turn, compression may be feasible, because in the 18 years since Oslo began, negotiations have dealt with all critical issues. The zone of agreement is known in advance, as are the chief necessary compromises.[30]

If polls pointing to majority support for a negotiated compromise among Israelis and Palestinians are any guide, both sides are more exhausted by the conflict now than in 1993. On the West Bank, the Palestinian Authority, under President Abbas and his Prime Minister Salam Fayyad, has been remarkably successful, not only in preventing Hamas attacks on Israel and in restoring security cooperation with the IDF, but also in providing Palestinians with efficient basic services, fighting corruption, promoting economic growth, and restoring confidence in the PA among ordinary citizens. By all accounts, these trends have joined strong economic growth on the West Bank—over 11 percent from early 2009 to early 2010—as well as in Gaza, to create a mood less nihilistic and despairing than in the early 2000s.[31] The tentative rapprochement between Hamas and Fatah, announced in April 2011, may draw Hamas away from military adventurism into a more pragmatic diplomatic process. If, as some polls suggest, even Gazans want an end to conflict, Hamas, always sensitive to Palestinian opinion, may have difficulty standing in the way.

Prime Minister Netanyahu's status as a man of the political right increases the possibility that he could sell a deal to his conservative base—provided, of course, that he himself commits to such a deal. That is to say, Netanyahu is potentially less subject to right-wing vilification than Labor leaders Rabin or Barak, who led the push for peace in the 1990s. Only Nixon, it is often said, could go to Beijing. A recent Knesset bill requiring that any return of territory in the Golan or East Jerusalem be ratified by 80 members of the Knesset or by national referendum may increase Netanyahu's latitude for negotiations, insofar as he can claim that concessions are provisional and subject to popular approval.

Finally, some regional dynamics may favor a resolution. Jordan, Saudi Arabia, Fatah, Israel, and the United States continue to share a strategic goal: to curb the influence of Iran and its local clients, Hamas and Hezbollah. To the extent that Iran's ideological trump card is its support for Palestinian irredentism, by ending the Israeli–Palestinian dispute, Israel and its pro-American counterparts could reduce at a stroke Iran's regional influence. Ironically, Egypt's decision, following the overthrow of President Hosni Mubarak in early 2011, to pursue a more independent, less

---

30   Martin Indyk, "For Once, Hope in the Middle East," the *New York Times*, Op–Ed page, August 27, 2010; Jeffrey Goldberg and Hussein Ibish, "Good News from the Middle East (Really)," *New York Times*, Op–Ed page, January 26, 2011; and p. 82, n. 12 *supra*.

31   Previous note.

pro-American stance could help the peace process in one or more of the following ways: a) by increasing diplomatic pressure on Israel to settle with the Palestinians, b) by bringing Hamas for the first time into negotiations, c) by allowing Egypt, in combination perhaps with Turkey and the United States, to serve as a neutral mediator more effectively than the United States alone has been able to do. Statements by Egypt's post-Mubarak military caretaker government suggest that it is committed not only to maintaining diplomatic relations with Israel, but to achieving a durable peace as rapidly as possible.

However, if these factors favor an accord, what may be more powerful considerations push in the opposite direction. First, the jury is still out as to whether Netanyahu is really any more interested in a deal that would satisfy the Palestinians now than he was in 1996–1999, when his only consistent objective seemed to be to stay in office, and when his equivocation alienated all sides in Israel and beyond. Second, even if he were sincerely interested, it is unclear if he can overcome opposition from Greater Israel sympathizers in his coalition. Netanyahu's failure in late 2010 to secure coalition support even for a further two-month freeze on West Bank construction—something President Obama urgently sought—illustrated this weakness. That right-wingers were willing to defy both their own Prime Minister and the President of the United States on an issue of merely symbolic significance also shows how bitterly they are likely to oppose substantive compromise further down the road. Given a choice between a Jewish-majority democratic state in the 1967 borders and a Jewish-minority regime over the entire Land of Israel, many on the Israeli right seem prepared to accept the latter—even though such a decision is certain to generate unprecedented international isolation. Netanyahu could try to escape the right's embrace by imitating Ariel Sharon and opting for a centrist alliance with Kadima. Lacking Sharon's security credentials, however, it is unlikely he could peel away enough Likud defectors to succeed.

The enormous energy of settlers and Greater Israel advocates, and the corresponding lassitude of pro-peace elements—even though the latter's numerical strength may be greater—reflect a basic psychological problem, namely the extreme distrust with which vast numbers of Israelis now regard Palestinians. As most Israelis see things, since 2000 their commitment to rational discussion and territorial compromise repeatedly has been met only with violence. In retrospect, in this view, Arafat's insistence on the right of return meant that his acceptance of the two-state solution was never any more than semantic camouflage for his long-cherished ambition to destroy the Jewish state. According to Olmert, in the aforementioned secret negotiations in late 2008, he not only offered to return the equivalent of 100 percent of the West Bank, to divide Jerusalem, and to surrender sovereignty over the Noble Sanctuary, but he and Abbas tentatively agreed on the return to Israel of somewhere between 5,000 and 100,000 refugees. And yet Abbas' fear that Hamas would charge him with a "sell out" joined with the Gaza war of 2008–2009 to destroy those negotiations before they could be completed. In early 2011, when news of the earlier discussions leaked out, Abbas—still fearing popular dismay—denied that he had ever been ready to abandon the right of return. In other words, to retain legitimacy, the truth is that even Abbas, the "moderate," still must look constantly over his right shoulder.[32] Many Israelis conclude from all this that there is nothing they can do—short of national suicide—to win Palestinian acceptance, and that a pro-Hamas imam in 2008 expressed truthfully what is still the dominant trend in Palestinian thinking when he declared, "It doesn't matter what the Jews do. We will not let them have peace. They can be nice to us or they can kill us. It doesn't matter. If we have a ceasefire with the Jews, it is only so that we can prepare ourselves for the final battle."[33]

This assumption of implacable hostility leads many Israelis to believe that they must weaken Palestinian positions in the West Bank, and that more settlements—which most non-Israelis

---

32   See p. 76, n. 29 and p. 82, n.12 *supra*.

33   Jeffrey Goldberg, "The Unforgiven," *The Atlantic Online*, May 2008.

regard as an impediment to Israel's long-term welfare—will enhance national security. Given such attitudes, which generally trump fears of international criticism, it should not be difficult for Palestinian extremists to spook the Israeli electorate and sabotage any impending deal with violent provocations, as they did in 1996 and 2008.

Yet more worrisome for peace advocates, in early 2011 the expectation that pro-American Sunni states would continue to favor a negotiated two-state settlement suddenly seemed shaky. The pro-Western government of Tunisia fell to a popular uprising. Hezbollah finally toppled the Sunni-led, pro-Western government of Lebanon. American-allied regimes in Yemen and Bahrain were beset. Monarchic Jordan, with its sizable Palestinian population, faced demands for democratization. Most critical, as noted, in Egypt, whose 1979 treaty with Israel provided the cornerstone of American and Israeli policy, huge demonstrations forced out Mubarak in February 2011, and obliged the army to schedule free elections for the fall.

In an immediate sense, these revolts responded to local problems: endemic corruption, political repression, nepotism, tepid economic growth, maldistribution of wealth, and pervasive youth unemployment. However, if the primary spurs were domestic, these upheavals also had anti-Western, anti-Israel implications. Although similar domestic problems plague Iran, so far the Iranian regime has faced no credible threat. In part, Iran's theocrats remain in power because disdain for Western criticism allows them—as well as their chief regional ally, Syria—to be more crudely repressive. But more basically perhaps, Iran benefits from a popular perception, justified or not, that its leaders uphold the dignity of the Arab/Muslim world after decades of Western-imposed humiliation, of which the creation of Israel is a prime example. Neither Ben Ali's Tunisia, nor the anti-Hezbollah alliance in Lebanon, nor Hashemite Jordan, nor Mubarak's Egypt could stake the same defiant claims.

Conceivably—at this stage, one can do no more than speculate—the eclipse of pro-American Arab regimes could prove no less historic than the collapse of Communism in the late 1980s. But whereas Communism's demise made possible the Oslo process, the current transformation could have precisely the opposite effect. Post-Mubarak Egypt has now restored diplomatic relations with Iran that were severed in 1979, ended Egypt's support for the blockade of Hamas-run Gaza, and sponsored what may be an historic reconciliation between Hamas and Fatah. Admittedly, these policies, as I already noted, could advance the peace process by increasing pressure on Israel, pushing Hamas toward moderation, and letting Egypt play the role of honest broker. But it is equally plausible that Egypt's about-face will strengthen radical elements in Hamas, intimidate Fatah, kill any lingering Israeli inclination to withdraw from the West Bank—and thus reduce the already limited chances for a two-state solution. The Egyptian parliament to be chosen in September 2011 almost certainly will be more hostile to Israel than the military caretaker regime. Polls show that most Egyptians want to annul the 1979 peace treaty. The traditionally anti-Semitic Muslim Brotherhood, widely recognized as Egypt's best organized political force, has indicated that it will seek to modify the treaty and to strengthen Hamas, which in fact grew out of the Brotherhood.[34] Salafist elements to the right of the Brotherhood are yet more outspokenly hostile to the Jewish state. Hezbollah's recent success in Lebanon, along with Turkey's decision to end its historic alliance with Israel (see below), can only reinforce Israel's isolation. If an Islamist movement were to replace the Ba'athist regime in Syria, it would further deepen that vulnerability.

Whether gradual or sudden, partial or complete, the accession of anti-Israeli forces in Egypt, Lebanon, and elsewhere, therefore, could resurrect the circle of Arab enmity that Israel faced from 1948 to 1974, supported now by Iran. In retrospect, we may find that the era of Israeli–Arab detente and land-for-peace formulas that began in 1974 was but an artifact of American

---

34 Along with Hamas, the Brotherhood in May 2011 condemned the U.S. assassination of Osama bin Laden, whom Hamas described as a "holy warrior."

hegemony in the Mideast, and that by 2011 that era had begun to fade. Symptom and cause of that transition, the essentially secular, autocratic order that defined Mideast politics for at least two generations may be yielding to a more populist, self-consciously Islamic phase, with both Iran and Turkey providing competing models.

But for argument's sake, let's say that these speculations are wildly overdrawn, that Israel–Palestinian negotiations resume, and that they succeed in creating an independent Palestine under some sort of Fatah–Hamas dyarchy. This still leaves open the possibility that through free elections or by force, Hamas will take over the West Bank as it did Gaza, and seek to create another base for operations against Israel—this time only nine miles from Tel Aviv. Given that many Palestinians already regard Fatah as a creature of Israel, any effort by Fatah to call on the IDF for help would only hasten Fatah's delegitimization. But any prospect of a Hamas seizure almost certainly would lead Israel to reoccupy the entire West Bank.

In short, it is by no means clear that a two-state solution can be achieved, or if it were signed that it would stick, because, despite a yearning for peace in the abstract, popular attitudes remain extremely volatile.

What about a **three-state solution**? In this schema, Egypt's current effort to reconcile Fatah and Hamas ultimately fails, and the division between Hamas in Gaza, and Fatah in the West Bank, becomes permanent. Gaza would then become independent or join Egypt, while the West Bank would become independent or federate with Jordan. Such a scenario is by no means impossible, because previous Hamas–Fatah reconciliation efforts have collapsed, and the Gaza–West Bank split has cultural as well as institutional and ideological roots.

Yet obstacles to the three-state scenario are at least as formidable as to the two-state solution. Virtually all Palestinians still regard themselves as members of one national community. Gaza is not viable as an independent country, and Egypt has no interest in annexing it. Moreover, if Israel were to vacate the West Bank and the West Bank

did not federate with Jordan, local security forces might not be able to prevent a Hamas takeover. This is the problem with the two-state solution all over again.

If the one- and three-state solutions are impractical, and if two-state negotiations fail, what options remain, other than resumed warfare? Various observers, including Hussein Agha and Robert Malley, argue that **the best solution is no solution**.[35] That is to say, since Israel and the Palestinians cannot reach an end-of-conflict deal, they should lower their sights to interim arrangements that will not prejudice a final treaty at some future date. Hopefully, this will calm tensions and disempower extremists on both sides. Such an interim approach may, in fact, be amenable to Hamas, which has talked about a ten-year truce, as well as to Israel's hard-right Foreign Minister, Avigdor Lieberman,[36] who has said that decades must pass before mutual confidence will support a peace treaty. According to Agha and Malley, interim steps should include IDF withdrawal from most or all of the West Bank, to be replaced temporarily by forces from Jordan; indefinite deferral of insoluble issues like refugees and Jerusalem; and an agreement by all sides to refrain from violence for ten years.

But the pitfalls are obvious. A temporary border in the West Bank is no less likely to spark dissension than a permanent border, because both sides will assume that any interim demarcation will heavily influence the final lines. Likewise, Palestinians are likely to object to deferring issues like refugees and Jerusalem, because postponement automatically strengthens the status quo—to Israel's advantage. Introducing Jordanian troops raises the prospect of a permanent Jordanian presence and eventual federation, which would blight Palestinian dreams of an independent state. But again, without Jordanian troops, there is no obvious way to prevent Hamas from engaging

---

35   Hussein Agha and Robert Malley, "Israel and Palestine: Can They Start Over?," *The New York Review of Books* 56 (December 3, 2009).

36   No relation to the present author.

in provocation and Fatah from losing control, neither of which Israel would accept.

A fifth and final scenario that the PA is considering is to have the **UN General Assembly recognize Palestine as an independent state** within the borders of the West Bank and Gaza as of June 4, 1967. This proposal is based on Kosovo's success in gaining recognition of its 2008 declaration of independence from Serbia. If the UN were to admit Palestine as an independent state, any Israeli presence in East Jerusalem or the West Bank automatically would become illegal, and the General Assembly could authorize an international boycott and divestment campaign to force Israeli compliance. At a minimum this would substantially increase Israel's isolation. In theory, it could also spark a war, in which Israel would be cast as an outlaw and Palestine would be authorized to call on military help from UN member states. In effect, the UN would repartition the old British mandate. But whereas in 1947, the Jews accepted and Arabs rejected the UN's decision, this time roles would be reversed. Israel would choose the same self-isolating strategy as the Palestinians adopted in the 1940s.

The problem with this plan is that, under UN rules, the Security Council must approve General Assembly recommendations for admission, and the US almost certainly would veto Palestine's application on the grounds that unilateral action cannot produce a peace agreement. Nonetheless, even if a General Assembly vote did not result in Palestine's formal admission, the PA would gain leverage and would be able to put additional, possibly unprecedented, political pressure on a recalcitrant opponent.

The Angel of History's Blessing

If negotiations ever do produce an enforceable peace agreement, the balance of forces between Israel and her adversaries will become moot. Both sides will rest securely, and any lingering competition will express itself in sports events, cultural rivalries, and perhaps a contest for new markets.

But if negotiations fail, or if they succeed and the deal unravels, we can expect that the struggle between Israel and her enemies not only will continue, but will intensify. No doubt this would include redoubled efforts to isolate Israel on the South African model. We also would be likely to see Israel involved in renewed warfare, if not conventional war against a new Muslim coalition, then asymmetric warfare with Hamas, Hezbollah, and West Bank militants.

Under such circumstances, one is obliged to ask: What are the long-term strengths and vulnerabilities of Israel and her opponents? Which side, if either, is likely to benefit from continued polarization? How will the current balance of forces shift in ten years? In twenty? In short, if this Hundred Years War moves toward its second century, on which side will the Angel of History ultimately bestow her blessing?

Some tendencies clearly strengthen Israel, while others favor Israel's opponents, although, of course, how they will play out—or what factors not mentioned here will prove critical—is anyone's guess. We begin with four long-term trends that have assisted Israel and that seem likely to continue.

First is historical inertia, which refers to the tendency for temporary arrangements to become permanent, and for facts on the ground gradually to acquire formal status. Israel's very existence and its halting integration into the system of Mideast politics is the prime example. Whereas in 1948 and again in 1967 the Arab world explicitly refused to accept the Jewish state, first Egypt and then Jordan broke the barrier to recognition. In 2002 and 2007 the Arab League as a whole promised recognition, in return for substantial withdrawal to 1967 borders. Barring institutional transformations all across the Arab world, the momentum toward regional accommodation—"legitimacy" may be too strong a term—probably will continue, if only because Israel's demography and its military and economic power are impossible to ignore. As of early 2011, the only parties who deny they will ever recognize Israel are Hamas, Hezbollah, and Iran, but the latter is distant, and the nonstate actors have no strategic credibility. Even if current efforts fail, one can imagine that within a few years, the search for diplomatic accommodation between Israel and its neighbors will resume.

Likewise, despite heroic efforts by Palestinian refugees to preserve their identity and their right of return, inertia renders those aspirations increasingly problematic. Every year the number of 1948 refugees dwindles, while their grandchildren and great-grandchildren, people who have never laid eyes upon Israel, grow more numerous. Without some sudden collapse in Israeli fortunes, this "refugee" population seems set to assimilate to their local environments and to assume ever more tenuous ties to their families' earlier habitation.

By a similar logic, Jewish settlement is probably becoming irreversible. Already, some 550,000 Jews live in the West Bank and East Jerusalem, serviced by an ever more self-sufficient system of roads, utilities, communal institutions, and security checks. The Jewish population of the West Bank is now growing almost three times more rapidly than that of Israel proper, spurred by government incentives, which in turn reflect security concerns mixed with Zionist nostalgia and studied defiance of Palestinian and international opinion. Of course, one could argue that the diplomatic costs of this expansion exceed any strategic benefit (see below). And yet, given their rising numbers and political influence, it is difficult to see how any Israeli government will have the guts or the power to abandon, much less to uproot, any significant number of settlers.

Alongside inertia, a second trend, more indisputably favorable to Israel, is the Jewish state's remarkable economic dynamism. A combination of first-class universities, technology clusters, military stimuli, abundant venture capital, and a culture of innovation helps to explain why Israel has the highest density of start-up companies in the world, more companies on the NASDAQ than all of Europe combined, the world's highest proportional expenditure on civilian research and development, and growth rates well in excess of most developed economies.[37] Although Israel also

has serious economic problems—most notably the reluctance of ultra-Orthodox Jewish men and Arab Israeli women to enter the workforce—its economy is particularly impressive by Mideastern standards. Recent UN reports by leading Arab intellectuals emphasize the Arab world's high unemployment rates, chronically low productivity, and woefully deficient rates of technological and scientific innovation.[38] Iran suffers from similar systemic deficiencies. Thus, the per capita GDP gap between Israel and its neighbors/competitors, already substantial, seems likely to widen. If Muslim poverty and rapid population growth threaten to feed Islamist extremism, Israel's widening economic lead promises to enhance its military edge. Economic-cum-technological vitality also has implications for international alliances. Israel, for example has recently replaced Russia as India's largest external arms supplier. And prosperity can buy a degree of quiescence from Israeli Arabs.

Closely related to economic performance, a third long-term feature aiding Israel is political democracy. With the debatable exception of Lebanon, Israel, recall, is the only Mideastern country with a tradition of free elections and guaranteed civil liberties. This system fosters government accountability, citizen identification with the state, private initiative, and all manner of economic, as well as political, innovation. By contrast, the political systems of most Arab states and Iran require a far higher degree of repression and crude manipulation than we find in Israel proper. If repression promises long-term stability, the upheavals during the "Arab spring" of 2011 show all too graphically that this often comes at the price of popular alienation, institutional ossification, and severe market distortions. Until and unless such societies, many of them now in turmoil, succeed

227–36; *Forward*, May 6, 2011.

38 *The Arab Human Development Report 2003* (New York: United Nations Development Programme, 2003); *The Arab Human Development Report 2005* (New York: United Nations Development Programme, 2006); *The Arab Human Development Report 2009: The Report in Brief* (New York: United Nations Development Programme, 2009).

37 Dan Senor and Saul Singer, *Start-Up Nation* (New York: Council on Foreign Relations, 2009), 11–20,

in developing more representative institutions, Israel will retain a very considerable advantage in efficiency, innovation, and popular mobilization.

A fourth trend that *may* strengthen Israel is demography. Now, at first glance, this is quite surprising, because conventional wisdom has long argued that higher Arab fertility threatens the Jews with a demographic time bomb. But recent work—much of which, it must be said, remains controversial—by Israeli and American demographers emphasizes that as Arabs in Israel and the West Bank have grown more prosperous, their birthrates have exhibited the same downward trend as other middle-class populations around the world. At the same time, Jewish birthrates have risen, because within the overall Jewish population the percentage of Orthodox Jews, who tend to have very large families, has constantly grown. These studies argue, furthermore, that Arab emigration from the West Bank is larger than has generally been recognized, and that earlier enumerations of Arabs suffered from extensive double counting. Two explicit conclusions follow: 1) In 2008 Jews constituted not 57 percent, as was often claimed, but 67 percent of people in the West Bank and Israel proper. 2) Over the next two or three decades, as the Palestinian birthrate continues to fall and the Jewish rate rises, the Jewish portion of the total population will stabilize and eventually increase. These studies also make two implicit claims: 1) The Greater Israel project may in fact be demographically viable. 2) Even if Israel chooses a two-state solution, in the long term, Israel need not fear either its Arab minority or the Arabs of the West Bank.[39]

However, if these historic trends benefit Israel, equally, if not more, powerful trends favor the Palestinians and anti-Zionists. For one thing, the same historical inertia that allows settlers to create facts on the ground may be creating some sort of one-state solution that ultimately will undermine Zionist goals. Although thickest along the Green Line and around Jerusalem, substantial settlements now dot the entire West Bank. Together with bypass roads and security barriers, they dissect areas of Arab habitation ever more extensively. If a peace treaty is not concluded soon, some argue, Jewish and Arab areas will be so intermingled as to make separation ultimately impossible. As one PA official put it, "The settlements mean that the egg is hopelessly scrambled. Basically it's already one state."[40]

Despite—or indeed because of—its popularity in Israel, continued settlement expansion may usher in one of three scenarios, all ultimately fatal to Zionist hopes: 1) An apartheid–like system in the West Bank, in which Arabs enjoy local autonomy, but only Jews have voting rights as citizens of Israel. This could produce such widespread opposition, from Israeli democrats within, and from Western and Muslim countries without, as to guarantee Israel the same fate as apartheid South Africa. 2) A Jewish-dominated state that actively promotes Arab transfer out of the country. This would spark opposition no less fierce than would racially-based citizenship. 3) A binational state in which Jews are a rapidly shrinking majority. In such a state, where an emboldened Hamas would enjoy wide support, but where current security controls no longer would be feasible, it would be difficult for Jewish, not to mention Arab, officials to stop terrorist attacks aimed at forcing Jewish emigration. Like the Palestinian exodus of 1947, such emigration would start with the wealthiest and most mobile, and as demoralization spread, would embrace progressively lower strata. Any of

---

39 Gaza, which has shown little, if any, downward trend in fertility, is another story. "West Bank: Demographics," *Wikipedia*; "Demographics of the Palestinian Territories," *Wikipedia*; Bennett Zimmerman and Michael Wise, "Defusing the Demographic Time Bomb," *Focus Quarterly Review*, Spring 2008; Shahar Ilan, "Big Drop in Israeli Arab Fertility Rates," *Ha'aretz*, June 16, 2006; Hillel Fendel, "Latest Stats: Israel's Demographic Trend Is Jewish, not Arab," *Ha'aretz*, April 2, 2008; "Arab Population in the West Bank and Gaza," *Eretz Yisroel.Org*, June 12, 2009; Ted Bellman, "Israel,

from the Mediterranean to the Jordan," *Israpundit.com*, January 16, 2007; Arnon Soffer, "Jewish Population in Israel is Declining," *Ha'aretz*, October 4, 2010.

40 Goldberg, "Unforgiven."

these three scenarios would mean the death of the Zionist project as defined since its inception.

But if the aforementioned predictions of a growing Jewish majority in Israel and the West Bank are accurate, would they not support the Greater Israel project? In the West Bank, such trends would do nothing to make ethnic separation or transfer palatable to the world community. In Israel proper, an expanding Jewish majority obviously would strengthen Jewish control. The problem, however, is that the above demographic projections are by no means shared by all experts, many, perhaps most, of whom argue that for the foreseeable future Arab fertility rates will continue to exceed Jewish rates. According to one University of Haifa geographer, as early as 2020, of 15.5 million people between the Jordan and the sea (including Gaza), only 6.4 million will be Jews.[41] By then, Israeli Arabs, now just over 20 percent of all Israelis, may be 25 percent; and by 2050, 35–40 percent. By mid-century, Arabs may be able to attract enough left-wing Jewish support in the Knesset to block security funding, or to secure a modified right of return. Before then, however, if the experience of Lebanon, Yugoslavia, and other multiethnic states is a guide, the threatened majority will resist minority demands, leading to civil war. In part because the issue is so politically fraught, no consensus on demographic trends has emerged. But assuming that traditional views of the matter are correct, Jewish hegemony is threatened not only in the West Bank, but in Israel proper.

If demography in the territory of the former mandate constitutes a second threat to Israel, population trends in the United States, Europe, and the Mideast represent a third. In both America and Europe, Islam is arguably the fastest growing religion, the result both of large-scale immigration and of high fertility rates. As the Muslim population increases and becomes more prosperous, educated, and politically active, its influence on Mideast policy can only grow at the expense of Jewish influence. This is especially true insofar as

the post-1945 Jewish population in Europe (small to begin with) and in the United States has been slowly declining through intermarriage, assimilation, low fertility, and an end to fresh immigration. To be sure, as we saw, American Jews are but one element in the pro-Zionist American coalition. Conceivably, anti-Muslim, anti-immigration sentiment will fan pro-Israel sympathy among conservative Europeans and/or Americans. And yet it is also reasonable to assume that, on balance and in the long term, declining Jewish and rising Muslim numbers will dilute Western support for Israel. This seems yet more likely since memory of the Holocaust is bound to fade over time, along with inhibitions on European anti-Semitism—another instance perhaps of inertia working against Israel.

Taking a long-term demographic perspective, one could argue that in some measure, Zionist and anti-Zionist fortunes are largely a function of shifting birthrates. In the 19th century, the Jewish population of central and eastern Europe grew extremely rapidly, apparently the result of plummeting maternal and infant mortality. That explosion in turn contributed, directly or indirectly, to: a) Jewish immiseration, the rise of Zionism, and substantial immigration to Palestine to 1939; b) large-scale Jewish immigration between 1880 and 1950 to the United States, where Jews began to gain political influence; and c) immigration to Israel of large numbers of Holocaust survivors. All three developments were crucial to Israel's early success. In this same period, c. 1880 to 1960, Muslim population growth in Palestine and much of the Mideast remained modest. But from 1960 to the present, trends have reversed. Improved health care, sanitation, and food security have allowed Muslim populations across the Mideast to expand dramatically, shifting the balance in Israel and the West Bank, and helping to propel large-scale Muslim immigration to the United States and Europe. At the same time, Jewish growth rates in Europe and America have assumed the downward trajectory typical of middle-class families. Obviously, politics cannot be reduced to a function of demography. But population trends certainly contributed in some measure to the

---

41   Morris, *One State, Two States*, 7–8; Soffer, "Jewish Population in Israel is Declining."

Zionist momentum of the period c. 1920 to 1970, and to what many would argue is an anti-Zionist momentum since then. Such trends look set to continue for at least one more generation.[42]

Finally, long-term global shifts also threaten Israel. As the economic power of Asia—China in particular—and of Latin America rises, while that of America and Europe declines, new political and military constellations must cohere. Historic ties to the Jews, guilt over the Holocaust, influential local Jewish communities, and a shared political culture have made Europe and America Israel's natural benefactors. But none of these elements have much purchase on China, India, Brazil, Indonesia, or Turkey—all of which are inclined in varying degrees to ally with oil-rich Iran and Arab countries unsympathetic or hostile to Israel. (In India, opposition to Islamic extremism and rivalry with China qualifies this orientation to an uncertain, but probably modest extent.) Turkey, once Israel's strongest regional ally, is now downgrading, or as Turks see it balancing, its ties to Israel and NATO, so as to increase Turkey's influence with Arabs and the wider Muslim world. This is a major strategic shift.[43] More ominously yet for Israel, as I emphasized earlier, the upheavals in Tunisia, Lebanon, Egypt, Jordan, Syria, and other Arab lands could recreate the circle of enmity that Israel faced from 1948 to 1973. If Egypt remilitarized the Sinai and allied with Lebanon and Syria, Israel would face the prospect of a two-front war for the first time since 1973. But in an age of missiles, the strategic threat would be substantially more serious.

As declining Western influence over the Mideast obliges America and Europe to accommodate to new regional realities, popular attitudes are likely to assume an ever more anti-Israel inflection. Israel's shift to the right and the settler movement's indifference to international opinion—Israel's inclination, in effect, to duplicate the Palestinians' self-destructive posture of the 1940s—can only accelerate a reduction in Western sympathy. Indeed, such a shift is already visible in much of western Europe.

Despite—or in some measure, because of—Western distaste for revolutionary Iran's political culture, Iran is emerging as a principal beneficiary of these global trends by virtue of its relatively large population, its huge oil reserves, its uncompromisingly anti-Israel ideology, and its pursuit of nuclear weapons. If, as seems likely, U.S. and European sanctions fail to stymie that nuclear quest, the mere acquisition of such weapons targeted against Israel could, in theory, induce the most talented and mobile Israelis to leave, paralyze immigration and investment in Israel, and inhibit Israel's response to provocations by Hamas, Hezbollah, or Syria. That scenario, of course, is entirely distinct from the actual detonation of a nuclear weapon within Israel by Iran or Iranian proxies, an event that, while leading inexorably to Iran's incineration, would obliterate tiny Israel.

More probable, but also deeply disturbing for Israel, is the possibility that the dispute with the Palestinians will morph from a national to a religious/civilizational conflict. So long as the issue was framed as rivalry between Israeli and Palestinian nationalism, many developing nations, although sympathetic to the Palestinians, had a limited emotional investment. But current trends may push in a new direction. The rise of Hamas and Hezbollah as expressly Islamist movements, their efforts to bridge the Sunni–Shi'ite divide, new openings for the Muslim Brotherhood in Egypt, Muslim people's growing access to the Internet, Iran's effort to define itself as leader of the Muslim world, the growing tie in Israel itself between religion and nationalism—all such developments make it more likely that Muslims beyond the circle of Arab countries will become more involved in the Israel/Palestine conflict.

So what will happen? Will mutual exhaustion and external pressure on Israelis and Palestinians finally produce a solution? If a two-state deal is

---

42   What is more, insofar as the poorest, least educated, most encapsulated sectors of both the Israeli and Palestinian population have the largest families, this pattern feeds religious–cum–political extremism in both communities.

43   For a trenchant prognosis of early–21st–century global political trends, see the special issue of *Foreign Affairs*, 89 (November/December 2010) entitled "The World Ahead."

ever reached, will it hold? Will conflict continue, indeed escalate as anti-Israeli forces reorganize? At the time of this writing, nothing is clear. One can only fall back on a truism, that a knowledge of the past is a precondition not for predicting the future, but for analyzing those forces likely to influence the future.

PART TWO
Readings

Section One
Origins of the Conflict to 1947

Introduction

The three readings in this section introduce the conflict by considering the rise of Zionism, the difficulties Palestinians faced in responding to Zionism, and the ways that World War Two transformed both Zionist and Palestinian fortunes.

Bernard Reich begins by sketching the social and intellectual origins of Jewish nationalism in late 19th-century Europe and the growth of political Zionism prior to World War One. He then discusses the decisive impetus Zionism derived from British patronage, as embodied in the Balfour Declaration of 1917, and from the League of Nations' decision to create a British mandate over Palestine at the war's end. Reich sketches the careers of seminal Zionist leaders—Theodor Herzl, Chaim Weizmann, David Ben-Gurion, and Vladimir Ze'ev Jabotinsky; the five waves (aliyot) of Jewish immigration from Europe to pre-1939 Palestine; and the internal development of the prewar Palestinian Jewish community, known as the Yishuv. Reich then considers rising Arab–Jewish tensions and ever more desperate—and ultimately unsuccessful—British attempts to reconcile Jewish and Palestinian aspirations. He ends in 1947, as the end of the mandate approached.

If Reich treats the growth of Zionism and the Yishuv as phenomena in Jewish history, Rashid Khalidi integrates those developments with the rise of Palestinian Arab nationalism. Khalidi's self-appointed task is to explain why, between 1918 and 1939, the balance of power in Palestine between Zionist and Arab forces shifted decisively against the latter. External support was critical, insofar as the Yishuv relied on foreign immigrants, finance,

and organizational and ideological models. A marked improvement in Yishuv fortunes following the arrival of large numbers of refugees from Nazi Germany in the 1930s made this particularly clear. Yet Khalidi goes further to ask why, with a demographic advantage of over 2:1 as late as 1939, Palestinian Arabs still failed to hold their own. He identifies a number of social patterns favoring the Jews, including higher levels of literacy and technical training, a more urban base, stronger ideological commitment, far greater cross-class cohesion, and a more dynamic and inclusive leadership. To these factors were added British policies on self-government that, until Britain changed course in the late 1930s, deliberately sought to prevent Arab majority rule in favor of continued Jewish immigration.

Benny Morris shows how World War Two brought these trends to fruition. On the one hand, the war diminished Palestinian prospects by exposing their principal leader's Nazi sympathies, and by weakening Britain, the Arabs' main patron after 1939, in favor of America, which, under President Harry Truman, was increasingly pro-Zionist. On the other hand, despite—or indeed because of—the war's horrendous physical toll on European Jewry, the war boosted Zionist political prospects. The Jews' agony dramatically increased Gentile sympathy. The Holocaust inspired Yishuv attacks on British outposts in Palestine designed to drive the British out and open the coast to refugees. Most fundamentally, as the enormity of the Holocaust became known, world Jewry, now centered in America, mounted a fierce campaign to turn Palestine into a refuge by establishing an independent Jewish state.

Morris examines the international politics leading to the UN General Assembly vote of November 29, 1947, which finally authorized the creation of a Jewish state, thereby setting the stage for the first Arab–Israeli war of 1947–1949.

A Brief History of Israel

By Bernard Reich

The Roots of Zionism

Israel's modern history begins before statehood, with the migration of Jews to Palestine (as the area was then called) in the 19th century from eastern Europe, primarily Russia and Poland, and with the establishment of the modern political Zionist movement.

In 1880, the total number of Jews in Palestine was estimated at under 25,000. Some two-thirds lived in Jerusalem with most of the remainder in other cities considered holy by the Jews, such as Safed, Tiberias, and Hebron. There were also small Jewish communities in Jaffa and Haifa. Most of the Jews were Orthodox and generally subsisted on charitable donations from Jews abroad.

In the early 1880s, a wave of *aliyah* (immigration to Palestine or Israel), known as the First Aliyah, brought Jews from Russia and eastern Europe who wanted to settle the land. The Second Aliyah, which began in 1904 and lasted until Word War I, brought additional immigrant settlers from eastern Europe. This increased the Jewish population in Palestine to approximately 85,000 (about 12 percent of the total population) by 1914, with about half of the Jews residing in Jerusalem.

During these waves of migration, Jews came to Palestine for a variety of reasons. Some came primarily for religious reasons and joined existing Jewish communities, primarily in Jerusalem, but also in other holy cities, where they could study and practice their religion. Others sought to escape the pogroms (organized massacres) prevalent in Russia or the generally poor economic and social conditions in eastern Europe and often were motivated by socialist ideas and concepts. Some were drawn by the Zionist ideology that sought the creation of a Jewish state as a response to anti-Semitism (discrimination against or hostility toward Jews) in their native lands.

Nineteenth-century western Europe provided some opportunities for Jews to move from the ghettos and be assimilated, or incorporated, into general society Some Jews prospered and were seen as an economic threat to the local populace, fueling anti-Semitism. Political Zionism was the nationalist response of the Jewry of western and central Europe to the pervasiveness of anti-Semitism. Its objective was the establishment of a Jewish homeland in any available territory—not necessarily in Palestine—through cooperation with Western powers (the Great Powers). These Zionists believed that the new state, which they envisioned as a secular nation modeled after the postemancipation European states, would attract large numbers of Jews and resolve the problem of anti-Semitism.

Bernard Reich, "The Prehistory of the State of Israel," *A Brief History of Israel*, 2nd ed., pp. 13–39, 41–42. Copyright © 2008 by Facts on File, Inc.

In the Russian Empire, the situation of the Jews was different. Under Czar Alexander II (1855–81), Jews gained access to educational institutions and professions previously closed to them, and a class of Jewish intellectuals began to emerge in some cities, as they had in western Europe. However, all hopes for emancipation were dashed when Alexander II was assassinated in 1881. His reign was followed by renewed anti-Semitism and pogroms throughout the Russian Empire as Alexander III instituted oppressive policies. This led to substantial emigration of Jews from the empire. Between 1881 and 1914, some 2.5 million Jews left Russia. Most went to the United States, but some chose Palestine, where they sought refuge in the idea of reconstituting a Jewish state—but a secular and socialist one.

Zionism as a Political Movement

Modern Zionist writings emerged in Europe in the mid-1880s. A number of Jewish writers were impressed by the nationalist fervor developing in Europe that led to the creation of new nation-states and also by the resurgence of messianic expectations among Jews that, some believed, might include the return of the Jews to the Holy Land. In *Rome and Jerusalem* (1862), Moses Hess, a German Jew, called for the establishment of a Jewish social commonwealth in Palestine as

THEODOR HERZL
(May 2, 1860–July 3, 1904)

Theodor Herzl, the founder of political Zionism, was an unlikely choice to create the ideology and movement that led to the creation of the modern Jewish state. An assimilated Jew, he was born in Pest, Hungary, in 1860. He later moved to Vienna and studied law but soon wrote short stories and plays. He worked as the Paris correspondent of the Viennese daily newspaper Neue Freie Presse *from 1891 to 1895. Growing anti-Semitism in France contributed to Herzl's interest in the "Jewish Question."*

As a journalist, he observed the trial of Captain Alfred Dreyfus and was affected by the false accusations of "traitor" leveled against the French–Jewish army officer and by the episodes of anti-Semitism that accompanied the trial and the disgrace of Dreyfus. Herzl wrote Der Judenstaat (The Jewish State), *in which he proposed the establishment of a Jewish state.*

Subsequently, Herzl traveled widely to publicize and gain support for his ideas. He found backing among the masses of eastern European Jewry and opposition among the leadership and wealthier segments of the western Jewish communities.

In 1897 Herzl convened the first World Zionist Congress, in Basel. Switzerland.The congress established the World Zionist Organization (WZO) and founded a Jewish national movement with the goal of establishing a home in Palestine for the Jewish people. Zionism rejected other solutions to the Jewish Question and was the response to centuries of discrimination, persecution, and oppression. It sought redemption through self–determination. Herzl died in Austria in 1904 and was buried in Vienna. In August 1949, his remains were reinterred on Mount Herzl in Jerusalem.

a solution to the Jewish problem. Leo Pinsker. a Russian physician living in Odessa, wrote in *Auto-Emancipation* (1881) that anti-Semitism was a modern phenomenon and that Jews must organize themselves to find their own national home wherever possible. Pinsker's work attracted the attention of Hibbat Zion (Lovers of Zion), an organization devoted to Hebrew education and national revival. It took up his call for a territorial solution to the Jewish problem and helped establish Jewish agricultural settlements in Palestine at Rishon le Zion, south of Tel Aviv, and Zikhron Yaaqov, south of Haifa. Although the numbers were small—only 10,000 settlers by 1891—the First Aliyah (1882–1903) was important because it established a Jewish position in Palestine espousing political objectives.

Theodor Herzl is widely recognized in Israel and elsewhere as the founder of political Zionism and the prime mover in the effort to found a Jewish state. Modern political Zionism as conceived by Herzl sought the creation of a Jewish state in Palestine as a solution to the "Jewish Question" (essentially anti-Semitism). In *Der Judenstaat* (*The Jewish State*), published in Vienna, Austria, on February 14, 1896, Herzl assessed the situation of the Jews and proposed a practical plan for a resolution by creating a state in which Jews would reconstitute their national life from biblical days in a territory of their own. His assessment of the problem saw anti-Semitism as a broad-scale and widespread phenomenon that appeared wherever Jews were located. He wrote: "Let sovereignty be granted us over a portion of the globe large enough to satisfy the rightful requirements of a nation" (Reich, ed., 1995, p. 18). He suggested that the preferred location was Palestine: "Palestine is our ever-memorable historic home. The very name of Palestine would attract our people with a force of marvelous potency" (ibid.). But initially, Palestine was not the only location considered by the Zionist movement.

On August 23, 1897, in Basel, Switzerland, Herzl convened the first World Zionist Congress, representing Jewish communities and organizations throughout the world. The congress established the World Zionist Organization (WZO),

BASEL PROGRAM
(August 23, 1897)

*T*he aim of Zionism is to create for the Jewish people a home in Palestine secured by public law. The [World Zionist] Congress contemplates the following means to the attainment of this end:

1. *The promotion, on suitable lines, of the colonization of Palestine by Jewish agricultural and industrial workers.*
2. *The organization and binding together of the whole of Jewry by means of appropriate institutions, local and international, in accordance with the laws of each country.*
3. *The strengthening and fostering of Jewish national sentiment and consciousness.*
4. *Preparatory steps towards obtaining Government consent, where necessary, to the attainment of the aim of Zionism.*

whose primary goal was enunciated in the Basel Program: "to create for the Jewish people a home in Palestine." Herzl believed the meeting to have been a success and wrote in his diary on September 3, 1897:

Were I to sum up the Basel Congress in a word ... it would be this: At Basel I founded the Jewish State. If I said this out loud today, I would be answered by universal laughter. Perhaps in five years and certainly in 50, everyone will know it.

Thus, by the beginning of the 20th century, there was a movement whose goal was a Jewish state in Palestine, and there was Jewish immigration to Palestine, primarily from eastern Europe and Russia. Herzl negotiated for land with a number of world leaders, including the pope, Germany's kaiser Wilhelm, the Ottoman sultan Abdul Hamid II, various princes, and other European political figures.

Herzl's political Zionism and the WZO that he established to secure a Jewish state in Palestine were not universally welcomed in the world's Jewish communities. Only a small number of individuals joined his cause at the outset, and the growth of the movement was slow, especially outside western Europe. The primary opposition to political Zionism came from Orthodox Jews who saw it as a rewriting of Jewish tradition. They rejected the idea that the Jews would return to the Holy Land before the coming of the Messiah. Zionism was seen as a secular (and socialist) movement that contradicted Jewish belief and tradition. Many Jews were also of the view that Zionism had altered Judaism by its focus on a political objective, a Jewish state, rather than sustaining a central sense of devotion and Jewish ritual observance.

World War I

The migration of Jews to Palestine from Europe and Russia continued in the earliest years of the 20th century, and the Jewish population of the Holy Land continued to grow both in the cities and in rural areas. Similarly the Zionist movement continued its growth and development despite the death of Herzl in 1904. Growth of population was not matched by progress toward the goal of a Jewish state, and Ottoman control of the area remained the primary obstacle to Jewish self-government.

By World War I (1914) there were some 85,000 Jews in Palestine, both longtime residents and recent immigrants. At that time, there were some 600,000 Arabs in Palestine. The war provided an opportunity for substantial political maneuvering by the great powers seeking enhanced positions in the region as well as by indigenous peoples and leaders. During the war, Palestine was an area of particular focus. Both the Zionist movement and its supporters on the one hand and the Arab populations of the region under the leadership of Sherif Hussein ibn Ali, the emir of Mecca, on the

BALFOUR DECLARATION
(November 2, 1917)

*D*ear Lord Rothschild,

I have much pleasure in conveying to you, on behalf of His Majesty's Government, the following declaration of sympathy with Jewish Zionist aspirations which has been submitted to, and approved by, the Cabinet:

'His Majesty's Government view with favour the establishment in Palestine of a national home for the Jewish people, and will use their best endeavours to facilitate the achievement of this object, it being clearly understood that nothing shall be done which may prejudice the civil and religious rights of existing non–Jewish communities in Palestine, or the rights and political status enjoyed by Jews in any other country.'

I should be grateful if you would bring this declaration to the knowledge of the Zionist Federation.

Yours Sincerely,
Arthur James Balfour

other hand sought eventual control over Palestine. As part of wartime maneuvering, the British and French, initially with their Russian ally and later without it, developed schemes for the division of the territories of the defeated Ottoman Empire after the war's end. In the Sykes–Picot Agreement, Britain sought a sphere of influence in those parts of the empire that became Palestine and Iraq, while the French focused on the more northern territories that became Syria and Lebanon.

In their victory over the Ottomans, the British sought assistance from various groups in the region and beyond. A basic strategy was to encourage an Arab revolt against the Ottomans thereby forcing the empire to divert attention and forces from the war in Europe to the conflict in the Middle East. The British concluded that this would facilitate the Allied war effort against its adversaries.

In exchange for Arab assistance, the British pledged support for Sherif Hussein ibn Ali and his plans for an Arab kingdom under his leadership. In an exchange of correspondence between Hussein and the British high commissioner in Egypt, Sir Henry McMahon, between July 14, 1915, and March 1916, Hussein claimed Palestine as part of that territory. Although the British excluded that area from Hussein's proposed domain, McMahon's remarks left this pledge somewhat ambiguous during the hostilities so as to ensure Arab support against the Ottomans. Indeed, the ambiguities continued in the various negotiations for the postwar settlement. It was not until 1922, in the so-called Churchill Memorandum (also known as the Churchill White Paper), that the British government clarified that the pledge by McMahon to Hussein excluded the area west of the Jordan River (in other words, the area that later became Israel, the Gaza Strip, and the West Bank).

World War I also provided opportunities for the Zionist movement to make progress toward its objectives. Material aid to the Allied cause was provided by Jewish fighters, with the notable contribution of Dr. Chaim Weizmann m aiding the British war effort. A Russian Jewish immigrant to Great Britain and a leader of the World Zionist Organization who gamed access to the highest levels of the British government, Weizmann helped secure the issuance of the Balfour Declaration by the British government in November 1917. The declaration's core point was that "His Majesty's Government view with favour the establishment in Palestine of a national home for the Jewish people ..." This declaration was seen as expressing support for the Zionist position and laying the basis for a Jewish state in Palestine. But it was a short and somewhat ambiguous document: The declaration suggested that the British government would view such an event "with favour"; furthermore, it spoke not of a state but of "a national home." There was no timetable, no clear articulation of the end result, and no description of the area in question beyond noting "in Palestine." The ambiguity allowed for numerous and various interpretations.

The British found advantages to a Jewish presence in Palestine. Some believed it was economically politically, and strategically desirable; others saw the Jews in the Holy Land as having religious significance, with the Jews rightfully in Zion. The combination of British political and strategic calculations and Zionist efforts led to the British government's decision.

The Balfour Declaration dramatically altered the Zionist movement's efforts to create a Jewish state in Palestine. It pledged British support for the primary Zionist objective and thereby generated widespread international recognition of the objective and additional support for the goal. U.S. president Woodrow Wilson personally endorsed the declaration and the U.S. Congress, in 1922, unanimously approved a joint resolution supporting the Balfour Declaration.

The Mandate for Palestine and the Prestate Period

On December 9, 1917, British troops under General Edmund Allenby took Jerusalem from the Turks, ending four centuries of Ottoman rule. Included in the British army were three battalions of the Jewish Legion, consisting of thousands of Jewish volunteers. An armistice was concluded with Turkey on October 31, 1918, and all of Palestine came under British military control.

The Ottoman Empire, defeated by the Western alliance of Great Britain, France, the United States, and others, was forced to relinquish much of its empire. Competing arguments, supporting either the Jewish (Zionist) claim or the Arab claim, were advanced at the various peace conferences and other venues where the postwar settlement and the future of Palestine was considered. Eventually, the British decided not to grant control of the area to either the Arabs or the Zionists and thereby incurred the displeasure of both parties. Instead of making the decision soon after the cessation of hostilities, the British effectively postponed it and instead took upon themselves to retain control of

CHAIM WEIZMANN
(November 27, 1874–November 9, 1952)

Chaim Weizmann was born in Motol, near Pinsk, Russia, in 1874 to an ardent Zionist family. He was educated at the University of Freiburg in Germany where he received a doctor of science degree in 1900.

Weizmann moved to England in 1904 and began his career as a faculty member in biochemistry at the University of Manchester. As director of the Admiralty Laboratories during 1919, he discovered a process for producing acetone, a vital ingredient of gunpowder.

Weizmann became the leader of the English Zionist movement and was instrumental in securing the Balfour Declaration. In 1919, Weizmann headed the Zionist delegation to the Paris Peace Conference. Following World War I, Weizmann emerged as the leader of the World Zionist Organization and served as its president from 1920 to 1946, except for the years 1931–35.

He helped found the Jewish Agency, the Hebrew University of Jerusalem, and the Sieff Research Institute (now the Weizmann Institute of Science) at Rehovot. In the fall of 1947, he addressed the United Nations General Assembly to plead for the establishment of a Jewish state. Weizmann also met with U.S. president Harry Truman and appealed for assistance in the effort to secure a Jewish state. Weizmann became president of Israel's provisional government in May 1948. and in February 1949. the first elected Knesset selected Weizmann as the first president of Israel. He was reelected in November 1951 but died a year later.

Palestine. At the San Remo Conference of April 1920, the details of the mandate system were structured. The British mandate for Palestine was approved by the Council of the League of Nations on July 24, 1922, and became official on September 29, 1923.

The mandate for Palestine provided the legal foundation and the administrative and political framework for the ensuing quarter of a century. The history of the modern Jewish state, from an administrative and bureaucratic perspective, begins with the creation of the mandate.

The mandate recognized the "historical connection of the Jewish people with Palestine," called upon the mandatory power to "secure establishment of the Jewish national home," and recognized "an appropriate Jewish agency" for advice and cooperation to that end. The WZO, which was specifically recognized as the appropriate vehicle, formally established the Jewish Agency in 1929. Jewish immigration was to be facilitated, while ensuring that the "rights and position of other sections of the population are not prejudiced." English, Arabic, and Hebrew were all to be official languages.

The objective of the British mandate administration was the peaceful accommodation of Arabs and Jews in the mandate and the development of Palestine by Arabs and Jews under British control. Sir Herbert Samuel, the first high commissioner of Palestine, was responsible for keeping order between the two antagonistic communities. He called for Jewish immigration and land acquisition, which enabled thousands of highly committed and well-trained socialist Zionists to enter Palestine between 1919 and 1923. The Third Aliyah, as it came to be called, made important contributions to the development of Jewish agriculture, especially collective farming.

The Jewish Community under the Mandate

The British mandate authorities granted the Jewish and Arab communities the right to run their own internal affairs. During the mandate period, the Jewish community in Palestine (known as the Yishuv) established institutions for self-government and procedures for implementing decisions. The organized Jewish community chose by secret ballot the Assembly of the Elected (Asefat Hanivcharim) as its representative body. It met at least once a year, and between sessions its powers were exercised by the National Council (Vaad Leumi), which was elected by the assembly. The mandatory government entrusted the National Council with responsibility for Jewish communal affairs and granted it considerable autonomy. Financed by local resources and funds provided by world Jewry, these bodies maintained a network of educational, religious, health, and social services for the Jewish population. The council and its component units were responsible for administration within the Jewish community and created institutions to perform the requisite functions.

In addition to the standard departments and agencies of the government, a clandestine force, the Haganah, was created in 1920 as a wide-ranging organization for the defense of Jewish life and property in Palestine following a series of serious Arab actions in Jerusalem and elsewhere in Palestine. After independence, the Haganah formed the core of the Israel Defense Forces (IDF), Israel's military. Arms were smuggled to the Haganah, and training was provided. The Haganah guarded settlements, manufactured arms, and built stockades and roads for defense.

Other political and social institutions were created within the framework of the Yishuv, and many of these continued to function long after the creation of the State of Israel. These included the Histadrut, the General Federation of Labor, which coordinated labor-related matters and engaged in various social welfare and economic endeavors. The Histadrut. established in 1920, was more than a traditional labor union. It established training centers, helped to absorb new immigrants, and funded and managed large-scale agricultural and industrial enterprises. It set up agricultural marketing cooperatives, banks, and the construction firm Solel Boneh.

Political parties, many of which continue to exist today. albeit after various reinventions of themselves, were also created withm the Yishuv structure. Among these institutions was also the Jewish Agency created by the terms of the Palestine mandate, which eventually became the basis for the foreign ministry and other agencies with diplomatic missions outside Israel and for the functions relating to immigrants and liaison with the Jewish Diaspora.

The central figure and the architect of the Yishuv administration throughout the period of the mandate and into the first decades of the new State of Israel was David Ben-Gurion. In 1919, he founded a Zionist labor party, Ahdut Ha'avodah (Unity of Labor). Ben–Gurion and Ahdut Ha'avodah dominated the Histadrut and, through it, the Yishuv. As secretary-general of the Histadrut, Ben-Gurion oversaw the Jewish economy in the mandate.

Division in Zionism

The Jewish community in the mandate was not wholly cohesive. Internal divisions over domestic and foreign policies periodically developed. Revisionist Zionism, led by Vladimir Ze'ev Jabotinsky, challenged the views and policies of Ben-Gurion and the Zionist leadership of the Yishuv on a number of levels. Jabotinsky espoused a less socialist economic structure and a more activist defense policy against Arab riots and demonstrations. He also disagreed over the British decision to divide the Palestine mandate and create a new Arab state in the territory of the mandate east of the Jordan River, then known as Transjordan.

DAVID BEN–GURION
(October 16, 1886–December 1, 1973)

David Gruen (or Green) was born in Ptonsk, Russia (present-day Poland), in 1886. Under the influence of his father and grandfather, he became a committed Zionist in childhood. He studied in Warsaw and arrived in Jaffa in September 1906. There, he was elected to the central committee of the Poalei Zion (Workers of Zion), a socialist party, and began organizing workers into unions.

Prime Minister David Ben-Gurion meeting with President Harry Truman on May 8, 1951.

In 1910, he joined the editorial staff of a new Poalei Zion paper, Ahdut (Unity), in Jerusalem and began publishing articles under the name Ben-Gurion (Hebrew for "son of the young lion"). In 1912, he went to study at the University of Constantinople, where he earned a law degree with highest honors. In 1914, he returned to Palestine and resumed his work as a union organizer but in 1915 was exiled by Ottoman authorities.

In May 1918, he enlisted in a Jewish battalion of the British Royal Fusiliers and sailed to Egypt to join the expeditionary force. After the war, from 1921 to 1935, Ben-Gurion was the secretary–general of the Histadrut (General Federation of Labor) and was instrumental in the founding of the Unity of Labor party (Ahdut Ha'avodah), in 1919, which eventually would merge with other labor factions in 1930 to become Mapai (Israel Workers Party).

In the 1920s and 1930s, Chaim Weizmann, the head of the World Zionist Organization and chief diplomat of the Zionist movement, ran overall Zionist affairs, while Ben-Gurion headed Zionist activities in Palestine, where his major rival was Vladimir Ze'ev Jabotinsky, leader of the Revisionist Zionists. Ben-Gurion was convinced that the Revisionists and their more militant stance were endangering the drive toward eventual statehood and sought to undermine and discredit Revisionism. When Menachem Begin replaced Jabotinsky as the leader of Revisionism in the 1940s and increased militant actions against the British. Ben-Gurion intensified these efforts. In 1935, Ben-Gurion defeated the supporters of Chaim Weizmann and was elected chairman of the Jewish Agency's executive committee, a post he held from 1935 to 1948.

After World War II, Ben-Gurion supported an activist policy against the British in Palestine and. later, the United Nations partition plan of 1947. He declared the independence of Israel in May 1948 and became prime minister. He led Israel during the War of Independence and encouraged immigration. He served as prime minister from 1948 to 1963, except for a period of two years from December 1953 to 1955, when he voluntarily retired to Sde Boker in the Negev to seek respite from the rigors of his long political career and to dramatize the significance of pioneering and reclaiming the desert.

In 1955, Ben–Gurion left Sde Boker to become minister of defense in the government headed by Moshe Sharett.

After the election of 1955, Ben–Gurion undertook to form a new government.The eruption of the Lavon Affair in 1960 brought disarray to Mapai, and Ben–Gurion's political strength eroded. He resigned as prime minister in June 1963, ostensibly to study and write, but remained in the Knesset. In 1965, he founded

a new political party, Rafi (Israel Labor List), which won 10 seats in parliament. Rafi rejoined the government in 1967 and soon thereafter became part of the Israel Labor Party, but Ben–Gurion did not participate. In the October 1969 Knesset elections, he and some followers contested the election as the State List party and won four mandates. He remained in the Knesset until he resigned in 1970. He died in 1973.

In the Revisionist conception, the Zionist aim was to provide an integral solution to the worldwide Jewish problem in all its aspects—political, economic, and spiritual. To attain this objective, the Revisionists demanded that the entire mandated territory of Palestine, on both sides of the Jordan River, be turned into a Jewish state with a Jewish majority. They stressed the necessity of bringing to Palestine the largest number of Jews within the shortest possible time. Revisionism met with increasingly strong resistance, particularly from labor groups. The World Union of Zionists–Revisionists was founded in 1925 as an integral part of the WZO with Jabotinsky as president. In 1935, a referendum held among Revisionists resulted in their secession from the WZO and the establishment of an independent New Zionist Organization (NZO). Eleven years later, when ideological and tactical differences between the NZO and the WZO had diminished, the NZO decided to give up its separate existence and participated in the elections to the 22nd World Zionist Congress in Basel in 1946.

During the Mandate

Successive waves of Jewish immigrants arrived in Palestine between 1919 and 1939, each contributing to different aspects of the developing Jewish community. Some 35,000 who came between 1919 and 1923, mainly from Russia, strongly influenced the community's character and structure. These pioneers laid the foundations of a comprehensive social and economic infrastructure, developed agriculture, established kibbutzim (communal settlements) and moshavim (cooperative settlements), and provided the labor for the construction of housing and roads.

The following influx, between 1924 and 1932, of some 60,000 immigrants, primarily from Poland, was instrumental in developing and enriching urban life. They settled mainly in Tel Aviv, Haifa and Jerusalem, where they established small businesses, construction firms, and light industry The last major wave of immigration before World War II took place in the 1930s, following Adolf Hitler's rise to power, and consisted of some 165,000 people, mostly from Germany. The newcomers, many of whom were professionals and academics, constituted the first large-scale influx from western and central Europe. Their education, skills, and experience raised business standards, improved urban and rural lifestyles, and broadened the community's cultural life.

During the British mandate, agriculture expanded, factories were established, the waters of the Jordan River were harnessed for the production of electric power, new roads were built throughout the country, and the Dead Sea's mineral potential was tapped. Furthermore, a cultural life was emerging. Activities in art, music, and dance developed gradually with the establishment of professional schools and studios. Galleries and halls were set up to provide venues for exhibitions and performances. The Hebrew language was recognized as one of the three official languages of the territory, along with English and Arabic, and was used on documents, coins, and stamps, and on the radio. Publishing proliferated, and Palestine emerged as the dominant center of Hebrew literary activity. Theaters opened and there were attempts to write original Hebrew plays. The Palestine Philharmonic Orchestra was also founded during this time.

Arab–Jewish Conflict under the Mandate

The history of the mandate period is one of tension and conflict between the Jewish and Arab communities in Palestine and between them and the British. Each community believed that it had the right to the entire territory and had been so promised by the British government and its World War I Allies, yet neither got it as the British retained control. The efforts of the Jewish community to build a country for themselves primarily through Jewish immigration and land purchases were opposed by the Arabs and led to unrest, in 1920 and 1921, that continued to escalate.

Violence erupted again in the late 1920s. In 1928 and 1929, there were disturbances and riots associated with the Western, or Wailing, Wall, and Jews were killed in Jerusalem, Hebron, and Safed, with more injured there and elsewhere. A tenth of the Jewish community in Hebron was massacred, and the remainder left the city. The British government established a commission in September 1929 to investigate the cause of the anti-Jewish riots and to suggest policies that might prevent such occurrences in the future.

The Shaw Commission report suggested that the disturbances resulted from Arab fears of Jewish domination of Palestine through Jewish immigration and land purchases. It recommended that the British government issue a clear statement of policy on the meanings of the mandate provisions and on such issues as land ownership and immigration. The British continued to debate the issue of immigration and land purchases in the early 1930s but reached no definitive policy. Nevertheless, for several years Palestine remained relatively calm.

In November 1935, the Arabs in Palestine petitioned the British authorities to halt land transfers to the Jews, to establish a form of democratic leadership, and to terminate further Jewish immigration until there was an evaluation of the absorptive capacity of the country. Their demands were rejected, and in April 1936, the Arab Higher Committee, which consisted of representatives from the major Arab factions or groups in Palestine, called for a general strike. The Arab revolt soon escalated into violence as marauding bands of Arabs attacked Jewish settlements and Jewish paramilitary groups responded. After appeals from Arab leaders in the surrounding states, the committee called off the strike in October 1936.

The British government appointed a commission under Lord Robert Peel to assess the situation. The Peel report, published in July 1937, noted that because the British had made promises to both the Arabs and Jews during World War I and in return had gained the support of both, each party had drawn its own expectations from those promises. Although the British had believed that both Arabs and Jews could find a degree of compatibility under the mandate, this belief had not been justified nor would it be in the future. However, Britain would not renounce its obligations; it was responsible for the welfare of the mandate and would strive to make peace:

> In the light of experience and of the arguments adduced by the Commission ... [the British government is] driven to the conclusions that there is an irreconcilable conflict between the aspirations of Arabs and Jews in Palestine, that these aspirations cannot be satisfied under the terms of the present Mandate, and that a scheme of partition on the general lines recommended by the Commission represents the best and most hopeful solution to the deadlock.

Cantonization (the division of Palestine into cantons, or territories) was examined as a possible solution and found not to be viable because it

VLADIMIR ZE'EV JABOTINSKY
(October 18, 1880–August 4, 1940)

Vladimir Ze'ev Jabotinsky was born in Odessa, Russia, in 1880. He studied law in Bern, Switzerland, and Rome, Italy, and became interested in the Zionist cause with the pogroms in Russia. After the beginning of World War I, Jabotinsky promoted the idea of a Jewish Legion as a component of the British army, and he later joined it. In March 1921, he was elected to the Zionist Executive, which carried out policies established by the World Zionist Congress, but resigned in January 1923 to protest the perceived lack of resistance on the part of the Zionist leadership to British Middle East policy, specifically the unilateral secession of Transjordan from the Palestine mandate in 1922.

In 1923, Jabotinsky founded the youth movement Betar, and in 1925 the World Union of Ziomsts–Revisiomsts was formed in Pans, with Jabotinsky as president. He later seceded from the World Zionist Organization and founded in Vienna in 1935 the New Zionist Organization (NZO), which advocated the establishment of a Jewish state, increased Jewish immigration to Palestine, and militant opposition to the British mandatory authorities. Jabotinsky became president of the NZO. His philosophy provided the ideological basis for the Herut Party. He campaigned against the British plans for the partition of Palestine. He died in New York in 1940: his remains were transferred to Israel and reburied on Mount Herzl in Jerusalem in July 1964. Jabotinsky's influence on Israel's history and politics is substantial as indicated by his role as the ideological forebear of the Herut and Likud political parties and especially the influence of his ideas on the thinking and policies of Menachem Begin, Yitzhak Shamir. Benjamin Netanyahu, and Ariel Sharon.

would not settle the question of self-government. The commission suggested the partition of Palestine into three zones: a Jewish zone, an Arab section, and a corridor that went from Tel Aviv–Jaffa to Jerusalem and Bethlehem, which was to be under a continued British mandate. The drawbacks of partition, it was believed, would be outweighed by the advantages of peace and security. The mandate would thus be dissolved and replaced by a treaty system identical to that of Iraq and Syria. Access to and the protection of the Holy Places in Jerusalem and Bethlehem would be guaranteed to all by the League of Nations. The principle guiding the partition of Palestine was the separation of Jewish areas of settlement from those completely or mostly occupied by the Arabs.

The partition plan proposed by Peel, the first recommendation for the partition of Palestine, was a reversal of British policy on the mandate and the Balfour Declaration. Anger and protest from both the Arabs and the Zionists ensued. The Arabs did not want to have to give up any land to the Jews, and the Zionists felt betrayed in their pursuit of all of Palestine as a national home.

Britain endorsed the Peel plan. After reviewing the Peel Commission report in July/August 1937, the League of Nations Permanent Mandates Commission in Geneva objected to the partition. The Jewish Agency accepted the plan even though it was not happy with the exclusion of Jerusalem

THE KIBBUTZ

Jewish immigrants to Palestine in the 19th and early 20th centuries sought to create conditions for a Jewish state to prosper in an area of limited economic potential. To facilitate their efforts, these early pioneers (halutzim) developed a new type of communal settlement called the kibbutz. The first kibbutz had its origins in the founding, in December 1909, of an experimental collective settlement in the Jordan River Valley near the Sea of Galilee.

Although the experiment proved successful, its original members dispersed, and it was taken over by a group of pioneers from Russia, who named it Degania. The kibbutz soon came to symbolize the pioneering spirit of Israel and even became synonymous with Israeli society although it never represented more than a small proportion of Israel's population.

The word kibbutz comes from the Hebrew for "group." The kibbutz is a socialist experiment: a voluntary grouping of individuals who hold property in common and have their needs satisfied by the commune. Every kibbutz member participates in the work. All the needs of the members, including education, recreation, medical care, and vacations, are provided by the kibbutz.

The earliest kibbutzim were founded by immigrant halutzim from eastern Europe who sought to join socialism and Zionism to build a new kind of society and have been maintained by successive generations as well as new members. Initially, the kibbutzim focused on working the land and became known for their crops, poultry, orchards, and dairy farming.

As modern, especially automated, techniques were introduced and as land and water became less available, many of the kibbutzim shifted their activities or branched out into new areas, such as industry and tourism, to supplement their agricultural pursuits. Kibbutz factories now manufacture electronic products, furniture, plastics, household appliances, farm machinery, and irrigation–system components. Some operate large shopping centers.

A type of cooperative agricultural settlement often confused with the kibbutz is the moshav, which allows its members to live individually and to farm their own land but cooperatively owns the heavy machinery and handles the purchasing of supplies and marketing products. The first moshav, Nahalal, was founded in 1921 in the Jezreel Valley.

The kibbutz, a social and economic framework that grew out of the pioneering society of the early 20th century, became a permanent rural way of life based on egalitarian and communal principles. It set up a prosperous economy and distinguished itself through the contribution of its members in the establishment, and building, of the state. Given the small percentage of the population who participated in kibbutzim, however, the kibbutz was over–represented in social importance and political strength.

Prior to Israel's independence and its initial years of statehood, the kibbutz assumed a number of important functions and activities dealing with settlement, immigration, agriculture and defense. This was important in creating both a new state and a new society. Later these became state functions and the role of the kibbutzim in society, especially since the 1970s, has declined, as has its political strength. Nevertheless, its role in the economic sphere has remained significantly greater than the percentage of the participating population.

THE IRGUN

In part in response to anti-Jewish riots in 1929, the newly formed Revisionist Zionist movement developed its own militia. The Irgun (short for Irgun Zvai Leumi, or National Military Organization, also known by its Hebrew acronym, Etzel) was a clandestine defense organization founded in 1931 by militant members of the defense forces, the Haganah, and others who believed that the Haganah was not sufficiently responsive to Palestinian Arab violence against the Jews in the mandate.

In 1936, the Irgun formally became the armed wing of the Revisionist movement. In 1937, an agreement with the Haganah for the merger of the two defense bodies led to a split in Etzel in April 1937. Until May 1939, the Irgun's activities were limited to retaliation against Arab attacks. After the publication of the British White Paper of 1939, the British mandatory authorities became the Irgun's target.

With the outbreak of World War II, the Irgun announced the cessation of anti-British action and offered its cooperation in the common struggle against Nazi Germany. The Stern Gang (Lohamei Herut Yisrael—Lehi—Fighters for the Freedom of Israel) was then formed due to disagreement within the Irgun over anti-British actions. Founder Avraham Stern and his followers sought continued anti-British action despite World War II.

Menachem Begin was the Irgun's commander from December 1943 to 1948. In January 1944, the Irgun declared that the truce with the British was over and renewed the state of war. The Irgun demanded the liberation of Palestine from British occupation. Its attacks were directed against government institutions such as immigration, land registry, and income tax offices and police and radio stations. Limited cooperation was established in the late fall of 1945 among the Irgun, Lehi, and Haganah and lasted, with occasional setbacks, until August 1946. On July 22 of that year, Etzel blew up the British army headquarters and the secretariat of the Palestine government, housed in the King David Hotel in Jerusalem.

After the United Nations adopted the Palestine partition plan on November 29, 1947, organized Arab bands launched anti-Jewish attacks; the Irgun vigorously counterattacked. One of these was the capture, on April 9, 1948, of the village of Deir Yassin by the Irgun–Lehi forces, which resulted in a large number of Arab civilian casualties.

When the State of Israel was proclaimed on May 14, 1948, the Irgun announced that it would disband and transfer its men to the Israel Defense Forces. For several weeks, however, until full integration was completed, the Irgun formations continued to function as separate units, especially in Jerusalem which the UN had declared to be an international city.

On June 20. 1948. a cargo ship, the Altalena. purchased and equipped in Europe by the irgun and its sympathizers and carrying 800 volunteers and large quantities of arms and ammunition, reached Israel's shores. The Irgun demanded that 20 percent of the arms be allocated to its still independent units in Jerusalem, but the Israeli government under David Ben–Gurion ordered the surrender of all arms and of the ship. When the order was not complied with, government troops opened fire on the ship, which consequently went up in flames off Tel Aviv. On September 1, 1948. the remaining Irgun units disbanded and joined the IDF.

and with the amount of territory allotted to the Jewish state. The Arab Higher Committee rejected the plan and the division of Palestine, and a new and more violent phase of the Arab revolt began.

Yet another commission was established. The Woodhead Commission published its findings in October 1938, which held that the Peel Commission's proposals were not feasible, primarily because it would leave a large Arab minority within the boundaries of a Jewish state, which also would be surrounded by other Arab states. The Woodhead Commission concluded that there were no feasible boundaries for self-supporting Arab and Jewish states in Palestine but suggested a number of partition plans. The British government responded on November 9, 1938, noting that partition was not feasible: "His Majesty's Government ... have reached the conclusion that. the political, administrative and financial difficulties involved in the proposal to create independent Arab and Jewish States inside Palestine are so great that this solution of the problem is impracticable."

On February 7, 1939, the British government convened the St. James Conference in London to see if a solution could be developed through negotiations with the Arabs and the Jews. The failure of the conference led to a White Paper of May 17, 1939, that called for severe restrictions on Jewish immigration: "His Majesty's Government believe that the framers of the Mandate in which the Balfour Declaration was embodied could not have intended that Palestine should be converted into a Jewish State against the will of the Arab population of the country." It called, therefore, for the establishment of a Jewish National Home in an independent Palestinian state. Jewish immigration would be restricted, as would be land transfers. The White Paper foresaw an independent Palestinian state within 10 years.

The House of Commons debated the White Paper on May 22, 1939, and it was approved. The House of Lords also approved it. The response was outrage in both Arab and Jewish communities. The Arabs wanted an immediate end to all Jewish immigration and the review of all immigrants who had entered Palestine since 1918. The Zionists felt

that the British had backed away from previous commitments to work toward a Jewish homeland and that this policy was a breach of faith. Peace in Palestine seemed improbable, as both the Arabs and the Jews rejected the White Paper.

On the eve of World War II, the British realized they could not end the conflict in Palestine and that their role in the country was over. The animosity and the violence between Jews and Arabs had become unmanageable.

World War II and the Holocaust

During World War II, the National Socialist (Nazi) regime under Adolf Hitler in Germany systematically carried out a plan to liquidate the European Jewish community. As the Nazi armies swept through Europe, Jews were persecuted, subjected to pain and humiliation, and herded into ghettos. From the ghettos, they were transported to concentration camps and murdered in mass shootings or in gas chambers. In 1939, some 10 million of the estimated 16 million Jews in the world lived in Europe. By 1945, almost 6 million had been killed, most in the major concentration camps. In Czechoslovakia, about 4,000 Jews survived out of 281,000; in Greece, about 200 survived out of 65,000-70,000. In Austria, 5,000 of 70,000 escaped death. Some 4.6 million were killed in Poland and German-occupied areas of the Soviet Union.

During World War II, the Yishuv generally pursued a policy of cooperation with the British in the war effort against Germany and other Axis powers. Some 32,000 Jews in Palestine volunteered to serve in the British forces. In 1944, the Jewish Brigade (composed of some 5,000 volunteers) was formed and later fought. As a consequence, the Yishuv leadership formed a mobile defense force to replace the Haganah members who had gone to fight with the British. The Plugot Mahatz (Shock Forces), or Palmach, were a mobile force designed to defend the Yishuv, and the British helped train them. The Jewish Brigade and Palmach veterans would later constitute the core of the IDF officer corps.

HEBREW

Hebrew is one of the oldest living languages. Its history spans a period of some 3,300 years, during which it has served as the language of the Bible and many other works of thought and ethics. In addition, Hebrew represents the only instance of a language successfully revived as a spoken language after it had ceased to be spoken.

Between the years 200 C.E. and 1880, Hebrew was not spoken in everyday life, although it was used as a means of communication between Jews of different countries who could not understand each other's native languages and among some pious Jews who spoke Hebrew on the Sabbath. The use of Hebrew in writing was however widespread throughout that period. In some parts of Jewry, Hebrew was used side by side with another written language. In eastern Europe, Hebrew was the language of the educated classes.

When, in the late 18th century, modern European civilization began to penetrate among the Jewish masses, it did so largely through the Hebrew writings of the Haskalah (Enlightenment) movement, which encouraged secularization and assimilation as a route of Jewish emancipation. In 1856, there appeared the first Hebrew newspaper, the weekly Ha–Maggid.

When it became clear that the solution to anti-Semitism would include the rebuilding of a Jewish state, the importance of a national language in this reconstruction was recognized. Hebrew became the language of Hibbat Zion, the forerunner of Zionism. The immediate result was a spectacular development of Hebrew literature after 1880. This period, which included such writers as Ahad Ha'am (Asher Ginzberg), Chaim Nachman Bialik, and Saul Tchernichowsky, is generally considered the classical age of Hebrew literature. It also saw the rise of a Hebrew daily press.

The connection between the language and national revival was drawn by Eliezer Ben–Yehuda, considered the father of the modern Hebrew language. In spring 1879. he published an article in which he proposed the foundation of a Jewish state in Palestine as a national center where the literary language would be Hebrew.

The Palestine mandate recognized Hebrew as one of the official languages of the country. Thereafter, it was used in the administration of the mandate and especially by the autonomous Jewish institutions. Numerous daily and weekly papers emerged, a network of schools was created, the Hebrew University was founded in 1925, and a vigorous literature developed.

In May 1948, when the State of Israel was established, Hebrew regained a position it had lost nearly 2,000 years earlier, when the Hasmonean dynasty fell. It became the official language of the state.

After World War II

World War II and its associated horrors created a greater need for a resolution to the Palestine issue, and the struggle for Palestine intensified. At the end of World War II, hundreds of thousands of desperate Jews who had populated Europe's concentration camps wanted relocation to Palestine, but the British were still unwilling to allow it. A change of government in Britain brought Ernest Bevin, widely regarded as anti-Semitic, into the position of foreign secretary, and he opposed any new Jewish immigration to Palestine. British policy united the various elements of the Yishuv leadership, who saw no alternative but to launch a full-fledged campaign against the British, which took several forms. One was diplomatic. Another was an appeal to the compassion of the world by launching an illegal immigration effort, bringing tens of thousands of refugees from Europe in refugee boats. The campaign against the British also used violence, with the first shots fired on British military and government facilities by armed underground groups.

On July 22, 1946, the southwest corner of Jerusalem's King David Hotel, headquarters of the British military and civilian command in Palestine, was destroyed by a bombing committed by the Irgun Zvai Leumi. A total of 91 people were killed in the attack: 41 Arabs, 28 British, 17 Jews, and five others. According to the Irgun's leader, Menachem Begin, the bombing was a political act, a demonstration that the Irgun could strike at the very heart of the British mandate in Palestine.

The attack was condemned by the Jewish Agency leadership. Nevertheless, it prompted a crackdown by British security authorities on Zionist activities in Palestine.

During World War II, the focus of the Zionist movement's activities and leadership shifted from Europe to the United States, creating a new set of opportunities to achieve the Zionist objective as well as a fortuitous linking of Zionism to the United States, which would emerge a superpower from World War II and help guide the creation of a new world environment. The Biltmore Conference of 1942 marked the public manifestation of the move in Zionist focus to the United States. Subsequently, Chaim Weizmann secured U.S. support for the creation of a Jewish state in

EXODUS

Exodus sailed across the Mediterranean, it was trailed by a British warship and became the subject of international media attention. When it approached Palestine on July 18, it was intercepted by the British navy. International controversy intensified when the British, instead of deporting the refugees to Cyprus, shipped them

*T*he Exodus was the best known of the many ships loaded with refugees that Zionist activists sought to bring to Palestine, in defiance of the British authorities. Originally known as the President Warfield, the Exodus was purchased by the Haganah expressly to transport immigrants to Palestine. It departed from France in July 1947 with a shipload of 4,500 Holocaust survivors who sought entrance to Palestine. As the

back to France; however, all but a handful of the passengers refused to disembark. Then on August 22, the British ordered the refugees sent to the British zone of occupied Germany. Media coverage of the struggle further galvanized international criticism of Great Britain's policies. The passengers of the Exodus finally reached Israel in late 1948, following the establishment of the State of Israel.

Palestine, paralleling his role with the British during World War I.

The Zionist movement had been primarily a European one until World War II when its membership and leadership was destroyed and dislocated by the Holocaust and by the war. In the United States, the Jewish community, whose focus generally had not been on Zionism as a solution to anti-Semitism but rather on the civil rights concerns of American Jews, emerged as interested in and concerned about the fate of their coreligionists in Europe and Palestine.

The Holocaust and World War II emerged as public policy issues in the United States at the end of the war. The practical and humanitarian problems were faced by U.S. military forces confronting large numbers of displaced European Jews and the problems associated with their survival and future. It was at this point that U.S. president Harry Truman determined that allowing some of these Jewish refugees to find refuge in Palestine would make good sense and good policy. Truman suggested the need to open the gates to Palestine for displaced Jews seeking refuge. The newly elected British government refused. In November 1945, an Anglo-American Committee of Inquiry, composed of representatives appointed by their respective governments, was charged with studying the question ot Jewish immigration to Palestine and the future of the British mandate. After numerous meetings and hearings in the region and elsewhere, it issued a report on April 20, 1946. Among the recommendations was the immediate issuing of 100,000 immigration certificates for Palestine to Jewish victims of Nazi and Fascist persecution. Truman accepted much of the report; the British government did not and refused to increase the limits on Jewish immigration to Palestine.

Faced with continued British opposition, the Yishuv decided to commence illegal Jewish immigration to Palestine. The goal was to move secretly, and primarily by ship, Jews from European camps for displaced persons to Palestine's ports. The Yishuv sought to evade the British navy and land in Palestine where the arriving immigrants were granted refuge among the Jewish community in Palestine. This alternative immigration was referred to as Aliya Bet (Immigration B). More than 70,000 Jews arrived in Palestine on more than 100 ships of various sizes between the end of World War II and the independence of Israel in May 1948.

The End of the Mandate and the Partition Plan

The enormous drain on human and economic resources of the Allied powers during and immediately after World War II forced significant rethinking of political and strategic policies for the postwar era in most of the major states of the world. In Britain, the crucial decision was taken to reexamine the empire and reevaluate positions "east of Suez." The British position in Palestine became increasingly untenable, and it soon became an obvious choice for British withdrawal: The costs of continuing the mandate far outweighed the benefits to Britain of remaining there, especially with the growing pressures accelerated by the war and its subsequent effects on the regional and external players. The British, reflecting on their inability over the previous decades to find a solution to the Palestine issue that would satisfv the conflicting views of the Jews and the Arabs, and reconsidering the cost m men and pounds sterling of their continuation as the mandatory power, made a decision to relinquish their control over the Palestine mandate.

On February 15, 1947, Great Britain turned the issue of the Palestine mandate over to the United Nations. In effect, the British gave up on the issues affecting Palestine and, rather than suggesting a serious resolution of the issue, chose to place the problem on the agenda of the international community. The United Nations Special Committee on Palestine (UNSCOP) was created to investigate the issue and suggest appropriate measures to be taken.

As part of the Zionist lobbying effort, WZO president Chaim Weizmann met with U.S. president Truman. These meetings were crucial to generate American support for the creation of a

ARAB OPPOSITION TO THE PARTITION OF PALESTINE
(November 29, 1947)

After the adoption of Resolution 181 (II) by the United Nations General Assembly, Saudi Arabia's chief delegate, Emir Faisal al–Saud, declared:

> [T]oday's resolution has destroyed the Charter and all the convenants preceding it.
>
> We have felt, like many others, the pressure exerted on various representatives of this Organisation by some of the big Powers in order that the vote should be in favour of partition. For these reasons, the Government of Saudi Arabia registers, on this historic occasion, the fact that it does not consider itself bound by the resolution adopted today by the General Assembly. Furthermore, it reserves to itself the full right to act freely in whatever way it deems fit, in accordance with the principles of right and justice. My Government holds responsible those parties that hampered all means of cooperation and understanding.

Jewish state in Palestine along the lines preferred by the Zionist movement. Direct and significant U.S. involvement in the Palestine question had developed since the shift of the Zionist movement from Europe to the United States during World War II. Toward the end of the hostilities, the United States was also involved in the question of the future of the displaced persons in the concentration camps liberated by the U.S. and Allied forces. Truman's interest and concern with this issue was among the earliest of the U.S. involvement in the Palestine matter.

After considerable deliberation, the UNSCOP proposed a plan that called for the partition of the British mandate of Palestine into an Arab state and a Jewish state, with an international regime (*corpus separatum*) for the city of Jerusalem and its environs, as the city was deemed too holy to be accorded to either. The partition plan proposed boundaries for a 4,500-square-mile Arab state that would be home to about 800,000 Arabs and 10,000 Jews. The Jewish state was to consist of some 5,500 square miles where some 498,000 Jews and 468,000 Arabs would live. The Jewish state was located in the coastal plain along the Mediterranean Sea from about Ashkelon to Acre, the eastern area of the Galilee, and much of the Negev desert. The Arab state included the remainder of the territory of the mandate west of the Jordan River, except for Jerusalem and the immediate area around it, which were included in the internationalized zone. All would be linked in an economic union. On November 29, 1947, the UN General Assembly, by a vote of 33 to 13, with 10 abstentions and one member absent, adopted Resolution 181 (II), the plan of partition for Palestine. Thus, the international system created a Jewish state of Israel, within the territory of the Palestine mandate.

The Zionist movement and other Jews were divided concerning the United Nations decision. Among the Zionist groups in Palestine and the Diaspora there were essentially two perspectives. Both believed that they had been offered less than they wanted, but the left-of-center Labor Zionists adopted a practical stance and believed that acceptance of the partition was the most logical and appropriate step. The right wing of the Zionists, primarily the Revisionists, believed that they should have been awarded all of the land west of the Jordan River as well as the territory east of the river that the British had severed from the original League of Nations mandate for Palestine to create the state of Transjordan. Nevertheless, there was little that could be done. Thus, the Yishuv, though unhappy with the exclusion of Jerusalem, and the Jewish Agency accepted the decision of the General Assembly as an important step toward independent statehood and a practical necessity for providing refuge for survivors of the Holocaust. When the new state of Israel declared its independence in May 1948, it was within the lines drawn by the United Nations.

Meanwhile, the Arab leadership in Palestine and the League of Arab States unconditionally rejected the UN partition plan on the grounds that all of Palestine should be awarded to a Palestinian Arab state. The Arab rejection was based on the position that the United Nations had no right to give away approximately half of Palestine to the Zionists and that Palestinian Arabs should not be made to pay for Europe's crimes against the Jews. The latter argument was advanced despite the fact that the Balfour Declaration had been issued before the Nazis rose to power in Germany.

These clashing perspectives provided a basis tor the ongoing Arab–Israeli conflict. The partition plan was supported by the United States and the Soviet Union, both of whom seemed to be courting the new Jewish state as an ally in the east-west struggle for regional mastery.

Fighting erupted in Palestine after adoption of the partition plan: the first Jewish buses were attacked the next morning; six passengers were killed; and many others were wounded. Armed Palestinian Arabs aided by volunteers smuggled in from neighboring Arab countries launched attacks on Jewish settlements and facilities. The forces of the Yishuv, especially the Haganah, were able to deal effectively with this threat in many areas. The civil war between the communities m Palestine was the prelude to full-scale hostilities after the British mandate ended on May 15, 1948.

The Iron Cage: The Story of the Palestinian Struggle for Statehood

By Rashid Khalidi

Comparing the Incomparable

Examinations of the troubled history of Palestine before 1948 frequently compare Palestinian Arab society with the burgeoning Jewish community in Palestine, the yishuv. This is especially the case where the events leading up to the 1948 war are concerned, but these comparisons are common for the entire period before 1948, and more infrequently, thereafter. Among the indices commonly compared are the two societies' respective levels of economic development, the growth of their political and cultural institutions, their ideological cohesion, and their military capabilities. These comparisons can be found in the social scientific literature and in historical accounts, as well as in popular treatments of both societies and of the conflict between them.[31] The rationale for making such comparisons between the two communities is obvious: until 1948, they uneasily shared the country and were in increasingly fierce competition with one another. In that year, they finally and formally became two distinct entities, as one of them after May 15, organized as the nascent state of Israel, decisively bested the other, the Palestinian people, establishing demographic dominance in Palestine, control over most of its land, and a sovereign, independent state. In so doing, Israel succeeded in instituting effective hegemony over Palestine that has lasted until the present day, and that has so far been instrumental in preventing the creation of a Palestinian state.

Engaging in some sort of comparison of the two communities before 1948 is therefore both necessary and worthwhile, if one is careful not to ignore crucial external factors, especially foreign political, military, and economic support. This is a particularly important consideration where a quintessentially transnational movement such as Zionism is concerned. Both communities in confrontation in Palestine had important links with communities outside the country. However, only one, the yishuv, and the Zionist movement that represented it, in consequence received powerful external support, both from many of its coreligionists elsewhere and from the greatest imperial power of the day, as well as from the League of Nations.

By contrast, the Palestinians were largely bereft of significant, practical external support. This was true although they enjoyed the increasingly strong sympathy of public opinion in the surrounding Arab countries: indeed, that popular sympathy in 1936–39 and 1947–48 produced numerous volunteers willing to fight alongside the Palestinians. This was mildly ironic, since manpower was not one of the Palestinians' pressing needs, and it translated into little in the way of arms, funds, or effective international diplomatic support.[32] The lack of such practical outside assistance was not surprising, since until well after 1948 most Arab countries were still under colonial rule. Most of those that were nominally independent in 1948 remained subject to neocolonial forms of control and foreign military occupation: British troops remained in Egypt, Iraq, and Jordan until the 1950s, and French troops were in Syria and Lebanon until 1946. The other two, Saudi Arabia and Yemen, were hardly organized as modern states. All other parts of the Arab world, from Morocco, Algeria, and Tunisia to Libya and the Sudan, as well as South Yemen, Oman, and the other four countries of the Gulf, were still fully subject to direct or indirect colonial rule.

Needless to say, the colonial powers, in particular Great Britain and France, did their best to prevent the Arab peoples under their control from supporting the Palestinians. Thus, the French archives for the interwar period are replete with cases in which the Foreign Ministry in Paris or officials in Morocco, Algeria, or Tunisia prevented the sending of funds from North African Muslims to Palestine, or the sending of emissaries from the Maghribi community (of North African origins) in Palestine to North Africa to request aid, for example after the 1929 Wailing Wall disturbances. In contrast, the French authorities allowed considerable sums to be raised for the yishuv among the large Jewish communities of North Africa, and themselves often transferred the funds immediately to Palestine, while Zionist representatives from Palestine were permitted to travel to French North Africa with little hindrance for these and other purposes.

The two sides were thus in very different positions as far as external support was concerned. If one avoids the pitfalls of glib comparisons, however, careful examination of the similarities and differences between the two societies can be particularly revealing in understanding what happened and why during the crucial period beginning in the 1930s, which witnessed a growing disparity in power between them and a decisive shift in favor of the yishuv. At the outset of the fateful decade of the 1930s—during which Palestine was effectively lost to its indigenous population, although the final denouement came only in the late 1940s—the Jewish population of Palestine amounted to only 17.8 percent of the total. Indeed, this proportion had been declining slightly for several years, in spite of unstinting external financial support. For several years at the end of the 1920s and early 1930s, annual Jewish immigration to Palestine came to only a few thousand, an insignificant figure in a total population of over 1 million, especially given that the Arab birth rate was much higher than that of the Jewish community. By the end of the 1930s, however, after the rise to power of Hitler spurred the annual arrival of many tens of thousands of refugees fleeing persecution in Germany and elsewhere in Europe, Palestine's Jewish population rose to more than 30 percent of the total. The year 1935 alone, the high point of Jewish immigration before 1948, witnessed over sixty thousand Jewish immigrants, as many as the country's entire Jewish population in 1919.

The Palestinian Arabs and the yishuv were acutely aware that the outcome of the struggle between them depended largely on which one would win the "demographic battle." This led both to pay extraordinary attention to questions related to immigration. Without massive immigration the Zionist movement could not hope to claim majority status, dominate the Palestinians demographically, and build a Jewish national home in Palestine. Far-sighted Zionist leaders such as David Ben-Gurion realized that the massive wave of immigration to Palestine sparked by the Nazis' rise to power in the early 1930s finally provided the critical demographic mass that would soon make it possible for the Zionist movement to achieve absolute Jewish hegemony and sovereignty over the entire country. He stated at the time that he could understand Arab fears: "immigration at the rate of 60,000 a year means a Jewish state in all Palestine." Dr. Wolfgang von Weisl, a representative of the Zionist Revisionist movement, the leading rivals to Ben-Gurion's Zionist Labour Party, Mapai, said much the same thing to a senior French official in 1935: after only a few more years of immigration at the current rate of sixty thousand per year, a Jewish state in all of Palestine and Jordan would be possible, it could not be seriously harmed by the Arabs, and would be "strong enough to defend itself all by itself."

Such an outcome was impossible to foresee when the Jewish population of Palestine as a proportion of the total population actually declined in the late 1920s and early 1930s. Economic difficulties in Palestine, followed by the Great Depression of 1929, together with other factors, led to a decrease in immigration rates and the emigration of many Jews from Palestine during this period. The resulting wave of pessimism affected even some of the most stalwart Zionist leaders. But when the immigration wave of the mid-1930s, which was accompanied by a major inflow of capital brought by German Jewish refugees fleeing Nazi Germany, reached Palestine, the situation changed dramatically. Thereafter, the possibility that they could be outnumbered in their own country came to be a growing concern for the Palestinians, even as that same outcome promised security, victory, and absolute sovereignty to the Zionists. Equally important, during the 1930s the Jewish sector of Palestine's economy came to have the larger share of the country's national income: by 1933 the part of the economy controlled by the considerably smaller Jewish community had already grown bigger than that belonging to the Arabs, although the disparity between them did not widen much further until 1948.

Comparisons between the two communities before 1948 are useful beyond comprehending the course of the conflict between them, including understanding some aspects of each side's political, economic, and social development. However, these comparisons are far less useful in other ways, and indeed they can be quite misleading, for reasons that are often ignored, such as the incommensurability of many things being compared. Five main factors of incommensurability seem particularly important in understanding the two societies' subsequent trajectories.

The first and perhaps most marked difference between Arabs and Jews in Palestine before

1948 was economic. It can best be understood in terms of capital investment, and in particular in terms of capital inflow per capita. According to the Israeli scholar Zeev Sternhell, during the entire decade of the 1920s, "the annual inflow of Jewish capital was on average 41.5% larger than the Jewish net domestic product (NDP) … Its ratio to NDP did not fall below 33% in any of the pre-World War II years and was kept at about 15% in all but one year since 1941." By another calculation, the contributions of American Jews alone to the Zionist project until 1948 totaled well over $375 million, a considerable sum when one considers that in the 1930s the average national income of the Jewish sector of the economy was $75 million. For a Jewish population that was less than two hundred thousand in 1930, and that by 1948 had barely reached six hundred thousand, these were phenomenal absolute, relative, and per capita rates of capital inflow.

In consequence of this massive inflow of capital, and the concomitant arrival of skilled immigrants, the Jewish sector of the Palestinian economy grew extraordinarily rapidly. During the quarter century between 1922 and 1947, it maintained an *annual* growth rate of 13.2 percent. By contrast, the Arab sector of the economy grew at less than half that rate during the same period: by the much less spectacular (but still respectable) figure of 6.5 percent annually. This translated into an annual growth rate in real income per capita over these twenty-five years—including the Great Depression—of 3.6 percent for the Arabs and 4.8 percent for the Jews. This meant that during the Mandate, while the Arab economy of Palestine had a vigorous average growth rate, the Jewish economy had one of the highest sustained growth rates in the world. Put in other terms, and considering the respective assets and starting points of the two economies, the result of these considerable capital and skilled-labor inflows and related disparities was that in relative terms one society was well off and the other remained comparatively poor. Thus in 1936, per capita national income in the Jewish sector was LP (Palestinian pounds) 44; in the Arab sector it was LP 17. Thereafter the broad disparity in per capita income stayed about the same, with individuals in the Jewish sector enjoying on average 2.6 times as much income as those in the Arab sector.

Beyond these major economic inequalities, there was a second related set of perhaps even more extreme disparities between the Arab and Jewish sectors: these lay in the sphere of what might be termed human capital. This was notably the case in terms of literacy, education, and technical and professional training, in all of which the Arab sector suffered from serious deficiencies by comparison with the Jewish community, especially when one considers that the latter came to be dominated by relatively well-educated new Jewish immigrants from Europe, who became the overwhelming majority of the population of the yishuv during the Mandate period. According to the 1931 census, the last such complete enumeration before the end of the Mandate, only about 22 percent of Palestinian Arabs were literate, as against 86 percent of the country's Jewish population. Even though Arab literacy rates rose markedly over the following decade and a half, the gap in this regard between the two communities remained wide. By the end of the Mandate, according to the best existing figures, while 77 percent of the Jewish school-age population (ages five to nineteen) received schooling, 44.5 percent of school-age Arab children were in school. The latter figure in fact represented a relatively high proportion for a Middle Eastern country like Palestine at this time. As one of the most astute students of the subject, the respected Israeli economist Jacob Metzer, has noted: "Arab school enrollment … though low, was not too low." … Compared with other countries in the same income range, including … Egypt and Turkey, the Arabs of Palestine did rather well." This relatively creditable performance paled, however, by comparison with the extraordinarily high level of education among Jews in Palestine.

The disparity in education in particular, and in human capital in general, was not simply a function of the fact that as time went on, immigration during the Mandate had the effect of swelling the yishuv with a growing literate population. Beyond this, a high proportion of these newcomers were young and active, with a generally high level of education, and a relatively high and widespread level of technical aptitude, as was to be expected given the central and eastern European countries from which most of them came, and the traditionally high regard for education among Jews. This can be seen from a number of other indicators, such as the number of physicians per ten thousand people. The ratio among the Jewish population of Palestine in 1940 of 40 doctors per 10,000 people was the highest recorded in the world at the time (Switzerland, the next highest, had only 17 per 10,000), whereas by contrast, the ratio among the Arabs of 2.4 per 10,000 was much lower, although it was higher than the most advanced countries in the region: Egypt (2.2), Iraq (1.7), and Turkey (0.9).

The disparity in doctors was a product of profound deficiencies in education in the Middle East as a whole by comparison with Europe, where most immigrants originated. While there had been extensive progress in education in the late Ottoman period, and that progress continued during the Mandate, the development of a modern Palestinian educational system started from a very low base. Arab society in Palestine thus suffered from severe inherited educational disadvantages. Beyond this, it was primarily rural and therefore had not been extensively exposed to modern technology. In terms of the United Nations Development Program's "Human Development Index," which is meant to be a "comprehensive, comparative measure of a society's all-inclusive state of development," around 1939 Palestine's Jews placed fifteenth out of thirty-six countries measured, behind Belgium and Finland and ahead of Czechoslovakia and Italy, while the Palestinian Arabs placed thirtieth, falling behind Brazil and Peru, but ahead of Egypt (thirty-third) and Turkey (thirty-fifth). In light of the advantages that the yishuv enjoyed in the realm of human capital, it can be imagined what a benefit its phenomenally high ratio of capital investment per capita gave it by comparison with Palestinian Arab society, a benefit reflected in the exceedingly high growth rate of the Jewish economy already mentioned.

A third factor of incommensurability between these two communities is that while before 1948, Palestinian society was predominantly rural, the yishuv was always overwhelmingly urban. This was the case notwithstanding the enormous emphasis that Zionist ideology and propaganda placed on rural settlement, and on an almost mystical connection with the land; relatively few Jews lived in rural areas during the Mandate period, before, or since. The highest proportion reached by the rural sector of the total Jewish population of Palestine before 1948 was under 27 percent. Notwithstanding this lopsided imbalance in favor of the urban population, there was clearly an important ideological purpose to the attachment of the Zionist movement to a "return to the soil" and to control of the land. Beyond this, the Zionist fixation on the land also had a crucial strategic motivation, for the establishment of heavily fortified rural settlements along several major geographic axes was instrumental in enabling the Zionist movement to take control of most of Palestine during the fighting of 1947–49. In the words of Kenneth Stein, by 1939 these settlements already provided "a geographic nucleus for a Jewish state … in Palestine."

Ideology and strategy aside, the Jewish population of Palestine during the Mandate (and afterward) was principally concentrated in the urban and semi-urban regions of coastal Jaffa/Tel Aviv and Haifa, and Jerusalem. It constituted a majority in each of these three urban centers, which (to revert briefly to strategy) ultimately helped give it military control of the country's three largest cities and of both its main ports. By contrast, Palestinian society was, and had always been, overwhelmingly rural. The events of 1948 were to change that reality drastically, turning most Palestinians into refugees, and ultimately city dwellers—or rather refugee camp dwellers, which in practice for most of them meant residence in some of the poorest quarters of the cities of Palestine and the rest of the Levant (the eastern Mediterranean coast). In the event, the strategic advantages that might have accrued to the Palestinians from their being spread out over

so much of the country were never realized, as we shall see in Chapter 4.

Even at the end of the Mandate, by which time a significant shift of the Arab population from country to city had taken place, Palestinian society was still predominantly rural: only 32.7 percent of the country's Arab population lived in cities and large towns, by contrast with the Jewish population, which was 76.2 percent urban. The related disparities in terms of occupation were also great: while only 13 percent of the Jewish population was dependent on agriculture (indicating incidentally that a large portion of the nonurban Jewish population was engaged in services and industry rather than agriculture), about half of the Arab population was involved in agricultural pursuits. In terms of communications, military mobilization and indoctrination, and many other factors, this concentration of the Jewish population in urban areas proved to be a great advantage, as it was strategically during the fighting of 1948, when the small yishuv benefited from being concentrated on interior lines, fighting first against the Palestinians and later against the more formidable Arab armies.

The fourth factor of incommensurability is the wide disparities between the politics of the two communities. All observers have agreed on the essentially European nature of Zionist ideology and of the major political currents within the yishuv. This contrasted strikingly with the diverse range of local, Arab, Islamic, European, and other sources influencing the political trends found within Palestinian Arab society, which in this respect was very similar to other societies in the Middle East. As Zeev Sternhell and others have convincingly shown, in the development of national identity and of "ethnic, religious and cultural particularity," Israel was "not dissimilar to other states in Central and Eastern Europe."

Moreover, the great majority of the population of the yishuv in effect constituted a self-selecting sample, united by the Zionist ideology that had brought most of them to Palestine. An overwhelming majority of the Jews leaving eastern Europe in the late nineteenth and early twentieth centuries were non-Zionist, and had made the conscious choice to avoid Palestine, with most of them preferring the United States as a destination. Thus, of the 3.3 million Jews estimated to have emigrated from Europe between 1881 and 1939, 2.6 million went to the United States, while less than a sixth of that number, 420,000, went to Palestine (and many of those later left). The bulk of this latter group came to Palestine only after the Immigration Act of 1924 effectively closed America's doors to further large-scale immigration from countries other than those of northern Europe. Nevertheless, most Jews who came to Palestine, at least before the horrors of the Nazi persecutions left many hundreds of thousands with no choice, had done so because they wanted to, and because they shared the Zionist ideology and aspirations of the yishuv. This self-regulating winnowing-out process made for a Jewish society in Palestine that was remarkably homogeneous at this early stage, at least in ideological terms.

By contrast, as I have argued at length elsewhere, the sense of Palestinian identity that emerged during approximately the same period as did modern Zionism included elements of Ottoman, Arab, Islamic and Christian, local Palestinian, and European ideologies and thought. While a certain synthesis of these elements eventually emerged to constitute modern Palestinian nationalist political consciousness, Palestinian politics nevertheless remained considerably less homogeneous ideologically than politics within the yishuv. The differences between the kinds of influences on Zionism and Palestinian nationalism could not be more obvious than in the realm of ideology, although both were ostensibly national movements. These disparities could be seen along the entire spectrum of the politics of the era, whether with regard to the divergent impact of communism, fascism, or any other ideology on the two communities, or in terms of phenomena that were unique to either polity. Thus, eastern and central European ideas about nationalism and socialism had a major impact on the yishuv; the impact of nationalism was less widespread among Palestinians, but those affected by it tended to be influenced by western European models. Communism had quite a different impact

on both societies, although it was relatively minor in both cases. The political influence of Islam was naturally felt only among Palestinians.

Along with these ideological and political differences, and the profound social and economic dissimilarities in which they were rooted, came great disparities in types of political formations and organizational capabilities. Put simply, Palestinian society during the Mandate period was completely different from the entirely new society being constructed out of a mainly European immigrant population on an ideological basis by the Zionist movement, and the political trends in the two societies reflected that enormous difference.

This brings us to the fifth and last factor of incommensurability between the two societies, illustrating why comparison between them should only be undertaken with great care, and with due regard for the specificities of each. Perhaps the most striking of these specificities to contemporary observers were the profound social differences, notably the divergent class structures and social formations of each society. On the one hand, the yishuv was for the most part an entirely new, largely secular society (there existed as well an "old yishuv" composed of Oriental Jews—originally from different parts of the Muslim world—and religious Ashkenazim—European Jews—both of which groups had long been in Palestine, some of them with family roots going back many centuries). This new society was drawn primarily from the secular elements of the Jewish communities of Europe, albeit with some Oriental Jewish and religious admixtures. It was composed of a relatively developed capitalist class, powerful para-state institutions dominated by the Zionist movement, and strong unions, cooperative movements, and socialist-oriented (albeit heavily subsidized) agricultural settlements, with the whole relatively free of strong social tensions.

On the other hand, Palestinian society was generally quite similar in most respects to those of the surrounding Arab countries. It was dominated by a sizable landholding class, which was largely made up of traditional notable families that had held high religious offices and served as intermediaries between the Ottoman authorities and the population, but increasingly also included new merchant entrepreneurs who had purchased land with their newfound wealth. It also included small but growing industrialist and merchant groups and professional elites, a small and rapidly expanding urban working class, and, by far the largest group, a mass of peasants, most of whom owned some land. These socioeconomic differences in turn produced greater income disparities on the Arab side by comparison with the relatively egalitarian yishuv, although the egalitarian rhetoric of Zionism was not always reflected in practice. Another major difference between the two societies was the contrast between their starkly different ethnic makeups. On the one hand, there was the highly diverse yishuv, which during the Mandate period came to be constituted mainly of immigrants from dozens of countries (most of whom came to share a single vernacular language and culture only after they arrived in Palestine), and on the other there was the generally quite homogeneous ethnic, cultural, and linguistic composition of Palestinian society. Thus, ironically, Palestinian society, which was divided internally by political and social differences and included both Muslims and Christians, was highly homogeneous in ethnic, cultural, and linguistic terms, while the more ideologically and politically unified Jewish society was much more diverse in terms of the places of origin and original languages and cultures of most of its members.

That Palestinian Arab society was radically different from, and had not developed to the same degree or in the same ways as, the growing Jewish society with which it uneasily shared the country should be obvious. The consequence of this disparity in terms of the capacity of the two polities for social, political, and, ultimately, military mobilization should be equally obvious. All the gauges of massive import of capital, the inflow of highly skilled human capital, the community's predominantly urban nature, its high degree of ideological homogeneity, its unique social makeup and governing structures—when taken together, indicate its capacity for generating considerable state power. This capacity was fully realized in 1948 and afterward, right up to the present day. Small though the Jewish population of Palestine was, and recent though the inception of the modern yishuv had been, by early 1948 it already contained within it many of the institutions characteristic of a fully developed modern society, headed by a highly developed state structure.

As a result of the untiring efforts of the yishuv, the international Zionist movement, and Great Britain, which for at least two decades faithfully carried out its mandatory responsibilities to build up the Jewish national home, these institutions included, notably, a completely formed government bureaucracy and representative institutions, together with the core of a modern European-style regular army. By 1948, all had grown far beyond the embryonic stage, and indeed were fully ready to be born into independent statehood. As was clear from the one-sided outcome of the conflict between the two peoples in 1948, Palestinian society had not developed in a similar fashion. In fact it generated neither a state structure, nor representative institutions, nor an army to match those of the yishuv, with disastrous consequences for its capabilities when the crisis of 1948 broke.

Righteous Victims: A History of the Zionist–Arab Conflict, 1881–2001

By Benny Morris

World War Two

As the pogroms in Russia in the 1880s had launched modern Zionism, so the largest pogrom of all, the Holocaust, was to propel the movement, almost instantly, into statehood; and much as World War I had issued in the first international support for a Jewish "National Home," so the aftermath of World War II was to result in that decisive international warrant, the United Nations Partition Resolution of November 29, 1947, which was to underpin the emergence of the State of Israel.

The Zionist leadership greeted the outbreak of war with unequivocal declarations of allegiance to Britain. On September 3, the day Britain declared war on Germany, the Jewish Agency Executive announced:

> At this fateful moment, the Jewish community has a threefold concern: the protection of the Jewish homeland, the welfare of the Jewish people, [and] the victory of the British Empire … The war which has now been forced upon Great Britain by Nazi Germany is our war, and all the assistance that we shall be able and permitted to give to the

British Army and to the British people we shall render wholeheartedly.

Even the Revisionists, who had embarked on an anti-British campaign of terrorism following the issuance of the White Paper, now offered a truce—and were soon to offer active military assistance. Only the minuscule Lohamei Herut Israel (Lehi, LHI, or the Stern gang), formed at this time by breakaways from the Revisionist Irgun, continued to adhere to a rigidly anti-British line.

The Zionists hoped that loyalty and wartime services would be repaid with the abrogation of the White Paper and support for Jewish statehood. But for the Arabs the war posed difficult choices. By tradition, they lacked any innate sympathy or affinity with democratic and Western values, but current realities also had to be considered: Britain physically controlled the Middle East and had large troop concentrations in Egypt, Palestine, and Iraq; adopting a forthright anti-Allied position could prove self-destructive. On the other hand, common sense dictated support for the future victor, and at least down to mid-1942 it appeared likely that Germany would win and perhaps overrun the Middle East. Hence calculations of expediency cut both ways.

Benny Morris, "World War II and the First Arab-Israeli War, 1939-49," *Righteous Victims: A History of the Zionist-Arab Conflict, 1881-2001*, 2nd ed., pp. 161–184, 186–189. Copyright © 1999, 2001 by Benny Morris. Reprinted with permission of Alfred A. Knopf, a division of Random House, Inc.

But there were other, more closely felt factors. The British were seen by the Arabs as the protectors of Zionism, and the bitter memory of the crushing defeat of the Palestinian uprising of 1936–39 was still fresh. Support for the Axis seemed only natural, especially as Italian and German propaganda promised the Arabs independence after Britain's defeat. And many Egyptians, Iraqis, Syrians, and Lebanese had the same desire to get out from under the Western imperial boot. True, German racist beliefs and behavior may have put off some Arabs. But Germany was a long way away, while the hated British and French were all too present. The cataclysm of world war appeared to be a good opportunity to achieve complete independence.

Khalil Sakakini was not unrepresentative when he noted in his diary, in mid-1941, that the Arabs of Palestine "had rejoiced when the British bastion at Tobruk fell to the Germans. Indeed: "Not only the Palestinians rejoiced … but the whole Arab world, in Egypt and Palestine and Iraq and Syria and Lebanon, and not because they love the Germans, but because they dislike the English … because … of their policy in Palestine."

The outbreak of war put the triangular struggle for Palestine on temporary hold. Of the major elements of the White Paper, only cessation of Jewish land purchases was fairly effectively implemented. Limiting immigration—to fifteen thousand per year for five years, starting in May 1939—proved more complicated. Since 1934 illegal immigrants had been smuggled into the country, mainly by sea. As the noose tightened around the neck of European Jewry, the Zionist leadership became increasingly desperate. It was not so much fear that the Jews faced annihilation as that the pool of potential *olim*—which could supply the critical mass needed to push on to statehood—was about to dry up, and that the whole Zionist enterprise might thus founder.

Ben-Gurion remarked in December 1938 (a month after the Nazis' pogrom against Germany's Jews, known as *Kristallnacht,* but two years before the start of the Holocaust): "If I knew it was possible to save all the [Jewish] children of Germany by their transfer to England and only half of them by transferring them to Eretz-Yisrael, I would choose the latter—because we are faced not only with the accounting of these children but also with the historical accounting of the Jewish People." Ben-Gurion viewed the Holocaust primarily through the prism of its effect on the Yishuv. "The catastrophe of European Jewry is not, in a direct manner, my business," he said in December 1942. And, "The destruction of European Jewry is the death-knell of Zionism." In the words of Yitzhak Gruenbaum, a member of the Jewish Agency Executive, "Zionism is above everything."

In mid-1941, after the Germans had started massacring Jews on a large scale but before it was known or, at least, *believed* in Palestine, Ben-Gurion spoke of the need to move three million Jews there over the next ten years. The Colonial Office spoke of a similar number of anticipated postwar refugees—but it opposed their resettlement in Palestine.

The last months of peace and the first months of the war saw a surge of rickety, Haganah-commanded, refugee-laden ships set sail from Balkan ports for Palestine, though such men as Chaim Weizmann, president of the World Zionist Organization, opposed the operation, believing that illegal immigration would do the cause more harm (by provoking the British) than good. In any event, due to the Zionists' meager means, the sealing off of large parts of Europe, and British interference, the campaign never amounted to much, though combating it caused Britain political embarrassment. During the period 1934–38 about forty thousand Jews had entered Palestine illegally, and another nine thousand by September 1939. But less than sixteen thousand made it during the following six years, when the need for sanctuary was at its most acute.

The British viewed illegal immigration as a challenge to the White Paper and to their rule in Palestine, and consequently, as a threat to their position in the Middle East. Given the conflict that already strained resources to the utmost, it is little wonder that Whitehall resorted to severe, sometimes brutal, measures to stop the campaign. At first, they attempted to deport captured individuals back to their countries of origin. This quickly proved impossible (in 1939 only forty-three Jews were so deported; in 1940, seventy-two). For a time, in 1939–40, they resolved to suspend legal immigration until the illegal traffic was stopped. Subsequently they deducted the known illegal entry totals from the annual legal quota of fifteen thousand. Pressure was applied to Balkan states, particularly Rumania and Turkey, to stop the ships from sailing.

In the end, however, Whitehall adopted a policy of capturing and deporting the immigrants en masse to special island camps, in Mauritius and eventually Cyprus. In November 1940 the Haganah tried to subvert the policy by blowing up the *Patria,* a tramp steamer docked in Haifa and crowded with more than 1,700 illegal immigrants from Rumania who were about to be shipped to Mauritius. Miscalculating the explosive charge, the sappers killed 252 of the refugees.

The following month the LHI bombed the immigration office in Haifa to protest Britain's policy. But thousands of Jewish refugees were to spend the war years and beyond in camps in Cyprus, reaching Palestine only after the establishment of the State of Israel. Given the circumstances of global war and strict censorship, the British proved able to weather the occasional tragedy or embarrassment. Thus, when the *Struma,* a ramshackle steamer out of Constantsa, Rumania, with 769 Jewish emigrants aboard, was torpedoed and sunk, probably by a Soviet submarine, in the Black Sea on February 25, 1942, with only one survivor, there were few political waves, though the incident was directly traceable to a British veto on the transshipment of these refugees to Palestine, and British pressure on Ankara. The only change it wrought in Whitehall was the formal cessation of the policy of returning refugees to Europe when caught.

From the Zionist viewpoint, the illegal immigration campaign was both a disaster and a boon. By September 30, 1941, the midpoint in the White Paper's five-year period, nearly 35,000 Jews had arrived in Palestine, legally and illegally—less than half the 75,000 stipulated.

By March 31, 1944, the number was still 20,000 short of the limit.

Very few people were saved from Hitler's death camps or added to the Yishuv's population register; but British policy was highlighted as inhumane, and the need for a sanctuary for the world's oppressed Jews was made clear to the community of nations, especially the United States. The Royal Navy and the security forces in Palestine had managed to keep Jewish immigration down and the Arabs quiescent, but the persistent, cumulative embarrassment that the policy engendered was among the factors that led to Britain's eventual withdrawal from Palestine after the war. Ben-Gurion is said to have greeted the outbreak of war by saying: "We shall fight the White Paper as if there is no war, and we shall fight the war as if there is no White Paper." But in fact the Yishuv confined its struggle against the British to the sphere of illegal immigration. In all else the Yishuv (save for the LHI) laid down its grievances and weapons and joined the war against the Nazis. "Above our regret and bitterness [toward Britain] are higher interests ... What the democracies are fighting for is the minimum ... necessary for Jewish life. Their anxiety is our anxiety, their war our war," explained Weizmann.

The implementation of the White Paper's call for constitutional change that would lead to eventual Arab self-government and dominance in Palestine was shelved for several reasons: internal Arab disarray, Zionist opposition, Whitehall's resentment of the pro-Axis actions of many Arabs, the more pressing tasks at hand, and the fact that the pro-Zionist Churchill was at the helm of government. In general, Britain was loath to do anything that might antagonize American Jewry and hence Washington. Whitehall never got around to appointing Arab heads of Mandatory government departments, the necessary first step on the road to self-government, and repeatedly postponed the establishment of an Executive Council (the mooted Arab-dominated advisory body to the high commissioner).

The Allied defeats in 1939–40 and the Axis gains in North Africa in 1940–41 had a dual effect. They tended to reinforce Britain's desire to appease the Arabs—anything to keep Palestine and the Middle East quiet. But they also tended to persuade the Arabs to support the Axis, creating antipathy among British officials toward them and their political aspirations. In May–June 1940 the exiled ex-mufti, Amin al-Husseini, reportedly sent agents to Palestine to look into the possibility of inciting a new revolt—but Palestine, which served as a rear base for the British Eighth Army, was awash with Allied troops, and the inhabitants were enjoying an unprecedented bout of prosperity.

Elsewhere in the Middle East, circumstances were more propitious. In Baghdad in April 1941 the Iraqi military, led by deposed Prime Minister Rashid 'Ali al-Kilani, rose in Axis-supported revolt. Britain's fortunes were at a low ebb: General Erwin Rommel's Afrika Korps, encamped in Libya, was potentially poised to invade the Nile Valley. Eclipsing the pro-British Hashemite regime, Rashid 'Ali returned to the premiership and offered Germany air bases and other facilities. But the Reich, husbanding its resources for the coming onslaught on Russia, sent only a squadron of fighter aircraft.

The rebels were assisted by hundreds of Palestinian exiles, including al-Husseini, who appears to have enjoyed subsidies from both the Iraqi government and Berlin. Once Baghdad had fallen to the rebels, he issued a *fatwa* (religious ruling), calling by radio on all Muslims to join in a *jihad* against Britain. But apart from some riots in Syria, he had little success in spreading the conflagration to the rest of the Levant. The British reacted with dispatch; oil and vital supply lines were at stake. On April 18 they landed troops at Basra and marched on Baghdad. At the same time a mixed force of Arab Legionnaires and British troops took the land route from Transjordan. By May 29 it was all over, save for extensive looting and a pogrom by locals on June 1–2 against Baghdad's Jews, in which 120 persons were killed.

Husseini fled to Berlin, where a Foreign Ministry spokesman greeted him as "a great champion of Arab liberation and the most distinguished antagonist of England and Jewry."

He had thrown in his lot with the Reich (even though Hitler had once called the Arabs "half-apes"). Amply financed, he was installed as one of the directors in Berlin of a new Arab Office, whose function was to broadcast propaganda and mobilize Arab and Muslim support for the Axis. He also traveled to Yugoslavia and Albania to recruit Muslim prisoners of war for an "Arab Legion" to fight alongside the Axis armies in the East. Occasionally he briefed Arabs about to be parachuted into the Levant as saboteurs. He was later to explain why the Germans had turned on the Jews:

> In return for the [Balfour] Declaration … the Jews filled a central role in acts of sabotage and destructive propaganda inside Germany [in World War I] … They acted in every way to bring about its destruction. This was the main reason for Hitler's war against the Jews and for his strong hatred of them. They brought catastrophe upon Germany [in World War I], even though it was winning militarily. Germany's revenge on the Jews was fierce: and it destroyed millions of them during World War II.

On November 28, 1941, al-Husseini met Hitler and promised to organize a new, pan-Arab revolt (similar to the one Hussein, the sharif of Mecca, had organized against the Turks in World War I); and like the British in World War I, Hitler promised the Arabs postwar independence (as well as the abolition of the Jewish National Home). Hitler apparently liked what he heard and saw, including Husseini's blue eyes; he said Husseini must have had "more than one Aryan among his ancestors and one who may be descended from the best Roman stock."

During 1943–44 Husseini wrote to Eastern European leaders asking that they bar the emigration to Palestine of hundreds of Jewish children and adults. In a letter to the Hungarian foreign minister, he suggested that the children be sent to Poland, under German supervision. Whether Husseini was fully aware of the Holocaust, approved of it, or directly aided the Nazis in its implementation, he had without doubt "cooperated with the most barbaric regime in modern times," even in the understated words of his generally sympathetic Arab biographer.

Husseini's activities would weigh against the Palestinians during the following years. Churchill, who replaced Chamberlain as prime minister on May 10, 1940, had never had any great liking for the Arabs, and repeatedly lambasted the "treacherous" Iraqi revolt and the Palestinian support it had enjoyed. Britain, he came to feel, owed the Arabs nothing in a postwar settlement. He found the White Paper's appeasement of them humiliating and politically self-defeating. In April 1943 he said: "I cannot agree that the White Paper is 'the firmly established policy' of the present Government. I have always regarded it as a gross breach of faith committed by the Chamberlain Government in respect of obligations to which I personally was a party."

The anti-Arab feeling in Whitehall was reinforced by the Zionists' readiness to help the war effort. In 1940–41, with the Italians and Rommel at the gates of Egypt, thousands of Palestinian Jews rushed to the colors. Their eagerness to join up was curtailed only by British reluctance to have them. (Eventually from 25,000 to 28,000 of them were to serve in the British Army during the war, with thousands more enlisting as special auxiliary policemen.) Jewish scouts from Palestine assisted the Allied advance into Vichy-controlled Syria and Lebanon in 1941 (it was there that Moshe Dayan lost an eye) and an IZL [Irgun] team, including its commander, David Raziel, assisted in the British push on Baghdad that spring (Raziel was killed by a strafing German aircraft during the campaign). British officials, however, remained acutely mindful of the need to keep the Arab areas of the Middle East—with their vital waterways and land routes—trouble-free, and the area's oil available and flowing.

In this context, during the first years of the war plans were put forward for an Arab "federation" to include Palestine, which might be divided into Arab and Jewish cantons, or ministates, as part of the postwar settlement. But the idea did not attract significant Arab support, and British officials noted the incompatibility of promoting Middle Eastern federation while supporting Jewish national aspirations.

The Palestinian Arab leadership, most of it still in exile, remained silent if not downright contrary about proposals for both constitutional change within the Mandate and a regional Arab "federation." Even more significant was the opposition of the high commissioner himself. Sir Harold MacMichael wrote to the Foreign Office: "I regard it as a fallacy to suppose that to give a few Heads of Departments to Palestinians is likely to turn the politicians of Egypt, Syria and Iraq into likely allies or do more than convince them that we are on the run. The only thing that will achieve the end desired is success in the field of war."

Indeed, MacMichael argued that, despite declining Allied fortunes, Palestine remained quiet; concessions would only whet pan-Arab appetites and cause renewed turmoil. By October 1942 British victories had substantially eroded the urgency for appeasement.

From the start of the war, the Zionists had pressed the British to organize and train a Jewish "army," a demand that enjoyed Churchill's support, at least on paper. In October 1939 he had proposed recruiting several thousand Palestinian Jews to keep law and order in the country and free the British garrison to fight in Europe. Both sides understood that the Jews' offer was partly motivated by the need for a corps of trained troops to protect the Yishuv against the Arabs after the war. And it was understood that, as Colonial Secretary Lord George Lloyd put it bluntly in 1940: "The conversion of Palestine into a Jewish State as a reward for Jewish military assistance is the objective." The Arabs, of course, opposed the creation of a Jewish army, and the British government therefore viewed the idea gingerly. MacMichael even argued that such a force after the war might be used against the Mandatory government itself.

In 1940 the Zionists won an initial, small victory: The British agreed to the raising in Palestine of two battalions—one Jewish, one Arab—to be deployed on guard duty around vital installations. But it was not until September 1944 that Churchill at last pushed down Whitehall's throat the decision to set up a Jewish Brigade, with its own distinct blue-and-white flag. The formation saw action in Italy during the dying months of the war.

The Biltmore Program

In October 1941 Churchill wrote in a secret Cabinet minute: "I may say at once that if Britain and the United States emerge victorious from the war, the creation of a great Jewish state in Palestine inhabited [sic] by millions of Jews will be one of the leading features of the Peace Conference discussions."

And two years later Churchill was said to have declared that he intended to see to it that there would be a Jewish state. For the Zionists the quest for statehood had quickened in the tragic circumstances of the Holocaust into a desperate resolve. In July 1942, the Polish government-in-exile in London reported that 700,000 of that country's Jews had already been murdered; in December, Eden told the House of Commons of "hundreds of thousands" of victims.

On September 8, 1939, Ben-Gurion had told the commanders of the Haganah: "The First World War … had given us the Balfour Declaration. This time we must bring about a Jewish State." The goal of statehood was thereafter to dominate his thinking. He was soon joined by Weizmann, still the formal head of the Zionist movement. In January 1942 Weizmann, in an article in *Foreign Affairs,* explicitly demanded the establishment of a Jewish state in all of the area west of the River Jordan.

In May 1942 an Extraordinary Zionist Conference in New York, attended by American and European leaders as well as three members of the Palestine Jewish Agency Executive, voted to support what became known as the Biltmore Program, for the hotel in which they met. The program was drafted by Meyer Weisgal, Weizmann's aide, but its essence was later always to be identified with Ben-Gurion. It called for "Palestine

to be established as a Jewish Commonwealth integrated in the structure of the new democratic world…"; the possibility that the state would be established only in part of Palestine was implicit. The Jewish Agency was to have control of immigration and the development of the country. Ben-Gurion hoped immediately to bring in two million Jews, a number Weizmann dismissed as unfeasible.

In the months before the conference both Weizmann and Ben-Gurion had expressed support for the transfer of the Arabs—preferably in a voluntary move, but by compulsion if necessary. On January 30, 1941, Weizmann met the Soviet ambassador to London, Ivan Maisky. The Zionist report on the meeting read, in part: "Dr. Weizmann said that if half a million Arabs could be transferred, two million Jews could be put in their place. That, of course, would be a first installment; what might happen afterwards was a matter for history. … Weizmann said that … they would be transferring the Arabs only into Iraq or Transjordan … conditions in Transjordan were not very different from those of the Palestine hill country."

In October 1941 Ben-Gurion set out his thinking on transfer in a memorandum entitled "Outlines of Zionist Policy." He paid the necessary lip service to the traditional Zionist position on the benefits Jews could bring to Palestine without displacing any Arabs, and how neighboring Arab states could easily absorb all of the country's Arabs in the event of transfer. But, he wrote: "Complete transfer without compulsion—and ruthless compulsion at that—is hardly imaginable." Some—Circassians, Druze, Bedouin, Shi'ites, tenant farmers, and landless laborers—could be persuaded to leave. But "the majority of the Arabs could hardly be expected to leave voluntarily within the short period of time which can materially affect our problem." He concluded that the Jews should not "discourage other people, British or American, who favour transfer from advocating this course, but we should in no way make it part of our programme." As to those Arabs remaining in the prospective Jewish State, they must be treated as equals, even though "our country may … suffer from the presence of a considerable illiterate and backward population, and so may our relations with the neighboring Arab countries."

With the support of the American Zionists, Ben-Gurion pushed the Biltmore Program through the Inner Zionist General Council in Jerusalem in August 1942, thus making it the official policy of the Yishuv. A state was now—at last, publicly—what Zionism was all about. Sharett may have dubbed the program "somewhat Utopian," but it was to remain the accepted agenda and, by fits and starts, was to guide the movement to the promised shores of statehood in 1947–48.

As the Peel Commission report had in 1937, the Biltmore Program triggered bitter controversies within the Zionist movement. The group called Faction B (Si'ah Bet), soon to become HaTnu'ah LeAhdut Ha'Avoda (the movement for labor unity), split with Ben-Gurion's mainstream Mapai after refusing to agree to the compromise implicit in Biltmore: that the state would encompass only part of Palestine. Others, such as Weizmann himself, preferred to soft-pedal the demand for statehood. Ben-Gurion resigned in October 1943 as chairman of the Jewish Agency Executive, with the aim of forcing Weizmann back on track, or out of office (he was president of the World Zionist Organization) altogether. In March 1944 Ben-Gurion "reluctantly" agreed to return to office, and in August 1944, in two sets of internal elections (for the Elected Assembly and the Histadrut Executive), finally won the contest. His supporters garnered from 58 to 66 percent of the votes.

But Weizmann's eclipse was not really caused by Biltmore. From its inception and until the mid-1930s, Europe had constituted Zionism's chief base, and Weizmann was the quintessential European. The destruction of European Jewry turned him into a leader without a constituency. The major power centers were now in Palestine and, to a lesser extent, the United States. It was thus natural for that consummate politician Ben-Gurion, head of the Jewish Agency Executive since 1935 and of mainstream Palestinian

Zionism, to gain pride of place in the movement as a whole.

Underlying all the disputes between the two men were Weizmann's continued faith in the power of diplomacy and, specifically, in British goodwill—especially after Churchill took the helm—and Ben-Gurion's distrust of those same factors. Ben–Gurion, who matured as a politician on the hard soil of Palestine, preferred action to faith, facts to talk. The clash between the two men finally ended with Ben-Gurion's complete victory in 1946. Ultimately it was Whitehall's rejection of Jewish statehood that undermined Weizmann. At the Zionist Congress of January 1946 he was removed by Ben-Gurion and his supporters from the presidency of the World Zionist Organization. And, not satisfied with victory, the vindictive Ben-Gurion was to hound him during the years that remained before his death in 1952. To be sure, the ailing elder statesman was installed in 1949 in the (politically neutered) presidency of the State of Israel; but he was firmly kept away from any exercise of influence and was even prevented from signing the new state's Declaration of Independence.

The British victory in North Africa in October 1942 and the Russian victories in Stalingrad and the Caucasus that winter dispelled the German threat to the Middle East, but Britain continued to appease its Arab clients, in order not to rock the boat before the war was won and, in the long term, to exclude American and/or Soviet influence from the region. The war had underlined the region's crucial importance: Oil reserves and production facilities were to become a major issue in the consideration of the postwar future. Moreover, its potential as a vast market for Western goods was beginning to emerge.

But there was a surge of sympathy for the Jews, precipitated by the information gradually leaking out of Europe since mid-1941, and culminating in a formal announcement by the Allies in December 1942, that Hitler was engaged in mass murder of the Jews. The news of the Holocaust seemed to render irrefutable the need for a Palestinian sanctuary. Moreover, American Zionists were gradually pushing a reluctant

Democratic administration toward support of Jewish statehood, something Whitehall could not ignore. When the war ended, the problem of the "displaced persons" (DPs) only aggravated the situation. Hundreds of thousands of Jewish survivors refused to remain anywhere near the killing fields, the Western European countries and the United States were unwilling to take them in, and the Zionists wanted them in Palestine.

During 1943–45 Washington continued to view Palestine as London's headache, while in Whitehall, the cumulative thrust of past policy, and a bevy of pro-Arab bureaucrats, prevented the formal abrogation of the White Paper. But in mid-1943 Churchill managed to put together a special cabinet committee, packed with pro-Zionists, to prepare for the postwar settlement. It resurrected the Peel Commission's principle of partition, which the full cabinet endorsed in January 1944, leaving the exact geographical details undefined.

The proposal was that partition "be implemented as soon as the necessary arrangements could be made." But implementation was stymied by a rearguard action in Whitehall. The Chiefs of Staff Committee argued that "the Arab States will object," and the Foreign Office maintained that "the solution to the Palestine question … should [not] be determined solely on the basis of world sympathy with the sufferings of the Jews, as contrasted with the alleged failure of the Arabs to assist the war effort." The new scheme, the Foreign Office felt, was a breach of good faith: "When we wanted to keep [the Arabs] quiet, in 1939, we produced the White Paper, but when, after the war, our international difficulties were eased, we decided to betray Arab interests."

Then, on November 6, 1944, Lord Moyne, the British minister resident in the Middle East, was shot dead by LHI terrorists in Cairo. Moyne had been a close friend of Churchill, who took the murder as a personal affront and told the House of Commons: "If our dreams for Zionism are to end in the smoke of assassins' pistols and our labours for its future to produce only a new set of gangsters worthy of Nazi Germany, many

like myself will have to reconsider the position we have maintained so consistently in the past."

And he personally prodded the Egyptian government to execute the assassins, who were duly hanged the following March, and withdrew his support of the partition scheme. On July 27, 1945, Churchill and the Conservatives were swept from office, and the Labour Party took over, led by Clement Attlee. The Zionists were now in a completely different ballgame. Though the Labour platform supported Jewish statehood and even transfer, decisionmaking remained in the hands of the new foreign secretary, Ernest Bevin—a man without a soft spot for Zionism and given, to anti-Semitic asides, who thought that Britain's vital interests required support for the Arabs—the cabinet, and the military chiefs.

But during the two-and-a-half years between the end of the war and the start of Arab–Jewish hostilities at the end of 1947, developments in the United States, Palestine, and continental Europe proved more important than the mindset of Whitehall. In Washington the battle for support was decisively won by the Zionists, because of the impact of the Holocaust, effective propaganda, and the electoral and financial clout of the five million American Jews. Until 1944 the administration of President Franklin D. Roosevelt had managed to desist from anything but insignificant expressions of sympathy for Zionism. True, the plight of European Jewry weighed heavily; but American global interests, primarily oil, clearly militated in the other direction. In May 1943 Roosevelt had assured King Ibn Saud that both Arabs and Jews would be heard before a decision was made on the postwar settlement in Palestine.

In March 1944 a shift of attitude began. The White House, under pressure from Arabist officials, persuaded Congress to withdraw a joint resolution calling on Britain to rescind the White Paper and supporting a Jewish state. But, at the same time, Roosevelt assured the Jews that "full justice will be done [after the war] to those who seek a Jewish national home, for which our Government and the American People have always had the deepest sympathy and today more than ever in view of the tragic plight of hundreds of thousands of homeless Jewish refugees."

At Yalta, in February 1945, Roosevelt described himself to Stalin as "a Zionist" (as did the Soviet dictator, though he added that Jews were "middle men, profiteers, and parasites"). The following month Roosevelt assured Ibn Saud that he would support "no action ... that would prove hostile to the Arab people," but the growingly Zionist orientation of American public opinion and officialdom proved inexorable. After Roosevelt's death in April, his marginally more pro-Zionist successor Harry S. Truman came out, at the Potsdam summit in August, in support of resettling Jewish DPs in Palestine, and asked Churchill to lift the restrictions on immigration (in response to which the new Arab League's secretary general, Abd al–Rahman Azzam, declared that this could touch off a new war between Christianity and Islam).

For Palestine's Arabs the war passed without significant change. Their financial assets grew substantially as a result of Allied spending and investment, but militarily and politically, things remained much the same. Few—perhaps five to six thousand men—joined the Allied armed forces or otherwise gained military experience; there was no increment in local military force or organization. And the political (and military) leadership that had been shattered and scattered in 1938–39 remained in exile, neutralized or *hors de combat*.

By mid-1943 it had become clear that the Allies would win the war. To gain anything Palestine's Arabs would require leadership and organization. The former heads of the Istiqlal Party launched an effort to reunite the nationalists, and in November, the fifteenth conference of the Palestinian Arab chambers of commerce met in Jerusalem and set in motion a process to elect new national representation. Owing to the Husseinis' opposition, matters were delayed. But they too began to reorganize. Their major figures were in exile—Hajj Amin in Berlin, serving the Nazis, and Jamal al–Husseini interned in Southern Rhodesia. But in April 1944 the remaining local leadership formally relaunched the

Palestine Arab Party; by September the Husseinis were once again the most active and powerful faction, and they led nationwide protests on November 2, Balfour Declaration Day.

This "repoliticization of the Palestinian community coincided with a British-supported drive for Arab unity. From September 25 to October 7, delegates from seven countries met in Alexandria to found the Arab League, and on March 22, 1945, its pact was formally signed in Cairo. The Palestinians sent Jericho notable Musa al–Alami to the gathering in Alexandria. At first he was designated an "observer," but by the end of the conference he was recognized as a "delegate," the Palestinian community thus enjoying, at least theoretically, an equal footing with the Arab states.

One section of the conference's "Alexandria Protocol" stated: "The rights of the Arabs [of Palestine] cannot be touched without prejudice to peace and stability in the Arab world." The Arab states declared that they were "second to none in regretting the woes which have been inflicted on the Jews of Europe. ...But the question of these Jews should not be confused with Zionism, for there can be no greater injustice and aggression than solving the problem of the Jews of Europe by ... inflicting injustice on the Palestine Arabs."

In early 1945 Egypt, Syria, Lebanon, and Saudi Arabia declared war on the Axis, thus assuring themselves membership in the nascent United Nations and a voice in the peace settlement.

The Arab League states collectively put their weight behind the basic demands of Palestine's Arabs but arrogated to themselves the right to select who would represent the Palestinians in their councils, so long as their country was not independent. This, coupled with the deadlock within Palestine, meant that "the initiative in Palestine Arab politics ... passed to the heads of the Arab states" and "major political decisions on the organization of Arab resistance to Zionism were thereafter taken not at Jerusalem but at Cairo."

And, indeed, it was at the initiative of the Arab League that in November 1945 the Arab Higher Committee was reestablished as the supreme executive body of the Palestine community. A twelve-member committee was appointed, with five Husseini representatives, two independents, and five other members representing the other (now resurrected) pre-1939 parties. But the return of Jamal al–Husseini precipitated quarreling and the disbanding of the committee in March 1946. The opposition set up its own Arab Higher Front (AHF) and Jamal reconstituted the AHC (Arab Higher Committee) with Husseini family members and affiliates. In June the Arab League foreign ministers imposed upon the Palestinians a new leadership body, the Arab Higher Executive (AHE), with Amin al–Husseini as (absentee) chairman and Jamal al–Husseini as vice-chairman. The Husseinis were now firmly back in the saddle, this time with the imprimatur of the Arab League. Hajj Amin returned to the Middle East and began directing Palestinian affairs from Cairo. In January 1947 he expanded the AHE—now again called the AHC—to nine members, all of them Husseinis or Husseini supporters. The Palestinian Arabs appeared once more to have a somewhat unified, if not particularly representative, leadership.

The Yishuv Rises

Developments in the Zionist camp proved far more significant. The approaching end of the war obviated the need to maintain solidarity with Britain. Moreover, a home had to be found for the survivors of the Holocaust, but the cabinet in London, the Royal Navy in the Mediterranean, and the security forces in Palestine stood between the DPs and the shores of the Promised Land. On September 27, 1945, the Zionist leadership proclaimed that the blockade was "tantamount to a death sentence upon … those liberated Jews … still languishing in the internment camps of Germany."

A revolt that had been postponed for six years was now about to break out.

In May 1943 General Harold Alexander, commander of Britain's forces in the Middle East, had warned of the "probability" of revolt after the war:

"[The] Jews mean business and are armed and trained." In mid-1942 MI6, Britain's foreign intelligence agency, had estimated, fairly accurately, that the Haganah had thirty thousand members, with arms for 50 to 70 percent of them. The IZL could field another one thousand trained men, with several thousand more supporters and auxiliaries. Jewish estimates put Haganah strength in 1944 at 36,000, with about 14,000 light weapons, including some two- and three-inch mortars and machine guns.

The Yishuv had not wasted the war years. Tens of thousands of its men had joined the Allied (principally, the British) armies and acquired a measure of military training; arms had been stolen or illegally purchased.by the Haganah from the vast British stockpiles in Palestine and Egypt. Most significantly, in May–June 1941 the Haganah—with British assistance—had established the Palmah (an abbreviation of *plugot mahatz*, "shock companies"), a fully mobilized strike force, headed by Yitzhak Sadeh, the veteran Red Army soldier and Haganah commando leader. The Jews regarded the Palmah as an instantly available crack torce to fend off Arab attacks and a commando unit to be used against the Nazis: the British saw it as the core of a guerrilla army to fight the Germans should Rommel succeed in conquering Palestine. By 1945 the Palmah comprised some two thousand men and women, its platoons dispersed among several dozen kibbutzim and two or three towns. For two weeks each month they worked in the fields to cover their upkeep. The rest of the month was devoted to military training.

The Haganah and Palmah were to join the simmering anti-British struggle, but only after the war ended. The first note had been struck years before by the LHI—led initially by Avraham ("Yair") Stern—which believed that Britain was Zionism's main obstacle and an accomplice in the Nazi crimes against the Jews and, paradoxically, even tried to establish an anti-British alliance with Germany. However, due to its meager resources and manpower, almost consensual Yishuv opposition to anti-British terrorism, and successive, effective British clampdowns, sometimes assisted by tip-offs from the Haganah and the IZL, the LHI's stance was never really translated into action during 1941–43.

On February 1, 1944, several days after Menachem Begin took over command of the IZL, it announced the resumption of the struggle against Britain. The Irgun felt that the war against the Nazis had been decided; London was now the problem. It immediately began blowing up or attacking government immigration and income tax offices and police buildings. The LHI also launched a number of spectacular attacks; on August 8 they even tried to assassinate the high commissioner, MacMichael.

The two groups were roundly condemned by the mainstream leadership and the press. The IZL members were labeled "misguided terrorists," "young fanatics crazed by the sufferings of their people into believing that destruction will bring healing." Efforts by the Jewish Agency Executive and the Haganah to dissuade them failed. Following the attempt on MacMichael and the assassination of Lord Moyne, the LHI agreed to suspend its war on Britain until the larger war ended. But the IZL defied the JAE and the National Committee and continued its attacks. The Haganah declared an "open season" (referred to in Zionist historiography as the "*Saison*," meaning hunting season) against the IZL, and Haganah intelligence and Palmah teams tracked down IZL members, confiscated their weapons, interrogated and beat them, and occasionally handed them over to the British police.

The *Saison* lasted from November 1944 to March 1945. But the changed international situation and growing activist rumblings within the Haganah itself eventually issued in a radical change of tack. The imminent end of the war in Europe signalled the reopening of the struggle for statehood. A memorandum from Weizmann to Churchill in May 1945 served as a prelude to the Haganah campaign: Whitehall should take steps at last to turn Palestine into a Jewish State and concede responsibility for the regulation of immigration to the Jewish Agency. In June a Jewish Agency memorandum pleaded that Britain allow 100,000 immigrants into Palestine immediately. In Ben-Gurion's phrase, the DPs could not be allowed to languish "among the graveyards of the millions of their slaughtered brethren"; their salvation lay in speedy resettlement in Palestine.

But Churchill and his cabinet were voted out of office. The new foreign secretary, Ernest Bevin, proposed that immigration to Palestine be allowed, even after the expiration of the White Paper's 75,000 quota, at a rate of fifteen hundred per month. Weizmann rejected the proposal out of hand, and Truman implicitly agreed with him. The president had been persuaded by Earl G. Harrison, his representative on the Intergovernmental Committee on Refugees, that Palestine was the best haven for Europe's remaining Jews and that that was what they wanted. Harrison specifically wrote of the need to grant "100,000" additional entry certificates. Truman forwarded the report to Prime Minister Attlee with his personal recommendation that "as many as possible of the non-repatriable Jews who wish it" be resettled in Palestine. Attlee and Bevin managed to dissuade Truman for a time from a public endorsement of the proposal, but the news of his support for it was eventually published, in mid-October.

In the face of British intransigence, the Yishuv resumed the struggle. The IZL's operations had fallen off considerably at the end of 1944 as a result of the British clampdown and the *Saison*. but in May 1945 the group bombed British targets, including police stations, telephone poles, and the IPC (Iraq Petroleum Company) pipeline that ran through the Jezreel Valley to Haifa. In July the LHI came out of hibernation, and. following an agreement with the IZL, a joint team of sappers blew up a bridge near Yavneh. Next, they turned their attention to Labor-affiliated Jewish targets, robbing banks and Histadrut affiliates of money and stocks of explosives.

The Haganah took a few more months to join in, having decided to await the results of the British general elections and, then, Labour's assumption of power. Bevin almost immediately hinted that he intended to push a pro-Arab line, and in early October, the Haganah, IZL, and

LHI negotiated an operational pact and formally launched the Hebrew Rebellion Movement (T*nu'at Hameri Ha'ivri*). The Palmah went into action even before the signing ceremony. On the night of October 9 they raided the British detention camp at Atlit and freed 208 illegal immigrants. In November, Palmah sapper squads sabotaged railway tracks at 153 points around Palestine; a British patrol vessel was sunk; and, in response to the capture of a ship carrying illegal immigrants by the Royal Navy, two British coast guard stations were blown up.

The British responded with raids on several coastal-plain settlements they suspected of harboring Haganah soldiers or illegal immigrants. The troops panicked and opened fire, killing nine civilians and wounding sixty-three. Anti-British emotions peaked. Periodically during the following months the Haganah, IZL, and LHI attacked British targets. The most spectacular action was by Palmah squads on the night of June 17, 1946, when eleven bridges, connecting Palestine to Transjordan, Syria, Lebanon, and the Sinai, were blown up simultaneously.

Meanwhile the illegal immigration campaign was resumed. All but one of the dozens of boats involved were organized and commanded by the Haganah's illegal-immigration branch, the Mossad Le'Aliyah Bet. Many boats were intercepted by the Royal Navy and their passengers interned; but others got through. Between August 1945 and May 14, 1948, about 70,700 illegal immigrants were landed on Palestine's shores.

But the British found themselves under simultaneous pressure from the Arab side. On November 2, 1945, Balfour Declaration Day, there were anti-Zionist demonstrations in Syria, Egypt, Lebanon, and Iraq. In Alexandria, crowds attacked Jewish shops, homes, and synagogues; in British-governed Libya, the mobs slaughtered about one hundred Jews. The dilemma was stark: To turn down Truman's proposal might jeopardize the cornerstone of British foreign policy, the Anglo–American alliance. But to allow 100,000 Jews into Palestine would enrage the Arabs and invite rebellion there and elsewhere in the Middle East.

Whitehall chose the path of least resistance—yet another committee of inquiry into the fate of the Jewish DPs, this one to work jointly with the Americans. The appointment of the committee on November 13 put a temporary halt to Haganah activities. It seemed that Bevin had succeeded in drawing the United States into the Palestine problem. Washington would now share in formulating a solution and might even end up partaking in the expense.

THE ANGLO–AMERICAN COMMITTEE OF INQUIRY

The committee was directed to determine how many of the remaining European Jews could be reintegrated in their native lands, and how many preferred to migrate to other countries. Both Jews and Arabs were to be consulted about the numbers that could be absorbed in Palestine.

Twelve men—naturally dubbed the "twelve apostles"—were named, six Britons and six Americans. In launching the committee Bevin publicly set out his Palestine policy: Britain would give up the Mandate, and Palestine would be converted into an international "trusteeship"; after a time an independent "Palestinian, not Jewish, state" would be established. He expected the committee to more or less endorse this solution. He warned the Jews not to push their way to "the head of the queue," lest they provoke an anti-Semitic reaction. Meanwhile, there would be a ceiling of fifteen hundred immigration permits per month. The Jewish Agency denounced Bevin's "prejudging" of the committee's findings and formally endorsed illegal immigration.

During February and March 1946 the committee studied the situation of the DPs, toured the Middle East, heard testimony from Arab and Zionist representatives and British officials, and received and read reports from agencies and movements in Palestine and from outside observers. The Palestinian Arab propaganda agency, the Arab Office, headed by Musa al–Alami, submitted a three-volume survey entitled *The Problem of Palestine*. It cautioned the committee against regarding "Jewish colonisation in Palestine and Arab resistance to it in terms of white colonization of North America and Australia and the resistance of the indigenous peoples." Nor would the prosperity Zionism would allegedly bring to Palestine persuade the Arabs to shelve their opposition to a movement that was bent on dispossessing them. The Jewish Agency submitted a thousand-page volume, *The Jewish Case Before the AAC of Inquiry on Palestine*, which contrasted Palestinian Arab backwardness with Zionism's role as a bearer of enlightenment and progress, backed up with reams of statistics and graphs.

Of particular effect was the month the committee spent touring DP centers, especially in Poland. Haganah and Jewish Agency representatives coached the DPs and made sure the AAC met only Jews propounding the Zionist solution. The committee found that the Jews in Poland lived in an "atmosphere of terror," with "pogroms ... an everyday occurrence." (Indeed, Poles had murdered over a thousand Jews since the end of the war.) The testimony of American and British officials on the spot confirmed this, and most of the committee members became convinced of the need for immigration of the DPs to Palestine.

Before reaching Palestine, the committee subdivided and visited several Arab capitals. At Riyadh, King Abdul Aziz ibn Saud told his visitors: "The Jews are our enemies everywhere. Wherever they are found, they intrigue and work against us. ...With the power of the sword, we drove the Romans out of Palestine. How, after all this sacrifice, would a merchant [that is, a Jew] come and take Palestine out of our hands for money?"

He then presented each member with a golden dagger and an Arabian robe and headdress, and showed them his harem. He offered to find the AAC chairman, Judge Sir John Singleton, a wife.

At the hearings in Palestine in March, the Jewish leaders presented the Zionist case forcefully, citing facts and figures. Ben-Gurion banned all but mainstream spokesmen from appearing (though, defying the leadership, Hebrew University president Yehuda Leib Magnes testified on behalf of a binational solution). The Arabs, according to

an American observer, preferred to impress the committee with "a sumptuous luncheon at Katy Antonius's or a ceremonial visit to a large estate rather than with any systematic marshaling of facts and figures to make a convincing presentation."

But perhaps more important than all the testimony were the committee's travels around the country. The diverse realities of the cities and countryside left an abiding impression. One American committee member, Frank Aydelotte, later wrote: "I left Washington pretty strongly anti-Zionist. ... But when you see at first hand what these Jews have done in Palestine ... the greatest creative effort in the modern world. The Arabs are not equal to anything like it and would destroy all that the Jews have done. ...This we must not let them do."

Frank Buxton, another American member, wrote: "How my Vermont father ... would have been amazed at the greater deeds of the Palestinian Jews. ...I came away from those farms less cocky and more humble and not quite so certain that American pioneers left no successors." Buxton later compared the Haganah to the American Revolutionary army, "a rabble in arms in the fine sense."

British committee member R. H. S. Crossman later recalled, by contrast, visiting "the stenchiest Arab village" he had ever seen. The main findings of the report, which was released on May 1, were that the great majority of DPs wished to settle in Palestine and that 100,000 visas should be issued and immigration expedited "as rapidly as conditions will permit." The committee rejected partition as unworkable; independence, when given, should be within a single, binational framework. But independence should be postponed for now, and the Mandate continued as a United Nations Trusteeship. If Bevin had hoped that the committee would produce an agreed Anglo–American policy, he was sorely disappointed. Truman again endorsed the passage of 100,000 DPs to Palestine and approved the scrapping of the White Paper's land sale provisions, which the committee had deemed discriminatory. Attlee ruled out mass immigration until the Jewish military undergrounds were disbanded and the Yishuv disarmed.

The Jewish Agency greeted the report with limited approval, endorsing the immigration recommendation. The Arabs rejected it completely. There were riots and demonstrations m Baghdad and Palestine, and in Beirut the United States Information Center was set on fire. The report was officially condemned by the Arab League Council, but it resisted calls for severe measures against Britain and the United States should the recommendations be implemented.

Publication of the report did nothing to stop Jewish attacks on British targets, culminating in the Palmah's "Night of the Bridges" (June 17). On June 29, in response, the British launched "Operation Agatha," aimed at seriously reducing Jewish military capabilities. Haganah intelligence had obtained advance warning, and most commanders escaped the dragnet. The operation, in which hundreds were arrested, including four members of the JAE, only marginally affected the Haganah's strength and did nothing to improve Britain's image in the United States. But on the political plane, it paralyzed the Yishuv decision-makers and persuaded the JAE (meeting in Paris in August 1946) to abandon the path of military confrontation with the British.

However, the operation also provoked a desire for revenge, as the IZL, rather ironically, took up the cudgels for its sometime enemy, the Haganah, on July 22. Without coordinating with the Haganah, sappers placed a number of bomb-laden milk containers in the basement of the King David Hotel in Jerusalem, which served as a British military and administrative headquarters. The resulting explosion, which demolished an entire wing of the building and killed ninety-one people—Britons, Arabs, and Jews—was the biggest terrorist action in the organization's history. The IZL subsequently claimed it had given the occupants ample warning, but they had failed to evacuate the building; the British maintained that no such warning had been issued. In response, the commander of the British forces in Palestine, Lt. Gen. Sir Evelyn Barker, issued a nonfraternization order in which he accused all of Palestine's Jews of complicity in the outrage. Personnel were barred from frequenting any Jewish home or business or

having "any social intercourse with any Jew" in order to punish "the Jews in a way the race dislikes as much as any, by striking at their pockets." Barker was subsequently rebuked by Attlee but was not removed from his command.

The Haganah, always opposed to terrorism (which it distinguished from legitimate anti-imperialist guerrilla warfare), condemned the attack, disbanded the Hebrew Resistance Movement, and called a halt to its anti-British military actions. Once again, each of the three Jewish underground organizations went its own way.

The upshot of the Anglo–American talks in the summer of 1946, and of the violence in Palestine, was Britain's floating of the Morrison–Grady, or Provincial Autonomy, Plan, London's last effort to find a compromise solution. It left defense, foreign affairs, and most economic matters in British—or "International Trusteeship"—hands, while, subdivided into four "provinces" or cantons, Jews and Arabs were offered a measure of local autonomy over municipal affairs, agriculture, education, and so on. Provision was made for the immediate transfer of 100,000 DPs and eventual independence for Palestine as a unitary (or binational) state.

In September, British officials and representatives of the Arab states met in London to discuss the plan. There was no Palestinian Arab or Jewish representation; British insistence on determining the composition of the two delegations resulted in a double boycott. Like all its predecessors, the Morrison–Grady Plan was rejected, both by the Zionists (who insisted on "Jewish statehood") and the Arabs ("immediate Arab independence") as well as by the United States. Indeed, on October 4, 1946, consummating a steady process that had begun in 1945, President Truman formally enunciated U.S. support of partition and Jewish statehood and called for an immediate start to "substantial" immigration. This statement, in large measure prompted by the heated contest for Jewish votes in New York in the upcoming midterm elections, was a bitter blow to Attlee. "I am astonished that you did not wait to acquaint yourself with the reasons" for the British plan, he cabled Truman. Within weeks his cabinet was to decide to abandon the Mandate: Britain understood that its position in Palestine was untenable without an Anglo–American understanding—and clearly no such accord was in the cards.

On January 27, 1947, the London Conference was reconvened. This time the AHC was represented—but the Jewish Agency continued its boycott and the United States refused even to send an observer. The British formally negotiated with Palestinian and other Arab representatives while informally meeting Zionist officials behind the scenes. But there was no basis for an agreement. The agency refused to consider anything less than partition; the Palestinians, anything less than majority-rule independence for all of Palestine.

UNSCOP

On February 14, 1947, the British cabinet decided, in effect, to wash its hands of Palestine and dump the problem in the lap of the United Nations. "We are unable to accept the scheme put forward either by the Arabs or by the Jews, or to impose ourselves a solution of our own," Bevin told the Commons on February 18. The Arabs were not averse to the matter going before the UN, where they anticipated a favorable outcome; the Zionists were wary of a "UN solution." These attitudes may well have affected Bevin's decision.

Some historians have suggested that by threatening the sides with the unknown and the unpredictable, Britain may have been aiming to force them to accept its latest proposals, or to accede in a prolongation of the Mandate. Others believe Britain was simply too weak and poor to soldier on. IZL and LHI adherents claim it was their constant attacks that persuaded the British to cast off the burden. The Haganah operations of 1945–46 have also been seen as portending a clash with the main Zionist militia that Whitehall was unwilling to contemplate, while the struggle against illegal immigration was a headache of major proportions. Most historians agree that given the Cold War context, in which the need for Anglo–American amity was seen as paramount, and Britain's insolvency, Whitehall could ill afford

to alienate Washington over a highly emotional issue that, when all was said and done, was not a vital British interest.

The political developments of 1947 were played out against a background of Jewish violence and reprisals spiraling almost out of control. Efforts to block and punish illegal immigration took on new, bloody dimensions, though by and large the British displayed restraint and humanity in face of terrorism. With evacuation only months away, Britain appeared no longer capable of properly governing Palestine and to have lost the will to continue. And, without doubt, the decision to withdraw heightened the terrorists' expectations. The British had close to 100,000 troops in Palestine, five times as many as had been used to crush the Arab Revolt of 1936–39 (a tribute, perhaps, to the greater efficiency and deadliness of the Jewish militants), but there were strict limits to what they could allow themselves to do in the way of effective counterterrorism.

On March 1, 1947, IZL gunmen killed more than twenty British servicemen, twelve of them in a grenade attack on their Officers Club in Tel Aviv, and injured thirty. On March 31 the LHI sabotaged the Haifa oil refinery; the fire took three weeks to put out. And on May 4 the IZL penetrated the British prison in Acre and set free two dozen of its incarcerated members (and, unintentionally, some two hundred Arab prisoners), but nine of the attackers were killed and eight captured. The latter were tried, and on July 8 death sentences were confirmed against three of them.

On July 12, the IZL abducted two British sergeants, Clifford Martin (apparently a Jew) and Mervyn Paice, and hanged them after their three comrades were executed on July 29. The Britons' bodies were booby-trapped and a British captain was injured when they were cut down. "The bestialities practised by the Nazis themselves could go no further," commented *The Times* of London. But bestiality was by no means a monopoly of the Jewish terrorists. On the evening of July 30 British troops and police went on a retaliatory rampage in Tel Aviv, destroying shops and beating up Jews. In one area, berserk security men sprayed pedestrians and shops with gunfire, killing five and injuring ten.

In Parliament, meeting in special session on August 12, there was an all-party consensus to quit Palestine, quickly; "no British interest" was safeguarded by staying on, said Churchill. The judgment of historians familiar with the British state archives is that "the IZL's draconian methods, morally reprehensible as they were, were decisive in transforming the evacuation option of February 1947 into a determined resolve to give up the burdens of the Mandate."

The British had by now dumped the problem in the lap of the UN. Responding, in April–May 1947 the General Assembly met in special session in New York and established yet another committee to examine the problem. Over Arab objections the UN Special Committee on Palestine (UNSCOP) was empowered to probe the DP problem, and also to determine guidelines for a settlement. The Netherlands, Sweden, Czechoslovakia, Yugoslavia, Canada, Australia, India, Iran, Peru, Guatemala, and Uruguay were asked to send representatives. The Arab states were not dismayed, expecting an easy victory at the UN.

With a Swedish judge, Emil Sandstrom, as its chairman. UNSCOP spent five weeks in Palestine that summer, hearing Jewish and British officials. Ben-Gurion at first spoke of a Jewish state in all of Palestine, then agreed to partition; Weizmann spoke of partition from the start. The Jews enjoyed a clandestine advantage: They had bugged the committee's rooms and knew what every committee member and witness was saying.

The committee toured the country and again, the face-to-face encounter with the two sides in the settlements and villages was to prove persuasive. The committee members were warmly welcomed by their Jewish hosts, and the Jewish Agency made sure they met with settlers who spoke their languages (Swedish, Spanish, Serbo-Croat, and so on). The Arabs, on the other hand, everywhere greeted them with sourness, suspicion, or aggressiveness. The committee was impressed by the cleanliness and development in the Jewish areas and, conversely, by the dirt and backwardness of the Arab villages and towns. The Jewish community appeared to be "European, modern, dynamic … a state in the making."

Though officially the AHC boycotted UNSCOP, the Arab position did not go completely unrepresented. Acting "independently," Musa al-Alami and Cecil Hourani, secretary of the Arab Office in Washington, submitted a memorandum setting out the Arab viewpoint. UNSCOP also heard representatives ot the Arab states who rejected partition and advocated a unitary, democratic state from which the illegal immigrants would be expelled, and where the remaining Jews would have no political rights.

A factor that dramatically influenced UNSCOP was the *Exodus* affair. Since August 1946 the British had been sending captured illegal immigrants to detention camps in Cyprus. But with about twelve thousand prisoners in the island's camps, there was no more room. In spring 1947, under the hammer blows of IZL terror and the Haganah illegal immigration campaign, the British decided to tighten the screws. MI6 unleashed a campaign of sabotage against the Haganah's ships in European harbors: The *Vrisi* was sunk in Genoa on July 11; the *Pan Crescent* was damaged and grounded near Venice on the night of August 30–31. Whitehall also decided to send captured illegal immigrants back to Europe.

On July 12, the *Exodus 1947* set sail from southern France, with 4,500 DPs aboard. On July 18 it was intercepted and boarded by Royal Marines some 30 kilometers off the coast of Palestine, opposite Gaza. A nightlong hand-to-hand battle followed, which the Haganah decided to exploit to show how poor and weak and helpless the Jews were, and how cruel the British. Three Jews died and twenty-eight were seriously wounded, but the desperate plight of the DPs had been highlighted and their fate linked to Palestine. As if to drive home the grim message, the British then proceeded to tow the boat into Haifa harbor, disembark the dead and wounded, and then transfer the bulk of the DPs to three seaworthy ships—under the watchful eye of UNSCOP chairman Sandstrom—and ship them back to France. Increasing Britain's embarrassment, the French refused to cooperate; the French Communist Party daily *L'Humanite* described the vessels as "a floating Auschwitz." The great majority of the passengers refused to leave the ships, and the British, maneuvered into a corner of their own making, sailed on to Hamburg, where the army on September 8 forcibly disembarked the passengers. Jews, this time shepherded by British troops, had been returned to the land of their persecution. The ordeal of the *Exodus* seemed to symbolize contemporary Jewish history and British insensitivity. Nothing could have done more to promote the Zionist cause at this crucial juncture. The almost simultaneous British execution of the three IZL operatives and the IZL hanging of the two sergeants apparently had a much smaller impact on the UNSCOP members—though perhaps the *Exodus* affair had indirectly cast light on the wellsprings of the IZL's behavior.

The committee moved to Europe in late July to interview DPs and officials dealing with the problem. The DPs—as with the AAC before—unanimously asserted that they wanted to immigrate to Palestine. UNSCOP's report, submitted to the General Assembly on September 1, was unanimous about the need to terminate the Mandate. A majority of eight proposed partitioning Palestine into Jewish and Arab states, with an international trusteeship for Jerusalem and Bethlehem. The two states would be bound in economic union, and Britain would continue to administer the country for two years, during which 150,000 Jews would be allowed in. The minority report—written by the Yugoslav, Iranian, and Indian representatives—proposed that Palestine be given independence as a "federal state," meaning a unitary entity under Arab domination.

The immediate British cabinet reaction was initially a secret decision, on September 20, to evacuate Palestine completely. Either the UN would set up the machinery for an orderly transfer of power or else the Arabs and the Jews would settle the problem on their own, by force of arms. In either case, it was no longer Britain's responsibility.

The General Assembly Partition Resolution, November 29, 1947

The Zionists mounted a powerful campaign in the United States to pressure President Truman into endorsing the UNSCOP majority report. As he had supported partition back in October 1946, and, moreover, the Soviets had recently adopted a propartition stance,[120] he could hardly do otherwise, despite a last-ditch struggle by the State Department. Two weeks after Britain announced its intention to evacuate, both the United States (October 11) and the Soviet Union (October 13) publicly reiterated their support for partition. On November 13 Britain announced that it would withdraw all its troops from Palestine by August 1, 1948.

Before the General Assembly vote on November 29, 1947, the State Department made frantic efforts to award the Negev—which the UNSCOP majority had earmarked for the Jews—to the Arabs. Only Weizmann's personal intervention with Truman saved the bulk of the desert for the Jews. In exchange the Jewish Agency reluctantly agreed to concede Beersheba and a strip of territory along the Sinai–Negev border—awarded to the Jews in the majority report—to the Arabs. Jaffa was made an Arab enclave in the Jewish state, while the Jews were given a little more land in the Galilee. With these changes the prospective Jewish state was to have 55 percent of Palestine and a population of approximately 500,000 Jews with an Arab minority of close to 400,000. (Another 100,000 Jews lived in Jerusalem.)

The UN Charter required that the resolution pass by a two-thirds majority. Despite the majority in UNSCOP and despite U.S. and Soviet support, the Zionists were initially far from optimistic. On November 26 three wavering nations—Haiti, Greece, and the Philippines—indicated that they would vote against the resolution. The desperate Zionists turned to the United States, realizing that without direct American pressure on its client states the vote might be lost. Zionist lobbying was crude and effective—as was the arm-twisting the Americans, in turn, applied to a dozen smaller nations. Truman's original instruction of November

24—"[not] to use threats or improper pressure of any kind on other Delegations to vote for the majority report"—was cast aside. Greece was threatened with a foreign aid cutoff, Liberia with a rubber embargo.

On November 28, in the hours before the crucial vote, the Arabs succeeded in obtaining a short delay. But only a serious compromise proposal could have warded off the vote for partition, and this the Arabs proved unable to put together. The AHC representatives made themselves scarce during the behind-the-scenes deliberations, as did the Pakistani delegate, Zufferallah Khan, the ablest of the Muslim spokesmen.

The voting was broadcast live on radio around the world. Nowhere was attention more riveted than in Palestine. When the tally was complete, thirty-three states had voted yes, thirteen no, and ten had abstained. Partition had passed, but not very comfortably (had three of the ayes voted nay, the resolution would have failed). The nays had consisted of the Arab and Muslim states, Cuba, and India; the ayes, of the United States, the British Commonwealth states, Western Europe, the Soviet bloc, and most of Latin America. Among the abstainers had been Britain, Argentina, Mexico, Chile, and China.

The Zionists and their supporters rejoiced; the Arabs walked out of the hall after declaring the resolution invalid. They could not fathom, a Palestinian historian was later to write, why 37 percent of the population had been given 55 percent of the land (of which they owned only 7 percent). And "the Palestinians failed to see why they should be made to pay for the Holocaust … they failed to see why it was *not* fair for the Jews to be a minority in a unitary Palestinian state, while it *was* fair for almost half of the Palestinian population—the indigenous majority on its own ancestral soil—to be converted overnight into a minority under alien rule." The Arab delegates asserted that any effort to implement the resolution would lead to war. Ben-Gurion knew that there would be war. But still, he said, "I know of no greater achievement by the Jewish people … in its long history since it became a people."

Resolution 181 was, in some way, "Western civilization's gesture of repentance for the Holocaust … the repayment of a debt owed by those nations that realized that they might have done more to prevent or at least limit the scale of Jewish tragedy during World War II."

The Zionists had effectively exploited the unusual situation, in which, for a brief moment, there was Soviet–American agreement on the Palestine problem. Helped to a great extent by the nations' feeling of guilt about the Holocaust, the Zionists had managed to obtain an international warrant for a small piece of earth for the Jewish people. What remained was for the Jews to translate the formal leasehold into concrete possession and statehood, in war—and for the Palestinians to pay the price.

When the Arabs walked out of the General Assembly declaring that partition would lead to war, it was not an idle threat. In June 1946 the Arab League had secretly pledged funds, arms, and volunteers to the Palestinians. On September 16, 1947, the league decided to establish an Arab Liberation Army (ALA), composed of Palestinians and volunteers from the Arab states. In November the Syrian army began registering volunteers and set up a training camp. Fawzi al–Qawuqji, who had sat out the war years in Germany, broadcasting the Nazi message to the Arab world, was named commander. Amin al–Husseini bitterly opposed the appointment. Since the Arab Revolt he had seen Qawuqji as a rival, and their animosity was to undermine the Palestinian war effort in 1948. The forces aligned with Husseini would operate without coordination with, and often at cross-purposes to, the ALA.

Even before the vote in the UN, the Arab League had set up a Military Committee, to be headed by Gen. Ismail Safwat, former chief of staff of the Iraqi army, to assist the Palestinians. To pressure Britain and the UN it decided to deploy troops along Palestine's frontiers. Damascus sent several battalions to the border, giving the British a scare and jolting the Yishuv into vigilance. Indeed, on October 20, 1947, a small Syrian force crossed the frontier at Tel al–Qadi, perhaps by mistake, perhaps with the intention of testing the British, who immediately drove them back.

In a bleak report to the League, General Safwat said that the Zionists possessed "political, military and administrative institutions and organizations, characterized by a very high degree of efficiency." They could field twenty thousand troops, and had forty thousand reserves, good lines of communication and well-defended settlements. The Palestinians had none of these things. The Arab states must mobilize and come to their aid, or, he implied, the Zionists would win.[132] But the other League members were not yet ready to be sucked into the conflict. Consistently it was the Iraqis who were the most militant, "breathing brimstone for home consumption." Being farthest from the prospective battlefield, they apparently felt free to exhibit less caution than the front-line states. A few days after the passage of the partition resolution and the start of hostilities in Palestine, Iraq proposed that the regular Arab armies intervene to "save" Palestine even before the Jews proclaimed a state and the British departed. This was rejected, but the League decided on indirect, minimal intervention, by sending ten thousand rifles[134] and three thousand "volunteers."

Husseini, forever showing up uninvited at Arab League meetings, forever saw his proposals rejected. He had been deeply unhappy with Safwat's proposal for intervention, understanding that it would provide an opportunity for land grabs by Jordan, Syria, and Egypt. The meetings were marked by disunity, mutual suspicion, and bitter enmities. Most of the Arab rulers had developed a strong antagonism toward Husseini, whom they regarded as an inveterate plotter, and this undermined any hope of realistic decision-making in their councils. Moderates—such as Abdullah of Jordan—allowed themselves to be pushed into extremist pronouncements, lest they be charged with showing insufficient zeal. All paid lip service to Arab unity and the Palestinian cause, and all opposed partition—but all were really at a loss about what to do to prevent it. Most knew their armies were weak and in no state to take on a serious enemy, certainly not while the British were still in Palestine. Still, the Arab

leaders felt that they had to do something. Some felt opposition politicians nipping at their heels; most, especially some of the monarchs, suffered from unpopularity and questionable legitimacy. Non-intervention in Palestine might well doom their regimes. The public bluster, the leaders' fear of their own populations, whom they had whipped up to a frenzy with militant rhetoric, and the pressure of their fellows all combined to egg them on. They had embarked on a course almost inevitably leading to war.

Ben-Gurion understood that the decisive battle for statehood would be waged not against the British or in the diplomatic arena but against the Arabs. Between 1936 and 1945 the Haganah grew by leaps and bounds, steadily improving its command structures and soldiering abilities, adding fresh units, particularly the Palmah, and enlarging its armory and arms-producing capabilities. In 1945 its agents in the United States had managed to buy war surplus arms-making machine tools and smuggle them into Palestine. By the end of 1947 Haganah arms factories were producing two and three-inch mortars, Sten submachine guns, and grenades and bullets in large numbers. The buildup extended also to the air. In the 1930s the Haganah had bought planes and, under civilian camouflage, had begun training pilots. In November 1947 the Air Service was formed, and some light civil aircraft were armed.

In May 1946 the Haganah General Staff put together its Plan C, a response to organized attacks and guidelines for retaliation. Plan B, devised in 1945, had outlined the defense of the Yishuv in the event of a renewed Arab rebellion, with the Haganah serving as an auxiliary to the British forces. In October and December 1946, in two addenda to Plan C, instructions were issued to regional commanders regarding retaliation against British forces should they come to the aid of the Arabs. Formerly an organization that saw itself as an appendage of the British Army, cooperating with the Mandate government, the Haganah now took on sole responsibility for the defense of the Yishuv, against the British if necessary.

In December the Zionist leadership made Ben-Gurion responsible for defense in addition to his function as Jewish Agency chairman—effectively, the prime minister of the state within a state. From the spring of 1947 he devoted most of his time and energy to preparing the Yishuv for war, leaving the conduct of the political-diplomatic battle to Moshe Sharett, Abba Hillel Silver in the United States, and others. He spent long hours with Haganah and Palmah officers and veterans of the Jewish Brigade, studying the Yishuv's strategic problems and defense needs.

During this period the Haganah–Palmah brass battled for dominance against the regular (mainly British) army veterans, who had returned to the Haganah after 1945 or were waiting for commissions. It was a matter of both military philosophies and personnel: What outlook and which group of commanders would fashion the emergent Jewish army? Each group sought to win Ben-Gurion over: the hit-and-run, informal, small-unit approach versus the big-unit, strict-regimen, regular army way.

Unlike most of his colleagues, Ben-Gurion believed:

> Until recently there was only the problem of how to defend [the Yishuv] against the Palestinian Arabs … But now we face a completely new situation. The Land of Israel is surrounded by independent Arab states … that have the right to purchase and produce arms, to set up armies and train them. Attack by the Palestinian Arabs does not endanger the Yishuv, but there is a danger, that the neighboring Arab states will send their armies to attack and destroy the Yishuv.

The preparations set in train by the Haganah in 1947 were for conventional war against a coalition of Arab states rather than for limited guerrilla warfare against the Palestinians. Ben-Gurion tended to belittle the Haganah and apparently doubted its ability to convert itself efficiently and quickly into a competent regular army. He surrounded himself with military advisers drawn largely from the pool of regular army veterans, as a counterweight to the existing Haganah leadership.[141] Nonetheless, apart from appointment to command posts of a few regular army veterans and the adoption of certain regular army norms in the fields of logistics, staff work, and intelligence, it was the Haganah that eventually expanded and in mid-1948 became the Israel Defense Forces (IDF).

This conversion was left until very late in the day, largely because Palestine remained under British control and the Haganah was by nature an illegal, underground organization. Only in November 1947 did Ben-Gurion and the Haganah command shift to an active mode and begin to reorganize for war. Even though Ben-Gurion believed as late as April 1948 that the British intended to manipulate events so that they could stay on in Palestine, the reorganization of the Haganah was based on the assumption that they were, indeed, leaving and that the Palestinians and the Arab states were the enemies the Haganah would have to face.

Section 2
Expanding the Conflict, 1947–1967

 Introduction

This section focuses on the wars of 1947–1949 and 1967. Both conflicts transformed the Mideast. The first war established Israeli independence at the same time as it collapsed Palestinian Arab society. Hence, the contrasting Israeli and Palestinian names for that conflict: the War of Independence and the Catastrophe (al–Nakba). The second clash, the Six Day War of June 1967, gave Israel control over all of what had been mandatory Palestine, as well as extensive Egyptian and Syrian territories.

The initial selection, by Ahron Bregman, considers opposing forces and strategies during the fighting of 1947 to 1949, which, in turn, fell into two phases: 1) the Jewish–Palestinian civil war, from November 30, 1947 to May 14, 1948; and 2) the war between the newly proclaimed state of Israel and invading Arab armies, from May 15, 1948 to March 1949. Each phase was precipitated by Arab attacks, in the first instance by Palestinian irregulars, and in the second, by state armies. But contrary to the Jewish David vs. Arab Goliath image, Bregman shows that Jewish forces frequently outnumbered and outgunned their foes.[1] Poor coordination among Arab forces joined with generally stronger Jewish motivation to magnify the Jews' physical advantages.

Benny Morris and Norman Stillman consider the anguished population movements set in motion by this fighting. Morris, who describes at the outset of his contribution the problems involved in researching the Palestinian exodus, is widely recognized as the principal authority on that topic. He claims, on the one hand, that the Jews had no predetermined program of expulsion, that they resorted to expulsion only after Arab attacks threatened to extinguish the Yishuv, and that expulsionist actions remained ad hoc and inconsistent. On the other hand, Morris argues that as an abstract concept, the idea of Arab dispossession was part of Zionist thinking long before 1948; that as soon as coexistence collapsed, most Jews wanted to see as few Arabs remain as possible; and that even after mid-1948, when there was no longer a plausible strategic justification for Arab expulsion, the IDF continued—indeed, deliberately increased—Arab displacement so as to minimize a suspect minority and to seize valuable property.

Without referring directly to the Palestinian expulsion, Stillman provides data by which to compare Arab and Jewish population movements. In some instances, Jewish flight was less coerced than that of the Palestinians: very few Palestinians wanted to abandon their homes, but Zionist organizers often encouraged Jews in Arab countries to leave for Israel. The two displacements differed as well in that the percentage of Jews who were expelled or fled from Arab lands was higher than the percentage of Arabs who were expelled or fled

---

1 Bregman, however, overstates Jewish numerical superiority during the second phase, because his troop totals for 1948–1949 *include* both Jewish front-line and rear-echelon forces, but *exclude* rear-echelon forces in Arab state armies. The ratio of support forces to front-line forces was usually at least 1:1. See Benny Morris, "And Now for Some Facts," *The New Republic*, May 8, 2006, p. 24.

from Israel. Jewish expulsion also had a less plausible security rationale, insofar as Jews—unlike Palestinians—represented no threat to their host societies. More basically, however, these movements resembled one another in that both reflected an impulse toward national homogenization and unification that demanded the exclusion of aliens. In size and lost property, the two displacements also were comparable.

The late Palestinian–American academic Edward Said turns to the impact of 1948 on political culture in the wider Arab world, an impact that he views as highly deleterious. Insofar as the West was seen as an accomplice in the Israeli victory, the war fostered a certain hostility to Western ideas and innovation, which, in turn, contributed to intellectual stultification. More specifically, 1948 bred a haunting sense of failure, while encouraging the compensatory militarization of Arab societies, the diversion of resources from economic investment to arms, and a search for redemption through military heroes. Together with a tendency to rhetorical excess, Said argues that these developments helped lead to the Six Day War of 1967.

This section concludes with writings by Morris and Bregman that analyze the origins and course of the Six Day War. Morris takes pains to deny that Israel before June 1967 sought war as a pretext for expansion. In his words, the war "triggered an expansionist, and even millenarian, upsurge; but the war was not prompted or preceded by one." In fact, Israeli society on the eve of war was in chaos. The conflict arose primarily through miscalculations by Egyptian President Gamal Abdel Nasser, who was egged on by deliberate Soviet misinformation. On the question of whether, as some have charged, the Soviets sought war so as to provide an excuse to destroy Israel's nuclear facilities, Morris is agnostic.

Reflecting a broad scholarly consensus, Bregman's analysis of the political origins of the 1967 war is not dissimilar to that of Morris. But as a military historian, Bregman offers intriguing details on Israel's implementation of its first-strike doctrine, and its successful prosecution of the conflict against three poorly coordinated enemy armies.

Israel's Wars: A History Since 1947

By Ahron Bregman

Civil War in Palestine

Although significant, the UN partition resolution did not envisage the immediate creation of either a Jewish or an Arab state on the land of Palestine. Yet, rather than easing tension, the resolution to partition the land and the subsequent British decision, made on 4 December 1947, to depart on Friday 14 May 1948, had increased tensions between the peoples of Palestine and 'it was as if on a signal Arabs and Jews squeezed the trigger and exchanged fire'. On 15 December 1947, Lieutenant General Sir Alan Cunningham, the British High Commissioner for Palestine, sent a top-secret memorandum to the British Colonial Secretary Arthur Creech–Jones, outlining the situation in Palestine in fearful detail. 'Situation now is deteriorating', he wrote, 'into a series of reprisals and counter-reprisals between Jews and Arabs, in which many innocent lives are being lost, the tempo of which may accelerate'.

The initial phase following the UN resolution to partition Palestine was characterized mainly by Arab attacks on Jewish convoys and street fighting on the Jaffa–Tel Aviv border and in the Old City of Jerusalem. This was not yet a full-blown civil war but rather skirmishes and a vicious circle where an action was followed by a reprisal with disturbances and clashes between Jews and Arabs spreading to all parts of Palestine.

With all its energy directed to the evacuation and removal of some 210,000 tons of stores and a huge retinue of colonial administrators, the British in Palestine, under the command of Sir Gordon Macmillan, chose to stand aside and to protect only their own evacuation routes. Britain now simply washed its hands of the problems of Palestine and refused to assume responsibility for implementing the UN partition plan. And with the 'policeman' standing aside, the condition of Palestine deteriorated into anarchy, with Jews and Arabs fighting out their differences in what gradually slid into an all-out civil war which was to last about five months.

The Opposing Forces at the Outbreak of the Civil War

On the eve of the civil war in Palestine, Jewish forces comprised Haganah, which was the largest underground organization of the Yishuv, the Jewish community, and two smaller dissident organizations: the Irgun Zvai Leumi, better known as 'the Irgun,' and *Lochamai Herut Yisrael*, known also as 'the Lehi' (or 'The Stern Gang'). The Haganah comprised 45,000 men and women, about 2,100 of them in the Palmach, making up the striking force of the organization. In the Irgun and the Lehi there were about 3,000 fighters and, although independent of Ben Gurion's Haganah, the two small organizations often coordinated their actions with the Haganah, as they did in the notorious battle at Deir Yassin. Expecting a strong Arab response to the UN resolution to partition the land of Palestine, the Jewish leadership under Ben Gurion began mobilizing the whole community, and just a day after the UN resolution it issued a decree calling on men and women between the ages of 17 and 25 (those born between 1922 and 1930) to service. On 22 January 1948, the Jewish leadership ordered that all those born between 1911 and 1932 were not to leave the country; a month later all those born between 1908 and 1932 were ordered to come forward and enlist. On 3 February, all Jews aged between 19 and 23 (born between 1925 and 1929) were called to serve. The new recruits were not ordered to join a specific underground organization—this could have caused an immediate controversy—rather to enlist to *Sherut Ha'am* (literally: 'Service of the Nation').

The Arab force in the civil war was made up of four components. First was the Arab Liberation Army (ALA), which had around 4,000 volunteers from Palestine and the neighbouring Arab countries, mainly Iraq and Syria. The ALA was organized and equipped by the Military Committee of the Arab League and was trained at the Syrian training centre, Katana. It marched into Palestine on 20 January 1948 from Jordan, and operated from two locations: Galilee, where it had two battalions comprising between 1,500 and 2,000 men; and Samaria, just west of the Jordan river, where it deployed about the same number of men.

The second element of the Arab force consisted of between 1,000 and 1,500 volunteers from the 'Moslem Brothers' and Egyptian youth organizations who had crossed from Egypt to Palestine, and operated in the southern part of the country and in and around Majdal (now called Ashkelon) and Yibne (now called Yebne).

The third element, some 5,000 men, was led by Abdall Quader al-Husseini, a relative of the Mufti of Jerusalem and perhaps the most charismatic and ablest Arab leader in Palestine; he was operating in the Jerusalem, Ramallah and Jericho areas. Husseini's force comprised irregular bands and masses of villagers—the Palestinian element was strong—and it also had some European elements, that is volunteers from Britain, Yugoslavia and Germany who had joined the Arab Palestinians in their fight against the Jews. Another Arab group, 3,000 at most, was led by Hassan Salemeh, who had been trained in Germany, had been parachuted into Palestine, and was operating in the Jaffa–Lydda–Ramleh area. All in all, the number of Arab para regulars, irregulars and volunteers can be estimated at 25,000-30,000 men; their weakness, though, was a lack of cooperation and central control.

Aims and Fighting

The principal aim of the Jews in Palestine in the period immediately after the UN resolution to partition Palestine, was to gain effective control over the territory allotted to them by the UN and to secure communication with thirty-three Jewish settlements which, according to the UN plan, fell outside the proposed Jewish state. For although the UN had partitioned the land between Jews and Arab Palestinians, there were still Jewish settlements which were to remain within the Arab area and, on the other hand, Arab villages on land allotted to the Jews. In contrast to Arab villages within Jewish areas, which were self-reliant, the Jewish settlements relied heavily on outside supplies, which made the keeping open of routes a necessity for them. Another aim of the Jewish forces was to prepare the ground for what seemed to be an inevitable invasion of neighbouring Arab regular armies the moment the British left Palestine. The General Staff of the Jewish forces devised what became known as 'Plan Dalet' (*Tochnit Dalet*), the principal objective of which was to consolidate control over areas allotted to the Jewish State and also to seize strategic positions to make it possible to block regular Arab armies in case they marched into Palestine. What is significant about 'Plan Dalet'—it was distributed to field commanders on 29 February and became a directive to all units on 10 March 1948 —is that, apart from envisaging the occupation of strategic positions, it also allowed for the occupation of Arab villages, towns and cities and, where necessary, the expulsion of their inhabitants. This, we should comment here, was a blank cheque for Jewish forces to expel Arab Palestinians, as indeed happened in the ensuing days of the war.

The Palestinians' strategic aim during the civil war was negative in nature, namely to prevent the implementation of the partition plan by disrupting and strangling Jewish lines of communication, and by cutting off Jewish settlements from localities and positions that were already occupied. These opposing aims of Jews and Arabs led to the 'battle of the roads' which raged in Palestine during the first half of 1948, with Jewish forces attempting to gain control of the communications roads and the Arabs of Palestine seeking to prevent them from achieving this.

In the initial stages of the civil war the Arabs gained the upper hand and succeeded in dictating the pattern of the struggle. By March 1948 they had cut off the entire Negev—allotted to the Jews by the UN—from the coastal plain, as well as most of Western Galilee and the Jerusalem area; they also succeeded in isolating many Jewish settlements within these regions from one another. So successful were these operations that the Arabs of Palestine came close to reaching their principal aim when, in March 1948, British Colonial Secretary Creech–Jones told the British House of Commons that the Palestine situation was 'rapidly becoming insoluble' and on 19 March proposed that the UN rescind partition in favour of trusteeship. The US administration, too, frustrated by the deteriorating situation in Palestine, had joined the British call and declared, in mid-March, that since partition was hard to establish, a trusteeship should replace it. Only the Soviet Union remained constantly in favour of partition possibly because Moscow calculated that the creation of a Jewish State would undermine Western relations with the Arab States and thus provide for the Soviet Union a means of extending its influence in the Middle East, or even that a socialist Israel would become an ally. Anyway, the British–American view, aimed at replacing partition with trusteeship, dismayed the Jews, who saw their dream of establishing a state on the land allotted by the UN slipping away.

But soon the civil war began to take a new shape. In April 1948, with the war at its height, an attempt by the Arab Liberation Army to cut off the Haifa region and the Valley of Jezreel from the coastal plain failed (4 April) and Jewish forces proceeded with their own offensive, which proved to be eminently successful. In central Palestine, they broke open the road to Jerusalem ('Operation Nachshon', 3–15 April) and this allowed supplies of food and ammunition to get through to the Jews in the city. Elsewhere, all Arab towns and villages, and the mixed cities within the territory designated for the Jewish state, were overrun in rapid succession. Tiberias was captured on 18 April, and the vital port of Haifa fell into Jewish hands on 22–3 April. Most of Haifa's 70,000 Arabs fled, many to Acre, others to Lebanon. Between 25 and 27 April, Irgun forces attacked the all-Arab town of Jaffa, which was meant to be included in the future Arab state. At first they were checked by British troops, but once the British had left, Irgun forces took the town (13 May 1948) whose original 90,000 inhabitants were reduced to only 5,000—most of them fled to Gaza by sea. In northern Palestine, the town of Safed was occupied, and on the night of 13–14 May all Western Galilee came under Jewish control. The all-Arab town of Acre—like Jaffa it was meant to be included in the future Arab state—was besieged by Jewish forces and capitulated on 17 May. The Arab forces in Palestine were now bewildered by defeat, and retreated, with their leadership confused and disorganized.

Massacres and Refugees

The civil war in Palestine was vicious, cruel and littered with atrocities. It involved immense human suffering and a degree of blatant brutality never before seen in Jewish–Arab relations in Palestine, which had usually seen the two peoples living side-by-side in relative peace. On 31 December 1947, taking revenge for the killing of six of their fellows by the Irgun, Arabs attacked and killed thirty-nine Jews at the Haifa oil refineries. The Haganah responded in kind, attacking the village of Blad–el–Sheikh, where it killed more than 60 Arabs, including women and children. At the beginning of February 1948, more than ten Arabs and two British policemen were killed in an explosion near the Jaffa Gate in Jerusalem and, on 22 February, 60 Jews were killed by a car-bomb explosion on Jerusalem's Ben Yehuda street. The Jewish leader David Ben Gurion, visiting the scene, blamed Jewish thugs for this. As he put it: 'Such a destruction ... I could not recognize the streets ... But I could not forget that our thugs and murderers (meaning members of the Irgun and the Lehi) had opened the way', that is, brought about this Arab reaction by their own terrorist actions. On 11 March, 17 Jews were killed and forty were injured by a bomb in the courtyard of the Jewish Agency in Jerusalem and, on 9 April, 110 Palestinians—men, women and children—were killed by Jews in the small village of Deir Yassin just west of Jerusalem, at least 25 of them being massacred in cold blood. Four days later, on 13 April, the Arabs took revenge by attacking a Jewish convoy of medical staff on its way to Mount Scopus, leaving 77 dead.

What is so significant about the civil war in Palestine is that it was then that what became known as 'the Palestinian refugee problem' started. With its leadership and the middle class —those who had the money to do so—leaving Palestine to take what they believed to be temporary refuge in neighbouring Arab countries, and with the Jews advising the poorer Palestinians to follow suit and using force to expel the others— the Arab Palestinians moved out of Palestine. Exaggerations by Arab leadership of Jewish atrocities, as happened after the events at Deir Yassin, was also a catalyst, leading the Palestinians to flee whenever a Jewish soldier was seen approaching their village.

The demographic scales were now tilting in favour of the Jews, and with the en masse departure of the Arabs, Jews became the majority in the land of Palestine. While there was no explicit decision by the Jewish leadership to expel the Palestinians, there was nevertheless a tacit agreement that this should be done. In a meeting with military commanders, Prime Minister Ben Gurion said: 'In each attack [against Arabs] it is necessary to give a decisive blow, ruining the place, kicking away the inhabitants'. It is estimated that about 750,000 Palestinians left Palestine during the war (160,000 remained behind) and their homes were taken by new Jewish immigrants; as Ben Gurion recorded in his war diary: 'New immigrants [we] put in Arab houses'. This was the method the Jewish leadership employed to absorb the new Jewish immigrants who, in spite of the ongoing civil war, poured copiously into Palestine.

Although highly successful, the period which had followed the UN partition resolution was for the Jews in Palestine, many of whom were European refugees, traumatic. During the six months from November 1947 to mid-1948, 1,308 Jewish soldiers and 1,100 civilians perished. This is a very high toll, given the relatively low number of Jews in Palestine and the relatively short duration of the fighting.

Proclamation, End of British Mandate, and Regional War

On 14 May 1948, Prime Minister David Ben Gurion recorded in his war diary: 'At four in the afternoon the Jewish independence was proclaimed and the state [of Israel] was established', and he added 'Its fate is in the hands of the armed forces'. From the thirty-two-minute ceremony where he had declared the establishment of Israel, Ben Gurion went straight to the 'Red House', the headquarters of the Israeli forces on Tel Aviv beach, to discuss with his military commanders the deteriorating situation. Declaring a state was a bold and courageous move, given the threat of Arab neighbouring states to prevent by force the establishment of a Jewish state, even on that part of Palestine which had been allotted to the Jews by the UN. It also seemed, at the time, a suicidal move, given that US Secretary of State George Marshall had warned the Jews that America would not consider itself responsible for the consequences of their declaring a state and would not 'bail you out' if attacked by Arab neighbours.

That Friday night, just half an hour before midnight, Lieutenant–General Sir Alan Cunningham, the seventh and last British High Commissioner for Palestine, sailed in HMS *Euryalus* from the bay of Haifa for England. The birth of the State of Israel and the end of more than thirty years of British rule in Palestine took place on a single day. In fact, the state of Israel was proclaimed even *before* the official termination of the Mandate. The reason being that the Mandate was due to expire on Friday at midnight, and because this was during the Jewish Sabbath, it was decided to bring forward the proclamation ceremony. These two events were significant for two main reasons. First, they came to symbolize the transformation of the status of Jews in Palestine from a community to an independent state, soon to be recognized by the international community. Second, these two events were the catalyst which transformed a strictly localized conflict—until the departure of the British and the proclamation of Israel the Jewish–Arab struggle had remained essentially a communal war—into a full-blown regional confrontation which also involved neighbouring Arab states and their regular armies.

That night, American President Harry Truman recognized the Jewish state. This was a major development, and vital for Israel, because neither the UN decision to partition Palestine nor Ben Gurion's unilateral declaration of independence gave any international status to the Jewish state. A recognition by a superpower—as the United States was after the Second World War—meant that, at least symbolically, the newly established state of Israel was accepted into the family of nations. At five in the morning on 15 May, while giving his positive reaction to the American recognition in a Tel Aviv radio studio, Ben Gurion could hear the Egyptian bomber planes overhead. By now the Arab Legion, consisting of four well-trained regiments, was already on the march into the West Bank, an area allotted to the Palestinians by the

UN. It was dispatched there personally by King Abdullah who just a few minutes before midnight arrived at the eastern, side of the Allenby bridge. With the formal expiry, at midnight of the British Mandate, the King took out his pistol, fired a shot into the air and shouting "Forward" he dispatched his troops across the Jordan river to the West Bank. That day, which was a Saturday, the Egyptian government sent a telegram to the President of the UN Security Council, announcing that Egyptian armed forces had entered Palestine and were engaged in 'an armed intervention'. On Sunday 16 May the Arab League sent a cablegram making similar statements on behalf of the Arab states.

By world standards the war which was now developing in Palestine–Israel was a small-scale, primitive confrontation conducted by poorly-equipped and ill-trained units. For his invasion of Russia—'Operation Barbarossa'—in 1941, Hitler had assembled 160 divisions; in the Palestine war the biggest unit to take part in battle was a brigade, and actual fighting often involved smaller units. The German armoured strength in the Barbarossa invasion totalled 3,550 tanks; in the Palestine war the Israelis had no tanks at all and the Arabs had only a few primitive ones. Nevertheless, for the parties involved, in particular for the Israelis, the war was perceived, rightly or wrongly, as a life-or-death struggle. It was a war fought all over the country in separate battles—a see-saw struggle with many changes of fortune.

It is worth looking at the forces, Israeli and Arab, which were now confronting each other in Palestine, to demolish what is perhaps the biggest myth with regard to this first all-out Arab–Israeli war.

Forces and weapons

Contrary to popular belief, the 1948 war between Israeli forces and the invading regular Arab armies was not one between 'the few [Israelis]' and 'the many [Arabs]', or, as it is often put, a clash between David (Israel) and Goliath (the Arabs). The root of this popular, though utterly erroneous, notion lay in the Israeli practice of referring to the potential of the Arabs rather than to the actual number of troops they put into the field. By confusing the issue, the Israeli leadership, in its war of words and attempts to gain the sympathy of the world and its own people, had for many years knowingly ignored the fact that ratios among adversaries do not merely reflect population ratios, and that a high degree of manpower mobilization can make up for the quantitative demographic inferiority of a small nation like Israel. Indeed, during the 1948 war, Israel had mobilized almost its entire resources and ablest population, while the more numerous Arabs had utilized only a small fraction of their huge potential.

The number of Israeli troops committed to battle on the eve of the Arab invasion was more or less equal to that of the Arabs, but then, while the number of Arab troops increased only slightly, the number of Israelis grew steadily and dramatically. A breakdown shows that the total strength of the invading Arab armies was about 23,500 troops, made up of 10,000 in the Egyptian army, 4,500 in the Arab Legion of Transjordan, 3,000 Syrians, 3,000 Iraqis and 3,000 Lebanese and Arab Liberation Army (ALA) troops; there was also a token contingent from Saudi Arabia. Compared with these numbers, Israel, as Ben Gurion notes in his diary of the war, had committed a total of 29,677 men and women to battle. But then, with the progressive mobilization of Israeli society and the average monthly arrival of 10,300 new immigrants, the number of available fighters steadily grew. On 4 June 1948, the number of Israeli troops was, according to Ben Gurion, 40,825; and on 17 July it grew to 63,586. On 7 October 1948, these numbers swelled to 88,033, and by 28 October reached more than 92,275. On 2 December the number of Israeli soldiers on the field was 106,900; on 23 December it stood at 107,652, and on 30 December the number had risen to 108,300 (10,259 of them women). Jewish volunteers from abroad—*Mahal*—also joined, and although their number was relatively low, at most 5,000, they nevertheless provided valuable technical expertise. By the end of the war Israel's fighting force was larger in absolute terms than that of the Arabs, and as John Bagot Glubb correctly observed:

> the common impression that the heroic little Israeli army was fighting against tremendous odds (one army against seven armies was one of the expressions used) was not altogether correct. The Israeli forces were, generally speaking, twice as numerous as all the Arab armies put together.

In weaponry and firepower, however, the Arabs had a clear edge. The total inventory of the Haganah at the start of the war consisted of 22,000 rifles of various calibres, 1,550 light and medium machine guns, 11,000 largely home-made submachine guns, 195 three-inch calibre infantry mortars, 682 two-inch mortars, 86 PIAT (Projector Infantry Anti-Tank—a crude man-portable device of armour-piercing explosive charges) and five old 65mm field guns. A few tanks and aircraft still awaited shipment in Europe. Egypt, according to Israeli estimates, had 48 field guns, 25-30 armoured cars, 10-20 tanks, and 21-25 aircraft. Iraq had 48 field guns, 25-30 armoured cars, and 20 aircraft. Syria had 24 field guns, 36 armoured cars, 10-20 tanks and 14 aircraft. Jordan had 24 field guns and 45 armoured cars; and Lebanon 8 field guns and 9 armoured cars.

But as in manpower, so with weaponry; as the war progressed the balance steadily tipped in favour of the Israelis. A fundraising mission by Golda Meir to America raised $50 million, which was used to buy arms, and ships loaded with weapons were purchased and sent to Israel by such people as Ehud Avriel. In New York, a team headed by Teddy Kollek—later the long-serving Mayor of Jerusalem—bought aeroplanes, took them to pieces and, with the help of the Mafia, and under the nose of the FBI, shipped the precious weapons to Israel. Israelis not only purchased weapons, but they also took measures to prevent the Arabs from adding arms to their own arsenals. In Bari, Italy, on 9 April 1948, Israeli agents executed 'Operation Booty 1' and sunk the ship *Lino*, which was packed with 8,000 rifles designated for

Syria. Also in Italy, on 18 September 1948, Israeli agents broke into a garage where they destroyed four aeroplanes which were awaiting shipment to Egypt. Additionally, Israel developed its own weapons industry, which included chemical and biological weapons.

There were, apart from manpower and equipment, other factors which affected the character of the battle. The invading Arab armies had the advantage of being fresh in comparison with the Israelis, who were exhausted after five months of bloody civil war in Palestine. Moreover, the invading armies were relatively homogenous, with commanders and troops communicating in the same language, while the Israelis suffered language difficulties, as many troops were new immigrants, who could not speak Hebrew. The weather also played an important part. The summer of 1948 was extremely hot and harsh, and Israeli troops, many of whom had just arrived from cold Europe, found it too oppressive. While the invading Arab armies had the tactical advantage of surprise, the Israelis had the advantage of interior lines of communications and fortified settlements which provided useful bases of operations.

Turning to the fighting itself, we see not only that the Arab invaders were inferior in numbers to the Israelis, but also that they failed to coordinate their moves and to prepare themselves properly for war. They also underestimated the determination of their opponents, all of which explains their total failure to dislodge the Israelis.

Fighting

The invading Arab armies of Syria, Iraq, Lebanon, Egypt, Transjordan and a contingent force from Saudi Arabia had started from different directions, heading towards the heart of the Jewish state and the lands allotted to the Palestinians by the UN in November 1947. Had they coordinated their operations better and concentrated their offensive, the outcome of the struggle could have been different. In the event, however, there was coordination neither of operational plans nor of movement and concentration of forces, reflecting both the lack of common interest of the invaders and the divided purposes in the minds of the Arab leaders, who were suspicious of each other's intentions. All regarded Jordan's King Abdullah with intense suspicion, and rightly so, for the King was far more concerned to seize the land west of the river Jordan, which had been allotted to the Palestinians, than to destroy Israel. Abdullah even dispatched his Prime Minister to the British Foreign Minister to explain that his intention was only to take the West Bank to which Bevin replied: 'It seems the obvious thing to do. But don't go and invade the areas allotted to the Jews'. The British commander of the Arab Legion later confirmed that the Jordanian troops were indeed instructed 'To occupy the central and largest area of Palestine allotted to the Arabs by the 1947 partition'. This is a most significant statement, for it shows that rather than five Arab armies attacking the Israelis, there had been only four—Egypt, Syria, Iraq and Lebanon—and rather than intending to destroy the newly born state of Israel, the Arab Legion had crossed the Jordan river with the aim of partitioning the land by seizing the territory allotted by the UN to the Palestinians.

Lack of coordination among the invading forces is reflected in testimonies of Arab troops who took part in this war. Mohsein Abdel Khalek, a captain in the Egyptian army and later a prime minister of that country, recalls how

> The Jews were attacking us from the flank that the Iraqis were supposed to be protecting. We discovered that the Iraqi army had withdrawn, without even telling us. We had to shorten our lines, else the Egyptian army would have been destroyed. It was the turning point in the war.

Thus, although Israel suffered war on three fronts, she fought in effect separate enemies among whom there was little coordination. The invading armies also suffered from lack of preparation—they had simply neglected to prepare themselves for such an operation. The Egyptian army, for example, which was considered the most powerful of all Arab regular armies, had less than two weeks to prepare itself for the war and everything had to be improvised in haste. Abdel Ghani Kanout, an Egyptian officer during that war, recalls: 'We went to the front on horseback … we did not have enough food for the horses so we had to send them back during the war. So overnight my unit was transformed from a cavalry unit to an infantry unit'. Worse still, the invading Arab armies had a poor opinion of the Jews and underestimated their strength and determination. Adel Sabit, a cousin of King Farouk and the liaison between the King and the Arab League, recalls: 'We were complacently expecting the Jews to run away the moment they saw us … we thought it would be a pushover'. And Mourad Ghaleb, another Egyptian officer: 'We thought that the Jews were not courageous … not fighters'. And Lieutenant-General John Bagot Glubb, the British commander of the Arab Legion: '[The Arabs] believed themselves to be a great military people, and regarded the Jews as a nation of shopkeepers. … [The Arabs] assumed that they would find no difficulty in defeating the Jews'. The Israelis, however, determined to win the war—for they felt themselves with their backs to the wall—exploited the confusion on the Arab side, and after less than four weeks of fierce fighting they had managed to withstand the initial critical moments of the invasion.

While the fighting was still raging, important organizational and structural changes were taking place in the Israeli forces. Mobilization was completed, and on 31 May 1948 Prime and Defence Minister Ben Gurion published an Order of the Day officially establishing the Israeli Defence Force (IDF, or *Tzhal* in Hebrew) as the sole armed force of the state. This meant that the Irgun and the Lehi—the dissident underground groups led, respectively, by Menachem Begin and a committee of Lehi members, Nathan Yelin Mor, Yisrael Eldad and Yitzhak Shamir—had to disband and its men and weapons to be incorporated into the IDF, the nucleus of which was the Haganah. Disarming the dissidents and restoring law-abiding habits—taking the law into one's own hands had become a custom hallowed by patriotism throughout the decades of British rule in Palestine—was not an easy task for Ben Gurion's government. Indeed, the attempt to dissolve the dissident groups and divert their weapons to the IDF led to a severe deterioration of relations between these organizations and the government, to the point where a Jewish civil war seemed imminent. But this was avoided thanks to the willingness of Irgun's commander, Menachem Begin, to call off his troops and agree to their complete integration with the IDF; the Lehi would be disbanded in September 1948.

The first three crucial weeks of fierce fighting between Arabs and Israelis ended in a truce which was negotiated by the Swedish UN mediator Count Folke Bernadotte. The Arabs had objected to stopping the fighting on the grounds that the Israelis might exploit the respite to regroup, strengthen their defences and obtain weapons. The Israelis, on the other hand, welcomed the possibility of a truce so that they could snatch a breathing space and reorganize themselves. Fearing UN sanctions, the Arabs reluctantly accepted the truce which came into effect on 11 June 1948 at 10 a.m. Four days later on 15 June Ben Gurion recorded in his war diary the arrival of ten 75mm guns, ten light tanks with 37mm guns, 19 65mm guns and four 20mm automatic guns. During the truce a highly centralized command system was also set up, and from his office in Tel Aviv, Ben Gurion's orders passed through GHQ to the four regional commands—North, Centre, East and South—which were functioning as operational fronts.

As the time approached for the truce to expire, the Arab League Political Committee met in Cairo and decided, under pressure from the Egyptian Prime Minister Nokrashy Pasha, to renew the fighting with the Israelis. Efforts by the UN mediator Count Bernadotte to renew the truce failed, and he recorded in his diary: 'They [the Arabs] totally rejected my proposal to agree to prolong the truce'. Upon realizing that the truce would not be renewed, the Israelis took the initiative and struck on 9 July, two days before the ceasefire was due to expire. Now—as the Arabs rightly feared when they objected to having a truce—the Israelis were even better organized and equipped with new weapons.

Fighting—particularly concentrated in the area of Tel-Aviv—was raging for ten successive days during which the battle clearly went in Israel's favour. Led by a young military commander, Moshe Dayan, later a chief of staff of the Israeli army and defence minister, Israeli forces occupied the Arab towns of Lydda (11–12 July) and Ramleh (12 July)—both of which had been allotted to the Arabs by the UN Partition Plan—expelling their 50,000 inhabitants and thus making more space for settling new Jewish immigrants. This major expulsion of Palestinians was carried out with the tacit approval of Premier Ben Gurion, as is recorded by Yitzhak Rabin—then a military commander who took part in the operation—in a piece which was censored from his published memoirs:

> We walked outside [the headquarters], Ben Gurion accompanying us. Allon [the commander of central command] repeated his question: 'What is to be done with the [Arab] population [of Ramleh and Lydda]?' Ben Gurion waved his hand in a gesture which said: 'Drive them out!' Allon and I had a consultation. I agreed that it was essential to drive the inhabitants out. We took them on foot towards Bet Horon road. … The population did not leave willingly. There was no way of avoiding the use of force and warning shots in order to make the inhabitants march the ten to fifteen miles to the point where they met with the Arab Legion.

One of those expelled was George Habash — years later the leader of the Popular Front for the Liberation of Palestine (PFLP):

> They directed us to a specific road ... there were road blocks manned by Israeli soldiers every 100 metres to make sure that no one diverted. This went on until we arrived at the outskirts of Lydda (now Lod). There we found a large number of [Israeli] soldiers. They put us in rows and started searching each person, a body search … they were not just looking for weapons but also tried to take money.

The expelled Arabs were not allowed back to their homes, for what the Israelis wanted was to have the land without its inhabitants so they could establish an exclusive Jewish community. In a meeting of the Israeli cabinet on 16 June 1948, Prime Minister Ben Gurion told ministers: 'War is war. We did not start the war. They did. Do we have to allow the enemy back so they could make war against us? They lost and fled and I will oppose their return also after the war'.

On 19 July 1948, a second UN truce came into effect, but by this time the Israelis were well on the offensive, while the Arabs were exhausted and demoralized and had no alternative but to sue for a truce. Military commander Rabin recorded in his memoirs: '[The Arabs] did not incline to renew the war … we estimated that the Egyptians were not interested in renewing it'. But to build on their previous successes, the Israelis now wished to continue the struggle and to fight on, especially in the Negev, which could provide Israel with much space to accommodate Jewish immigrants.

On the night of 15 October, under the command of Yigal Allon, an Israeli army launched—in breach of the truce—'Operation Yoav' which was aimed at breaking into the Negev. Beersheva, the capital of the Negev, fell into their hands on 21 October, and two months later, on the night of 22–3 December, they attacked again; and later, on 5–10 March 1949, they struck again in the Negev, reached Eilat and occupied it. This was significant for, by seizing Eilat, Israel had driven a wedge between the east and the west Arab world, thus preventing Egypt from having a direct land bridge to Jordan. In the north of the country during 29–31 October 1948, four Israeli brigades had penetrated into Lebanon and moved up to the Litani river, destroying on its way the Arab Liberation Army, as well as Lebanese and Syrian units—this was 'Operation Hiram'.

All in all the war lasted one year, three months and ten days and cost Israel $500 million, compared with $300 million for the Arabs. There had been three separate rounds of fighting between December 1947 and March 1949, interrupted by two truces imposed by the UN. The Israeli forces occupied about 2,500 square miles of Arab land, which was added to the 5,600 square miles allocated to them by the UN in November 1947. According to the UN partition resolution, about 55 per cent of the land was to be given to the Jews and 45 per cent to the Arabs, but when the war ended Israel controlled almost 80 per cent of the land. Israel—odd thought it seems—had managed to keep these occupied territories without serious protest or international outcry—this was not to happen again in future wars. Egypt retained the Gaza Strip, and Jordan's King Abdullah the West Bank of the river Jordan, which he annexed to his kingdom in 1950. For all practical purposes Palestine was partitioned; not, however, as the UN had envisaged, between Jews and Arab–Palestinains, but rather between the Israelis and the Arab states which had, apparently, invaded the land in support of the Palestinians. These last were the big losers in this war, for they had become refugees in camps in Gaza, the West Bank, and other neighbouring Arab states.

When the war ended, Israelis and Arab representatives of the invading armies met on the island of Rhodes where, as Moshe Dayan of the Israeli delegation later recalled, 'Good food, spring weather, enchanting scenery ... hundreds of butterflies of all sizes and colours' lent a 'fairy tale air' to the tough negotiations on achieving armistice agreements between the opposing parties. The talks were tough because there was no clear victor in this war. Israel had withheld the Arab invasion and beaten Lebanon and Egypt, but both Syria and Jordan had done well. The Syrian army had managed to cross the international border—agreed between France and Britain in 1923—and occupy land which had been allotted by the UN to the Jewish state. The Arab Legion, as has been shown, seized the West Bank and kept East Jerusalem. Thus in contrast, for instance, to the situation after the First World War, where the

victors were able to impose 'peace' on Germany at Versailles, here there had been no clear winner, and reaching an agreement had to involve give-and-take between the parties.

Nonetheless, on 24 February 1949, Egypt was the first to sign an armistice agreement with Israel, and on 23 March 1949, after Israel agreed to pull out of 14 Lebanese villages it had occupied during the last stage of the war, Lebanon signed on the dotted line. On 3 April 1949, after four weeks of negotiations, Israel and Transjordan signed an agreement. Negotiations between Israel and Syria ended when, under international pressure, Syria was forced to agree to withdraw its forces from the land it had occupied west of the international border, which now became a demilitarized zone; Israeli and Syrian representatives signed on 20 July 1949. Iraq, however, refused to sign an armistice agreement with Israel, and its forces on the West Bank were replaced by those of the Transjordan Arab Legion, with some of the land under Iraqi occupation being transferred to Israeli hands.

The armistice agreements were seen as temporary settlements which would later be replaced by permanent peace agreements. But the conflict between Israel and the Arabs and Palestinians was bound to continue, for the great problem which had caused the war in the first place—the struggle between Jews and Arab Palestinians for mastery of the land—was still unresolved at the war's end. Worse still, the war had created a particular problem that was to fester and provoke unrest for more than 50 years: the Palestinian refugees.

The Impact of War on the Israelis

'The War of Independence' or 'The War of Liberation', as the Israelis refer to the 1947–9 war, was perceived by them as a life-or-death struggle. But with the benefit of hindsight we can state that if any danger of extinction did exist—when the country's fate was still in the balance—it was only during the very short period between 15 May 1948, the day the regular Arab armies invaded, and 11 June, the day the first UN truce came into effect. This three-week period was the time when there was still a clear Arab superiority in weaponry and firepower—though as we have shown, not in manpower—and when it was also unclear how the freshly recruited Israeli soldiers, many of whom were newly arrived immigrants, would perform. However, once the Israeli forces had checked the Arab onslaught, absorbed new weapons, increased their own weapons production, and trained immigrants and volunteers, the worst was over and Israeli superiority in manpower and weapons combined with short internal lines of communication and high motivation to defeat the Arabs.

That said, this bloodiest of all Israel's wars was to have a most profound and longstanding impact on the psyche of the people of Israel. A particularly significant effect of the war on the collective spirit of the Israelis concerned the fact that it was fought only a short time after the terrible tragedy that had befallen the Jewish people in Europe, with the massacre of 5.4 million of them at the hands of the Nazis. Moreover, in sharp contrast to most of Israel's future wars, the majority of the Israeli population was effectively on the frontline, facing war on its doorstep and exposed to bombardment by enemy aeroplanes; Tel Aviv was bombed 15 times, with several hundred civilian casualties.

The war cost Israel 5,682 dead, 20 per cent of them civilians and about 8 per cent women. This amounts to about 1 per cent of the total Jewish population in Palestine–Israel, and is indeed a high ratio if compared, for example, to the number of casualties in the First World War, where France lost 34 per thousand, Germany 30 per thousand, Austro–Hungary 10 per thousand, Britain and Italy 16 per thousand, and Russia 11 per thousand. Taking into consideration that the First World War was nearly three and a half times as long as the 1948 war—51 months compared with 15—then it can be said that the ratio of Israeli dead compared with the population was more than Germany's and closer to France's. There were 1,260 women widowed, 2,290 children orphaned and 3,000 soldiers wounded, of whom as many as 360 became mentally ill, which is as high as Britain during the First World War.

The loss of so many young men—the fittest of their society—was perhaps the main feature of this war, but ironically, it had very little long-term effect on the growth of the Israeli population. A war like this, in which many perish, often causes a reduction in the number of marriages and inevitably leads to a sharp dip in the birth rate. But in Israel, the destruction of an entire generation did not lead to what had happened in Europe after the First World War—a 'surplus of women', or rather a 'deficit of men'. The reason for the absence of this problem after the 1948 war was that the death of so many men was compensated for by the waves of new immigrants arriving in Israel, which in 1948 amounted to 118,000, in 1949 to 239,000 and in 1950–1 to 343,000. In crude terms, for every Israeli killed, several more Jews had come. And thus although in 1948, the most hard-fought year of the war, the number of marriages went down to 10.85 per thousand—compared with 12.98 per thousand in 1947—it went up (and again in spite of the sheer number of young men who died) in 1949 to 13.40 per thousand (even higher than in 1947!), and up again to 14.54 per thousand in 1950. The annual birth rate, which between 1947 and 1948 went down from 30.55 per thousand to 26.31 per thousand, had risen in 1949 to 29.95 per thousand and went up further in 1950. The young Israeli nation demonstrated its resilience, and a closer look shows that in all walks of life there had been little change, even during the most intensive months of the war. The number of deaths in the Jewish population (excluding deaths resulting directly from the war) was stable: 6.36 per thousand in 1946; 6.58 per thousand in 1947; 6.46 per thousand in 1948; this shows that in spite of the dreadful war the standards of medical care remained intact. Jerusalem was under siege, but there was no hunger, and social life continued to function more or less normally.

Nevertheless, the war provided succeeding generations of Israelis with plenty of material for mythology and legend with which to nourish their future. But not all that was told was strictly true. The Israeli soldier emerging from this war was portrayed as a fighter always playing a fair game—a sort of an English gentleman who even in the heat of the battle never stabs his enemy in the back. In reality, however, the Israeli soldiers, contrary to the myth, had behaved no differently from many other armies—they looted, expelled, massacred and raped. In Acre a group of Israeli soldiers raped an Arab woman, killed her father and injured her mother; and this, as we learn from the war diary of Prime Minister Ben Gurion, was not an isolated case.

The experience of the war stamped a sense of unity and common destiny on the psychic fibre of the Israelis, who had emerged from it with a new national consciousness, a unity of purpose overriding party conflict and internal feuds. What further cemented unity and emphasized the common destiny of the people of Israel was the huge effort which had followed the war to commemorate those who had died. The Ministry of Defence assembled details of those who perished and produced 4,520 obituaries, collected in a book entitled *Yizkor* ('Remembrance'). Another official memorial was *Gevilei Esh* ('Scrolls of Fire'), which included 455 items: poetry and stories written by those who had died. It was after this war that the term *Mishpachat Ha'schol*, meaning 'The Family of Breavement', was coined to emphasize that the entire nation was one family grieving its dead. The number of memorials erected to commemorate the dead had reached 1,321 by the mid-1950s; at least one out of every three dead soldiers was individually commemorated.

Gunther Rothenberg, in *The Anatomy of the Israeli Army*, summarizes the story of the 1948 war of independence in a fine passage: 'Both the realization that his life and that of his family literally were at stake … fuelled by the pronouncements of Arab politicians about a "war of extermination" stiffened the will [of Israelis] to fight'. And this will to fight was further strengthened by the dominant presence of the Holocaust generation. For as Bernard Lewis correctly observed in *Semites and Anti-Semites*:

> For most Jews, that genocide was the most shattering event in their history … the central experience of their personal lives, and their thoughts and actions are dominated by the knowledge that what has happened once can happen again, and by the determination that it must not.

Indeed, feeling that they were with their backs to the wall facing enemies determined to destroy them, and with the experiences of the Holocaust still fresh in mind, Israelis in the coming years would continue—as they had done during the first war with the Arabs—to rally behind the flag and its leadership, to take up arms when asked, and to fight with determination and desperation, believing themselves to be fighting for their very survival.

The Birth of the Palestinian Refugee Problem Revisited

By Benny Morris

Introduction

In 1988 Cambridge University Press published the first edition of this work, which sought to describe the birth of the Palestinian refugee problem that, along with the establishment of the State of Israel, was the major political consequence of the 1948 war. The study examined how and why, over November 1947–October 1950, an estimated 600,000 to 760,000 Palestinian Arabs departed their homes, moving to other parts of Palestine (i.e., the West Bank and Gaza Strip) or abroad, primarily to Jordan, Syria and Lebanon. There are today on the United Nations rolls close to four million Palestinian refugees (the Palestinian Authority says five million). About one third live in so-called refugee 'camps,' which in reality are concrete-structured slum neighbourhoods on the peripheries of cities (Nablus, Gaza, Ramallah, Beirut, Damascus, Amman, etc.).

Perhaps curiously, little serious historiography had been produced, both in the four decades before the publication of the original version of this book or since, on why and how these Palestinians became refugees. Soon after 1948, several chronicles were published by Palestinian exiles, including Arif al Arif's *Al–Nakba, 1947–1952 (The catastrophe, 1947–1952)* and

Haj Muhammad Nimr al Khatib's *Min Athar al Nakba* (following the catastrophe). About a decade after the event, Walid Khalidi, a Palestinian scholar, published two academic essays, 'The Fall of Haifa' and 'Why Did the Palestinians Leave?', that shed fresh light on aspects of the subject. The first major piece of research on the origin of the refugee problem, based mainly on open United Nations documentation and newspapers, was a doctoral study by an Israeli scholar, Rony Gabbay, *A Political Study of the Arab–Jewish Conflict: The Arab Refugee Problem (a Case Study)*, published in 1959. Two decades later, a Palestinian scholar, Nafez Nazzal, published *The Palestinian Exodus from Galilee 1948*, a path-breaking regional study but based almost completely on interviews in the Beirut-area refugee camps conducted in the early 1970s. A few years later, Israeli sociologist Baruch Kimmerling's published *Zionism and Territory: The Socio-Territorial Dimensions of Zionist Politics*, which contributed to understanding what had happened. During the decades after 1945, a number of Israelis and Palestinians produced serious essays and stories that illuminated the exodus, combining personal recollection and objective analysis—most prominently, Ephraim Kleiman's "Khirbet Khizah and Other Unpleasant Memories," S. Yizhar's "The Story of

Khirbet Khiza," and Elias Shoufani's "The Fall of a Village."

All had suffered from the relative paucity of archival materials. In recent years, a number of young Israeli scholars produced MA and PhD theses and articles on the exodus in particular areas of Palestine and Yoav Gelber published *Palestine 1948: War Escape and the Emergence of the Palestinian Refugee Problem*, which in part dealt with the subject under discussion.

The Palestinian refugee problem and its consequences have shaken the Middle East and acutely troubled the world for more than five decades. Terrorist or guerrilla incursions into Israel by these refugees have helped trigger at least three conventional Arab–Israeli wars, in 1956, 1967 and 1982, and Palestinian terrorism, especially attacks on airline passengers and aircraft hijackings during the 1970s and 1980s, have caused chaos and instability worldwide. More recently since 2000, Palestinian rebellion (the Second Intifada), largely powered by the refugee camps, has scuppered the Israeli–Arab peace process and destabilised the Middle East.

The centrality in the conflict of the refugee problem was convincingly demonstrated in the Israeli–Palestinian–American negotiations of July 2000–January 2001 (Camp David and after), when the refugees emerged as the single most important and intractable issue, with the Arabs insisting on their right to return to their lost homes and lands and Israel rejecting that demand, arguing that its implementation would bring about the Jewish State's demise.

The question of what in 1948 turned hundreds of thousand of Palestinians into refugees has been a fundamental propaganda issue between Israel and the Arab states ever since The general Arab claim that the Jews expelled Palestine's Arabs with predetermination and preplanning, as part of a systematic, grand political-military design, has served to underline the Arab portrayal of Israel as a vicious, immoral robber state. The official Israeli narrative, that the Palestinians fled voluntarily (meaning not as a result of Jewish compulsion) or that they were asked or ordered to do so by their leaders and by the leaders of the

Arab states, helped leave intact the new state's self-image as the haven of a much persecuted people, a body politic more just, moral and deserving of the West's sympathy and help than the surrounding sea of reactionary semi-feudal, dictatorial Arab societies.

The publication of the first edition of this book in 1988 provoked a great deal of anger and controversy. My conclusions appeared to satisfy no one (except the few who like their history complex and nuanced). The book tailed to endorse either the official Palestinian or Israeli narratives and. indeed, tended to undermine both. I was vilified alternatively as a "propagandist for the Palestine Liberation Organisation" and as a "sophisticated Zionist propagandist"; more rarely as merely a bad historian.

I embarked upon the research not out of ideological commitment or political interest. I simply wanted to know what happened. Often, at some point in their career, journalists get an urge to write "a book" and I had decided on a history of the Palmah, the strike force of the Haganah, the main militia of the Jewish community in Palestine, and, later, of the Israel Defence Forces (IDF) in 1948. I had always wanted to do military history and nothing serious had been done on this subject. In late 1982 I was privileged to be given access to the still classified papers of the Palmah's headquarters by the association of Palmah veterans, 'Dor Hapalmah'. But a few months later, perhaps sensing trouble, the veterans abruptly withdrew this access, and I realised I would be unable to write the planned history. Yet I had seen and read batches of documents, often marked 'top secret,' that shed light on the creation of the refugee problem. I felt that there might be a good story there. Serendipity would have it that my interest in the subject had been ignited a few weeks earlier when, as a reporter, I had been sent to cover the Israeli invasion and occupation of southern Lebanon. It was there, in the ruins of Rashidiye Refugee Camp, outside Tyre, in June 1982, that I first met and interviewed refugees, originally from al Bassa, in the Galilee.

Historians, like generals, need luck. 1982 proved to be a pivotal year in the Israeli archives.

The government began opening large amounts of documentation on 1948 at the Israel State Archive (ISA). Simultaneously, local and party political archives began organising and releasing materials. When I added these to the material I had seen in the Palmah Archive (PA), and material I was later to see in British and American archives and the United Nations Archive, I had a solid documentary basis on which to write the contemplated study.

But a major problem remained: Arab documentation. Unfortunately, the Palestinians failed to produce and preserve 'state papers' from 1947–1949, and the Arab states—all dictatorships of one sort or another (military juntas, absolute monarchies, etc.)—refused and continue to refuse access to their papers from the 1948 war, which they regarded and still regard as a humiliating catastrophe. In the course of the research and writing, I did my best to illuminate this 'area of darkness' by culling heavily from Jewish or Israeli intelligence material and British and American diplomatic dispatches dealing with the Arab world and, specifically, with the evolving refugee problem. The intelligence and diplomatic material went some way towards filling out the picture of what was happening in the field, in the towns and villages of Palestine, in 1948. They were less enlightening about policy-making in the Arab capitals and military headquarters. But given the disarray, confusion and general absence of clear policy in those capitals concerning the evolving problem over November 1947–June 1948, this paucity of information was not as important as at first seems. As it turned out, with regard to the refugees there was very little connection between what was happening in the field and what was discussed and, even, decided by the Arab leaders inside and outside Palestine.

I also made use of some Arab diaries, memoirs, and books based on interviews, to round out the picture. A number of Israeli orientalists (though, strangely enough, no Arabs) later took me and the book to task for failing to cull Arab memoirs more thoroughly But none was able to show how use of this ignored material would have substantially or even marginally altered or

enhanced the picture that I was able to draw on the basis of the Israeli and Western archives.

After careful thought, I refrained almost completely from using interviews, with Jews or Arabs, as sources of concrete information. My brief forays into interviewing had persuaded me of the undesirability of relying on human memories 40-50 years after the event to illuminate the past. The clincher came when I asked Yigael Yadin. the famous professor of archaeology who in 1945 had served as the Haganan\IDF head of operations (and often de facto chief of general staff), about the expulsion of the Arabs from the towns of Lydda and Ramle. What expulsion? he asked about what had been the biggest expulsion of the war. He did not deny that an expulsion had taken place: he merely said that he could not remember.

I believe in the value of documents. While contemporary documents may misinform, distort, omit or lie. they do so. in my experience, tar less than interviewees recalling highly controversial events some 40-50 years ago. My limited experience with such interviews revealed enormous gaps of memory and terrible distortion and selectivity born of adopted and rediscovered memories, ideological certainties and commitments and political agendas. I have found interviews occasionally of use in providing colour and in reconstructing a picture of prevailing conditions and, sometimes, feelings. But not in establishing facts.

The value of oral testimony about 1948, if anything, has diminished with the passage of the 20 years since I first researched the birth of the Palestinian refugee problem. Memories have further faded and acquired memories, ideological precepts, and political agendas have grown if anything more intractable; intifadas and counter-intifadas have done nothing tor the cause of salvaging historical truth.

But, thankfully, the liberalisation of Israeli archival practices has led during the past decade and a half to the release of an enormous amount of archival material that was closed when I wrote the first version of this study. More specifically, the ISA has declassified almost all the Israeli Cabinet protocols for 1948-1949, and the IDF

Archive (IDFA) and the Haganah Archive (HA), which were both completely closed to anyone not employed by the Defence Ministry, have opened their doors and declassified hundreds of thousands of documents, a true boon for historians. While the IDFA, HA and ISA continue to keep sealed a certain amount of sensitive documentation, enough has recently been declassified and made available—including much if not most of the IDF operational and intelligence material from 1948—to warrant a fresh look at what brought about the refugee problem.

I have no doubt that the eventual declassification of the material still untouched or newly sealed by the IDFA declassifiers, and the materials stored in the still-closed Israeli intelligence archives at Gelilof, will supply further revelations and new insights. But enough has been opened to give a good idea of what at least the materials in the IDFA and HA can reveal about what happened. The newly-opened documentation very substantially enriches the picture, and our understanding, of what happened in various parts of Palestine during 1948—what happened week by week and month by month in Jaffa and Haifa and Jerusalem, and in the countryside; and, on the other hand—and this is a paradoxical conclusion which won't sit well with either Israeli or Palestinian propagandists and 'black-or-white historians'—they substantially increase both Israeli and Palestinian responsibility for the creation of the refugee problem. For what the new documents reveal is that there were both far more expulsions and atrocities by Israeli troops than tabulated in this book's first edition and, at the same time, far more orders and advice to various communities by Arab officials and officers to quit their villages or to at least send away their women, old folk and children, substantially fuelling the exodus. I have added a great many passages based on this material to this edition.

The other major innovation here is the addition of a new chapter on Zionist thinking about 'Transfer'—i.e. the organised, compensated, mutually agreed shift, or one-sided expulsion, of Arab communities out of Palestine—a subject accorded only four pages in the 1988 edition.

Over the intervening years, I have concluded that pre-1948 'Transfer' thinking had a greater effect on what happened in 1948 than I had allowed for and, hence, deserved deeper treatment and more space. An additional reason for this deeper treatment was criticism of my original handling of the subject by both Arab and Israeli scholars: Arab historians like Nur Masalha argued that the pre-1948 Zionist 'Transfer' thinking was a pillar of Zionist ideology and was tantamount to a master plan—which was then systematically implemented in 1948. Masalha was eager to prove that Zionism was a robber ideology and Israel, an innately expansionist robber state. From the Israeli side, Shabtai Teveth, David Ben–Gurion s biographer, and Anita Shapira, an historian of Zionism, argued that the Zionist leadership—including Ben–Gurion—had never supported the idea of transfer and had never taken the idea seriously, and that, therefore, there was no connection between the occasional propagation of the idea in the 1930s and 1940s and what happened to the Palestinians in 1947-1949. Both were driven by a desire to clear Israel of the charge of premeditation in what befell Palestine's Arabs.

As readers of the new chapter will see, the evidence for pre-1948 Zionist support for Transfer really is unambiguous; but the connection between that support and what actually happened during the war is far more tenuous than Arab propagandists will allow.

I have also tried, in this revision, to integrate fresh insights and evidence published by a number of Israeli historians during the past 15 years. Unfortunately, no worthwhile historiography on 1948—comparable to that of, say, Urs Milstein and Yoav Gelber—has been produced by Palestinians, though I have occasionally referred to the essentially anthropological 'village series' produced by Bir Zeit University Press during the past two decades.

The Arab exodus from the areas that became the Jewish State at the end of the war occurred over the space of 20 months, from the end of November 1947 to July 1949, with several small appendages during the following months and years, it occurred in the course of a war marked by radically shifting circumstances and conditions in the various areas of the country. The exodus of the rich from Jaffa and Haifa over December 1947 to March 1945 was vastly different from the mass urban flight of April and early May; indeed, the multi-layered flight from Jaffa was markedly different from that from Haifa; and both had little in common with the expulsion and flight from Lydda and Ramle in July or from Eilabun Dawayima and Kafr Birim in October–November 1948. To describe and explain the exodus I have had to describe and explain events and circumstances during the war's various stages and in different areas. Where necessary, and this is truer of this edition than of its predecessor. I have gone into considerable detail. Fortunately or unfortunately, the devil is in the details and an historian cannot avoid the devil.

The study generally proceeds chronologically, from the United Nations General Assembly Partition Resolution (No. 181) of 29 November 1947 to the collapse of the Lausanne peace conference in September 1949. In examining the exodus, the study proceeds geographically, from area to area. But the chronological-geographical flow is interrupted by a number of horizontal chapters dealing with specific subjects ('Transfer' and 'Blocking the return of the refugees').

A major criticism of the 1988 edition, especially by Israelis, was that the book lacked 'context'—that I had not given sufficient weight to the Holocaust, which had ended less than three years before the events described, and, more importantly, to the events of the 1948 war itself, which had in many ways shaped and moulded Israeli decision-making and actions, at local and national levels. Some critics noted that I devoted little space to describing Arab massacres of Jews in the course of 1948 (there were three such massacres). My response to this is twofold. First, this is not a history of the 1948 war or a history of what the Arabs did to the Jews but a history of how and why the Palestinian refugee problem came about. In this context, what Jews did to Arabs, including massacres, played a role: what Arabs did to Jews was barely relevant. Second, where possible. I did try to describe the context

of hostilities—specific battles—that resulted in Palestinian flight or expulsion. In any event, in this current edition I have slightly expanded the discussion of the varying contexts in which the refugee problem was created.

In general, it cannot be stressed too strongly that, while this is not a military history, the events it describes, cumulatively amounting to the Palestinian Arab exodus, occurred in wartime and were a product, direct and indirect, of that war. a war that the Palestinians started. The threat of battle and battle itself were the immediate backdrop to the various components of the exodus.

Throughout, when examining what happened, the reader must also recall the wider context—the clash of arms between Palestine's warring Jewish and Arab militias and. later, the armies of the Arab states and Israel; the intention of the Palestinian leadership and irregulars and. later, of most of the Arab states leaders and armies in launching the hostilities in November–December 1947 and in invading Palestine in May 1948 to destroy the Jewish state and possibly the Yishuv (the Jewish community in Palestine) itself; the fears of the Yishuv that the Palestinians and the Arab states, if given the chance, intended to re-enact a Middle Eastern version of the Holocaust; and the extremely small dimensions, geographical and numerical, of the Yishuv (pop. 650,000) in comparison with the Palestinian Arabs (1.25 million) and the infinitely larger surrounding Arab hinterland, with tens of millions of people. At the same time, it is well to recall that, from late July 1948, it was clear to the Yishuv's leaders (and probably to most Arab leaders) that Israel had won its war for survival at least in the short term, and that the subsequent IDF offensives were geared to securing the political-military future of the Jewish state in what continued to be a highly hostile and uncomfortable geopolitical environment and to rounding out its borders.

I believe this revised edition adds substantially to our understanding of what happened in 1948 and of the deep roots of Israeli–Arab enmity in our time.

Conclusion

The first Arab–Israeli war, of 1948, was launched by the Palestinian Arabs, who rejected the UN partition resolution and embarked on hostilities aimed at preventing the birth of Israel. That war and not design, Jewish or Arab, gave birth to the Palestinian refugee problem.

But the displacement of Arabs from Palestine or from the areas of Palestine that would become the Jewish State was inherent in Zionist ideology and, in microcosm, in Zionist praxis from the start of the enterprise. The piecemeal eviction of tenant farmers, albeit in relatively small numbers, during the first five decades of Zionist land purchase and settlement naturally stemmed from, and in a sense hinted at, the underlying thrust of the ideology, which was to turn an Arab-populated land into a State with an overwhelming Jewish majority. And the Zionist leaders' thinking about, and periodic endorsement of, 'transfer' during those decades—voluntary and agreed, if possible, but coerced if not—readied hearts and minds for the denouement of 1948 and its immediate aftermath, in which some 700,000 Arabs were displaced from their homes (though the majority remained in Palestine).

But there was no pre-war Zionist plan to expel the Arabs from Palestine or the areas of the emergent Jewish State: and the Yishuv did not enter the war with a plan or policy of expulsion. Nor was the pre-war 'transfer' thinking ever translated, in the course of the war, into an agreed, systematic policy of expulsion. Hence, in the war's first four months, between the end of November 1947 and the end of March 1948 there were no preparations for mass expulsion and there were almost no cases of expulsion or the leveling of villages; hence, during the following ten months, Haganah and IDF units acted inconsistently, most units driving out Arab communities as a matter of course while others left (Muslim as well as Christian and Druse) villages and townspeople in place; and hence, at war's end, Israel emerged with a substantial Arab minority, of 150,000 (a minority that today numbers one million—and still constitutes (a restive and potentially explosive) one fifth of the State's population).

At the same time, largely as a result of Arab belligerence and the Yishuv's sense of siege, fragility and isolation, from early April 1948 on, 'transfer' was in the air and the departure of the Arabs was deeply desired on the local and national levels by the majority in the Yishuv, from Ben-Gurion down. And while this general will was never translated into systematic policy, a large number of Arabs were expelled, the frequency of expulsions and the expulsive resolve of the troops increasing following the pan-Arab invasion of mid-May 1948 that threatened the Yishuv with extinction. Yet, still, in July and again in October–November 1948, IDF troops continued to leave Arab communities in place; much depended on local circumstances and on the individual Israeli company, battalion and brigade commanders.

But if a measure of ambivalence and confusion attended Haganah IDF treatment of Arab communities during and immediately after conquest, there was nothing ambiguous about Israeli policy, from summer 1948, toward those who had been displaced and had become refugees and toward those who were yet to be displaced, in future operations: Generally applied with resolution and, often, with brutality, the policy was to prevent a refugee return at all costs. And if, somehow, refugees succeeded in infiltrating back, they were routinely rounded up and expelled (though tens of thousands of 'infiltrators' ultimately succeeded in resettling and becoming Israeli citizens). In this sense, it may fairly be said that all 700,000 or so who ended up as refugees were compulsorily displaced or 'expelled'.

Yet it is also worth remembering that a large proportion of those who became refugees fled their towns and villages not under direct Israeli threat or duress. Tens of thousands—mostly from well-to-do and elite families—left the towns in the war's early months because of the withdrawal of the British administration, the war-filled chaos that followed, and the prospect of Jewish rule. And, in the following months, hundreds of thousands fled not under Jewish orders or direct coercion though, to be sure, most sought to move out of harm's way as Zionist troops conquered town after town and district after district. And most probably believed that they would be returning home in a matter of months if not weeks, perhaps after the Arab armies had crushed Israel.

From the first, the AHC (Arab Higher Committee) and the local National Committees opposed the exodus, especially of army-aged males, and made efforts to block it. But they were inefficient and, sometimes, half-hearted. And, at the same time they actively promoted the depopulation of villages and towns. Many thousands of Arabs—women, children and old people, from villages around Jerusalem, the Coastal Plain and the Jezreel and Jordan valleys, and from various towns—left, well before battle was joined, as a result of advice and orders from local Arab commanders and officials, who feared for their safety and were concerned that their presence would hamper their militiamen in battle. Indeed, already months before the war the Arab states and the AHC had endorsed the removal of dependents from active and potential combat zones. And, starting in December 1947, Arab officers ordered the complete evacuation of specific villages in certain areas, lest their inhabitants 'treacherously' acquiesce in Israeli rule or hamper Arab military deployments. There can be no exaggerating the importance of these early, Arab-initiated evacuations in the demoralisation, and eventual exodus, of the remaining rural and urban populations.

The creation of the Palestinian refugee problem was almost inevitable, given the geographical intermixing of the Arab and Jewish populations in what is a minute country (10,000 sq. miles), the history of Arab–Jewish hostility over 1881–1947, the overwhelming opposition on both sides to a binational state, the outbreak and prolongation of the war for Israel's birth and survival, the major structural weaknesses of Palestinian Arab society, the depth of Arab animosity towards the Yishuv and Arab fears of falling under Jewish rule, and the Yishuv's fears of what would happen should the Arabs win or of what would befall a Jewish State born with a very large and hostile Arab minority.

The exodus unfolded in four or four and a half stages, closely linked to the development of the war itself. It began during December 1947–March 1948—the first stage—with the departure of many of the country's upper and middle class families, especially from Haifa and Jaffa, towns destined to be in, or at the mercy of, the Jewish state-to-be, and from neighbourhoods of Jewish west Jerusalem. Flight proved infectious. Household followed household, neighbour, neighbour, street, street and neighbourhood, neighbourhood (as, later, village was to follow neighbouring village, in domino clusters). The prosperous and educated feared death or injury in the ever-spreading hostilities, the anarchy that attended the gradual withdrawal of the British administration and security forces, the brigandage and intimidation of the Arab militias and irregulars and, more vaguely but generally, the unknown, probably dark future that awaited them under Jewish or, indeed, Husseini rule. Some of these considerations, as well as a variety of direct and indirect military pressures, also caused during these months the evacuation of most of the Arab rural communities in the predominantly Jewish Coastal Plain.

Most of the upper and middle class families, who moved from Jaffa, Haifa, Jerusalem, Ramle, Acre and Tiberias to Damascus, Nablus, Amman, Beirut, Gaza and Cairo, probably thought their exile would be temporary. They had the financial wherewithal to tide them over; many had wealthy relatives and accommodation outside the country. The urban masses and the *fellahin*, however, had nowhere to go, certainly not in comfort. For most of them, flight meant instant destitution; it was not a course readily adopted. But the daily spectacle of abandonment by their 'betters,' with its concomitant progressive closure of businesses, shops, schools, law offices and medical clinics, and abandonment of public service posts, led to a steady attrition of morale, a cumulative sapping of faith and trust in the world around them: Their leaders were going or had gone; the British were packing. They were being left 'alone' to face the Zionist enemy.

Daily, week in, week out, over December 1947, January, February and March 1948, there were clashes along the 'seams' between the two communities in the mixed towns, ambushes in the fields and on the roads, sniping, machine-gun fire, bomb attacks and occasional mortaring. Problems of movement and communication, unemployment and food distribution intensified, especially in the towns, as the hostilities drew out. There is probably no accounting for the mass exodus that followed without understanding the prevalence and depth of the general sense of collapse, of 'falling apart' and of a centre that 'cannot hold', that permeated Arab Palestine, especially the towns, by April 1948. In many places, it would take very little to nudge the masses to pack up and flee.

Come the Haganah [and Irgun and Stern Gang] offensives and counteroffensives of April–June, the cumulative effect of the fears, deprivations, abandonment and depredations of the previous months, in both towns and villages, overcame the natural, basic reluctance to abandon home and property and flee. As Palestinian military power was swiftly and dramatically crushed and the Haganah demonstrated almost unchallenged superiority in successive battles, Arab morale cracked, giving way to general, blind, panic or a 'psychosis of flight', as one IDF intelligence report put it. This was the second—and crucial—stage of the exodus. There is a clear, chronological, one-to-one correspondence between the Jewish offensives and the flight of the bulk of the population from each town and district attacked.

Often, the fall of villages harmed morale in neighbouring towns (vide the fall of Khirbet Nasir ad Din and Arab Tiberias). Similarly, the fall of the towns—Tiberias, Haifa, Jaffa, Beisan, Safad—and the flight of their population generated panic in the surrounding hinterlands: After Haifa, came flight from Balad al Sheikh and Hawassa; after Jaffa, Salama, Kheiriya and Yazur; after Safad, Dhahiriya Tahta, Sammu'i and Meirun. For decades the villagers had looked to the towns for leadership; now, they followed them into exile.

If Jewish attack directly and indirectly triggered most of the exodus up to June 1948, a small but significant proportion was due to direct expulsion orders and to psychological warfare ploys ('whispering propaganda') designed to intimidate people into flight. Several dozen villages were ordered or 'advised' by the Haganah to evacuate during April–June. The expulsions were usually from areas considered strategically vital and in conformity with Plan D, which called for clear main lines of communications and border areas. But, in general, Haganah and IDF commanders were not forced to confront the moral dilemma posed by expulsion; most Arabs fled before and during battle, before the Israeli troops reached their homes and before the Israeli commanders were forced to confront the dilemma.

Moreover, during April–July, Arab commanders and the AHC ordered the evacuation of several dozen villages as well as the removal of dependents from dozens more. The invading Arab armies also occasionally ordered whole villages to depart, so as not to be in their way.

In April–May, and indeed, again in October–November, the 'atrocity factor' played a major role in flight from certain areas. Villagers and townspeople, prompted by the fear that the Jews, if victorious, would do to them what, in the reverse circumstances, victorious Arab fighters would most probably have done (and, occasionally, did, as in the Etzion Bloc in May) to the Jews, took to their heels. The actual atrocities committed by the Jewish forces (primarily at Deir Yassin) reinforced such fears considerably, especially when magnified loudly and persistently in the Arab media for weeks thereafter. Apart from the 20-odd cases of massacre, Jewish troops often randomly killed individual prisoners of war, farm hands in the fields and the occasional villager who had stayed behind. Such actions could not but amplify flight. There were also several dozen cases of rape, a crime viewed with particular horror in Arab and Muslim societies. The fear of rape apparently figured large in the Arab imagination, and this may in part account for the dispatch of women and girls out of active or potential combat zones and, in some measure, for the headlong flight of villages and urban neighbourhoods from April on.

To what extent was the exodus up to June 1948 a product of Yishuv or Arab policy?

To be sure, the Haganah's adoption and implementation during December 1947–March 1948 of a retaliatory strategy against Arab militia bases—meaning villages and urban neighbourhoods—resulted in civilian flight. But the strategy, to judge from the documentation, was designed to punish, harm and deter militiamen, not to precipitate an exodus.

In early March, the prospect of pan-Arab invasion gave rise to Plan D. It accorded the Haganah brigade and battalion-level commanders *carte blanche* to completely clear vital areas of Arab population. Many villages served as bases for bands of irregulars; most had militias that periodically assisted the irregulars in attacks on settlements and convoys. During April–May, Haganah units, usually under orders from the General Staff, carried out elements of Plan D, each unit interpreting and implementing the plan as it saw fit in light of local circumstances. The Haganah offensives were in large measure responses to Arab attacks. In general, the Jewish commanders preferred to completely clear the vital roads and border areas of Arab communities—Allon in Eastern Galilee, Carmel around Haifa and in Western Galilee, Avidan in the south. Most villagers fled before or during the fighting. Those who stayed put were almost invariably expelled.

During April–June, neither the political nor military leaderships took a decision to expel 'the Arabs'. As far as the available evidence shows, the matter was never discussed in the supreme decision-making bodies. But it was understood by all concerned that, militarily, in the struggle to survive, the fewer Arabs remaining behind and along the front lines, the better and, politically, the fewer Arabs remaining in the Jewish State, the better. At each level of command and execution, Haganah officers, in those April–June days when the fate of the State hung in the balance, simply 'understood' what was required in order to survive. Even most Mapam officers—ideologically committed to coexistence with the Arabs—failed to 'adhere' to the party line: Conditions in the field, tactically and strategically, gave precedence to immediate survival-mindedness over the long-term desirability and ethos of coexistence.

The Arab leadership inside and outside Palestine probably helped precipitate flight in the sense that, while doctrinally opposed to the exodus, it was disunited and ineffectual, and had decided, from the start, on no fixed, uniform policy and gave the masses no consistent guidelines for behaviour, especially during the crucial month of April. The records are incomplete, but they show overwhelming confusion and disparate purpose, 'policy' and implementation changing from week to week and area to area. No guiding hand or central control is evident; no overarching 'policy' was manifest.

During the months before April 1948, especially in March, the flight of the middle and upper classes from the towns provoked condemnations from local NCs and the AHC (while NC members, and their families, were themselves busy fleeing iheir homes or already living abroad). But little was effectively done to prevent flight. And the surrounding Arab states did little, before late March, to block the entry or the evacuees into their territory The rich and middle class arrived in Nablus, Amman, Beirut, and Cairo in a trickle and were not needy; it seemed to be merely a repeat of the exodus of 1936–1939. No Arab country effectively closed its borders though, at the end of March. Syria and Lebanon severely curtailed the issue of entry visas. The Husseinis were probably happy that many Opposition-linked families were leaving Palestine. The AHC, almost all its members already dispersed abroad, issued no forceful, blanket, public condemnations of the exodus, though occasionally it implored army-aged males to stand, or return, and fight. At the local level, some NCs (in Haifa and Jerusalem, for example) and local commanders tried to stem the exodus, even setting up people's courts to try offenders and threatening confiscation of the departees property. However, enforcement seems to have been weak and haphazard; the measures proved largely unavailing. And bribes could overwhelm any regulation. Militiamen and irregulars often had an interest in encouraging flight—they needed the houses for quarters and there was money to be made out of it (departees paid to have their empty homes 'protected', abandoned houses were looted, and money was extorted from departees).

Regarding April–May and the start of the main stage of the exodus, I have found no evidence to show that the AHC or the Arab leaders outside Palestine issued blanket instructions, by radio or otherwise, to the inhabitants to flee. However, in certain areas, women, children and old people continued to be evacuated and specific villages were instructed to leave, lock, stock and barrel. Moreover, it appears that Husseini supporters in certain areas ordered or encouraged flight out or political calculation, believing that they were doing what the AHC would want them to do. Haifa affords illustration. While it is unlikely that Husseini or AHC members from outside Palestine instructed the Haifa Arab leadership on 22 April to opt for evacuation rather than surrender, local Husseini supporters, led by Sheikh Murad, certainly did. They were probably motivated by fear that staying in Haifa would be interpreted as acquiescence in Jewish rule and 'treachery' and by the calculation that Palestinian misery, born of the exodus, would increase the pressure on the Arab states to intervene. Local and AHC leaders believed that the evacuation was temporary and that a mass return would soon follow. In any event, the AHC encouraged the continuing exodus after it had begun. The case of Haifa in late April–early May is supremely instructive about the ambivalence of the national and local Palestinian leaderships toward the exodus.

The Arab states, apart from appealing to the British to halt the Haganah offensives and charging thai the Jews were expelling Palestine s Arabs, seem to have taken weeks to digest and understand what was happening. They did not appeal to the Palestinian masses to leave, but neither, in April, did they publicly enjoin the Palestinians to stay put. Perhaps the politicians in Damascus, Cairo and Amman, like Husseini, understood that they would need to justify their armed intervention—and the exodus, presented as a planned Zionist expulsion, afforded such justification.

But the dimensions and burden of the problem created by the exodus, falling necessarily and initially upon the shoulders of the host countries, quickly persuaded the Arab states—primarily Jordan—that it were best to halt the floodtide. The AHC, too, was apparently shocked by the ease and completeness of the exodus. Hence the spate of appeals to the Palestinians in early May by Jordan, the AHC and the ALA to stay put or, if already in exile, to return home. But, given the ongoing hostilities and the expectation of a dramatic increase in warfare along the fronts, the appeals had little effect: The refugees, who had just left active combat zones, were hardly minded to return to them, especially on the eve of the invasion. Besides, in most areas the Haganah physically barred a return. Later, after 15 May, the pan-Arab invasion and the widespread fighting made any thought of a return impracticable. At the same time, the invasion substantially increased the readiness of Haganah commanders to clear border areas of Arab communities. (And given the narrow, elongated shape of the new State, every area was in effect a border area.)

Already in April–May, on the local and national levels, the Yishuv's leaders began to contemplate the problem of a return: Should the refugees be allowed back? The approach of the First Truce in early June raised the problem as one of the major political and strategic issues facing the new State. The Arab states, on the local level on each front and in international forums, had begun pressing for Israel to allow back the refugees. And the UN Mediator, Bernadotte, had vigorously taken up the cause.

However, politically and militarily it was clear to most Israelis that a return would be disastrous. Militarily—and the war, all understood, was far from over—it would mean the introduction of a large, potential Fifth Column; politically, it would mean the reintroduction of a large, disruptive, Arab minority. The military commanders argued against a return; so did political common sense. Both were reinforced by strident anti-return lobbying by settlements around the country.

The mainstream national leaders, led by Ben-Gurion, had to confront the issue within two problematic political contexts—the international context of future Israeli–Arab relations,

Israeli–United Nations relations and Israeli–United States relations, and the local context of a coalition government, in which the Mapam ministers (and, less insistently, other ministers) advocated future Jewish–Arab coexistence and a return of 'peace-minded' refugees after the war. Hence the Cabinet consensus of June–August 1948 was that there would be no return during the war and that the matter could be reconsidered after the hostilities. This left Israel's diplomats with room for manoeuvre and was sufficiently flexible to allow Mapam to stay in the government, leaving national unity intact.

On the practical level, from spring 1948, a series of developments on the ground increasingly precluded any possibility of a refugee return. These were an admixture of incidental, 'natural' processes and steps specifically designed to assure the impossibility of a return, including the gradual destruction of the abandoned villages, the destruction or cultivation and long-term takeover of Arab fields, the establishment of new settlements on Arab lands and the settlement of Jewish immigrants in abandoned villages and urban neighbourhoods.

The months between the end of the First Truce (8 July) and the signing of the Israeli–Arab armistice agreements in spring-summer 1949 were characterised by short, sharp Israeli offensives interspersed with long periods of ceasefire. In these offensives, the IDF beat the Jordanian and Egyptian armies and the ALA in the Galilee, and conquered large parts of the territory earmarked by the UN for a Palestine Arab state. During and after these battles in July, October–November and December 1948–January 1949, something like 300,000 more Palestinians became refugees.

Again, there was no Cabinet or IDF General Staff-level decision to expel. Indeed, the July fighting (the 'Ten Days')—the third stage of the exodus—was preceded by an explicit IDF General Staff order to all units and corps to refrain from destruction of villages and expulsions without prior authorisation by the Defence Minister. The order was issued as a result of the cumulative political pressure during the summer by various softline ministers on Ben-Gurion and, perhaps,

was never intended to be taken too seriously. In any event, it was largely ignored.

But the overarching operational orders for operations Dekel, Dani, Yoav and Hiram—the main July–November offensives that resulted in Arab displacement—did not include expulsory clauses. However, from July onwards, there was a growing readiness in the IDF units to expel. This was at least partly due to the feeling, encouraged by the mass exodus from Jewish-held areas to date, that an almost completely Jewish State was a realistic possibility. There were also powerful vengeful urges at play—revenge for the Palestinian onslaught on the Yishuv during December 1947–March 1948, the pan-Arab invasion of May–June, and the massive Jewish losses. In short, the Palestinians were being punished for having forced upon the Yishuv the protracted, bitter war that had resulted in the death of one, and the maiming of two, in every 100 in the Jewish population. The Arabs had rejected partition and unleashed the dogs of war. In consequence, quite understandably, the Yishuv's leadership—left, centre and right—came to believe that leaving in place a large hostile Arab minority (or an Arab majority) inside the State would be suicidal. And driving out the Arabs, it emerged, was easy; generally they fled at the first whiff of grapeshot, their notables and commanders in the lead. Ben-Gurion said that this revealed a collective lack of backbone. In general, the advancing Haganah and IDF units were spared the need to face morally painful decisions to expel communities; to a large degree, Arab flight let the commanders off the moral hook, though, to be sure, many were subsequently, at the very least, troubled by the need to confront, and repel, would-be returnees.

The tendency of IDF units to expel civilians increased just as the pressures on the remaining Arabs by their leaders inside and outside Palestine to stay put grew and just as their motivation to stand fast increased. During the summer, the Arab governments intermittently tried to bar the entry of new refugees into their territory. The Palestinians were encouraged to stay in Palestine or to return to their homes. At the same time, those Palestinians still in their villages, hearing of the misery that was the lot of their exiled brethren and despairing of salvation and a reconquest of Palestine, generally preferred to stay put, despite the prospect of Israeli rule. After July, Arab resistance to flight was far greater than in the pre-July days. There was to be much less 'spontaneous' flight; villagers tended either to stay put or to leave under duress.

Ben-Gurion clearly wanted as few Arabs as possible in the Jewish State. From early on he hoped that they would flee. He hinted at this in February 1948 and said so explicitly in meetings in August, September and October. But no expulsion policy was ever enunciated and Ben-Gurion always refrained from issuing clear or written expulsion orders; he preferred that his generals 'understand' what he wanted. He probably wished to avoid going down in history as the 'great expeller' and he did not want his government to be blamed for a morally questionable policy. And he sought to preserve national unity in wartime.

But while there was no 'expulsion policy,' the July offensives were characterised by far more expulsions and, indeed, brutality than the first half of the war. Yet events varied from place to place. Ben-Gurion approved the largest expulsion of the war, from Lydda and Ramle, but, at the same time, IDF Northern Front, with Ben-Gurion's authorisation, left mostly-Christian Nazareth's population in place; the 'Christian factor' outgunned security and demographic concerns and was allowed to determine policy. And, in the centre of the country, three Arab villages sitting astride vital axes—Fureidis, Jisr az Zarka and Abu Ghosh—were allowed to stay, for economic and sentimental reasons.

Again, the IDF offensives in October–November—the fourth stage of the exodus—were marked by a measure of ambivalence in all that concerned the troops' treatment of overrun civilian populations. In the south ('Yoav'), where Allon was in command, almost no Arab civilians remained. Allon preferred Arab-clear rear areas and let his subordinates know what he wanted. In the north ('Hiram'), where Carmel was in charge, the picture was varied. Many Arabs declined to budge, contrary to Ben-Gurion's

expectations. This was partly due to the fact that before October, the villagers had hardly been touched by the war or its privations. Again, Carmel's hesitant, inexplicit expulsion orders, issued after the battles were over, contributed. So did the varied demographic make-up of the central-upper Galilee pocket. The IDF generally related far more benignly to Christians and Druse than to Muslims. Most Christian and Druse villagers stayed put and were allowed to do so. Many of the Muslim villagers fled; others were expelled. But many other Muslims—in Deir Hanna, 'Arraba, Sakhnin, Majd al Kurum and other villages—stayed put, and were allowed to stay. Much depended on specific local factors.

During the following months, with the Cabinet in Tel Aviv gradually persuaded by Arab rhetoric and actions that the conflict would remain a central feature of the Middle East for many years, the IDF was authorised to clear Arab communities from Israel's long, winding and highly penetrable borders to a depth of 5-15 kilometres. The result may be seen as 'stage four and a half' of the exodus. One of the aims was to prevent infiltration of refugees back to their homes. The IDF was also afraid of sabotage and spying. Early November saw a wave of IDF expulsions and transfers inland of villagers along the northern border. Some villagers, ordered out, were 'saved' by last-minute intervention by softline Israeli politicians. The following months and years saw other border areas cleared or partially cleared of Arab inhabitants.

In examining the causes of the Arab exodus from Palestine over 1947–1949, accurate quantification is impossible. I have tried to show that the exodus occurred in stages and that causation was multi-layered: A Haifa merchant did not leave only because of the weeks or months of sniping and bombings; or because business was getting bad; or because of intimidation and extortion by irregulars; or because he feared the collapse of law and order when the British left; or because he feared for his prospects and livelihood under Jewish rule. He left because of the accumulation of all these factors. And the mass of Haifaites who fled in his wake, at the end of April–early

May 1948, did not flee only as a result of the Arab militia collapse and Haganah conquest of 21–22 April. They fled because of the cumulative effect of the elite's departure, the snipings and bombings and material privations, unemplyment and chaos during the previous months; and because of their local leaders' instructions to leave, issued on 22 April; and because of the follow up orders by the AHC to continue departing; and because of IZL and Haganah activities and pressures during the days after the conquest; and because of the prospect of life under Jewish rule.

The situation was somewhat more clear-cut in the countryside. But there, too, multiple causation often applied. Take Qaluniya, near Jerusalem. There were months of hostilities in the area, intermittent shortages of supplies, severance of communications with Arab Jerusalem, lack of leadership or clear instructions about what to do or expect, lack of sustained help from outside, rumours of impending Jewish attack, Jewish attacks on neighbouring villages and reports of Jewish atrocities, and, finally, Jewish attack on Qaluniya itself (after most of the inhabitants had left). Again, evacuation was the end product of a cumulative process.

Even in the case of a Haganah or IDF expulsion order, the actual departure was often the result of a process rather than of that one act. Take Lydda, largely untouched by battle before July 1948. During the first months of the war, there was unemployment and skyrocketing prices, and the burden of armed irregulars. In April–May, thousands of refugees from Jaffa and its hinterland arrived in the town, camping out in courtyards and on the town's periphery. They brought demoralisation and sickness. Some wealthy families left. There were pinprick Haganah raids. There was uncertainty about Abdullah's commitment to the town's defence. In June, there was a feeling that Lydda's 'turn' was imminent. Then came the attack, with bombings and shelling, Arab Legion pullout, collapse of resistance, sniping, massacre—and expulsion orders. Lydda was evacuated.

What happened in Palestine/Israel over 1947–1949 was so complex and varied, the situation radically changing from date to date and place to place, that a single-cause explanation of the exodus from most sites is untenable. At most, one can say that certain causes were important in certain areas at certain times, with a general shift in the spring of 1948 from precedence of cumulative internal Arab factors—lack of leadership, economic problems, breakdown of law and order—to a primacy of external, compulsive causes: Haganah/IDF attacks and expulsions, fear of Jewish attacks and atrocities, lack of help from the Arab world and the AHC and a feeling of impotence and abandonment, and orders from Arab officials and commanders to leave. In general, throughout the war, the final and decisive precipitant to flight in most places was Haganah, IZL, LHI or IDF attack or the inhabitants' fear of imminent attack.

During the second half of 1948, international concern about the refugee problem mounted. Concern translated into pressure. This pressure, initiated by Bernadotte and the Arab states in the summer of 1948, increased as the months passed, as the number of refugees swelled, as their physical plight became more acute and as the discomfort of their Arab hosts grew. The problem moved to the forefront of every discussion of the Middle East crisis and the Arabs made their agreement to a settlement, nay, even to meaningful negotiations, with Israel contingent on a solution of the problem by repatriation.

From summer 1948, Bernadotte, and from the autumn, the United States, pressed Israel to agree to a substantial measure of repatriation as part ot a comprehensive solution to the refugee problem and the conflict. In December, the UN General Assembly endorsed the (peace-minded) refugees' 'right of return'. But, as the abandoned villages fell into decrepitude or were bulldozed or settled, and as more Jewish immigrants poured into the country and were accommodated in abandoned Arab houses, the physical possibility of substantial repatriation grew more remote. Allowing back Arab refugees, Israel argued, would commensurately reduce Israel's ability to absorb Jewish refugees from Europe and the Middle East. Time worked against repatriation. Bernadotte and the United States wanted Israel to make a 'gesture' in the coin of repatriation, to get peace negotiations off the ground.

In the spring of 1949, the thinking about a 'gesture' matured into an American demand that Israel agree to take back 250,000, with the remaining refugees to be resettled in the neighbouring countries. America threatened and cajoled, but never with sufficient force or conviction to persuade Tel Aviv to accede.

In the spring, in a final major effort, the United Nations and United States engineered the Lausanne Peace Conference. Weeks and months of haggling over agenda and secondary problems led nowhere. The Arabs made all progress contingent on Israeli agreement to mass repatriation. Under American pressure, Tel Aviv reluctantly agreed, in July, to take back 65,000-70,000 refugees (the '100,000 Offer') as part of a comprehensive peace settlement. But by summer 1949, public and party political opinion in Israel—in part, due to conditioning by the government—had so hardened against a return that even this minimal offer was greeted by a storm of public protest and howls within Mapai. In any case, the sincerity of the Israeli offer was never tested; the Arabs rejected it out of hand. The United States, too, regarded it as insufficient; as too little, too late.

The insufficiency of the '100,000 Offer', the Arab states' continuing rejectionism, their unwillingness to accept and concede defeat and their inability to publicly agree to absorb and resettle most of the refugees if Israel agreed to repatriate the rest, the Egyptian rejection of the 'Gaza Plan', and America's unwillingness or inability to apply persuasive pressure on Israel and the Arab states to compromise—all meant that the Arab–Israeli impasse would remain and that Palestine s displaced Arabs would remain refugees, to be utilised during the following years by the Arab states as a powerful political and propaganda tool against Israel. The memory or vicarious memory of 1948 and the subsequent decades of humiliation and deprivation in the refugee camps would ultimately turn generations of Palestinians into potential or active terrorists and the 'Palestinian problem' into one of the world's most intractable. And at the core of that problem remain the refugees.

The Jews of Arab Lands in Modern Times

By Norman Stillman

Rising Tensions in the Post War Era

At the end of World War II, a concatenation of forces and events was set in motion that in relatively short order would totally undermine the position of the Jewish communities in the Arab world and result in their almost total dissolution. Within a decade, the overall Jewish population in the Arab countries was reduced by half through emigration. In several countries the decline was far greater. By the end of 1953, Iraq, Yemen, and Libya had lost over 90 percent of their Jews, and Syria approximately 75 percent. Most of the Jews who remained in the Arab world were in the French-ruled Maghreb. It was not long, however, before the three countries of that region achieved their independence. Within little more than two decades after the end of World War II, most of the North African Jews were gone as well.

The postwar years witnessed a renewed surge of Arab and Jewish nationalism. The Jews in the various Arab countries found themselves buffeted by centrifugal and centripetal forces. If, as has already been noted, the Jews on the whole emerged from the war years with a heightened sense of self-awareness, so too did the Arabs. Arab national aspirations had been frustrated during the war. Even independent states like Egypt and Iraq had

found themselves unable to get free of British interference in their affairs. Overt political activities had been sharply curtailed everywhere in the Arab world during the war. By 1943, it was clear that the Allies would prevail and that any hopes placed on the Axis for deliverance from British and French colonialism or from Zionism were in vain. Those Arab leaders who had not made the mistake of hitching their fortunes to the losing side, as the Mufti and Rashīd ᶜĀlī had done, looked forward to a new geopolitical order that seemed sure to come. The tight political controls of the war years had led to a mounting of pent-up pressure among the Arab masses, whose rising expectations were coupled with deep dissatisfaction with the social and economic inequities that were heightened by the wartime experience. In Egypt, for example, the militant Muslim Brotherhood (al–Ikhwān al–Muslimūn) had become a great popular force by the end of the war, with a following of about 1 million members and sympathizers. Popular animus was directed against the wealthy ruling class, foreigners, and the non-Muslim minorities that were closely associated with the foreigners in the popular mind. Even more ominous for the Jews was the fact that the Palestine question, which had been temporarily dormant during most of the war years, returned to the forefront among the issues of primary Arab political concern.

Anti-Zionist agitation, with its corollary of anti-Jewish incitement, began to increase markedly after 1943, at the very time when Zionism was enjoying a resurgence among Jews throughout the Arab world and when Zionists in the West, especially in the United States, were pressing for unlimited immigration of Jewish refugees into Palestine when the war ended. The economic grievances of the masses, their xenophobia, and their anti-Zionism came to a head in November 1945 in a series of anti-Jewish riots that broke out in several Arab countries.

The first of these riots occurred in Egypt. Anti-Zionist demonstrations had been called for by such groups as Misr al–Fatāt, the Muslim Brotherhood, and the Young Men's Muslim Association. A few days before the demonstrations were to take place, the British assistant commandant of the Cairo city police noted an atmosphere of "considerable ill-feeling in Cairo against Jews." However, he believed that with proper security precautions, there was no need for undue concern. Events proved otherwise, however. Mass demonstrations took place on November 2 (Balfour Declaration Day) in Cairo and Alexandria, with smaller ones in Port Said, Mansura, and Tanta. In Cairo, mobs pillaged Jewish businesses in the main part of town, in the Muski, and in the Jewish Quarter. The Ashkenazi synagogue was ransacked and burned. As often has been the case in the history of the Islamic world, violence initially directed against one non-Muslim minority easily spilled over into a generalized anti-dhimmī violence.

Coptic, Greek Orthodox, and Catholic institutions were also attacked, as well as shops owned by foreigners. Some 500 businesses were looted, 109 of these belonging to Jews. Damage was estimated to be in excess of 1 million Egyptian pounds. Injuries numbered in the hundreds, but amazingly only one person, a policeman, was killed. In Alexandria, the rioting claimed six lives, five of them Jewish, and another 150 persons were injured. Some disturbances continued on the following day. The king and some prominent public figures expressed their regrets at what had happened, and the government offered to bear the expenses for rebuilding the ruined synagogue. At the same time, however, there were calls from the Islamic religious establishment for Chief Rabbi Hayyim Nahum to issue a public statement repudiating Zionism. The chief rabbi responded with a letter to Prime Minister al–Nuqrashī Pasha, in which he included an earlier note that he had sent to the World Jewish Congress declaring the loyalty of the Jewish community to Egypt, observing the need for finding some less confined refuge than Palestine for the survivors of the Holocaust, and expressing the hope that Jews and Arabs would cooperate in solving the problem "in an atmosphere of complete accord."

Neither the protestations of loyalty by the chief rabbi nor the expressions of regret and sympathy by government officials could restore Egyptian Jewry's sense of security, since the general atmosphere of hostility continued unchanged. As Thomas Mayer has rightly pointed out, "the critics of the riots did nothing to prevent the distribution of anti-Jewish propaganda in Egypt," and "the Egyptian Jews continued to be harassed by Pan–Arab and Islamic societies, as well as by Government officials, and pressed to make anti-Zionist declarations."

Far more devastating anti-Jewish violence erupted in Libya only one day after the Egyptian rioting had quieted down. Early Sunday evening, November 4, attacks against Jews broke out in various parts of Tripoli after a minor altercation between a gang of Arab toughs and some Jews near the electric power station outside the Jewish Quarter. The riot took on major proportions on the following day when mobs numbering in the thousands poured into the Jewish Quarter and the Sūq al–Turk (the bazaar where many Jewish shops were located) and went on a rampage of looting, beating, and killing. According to one confidential report, weapons were distributed to the rioters at certain command centers, one of which was the shop of Ahmad Krawī, a leading Arab merchant.

Unlike the earlier disturbances in Egypt, the Tripolitanian incidents had no overt political coloring whatsoever, although some of the provocateurs may well have had political motives. Again unlike in Egypt, in Libya only Jews and

Jewish property were attacked. The rioters had no difficulty in distinguishing Jewish homes and businesses because prior to the attack, doors had been marked with chalk in Arabic indicating "Jew," "Italian," or "Arab." Mob passions reached a fever pitch when a rumor spread that the Chief Qadl of Tripoli had been murdered by Jews and the SharFa Court burned. The terror then spread to the nearby towns of Amrus, Tagiura, Zawia, Zanzur, and Qusabat. Only in the Berber area of Yafran were there no attacks against Jews.

Throughout the first three days of the riots, the civil police stood by for the most part and did nothing, except in some cases relieving individual looters of their booty. Despite repeated pleas by leaders of the Jewish community, soldiers in the Palestine units of the British army, and American Jewish servicemen stationed on the outskirts of Tripoli, the British Military Authority waited inexplicably until Tuesday afternoon before sending in troops with orders to shoot rioters and impose a curfew in Tripoli.

When the pogroms—for that is what the riots essentially were—were over, 130 Jews were dead, including thirty-six children. Some entire families were wiped out. Hundreds were injured, and approximately 4,000 people were left homeless. An additional 4,200 were reduced to poverty. There were many instances of rape, especially in the provincial town of Qusabat, where many individuals embraced Islam to save themselves. Nine synagogues—five in Tripoli, four in the provincial towns—had been desecrated and destroyed. More than 1,000 residential buildings and businesses had been plundered in Tripoli alone. Damage claims totaled more than one quarter of a billion lire (over half a million pounds sterling).

Many Libyan Jews, Jewish servicemen in the American and British armies, Italian colonists, and even some Arab notables believed that the British themselves were behind the pogroms. Renzo de Felice, after carefully weighing the known facts and allegations, comes to the highly persuasive conclusion that one cannot seriously believe the British organized the pogroms, but he also rejects the notion that the. inaction of the British authorities during the early days of the

rioting could be attributed merely to incompetence. Rather, he concludes:

> One can only think that the BMA's [British Military Administration's conduct was strongly affected by a *political* concern not to adopt too harsh a position and not to annoy the Arab masses or alienate them, thereby playing into the hands of the nationalists. ... This political concern is indirectly confirmed by the fact that, even though the British military authorities did not have large forces available and had to bring the whole region under control, they were careful not to deploy the soldiers of the Palestinian Brigade in restoring order, keeping them closely consigned to barracks.

Arab–Jewish tensions reached new heights in the fall of 1947 as the United Nations debated the future of Palestine. Dr. Muhammad Husayn Haykal, the chairman of the Egyptian delegation, warned the Palestine Committee of the General Assembly that "the lives of 1,000,000 Jews in Moslem countries would be jeopardized by partition." Jamāl al–Husaynī, representing the Palestinian Arab Higher Committee, was even blunter:

> It must be remembered, by the way, that there are as many Jews in the Arab world as there are in Palestine whose positions, under such conditions, will become very precarious, even though the Arab states may do their best to save their skins. Governments, in general, have always been unable to prevent mob excitement and violence.

Such threats were not idle. In the wake of the General Assembly vote in favor of the partition of Palestine on November 29, 1949, a new wave of anti-Jewish violence spread through the Middle Eastern Arab countries, where demonstrations against the United Nations vote were called for

December 2–5. As in the 1945 disturbances, mobs in Cairo turned upon Jewish, minority, and foreign businesses and other institutions. This time, however, the police prevented the attackers from storming the Jewish Quarter, and on December 5, the government clamped down by declaring a state of emergency and banning all demonstrations.

In Bahrain, the first two days of demonstrations were marked only by some minor stone throwing at individual members of the small Jewish community. Beginning on December 5, however, crowds in al–Manama, the capital, began looting Jewish homes and shops, destroyed the synagogue, and beat up any Jews they could lay their hands upon. Miraculously, only one elderly woman was killed.

– The rioting in Aleppo, Syria, took a far greater toll. The venerable Jewish community was physically devastated. At least 150 homes, 50 shops, all of the community's 18 synagogues, 5 schools, its orphanage, and a youth club were destroyed. Property damage was estimated at $2.5 million. Many people were reported killed, but no figures have ever been advanced. More than half of the city's 10,000 Jews fled across the borders into Turkey, Lebanon, and Palestine.

Similar devastation engulfed the Jewish community in the British-controlled protectorate of Aden. As in the Tripolitanian pogroms of 1945, the police, composed mainly of natives, proved unable to contain the rioting and in some cases took part in it themselves. Troops had to be called in to quell the violence. By the time order was finally restored on December 4, 82 Jews had been killed and a similar number injured. Of the 170 Jewish-owned shops in the Crater (the main town of Aden), 106 were totally destroyed and 8 more partially sacked. Hundreds of houses and all of the Jewish communal institutions, including the synagogue and the two schools, were burned to the ground. Many people had lost everything. Four thousand Jews had to be fed by the authorities. Rioters also wrought havoc upon the small Jewish communities in the surrounding towns and in the Hashed camp housing Yemenite Jewish refugees. The Adeni Jewish community claimed

that the damage it had suffered exceeded over 1 million pounds.

The wave of violence that followed the United Nations vote for the partition of Palestine had a demoralizing effect upon the Jews living in the eastern Arab countries. Expressions of sympathy from political leaders and reassurances that they had nothing to fear as long as they were not associated with Zionism offered little solace. The press, students, members of the political opposition, and religious leaders rarely maintained the fine distinction between Jews and Zionists. Calls for *jihad,* or holy war, heightened interreligious tensions. Prominent Jews were increasingly called upon to make declarations of solidarity with the Palestinian Arab cause, not to mention generous contributions.

The Jews of the French-ruled Maghreb had been spared the fury of the latest storm. There certainly was tension between Arabs and Jews over the Palestine issue, but for the most part it remained beneath the surface at this time. This was due to a number of factors. The French still exercised tight, even repressive, control over the population. Palestine was geographically far removed and, no less important, was not the central issue of North African nationalist concern. Maghrebi Arab leaders consistently eschewed the kind of anti-Jewish rhetoric that had become commonplace in Middle Eastern political discourse. As André Chouraqui has noted, there was "a tacit understanding" between the Muslim and Jewish communities in North Africa "that the conflicts which plagued their coreligionists in the Holy Land were to be avoided." Thus Maghrebi Jewry, although anxious about the future, maintained a much higher morale than its brethren in the East during this period.

The Irrevocable Split

By the time Israel was established on May 15, 1948, and war was declared by the members of the Arab League against the newborn state, the very foundations of the Jewish communities in the Arab world had already been severely weakened. The waves of anti-Jewish violence that had struck almost every major Jewish community from Libya to Iraq, beginning with the Baghdadi Farhud of 1941 and culminating in the widespread rioting of 1945 and 1947, had eroded the Jews' confidence in these countries. The Palestine issue was, of course, a major contributing factor in all of this, but it was by no means the only one. Indeed, it was more of a catalyst precipitating and sharpening other problematic issues.

More and more, Jews were finding themselves in the position of "odd man out" as the societies around them cultivated nationalisms with a strong ethnic and religious component (namely, Arab and Islamic), as well as what Bernard Lewis has characterized as "a new militancy that [left] no place for those who deviate from the rule." This was as true in Iraq, where most of the Jews had roots going back two and a half millennia, as it was in Egypt, where most of them were of relatively recent foreign origin. Already in the late 1930s, Jewish civil servants were being weeded out of the Iraqi bureaucracy, utilities, and public corporations to make room for "real Iraqis." Throughout the late 1930s and 1940s, Egypt enacted a series of legislative measures aimed at Egyptianizing the economy. The Company Law of 1947, for example, specified that at least 75 percent of the employees, 90 percent of the laborers, and 51 percent of the capital in companies incorporated in the country had to be Egyptian. Since the majority of Jews in Egypt either held foreign nationalities or were technically stateless persons, they could not help but be adversely affected by the Company Law. The president of Cairo's Jewish community estimated privately that the Company Law jeopardized the jobs of perhaps as many as 50,000 Jews. Already in 1945, Minister of Commerce and Industry Hafnl Mahmud was differentiating between "nominal Egyptians" and "real Egyptians" with regard to employment.

The first Arab–Israeli war greatly accelerated the process whereby the Jewish minorities in the Arab countries were being alienated and isolated from the larger societies in which they lived. Compared with the violent mob reactions against them following the United Nations partition vote in 1947, the overall response at the outbreak of the war in May 1948 was relatively subdued. This was due perhaps to the universal popular expectation of a speedy and decisive Arab victory that was fostered by the unrealistic rhetoric of their leaders and the grossly exaggerated reports of early successes in their media. "The Zionist fortress will fall after the first attack," predicted King 'Abd Allāh of Transjordan, and 'Azzām Pasha, the secretary of the Arab League, declared, "[T]his will be a war of extermination and a momentous massacre which will be spoken of like the Mongolian massacres and the crusades." Egypt's leading newspaper *al–Ahrām* observed, "The history of the Egyptian army is one long list of victories." Much of the attention and the passion of the Arab masses was directed almost exclusively toward Palestine and temporarily, at least, away from the local Jewish communities and, it might be added, from the serious internal problems plaguing their individual countries. The governments of Egypt, Iraq, Lebanon, and Syria also took concerted steps to prevent mob violence from erupting during the early days of the war by imposing a state of emergency and martial law. In Morocco, the popular Sultan Muhammad V, addressing his Muslim and Jewish subjects as "all of you, Moroccans, without exception," publicly appealed for calm and the preservation of order. Egypt's King Faruq, meeting with a delegation of Jewish leaders on the eve of the war, assured them of his protection.

While protected from the danger of mob actions, the Jewish communities in the Arab League states found themselves subject to a variety of harsh and intimidating administrative impositions. Known or suspected Zionist activists were arrested everywhere. In Egypt and Iraq, the governments took advantage of the state of emergency to round up communists, which in both countries included a considerable number of Jews. In fact, as far as Egyptian Premier al–Nuqrashī Pasha was concerned, "all Jews were potential Zionists," "all Zionists were Communists," and all communist activities "were directed exclusively by Jews." Some of Iraq's veteran politicians, like Nūrī al-Saʿīd, were of a similar mind. In all, between

600 and 1,000 Jews in Egypt and around 310 Jews (nowhere near the figure of 2,000 charged by Israel at the time) in Iraq were taken into custody during the early days of the war. Most were held in prisons and internment camps for weeks. The treatment meted out to the internees was generally far better in Egypt than in Iraq. Many more non-Jews were also arrested at this time since the two governments took advantage of the imposition of martial law to suppress internal opposition. In addition to the communists, for example, many Muslim Brethren were rounded up in Egypt. The property of those arrested, both Jewish and non-Jewish, was placed under special stewardship during their incarceration. Most of the Egyptian Jews who were interned were eventually released and their property restored. In Iraq, most of the Jews arrested were brought before courts-martial and received fines, prison sentences of varying lengths, or both. The only individual to receive the death penalty was Shafiq 'Adas, Iraq's richest Jew, who was condemned on the unlikely charge of having supplied scrap metal to the Zionist state. (Even more farfetched, he was accused of having communist ties.)

'Adas was fined 5 million pounds and publicly hanged in front of his palatial home in Basra on September 23, 1948.

It was not until several weeks after the war began, when it was becoming clear that the Arab offensive in Palestine was encountering serious difficulties, that incidents of anti-Jewish violence began to break out in the Arab countries. The first such incidents took place on June 7 and 8 in the northeastern Moroccan towns of Oujda and Jerada. Forty-two Jews were killed and approximately 150 injured, many of them seriously. Scores of homes and shops were sacked.

On June 12, the day after the first truce was declared between the Israeli and Arab forces in Palestine, mobs attacked the Jewish Quarter in Tripoli, Libya. (Thousands of Moroccan and Tunisian volunteers had been streaming through the city on their way east to join the Arab armies fighting in Palestine.) However, Jewish self-defense units, which had been organized here as in other cities that had suffered pogroms in recent years, repelled the attackers with stones, handguns, grenades, and Molotov cocktails, inflicting heavy casualties. The rioters then turned upon undefended neighborhoods outside the Hara. Only thirteen or fourteen Jews were killed and twenty-two seriously injured, but property damage was very high. Approximately 300 families were left destitute. There were also attacks against Jews in the surrounding countryside and in Benghazi.

Following the Israeli air force bombing raids over Cairo and Alexandria, which had resulted in heavy civilian casualties on July 15, and the declaration of a second truce in Palestine on July 18, anti-Jewish and anti-foreign agitation in the mosques and in the press reached a fever pitch. The atmosphere was even more highly charged by the coincidence of Ramadan, the holy month of fasting. There were sporadic assaults against Jews and foreigners in the streets in the days immediately following the air raids.

A large explosion severely damaged the Circurel and Oreco department stores in the heart of Cairo's modern business district on July 19. Twenty minutes after the blast, an air raid alert was sounded. The explosion was officially blamed on "an aerial torpedo from a Jewish aircraft," although a truce was in effect, no plane had been sighted, and a former under secretary of the interior, Hasan Rifa'at Pasha, who was one of Circurel's Muslim board members, affirmed that the explosion "could not possibly have been caused by a bomb from the air." The attack on Circurel's was the signal for what British Ambassador Campbell described as "an orgy of looting" and stepped-up assaults upon Jews and foreigners.

Over the next three months, bombs destroyed Jewish-owned movie theaters and large retail businesses, including the Adès, Gattegno, and Benzion establishments. In all, attacks on Jews claimed approximately fifty lives during the summer of 1948, with tremendous property losses. The injured homeless, and unemployed numbered in the hundreds. Public protestations of loyalty and condemnations of Zionism by Jewish notables and large contributions totaling nearly a quarter of a million dollars to the Welfare Fund for Egyptian troops fighting in Palestine did not bring security. A series of bombs in the Jewish Quarter killed 29 people on September 22, and fifty Jews were arrested on trumped-up charges. Morale in the community reached a particularly low ebb during this period, and according to a confidential American Jewish Committee report, there was a marked increase in conversions to Islam and Christianity.

The Israeli victory and the Arab defeat in Palestine had enormous political consequences throughout the Middle East in both the short and the long run. No less important were the psychological consequences for the minority Jewish communities and for the Muslim majorities in the various Arab countries. But just what were these consequences was by no means immediately clear as the cease-fire agreements were being signed by the belligerents in the spring and summer of 1949.

Despite their feelings of insecurity, which had existed long before the first Arab–Israeli war, many Jews of the upper classes and some of the middle classes in several Arab countries still hoped that they could make the best of the new situation and return to some semblance of life as usual. In Egypt, Iraq, and even Syria for a brief time during the short-lived regime of Husnī al–Zaʿīm, these hopes were fostered by the easing of some restrictions imposed during the war and the release of many individuals who had been imprisoned on flimsy charges. In Egypt, hope was reinforced by the restoration of much of the property that had been placed under government stewardship. Furthermore, it was clear that much of the violence against Jews had not been government sponsored, although the authorities were certainly responsible for allowing the development of (and in part fostering) an atmosphere conducive to such violence and for taking inadequate steps to protect their Jewish minorities. For their part, government officials saw that, once unleashed, popular violence could get dangerously out of hand for all concerned, as the assassination of Egypt's Prime Minister al–Nuqrashl Pasha by the Muslim Brotherhood proved in December 1948. (This was only the first

in a long series of political assassinations in the Arab world that may be viewed at least in part as a consequence of the Arab–Israeli war.)

The Mass Exodus Begins

The momentary optimism quickly evaporated in Syria and Iraq. In Libya, there had been none at all. Libyan Jewry had been thoroughy demoralized by the pogroms and saw no hope for the future in the country. Some members of the community, in an impassioned letter to the United Nations Security Council, described their collective plight as "unbearable materially, economically, as well as morally" and asked to "be free of this hell." According to the same letter, 60 percent of the community was living on welfare provided by Jewish philanthropy from abroad. The Libyan Jews detested both the British and the Arabs and were totally unwilling to remain in an independent Libya under Arab rule. By 1949, many Libyan Jews were becoming desperate, feeling trapped by the British Military Administration, which would not allow them to emigrate either to Israel, where the vast majority desired to go, or to Italy, the refuge of choice for some of the more assimilated members of the elite. As in other Arab countries during this period, a considerable number of individuals resorted to clandestine emigration, much of it organized by emissaries from Israel. During the second half of 1948, 1,041 young people departed in this way.

When the British Military Administration lifted travel restrictions on February 2, 1949, thousands of Jews lined up for exit permits. In Tripoli alone, over 8,000 were issued within a few days. Within a few months, approximately 2,000 individuals had left the country on their own— most of them for Italy, and from there, Israel. The rest of the community waited impatiently to be evacuated in a mass ʿaliya. Between April 1949 and December 1951, over 31,000 of a total of 35,000 to 36,000 Jews left the country on Israeli ships, the last two of which sailed out of Tripoli harbor shortly after Libya gained its independence at the end of 1951.

Practically the entire Jewish population of Yemen had also been gripped with a messianic enthusiasm after the establishment of the State of Israel. Already during the preceding five years, several thousand Yemenite Jews had made their way to Palestine individually and in small groups. The great majority came through the British protectorate of Aden, where most ended up for shorter or longer periods in refugee camps. The largest camp at Hashid, known in Hebrew as Mahane Ge'ula (Camp Redemption), was maintained by the American Joint Distribution Committee and the Jewish Agency. By the early autumn of 1948, the camp's population had swollen to nearly 7,000, far beyond its intended capacity.

The British authorities in Aden, as elsewhere in the Middle East, were generally unsympathetic to Zionism and to 'aliya. They also feared a repetition of the disorders that had rocked the protectorate a year earlier and tried to stanch the flow emanating from Yemen and to repatriate the refugees. However, the lobbying efforts of Jewish organizations in London and the sudden, unprecedented, and completely inexplicable decision of the new Zaydī Imam Ahmad to allow his Jewish subjects to leave Yemen unimpeded set in motion a mass migration from every corner of the country into Aden via the neighboring sultanates.

The Yemenite refugees poured into Aden at a rate and in numbers that were beyond anything that had been expected and overwhelmed the camp facilities, and relief efforts. Many refugees arrived undernourished and in frightful physical condition after having trekked hundreds of miles over rough terrain, in many cases entirely on foot. Several thousand individuals were stricken with malaria, and 70 to 80 percent of all refugees were suffering from eye diseases. Approximately 600 people died in the camps, nearly half of these during September and October 1949, when the influx of refugees was at its height. Fearing the outbreak of an epidemic, the British authorities in Aden closed the border for five weeks during this peak period, causing near starvation among the hapless refugees stranded on the other side. The situation demanded that the facilities be expanded and the refugees transferred as quickly

as possible. Between June 1949 and September 1950, approximately 44,000 Yemenite Jews were brought from Aden to Israel in a dramatic airlift, dubbed Operation On Wings of Eagles (see Exod. 19:4), later renamed Operation Magic Carpet. The airlift was carried out by a specially formed American charter airline, the Near East Air Transport Company, in 430 flights, with at times as many as eleven planes flying around the clock during the height of the exodus in the fall of 1949.

Jews continued to trickle out of Yemen during the early 1950s. Many of these last emigrants were craftsmen who had been required by the Imam or by local tribal shaykhs to remain behind until they had taught their skills to Arabs who could replace them. (The Jews had traditionally been the principal artisans in the country.) By 1955, the exodus had ended. Less than 1,000 Jews were estimated to have remained behind, mainly in the remoter mountain regions of northern Yemen.

The Jews of Iraq were considerably more divided as to where their future lay after the birth of Israel than either their Libyan or Yemenite coreligionists. Many members, though by no means all, of the wealthy mercantile elite and most of the official communal leadership in Baghdad headed by Rabbi Sassoon Khadduri, a longtime and outspoken opponent of Zionism, still hoped that despite the intensely hostile atmosphere that prevailed in the country they could ride out the storm and eventually, with the easing of restrictions, continue their comfortable lives as before. Most other segments, of Jewish society, however, were far less optimistic about their future in Iraq. In addition to the committed Zionists, who numbered only a few thousand, were many Zionist sympathizers, especially among young people. A secret British diplomatic report sent to the American secretary of state in March 1949 estimated that "many younger men, of the 'white collar' class, roughly those aged 30 and younger, would be interested in emigrating to Israel, in the belief that they would have better opportunities there than in Iraq." Growing numbers of primarily young Jews began crossing the frontier illegally into Iran either individually or in small groups. Despite martial law, which was in force until

December 1949, at least 1,500 of them succeeded in making the crossing. About two thirds of these went on to Israel.

Throughout 1949, the general disaffection of Iraqi Jewry was exacerbated by frequent calls of the extreme nationalists for the wholesale expulsion of the Jews as a disloyal element from the country. This idea was even picked up briefly by veteran politician Nūrī al–Saʿīd as a possible retaliation for the expulsion of Palestinian Arabs from Israel. Such threats were complemented by broadcasts on the Voice of Israel promising the Iraqi Jews salvation and by the distribution of underground publications urging resistance. Just how alienated the rank and hie of the Jewish community was from its official leadership became apparent on October 23, 1949, when a large demonstration of Jews protesting arrests and other harassments took place in Baghdad, and the president of the communal council, Rabbi Khadduri, was dragged from his home and manhandled by the crowd before being extricated by the police. He resigned a few days later (although his resignation was not officially announced by the government until mid-December). On October 25, most of the Jews of Baghdad stayed home from work to observe a day of special fasting and prayer and to express their general sense of grievance.

Promises by Acting Premier ʿUmar Nazmī to a group of Jewish notables a few days after these incidents that some of the restrictions would soon be lifted had little effect on the Jewish masses. When martial law was finally lifted in December 1949 and the punishment for attempting to emigrate illegally was accordingly lightened, clandestine crossings of the Iranian border began to assume major proportions. Within the first few months of 1950, at least 10,000 Jews fled Iraq in this way. Only a small portion of these emigres were spirited out of the country by the Zionist organization. The majority simply went on their own, often with the aid of Arab smugglers, bribed policemen, and other officials. Once in Iran, most Iraqi Jews were directed to the large refugee camp administered by the Joint Distribution Gommittee near Teheran, and from there they were airlifted to Israel. All of this was done in cooperation with the Iranian authorities.

The government of Iraq was being caused considerable embarrassment both domestically and internationally by the flood of illegal emigration. It also considered the continued presence of large numbers of disaffected people who remained in the country against their will to be a risk to security and economic stability. Because of the uncertain climate, many Jewish businessmen had stopped reinvesting their capital in local enterprises. Many more Jews were trying to dispose of their assets and to transfer funds out of the country. The national economy had also been seriously affected by a decline in oil revenues caused by the closing of the pipeline terminating at Haifa.

In an attempt to stabilize the situation and to solve its Jewish problem once and for all, the government of Prime Minister Tawfīq al–Suwaydī introduced a bill in the Iraqi Parliament at the beginning of March 1950 that would in effect permit Jews who desired to leave the country for good to do so after renouncing their Iraqi citizenship. The bill also provided for the denaturalization of those Jews who had already left the country. During the parliamentary debate, the elderly Jewish Senator Ezra Menahem Daniel urged the government to reassure the Jews who wished to remain in Iraq by removing the severe official restrictions and the no less debilitating unofficial discrimination to which they had been subject. Interior Minister Salih Jabr, who had introduced the bill, replied that Jews who remained in the country would be considered "as Iraqis equal with Muslim and Christian Iraqis so long as they obeyed the law and acted in accordance with the national interest," adding perhaps somewhat disingenuously, "the constitution was a guarantee of this." The measure was duly passed in the Chamber of Deputies on March 2 and in the Senate on March 4 as Law No. 1 of 1950 (Annexure to the Ordinance for the Cancellation of Iraqi Nationality, Law No. 62 of 1933). It was to remain in force for one year.

Iraqi government officials thought that only about 6,000 or 7,000—and at most 10,000—Jews would take advantage of the new law and that most of these would come from the poorer classes. This view was shared at the time by the British diplomats in Baghdad and by a few Israelis as well. During the first few weeks following the enactment of the law, only a few dozen individuals presented themselves for denaturalization. Representatives of the Zionist organization in Iraq spread the word for Jews to hold back, while many unclarified details as to just how they would be gotten out of the country were being clarified. (There was in fact a debate in Israel whether the financially beleaguered state, which was already overwhelmed with immigrants, would even be able to accommodate large numbers of Iraqi refugees.)

When arrangements for an airlift of those Jews wishing to leave the country were finalized between Near East Transport, the same American company (now secretly a partner with El Al) that had carried out Operation Magic Carpet, and the Iraqi government, the Zionist organization in Iraq issued the call at the end of Passover (April 8, 1950) for Jews to come forward and register for emigration. By the end of the month, 47,000 people had appeared at registration centers set up at the major synagogues and had signed the following declaration:

> I declare willingly and voluntarily that I have decided to leave Iraq permanently and that I am aware this statement of mine will have the effect of depriving me of Iraqi nationality and of causing my deportation from Iraq and of preventing me forever afterward from returning.

By January 13, 1951, a total of 85,893 people, or about two thirds of all Iraqi Jews, had registered for emigration to Israel. Because of the slowness of the airlift, dubbed Operation Ezra and Nehemiah (popularly called Operation Ali Baba), only a little over 23,000 of the would-be emigrants had been flown out of the country. The plight—not to mention the morale—of those who were still waiting to leave was becoming increasingly precarious. The number of stateless individuals without employment, and in many instances without homes, was growing daily. (It

could take up to two months for a person to be officially denaturalized after having signed the preceding declaration.) The newly installed government of Nuri al–Sa'id increased the pressure to speed up the emigration process by threatening to drive the stateless Jews across the border into neighboring Kuwait, if they were not out of the country by the March deadline.

Tensions in Iraq mounted further after a hand grenade was thrown on January 14, 1951, into a group of Jews in the courtyard of the Mas'ūda Shemtov Synagogue, one of the main registration centers in Baghdad. Five people were killed and at least fourteen injured as they were about to leave for the airport. The incident remains unsolved to this day. Jewish sources tend to blame Arab extremists, whereas Arab sources and pro-Arab sympathizers blame the Zionist underground, whose caches of arms were discovered later that same year. The Iraqi government accused the Zionists variously of wishing to discredit Iraq, to pressure Israel into speeding up the protracted airlift, and to sow panic among the Jewish population in order to stampede those who had not registered for emigration into doing so. Much of the evidence for these accusations by Iraq came from the show trials of Zionists held in December 1951. Both sides in this historical dispute, over which a considerable amount of ink has been spilled, are certainly plausible. Neither side, however, has provided truly convincing evidence, and for any detached observer the point must remain moot.

Whoever was behind the bomb attack, and whatever the motive may have been, it is an undisputed fact that over the following seven weeks leading up to the March 9 deadline, after which registration for emigration would no longer be accepted, nearly 30,000 additional Jews signed up for departure, and the pace of the airlift was accelerated dramatically. The Iraqi authorities even dropped their earlier insistence that the departing Jews fly first to Cyprus and, as of March 12, permitted the planes to carry them directly from Baghdad to Lod Airport in Israel.

Only one day after the registration deadline passed, the Iraqi Parliament, convened in secret session by Prime Minister Nūrī al-Sa'īd, passed

Law No. 5 of 1951, which froze the assets of all departing Jews and placed them under the control of a government bureau, in effect stripping the emigres of all they possessed. The Parliament also passed a second law (Law No. 12 of 1951), which declared that all Iraqi Jews who were abroad and did not return home within a specific period would forfeit both their nationality and their property. It is clear that Nūrī had waited until after the expiration of the registration deadline in order not to frighten off any prospective emigrants and thereby maximize the government's windfall. Estimates of the total value of the frozen Jewish assets at the time ranged from as low as the Iraqi government s figure of $50 million to as high as $436 million put forward by the Israelis. Less politically inspired estimates of $150 million to $200 million do not seem unreasonable. Although some individuals succeeded in smuggling out considerable sums after March 10, 1951 (often via the Beirut black market), many more were reduced to paupers, being allowed to take out only 50 dinars ($140) per adult and 20 to 30 dinars ($56 to $84) per minor depending upon age. Most émigrés were thoroughly searched—and frequently subjected to all sorts of abuse—upon departure.

By the end of 1951, only about 6,000 Jews remained in Iraq. Operation Ezra and Nehemiah had evacuated 113,545 people. Another 20,000 had left the country illegally. Most of those who chose to remain in Iraq were prosperous and despite some restrictions and inconveniences were able, after the fury of the late 1940s and early 1950s had died down, to return to relatively normal, comfortable lives for at least another decade.

The exodus from Syria was of mass proportions in relation to the smallness of the community, but it was in no way organized. Most Syrian Jews simply melted across the country's borders individually or in small groups despite the considerable personal risks. (In November 1950, for example, thirty Syrian Jews were murdered at sea by a band of smugglers who had agreed to ferry them to Israel.) The outward flow had been going on steadily since the last years of World War II and gathered momentum just before and after the creation of the State of Israel. Reports emanating from Beirut in May 1950 indicated that the Syrian authorities were considering following Iraq's example of permitting Jews to emigrate freely upon their renunciation of citizenship. However, nothing came of these reports, and the illegal emigration continued. From 1948 to 1953, approximately 4,000 Syrian Jews succeeded in making their way to Israel. Many Syrian Jews settled in neighboring Lebanon, where they became the majority of the Jewish community of 11,000. Lebanon, with its generally tolerant, laissez-faire atmosphere and multiethnic composition, was in fact the only Arab country whose Jewish population increased after the first Arab–Israeli war.

By the mid-1950s, only about 5,300 Jews remained in Syria. Don Peretz, who visited there in 1957, describes the remnant of Syrian Jewry as living, "if not in terror, certainly in constant fear, bedeviled by the Syrian security forces. He also depicted the Jews in the three remaining communities of Damascus, Aleppo, and Qamishli as generally poor and dependent upon charity from abroad.

The Second Stage of the Exodus

The initial waves of Jewish emigration from the Arab world were followed by a period—longer in some places, shorter in others—of relative tranquillity and security.

The new revolutionary regime in Egypt, which came to power in July 1952, went out of its way to reassure Jews and other minorities that had been badly shaken by the events of the late 1940s and early 1950s. General Muhammad Najib, the popular figurehead of the ruling Revolutionary Command Council, made public visits to Jewish communal institutions in Cairo and Alexandria, including an unprecedented appearance for an Egyptian head of state at Cairo's Great Synagogue on Yom Kippur, just two months after coming to power. The new government pointedly refused to identify the local Jewish community with the Zionist enemy and vigorously rejected calls within the Arab League for freezing Jewish property in all the member states. As Jewish confidence began to be restored, some Jews began to hearken to Najīb's call and began bringing back capital they had abroad for reinvestment in Egypt.

This brief halcyon period began to end in 1954, when Jamal 'Abd al–Nāsir, the real force behind the revolution, deposed General Najīb. During that same year, an espionage and sabotage ring composed of young Egyptian Jews working for Israel was uncovered. Two of the defendants, Dr. Moses Leito Marzouk and Samuel Azar, were hanged in January 1955 and six others sentenced to prison. This fiasco could not help but undermine efforts to stabilize the position of the Jewish community in Egypt.

The October. 1956 war, in which Great Britain, France, and Israel attacked Egypt following the nationalization of the Suez Canal, provided the coup de grace to Egyptian Jewry. In marked contrast to 1948, there was no mob violence against Jews or their property. The government, however, responded swiftly with harsh measures aimed at Jews and foreigners. Most of the Jewish leaders of Cairo and Alexandria were rounded up in a wave of mass arrests. At least 900 Jews were detained or imprisoned. More than half of them were interned in the Jewish Sybil School in Cairo's Abbasiyya suburb. An additional 500 heads of households were summoned to police stations and summarily ordered to leave the country, either alone or together with their families within two to seven days. Proclamation No. 4 of November 1, 1956, provided for the freezing of bank accounts and the sequestration of property of both internees and suspects. Among those whose property was seized was Salvatore Circurel, president of the Cairene Jewish community and owner of one of Egypt's leading department stores. There were mass dismissals of Jewish employees everywhere. The undefined crime of "Zionism" was now specifically mentioned in the penal code and was grounds for loss of citizenship.

Panic spread rapidly through Egyptian Jewry. During the twelve months that followed the war, approximately 30,000 Jews, about 60 percent of the entire community, left Egypt. Most of the emigres were required to leave behind almost everything they possessed except for a few items of clothing.

The International Red Cross played a major role in facilitating this exodus with behind-the-scenes funding by the American Joint Distribution Committee. Most of the stateless individuals and Egyptian citizens who had been stripped of their nationality went to Israel. Although the pace of emigration eased considerably by mid-1957, the departure of Jews continued unabated. Three years later, only about 10,000 Jews remained in the country, and by the time the third Arab–Israeli war broke out in 1967, their number had shrunk to a mere 2,500 to 3,000 souls.

It was not the repercussions of the Suez conflict but the disengagement of France from its colonial empire in North Africa and the reintegration of the region into the Arab world that set in motion a great wave of Jewish emigration from that region. Already in 1954, there was mounting anxiety both within Maghrebi Jewry and within world Jewish organizations after French Premier Mendès–France proposed granting greater autonomy for Tunisia and gradual internal reforms for Morocco. Mendès–France's controversial initiative, which led to the fall of his government, was taken in response to a rising tide of nationalist agitation in the two protectorates. Most of the violence in North Africa during the early to mid-1950s was aimed at the French, not at the Jews. (It has even been claimed that the Moroccan resistance deliberately chose to throw a bomb into Fez's popular Cafe de la Renaissance on the eve of Yom Kippur because it knew that no Jews would be there at that time.)

Most Jews stood on the sidelines during the years of nationalist agitation, observing a studied neutrality, torn by conflicting feelings for their native land, for their French mentors, and for their reestablished Jewish homeland in the Middle East. Only a small handful of individuals, like Andre Barouche in Tunisia, Joseph Ohana in Morocco, and some leftist students at French universities, were actually attracted to the active ranks of the nationalists.

In Algeria, where the long, bloody national revolution was only just beginning in 1954, "a significant proportion" of Jewish intellectuals was at first sympathetic to the FLN (Front de

Liberation Nationale), while the communal leadership maintained its traditional stance that the Jewish community was not a political entity and that individual members could only speak for themselves. At the same time, though, the leadership pointed out that the members of the Jewish community were French citizens. Jews on the whole kept their distance from both the Muslims and the European colonists. However, as Jews began to become the victims of FLN terrorist attacks from 1956 on, a small number were attracted to the counterrevolutionary OAS (Organisation Armée Secrète).

Jewish emigration rose dramatically as Morocco and Tunisia neared independence despite frequent public and private assurance by the nationalists that Jews would be equal citizens in the new independent, democratic states. Most Jews were not convinced by these statements. The tense atmosphere, the sagging economy, increased competition between Muslims and Jews for jobs, and opposing sympathies with regard to the Middle East conflict made for considerable inter communal friction. The smaller Jewish communities outside the main population centers felt especially isolated and vulnerable. So too did the Jewish urban poor who overwhelmingly wished to go to Israel. With an easing of the policy of restriction, nearly 25,000 Jews left Morocco for Israel in 1955, and over 36,000 in the first half of 1956. More than 12,000 Tunisian Jews also went on 'aliya during the same two-year period.

Much larger numbers would have left Morocco had not the new Moroccan government placed a ban on organized emigration and ordered the local Zionist organization Cadima to dissolve itself in June 1956. This move by the authorities left stranded some 50,000 Jews who had already registered for 'aliya, as well as an equal number who had expressed interest in registering. Although Jews were still legally allowed to leave the country individually, the government ban on organized departures effectively put an end to the mass flight since, as one British diplomat in Rabat observed, "in practice … the type of Moroccan Jew who wishes to emigrate cannot do so without the aid of some organisation such as Cadima." As of

1957, it became difficult for individuals—Jewish or Muslim—to obtain passports.

In contrast to the Moroccan governments restrictive policy, Tunisia continued to allow free emigration under the aegis of the Jewish Agency, although Tunisian officials openly deplored the steady outflow of the Jewish population to France (approximately one third of the country's Jews had French citizenship) and Israel. During the year following independence alone, more than 10,000 Jews left Tunisia. About two thirds of these went to Israel.

When Morocco and Tunisia achieved independence in March 1956, genuine efforts were made by the respective leaders of the two countries, Muhammad V and Habib Bourguiba, to show goodwill and win over their anxious Jewish communities. In each country a Jew was appointed to the cabinet. Dr. Léon Benzaquen was named minister of posts, telephone, and telegraph in Morocco, and Andre Barouche was appointed minister of planning and construction in Tunisia. Jews were also given positions in the government bureaucracy in both countries. In Morocco, an elite group for promoting mutual understanding between Muslims and Jews, called al–Wifāq (Entente), was formed within the Istiqlal party under the leadership of Jewish political activists like Marc Sabbah, a follower of Mahdi Ben Barka.

These initial gestures of goodwill, sincere though they may have been, were ultimately unsuccessful. They were quickly overshadowed by events and trends that further undermined the confidence of most Jews regarding their future in postcolonial North Africa. Neither Jewish minister survived the first reshuffling of their respective cabinets. More significantly, no Jew was appointed again to a ministerial post in either Morocco or Tunisia. The proponents of intercommunal entente made little impression on the Jewish and Muslim masses from whom they were totally removed. The cordiality shown to Jews in some of the highest echelons of government did not percolate down to the lower ranks of officialdom, which exhibited attitudes that ranged from traditional contempt to outright hostility. The natural progression in both countries toward increased identification with the rest of the Arab world (first Morocco, then Tunisia, entered the Arab League in 1958) only widened the gulf between Muslims and Jews. Furthermore, government steps to reduce Jewish communal autonomy, such as Tunisian Law No. 58-78 of July 11, 1958, which dissolved the Jewish Communal Council of Tunis and replaced it with the Provisional Commission for the Oversight of Jewish Religious Matters, having far more circumscribed authority, had negative psychological consequences for Jews, who saw their traditional structures under siege. The official pressure on Jewish educational institutions for arabization and cultural conformity only succeeded in feeding the Jews' worst fears, rather than fostering their integration.

Jewish emigration from Tunisia continued steadily and gained momentum after the crisis of 1961, when France and Tunisia became embroiled in violent confrontations over the continued presence of the French naval base at Bizerte. At the height of the crisis, Jews were accused in the nationalist press of being sympathetic to France and a potentially disloyal element. By the time the Six–Day War broke out between Israel and the Middle Eastern Arab states in June 1967, Tunisian Jewry had dwindled to about 23,000 persons.

The third Arab–Israeli war proved to be the final blow to the still not insubstantial remnant of Tunisian Jewry. On June 5, 1967, widespread anti-Jewish rioting in Tunis, the capital, where the vast majority of Jews lived, resulted in the looting of most Jewish shops and businesses and the desecration and burning of the Great Synagogue. A sense of almost total despair took hold of the community despite President Bourguiba's strong condemnation of the riots and government promises to punish the perpetrators and make restitution. In the words of one eyewitness, "It is the unanimous opinion of Jews one talks to that if there was any doubt about the question previously, it is quite clear now that there is no future for them in Tunisia." Most fled to France. Within a year, only about 7,000 to 8,000 Jews remained in the country.

Although legal mass emigration from Morocco had been halted by the authorities in 1956, clandestine departures organized by agents of the Israeli Mōsād continued throughout the remainder of the decade and into the early 1960s. In the four years following the dissolution of Cadima and the imposition of the ban on 'aliya activities, nearly 18,000 Moroccan Jews were spirited out of the country. Moroccan officials frequently looked aside as this underground exodus was taking place. Only during the premiership of 'Abd Allah Ibrāhīm (December 1958 to May 1960), who represented the radical wing of the Istiqlal party, was there a serious attempt to clamp down on illegal movement, and a special emigration section was established in the police department that carried out numerous arrests of Jews attempting or even suspected of planning to emigrate illegally.

Shortly before his sudden death in February 1961, King Muhammad V decided to reverse the policy banning Jewish emigration. This decision was prompted by a genuine desire—both pragmatic and benevolent—to settle the Jewish problem once and for all, to reverse the growing influence of Nasserism in the country, which had become painfully evident during the Casablanca Conference of African States in January of that year, and to counter the negative international publicity that had been generated by the drowning of forty-four Jews, whose small boat, the Pisces, foundered off the northern Moroccan coast on the night of January 10, 1961, as they were attempting to flee the country. With the door to emigration now opened, 70,000 more Jews left Morocco over the next three years under the aegis of American United HIAS Service, which was permitted by King Hasan II, who had ascended the throne upon his father's death, to operate discreetly in the country.

Throughout the 1960s and 1970s, the Jewish community in Morocco steadily ebbed away, with the rate of departures increasing after the Arab–Israeli wars of 1967 and 1973 and the attempts against King Hasan's life in 1971 and 1972. Unlike those who had gone in the earlier waves, many of those who left after 1967 belonged to the well-to-do and professional classes. Most of them immigrated to France, Belgium, Spain, and Canada rather than to Israel. By 1967, Moroccan

Jewry, which had numbered close to a quarter million souls after World War II had declined to approximately 50,000. By the early 1970s, that number had been reduced by half to only about 25,000 as emigration continued inexorably.

The decline of Algerian Jewry was far more precipitous and more complete than that of either its Moroccan or Tunisian counterparts. As the revolution began, approximately 140,000 Jews were living in Algeria. All of them were French citizens except for those few thousand living in the Saharan Mzab province. For the most part, Algerian Jews could identify with neither the Islamic nationalism of the revolutionaries nor the extreme right-wing, racist politics of the anti-Semitic *colons*. Caught in the cross fire, Jews began leaving the country for France as the savagery mounted on all sides during the late 1950s. Perhaps most symbolic of their predicament was the tragedy of the William Lévy family of Algiers. The father, a socialist leader, was murdered by the OAS in 1961, and his son was murdered by the FLN.

On the eve of Algerian independence m July 1962, virtually the entire Jewish community joined the flood of European refugees going to France. (Only about 5,000 chose to go to Israel.) By the time of the Six–Day War, there were only 3,000 Jews in all of Algeria, most of whom were involved with the French Technical Cooperation Project. Two thirds of these had left by 1970, and most of those who remained behind were elderly. Organized Jewish life in the country had almost entirely ceased to exist.

Epilogue

The long history of the Jews of Arab lands, a history that is only a few centuries shorter than the entire post-Second Temple Diaspora, is now virtually ended. The collapse and dissolution of the Jewish communities in these lands had been rapid. Within two decades, beginning at mid-century, the overwhelming majority of Jews from Iraq in the east to Morocco in the west abandoned their countries of origin, primarily for Israel and

France. Only a small, vestigial, and moribund remnant is left behind. No more Jews are left in Aden (now the People's Democratic Republic of Yemen). Perhaps half a dozen individuals remain in Libya, some sixty in Lebanon, about 300 each in Iraq and Algeria, and less than 200 in Egypt. Only four Arab countries can boast of a Jewish population of more than a thousand people—Morocco (less than 10,000), Tunisia (a little over 2,000), Yemen (perhaps over 2,000), and Syria (with 4,000). In the first two, life is rather tolerable, if somewhat tenuous, for the Jews who have chosen to remain. However, many Moroccan and Tunisian Jewish parents send their children to study abroad for their secondary or advanced education, and few return. These communities are declining slowly but steadily. In Syria and Yemen (now the Yemen Arab Republic), the Jews are virtual prisoners, living in a state of constant terror under strict surveillance in Syria, and under considerably less oppressive, if no less isolated, conditions in Yemen.

The Arab–Israeli conflict may have been the catalyst for the mass exodus of Jews from most of the Arab countries (in the Maghreb, the end of French colonial rule was also a major contributing factor), but it was by no means the sole cause. The underlying forces that paved the way and contributed to this seemingly sudden rupture had been at work since the dawn of the modern era and were part and parcel of the impact of the West and the process of modernization that affected both Jews and Arabs, albeit in different ways.

The growing economic, political, and cultural intrusion of the West into the Islamic world during the course of the nineteenth century and well into the twentieth was perceived as a serious threat by the dominant Muslim community, whereas by the Jews and most native Christians, it was viewed as a liberation from their traditional humble and subordinate *dhimmī* status, which since the later Middle Ages had been rigorously imposed upon them. The Jews and Christians of the Muslim world were quick to see that increased European interference and penetration into the affairs of their region meant a weakening of the traditional

Islamic norms of society and could only better their own position, which was one of religiously and legally defined inferiority.

Non-Muslims in the Islamic world had for centuries served as the intermediaries between European commercial interests in the Middle East and North Africa and the surrounding Muslim society. In the nineteenth century, they began to take advantage of the protection these ties might afford them under the capitulations. They were encouraged in this by the European powers that had begun to take an interest in their welfare at this time for both humanitarian and imperialistic reasons. For their part, the European powers lobbied with the Islamic states—and particularly with the Ottoman Empire—to extend greater civil rights to their non-Muslim subjects.

Non-Muslims also began during the last century eagerly to avail themselves of the benefits of a modern European education provided by the various cultural and religious missionaries who flocked into the Middle East and North Africa. For the Jews, the Alliance Israelite Universelle became the chief provider of modern education in the major towns and cities of most Arab countries from the 1860s onward. French, rather than Arabic or Turkish, became the primary language of high culture for thousands upon thousands of Jews. The Alliance gave its pupils far more than an education. It gave them a new self-image, created new expectations within them, and helped to arouse a sense of international Jewish solidarity. It also produced cadres of westernized native Jews who now had a distinct advantage of opportunity over the largely uneducated Muslim masses as the Islamic world was drawn ineluctably into the modern world economic system.

Together with the rapidly evolving native Christians who benefited from missionary schools, Jews came to have a place in the economic life of the Middle East and North Africa that was far out of proportion to their numbers or their social status in the general population. Their foreign ties, Western acculturation, and economic success were deeply resented by the Muslim Arab majority. This conspicuous overachievement by some Jews and Christians would contribute to

their undoing as a group in the twentieth century with the rise of nationalism in the Arab world.

Rapid acculturation, overachievement in certain economic spheres, and a weakening of tradition may seem to parallel the emergence of European Jewry from the ghetto. However, in Europe, the emancipation and modernization of the Jews resulted in greater assimilation into the surrounding culture. In the Islamic world, the result was quite the opposite. Jews there became further alienated from the society around them. Although Arabic-speaking Jewry had never been totally a part of Arab culture, it nevertheless shared many more cultural elements with its Muslim neighbors prior to the modern era than did its European brethren with their Christian compatriots.

The Jews of Arab lands had no vested interest in the old social and political order of their traditional Muslim overlords. Therefore, they welcomed European political domination that began with the French conquest of Algeria in the 1830s and culminated in the carving up of the Ottoman Empire at the end of World War I. It was their misfortune to discover that the hopes they placed in their British, French, and Italian masters would be disappointed again and again. In the nineteenth century, the European powers had sought to extend their protection to the non-Muslim minorities, in part, to gain greater influence in the region. Once much of the Middle East and North Africa were under European control in the twentieth century, the colonial and mandatory authorities were frequently more concerned with appeasing, or at least not offending, the Muslim majority than in protecting the Jewish and Christian minorities, especially as the tide of Arab nationalism began to rise and swell. It was this powerful tide that would eventually engulf and destroy the Jewish and some of the Christian communities in the Arab world.

It is at times suggested that the Jews failed to hear the call of Arab nationalism when they had the chance. On the contrary, they heard it only too well. There never really was a place for them in the militant national movements with their strong

Pan–Arab and Islamic overtones. Furthermore, from 1929 onward, Arab nationalism became increasingly anti-Zionist. Despite frequent disclaimers, it became increasingly difficult for either nationalist leaders or the population at large to differentiate between Jews and Zionists. Growing Arab admiration of German National Socialism and Italian Fascism in the 1930s and 1940s and a concomitant receptivity to their anti-Semitic rhetoric also ensured that Jews would find no place for themselves in the Arab nationalist camp and the society it would create.

World War II demonstrated to the Jews of Arab lands with painful clarity just how vulnerable they were. In Iraq during the Farhud, Jews had seen the kind of violence that could be visited upon them under a native regime. In Italian Libya and the French Maghreb, they saw what anti-Semitic European colonial rule could do to them while much of the native Arab population looked on with indifference. In Egypt, they could only imagine what might have befallen them if King Fārūq had been able to welcome Rommel into the country as he had hoped to do. The lesson of the European Holocaust was not lost upon most of the Jews of the Arab world either. They emerged from their wartime experience with a heightened sense of Jewish consciousness and esprit de corps. Among young people in particular, there was an increased receptiveness to Zionism as the ultimate answer to the anti-Semitism of both the European colonialists and the Arab nationalists.

Events moved rapidly in the years immediately after World War II, and in short order totally undermined the already weakened underpinnings of the Jewish communities in the Arab world. It made little difference whether Jews abjectly mouthed the Arab anti-Zionist line as in Syria, donated generous sums of money to the Palestinian cause as in Iraq, publicly proclaimed their loyalty as in Egypt, openly declared their allegiance to Zionism as in Tunisia and Libya, or completely identified themselves with a colonial power as in Algeria. In the end, they all shared a similar fate and chose to emigrate or flee from the lands of their birth.

Afterword: The Consequences of 1948

By Edward W. Said

I might as well begin with my own experience of 1948, and what it meant for many of the people around me. I talk about this at some length in my memoir *Out of Place*. My own immediate family was spared the worst ravages of the catastrophe: we had a house and my father a business in Cairo, so even though we were in Palestine during most of 1947 when we left in December of that year, the wrenching, cataclysmic quality of the collective experience (when 780,000 Palestinians, literally two-thirds of the country's population were driven out by Zionist troops and design) was not one we had to go through. I was 12 at the time so had only a somewhat attenuated and certainly no more than a semi-conscious awareness of what was happening; only this narrow awareness was available to me, but I do distinctly recall some things with special lucidity. One was that every member of my family, on both sides, became a refugee during the period; no one remained in our Palestine, that is, that part of the territory (controlled by the British Mandate) that did not include the West Bank which was annexed to Jordan. Therefore, those of my relatives who lived in Jaffa, Safad, Haifa, and West Jerusalem were suddenly made homeless, in many instances penniless, disoriented, and scarred forever. I saw most of them again after the fall of Palestine but all were greatly reduced in circumstances, their

faces stark with worry, ill-health, despair. My extended family lost all its property and residences, and like so many Palestinians of the time bore the travail not so much as a political but as a natural tragedy. This etched itself on my memory with lasting results, mostly because of the faces which I had once remembered as content and at ease, but which were now lined with the cares of exile and homelessness. Many families and individuals had their lives broken, their spirits drained, their composure destroyed forever in the context of seemingly unending, serial dislocation: this was and still is for me of the greatest poignancy. One of my uncles went from Palestine to Alexandria to Cairo to Baghdad to Beirut and now in his 80s lives, a sad, silent man, in Seattle. Neither he nor his immediate family ever fully recovered. This is emblematic of the larger story of loss and dispossession, which continues today.

The second thing I recall was that for the one person in my family who somehow managed to pull herself together in the aftermath of the *nakba*, my paternal aunt, a middle-aged widow with some financial means, Palestine meant service to the unfortunate refugees, many thousands of whom ended up penniless, jobless, destitute, and disoriented in Egypt. She devoted her life to them in the face of government obduracy and sadistic indifference. From her I learned that whereas everyone was willing to pay lip service to the cause, only a very few people were willing to do anything about it. As a Palestinian, therefore, she took it as her lifelong duty to set about helping the refugees—getting their children into schools, cajoling doctors and pharmacists into giving them treatment and medicine, finding the men jobs, and above all, being there for them, a willing, sympathetic and above all selfless presence. Without administrative or financial assistance of any kind, she remains an exemplary figure for me from my early adolescence, a person against whom my own terribly modest efforts are always measured and, alas, always found wanting. The job for us in my lifetime was to be literally unending, and because it derived from a human tragedy so profound, so extraordinary in saturating both the formal as well as the informal life of its people down to the smallest detail, it has been and will continue to need to be recalled, testified to, remedied. For Palestinians, a vast collective feeling of injustice continues to hang over our lives with undiminished weight. If there has been one thing, one particular delinquency committed by the present group of Palestinian leaders for me, it is their supernally gifted power of forgetting: when one of them was asked recently what he felt about Ariel Sharon's accession to Israel's Foreign Ministry, given that he was responsible for the shedding of so much Palestinian blood, this leader said blithely, we are prepared to forget history—and this is a sentiment I neither can share nor, I hasten to add, easily forgive.

One needs to recall by comparison Moshe Dayan's statement in 1969:

> We came to this country which was already populated by Arabs, and we are establishing a Hebrew, that is a Jewish state here. In considerable areas of the country [the total area was about 6 percent-EWS] we bought the lands from the Arabs. Jewish villages were built in the place of Arab villages, and I do not even know the names of these Arab villages, and I do not blame you, because these geography books no longer exist; not only do the books not exist, the Arab villages are not there either. Nahalal [Dayan's own village] arose in the place of Mahalul, Gevat in the place of Jibta, [Kibbutz] Sarid in the place of Haneifs and Kefar Yehoshua in the place of Tel Shaman. There is not one place built in this country that did not have a former Arab population.

What also strikes me about these early Palestinian reactions is how largely unpolitical they were. For twenty years after 1948 Palestinians were immersed in the problems of everyday life with little time left over for organizing, analyzing, and planning, although there were some attempts to infiltrate Israel, try some military action, write and agitate. With the exception of the kind of work produced in Mohammed Hassanein Haykal's Ahram Strategic Institute, Israel to most Arabs and even to Palestinians was a cipher, its language unknown, its society unexplored, its people and the history of their movement largely confined to slogans, catch-all phrases, negation. We saw and experienced its behavior towards us but it took us a long while to understand what we saw or what we experienced.

The overall tendency throughout the Arab world was to think of military solutions to that scarcely imaginable country, with the result that a vast militarization overtook every society almost without exception in the Arab world; coups succeeded each other more or less unceasingly and, worse yet, every advance in the military idea brought an equal and opposite diminution in social, political, and economic democracy. Looking back on it now, the rise to hegemony of Arab nationalism allowed for very little in the way of democratic civil institutions, mainly because the language and concepts of that nationalism itself devoted little attention to the role of democracy in the evolution of those societies. Until now, the presence of a putative danger to the Arab world has engendered a permanent deferral of such things as an open press, or unpoliticized universities, or freedoms to research, travel in, and explore new realms of knowledge. No massive investment was ever made in the quality of education, despite largely successful attempts on the part of the Nasser government in Egypt as well as other Arab governments to lower the rate of illiteracy. It was thought that, given the perpetual state of emergency caused by Israel, such matters, which could only be the result of long-range planning and reflection, were luxuries that were ill-afforded. Instead, arms procurement on a huge scale took the place of genuine human development with negative results that we live with until today. Thirty percent of the world's arms were still bought by Arab countries in 1998–99. Along with the militarization went the wholesale persecution of communities, preeminently but not exclusively the Jewish ones, whose presence in our midst for generations was suddenly thought to be dangerous. I know that there was an active Zionist role in stimulating unrest between the Jews of Iraq, Egypt, and elsewhere on the one hand, and the governments of those Arab countries were scarcely democratic, on the other, but it seems to me to be incontestable that there was a xenophobic enthusiasm officially decreeing that these and other designated "alien" communities had to be extracted by force from our midst. Nor was this all. In the name of military security in countries like Egypt there was a bloody minded, imponderably wasteful campaign against dissenters, mostly on the left, but independent-minded people too whose vocation as critics and skilled men and women was brutally terminated in prisons, by fatal torture and summary executions. As one looks back at these things in the context of 1948, it is the immense panorama of waste and cruelty that stands out as the immediate result of the war itself.

Along with that went a scandalously poor treatment of the refugees themselves. It is still the case, for example, that the 40,000-50,000 Palestinian refugees resident in Egypt must report to a local police station every month; vocational, educational, and social opportunities for them are curtailed, and the general sense of not belonging adheres to them despite their Arab nationality and language. In Lebanon the situation is direr still. Almost 400,000 Palestinian refugees have had to endure not only the massacres of Sabra, Shatila, Tell el Zaatar, Dbaye, and elsewhere, but have remained confined in hideous quarantine for almost two generations. They have no legal right to work in at least sixty occupations, they are not adequately covered by medical insurance, they cannot travel and return, they are objects of suspicion and dislike. In part—and I shall return to this later—they have inherited the mantle of opprobrium draped around them by the PLO's presence (and since 1982 its unlamented absence) there, and thus they remain in the eyes of many ordinary Lebanese a sort of house enemy to be warded off and/or punished from time to time. A similar situation in kind, if not in degree, exists in Syria. As for Jordan, though it was (to its credit) the only country where Palestinians were given naturalized status, a visible fault line exists between the disadvantaged majority of that very large community and the Jordanian establishment for reasons that scarcely need to be spelled out here. I might add, however, that for most of these situations where Palestinian refugees exist in large groups within one or another Arab country—all of them as a direct consequence of 1948—no simple, much less elegant or just, solution exists in the foreseeable future. It is also worth asking why it is that a destiny of confinement and isolation has been imposed on a people who quite naturally flocked to neighboring countries when driven out of theirs, countries which everyone thought would welcome and sustain them. More or less the opposite took place: no welcome was given them (except in Jordan)—another unpleasant consequence of the original dispossession in 1948.

This now brings me to a specially significant point, namely the emergence since 1948 in both Israel and the Arab countries of a new rhetoric and political culture. For the Arabs this was heralded in such landmark books as Constantine Zurayk's *Ma'nat al-Nakba*, the idea that because of 1948 an entirely unprecedented situation had arisen for which again, an unprecedented state of alertness and revival was to be necessary. What I find more interesting than the emergence of a new political rhetoric or discourse—with all its formulas, prohibitions, circumlocutions, euphemisms, and sometimes empty blasts—is its total watertightness (to coin a phrase) with regard to its opposite number. Perhaps it is true to say that this occlusion of the other has its origin in the *irreconcilability of Zionist conquest* with *Palestinian dispossession*, but the developments out of that fundamental antinomy led to a separation between the two on the official level that was never absolutely real even though on a popular level there was a great deal of enthusiasm for it. Thus we now know that Nasser, whose rhetoric was next to none in implacability and determination, was in contact with Israel through various intermediaries, as was Sadat, and of course Mubarak. This was even more true of Jordan's rulers, somewhat less so (but nevertheless the case) with Syria. I am not advancing a simple value judgment here since such disparities between rhetoric and reality are common enough in all politics. But what I am suggesting is that a sort of orthodoxy of hypocrisy developed inside the Arab and Israeli camps that in effect fueled and capitalized the worst aspect of each society. The tendency towards orthodoxy, uncritical repetition of received ideas, fear of innovation, one or more types of double-speak, etc. has had an extremely rich life.

I mean, in the Arab case, that the rhetorical and military hostility toward Israel led to more, not less ignorance about it, and ultimately to the disastrous politico-military performances of the 1960s and 1970s. The cult of the army which implied that there were only military solutions to political problems was so prevalent that it overshadowed the axiom that successful military action had to derive from a motivated, bravely led, and politically integrated and educated force, and this could only issue from a citizens' society. Such a desideratum was never the case in the Arab world, and was rarely practised or articulated. In addition, a nationalist culture was consolidated that encouraged rather than mitigated Arab isolation from the rest of the modern world. Israel was soon perceived not only as a Jewish but as a Western state, and as such was completely rejected even as a suitable intellectual pursuit for those who were interested in finding out about the enemy.

From that premise a number of horrendous mistakes flowed. Among those was the proposition that Israel was not a real society but a makeshift quasi-state; its citizens were there only long enough to be scared into leaving; Israel was a total chimera, a "presumed" or "alleged" entity, not a real state. Propaganda to this effect was crude, uninformed, ineffective.

The rhetorical and cultural conflict—a real one—was displaced from the field so to speak to the world stage, and there too with the exception of the Third World, we were routed. We never mastered the art of putting our case against Israel in human terms, no narrative was fashioned, no statistics were marshalled and employed, no spokespersons trained and refined in their work emerged. We never learned to speak one, as opposed to several contradictory languages. Consider the very early days before and after the 1948 debacle when people like Musa al–Alami, Charles Issawi, Walid Khalidi, Albert Hourani, and others like them undertook a campaign to inform the Western world, which is where Israel's main support derived from, about the Palestinian case. Now contrast those early efforts, which were soon dissipated by infighting and jealousy, with the official rhetoric of the Arab League or of any one or combination of Arab countries. These were (and alas continue to be) primitive, badly organized and diffused, insufficiently thought through. In short, embarrassingly clumsy, especially since the human content itself, the Palestinian tragedy, was so potent, and the Zionist argument and plan *vis-à-vis* the Palestinians so outrageous. By impressive contrast, the Israeli system of information was for the most part successful, professional, and in the West, more or less all-conquering. It was buttressed in parts of the world like Africa and Asia with the export of agricultural, technological, and academic expertise, something the Arabs never really got into. That what the Israelis put out was a tissue of ideological half-truths is less important than that as a confection it served the purpose of promoting a cause, an image, and an idea about Israel that both shut out the Arabs and in many ways disgraced them.

Looking back on it now, the rhetorical conflict that derived from and was a consequence of 1948 was amplified well beyond anything like it anywhere else in the world. For part of the time it took on some of the vehemence and prominence of the Cold War which framed it for almost thirty years. What was strange about it is that like the events of 1948 themselves there was no real Palestinian representation at all until 1967, and the subsequent prominence of the PLO. Until then we were simply known as the Arab refugees who fled because their leaders told them to. Even after the research of Erskine Childers and Walid Khalidi utterly disputed the validity of those claims and proved the existence of Plan Dalet thirty-eight years ago, we were not to be believed. Worse yet, those Palestinians who remained in Israel after 1948 acquired a singularly solitary status as Israeli Arabs, shunned by other Arabs, treated by Israeli Jews under a whip by the military administration and, until 1966, by stringent emergency laws applied and assigned to them as non-Jews. The queerness of this rhetorical conflict in comparison say, with the war between American and Japanese propagandists during World War Two as chronicled by John Dower is that Israeli misinformation, like the Zionist movement itself, allowed no room for an indigenous opponent, someone on the ground whose land, society, and history were simply taken from him/her. We were largely invisible, except occasionally as fedayin and terrorists or as part of the menacing Arab hordes who wanted to throttle the young Jewish state, as the expression had it.

One of the most unfortunate aspects of this state of affairs is that even the word "peace" acquired a sinister, uncomfortable meaning for the Arabs, at just the time that Israeli publicists used it at every opportunity. We want peace with the Arabs, they would say, and, sure enough, the echo went around that Israel fervently desired peace, while the Arabs—ferocious, vengeful, gratuitously bent on violence—did not. In fact, what was at issue between Israelis and Palestinians was never peace but the possibility for Palestinians of restitution of property, nationhood, identity—all of them blotted out by the new Jewish state. Moreover, it appeared to Palestinians that peace with Israel was a form of exterminism that left us without political existence: it meant accepting as definitive and unappealable the events of 1948, the

loss of our society and homeland. So, even more alienated from Israel and everything it stood for, the whole idea of separation between the two peoples acquired a life of its own, though it meant different things for each. Israelis wanted it in order to live in a purely Jewish state, freed from its non-Jewish residents both in memory and in actuality. Palestinians wanted it as a method for getting back to their originary existence as the Arab possessors of Palestine. The logic of separation has operated since 1948 as a persistent motif and has now reached its apogee and its logical conclusion in the hopelessly skewed and unworkable Oslo accords. At only the very rarest of moments did either Palestinians or Israelis try to think their histories and cultures—inextricably linked for better or for worse—together, contrapuntally, in symbiotic, rather than mutually exclusive terms. The sheer distortion in views both of history and of the future that has resulted is breathtaking and requires some example and analysis here.

I don't think that anyone can honestly disagree that since 1948 the Palestinians have been the victims, Israelis the victors. No matter how much one tries to dress up or prettify this rather bleak formulation, its truth shines through the murk just the same. The general argument from Israel and its supporters has been that the Palestinians brought it on themselves: why did they leave? Why did the Arabs declare war? Why did they not accept the 1947 plan of partition? And so on and on. None of this, it should be clear, justifies Israel's subsequent official behavior both toward itself and its Palestinian victims, where a hard cruelty, a dehumanizing attitude, and an almost sadistic severity in putting down the Palestinians has prevailed over all the years. The frequently expressed Israeli and general Jewish feeling, that Israel is in serious peril and that Jews will always be targets of anti-Semitic opportunity, that is buttressed by appeals to the Holocaust, to centuries of Christian anti-Semitism, and to Jewish exile, is a potent and in many ways justifiable sentiment. I have gone on record as saying that *it is* justified for Jews—even for American Jews whose experiences have been nowhere near as traumatic as their European counterparts—to feel the agonies of the Holocaust as their own, even unto the present, but I keep asking myself whether the use of that feeling to keep Palestinians in more or less permanent submission can repeatedly be justified on those grounds alone? And are the official and intemperate (to say the least) harangues about Israeli security justified, given what a miserable lot has been the Palestinians'? Are the huge numbers of soldiers, the obsessive, excessive, measures about terrorism, the endless fencing in, the interrogations, the legal justification of torture for twelve years, the nuclear, biological, and chemical options, the discriminations against Israeli Palestinians, the fear and contempt, the bellicosity—one could go on and on—are all these things not a sort of massive distortion in perception and mode of life, all of them premised on and fueled by the extreme separatist, not to say xenophobic sentiment that Israel must be, must remain at all costs an endangered, isolated, unloved Jewish state? Doesn't one have the impression that the language and discourse of Israel—there are exceptions, of course—generally signify a refusal to engage with the common regional history except on these extreme separatist terms?

Here is Adorno discussing distortions of language in the dominated and the dominating:

> The language of the dominant turns against the masters, who misuse it to command, by seeking to command them, and refuses to serve their interests. The language of the subjected, on the other hand, domination alone has stamped, so robbing them further of the justice promised by the unmutilated, autonomous word to all those free enough to pronounce it without rancor. Proletarian language is dictated by hunger. The poor chew words to fill their bellies. From the objective spirit of language they expect the sustenance refused them by society; those whose mouths are full of words have nothing else between their teeth. So they take revenge on language. Being forbidden to love it, they maim the body of language,

and so repeat in impotent strength the disfigurement inflicted on them.

The compelling quality of this passage is the imagery of distortion inflicted on language, repeated, reproduced, turning inward, unable to provide sustenance. And so it seems to me has been the interplay since 1948 between the official discourses of Zionism and Palestinian nationalism, the former dominating but in the process twisting language to serve an endless series of misrepresentations which does not serve their interests (Israel is *more* insecure today, less accepted by Arabs, more disliked and resented), the latter using language as a compensatory medium for the unfulfillment of a desperate political self-realization. For years after 1948 the Palestinians are an absence, a desired and willed nonentity in Israeli discourse, on whom various images of absence have been heaped—the nomad, the terrorist, the fellah, the Arab, the fanatic, and so forth. For Palestinians their official discourse has been full of the affirmation of presence, yet a presence mostly dialectically annulled in the terms of power politics and hence affirmed in a language like that of Darwish's poem *Sajjil Ana 'Arab?*—"I am here, take note of me"—or in the ludicrous trappings including honor guard and bagpipes of a head of state allowed himself by Yasir Arafat. Over time it is the distortions that are increased, not the amount of reality in the language.

This is a difficult point to try to express, so let me give it another formulation. The modern history of the struggle for Palestinian self-determination can be regarded as an attempt to set right the distortions in life and language inscribed so traumatically as a consequence of 1948. There has never been any shortage of Palestinian resistance, and while it is true that there have been some advances here and there in Palestinian struggle—the intifada and the invigorations provided by the PLO before 1991 being two of the most notable—the general movement either has been much slower than that of Zionism, or it has been regressive. Where the struggle over land has been concerned there has been a net loss, as Israel through belligerent as well as pacific means has asserted its actual hold on more and more of Palestinian land. I speak here of course of sovereignty, military power, actual settlement. I contrast that with what I shall call Palestinian symptoms of response, such as the multiple rhetorical attempts to assert the existence of a Palestinian state, to bargain with Israel over conditions of Israeli (and not Palestinian) security, and the general untidiness, sloppiness, and carelessness—absence of preparations, maps, files, facts, and figures among Palestinian negotiators in the Oslo process—that have characterized what can only be called a lack of ultimate seriousness in dealing with the real, as opposed to the rhetorical, conditions of dispossession. These, as I said earlier, multiply the distortions stemming from the original condition of loss and dispossession: rather than rectifications they offer additional dislocations and the reproduction of distortions whose widening effects extend the whole range, from war, to increasing numbers of refugees, more property abandoned and taken, more frustration, more anger, more humiliation, and so on. From all this derives the force of Rosemary Sayigh's startlingly appropriate, and even shattering phrase, "too many enemies"—the poignancy is that Palestinians, by a further dialectical transformation, have even become their own enemies through unsuccessful and self-inflicted violence.

For Israel and its supporters—especially its Western liberal supporters—none of this has mattered very much, even though the encomia to Israel and/or a generalized embarrassed silence when Israel has indulged itself in ways normally not permitted any other country have been unrelenting. One of the main consequences of 1948 is an ironic one: as the effects of that highly productive dispossession have increased, so too the tendency has been to overlook their source, to concentrate on pragmatic, realistic, tactical responses to "the problem" in the present. The present peace process is unthinkable without an amnesiac official abandonment, which I deplore, by the Palestinian leaders of what happened to them in 1948 and thereafter. And yet they could not be in the position they are in without that entirely concrete and minutely, intensely lived experience of loss and dispossession for which 1948 is both origin and

enduring symbol. So there is an eerie dynamic by which the reliving of our mistakes and disasters comes forward collectively without the force or the lessons or even the recollection of our past. We are perpetually at the starting point, looking for a solution now, even as that "now" itself bears all the marks of our historical diminishment and human suffering.

In both the Israeli and Palestinian cases there is, I think, a constitutive break between the individual and the whole, which is quite striking, especially in so far as the whole is, as Adorno once put it, the false. Zeev Sternhell has shown in his historical analysis of Israel's founding narratives that an idea of the collective overriding every instance of the particular was at the very heart of what he calls Israel's nationalist socialism. The Zionist enterprise he says was one of conquest and redemption of something referred to almost mystically as "the land." Humanly the result was a total subordination of the individual to a corporate self, presumed to be the new Jewish body, a sort of super-collective whole in which the constituent parts were insignificant compared to that whole. Many of the institutions of the state, specially the Histadrut and the land agency, overrode anything that might smack of individualism, or of individual agency since what was always of the utmost importance was the presumed good of the whole. Thus, according to Ben-Gurion, nationhood mattered more than anything else: consequently, frugality of lifestyle, self-sacrifice, pioneer values were the essence of the Israeli mission. Sternhell traces out with more detail than anyone I know what sorts of complications and contradictions were entailed by this vision—how, for example, Histadrut leaders and military men got higher pay than the laborers who were, in the going phrase, conquering the wasteland, even though an ideology of complete egalitarianism (often referred to abroad as "socialism") prevailed. Yet this did not evolve once Israel became an independent state. "The pioneering ideology, with its central principles—the conquest of land, the reformation of the individual, and self-realization—was not an ideology of social change; it was not an ideology that could establish a secular, liberal state and put an end to the war with the Arabs." Nor, it must be added, could it develop a notion of citizenship since it was meant to inform a state of the Jewish people, not of its individual citizens. The project of Zionism therefore was not only this entirely new modern state but, as Sternhell puts it, the very negation of the diaspora.

It would be extremely difficult to find within the parallel Arab dominant ideology or practice of the period after 1948—whether we look in the annals of Ba'thism, Nasserism, or general Arab nationalism—anything like a concerned attention paid to the notion of citizenship. Quite the contrary, there was if anything a mirror image of Zionist corporatism except that most of the ethnic and religious exclusivity of Jewish nationalism is not there. In its basic form Arab nationalism is inclusive and pluralistic generally, though like Zionism there is a quasi-messianic, quasi-apocalyptic air about the descriptions in its major texts (of Nasserism and Ba'thism) of revival, the new Arab individual, the emergence and birth of the new polity, etc. As I noted earlier, even in the emphasis on Arab unity in Nasserism one feels that a core of human individualism and agency is missing, just as in practice it is simply not part of the national program in a time of emergency. Now the Arab security state already well described by scholars, political scientists, sociologists, and intellectuals, is a nasty or sorry thing in its aggregate, repressive, and monopolistic in its notions of state power, coercive when it comes to issues of collective well-being. But, once again, thunderingly silent on the whole matter of what being a citizen, and what citizenship itself, entails beyond serving the motherland and being willing to sacrifice for the greater good. On the issue of national minorities there are some scraps of thought here and there, but nothing in practice, given the fantastic mosaic of identities, sects, and ethnicities in the Arab world. Most of the scholarly, scientific literature that I have read on the Arab world—the best and most recent of which is critical and highly advanced—speaks about clientelism, bureaucracies, patriarchal hierarchies, notables, and so on, but spends depressingly little time talking about *muwatana* (citizenship) as a key to the sociopolitical and economic morass of

recession and de-development that is now taking place. Certainly, accountability is left out of the critical picture more or less totally.

I am not the only one to have said, though, that one of the brightest consequences of 1948 is the emergence of new critical voices, here and there, in the Israeli and Arab worlds (including diasporas) whose vision is both critical and integrative. By that I mean such schools as the Israeli "new historians," their Arab counterparts and, among many of the younger area studies specialists in the West, those whose work is openly revisionist and politically engaged. Perhaps it is now possible to speak of a new cycle opening up in which the dialectic of separation and separatism has reached a sort of point of exhaustion, and a new process might be beginning, glimpsed here and there within the anguished repertoire of communitarianism which by now every reflecting Arab and every Jew somehow feels as the home of last resort. It is of course true and even a truism that the system of states in the region has done what it can do as a consequence of 1948, that is, provide what purports to be a sort of homogenized political space for like people, for Syrians, Jordanians, Israelis, Egyptians and so on. Palestinians have and continue to aspire to a similar consolidation of self-hood with geography, some unity of the nation, now dispersed, with its home territory. Yet the problem of the Other remains, for Zionism, for Palestinian nationalism, for Arab and/or Islamic nationalism. There is, to put it simply, an irreducible, heterogenous presence always to be taken account of which, since and because of 1948, has become intractable, unwishable away, *there*.

How then to look to the future? How to see it, and how to work towards it, if all the schemes either of separatism or exterminism, or of going back either to the Old Testament or the Golden Age of Islam or to the pre-1948 period, simply will not do, will not work? What I want to propose is an attempt to flesh out the emergence of a political and intellectual strategy based on just peace and just coexistence based on equality. This strategy is based on a full consciousness of what 1948 was for Palestinians and for Israelis, the point being that no bowdlerization of the past, no diminishment of its effects can possibly serve any sort of decent future. I want to suggest here the need for a new kind of grouping, one that provides a critique of ideological narratives as well as a form that is compatible with real citizenship and a real democratic politics.

1. We need to think about two histories not separated ideologically, but together, contrapuntally. Neither Palestinian nor Israeli history at this point is a thing in itself, without the other. In so doing we will necessarily come up against the basic irreconcilability between the Zionist claim and Palestinian dispossession. The injustice done to the Palestinians is essential to these two histories, as is also the effect of Western anti-Semitism and the Holocaust.

2. The construction of what Raymond Williams termed an emergent composite identity based on that shared or common history, irreconcilabilities, antinomies and all. What we will then have is an overlapping and necessarily unresolved consciousness of Palestine/Israel through its history, not despite it.

3. A demand for rights and institutions of common citizenship, not of ethnic or religious exclusivity, with its culmination in a unitary state, as well as rethinking the Law of Return and Palestinian return together. Citizenship should be based on the just solidarities of coexistence and the gradual dissolving of ethnic lines.

4. The crucial role of education with special emphasis on Other. This is an extremely long-term project in which the diaspora/exilic and research communities must play a central role. There are now at least two or perhaps more warring research paradigms: to its credit this series of interventions acknowledges the transitional state of research on Israel/Palestine, its precarious, rapidly evolving, and yet fragmentary and uneven character.

Ideally of course the goal is to achieve consensus by scholars and activist intellectuals that a new, synthetic paradigm might slowly emerge which would re-orient the combative and divisive energies we've all had to contend with into more productive and collaborative channels. This cannot occur, I believe, without some basic agreement, a compact or entente whose outlines would have to include regarding the Other's history as valid but incomplete as usually presented, and second, admitting that despite the antinomy these histories can only continue to flow together, not apart, within a broader framework based on the notion of equality for all. This of course is a secular, and by no means a religious, goal and I believe it needs to start life by virtue of entirely secular, not religious or exclusivist, needs. Secularization requires demystification, it requires courage, it requires an irrevocably critical attitude towards self, society, and other. But it also requires a narrative of emancipation and enlightenment for all, not just for one's own community.

For those who challenge all this and call it Utopian or unrealistic, my answer is a simple one: show me what else is available today. Show me a scheme for separation that isn't based on abridged memory, continued injustice, unmitigated conflict, apartheid. There just isn't one, hence the value of what I've tried to outline here.

Provocations

By Benny Morris

1967: Israel, The War, And The Year That Transformed The Middle East
By Tom Segev
Translated by Jessica Cohen
(Metropolitan Books, 673 pages)

Foxbats Over Dimona: The Soviets' Gamble In The Six-Day War
By Isabella Ginor and Gideon Remez
(Yale University Press, 287 pages)

In all modesty, I know a thing or two about historical revisionism. The desire to innovate, to surprise, to overthrow conventional wisdom and to subvert the well-worn tale—I, too, have acted on these impulses. And I have no apologies for the disturbances that I caused. In the 1980s, the history of Zionism and Israel sorely required critical review and scholarly emendation. For decades, too much nationalist propaganda had passed without scrutiny and been imbibed by Israeli society.

The official history—from the outlandish, skimpy beginnings of Zionism in the 1880s, when a handful of poor Jewish settlers struck roots in a semi-arid patch of ground ruled by hostile Muslim governors, through the succession of victories over much larger and potentially far more powerful surrounding Arab states—was a tale of triumph and glory, veritably miraculous in concept and in experience. This history seemed, to myself and to some others, to call out for cool, objective study—and, in the process, to be pricked and deflated. In the course of the 1980s and 1990s, large themes and central episodes of the hallowed narrative were revised and retold with some persuasiveness and success, if not to universal approbation. Tom Segev had a small part in this revisionism with his *1949: The First Israelis*, which appeared in English in 1986, but the book vanished without leaving much of a trace on Israeli scholarship or Israeli consciousness, because in tackling too many themes—the "Sephardi Problem," the religious-secular divide, the Israeli–Palestinian conflict—he contributed significantly to none.

But not all revisionism is good. Historical revisionism should aim at presenting a clearer and more accurate picture of the past than that served up by the previous generation of historians—a more truthful picture of what happened, and why, and how; of what motivated the protagonists and what were the reasons for, and consequences of, a given action or episode. Good revisionist historiography is no different from good historiography. It should not be written with a political purpose, or with the aim of shocking for shock's sake. (That is not revisionist historiography, it is tabloid historiography.)

Now, following the opening of many of the relevant major collections of papers in Israeli and American archives, we are in the throes of a revisionist surge regarding the Six Day War, whose fortieth anniversary has just been marked with a mixture of celebration and anxiety. Both *1967*, by Tom Segev, and *Foxbats Over Dimona*, by Isabella Ginor and Gideon Remez, are explicitly revisionist. Ginor and Remez aim to correct our understanding of a crucial aspect of the origins of the crisis in May 1967, giving a radically new spin to the war that took place the following month, and specifically Soviet behavior during the war; while Segev subjects the war, including its origins and its aftermath, and specifically the question of Israeli behavior during the war, to the full flail of newly released documentation, turning the whole story on its head. Six Day War revisionism is not a purely local emendation of history: in Ginor and Remez's case, it has important global ramifications, and in Segev's case, it has deep moral implications regarding the conduct of the Jewish state.

I will begin with Ginor and Remez—who write that they "fell into this role of historical revisionists like Alice into her rabbit hole"— because they have written the more important book, if proximity to the truth is a measure of importance. One of the abiding mysteries of the Six Day War is why, during the second week of May 1967, the Soviets officially and persistently, and through a host of channels, misinformed the Egyptians that Israel was massing troops, ten to twenty brigades, to invade Syria and conquer Damascus and topple its (pro- Soviet) Baathist regime. The Soviets knew this to be a lie, as Ginor and Remez demonstrate. Indeed, in mid-May Israel's prime minister, Levi Eshkol, repeatedly invited Dmitri Chuvakhin, the Soviet ambassador to Israel, to inspect the border area for troops concentrations. Chuvakhin declined, remarking that "it isn't a diplomat's assignment to tour frontiers and see whether forces are being massed there." The Egyptians also knew that this was a lie. They sent their army chief of staff,

Muhammad Fawzi, to Damascus to check, and he reported back to Cairo, on May 14 or 15, that "there was no sign of Israeli troop concentrations and the Russians must have been having hallucinations." The Syrians also knew it was a lie; and so did UNTSO, the U.N. truce force that supervised the borders.

Yet the Soviet move set the cat among the pigeons, leading directly to the sequence of Egyptian moves that resulted in the war. Starting on May 14, Egypt sent into the Sinai Peninsula four army divisions, undoing the de facto demilitarization of the peninsula that had prevailed since 1957. On May 16-18, the Egyptians expelled UNEF, the U.N. peacekeeping force deployed along the Egyptian side of the border between Sinai and the Negev. And on May 22-23, they closed the Straits of Tiran, at the northern end of the Red Sea, to Israeli shipping and aircraft, thus substantively cutting Israel off from Africa and Asia.

In 1957, the United States had given Israel a guarantee that the straits would remain open. And so, at a stroke, Egypt's president, Gamal Abdel Nasser, had canceled Israel's three major accomplishments from the Sinai-Suez War of 1956. Each of his steps was a clear casus belli—the remilitarization of a buffer area, which threatened the south of Israel and forced it to mobilize its reserves, the bulk of the Israel Defense Forces (thus partially paralyzing the economy); the removal of the U.N. tripwire that afforded Israel sufficient time and notice to mobilize should Egypt intend war; and the closure of a vital international waterway and lifeline.

Nasser capped these moves, on May 30, by signing a defense pact with Jordan's King Hussein that subordinated Jordan's army to the Egyptian high command and provided for the deployment of Egyptian troops on Jordanian soil. (Two battalions of Egyptian commandos were immediately positioned in the West Bank.) And then, after signing a defense pact with Egypt, the Iraqis sent their Eighth Brigade into Jordan—but, tardy as always, the Iraqis were interdicted and bombed by the Israeli Air Force on the afternoon of June 5, before they managed to cross the river and join the fray.

Nasser's actions were preceded by rising tension along the Israeli- Syrian border, which, during the previous two years, had seen the start of Fatah guerrilla-terrorist raids against Israel originating in refugee camps in Syria (though usually carried out across the Jordanian-Israeli and Lebanese–Israeli frontiers); and Syrian efforts to divert the headwaters of the Jordan River (which, along with the Sea of Galilee, is Israel's main water resource); and intermittent Syrian harassment, with small arms and artillery fire, of Israeli farmers and border kibbutzim. During the first months of 1967, Israel retaliated a number of times—six Syrian MiG-21 fighters were downed around Damascus in April 1967—and Israel's military and political leaders threatened Syria with further reprisals if it persisted.

The conventional wisdom had been (and still is) that Moscow 'warned" Egypt of the massing of Israeli troops along the Syrian border in order to push the Egyptians into making a show of strength in Sinai that would deter the Israelis from attacking their Syrian allies. The Russians had not intended war. But the muscle-flexing got out of hand. Nasser, the eternal gambler (in 1956 he had nationalized the Suez Canal, bringing the Anglo-French invasion down on his head, and in 1963 he had intervened with his army in Yemen's civil war, suffering a bloody nose), pushed his army into Sinai; and, encountering no Israeli or international response, he ordered out the U.N. peacekeepers. Still there was no response—so he closed the straits. By then Nasser had gone too far to reverse course, at least without a loss of political and strategic prestige; and after a two-week delay, in which Israel allowed the diplomats and Washington time to resolve the problem but nothing happened, the IDF unleashed its assault on Egypt.

Ginor and Remez argue that the war was not a result of Egyptian (and Soviet) miscalculation, but the deliberate outcome of Soviet (or Soviet-Egyptian- Syrian) design and policy. As Israel's nuclear weapons project at Dimona neared fruition, the Soviets (and Egyptians) grew increasingly alarmed. Nasser had already declared back in 1960 that if Israel were to

achieve nuclear weapons capability, he would launch a pre-emptive attack. Now, in May 1967, the Soviets decided to destroy Dimona. But they would do so not out of the blue (as the Israelis later did with Saddam's nuclear reactor outside Baghdad in 1981). They would instead provoke Israel into attacking Egypt (and Syria), thus setting the stage—and providing cover and political justification— for a pinpoint strike on Dimona.

They argue also that the Soviets and Egyptians had conceived the "Grechko–Amer Plan" (named for Andrei Grechko, the Soviet defense minister, and Marshal Abdel Hakim Amer, Egypt's vice president and defense minister), which was to include the initial provocative Egyptian push into Sinai, in November 1966, shortly after the signing of the Egyptian- Syrian defense pact. The Egyptians and the Soviets believed that the Egyptian army, properly deployed, would manage to contain and to halt the initial Israeli attack in Sinai, and they would then follow it up, after the world branded Israel the aggressor, with the counter-stroke that would include Dimona. The Arabs, they believed, would win, and Israel might well go under. "The goal of eradicating Israel, while never formally stated as official policy, was widespread in Soviet thought and parlance," Ginor and Remez write. Chuvakhin reportedly told one Israeli communist interlocutor that "the war will last twenty-four hours only and no trace of the state of Israel will be left." In addition to destroying Dimona from the air, the Soviets, according to Ginor and Remez, planned small amphibious landings on Israel's Mediterranean coastline.

But the Soviet (or Soviet-Egyptian- Syrian) plan came a cropper because Israel's opening air strike against the Egyptian Air Force on the morning of June 5, code-named Operation Moked, was so devastating that the hours and days that followed failed to provide the cover (and the bases) that were needed for a Soviet attack on Dimona. After 11 a.m. on June 5, there were no functioning Egyptian air bases, and by the end of day one—or, at the latest, day two—of the war, there was nothing much left of Egypt's ground forces either. The Soviets dropped the plan.

The problem with Ginor and Remez's thesis is that it rests on very flimsy evidence. More bluntly, they have no real documentation to back it up. They may well be right, but they do not prove their case. They argue, correctly, that the relevant Soviet documentation—from the KGB, the Communist Party presidium, the GRU, the Soviet Air Force and Navy—is closed; and they add, for good measure, that it is quite possible that the whole design may well never have been recorded on paper. (I doubt that: modern armies cannot march against foreign countries, nor can air and naval fleets deploy to attack them, without a great deal of political, logistical, intelligence, and operational paperwork.) Almost the only backup that Ginor and Remez have is a handful of Soviet memoirs or interviews with former soldiers that allege Soviet preparations for ramshackle, two-bit commando landings (by units including ships' "cooks and medics," without maps or specific targets) on Israel's shores, and some circumstantial evidence that may or may not be relevant (such as the Soviets' reinforcement of their Mediterranean fleet in the months before the war).

But the "almost" is important. Ginor and Remez do adduce one (almost) hard and troubling piece of evidence: aircraft flying out of Egypt did, on May 17 and May 26, fly over the Dimona reactor site on photography and intelligence-gathering missions, and Israel's Hawk anti-aircraft batteries and Mirage III fighters failed to intercept, catch, or shoot down the intruders. The planes flew too high and too fast; and this fact, combined with several additional snippets of information, leads Ginor and Remez to conclude, persuasively, that at least some of the intruding aircraft were MiG-25 Foxbats, advanced aircraft that only Soviet pilots could have flown—and, let me add, that only Soviet ground crews could have serviced and only Soviet ground control officers could have directed to target. These overflights, along with Amer's order to the Egyptian Air Force to attack Israel, including Dimona, on May 26 (an order immediately rescinded by Nasser), caused consternation, almost panic, in the Israeli General Staff and Cabinet.

Ginor is a Ukrainian-born researcher who immigrated to Israel in 1967; Remez, her spouse, is an Israeli radio journalist. They stress that their book "has no present-day political agenda"—though, curiously, they compare Russia's "dilemma" in 1967, when facing Israel's imminent acquisition of nuclear weapons, with that faced by "the United States in 2006" when confronting Iran's nuclear ambitions. Still, this book goes a way toward further blackening the image of the Evil Empire in the heyday of the cold war, portraying a mendacious regime that would stop at nothing to instigate a proxy war so as to achieve its military and political purposes.

Ginor and Remez state, almost as an aside, that "our work does confirm that the Six-Day War was definitely not premeditated by Israel for expansionist purposes." This has seemed obvious to most reasonable observers almost since the guns of June 1967 fell silent. But perhaps the point does require reiteration, because it is precisely one of Tom Segev's contentions in 1967 that the war was a result, in large part, of Israeli expansionist drives and ideologies, religious and secular. (This argument was recently heard also in the punditry that was provoked by the fortieth anniversary of the war.) It was also, Segev further argues, a result of an Israeli economic crisis, a downturn in immigration, social turmoil, a weak political leadership unable to oppose muscular generals, and a pervasive paranoia—which is not the same thing as a legitimate fear—bred by the memory of the Holocaust.

Segev's book appeared in Hebrew almost two years ago, and the English-language version contains several additions, though no substantive alterations that I could detect. In both versions, it is Segev's contention that Israel—more precisely, Israeli "insanity"—was to blame for the Six Day War:

> It was not Nasser's threats...but the
> quicksand of [Israeli] depression. ...
> It was the ... feeling that the Israeli
> dream had run its course. It was the
> loss of David Ben-Gurion's leadership
> ... coupled with the lack of faith in

Eshkol. ... It was the recession and the unemployment; the decline in immigration and the mass emigration. It was the deprivation of the Mizrahim [Jews from Arab countries], as well as the fear of them. ... It was the boredom. It was the terrorism; the sense that there could be no peace.

Here Segev seems to be projecting 2000-2007 onto 1967. "All these feelings welled up in the week[s] before the war, sweeping through the nation in a tide of insanity. ... So the ideas [for a diplomatic solution] being put forth ... by more stable minds in Israel, Washington, and New York never had much of a chance."

This portrait of Israel in 1966 and early 1967 is skewed. The economic downturn was a minor recession, nothing like the American or German depressions. (Indeed, the early 1960s saw the establishment of the foundations of the modern industrial economy.) There was greater immigration to Israel than emigration. The Sephardi–Ashkenazi gap, while extant, was hardly in crisis mode (there were no riots to compare with 1959 or the early 1970s); and the same applies to the religious-secular divide—hardly a period of violence or fireworks. Palestinian terrorism was meager and trivial compared with the standards set in the 1970s and 1990s. The country's political leadership, while not flamboyant or "great," was certainly composed of capable and honest people. Israelis were no more "bored" then than in any other time. In other words, the picture that Segev paints of Israel's internal condition in 1966 and early 1967, with which he tries to "explain" the war, is essentially false. Segev, a journalist, is overly impressed by newspaper headlines.

And there was also, he instructs, the expansionist mentality of Zionism. "Many Israelis refused to give up the original Zionist dream, hoping for the day when Israel would embrace both sides of the Jordan [not just all of Palestine from the Mediterranean to the river]," Segev tells us in the beginning of his book. "Some Israeli politicians, including Ben-Gurion, as well as some IDF generals did not rule out military action to expand the state over the Green [1949 armistice] Line[s]." A few pages later we learn that "while war with Egypt [in June 1967] was the outcome of Israel's demoralization and a sense of helplessness, the fighting with Jordan and Syria expressed a surge of power and messianic passion."

And finally there was the bellicosity born of the memory of the fate of Europe's Jews. (Some years ago Segev wrote a book called *The Seventh Million*, about Zionist and Israeli attitudes toward the Holocaust.) It is true, as Segev argues, that Israelis—indeed, Jews everywhere—were traumatized by the Holocaust (how could they not have been?), and that in those waiting days between May 15 and June 4 many Jews thought there would be thousands of casualties in the war and feared a genocidal slaughter. (As it turned out, Israel suffered less than eight hundred dead, several dozen of them civilians.) With the benefit of hindsight, Segev feels able to argue that Israeli fears were irrational, indeed paranoid: the Arabs were weak and Israel was strong, and Nasser and the others did not really mean it when they spoke of throwing the Jews into the sea.

And yet Segev himself provides the counter to this when he quotes Ben-Gurion: "None of us can forget the Nazi Holocaust, and if some of the Arab leaders, with the leader of Egypt at their head, declare day and night that Israel must be destroyed ... we should not take these declarations lightly." (Later Segev offers a counter to this counter by quoting King Hussein: "With the Arabs, words don't have the same value as they do for other people. Threats mean nothing." So, in the end, Israel should not have taken Nasser's threats, or moves, seriously?)

In Segev's view, to understand the Six Day War one needs to understand more than the "diplomatic and military background. What is needed is deep knowledge of the Israelis themselves." Not of the Arabs—of Nasser and his generals, who sent in their tank divisions and closed the straits in defiance of the agreements of 1956-1957; or of the Jordanians, who ignored Israeli appeals on the morning of June 5 not to open fire or, later, to stop firing artillery into downtown West Jerusalem, the suburbs of Tel Aviv, and the Ramat David air base in lower Galilee (the IDF began responding only at around noon, after Jordanian troops stormed the U.N. headquarters compound in southern Jerusalem); or of the Syrians, who rained down shells on Israel's Jordan Valley settlements starting on the evening of June 5 (the IDF assaulted the Golan on June 9-10). No, there is no need to look at or understand Nasser, Hussein, or the Syrian leadership—or the hundreds of thousands of Arabs who took to the streets of Cairo, East Jerusalem, Damascus, and Baghdad shouting "Idhbah al Yahud!", "Slaughter the Jews!"

For Segev, Arab politics and Arab society have no bearing upon the proper understanding of the origins of the war. In 1967, the Arabs are mere props—mindless, thoughtless, motiveless extras, and in no meaningful sense historical agents. Segev expends hardly a line on them. There is no trace of any effort to get into their heads or under their skin. The book has massive footnotes, with thousands of references (almost every footnote refers to half a dozen or a dozen or more sources, which is itself annoying to anyone wishing to trace the origin of a quote), but none, as far as I could tell, refers to an Arab source. Granted, the Arab states' archives are all closed since they are located within the sway of dictatorships—but this does not entirely excuse Segev's delinquent lack of interest in the Arab side of the story. There are Arab memoirs and newspapers; and there are living Arab politicians, officials, and officers from 1967 who might have been willing to talk. And yet all the references are to Israeli and, to a lesser extent, American sources. It is almost as if Israel fought the war with itself.

Even when Segev briefly mentions Nasser and his actions between May 14 and May 23, it is, curiously, not what Nasser thought and did that is presented, but what Israelis reported and thought about what Nasser did. The reader first encounters the Egyptian thrust into Sinai thus: "[IDF Chief of Staff Yitzhak] Rabin had come by to tell the prime minister [Levi Eshkol] that information from Cairo indicated the Egyptians were moving forces into the Sinai Desert. ... Eshkol was surprised." The only Arabs who actually make an appearance (again, via Israeli sources) are the

Palestinians, after the West Bank and Gaza Strip have been conquered. But here, too, the focus is on Israel and Israelis: Segev cares only about what Israelis saw and thought and proposed and did about or to these Arabs.

Some Israelis—David Kimche, Arie Lova Eliav, Dan Bavli, and others—did try to formulate some type of two-state accord with Palestinian notables or to initiate a rehabilitation of refugee camp dwellers, but without success. Others—this is one of the book's more illuminating passages—worked on plans for transferring Arabs out of the West Bank and Gaza to South America or elsewhere. Segev devotes long pages to describing the attempted destruction of the town of Qalqilya and the expulsion of villagers from the Latrun Salient and the western edge of the southern West Bank. Some of this material, including many of the references, is new.

The picture of 1967 left with Segev's reader is of trigger-happy, mindless Israeli politicians, bureaucrats, and generals cynically and hysterically seeking a casus belli to enlarge the state. Page after page, quote after quote, this is the picture. No, that is not quite fair: in throwaway sentences, Segev also provides his readers with an inkling of the truth. These sentences contain the essence of the story of the period between May 14 and June 4. Describing the Israeli Cabinet meeting on May 23, Segev writes: "But most of the ministers were loath to take action. Minister of Health Israel Barzilai suggested waiting two or three weeks. Avraham Shapira maintained that Egypt did not want war. They all agreed that closing the Straits was 'an act of aggression' and decided to send Foreign Minister Eban to the United States." So Israel did wait "two weeks." Those are not the animadversion of trigger-happy people.

As for Israeli expansionism, it is true that after the war of 1948- 1949, many Israelis, including Ben-Gurion and most of his generals, felt that a great opportunity had been missed and that it would have been better to have ended the war with the country's border on the Jordan River. (Their reasons were more military and strategic, and less ideological and historical.) But over the following years, an overwhelming majority of Israelis came to accept that war's results, including its strategically problematic borders, and restrained any expansionist inclinations. By 1967, only the messianic–religious and the secular far right dreamed and talked about expansion to the West Bank, or Judea and Samaria, the historical heartland of the Jewish people and faith. For the vast majority of the citizenry, led by the successive Mapai-dominated governments, such thinking was alien. Many examples can be offered in proof of this claim. Consider only this exchange, published in early May 1967 in an Israeli newspaper, between the expansionist right-winger Geula Cohen and the Grand Old Man, David Ben-Gurion.

Cohen: "What are the borders of my homeland?"

Ben-Gurion: "The borders of your homeland … are the borders of the State of Israel, as they are today."

(After the war, incidentally, Ben-Gurion advocated complete Israeli withdrawal from the territories, except from East Jerusalem, though occasionally he also spoke covetously of the Golan Heights.)

Yes, the IDF general staff—certainly after May 22-23, when Nasser closed the Straits of Tiran—pressed for war. By the end of the month they were even chafing at the bit, arguing that every day's delay would multiply the number of Israeli dead. But their political bosses, the Cabinet and the prime minister, refused to knuckle under. For almost three weeks, from May 15 to June 4, the politicians—led by Eshkol—held out, hoping against hope that war would be averted; that the Americans or the United Nations would manage a diplomatic solution or that an international flotilla would somehow force open the straits and force Nasser to back off. The full story of the Israeli side in those unbelievably tense weeks is of a democratic polity under external military siege, feeling gradual asphyxiation but firmly under the control of the political echelon, which was doing its damnedest, in the face of mounting Arab provocation, to stave off war.

And the picture is similar in microcosm—this is apparent even from Segev's book—regarding the conquest of the West Bank and Jerusalem. For long hours, while the Jordanians, unprovoked, were shelling Jerusalem, the Israeli Cabinet held off on unleashing the IDF against the Hashemite kingdom. And for two days it deferred and delayed, contrary to military logic, the decision to conquer East Jerusalem, with the Old City and the Temple Mount at its heart. Israel went to war reluctantly and it conquered the Palestinian territories reluctantly. It won decisively, to be sure; but that decisiveness was owed to Arab weaknesses on the ground. And in the end, even the Golan Heights was almost not taken. The IDF Northern Command and the Jordan Valley kibbutzim lobbied and lobbied for Israeli military action in the north on June 5 through 8—not because they coveted the tracts of land on the Golan, as Segev would have it, but because they were sick of the intermittent shelling they had suffered at Syrian hands during the previous decade—and still the Cabinet, including Defense Minister Moshe Dayan, held off. It was not until June 9 that Dayan gave the green light. (It appears that he was deterred during the war's first four days by the fear of Soviet intervention, and also by the shortage of available units to take the Golan. But the fact is that he held off.)

It is true that, following the war, an expansionist messianic spirit gripped much of the Israeli population. The deep fear of catastrophe and slaughter was replaced by an overwhelming elation, which translated for many into a sense that Israel had been given a divine warrant to expand its borders. The consequences of these dangerous enthusiasms are now well known. But as a historical matter, it is worth noting that on June 19 the Israeli government secretly offered the Syrians the return of the Golan Heights in exchange for peace (and a demilitarized Golan), and offered the Egyptians the whole Sinai Peninsula (demilitarized) in exchange for peace. Of this, Segev writes: "Israel thus created the impression that it had offered to return the territories in exchange for peace." He is, of course, right that Israel failed to offer to return the West Bank and the Gaza Strip to Arab sovereignty. The Israeli Cabinet was deadlocked about the fate of these territories. But to dismiss the Israeli offer—to two states that had just in effect tried to destroy it—as mendacious or meaningless is absurd. It is also worth recalling that the Israeli offer and its rejection by Cairo and Damascus were in short order followed by a terse, comprehensive pan-Arab response at the summit in Khartoum—the famous "Three No's": no recognition, no negotiation with Israel, no peace.

Again, a wild, somewhat mindless expansionist spirit did overcome the Israelis after the victory, with religious extremists calling for the destruction of the two mosques on the Temple Mount and their replacement with the Third Temple. Ben-Gurion proposed pulling down the Old City's walls. And the government immediately destroyed Jerusalem's small Maghrebi Quarter to make way for a large plaza in front of the Wailing Wall. Within weeks, the government began settling parts of the West Bank and the Golan Heights, setting in motion the first wave of the vast settlement venture that implanted, within four decades, more than 400,000 Israelis in the West Bank and the Jerusalem area. The war certainly triggered an expansionist, and even millenarian, upsurge; but the war was not prompted or preceded by one.

One could argue that after defeating the Jordanian army and after Khartoum, Israel should immediately and unilaterally have withdrawn from the West Bank and restored it to Hussein's rule, and perhaps done something similar with the Gaza Strip and Sinai and the Golan Heights (as perhaps the Americans should have done after toppling Saddam Hussein in Iraq in 2003), though the immediate return of the Sinai Peninsula would have given away the card that proved necessary for trading land for peace with Egypt in 1979. But to argue, as Segev does, that Israel, locked in battle with the Egyptians in the south, should have refrained from going into the West Bank from which the Jordanians were shelling Israel's cities (and from which further attack by Iraqi and Egyptian troops was imminent) makes no sense. It is pure ahistorical thinking. Segev declares that "Israel could have responded by defeating the Jordanian army without taking the West Bank and Jerusalem." Really? Perhaps by carpet- bombing and massively shelling the

West Bank and Jerusalem? Would Segev have later approved of such actions, which would have resulted in thousands of civilian casualties? (As it happened, the Israeli conquest of the territory caused very few civilian casualties.)

Segev's 1967 is studded with such politically correct posturing, and riddled with perverse and high-minded asides and aphorisms. Consider this one: the struggle to throw off the "various restrictions" under which Israel's Arab minority lived after 1948 "was a civil rights cause, not unlike the campaign against racial discrimination in the United States." "Not unlike"? Surely there is a difference. Israel's Arabs were part of a people that had launched a war to destroy Israel in 1948 and continued guerrilla and terrorist warfare against Israel during the following decades. Is this really comparable to the plight of the African Americans? Is Africa besieging the United States and engaged in a war against it, with a putative African American fifth column within? The analogy is ridiculous. And one shouldn't forget that while suffering certain types of discrimination and enjoying certain "affirmative" benefits—they do not need to "waste" three years of young adulthood in military service—Israel's Arabs do enjoy full rights of citizenship (voting rights, election to the Knesset, an Israeli Arab sits in the Cabinet, and so on).

The book's final two hundred pages, covering the war's aftermath, contain some wonderful passages. Segev devotes five pages to the story of the influential book *Siah Lohamim*, or *The Talk of Soldiers* (which appeared in abridged form in English in 1971 as *The Seventh Day: Soldiers Talk About the Six-Day War*), in which some 140 kibbutznik veterans of the fighting discussed, in group interviews or conversations, their experiences and their moral repercussions.

It was most certainly not a victory album, with which Israel was awash within weeks of the war. The young Amos Oz co-edited the book. The soldiers spoke of fear, of death and mutilation, of the horror and pain of war. The book, a major bestseller, sold 100,000 copies in Hebrew and was received, as Segev rightly notes, as an "authentic document."

But that is not the whole of the tale. Using research by a young scholar at Tel Aviv University, Segev describes how the original transcripts were altered and censored by the editors; how graphic descriptions of atrocities against Arabs were deleted; how expansionist meditations by sons of Palmach commanders from the 1948 war were omitted; how messianic reveries by religious kibbutzniks were left out. Also deleted were veterans' references to orders to shoot wounded soldiers or civilians and comparisons between Israeli and Nazi behavior. In short, the editors managed to create a "candid," moving, liberal anti-war text that bore only a partial resemblance to what was actually said in the original conversations.

But apart from the descriptions of various aspects of the war's aftermath, 1967 is one vast, tendentious historical misjudgment. Unfortunately, this has become one of Segev's calling cards (alongside great readability). Examples could be multiplied. In his previous book *One Palestine, Complete*, a history of the British Mandate, Segev wrote of the origins of the Balfour Declaration of 1917, in which Britain expressed support for the creation in Palestine of a Jewish "national home": "The declaration was the product of neither military nor diplomatic interests but of prejudice, faith, and sleight of hand. The men who sired it were Christian and Zionist and, in many cases, anti-Semitic. They believed the Jews controlled the world." In short, first and foremost, according to Segev, the declaration was a product of British anti-Semitism. Most historians would say—along with what Lloyd George and Balfour themselves said, repeatedly—that the declaration was a product of the philo-Semitism of most of the Imperial War Cabinet members (including Jan Smuts, Lord Milner, Balfour, and Lloyd George), and also, more coldly, of British imperial interests.

Or consider *The Seventh Million*, in many ways an important book, full of valuable insights into Israeli and Zionist history. At the end of its second chapter, for example, Segev explains why and how three million of Europe's pre-World War II nine-million-strong Jewish community survived the war. "Most"—I am translating from the Hebrew edition—"were saved as a result of Germany's defeat in the war, some thanks to help from various governments and institutions... and several thousand in each country by good people, righteous gentiles....Only a relatively small number from among the survivors owed their lives to the redemptive efforts of the Zionist movement." A heavy accusatory cloud hangs over this sentence (and others like it), the implication being that the Zionist movement did not do all it could have done to save Europe's Jews and that, had it done so, more, perhaps many more, would have been saved.

This is nonsense. Various Zionist organizations did try to lobby the combatant Western powers to do more—to bomb Auschwitz, to deal with Hitler—but to no avail. America and Britain were focused on winning the war and destroying the Nazi regime, not on saving Jews. The only branch of the movement with any real power was the Yishuv, but it, too, lacked any capability to project power into Nazi-occupied Europe and, in any case, under British mandatory rule it lacked any possibility of independent military action, in the circumstances of 1941-1945, outside Palestine. So in fact it had no capacity to save European Jews—though it symbolically sacrificed a dozen parachutists, who were dropped into Europe, to demonstrate that it at least cared. To imply, or even to hint, that the Yishuv could have saved Jews but chose not to save them is cheap sensationalism, and testifies to an astonishing lack of judgment and a deep desire to blacken the reputation of the Yishuv's leadership.

So there is revisionism and there is revisionism. Isabella Ginor and Gideon Remez's book opens a door for further research. Its thesis deserves to be beaten like bushes by hunters outing their prey—and the prey will indeed be trapped, one way or another, at the moment the Russian archives open the relevant files. And if what the authors suggest is true, the Six Day War will end up illumined in a completely fresh light. As for Tom Segev, his book points readers and scholars in no worthwhile direction. Its argument is not merely wrong; it also makes a small contribution of its own to the contemporary delegitimation of Israel.

Israel's Wars

By Ahron Bregman

A Powder Keg

The outbreak of war in the spring of 1967 shocked Israelis to the core, for it came, to speak bluntly, as a bolt from the blue. And it is only because this war was so remarkably successful that no demand was ever made—as was to be the case after the 1973 war—to investigate the politico-military establishment, whose superficial optimism and complacency had led Israelis to believe that war was a remote and unlikely event. That the Israeli leadership was totally relaxed about the security situation in the period just before this war, is well illustrated in the following extract from a report written by Walt Rostow, National Security Adviser in Lyndon Johnson's administration, of his meeting with Israeli Ambassador Abraham Harman on 31 January 1967:

> Israeli ambassador Harman came in yesterday … to share his observations on the mood in Israel. His theme was basically that Israel faces an economically difficult situation over the next three years or so … he said most Israeli leaders feel the long-term security situation is under control.

The view in Israel in the first half of 1967 was that its most implacable foe, President Nasser of Egypt, was unlikely to embark on a full-scale war. This opinion rested upon a theory that proved to be utterly erroneous; it was that as long as *la crème de la crème* of Nasser's forces, eight brigades in all, was still involved in the civil war in Yemen, supporting the Republicans against the Royalists, he would not dare to attack Israel. Complementary to this assessment was the view that neither Syria nor Jordan would open fire without the active participation of Egypt, which not only had the most powerful army but which was also in a geographical position to impose on Israel its traditional nightmare—a war on more than one front. And because the Israeli theory that war was remote was based heavily on the continuing Egyptian presence in the Yemen, the eyes of its intelligence services were fixed on airfields in Yemen and Egypt to check whether Egyptian troops were being brought back home, for their return to Egypt would be a strong indication that the prospects of war were higher than before. But in the first half of 1967 the Egyptian elite forces were still bogged down in the Yemenite civil war—they would return to Egypt only after the 1967 war—and in Israel it seemed as if the relatively calm situation along the Israeli–Egyptian border would continue unabated.

In stark contrast with the relatively calm relations between Egypt and Israel, the latter's relations with Syria were volatile and, in the period up to the 1967 war, characterized by a series of mounting tensions and skirmishes. There were three bones of contention between Israel and Syria. The first of these was over water. Israel wished to divert water from Lake Kinneret (also known as the Sea of Galilee) down south to the Negev desert where water was scarce. It was vital for Israel to develop the Negev, because this was its most unpopulated area, and it contained valuable resources such as uranium. Perhaps more important was the fact that a Negev which was dotted with Jewish settlements and factories would, so the Israelis hoped, put an end to the persistent calls on Israel to cede parts of the desert to the Arabs and allow Egypt to establish a land bridge with Jordan. But without water Israel could not develop the desert, and this is why she built a pipeline, partly open, called Ha'movil Haartzi (National Water Carrier) to divert water from the north to the south. The Syrians, however, objected to this project—their aims, after all, were opposite to those of Israel—and as the water sources, mainly from the Hatzbani and Banyas rivers, were in their territory, they attempted to divert the water before it reached Israel. This in turn had led to exchanges of fire in which Israeli tanks and aeroplanes hit and destroyed Syrian tractors and other machinery assembled to divert the water. This happened in four major border clashes: 17 March 1965, 13 May 1965, 12 August 1965 and 17 July 1966. Israel did manage to transfer water to the Negev, but the water project was a constant source of tension between the two countries.

The second bone of contention between Israel and Syria, and a persistent source of trouble in the region, was the support which the Syrian regime was giving to Palestinian paramilitary groups to cross into Israel and terrorize its citizens. This often led to Israeli military retaliatory actions aimed at forcing Syria to curb incursions from her territory. But while the authorities in both Jordan and Lebanon had taken tough measures to curb such infiltrations from their own countries into Israel, the Syrian leadership had extended its support to the Palestinian paramilitary groups. This led Yitzhak Rabin—he had taken over as Israel's Chief of Staff in January 1964—to state on 12 May 1967 that the retaliatory actions Israel had directed against Jordan and Lebanon to force them to curb terrorist attacks on Israel, were not an effective measure as far as Syria was concerned because, as Rabin put it, 'In Syria … the authorities themselves activate the terrorists'. He went on: 'therefore, the aim of any [future Israeli military] action against Syria will be different from the actions which Israel has taken against Jordan and Lebanon'. This statement—although given to the small and unimportant IDF Magazine *Ba'machane*—was regarded in Arab circles as an Israeli intent to harm Syria. As Nasser later put it: 'Israeli commanders (meaning Rabin) announced they would carry out military operations against Syria in order to occupy Damascus and overthrow the Syrian government'. Although Premier and Defence Minister Levi Eshkol—he had taken over from Ben Gurion in June 1963—criticized Rabin for issuing statements which increased tensions in the region, he had himself fuelled Arab anxiety by issuing similar declarations (Nasser: 'on the same day … Eshkol made a very threatening statement against Syria'). Eshkol's bizarre behaviour had little to do with Israeli–Arab relations, but rather with his own relationship with Chief of Staff Rabin and the attempts of each of them to outdo the other and impress upon the Israeli people that they were tough on the Arabs. Such declarations put President Nasser under strong pressure because of the defence pact between Egypt and Syria—signed on 4 November 1966—which committed Egypt to helping Syria if it was attacked by Israel.

The third bone of contention between Israel and Syria was over control of the demilitarized zones (DMZs). These were three areas west of the international border (agreed in 1923 between French mandatory Syria and British mandatory Palestine) which Syria had occupied during the 1948 war. Under intense international pressure, the Syrians were obliged to withdraw and to agree to these lands becoming demilitarized zones without defining their sovereignty. The Israelis—who had signed up to this arrangement voluntarily rather than under a *Diktat*—later regretted this, and attempted to regain control over these lands by provoking the Syrians and then taking advantage of military clashes to expand control over the DMZs. In a candid interview, former Chief of Staff Moshe Dayan had openly admitted that Israel, rather than Syria, was responsible for 'at least 80 per cent' of the clashes that had occurred in the DMZs between 1949 and 1967. Perhaps the most serious clash between Israeli and Syrian forces just before the June 1967 war occurred on 7 April 1967. On that day an exchange of fire in the DMZs escalated into an air battle in which Israeli planes shot down six Syrian MiG fighter planes, two of them on the outskirts of the capital Damascus. This was a humiliating defeat for Syria and, again, it put Nasser of Egypt under intense pressure to come to Syria's assistance.

To sum up, in the spring of 1967 Israeli–Egyptian relationships were relatively calm, in contrast with the tense Israeli–Syrian situation. As we shall now see, what ignited the Israeli–Syrian powder keg into a full-blown war which would also involve other Arab states, notably Egypt, was a Soviet lie.

The Spark—A False Soviet Report

In the literature, there are two competing views on relationships between the superpowers—the USSR and the USA—and the local states in the Middle East during the period of the Cold War (1945–89). One view maintains that throughout these years the local states had their own domestic and regional agendas which they tried, in their different ways, to make the Cold War serve. The other view is that the Middle Eastern powers had been mere pawns in a game played by the superpowers. The 1967 war has often been explained in terms of the first view, and the answer to the question of who first raised the storm and launched the march of events which ended in the short but decisive confrontation between Israelis and Arabs and which almost led to direct US and Soviet intervention, was clear: it was Nasser. New evidence, however, shows that this was not the case, and in fact what really sparked this confrontation was a Soviet attempt to exploit the local states in order to score points in its confrontation with the US.

To understand how this came to happen we should go back to 13 May 1967, the date on which Anwar el-Sadat, speaker of the Egyptian parliament, was on an official visit to Moscow. When the visit was over Sadat was seen off at Moscow airport by Vladimir Semnov, the Soviet Deputy Foreign Minister, and it was then that Sadat heard from Semnov that according to Soviet intelligence, 'Ten Israeli brigades had been concentrated on the Syrian border' ready to strike at Syria; in Cairo the same message was delivered to President Nasser by the Soviet ambassador. Against mounting tension between Israel and Syria—which, as we have seen, was caused by statements from Israeli leaders and troubles in the DMZs, notably the shooting down of six Syrian fighter planes on 7 April—the Russian information was taken very seriously indeed. Nasser now felt he had to act, for he had long been under intense pressure and criticism from Jordanian and Saudi Arabian radio stations for not doing enough to support fellow Arab states. This is why, at a late-night meeting with his deputy and commander of the Egyptian armed forces, Field Marshal Abd el-Hakim Amer, and Sadat, who had just returned from Moscow, Nasser ordered to dispatch two divisions across the Suez Canal and into the Sinai, with the aim of distracting Israel from what seemed to be, according to the Soviet report, an imminent strike at Syria. It is important to note here that Sinai was Egyptian territory, and although the move was unusual there was nothing wrong with sending Egyptian troops there. In fact, seven years earlier, on 18 February 1960, Nasser had taken similar action, dispatching an armoured division and three infantry brigades—quite a substantial force at the time—into the Sinai to hint to the Israelis that they should leave Syria alone after they had attacked it at a place called Tawfik. But the difference between the two occasions was that in 1960 the Egyptian mobilization into the desert had been quiet and secret, whereas this time Egyptian troops on their way to Sinai marched through the streets of Cairo chanting: 'We are off to Tel Aviv.'

In addition to dispatching troops into the desert, Nasser sent his Chief of Staff Mohammed Fawzi to Damascus, entrusting him with two missions: first to confirm the Soviet information about the apparent Israeli mobilization, and second to coordinate moves with Damascus. In Syria, Chief of Staff Fawzi went with Syrian General Anwar Al–Kadi to inspect the border, but found nothing unusual. He later recalled: 'I was seeking confirmation about the Israeli troops, but when I arrived on the border I didn't find anything unusual … I looked at the latest aerial photos, but again I didn't find anything unusual.' The Syrians—they too had been informed by the Russians of the apparent Israeli mobilization—had sent reconnaissance planes which reported back that 'there was no massing [of Israeli troops] on the border [with Syria]'. The Israelis, in turn, dismissed reports of mobilization as false, and Prime Minister Eshkol even suggested that the Soviet ambassador in Tel Aviv, Leonid Chuvyakin, join the head of the Mossad, Meir Amit, in touring the border between Israel and Syria to see for himself that the Soviet allegations were unfounded; Chuvyakin, however, declined the offer. Neither in Israel nor in Syria had the foreign press reported any mobilization, which, as Abba Eban at the time, found odd, for:

> The mobilization of 'Eleven to thirteen Israeli brigades', to say nothing of their concentration on a narrow front, would have had a conspicuous effect on Israel's life. No newspaperman or foreign mission in Israel could have been unaware of it. The disruption of normality in so many families would have been registered in all the chanceries and newspapers of the world.

Israel, as everyone now knows, did not move any forces to its border with Syria, and it is widely acknowledged that the Soviet report, which for a long time has been one of the most puzzling features of the run-up to the 1967 war, was false.

An explanation of Soviet motives in issuing a false report is now possible, thanks to recent testimonies of such people as Evgeny Pyrlin, head of the Egypt department in the Soviet foreign ministry at the time the report was released. According to Pyrlin the reason why this crucial and most damaging report was issued was because the Soviets wanted to spark a war between Israel and its Arab neighbours, believing that

> even if the war was not won by our [Arab] side a war would be to our political advantage because our side would demonstrate its ability to fight with our weapons and with our military and political support.

That this was all part of the ongoing Cold War between the superpowers is also confirmed by the extraordinary report of a CIA agent, who had heard from a KGB agent that by releasing the report and instigating a full-scale Arab–Israeli war,

> The USSR wanted to create another trouble spot for the United States in addition to that already existing in Vietnam. The Soviet aim was to create a situation in which the US would become seriously involved economically, politically, and possibly even militarily and would suffer serious political reverses as a result of siding with the Israelis against the Arabs.

This evidence provides striking proof that, contrary to popular belief, the 1967 war was not instigated by the local states—neither Egypt nor Israel—but rather by the USSR as part of its competition with the US for world influence and supremacy.

Oddly enough, and in spite of Fawzi's findings that Israel had not mobilized troops on its border with Syria, Nasser did not call his divisions back from the Sinai—in fact he went so far as to reinforce them by dispatching more troops to the desert. Furthermore, on 16 May he instructed UN troops, which since the 1956 war had been deployed on the Egyptian side of the border (Israel would not allow them to deploy on her side of the border) and in Gaza and Sharm el–Sheikh, to leave their posts. Even though these UN troops were not strong enough to prevent either Israel or Egypt attacking the other, they were a symbol of non-belligerence and their removal was seen, and rightly so, as a further escalation of an already critical situation. We should point out, however, that Nasser's action was qualified, for what he did was order the removal of UN troops solely from their positions along the Egypt–Israel border, and not from Gaza or Sharm el–Sheikh, which controls passage through the Straits of Tiran. As Nasser put it in a later interview: 'I did not ask U Thant [the UN Secretary General] to withdraw UN troops from Gaza and Sharm el–Sheikh … but only from a part of the frontier from Rafah to Eilat'. Here, however, U Thant acted hastily and foolishly, insisting that either all UN troops remain in their positions, or that they leave altogether. Nasser—he could not back down on the UN issue without loss of face in the eyes of the world and his own people—took the latter option.

A week later, on 23 May, Egypt's president took yet another step, which raised the temperature of an overheated situation to boiling point, by ordering the closure of the Straits of Tiran to Israeli shipping. At a meeting with pilots at Bir Gafgafa air base, Nasser said:

> The armed forces yesterday occupied Sharm el–Sheikh … under no circumstances will we allow the Israeli flag to pass through the Gulf of Aqaba … if Jews threaten war we tell them 'you are welcome, we are ready for war. Our armed forces and all our people are ready for war' … This water is ours.

As has already been shown, the Straits of Tiran were perceived by Israel as a vital interest, and closing them meant bottling up Israel and hampering both vital imports—mainly oil from Iran—and exports. Closing the Straits, as we have made clear, also threatened Israel's ability to develop the Negev. The issue, however, was not only economic but also political, for the Straits had become a test of prestige for both Israel and Egypt. We should recall that after the 1956 campaign in which Israel occupied Sharm el–Sheikh and opened the blocked Straits, it was forced to withdraw and return the territory to Egypt. At the time, members of the international community pledged that Israel would never again be denied use of the Straits of Tiran. The French representative to the UN, for example, announced that any attempt to interfere with free shipping in the Straits would be against international law, and American President Dwight Eisenhower went so far as publicly to recognize that re-imposing a blockade in the Straits of Tiran would be seen as an aggressive act which would oblige Israel to protect its maritime rights in accordance with Article 51 of the UN Charter. Reluctantly, Israel accepted these diplomatic guarantees as a bad second-best substitute for the material security of actual occupation of the Straits. But on 1 March 1957, prior to the withdrawal of Israeli troops, Foreign Minister Golda Meir stated Israel's position before the UN General Assembly in unmistakably clear terms. She said:

> Interference by armed force, with ships of Israeli flag exercising free and innocent passage in the Gulf of Aqaba and through the Straits of Tiran will be regarded by Israel as an attack entitling it to exercise its inherent right of self-defence under Article 51 of the Charter and to take all measures as are necessary to ensure the free and innocent passage of its ships in the Gulf and in the Straits.

Yet in May 1967 Nasser ignored all this, and in the full knowledge that the Israelis were likely to react violently, he declared the Straits closed to her shipping. That he did so with open eyes we know from Anwar Sadat, who later testified how Nasser had said to his colleagues, whom he had brought together to decide on the closure of the Straits: 'Now, with the concentration of our force in Sinai the chances of war are fifty-fifty but if we close the Straits, war will be 100 per cent certain'.

What is also puzzling is that Nasser took such a drastic move without consulting either Syria or Jordan.

The historian A. J. P. Taylor once said that 'the greatest decisions are nearly always the ones most difficult to explain', and indeed, Nasser's fateful decision to close the Straits will long remain one of the most puzzling features of the 1967 war, and it may never be possible to learn for certain what his motives were. Nevertheless, two possible explanations can be offered to the question why he had decided on this action in the knowledge that for Israel this was a *casus belli* and the Straits represented a supreme national interest, their use being a right which it would assert and defend whatever the sacrifice. The first explanation, simple and straightforward, was probably best stated by Sadat—he would succeed Nasser in 1970—who wrote that 'Nasser was carried away by his own impetuosity'. Yet there may be a deeper explanation, and that is that in a matter of days Nasser's motive had changed from that at the start of the crisis, which was, following the false Soviet report, the attempt to distract the Israelis from attacking Syria, to a totally different aim, which was to take advantage of the growing crisis to reverse the post-1948 situation in the southern Negev and Eilat.

We should remember that at the end of the 1948 war, and after armistice agreements between Israel and Egypt (but not with Jordan) were concluded and signed, Israel breached these agreements by sending troops to Eilat and occupying it. This was significant, for by seizing Eilat Israel prevented Egypt and Jordan from having direct land access to each other. In *Al Ahram* on 7 January 1966, Mohamed Hassanian Heikal, a versatile journalist and intimate of Nasser whose writing frequently reflected the thinking of his president, wrote that it was most regrettable that in 1948 Israel had taken Eilat and thus created a 'wall' between the east and the west Arab world. He then added that in any future war with Israel, Egypt must attempt to pull down this wall and restore the pre-1948 situation in the vicinity of Eilat. It seems that now, with a crisis under way, Nasser decided to take advantage of the situation and achieve his long-held aim of reversing the situation in Eilat. What supports this interpretation is that the specific deployment of Egyptian forces in the desert appear instrumental to achieving such a task. We shall now examine this.

On the Brink of War: The Opposing Forces and Their Objectives

By 1 June—roughly two weeks after Nasser's first mobilization of troops into the desert—the Egyptian forces in the Sinai comprised seven divisions and a strength of 100,000 men. In addition, an infantry brigade was deployed at Sharm el-Sheikh, in control of the Straits of Tiran but not physically blocking it. It is a puzzling but little-known fact that Egyptian troops never blocked the Straits, which remained open before and throughout the crisis. As regards weaponry, the Egyptian forces were equipped with nearly 1,000 tanks, 900 guns of various calibres, 419 aircraft, four missile boats and two submarines. Yet contrary to popular belief, these forces were not deployed in attacking positions but rather on strictly defensive lines. That said, the one force which was ready to strike in the event of war, and thus was deployed in jump-off places, was Saad el-Shazli's, which was not, however, aimed at moving on Tel Aviv, but rather at striking in the direction of the southern tip of the Negev and Eilat in order to pave the way to establishing a land bridge between Egypt and Jordan. All other Egyptian forces in the Sinai were required to seal and isolate the operational area by blocking potential Israeli thrusts and thus enabling the Shazli force to accomplish its mission.

The Syrian army, which was also now fully mobilized, comprised between 50,000 and 60,000 men with at least 200 tanks of operational capacity and 100 Soviet aircraft, including thirty-two modern MiG–21s. The military aim of the Syrian forces was to occupy eastern Galilee and defend the Golan Heights from any Israeli attempt to seize them.

Jordanian forces were also fully mobilized and deployed. King Hussein's army was 56,000 strong and its main strength lay in its two armoured brigades—the 40th and 60th—mustering some 200 Patton tanks. These were deployed in a counter-attack role in the Jordan valley around the Damiya bridge in the north and near Jericho in the south; their aim was to defend the West Bank and East Jerusalem. A Jordanian–Egyptian force was also deployed in the salient of Latrun, just west of Jerusalem on the way to Tel Aviv. On 30 May, the King and President Nasser signed a joint defence pact. It meant that an attack on one country was seen as an attack on the other, which was required to come to the rescue. The King and the President also agreed that, in the event of war, Jordan's forces would be placed under Egyptian command.

Other Arab forces which were assembling against the Israelis included an Iraqi division, which took up positions on Jordanian territory, and two Iraqi squadrons which were advanced towards the Jordanian border and were thus closer to Israeli territory. Small token forces from other Arab countries, including Algeria and Kuwait, were sent to Egypt, and a small Lebanese army was also deployed.

Israel—whose main strength was its reserve force—had started mobilizing on 16 May and moved to full mobilization on 19 May; this was completed by the 20th. The forces were deployed in line with operational plan 'Anvil', which was a defensive posture, but one also designed for a speedy switch from defence to counter-offensive. Regarding Egypt as its main adversary and hoping that both Syria and Jordan would keep out of the battle, Israel had concentrated the bulk of its armed forces in the desert, leaving only scanty forces to fend off any attack on other fronts.

Israel's forces in the Sinai were organized into three divisions; the most northern was commanded by the diminutive Yisrael Tal, and consisted of two armoured brigades in which there were a total of between 250 and 300 tanks. Also under Tal's command and led by Colonel Rafael ('Raful') Eitan was a paratroop brigade supported by a battalion of Patton tanks. The second Israeli division in the Sinai, based entirely on reserves, was commanded by the veteran Abraham Yoffe

and consisted of two armoured brigades equipped with Centurion tanks. The third and most southern division was a mixed force which included an armoured brigade, two paratroop battalions, an infantry brigade, six battalions of artillery and a combat engineer battalion. It was commanded by the robust Ariel Sharon. In addition to these forces there were several independent combat groups: a mixed infantry armoured brigade in the rear of El Kuntilla; the 55th paratroop brigade headed by Mordechai Gur, and a naval task force. Totting up the balance sheet (Table 3.1), it can be seen that the Arab armies had clear superiority both in human and material resources.

The crux of all Israeli military operations in the desert was the offensive, for the strength of the Israeli Defence Force—despite its name—was in attack. Since the 1956 campaign, the IDF had been trained as an assault force whose doctrine of warfare was based on two principles: first, a pre-emptive strike by the air force, and second, the transfer of the war into enemy territory.

Comparison of IDF and Arab forces

	IDF	Arabs
Armoured brigades	10	18
Paratroop brigades	9	53
Tanks	1,300	2,500
Artillery pieces	746	2,780
Fighter jets	247	557
Ground-to-air batteries	5	26

The first military plan, drawn up immediately after Nasser's closure of the Straits of Tiran, visualized the movement of Israeli troops into the Gaza Strip with the aim of seizing it and then using it as a bargaining card to compel Nasser to open the Straits of Tiran. But opinions were divided as to the merits of such a plan. Moshe Dayan—he would later become Defence Minister—strongly opposed it on the ground that the Gaza Strip was not important enough for Nasser to be willing to trade it for ending the blockade of the Straits. In a private meeting with the Chief of Staff, Dayan told Rabin that the plan to capture the Gaza Strip in order to compel Nasser to open the Straits would not work, and added 'What will we then do with all these Arabs (meaning the Palestinian refugees of the Gaza Strip)?"

Under Ezer Weizman—he was then chief of operations, and on 24 May temporarily replaced the sick Chief of Staff Rabin—this plan was substantially modified. Now codenamed 'Atzmon Murchav', it visualized the occupation of the Gaza Strip and from there an advance of troops to occupy El Arish, and thence along the northern coastal axis to reach the Suez Canal. When Rabin returned to full service—he was absent for forty-eight hours and rumours said he had suffered a nervous collapse under the intense strain of the previous few days—he ordered the war plans to be recast. The air force was now to launch a preemptive strike to be followed by a simultaneous thrust of the three divisions in the northern part of the Sinai, in the area between Rafah and Umm Kataf, to break through into the desert and engage the Egyptian forces. Tal's forces operating in the northern sector were to occupy Gaza, El Arish and Rafah, which—controlling a natural passage of approximately ten miles between the sea and the dunes to the south—was considered a critical location as the jumping-off point for other forces into the heart of the Sinai. In the southern sector, Sharon's forces would take Abu Ageila and the Kuseima strongholds, two separate but mutually supporting bases. Sandwiched between Tal's forces in the north and Sharon's in the south, Yoffe would advance over dunes that had been considered to be almost impassable for tanks, and engage the major Egyptian armoured formations in central Sinai before moving deeper into the desert to seal the Mitla and Giddi passes against retreating Egyptian forces. From there the divisions would be ready to move up to the Suez Canal upon receiving new orders.

Israel—A Society Under Pressure

In Israel, meanwhile, the danger of war aroused increasing anxiety, and what came to be known as the 'waiting period', where forces were fully mobilized and the country came almost to a standstill, was nothing but a war of nerves. With news of the closure of the Straits of Tiran, anxiety turned to panic because after years of warnings by its leaders that a closure of the Straits meant war, Israelis could expect nothing but war. Threatening declarations by Arabs fuelled Israeli anxiety. In a speech before unionists on 26 May—just three days after announcing the closure of the Straits of Tiran—Nasser declared: 'The battle [with Israel] will be a general one and our basic objective will be to destroy Israel', and later:

> I was told at the time that I might have to wait seventy years. During the cru-saders' occupation, the Arabs waited seventy years before a suitable oppor-tunity arose and they drove away the crusaders … The whole question then, is the proper time to achieve our aims. We are preparing ourselves constantly.

In Damascus in the meantime it was announced that the time was ripe 'to liberate Palestine', and a Syrian delegation was reported to be heading to Cairo to coordinate military plans. The defence pact signed between Egypt and Jordan on 30 May—despite the inveterate hostility between the two countries—indicated to the anxious Israelis that this time the Arabs meant war and that Israel was totally isolated and faced a disaster. This all had a strong effect and awakened old memories of the Holocaust; as military commander Uzi Narkiss—he would later lead his forces to occupy Jerusalem—recalled: 'Auschwitz (the death camp where Jews were executed) came up. It never happened before. [Israelis] said … "we are surrounded, no one will help us, and God forbid if the Arabs armies invade, they'll kill us". Such was the panic that it was reported that Holocaust survivors were rushing to pharmacies to buy poison tablets lest they fell into the hands of the enemy. Rumours were rife, and we now know that these were based on fact, that the authorities had estimated 10,000 dead and, as we also now know, the Chief Rabbi, Shmuel Goren, demanded the preparation of coffins and sent his men to inspect public parks which would potentially become huge cemeteries in the event of war. In *My Country*, Abba Eban describes the mood in Israel at that moment in time: 'A sense of vulnerability penetrated every part of the Israeli consciousness like an icy wind. As Israelis looked around, they saw the world divided between those who were seeking their destruction and those who were doing nothing to prevent it'.

With tensions mounting and the mood becoming desperate, there was strong public pressure on Premier Eshkol to allow Ben Gurion back as either Prime Minister or Defence Minister. This was because Ben Gurion, the father of modern Israel, had led Israel through the 1948 and 1956 wars and was considered an expert in military affairs, while Eshkol was more of a finance expert. It did not matter to the Israelis that by now Ben Gurion was relatively out of touch, for what they sought was a strong, charismatic leader, and it seemed that Ben Gurion was the right man for this role. But relationships between Eshkol and Ben Gurion were at a low ebb, and Eshkol—an earthbound man and realist by nature, who had invested heavily in buying arms for the IDF in the years before this crisis—bitterly opposed having his predecessor in the cabinet. He said to those who pressurized him to invite Ben Gurion into his cabinet: 'These two horses can no longer pull the same cart'.

But on 28 May came an event which forced Eshkol to give way to public demand and political pressure. That Sunday he personally took to the airwaves to address the nation, and as he delivered his speech and as Israel heard it over the radio—there was not yet television in Israel—Eshkol stumbled over the words. He read his speech so badly and gave so poor a performance that it left the worst impression. It should be pointed out, however, that Eshkol's was more a failure of presentation and delivery than of substance, for there was nothing wrong with the speech itself—but such was the national mood that the effect of such a poor delivery was devastating. After his speech, which came to be known as *Ha'neum Ha'megumgam* ('the stammering speech'), Eshkol was widely criticized.

Now under growing pressure, Eshkol had no other option but to relinquish the defence post and offer it to Moshe Dayan, former chief of staff of the IDF and now a politician in Ben Gurion's small Rafi party. With the nomination of Dayan, it seemed as if the brake had been released and that the IDF—it could not remain mobilized indefinitely without wrecking Israel's economy—would be ordered to take action.

The Eve of War

On 2 June, Dayan met the IDF high command, and after being presented with the latest war plans he introduced three changes; the first related to the Straits of Tiran. We should recall that the last straw for Israel had been Nasser's decision to close the Straits to Israeli shipping; therefore Dayan held that in the event of a war breaking out, the Straits of Tiran must be opened. His instructions were that while the decisive thrust should be—as already planned by the military—in the direction of the heart of the Sinai desert, there should also be a thrust towards Sharm el–Sheikh to open the Straits. It was necessary to give such an instruction, for although the Straits were the main issue during the 'waiting period', by now the military planners preferred to concentrate on deciding how to engage the bulk of the Egyptian army in the desert and break its backbone. Dayan's second change to the operational plans dealt with the Gaza Strip. According to the military plans which were originally approved by Eshkol before the nomination of Dayan to the post of Defence Minister, Israeli forces were tasked with occupying the Gaza Strip. It was, in fact, Minister of Labour Yigal Allon—who was normally on the worst of terms with Dayan—who persuaded Eshkol that Israel should take the Gaza Strip and transfer its Palestinian refugees to Egypt. But to this Dayan objected strongly, for he held that the entire international community would turn against Israel if it attempted to transfer the Palestinians. Perhaps more importantly, he considered the Gaza Strip to be a place that 'bristled with problems ... a nest of wasps', a place which Israel should not occupy if it did not want to be 'stuck with a quarter of million Palestinians'. Therefore, in this crucial meeting with the military high command, Dayan ordered that the Gaza Strip should not be occupied, and as he later wrote in his memoirs: '[the plan] now before us received my approval … there would be no conquest of the Gaza Strip'. It is of historical interest to note here that Dayan was not the first to warn of the danger of occupying the Gaza Strip. In 1956, after Israeli troops had occupied the densely populated Strip, Prime Minister Ben Gurion said that he regarded Israel's rule over this compact mass of 'unreconciled people' as being 'as dangerous as dynamite placed at the foundation of the state'. The third element in the war plan which Dayan recast was the Suez Canal. Dayan held that if Israel occupied the Canal and deployed forces on its eastern bank, a mere 180 metres from Egyptian troops, Nasser could not operate the Suez Canal and he would resume the war against Israel; Dayan therefore gave orders that the troops should stop short of the Suez Canal. The restrictions which Dayan had imposed with regard to the Gaza Strip and the Suez Canal were clear and precise; as Aharon Yariv, then director of military intelligence later told the author: 'Dayan said to the General Staff: "I give you now the instruction of the defence minister: 1. To hit the Egyptian army. 2. *Not* to reach the [Suez] Canal. 3. *Not* to enter [the] Gaza [Strip]."' Dayan's observation that if Israel occupied the Suez Canal the war would continue and if it took the Gaza Strip it would 'be stuck' with too many Palestinian refugees was, as we now know, a deadly accurate forecast of the shape of things to come. One wonders why no one other than Dayan had similar insights, and furthermore how, given such a prophetic sense, Dayan later, as will be shown, gave way and agreed to allow the generals to occupy the Gaza Strip and reach the bank of the Suez Canal.

But still, on that crucial night of 2 June 1967, in the light of Dayan's instructions, a new plan codenamed 'Nachshonim' was prepared and its object was defined as 'Occupying Sinai up to the line of El Arish–Jabel Libini–Bir Hasna–Kuseima

… eliminating the Egyptian forces in this zone and being ready to continue development of the offensive into the heart of the Sinai'. From this newly devised plan two previous military aims were omitted: occupying the Gaza Strip and reaching the Suez Canal.

Back to the Superpowers

On 25 May, Nasser dispatched his Minister of War, Shams el–Din Badran, to Moscow to head an Egyptian delegation. Its mission was to obtain Soviet approval for Egypt to strike at Israel, and also to request a supply of war material. Nasser rightly assumed that whoever struck first would enjoy the advantage of surprise and hold the initiative, but he also recognized that acting without Soviet permission would be risky; Moscow might refuse to restock his arsenal after the war, and might also refuse to extend much needed political support. Badran and his delegation met Prime Minister Alexei Kosygin and explained that Egypt wished to strike at Israel. To this Kosygin replied: 'We, the Soviet Union, cannot give you our consent for your pre-emptive strikes against Israel. … Should you be the first to attack you will be the aggressor … we are against aggression … we cannot support you'. It is indeed puzzling that the Soviets, who had instigated the crisis in the first place by spreading the lie that Israel was mobilizing her forces on its border with Syria, were now attempting to control the situation and rein back Egypt.

On his return to Cairo, Badran reported to Nasser that the Soviets would not allow Egypt to strike and would not provide it with much-needed war material, but would intervene in the war on Egypt's side if America were to intervene on behalf of Israel. Nasser was careful to abide by the Soviet instructions and told his military commanders that Egypt would have to absorb a first strike by Israel. He insisted on this in the face of strong opposition, especially from the commander of the air force, General Sudki Mahmoud, who pleaded with him that such a policy 'will be crippling. … It will cripple the armed forces'.

Israel was also warned by the US not to take military action. In a tough conversation with Israel's Foreign Minister, US President Lyndon Johnson warned Abba Eban that: 'Israel will not be alone unless it decides to go it alone'. And in a late night meeting in Tel Aviv John Haydon, the CIA representative in Israel, warned Mossad Chief: 'If you strike, the United States will land forces in Egypt to defend her'.

On 30 May Israel sent former general and head of the Mossad, Meir Amit, to Washington. His mission was to see how Israel's view of the crisis compared with that of the American intelligence community (mainly the CIA), to see what would be Washington's response if Israel took action, and also to find out if any preparations had been made to put together an international armada—this had been proposed by British Prime Minister Harold Wilson—which would attempt to sail through the Straits of Tiran in defiance of Nasser's blockade. By this time the sole chance of preventing a general war lay in such an action, and given that, as we have already mentioned, the Straits were declared closed but were not in fact physically blocked (this of course was not known at the time), it might well be that such an armada could have passed without being fired on or even stopped, and war could have been averted. But this was a vain hope. In Washington, Amit found that the plan to set up a joint task force, composed of the principal maritime powers committed to the freedom of passage through the Straits of Tiran, had not even reached the launching stage. He also met Dean Rusk, American Secretary of State, who 'could not agree more' with Amit's assessment of the gravity of the situation. Amit also had three private meetings with James Angleton, the CIA's longtime liaison with the Mossad, from whom he learnt that the Americans would welcome it if Israel were to 'strike [at Egypt]'. To Robert MacNamara, Amit said that he intended to recommend to his government that they launch an attack, to which the American Secretary of Defence replied: 'I read you loud and clear'.

Thus it all came back to the superpowers. The USSR, which had instigated the crisis in the first place by issuing a false report, now showed the 'red light' to the Egyptians, warning them not to be the first to strike, though promising to intervene if America joined the war. As for the Americans, they had shown an 'amber light' to the Israelis ('I read you loud and clear'), which was interpreted by the head of the Mossad as a 'green light' to go to war. Following Amit's report, the Israeli cabinet decided to order the IDF to attack Egypt.

The Attack on Egypt

A successful air strike was crucial for the overall victory of the Israelis. This was aimed at curbing Egypt's capability to strike at Israeli cities and, perhaps more importantly, to achieve air supremacy over the desert, which would make Egyptian defeat certain. The air operation, code-named 'Moked', began at 7.45 a.m., as Egyptian pilots were having their breakfast, on Monday 5 June 1967. The air strike took a very roundabout approach, flying via the sea and coming in from the west. While the first wave of Israeli aeroplanes—183 in all—was making its way to Egypt, the entire command of the Egyptian armed forces, including Marshall Amer and Minister of War Shams el–Din Badran, were also in the air on their way to inspect Egyptian units in the Sinai; to ensure their safe passage and that they were not fired at by their own people, the radar system in Egypt was shut down. This tragi-comic episode, in which the Egyptian command is airborne, the radar system is shut down and Israeli fighter-bombers are on their way to targets in Egypt, symbolizes, perhaps more than anything else, the inefficiency of the Egyptian command, and demonstrates that part of Israel's stunning success resulted from the recklessness, blind folly and ineptitude of the enemy's political-military leadership.

'Operation Moked' was extraordinarily successful and led to a sensational and dramatic victory for the Israeli Air Force (IAF). Within 190 minutes the backbone of the Egyptian air force was broken—189 Egyptian aeroplanes were destroyed, mostly on the ground, in the first wave of attack, and by the end of the first day of war a stunning 298 Egyptian planes lay in ruins. Back in his headquarters Marshall Amer was trying to piece together a new plan from the wreckage. He ordered the air force to hit back at the Israelis, but the reply he received was that the little that remained of the air force was unable to carry out any meaningful operation. Nasser was later to complain bitterly that the Israeli air strike eventually came not from the direction his guns were pointing, but from behind: 'They came from the west', he said, 'when we expected them to come from the east'.

Backed by complete air superiority, the three Israeli divisions thrust into the desert to engage the Egyptian forces, which were incessantly pounded by Israeli planes and were no match for the Israeli ground forces. Meanwhile, the spokesman of the IDF announced that since the early hours of the morning Israeli forces had been engaged in fierce fighting with Egyptian forces which had started 'advancing towards Israel'; this was not quite true for, as we now know, the Israelis rather than the Egyptians were the first to open fire.

The retreat of the Egyptian army, though unavoidable, was hasty and chaotic. A skilfully conducted step-by-step withdrawal could have saved lives, or at least proved less costly, but in the event the retreat was very disorderly, with small and uncoordinated groups of troops trying to escape on foot through the desert dunes in the direction of the Suez Canal. The end result was disastrous—for while 2,000 Egyptian troops were killed fighting the Israelis, 10,000 perished in the retreat.

As Israeli forces gave chase in an attempt to cut the Egyptian lines of retreat, they drew closer to the Suez Canal, which Defence Minister Dayan had on the eve of the war ordered them not to occupy. At one point Dayan, thinking that his troops had already reached the Canal, issued orders to pull back. But then, under strong pressure from his Chief of Staff, who argued that militarily it was better to stop at the Canal, Dayan reversed his decision and allowed the troops to resume their advance and reach the bank of the Suez Canal. Furthermore, following the shelling of the Israeli settlements of Nachal Oz, Kisufim and Ein Ha'shlosha from inside the Gaza Strip, Dayan was requested to allow troops to enter the Strip and silence the enemy's fire. Again, Dayan gave way and allowed forces to enter Gaza, even though a few days before he had said that it 'bristled with problems', was 'a nest of wasps', and was a place which Israel should not occupy if it did not want to be 'stuck with a quarter of million Palestinians'.

Why Dayan gave way and allowed the armed forces to dictate the stopping line is a question to which there will never be a definite answer. But any clues may lie more in the character of Dayan than in any strategic consideration. For although Dayan was renowned as a brave soldier and almost a prophet because of his foresight, he was, on the other hand, too much the pessimist, often failing to fight for his ideas with colleagues or to impose his will on his subordinates; as was the case in the war in the Sinai, where he allowed short-term tactical considerations to disrupt his realistic policy.

Jordan

On the Jordanian front war started at 9:45 a.m. on 5 June, as King Hussein's guns opened fire along the border with Israel and Jordanian troops attempted to occupy the United Nations headquarters and other positions in Jerusalem. On this morning the Israelis delivered a message to the King, saying: 'This is a war between us and Egypt. If you stay out we will not touch you'. Upon receiving this message, the King—he was at air force headquarters—said: 'Jordan is not out. Jordan is already engaged'. This is understandable, for with Palestinians making up half of his population, if Hussein had stood aside his kingdom could have disintegrated. In addition, the King may have feared that he would miss the boat if he did not join the war, for in the early hours of 5 June, a message was received from Egypt's Marshall Amer, saying: 'approximately 75 per cent of the enemy's aircraft have been destroyed or put out of action … our troops have engaged the enemy and taken the offensive on the ground'.

This of course was a lie, but the King could not have known that. After all, Nasser had also called to say that Egypt was doing well. He said to the King—and we know exactly what he said because his conversation was intercepted and recorded by the Mossad—'We have sent all our aeroplanes against Israel. Since early this morning our air force has been bombing the Israeli air force'. This too was a lie, for while talking with King Hussein, Nasser already knew that his air force was totally destroyed. We know this because just before calling the King, Nasser had talked with President Boumedienne of Algeria, to whom he announced that the Egyptian air force was totally destroyed, and asked if he could spare a few aircraft. In his talk with the King, Nasser also urged that he join him in issuing 'an announcement concerning the British and American participation' in the war. This was clearly aimed to drag in the Soviets, for, as we should remember, the USSR had promised Egyptian Minister of War Badran that, if America joined the war, Russia would come in on Egypt's side.

Israel's response to the Jordanian attack was immediate and devastating—it destroyed Jordan's two air force bases and in 51 sorties totally crippled its small air force, before moving to occupy the West Bank and Jerusalem. This was a terrible defeat to King Hussein. He later recalled how he was standing on a hill watching his defeated troops:

> My troops were coming back in small groups, very tired. Many of them were saying: 'Please, your Majesty, find us some air cover and we'll go right back'. Of course, everything was over by then and I remember asking all these boys to move on to Zarka, so we could begin to reorganize whatever remained ... I saw all the years that I had spent since 1953 trying to build up the country and army, all the pride, all the hopes, destroyed ... I have never received a more crushing blow than that.

Elsewhere, on the Golan Heights, war did not start until 8 June. In fact the Syrians, after perceiving the fate of Egypt and Jordan, preferred to keep out of the battle, and when asked by the King of Jordan to provide air support they replied that all their aircraft were on training missions and not a single aircraft was available.

At first Israel refrained from attacking Syria because Defence Minister Dayan felt that if Israel struck, the Soviets might intervene on behalf of the Syrians. He also felt that if Israel occupied the Golan Heights it would never be willing to give it back and the conflict with Syria would continue for years. In the end, however, Dayan gave way, reversed his previous order not to attack, and authorized the occupation of the Golan Heights; in fact he did not even contact the Chief of Staff, who was sleeping at home in the belief that the war was over, but picked up the phone and issued an order to strike. We will probably never know why Dayan reversed his decision; it may be that he feared that after the war he would be blamed for not taking advantage of the situation to hit at Syria, with whom Israel had hostile border relationships. According to Dayan, his change of mind was made following intelligence information indicating that the Syrians would not resist if Israel struck. We now know what was not known even to Dayan at the time—that his prediction, that the Soviets might intervene alongside the Syrians to stop the Israeli advance on the Golan, almost materialized; Soviet planes in the Ukraine were preparing to attack Israeli military targets and Soviet submarines were approaching the shores of Israel. We do not know why they did not attack.

With Egypt and Jordan crippled, the IDF could concentrate all its strength on Syria, which was clearly no match for the Israeli air and ground forces. 'We dropped everything on the Golan Heights', recalls former IAF commander Mordechai Hod: In two days we dropped more tha[n] we had dropped on all Egyptian airfields [throughout the war]'. According to Syrian General Abdel Razzak Al–Dardari, who commanded four Syrian brigades on the Golan Heights,

> On that morning the Israelis moved ahead. … There was a sudden panic and there was an order to withdraw to the south. The pull-out was done in total chaos … the retreating soldiers had left their weapons behind and were almost running home. Some were running home even before the Israeli soldiers had come anywhere near their positions … there was no air cover nor an Egyptian front to distract the Israelis.

In spite of UN pressure on Israel to stop the war, and rising tensions between Washington and Moscow—the latter threatening to 'take any measures to stop Israel, including military'—the Israelis had managed to occupy the Golan Heights.

Euphoria and Division

The speed of the operation staggered the world, and the Israelis, whose immediate reaction to the stunning victory was euphoria and jubilation as a spontaneous expression of relief that the worst—what seemed to be an imminent second Holocaust—had not materialized and instead Israel had gained a victory with relatively few casualties. Indeed, in six days the battle was over, and by then Israeli troops were less than 50km from Amman, 60km from Damascus and 110km from Cairo. Israel now controlled an area of 88,000 square kilometres compared with 20,250 before the war, or 18 times the area which was allotted to the Jews by Lord Peel in the first partition plan for Palestine of 1937. The Sinai desert, the Gaza Strip, the Golan Heights and the West Bank now provided Israeli cities with a buffer zone, dramatically reducing the danger of Israel's extinction by a surprise Arab attack.

The victory had a special historic meaning because of the capturing of territories central to the religious mythical past: the Old City of Jerusalem with the Western Wall, which is the remnant of the ancient Jewish temple destroyed by the Romans; and the West Bank, which is part of biblical Eretz Yisrael and where such sites as Machpela are situated. For Israel's religious community, the occupation of these territories established the relationships between what they define as 'People, God and Promised Land', strengthening their sense of Jewish identity.

But the occupation of Arab lands also sowed the seeds of conflict and division within Israeli society; this was apparent immediately after the war, when a fierce debate regarding the future of the occupied lands broke out. A society, which only three weeks before was huddling together and fearing for its very existence, was now beginning to split between those who wished to cling to the occupied lands and those calling for it to be given back in return for peace and reconciliation. But it was more than a debate regarding occupied territories, for in the postwar era, with what seemed to Israelis to be a reduction of external danger because of their newly acquired strategic depth, a whole range of problems began to surface. As Abba Eban, a diplomat and a good observer, has written:

> As the pressure of war … died down, some of the latent tensions in Israeli society came to the surface. The turbulence took many shapes and expressions but the common factor was the growth of dissent … [Israelis now] rejected the idea that external dangers justified inertia or apathy towards domestic imperfections.

What became crystal clear in the post–1967 war period was that Israeli society was essentially a diverse, turbulent organism which tended to have a monolithic aspect only when facing urgent external danger. And this is precisely what made the 1967 war such a turning point in the life of the Israeli nation and society. For while the war seemed to remove a great external danger to Israel—whose cities were now far from the front—it also, ironically, removed the cement which had kept the people of Israel together.

And although, in the postwar era, opinion polls indicated the overwhelming popularity of the national leaders, with those in charge of defence policies supported by staggering percentages, the government was challenged as never before by its citizens. This criticism quickly gathered momentum and reached an unprecedented peak during the War of Attrition along the Suez Canal.

Section 3
Sparring for Advantage, 1967–1992

# Introduction

On Israel's southwestern frontier, following a costly but indecisive War of Attrition from 1968 to 1970 and the yet more painful—but equally indecisive—War of October 1973, Egypt and Israel both came to see the folly of continued hostilities. The result was a U.S.-mediated negotiating process leading to a formal Egyptian–Israeli peace treaty in March 1979. These agreements made possible inter alia the establishment of diplomatic relations between Israel and Egypt, Israeli withdrawal from all of Sinai, and Sinai's effective demilitarization.

On Israel's eastern and northern frontiers, however, no such accommodation developed, in part because Syria declined to follow Egypt's example of disengagement, but more basically because Palestinian and Israeli ambitions to control the same small bit of land remained irreconcilable. While Israel and Egypt moved toward compromise, Israel and its eastern foes thus pursued their struggles with undiminished vigor and imagination. Indeed, Egypt's neutralization inspired Israel, led by the newly formed right-wing Likud Party for most of the period from 1977 to 1992, to attempt to impose a solution, not only on the West Bank and Gaza, but on Lebanon, which after 1970 became the Palestinians' chief redoubt.

The two readings in this section describe the determined—and largely unsuccessful—search for unilateral advantage by both Palestinians and Israelis in the decades following the Six Day War. Given their paltry material resources, geographic dispersion, and initial fragmentation, the Palestinians' success in turning the Palestinian Liberation Organization (PLO) into a respected and influential political force was remarkable. Under Yasser Arafat's often brilliant leadership, the PLO directed world attention away from the conflict between the Arab states and Israel—which had dominated headlines from 1948 to 1967—back toward the central rivalry between Palestinian and Jewish nationalisms. The PLO's interpretation of Mideast tensions as an enduring competition between two national communities to control all or part of the same territory is now universally accepted.

Baruch Kimmerling and Joel Migdal describe this post-1967 transformation, starting with the development of a Palestinian self-image of heroism and sacrifice to supplant the image of Palestinians as wards of international charity. At the same time, Kimmerling and Migdal discuss the organizational conversion of the PLO from a docile tool of Arab states into an independent and innovative body with fervent support among Palestinians in the occupied territories, Jordan, Lebanon, and in the broader diaspora. If there is a unifying thread in the dizzying shifts in the PLO's political fortunes from 1967 to 1992, it is the Palestinians' constant search for strategic and political leverage with which to move the Israeli colossus. Central to these revised hopes was the PLO's insistence that Palestinians had to take responsibility for their own future, and that armed struggle was the only means to ultimate liberation. Yet, as we shall see, despite the PLO's creativity—and despite the its success in shaking Israeli complacency—by 1992 the PLO was obliged to abandon this foundational insistence on forcibly reclaiming all of Palestine. Instead, Arafat agreed *to consider negotiations under the aegis of the Americans toward some sort of two-state solution.*

But before Israel would enter negotiations, it too had to experience sustained frustration and partial defeat. This is the theme of Avi Shlaim's discussion of Israel's invasion of Lebanon in 1982 and its ineffectual response to the first intifada. *After describing the rather self-deluding plans for Lebanon developed by Prime Minister Menachem Begin and his Defense Minister Ariel Sharon, Shlaim shows how their ambitions were shattered by Lebanese sectarian politics, Syrian maneuvers, and mounting international criticism of Israeli actions.*

Although Israeli forces would remain in southern Lebanon, by late 1982 Sharon's gamble had failed. Nor was the IDF much more successful five years later in dealing with the intifada. *Again, popular resistance did great damage to Israel's international image and undermined Israeli confidence in military solutions. What is more, Shlaim emphasizes, the* intifada *destroyed any lingering hope that Israel could decide the future of the West Bank through a deal with Jordan's King Hussein rather than with the PLO. In short, by 1992 mutual frustration was edging both Israel and the Palestinians toward negotiations.*

The Palestinian People: A History

By Baruch Kimmerling and Joel S. Migdal

I am against boys becoming
heroes at ten
Against the tree flowering explosives
Against branches becoming scaffolds
Against the rose-beds turning to
trenches
And yet
When fire cremates my friends
            my youth
    and country
How can I
Stop a poem from becoming a gun?
—Rashid Hussein, "Opposition"

Israel's lightning victory in the Six Day War followed a month of dejection and demoralization in face of Nasser's bellicose maneuvers. Immediately afterward, things of course looked very different: In addition to taking the Golan Heights from Syria and the Sinai from Egypt, Israel's forces had driven Jordan's Arab Legion from the West Bank and the Egyptian army from the Gaza Strip, uniting the territory of the old Palestine mandate and bringing the majority of Palestinians under Israeli control (see Map 6). Over 600,000 West Bankers could now resume contact with the more than 300,000 Palestinians in the Strip and with a similar number living in Israel's pre-1967 boundaries. The war also precipitated another exodus of Palestinians from Palestine. Approximately 250,000 fled for the remnant of Jordan, the East Bank. The war is one of several events in the latter half of the twentieth century (others being the dissolution of the French and British empires and the Soviet Union, and the reunification of Germany) that radically transformed the world map. Its results were correspondingly momentous for both Israeli Arab citizens and Palestinians in the newly occupied territories.

To everyone's surprise, the nature of the conflict in which Jews and Arabs were embroiled was now different. After 1948, the conflict had seemed largely international—the armistice agreements, continuing border tensions, the Suez war in 1956, all involved sovereign states. From this perspective, both to its own Jewish citizens and to a larger world public, Israel seemed small and beleaguered, surrounded by much larger, hostile states that refused to accept its right to exist.

Following the 1967 war, the focus gradually drifted back to the communal problem, as in the days of the mandate: two peoples—Jews and Palestinians—claiming the same piece of soil. Israel's image thus shifted, much to the frustration of its supporters, from beleaguered to all-powerful.

With the territory of historical Palestine reassembled under a single authority for the first time since 1948, the bulk of the Palestinians once more stood face to face with the Jews, their longstanding enemies, representing an alien culture and religion. The reality of what was an almost perfect reversal of the two communities' proportions in the last years of the mandate—three million Jews now ruling slightly more than one million Palestinians—has been shrewdly and succinctly captured by poet Samih al-Qasim:

> Ladies and Gentlemen.
> We are here
> On a crossroad.

The Palestine Liberation Organization, led by Yasser Arafat and his Fatah faction, would now become the institutional vehicle for attracting and directing the charged emotions of the Palestinians. It would shape their self-understanding, although stumbling when it tried to mobilize their society under the single ideological umbrella of Palestinism—and under the noses of hostile governments. But despite its centrality, it was the resources of that society that would enable the organization to play such a prominent role.

Reflecting this interplay of leaders and followers, the Palestinians developed three heroic images in the face of the difficult post-1967 conditions: The *feday* (lit.: "one who sacrifices himself") was a modern metamorphosis of the holy warrior. Sacrificing himself in the battle against Zionism, he was portrayed with head wrapped in the distinctive checkered Palestinian kafiya, gripping a Kalishnokov. The image drew on memories of those who had manned the rebel groups from 1936 to 1939 and on idealized portraits of peasants as salt of the earth—even though the membership of the PLO, which heavily promoted the image, was primarily cosmopolitan and from the cities; its early popularity bolstered the PLO claim to be the sole legitimate Palestinian representative.

The image of the survivor also evoked the fast-disappearing fellah. But this was a more passive hero, demonstrating *sumud*, or steadfastness. Enduring the humiliations imposed by the conqueror, he confirmed his sumud by staying on the land at all costs—a bitter lesson learned

from 1948. Eventually, even those not tilling the land but simply staying in the occupied territories came to epitomize sumud. Finally, the survivor's counterpart was "the child of the stone," often exemplified through portraits of the *shahid*, or martyr, offering his life for the national cause by fighting against all odds. Modelled partly on the role of the shabab in the 1936–39 revolt, this was the adolescent willing to confront the enemy through rock throwing, tire burning, manning shoulder-mounted antitank rockets, and so forth.

At the end of the 1960s and in the 1970s, the feday dominated the Palestinian symbolic universe, as Palestinians groped for a response to the new conditions wrought by the June war. In the 1980s, images of the survivor and the child of the stone became more prominent, challenging what had become basic tenets of Palestinian society.

Fatah

As two of his biographers put it recently, "The ordinary facts of Arafat's life—his place of birth, his parents, his childhood, his adolescence—lay buried in the soil of his distant homeland."[3] Later, this vagueness would fuel myths among the Palestinians, hungry for a larger-than-life leader. One common story is that Arafat was born in Jerusalem, although more reliable evidence indicates he was actually born in Gaza and grew up in Egypt; another is that he was part of the Husseini clan—a connection that might have benefited him at one point, but became a liability as the ayan were discredited. He is also said to have been a member of the Muslim Brotherhood, and in fact, the Egyptians arrested him on such grounds in 1954, in connection with an attempt on Nasser's life. What is certain is that he ended up in Cairo in the early 1950s, studying to be a civil engineer and working hard as the head of the Palestinian Students' Union, which he founded with a small group of collaborators.

In the 1950s, the political and cultural center of gravity in the Arab world, and an ideal site for the Union, was Cairo. Nasser swept to power, drastically altering the tenor of Egyptian and

Arab politics. In the midst of Cairo's intellectual currents and crosscurrents, Arafat and his trusted colleague Salah Khalaf (who, under the name Abu Iyad, would remain Arafat's chief aide-de-camp until his assassination in 1991, probably at the hands of Iraqi agents) fashioned an agenda for the Palestinian people. Their thinking can be summed up as follows: First, the Palestinians had to take responsibility for their future—only an autonomous organization of their own could reverse their fortune. Second, their chief aim needed to be the liberation of Palestine, taking precedence over the goal of Arab unity (the key to the Nasserite revolution). Indeed, the liberation was a necessary precondition for that unity. Third, the key means to achieve liberation was armed struggle, undertaken by Palestinians themselves. And finally, Palestinians would work hand-in-hand with other Arabs and international forces on the basis of equality to help achieve the goal.

Despite the fact that the British kept their protectorate in Kuwait until 1961, Arafat and his colleagues found its Arab leaders offering them a relatively free hand to establish an organization based on the Cairo principles. They also found the growing oil wealth providing resources unimaginable in Egypt. Their underground cell, which in 1959 became *Fatah*—officially, the Palestine National Liberation Movement—began to take shape a few months after Arafat's arrival. Khalid al–Hassan, a Palestinian who had risen in Kuwaiti politics, joined the cell, giving it badly needed organizational skills. In time, Hassan became the leading ideologue of the right wing of the Palestinian movement.

The cell also began publishing a magazine, *Filastinuna* (Our Palestine: The Call to Life), which appeared every six weeks or so for the next five years. Its primary purpose was to put forth Fatah's strategy of provoking the Arab states into a war that Arafat was certain would eventually end Israeli control of Palestine. In a less ambitious vein, editor Khalil al–Wazir (Abu Jihad)—Arafat's long-time aide and close companion—also saw the publication as a critical forum for diverse ideas about how to promote the Palestinian cause.[9] This worked well, and the magazine's

success distinguished Arafat's small clandestine group from countless others forming in various Palestinian communities.

Both Fatah and the other groups drew their strength from the deep misery of the Palestinian situation, and from points of resistance elsewhere in the Arab world. Nasser's successful challenge to British control of the Suez Canal and the anti-French agitation of Algeria's FLN suggested it was possible to reverse the verdict of history. For all the clandestine groups, the FLN was a model of how to fashion a national liberation organization, and Arafat's own position was in fact greatly strengthened by the Algerian decision, immediately after independence in 1962, to recognize and support Fatah alone.

With Nasser beginning to use the term Palestinian entity, and Iraq's new revolutionary leader, Qasim, talking of the creation of a Palestinian republic, Palestinian militants gained confidence, despite limited resources and opportunities. In the late 1950s and early 1960s a sentiment seemed to emerge among the Arab republics to give the Palestinians an active role in the struggle against Israel—at least that is what the rhetoric suggested; actually, leaders such as Nasser and Qasim displayed extreme ambivalence towards Palestinian activists, regarding with the deepest suspicion any attempt to take the initiative or set the tone.

Along with the other groups, Fatah set out to sink roots in Palestinian society. But the task was difficult, partly because of its insistence that the sole realization of Nasser's wildly popular call for Arab unity was through Palestinian repatriation. This position did not find favor among Nasser or his avid followers—many of whom were young Palestinians. Nasser felt the Fatah militants were putting the cart before the horse. At the time, even George Habash, who subsequently became the leading Palestinian ideologue of the left, advocated working for unity of the Arab masses through revolutionary regimes as a prelude to the liberation of Palestine.

Arafat found himself moving against the current of popular feeling in the Arab world— Nasserism was pushing the entire Palestinian issue to the margins. His circumstances would eventually change, partly due to larger events—such as the failure of Egyptian–Syrian unity in 1961, and the Arab catastrophe in the 1967 war—and partly due to his own tenacity. Hassan notes how his unswerving dedication to the Palestine problem, before all else, paid off: "We reversed the slogan [of Arab unity first], and this is how we reversed the whole tide of thinking. And we managed to do that. Because when you want to talk about unity, then you have to work against the [present Arab] regimes. When we want to talk about liberation, we have to work on liberation."

The 1960s catapulted Fatah and Arafat from obscurity to overall leadership of the Palestinian people. The evolution from a clandestine political cell, tucked away in a remote corner of the Arab world, to an international organization, involved several important steps. In 1963, Fatah moved towards some permanence by creating a central committee, consisting of Palestinians who eschewed the party and factional conflicts wracking the Arab world. With Arafat as chief and Wazir as second in command, the committee consolidated power and directed the organization and its membership. At the same time, in the face of objections by Khalid al–Hassan and others on the committee, Arafat pushed Fatah into a strategy calling for immediate military action against Israel.

Probably nothing but armed violence could have established the organization so quickly among the various Palestinian communities, after almost two decades of inaction and growing despair. Still, the nature of the dispersal and the disdain of Fatah's leaders for traditional party organization—cells, local committees, and the like—made it difficult for the group to educate, recruit, or consistently mobilize the larger population. The committee succeeded in coordinating the organization's own actions, less so in infusing Fatah into the everyday lives of the Palestinians. When Fatah did create some rudimentary regional subgroups, it found itself hemmed in by the governing Arab regimes.

For all these organizational liabilities, the group did capture the Palestinians' imagination, but not in ways that could have been the basis for

systems of control and mass mobilization. This remained true after the 1967 war, when it built a complex central apparatus, covering areas from financial control to relations with Arab parties. Over the years, Arafat tried to make Fatah (and later the PLO, which Fatah came to dominate) into what the Jewish Agency had been for the Jews during the Palestine mandate—a state-in-the-making—but without the equivalent of the political parties and the Histadrut, which had given the Jewish Agency a firm foundation in the Jewish population.

Fatah's turn to violence came after the first Arab summit meeting, held in Cairo in January, 1964, voted to establish the Palestine Liberation Organization, the culmination of almost five years of ground-laying work by Nasser. The new PLO held its first convention in East Jerusalem's Palace Hall movie theater that spring. The motivation was Israel's completion of its National Water Carrier, diverting water from the Jordan River. Support for a Palestinian organization was a way for the Arabs to give the appearance of counteracting Israel without precipitating a direct confrontation. Nasser certainly did not intend the PLO to gain much autonomy—he wanted its semblance, while insuring that no underground groups dragged Egypt into war before it was ready.

Nasser selected a figure who had worked closely with individual Arab states and with the Arab League, Ahmad Shukayri, to build the new organization. Shukayri came from impeccable Palestinian lineage. His father had been a supporter of the Young Turks in 1908 and after being exiled by the sultan, had returned to Acre where he became a learned Muslim dignitary and an activist in the emerging Palestinian movement. Shukayri took the same route as spokesman for the Arab Higher Committee, the Arab League, and the Syrian and Saudi delegations to the United Nations. In his memoirs, he also claims a connection to al-Qassam, the Palestinian hero of the 1930s, noting that he offered his services as a lawyer to defend the surviving members of the Sheikh's group in 1935.

Shukayri had been advocating an organization to "liberate" Palestine for more than a year, but due to his bluster and self-promotion, few took him seriously. Alan Hart, Arafat's sympathetic biographer, vilifies Shukayri as the Puppet-in-Chief—a political mercenary selling himself to the highest bidder, and a demagogue who was a cross between Adolf Hitler and Ian Paisley. The claim ot Shukayri's opponents was that he was simply doing Nasser's bidding in creating an illusion of Palestinian autonomy while keeping the organization under tight wraps. But to the surprise of many, Shukayri was far more effective than his enemies (or their biographers) let on. To establish the PLO, he overcame the opposition of feisty old Haj Amin al–Husseini, despite the fact that his father had been an outspoken opponent of the Mufti, as well as the deep suspicions of the Jordanians and several other key regimes. His other efforts were undermined by unceasing hyperbole and demagogic statements: A "bombastic orator,"[12] perhaps best remembered for his purported threat before the 1967 war to drive the Jews into the sea, he had the temerity while in Amman to proclaim that all of Jordan, including the East Bank, was an integral part of Palestine.

The spring convention disgusted many of the Fatah activists, although several attended—Arafat, whose name was on the list of invitees, did not. They saw what they considered quiescent, hand-picked delegates ratify every proposal that Shukayri put before them. Some of those proposals, however, had long-term ramifications: the Palestinian National Covenant (revised in 1968 as the Palestine National Charter) was ratified, with its strong condemnation of Zionism and Israel—a bone in the throat of Israelis to this very day. "Zionism," the Covenant declared, "is a colonialist movement in its inception, aggressive and expansionist in its goals, racist and segregationist in its configurations and fascist in its means and aims. Israel in its capacity as the spearhead of this destructive movement and the pillar for colonialism is a permanent source of tension and turmoil …." The convention also emphasized the need for Palestinians to amass forces, mobilize their efforts and capabilities, and engage in holy war until complete and final victory has been attained.

Toward those ends, the PLO created the Palestine Liberation Army (PLA) two years later.

For Fatah, the PLO proved a formidable competitor. A real army of their own seemed highly attractive to destitute refugees and political exiles. Droves of Fatah members abandoned ship, hoping to join the projected new PLA. With almost no levers of influence and control among its own members, let alone in the wider Palestinian population, the PLO needed some audacious acts as a means of restoring its most important asset—its image. Khalid al–Hassan put it this way:

> You can say because it is the truth, that we were pushed down a road we did not want to take by the coming into being of the P.L.O. Because of its existence, and the fact that it was not the genuine article that so many Palestinians were assuming it to be, we decided that the only way to keep the idea of real struggle alive was to struggle.

The road that Hassan had not wanted to take was, of course, that of direct violence against Israel. Notions of armed struggle and popular liberation were in the air in the 1960s, leading some in Fatah to believe that they were part of a larger, inexorable world force. The success of Algeria's FLN in expelling the deeply rooted *pieds noirs* was but one of several important models. Jomo Kenyatta's triumph against British colonialism in Kenya and the efforts of the National Organization of [Greek] Cypriot Struggle (EOKA) were others. Farther away, but still extremely important in the minds of Fatah members, were the Cuban and Vietnamese revolutions. The writings of General Giap in Vietnam, Che Guevara in Cuba, and Mao Zedong, were all appearing in Palestinian refugee camps, newly translated into Arabic. Perhaps most influential of all was Franz Fanon's *The Wretched of the Earth*, which, in the Algerian context, talked of the cathartic benefits of violence against the occupier; Fanon himself was a psychiatrist who had joined the FLN.

The new strategy of armed violence had roots in Palestinian society as well. Some of the key figures involved in the early raids in 1965 had had direct experience in the 1936–39 revolt. Ahmad Musah, who led Fatah's first raid, had been part of Arab fighting groups carrying out action against Jewish settlements during that revolt. Another key figure in these years was Subhi Yasin, who had been a member of the Black Hand group during the mandate period, as well as a direct disciple of al–Qassam. Yasin alternately competed and cooperated with Fatah, finally merging his own group, the Organization of the Vanguard of Self–Sacrifice for the Liberation of Palestine, with Arafat's in 1968.

Fatah's decision was not the first time that the Palestinians had resorted to violence since 1948. Individuals such as Ahmad Musa had periodically slipped across the border to undertake personal acts of vengeance. Also, the Suez war of 1956 stemmed in no small part from the cycle of organized guerrilla raids from the Gaza Strip on Jewish settlements and Israel's strong retaliatory actions. In fact, in later years Arafat claimed some responsibility for those Gaza-based raids through his role as student leader at the time.

But Arafat's real military role began when a Fatah team operating under the name *Assifa* (The Storm) slipped into Israel and placed an explosive charge in the Beit Netopha canal. In some ways, the action was more a comedy of errors than a serious military expedition. The Lebanese arrested the group slated to carry out the attack on the last day of 1964, but, unaware of what had occurred, Arafat and his colleagues sped through Beirut distributing a military communique reporting the purported action. Later, laden with explosives, he was arrested and held for a short time by the Syrians, even though a high-ranking Syrian officer had pledged unfailing cooperation. When a group finally did plant the explosive charge on January 3, 1965, it set the timer so late that Israelis discovered and dismantled the bomb before it went off. And on its return from the action, the Palestinian unit ran into a Jordanian patrol that killed its leader, Ahmad Musa, and arrested the others.

What made the action more than merely a series of mistakes was the reaction to it. Fatah may have learned here that it is not how much actual damage they inflict on Israel that counts as how it perceives their actions. The Israelis publicized the attack and several others that Assifa undertook in early 1965, both in their Arabic radio broadcasts and in a speech by Prime Minister Levi Eshkol. Nothing could have better demonstrated the underground group's readiness to confront the enemy directly. After a second unit infiltrated into Israel, Fatah took public responsibility. Arab regimes also helped by branding Assifa the venal creation of Western intelligence agencies seeking to push the Arabs into war before they were fully prepared (Egypt) or as "communists bent on subversion" (Jordan). Egypt's army even declared itself at war with Assifa.

Wide publicity about the execution of real acts of violence and the furor they precipitated captured the attention and respect of the frustrated Palestinians around the Arab world. From an initial act of sabotage, Palestinians thus gained a new understanding of themselves as *jil al-thawra,* the revolutionary generation. At the same time, Fatah leaders learned the difficulty of making their way through minefields—not only those laid by the Israelis but also the political minefields set out by Arab regimes. Egypt; Syria, Jordan, Lebanon—all the states bordering Israel—either hunted down the underground group's members or, when professing cooperation, constrained their every move. Nonetheless, by the outbreak of the 1967 war, Assifa, which was by now the official military arm of Fatah, had undertaken nearly 100 acts of sabotage in Israel, killing eleven Israelis and wounding sixty-two. Indeed, Israeli spokesmen cited these provocations as an important catalyst of the cycle of violence leading to the war.

Recreating the PLO

As humiliating as the 1967 war had been for the Arabs, it gave Fatah new opportunities in two important areas. First, the humiliation quieted the gales of Nasserite pan-Arabism. Fatah's opposition to Nasser's philosophy—i.e., Arab unification as a prelude to the liberation of

Palestine—had previously seemed a form of spitting into the wind. Now the opportunity existed for alternatives to Nasser's discredited vision, to his handpicked PLO leadership, to his insistence on control.

Second, by reuniting the Palestinian majority—this time under Israeli occupation—the war made it much easier for Fatah to penetrate Palestinian society. The combination of its universal antipathy towards the Israelis with this shift from a logistically difficult fragmentation seemed to open the way for tactics reminiscent of Mao Zedong's or Ho Chi Minh's: Fatah could provide key social services and organizations to the people and, in turn, finally develop its means of mobilization and control. And such control would be a significant innovation in Palestinian society. While before 1948, the Husseinis had insinuated themselves into people's daily lives through landholding, the Supreme Muslim Council, and clan ties, neither they nor any other claimants to Palestinian leadership had created networks of influence that were truly national in scope.

In fact, Fatah was only able to capitalize on one of the opportunities, control of the PLO turning out to be its most far-reaching political achievement. Even with Nasser's firm backing, Shukayri had never managed to establish his own control over the organization, despite his claims that the PLO he led represented the general will of the Palestinians: He ended up precipitating and dealing with one factional split after another. His crowning accomplishment was the creation of the Palestine Liberation Army—in 1959, the Arab League had resolved to put such an army in the field, but little came of the effort or of several subsequent ones. Eventually, Shukayri deployed several units in Gaza. But this did not save the PLO from overall ineffectiveness, and Shukayri from political demise. The army, which did not amount to more than four or five thousand men, came under the command of each host country, rather than the PLO's appointed commander-in-chief. Shukayri simply could not achieve even the most rudimentary form of autonomy, for either the army or the PLO as a whole. Jordan, in particular, fought to erode even the slightest gains by

the PLO. This problem would later plague Arafat, as well.

The 1967 war recast relations among the Arabs as no other event would until Iraq's invasion of Kuwait. Pan-Arabism, which had electrified the Arab world from North Africa to the Fertile Crescent, slowly gave way to state relations reminiscent of those in other regions, based on standard diplomacy and international negotiation. Nasser's calls for unity, directed to the peoples of neighboring Arab countries above their rulers' heads, were replaced by conciliatory steps among kings and presidents. Even the dinosaur-like monarchs became legitimate nationalist leaders in this new diplomacy.

The result was a flagging interest by Arab heads of state in the PLO. At the Khartoum summit conference in the summer of 1967—the famous meeting in which the Arab League issued its notorious three no's to Israel: no negotiations, no recognition, no peace—the final communique did not even mention the PLO. Shukayri, who had enjoyed Nasser's support before the war, now felt his bone-chilling disinterest.

With the 1967 defeat, Palestinians felt the pan-Arab foundations of their hopes disintegrated. In the war's wake, many turned to the feday—especially as represented by Fatah and its record of direct, violent action against Israel—as their only chance for salvation. Fatah in turn, nourished by the new Palestinian support, used the growing disinterest of the Arab states to create some space for itself. Sending representatives to Arab capitals, it won both financial and rhetorical support. With Fatah thus catapulting into Arab consciousness, the PLO faded. By Christmas eve, 1967, Shukayri had resigned.

Arafat moved deliberately to replace Shukayri and revive the PLO. Probably no act furthered his aims more than the battle of Karamah (a refugee camp on the East Bank) on March 21, 1968. Nettled by Fatah guerrilla attacks, the Israeli government dispatched a large military force into Jordan, in order to destroy its local headquarters. In what turned out to be the first open battle between Jews and Palestinian irregulars since 1948, the Palestinians (aided by Jordanian artillery) ambushed the Israelis, killing as many as 25 soldiers in the course of a day-long fire-fight. The Israelis retreated without achieving their objective. While the Palestinians lost five times as many fighters as the Israelis, the psychological effect of the battle was overwhelming: Almost immediately assuming mythic proportions (Karamah means honor in Arabic), it confirmed the primacy of the feday, propelling thousands of teenagers into Assifa and Arafat to the top of the Palestinian national movement.

Within a year of the battle, he had assumed the chairmanship of the PLO, with Fatah the dominant group in the reconstituted organization. The PLO became an umbrella organization, enveloping a number of smaller ones dedicated to armed struggle and Palestinian autonomy, of which Fatah was by far the most important. It now controlled half the seats of the Palestine National Council (PNC), the PLO's emerging parliament-in-exile. Arafat and his associates controlled the 15-member Executive Committee, while keeping rival organizations fragmented and in sight as part of the Committee and the larger Council.

For substantial periods, Arafat insisted on standing clear of Arab political in-fighting, his single-minded preoccupation with Palestine making it possible for Fatah to maintain the political, moral, and financial support of a wide variety of Arab regimes. (He paid a price for deviating from this policy—the most dramatic recent example being his support for Iraq's Saddam Hussein.) In general, Fatah also spurned questions regarding the future makeup of Palestinian society or arcane ideological debates over the need for social revolution, thus enabling it to gain a broad base of support. Such choices clearly differentiated it from other Palestinian groups now committed to striking against Israel, none of which managed to establish extensive Palestinian and Arab support.

Nonetheless, such groups did have a significant impact on the movement, setting much of the tone and tenor of the PLO, indeed of the entire Palestinian national movement. In July, 1968, Palestinians hijacked an El Al Israeli airliner to Algeria, the first of a spate of hijackings and other acts aimed at the vulnerable international air transportation system. Terrorism now became a key element of the struggle against Israel. Until 1988, Palestinian groups never admitted to it, using the term "external operations" for all armed action outside Israel and the occupied territories. In 1988, the possibility of a direct dialogue with the United States hanging in the balance, Arafat denounced—and seemed to renounce—it.

Behind many such acts stood the Popular Front for the Liberation of Palestine (PFLP). Like those of Fatah, its leaders came from the student movement—but in this case from the American University in Beirut. There George Habash—its preeminent figure—and colleagues had established the clandestine Arab Nationalists' Movement; shortly after the 1967 war it merged with other groups to become the PFLP, finally joining the PLO in 1970. The Arab Nationalists' Movement's activists had originally advocated Nasserism. In the mid-1960s, it moved towards a Marxist perspective, demanding social revolution as a precondition for true Arab unity. After 1967 the Front took on a Palestine-first orientation.

Direct violent action was always at the center of its concerns. By 1964, even before Fatah, members of the Arab Nationalists' Movement's guerrilla unit had attacked Israel. But even while furnishing enough notoriety to challenge Fatah among the Palestinian population, the themes of violence and ideology divided and redivided the organization.

The first acrimonious split came when Naif Hawatma demanded a more radical approach: to break the Popular Front's relations with the inherently conservative Arab regimes and to align itself instead with popular revolutionary forces throughout the Arab world. Out of the ensuing, sometimes bloody battle came a splinter group, the Popular Democratic Front for the Liberation of Palestine, headed by Hawatma. The split with the Popular Front in 1969 was finally brokered by Fatah, which in turn got the Popular Democratic Front to join the PLO. Interestingly, the new group took the lead, after long polemical debates, in distinguishing between Israel proper (as defined by the armistice agreements following the 1948 war) and the territories it captured in 1967. By the early 1970s, these debates moved many within the PLO away from the Charter's insistence on expulsion from Palestine of post-1917 Jews and their descendants to advocacy of a secular, democratic state including Jews and a majority of Arabs. Under Hawatma's prodding, this position evolved even further; by the 1980s, the Popular Democratic Front had persuaded most of the national movement to accept the principles of (a) more flexibility regarding what had formerly been considered the absolute right of Palestinian repatriation in their original homes and (b) an Arab Palestinian state in the West Bank and Gaza, rather—at least at first—than the democratic secular state in all of Palestine.

The idea of creating a Palestinian state in the occupied territories had developed slowly, one of the first to raise the possibility being Mustaffa Akhmais, imprisoned by the Israelis shortly after the 1967 war. The PLO has consistently emphasized three demands—the right of return, the right to self-determination, and the right to be an independent state. The 1947 partition was seen by PLO leaders as abrogating the right to self-determination. The decision to found a Palestinian state in any "liberated" part of the country (i.e., the West Bank and Gaza) was finally taken at the eleventh PNC meeting (Cairo, June 9, 1974), and marked a major tactical turning point. Many Palestinians saw it as a withdrawal in principle from the idea of liberating the entire country and a movement towards the option of a "mini-state"—the backdrop to George Habash's resignation from the PLO Executive Committee on October 26 and the establishment of a "Rejection Front."

Ahmad Jibril provoked another split. He had been a member of Fatah's Central Committee before joining the Popular Front but was dissatisfied in both cases with the insufficient commitment to direct violent action. He, too, founded a new organization, the Popular Front for the Liberation of Palestine—General Command. With an emphasis more narrowly focused on guerrilla tactics, especially across Israel's northern border, it has been implicated in scurrilous acts of violence, including the blowing up of Pan Am flight 103

over Lockerbie, Scotland, in December, 1988. Even after Jibril withdrew his group from the PLO in the early 1980s, he retained considerable influence over the worldwide image of the Palestinian national movement.

Drawing on theories of urban guerrilla warfare and cooperating with a terrorist network including Japan's Red Army, the IRA, and the Baader–Meinhof group, the Popular Front and its splinter organizations initiated a series of "external operations." The most spectacular by far were the airplane hijackings. These and other acts—the mass murder of passengers by the Red Army in Israel's principal airports; the murder of Israeli athletes in the 1972 Olympics—made the Palestinian issue a media event, pushing it to the top of the world political agenda. Within Palestinian society, they offered new heroes and a sense of power. In the popular imagination, the feday was someone who, like Joshua, could stop the sun in the sky. Among Palestinians everywhere, there was a renewed sense of pride and autonomy, helping to rekindle a Palestinian national consciousness, battered in the decades since the Arab Revolt.

The emphasis on terror had its costs, as well, fostering a bloodthirsty stereotype, both internationally and among those Israelis who might have sought accommodation. Israeli leaders pointed to the terrorism as proof that the Palestinian Covenant involved not only the elimination of Israel but of Jews generally. And the world's revulsion enabled these leaders to delegitimize Palestinian national claims. As indicated, Arafat and Fatah over time distanced themselves from terrorist tactics, even while apparently creating their own deadly terrorist branches, Force 17 and Black September, for a while the world's most formidable terror organization. The latter was responsible for many operations, including the assassination of Jordanian Prime Minister Wasfi al-Tal in Cairo (November 28,1971) and the attack on the Munich Olympics (September 5, 1972; death toll: eleven Israeli athletes, a German policeman, five guerrillas). It is clear, then, that while Fatah now headed the PLO, it could not control many of the organization's parts; also, the reputation and image of the PLO derived as much from acts of the smaller groups as from Arafat's and Fatah's leadership.

Arafat's new stature, and that of the reorganized PLO, were recognized implicitly at the Arab League's Rabat conference in December, 1969. To the surprise of many, the PLO—now the umbrella for a slew of guerrilla groups and much more consistent on freedom of action than Shukayri ever had been—won Nasser's enthusiastic support for engaging in direct resistance to Israeli rule. He even gave Fatah some military aid and a special broadcasting station annexed to Cairo Radio.

Other states such as Syria and Iraq fell into line as well. Strains between them and the PLO did not disappear altogether: They appeared, for example, when Nasser agreed to the so-called Rogers initiative in 1970 (i.e., a cease-fire in Egypt's War of Attrition against Israeli forces dug in along the Suez Canal) or when Syria set up its own guerrilla group, Saiqa (along with Jibril's Popular Front for the Liberation of Palestine–General Command, it would quit the PLO altogether for most of the 1980s). But the overall situation was quite clear: Arafat and his Fatah colleagues had ridden the wave of Israeli success in the 1967 war, using the humiliation of the Arab states and the failure of their grand designs for Arab unity to seize leadership of the Palestinian national movement.

The PLO's Search for Roots

Modelling his effort on those of the Chinese, Vietnamese, and Cuban revolutionaries, Arafat began a push immediately after the June war to establish a permanent, popular base for resistance and revolt in the occupied territories. His dramatic failure—the Israelis forced his and his entourage's ouster at the end of the summer of 1967—was a crucial development for the guerrillas and for Palestinian society in general. Ironically, Fatah's success in the battle of Karamah a year later was a result of this failure: Once driven from the occupied territories, it established its headquarters there. Nevertheless, the forced physical distance from the centers of Palestinian settlement would prove to be a persistent liability. Fatah did try to

compensate for that liability with a Department of Popular Organizations, governing affiliated groups of students, doctors, peasants, and so forth, meant to mobilize the Palestinian population. Compared with Shukayri's feeble efforts, Arafat's seemed quite robust.

Khalid al–Hassan has argued that the new PLO might have been all too robust: "After Karamah we were forced to make our mobilisation and ideological education [of] ... the people in the camps by masses, by lectures, not by cells: and there is a big difference in both ways. There we deal with an individual; here we deal with the masses, with 100 at one time." Within a year of Karamah, Fatah had members in eighty countries, but the cost of this growth was loss of organizational cohesion. Embraced as the symbolic representation of the national movement, the PLO found itself in a symbiotic relationship with the Palestinian people: On the one hand, it promoted—despite extreme dependence upon various host countries—a sense of their distinctiveness, autonomy, and empowerment. On the other hand, Palestinian refugees and others gave the PLO a foundation for action and a coherent audience by developing a shared culture, drawing on their memories of Palestine and the myths of the Lost Garden that they had created. But such emotional closeness notwithstanding, the Palestinians found the PLO rather distant from their practical needs and way of life.

Arafat thus spent much of his time trying to preside over unruly groups and overcome frictions among them. Filling the seats of the Palestine National Council, which was seen as both a functioning parliament and a state-in-the-making, came only after intense and prolonged bargaining about precisely how much representation each group would have. Another formidable diversion involved the ever-more complicated world of Arab interstate relations, ensnaring the PLO in devastating, direct confrontations with the Jordanian and Syrian armies, as well as with numerous Lebanese militias.

Two factors led to such confrontations. First, the Palestinian communities located in Arab states often turned into points of contention between these states and the PLO. Local Palestinians frequently lacked basic rights and faced discrimination in their daily dealings. Attempts by the PLO to shield them from abuses meant a collision course with Arab regimes. Second, the PLO worked under a nigh-impossible dilemma. Among its most basic goals was autonomy in pursuing Palestinian interests—its own foreign policy, the right to initiate military action and develop unmediated relations with local Palestinians, and so forth. From the Palestinians' perspective, such autonomy was important, helping to define them in the Arab world as something other than refugees and victims. More concretely if the PLO were to succeed in building viable institutions among them, autonomy could mean acquiring services that local governments would not or could not provide.

But that potential independence rankled Arab governments, none, in the postcolonial period being ready to give even a hint of relinquishing any part of sovereignty within its assigned borders. This sentiment notwithstanding, Arafat had some success carving out areas of autonomy in particular states, but such cases were limited. One example was in Kuwait between 1967 and 1976, when the government, after greatly restricting the admission of non-Kuwaitis into the educational system, allowed the PLO to run schools for Palestinian children. Despite difficulties in keeping the schools afloat financially and in maintaining academic standards,

> The PLO school experience contributed immeasurably to the development of national consciousness among Palestinian students. Children saluted the Palestinian flag each day, participated regularly in Palestinian cultural and social activities, and joined scouting troops as well as the Zahrat and Ashbal (associations that provided children with paramilitary and political training).

This sort of success was rare. As we shall see below, the PLO managed to create broad zones of autonomy and independence for itself only in Lebanon. But there as elsewhere, its efforts led to disastrous conflict—perhaps none more so than the war with Jordan in 1970: what Palestinians came to call Black September.

After Fatah's failure to establish cells in the West Bank, Jordan became the center of its activities. Starting in the summer of 1967, first Fatah, then the PLO more generally, achieved a freedom of action calling King Hussein's control of his own territory into question. After the June war, Palestinian guerrilla suspects were released from Jordanian jails, and many fighters entered Jordan from across the Syrian border. Palestinian military units, which had been stationed in Egypt, also relocated in the Hashemite kingdom, coming under the PLOs direct command. For the first time, the feday appeared in refugee camps wearing his uniform and proudly bearing his arms.

A short honeymoon with the regime took place after the heady battle of Karamah, King Hussein proclaiming, "We shall all be fedayeen." But soon, rifle-toting guerrillas, unauthorized roadblocks they were manning, and related gestures prompted Jordanian officials to question whether the price for allowing the PLO free reign was worth it. Heavy Israeli artillery retaliation against Jordan's richest agricultural region, the Jordan Valley, only complicated the problem.

The smaller guerrilla groups heightened the tensions, some openly calling for the establishment of a "progressive regime" in Amman; the Popular Democratic Front for the Liberation of Palestine even tried to build local Soviets of workers and peasants among concentrations of Palestinians in the north of the country. Fatah activists spoke of converting Amman into the Palestinian Hanoi, to be used as the headquarters for an assault on the Israeli Saigon, Tel–Aviv. King Hussein and his army became increasingly anxious about all of this.

Anxiety turned into humiliation on September 6, 1970. George Habash's Popular Front for the Liberation of Palestine hijacked three international airliners and forced them to land at the stark Jordanian desert airport in Zarqa. After the Popular Front blew up the aircraft, Jordan's army, the descendant of the British-trained Arab Legion, left its barracks to disarm the guerrillas. Several of the Palestinian organizations countered by declaring the northern part of the country a "liberated Palestinian area." Full warfare ensued; using heavy armor, artillery, and air attacks, the Jordanians inflicted a shattering defeat, around three thousand Palestinians dying in the fighting. Some units preferred crossing the Jordan River and surrendering to the Israelis rather than falling into Jordanian hands. When Syrian tanks threatened to intervene, Israeli forces, acting in coordination with the United States, redeployed to deter a southern thrust into Jordan.

In the aftermath of this episode, the Hashemites closed all PLO institutions and arrested those leaders who had not managed to flee. The organization's prospects seemed bleak. In the course of three years, it had failed, first, in its efforts to gain direct access to the large Palestinian population in the occupied territories, and now to that in Jordan.

In subsequent decades, relations between the PLO and Jordan fluctuated. For fifteen years they were very poor; the Amman Agreement of 1985 then envisioned a confederation between Jordan and a future Palestinian state, but a year later the agreement dissolved into bitter mutual recriminations. Alternating cooperation and disputes followed regarding whether Palestinian representatives could be incorporated into a Jordanian delegation for possible talks with Israel. Relations warmed again in 1990 and 1991, when both parties supported Saddam Hussein in the Gulf War. The new Jordanian government approved by the King in June, 1991, included seven Palestinian ministers, a clear signal of readiness to return to the confederation plan. The renewed cooperation laid the basis for the joint Jordanian–Palestinian delegation to the U.S.-sponsored peace talks that began in Madrid in the fall of 1991.

Hovering behind all the vicissitudes in the relationship between Palestinians and Jordanians after 1970 was a continued presumption of complete Jordanian sovereignty within its borders— including sovereignty over Jordan's Palestinian population. When in 1988 Jordan severed the tie forged with the West Bank forty years earlier, declaring the PLO the sole representative of the Palestinian people, the move's primary purpose was to underscore this presumption by excluding Palestinians in the East Bank. (The move was, in any event, hedged somewhat—West Bank civil servants, for example, continued to receive Jordanian salaries.)

In any event, the PLO's grim circumstances in September, 1970, were to undergo a remarkable metamorphosis over the following five years—the greatest period of PLO success. With the uprooting from Jordan came the development of a state-within-a-state in Lebanon, that patched-together country with a large number of Palestinians (235,000). Arafat set up his headquarters in Beirut, but the real feday presence was in the southern part of the country close to Israel's border, where much of this population lived without the political and civic rights of refugees in Jordan, or even Syria and Egypt: "Lacking work permits and generally employed in small enterprises most Palestinians thus labored for low wages under poor working conditions with no fringe benefits, devoid of protection under Lebanese law."

For the chronically weak Lebanese regime, carved up as it was among various religious sects, the presence of the PLO brought new risks. The Israelis had already made it clear in 1968 that Lebanon was running such risks, responding to the Popular Front's El Al hijacking, with an attack on Lebanon's main airport that destroyed thirteen civilian airplanes. The I.D.F. also initiated retaliatory attacks in southern Lebanon in response to Palestinian hostilities, leading droves of Shi'ite Muslims from the south to flee north to Beirut.

Battered from all directions—Israel, the PLO, Lebanese Muslim students sympathetic to the Palestinians, camp-dwelling Palestinians who undertook their own spontaneous uprising—the Lebanese government tried to contain the guerrillas, but with only marginal success. In 1969, Nasser brokered the apparently paradoxical Cairo Agreement, offering the PLO ample autonomy and latitude in southern Lebanon while somehow promising Lebanon "sovereignty and security." For the first time, Arafat had an opportunity to carve out institutional autonomy, seemingly free of interference by jealous Arab states.

Once they entered the camps, the guerrilla groups established courts, imposed taxes, conscripted young men. They revised the curriculum in the schools, which were funded and run by UNRWA, so as to offer paramilitary training and change the tenor of social relationships in the camps. The entire spirit in them changed: The first appearance of the feday was received in mythological terms, as that of "giants [who] rose from the sea." One man in the Tal al–Zaatar camp exclaimed,

> The first moment I got down from the car I saw the Palestinian flag instead of the Lebanese flag, and a group of Palestinians in fedayeen clothes instead of the Lebanese police. As I moved through the camp I saw happiness on people's faces. … The *sheikh* in the mosque now spoke clearly about the homeland. … In the homes, mothers spoke clearly with their children about Palestine—before this was only done in whisper. There were many new projects which weren't there before: social activities, sports, meetings where people could say what they thought clearly, without censorship.

Service and administrative organizations quickly followed. By the early 1980s, the Palestinian Red Crescent Society had built 10 hospitals and 30 clinics, another 47 of the latter being run by the non-Fatah guerrilla groups. Two organizations with tens of thousands of members, the General Union of Palestine Workers and the General Union of Palestinian Women, gained most of their strength in Lebanon. The PLO and its allies also set up the Voice of Palestine radio network, several newspapers, a news agency (WAFA), and a research institute. The organization "had grown from a loosely organized collection of *fida'iyyin* to a vast bureaucratic network, centered in Lebanon, employing perhaps 8,000 civil servants and a budget (including that of

constituent organizations) in the hundreds of millions of dollars, three-quarters of which went to support the PLO's social and administrative programs." In addition, it had gained diplomatic recognition from over 50 states, established more than 100 foreign missions of its own, and won observer status in the United Nations (the platform for Arafat's well-known 1974 speech toting a partially visible, bolstered pistol). Rashid Khalidi describes the turn of fortune:

> PLO Chairman Yasser Arafat was now a head of a state in all but name, more powerful than many Arab rulers. His was no longer a humble revolutionary movement, but rather a vigorous para-state, with a growing bureaucracy administering the affairs of Palestinians everywhere and with a budget bigger than that of many small sovereign states.

Over time, the financial resources to sustain such a complex structure also developed, largely through aid from the Gulf states. Adam Zagorin estimates that the main financial body of the PLO, the Palestine National Fund, had yearly expenditures of approximately $233 million by the late 1980s, including over a third of that to support a standing army.

While at the beginning, competition among the guerrilla organizations to control camp life was intense, by 1978 Fatah had achieved dominance. It appointed popular committees that looked after the most mundane human problems—road maintenance, the building of bomb shelters (for protection from both Israeli bombing and Arab militias) and providing proper hygiene. Fatah was especially successful in forming the youth groups mentioned above by Brand—the Zahrat (flowers) for girls and Ashbal (lion cubs) for boys—that stressed military training and the building of a revolutionary culture. This new culture emphasized the difference between the jil al-thawra—the assertive revolutionary generation—and the desolate, humiliating identities of the children's parents, the jil al–Nakba.

Some residents complained that these activities eroded the Palestinians' normally high academic motivation as well as the standing of the regular schools, but there was no doubting the electrifying effect that the feday had on the Lebanese camps:

On dark alley walls
our comrades' deaths are announced
posters show their smiling faces

Such posters plastered the walls of the camps, and graffiti, folk songs, poetry, and stories all grew around the quasi-mystical icon of the feday, recognized as one who would gladly offer his (or in some versions, her) life to liberate Palestine. These idolized recruits earned relatively high salaries, and their families gained preferred access to PLO services and jobs. Families of martyrs received special pensions.

The PLO's control went far beyond the Palestinian camps. The guerrillas had nearly free reign in a wide swathe of Lebanese territory, including the coastal cities of Tyre and Sidon. Over time, the Lebanese police all but disappeared from the streets (they simply removed their uniforms, while continuing to receive their salaries from the central government); Lebanese courts and administrative services gave way to "revolutionary" courts and to private arrangements with the guerrilla groups, especially Fatah. Naturally, this power and success came with a variety of dangers, fears, and resentments, hidden and not-so-hidden. Within the camps, the old leadership felt particularly vulnerable. Sayigh quotes a camp school director:

Most of the *wujaha* [traditional notables or leaders] collaborated with the authorities and informers, not because they were unnationalistic, but because they feared the new generation which was threatening their influence. These were the people on whom the Mufti depended—they worked together against the new current.

A number of ordinary Palestinians also came to bridle under the rule of the feday. A few had established close relations with their Lebanese neighbors, even intermarrying, and opposed the wedge now dividing the two peoples. Others saw the guerrillas, many of whose families had come from the Hebron mountains and Gaza, as socially and intellectually inferior to the Haifa and Galilee Palestinians in southern Lebanon. For their part, guerrillas spoke of the Lebanese Palestinians as uncommitted to the revolution, as they called their new order, and as "embourgeoised." And to complicate matters even more, the various factions of the PLO often squabbled among themselves for control. The popular committees that they appointed were frequently underskilled, disorganized, and ineffective.

The greatest dangers, however, did not come from resentful Palestinians—most of whom gladly put up with inefficiences or even occasional indignities in return for a true Palestinian leadership—but from the Lebanese, who, like the Jordanians, feared that the guerrillas' autonomy would bring disaster. From the signing of the Cairo Agreement on, powerful elements in Lebanon were convinced that the Palestinian state-within-a-state could not coexist with Lebanese sovereignty—a conviction sharpened by Israeli retaliation for any Palestinian armed incursions, based on a faith that Lebanese pain would translate into restrictions on the PLO. The Phalangist party of the dominant Maronite sect—the religious group most closely identified with the modern Lebanese state—led the outcry. It watched Palestinian control expand from, what the Israeli media called Fatahland in the south to territorial enclaves in the north and the Biqa valley, as well as to the PLO's "capital" in the Kaka–khani district of West Beirut.

In March, 1970 (that is, before the expulsion of the PLO from Jordan) armed clashes broke out between units of the Lebanese army and guerrilla groups. A few years later (spring 1973), an Israeli raid in Beirut's rue Verdun, killing three leading PLO figures, provoked wide-scale fighting between Lebanese and Palestinian forces. The Milkart Protocols, signed in May, 1973, temporarily put an end to the warfare by precisely spelling out the boundaries for guerrilla forays and enjoining them to self-restraint. But in the end those agreements may have made the situation worse by prompting certain Lebanese factions, particularly among the Christian sects, to create their own militias. In the context of deteriorating relations among Lebanese confessional groups, the tensions helped generate one of the bloodiest communal conflicts of the twentieth century: the Lebanese civil war, lasting from 1975 until 1990 and resulting in well over 100,000 fatalities and endless human tragedy.

For the PLO and the Palestinians, this war would bring previously unimagined brutality and disasters, some of which would make Black September seem relatively benign. They would end up facing two Israeli invasions—a limited incursion in 1978 (the Litani Operation) and a full-scale attack in 1982—besides battles with numerous Lebanese militias. Encountering periodic hostility from the Syrian army, they would suffer a devastating defeat at its hands in 1976.

Confronting such ordeals, Arafat and the PLO tottered badly. The 1982 Israeli invasion routed the 15,000-strong PLO fighting force and put its entire infrastructure under siege for nearly the entire summer. At the end of August, Palestinian military, administrative, and political forces were evacuated from Lebanon under U.S. supervision—their only shred of honor being the ability to hoist their weapons as they boarded ship in Beirut port. Arafat's personal exit on August 30 marked an end to *ayam Beirut*, the era of PLO political and military presence in Lebanon.

Reestablished in Tunis, the organization moved some of its branches and training centers to Saddam Hussein's Iraq—paving the way for Arafat's support of that country in the 1991 Gulf War—after an Israeli bombing attack. By the late 1980s, the PLO was again engaging in international initiatives. Arafat engineered a short-lived dialogue with the United States, denouncing the use of terrorism and publicly recognizing the right of Israel to exist—both major concessions on his part. He also managed to reestablish his own tattered image among Palestinians and to have the Palestine National Council finally declare a state

that would eventually rule in the West Bank and the Gaza Strip. Without defining its borders or establishing a government, the extraordinary 19th session of the Council, convened near Algiers from November 12 to 15, 1988, authorized a declaration of independence bearing a striking resemblance to that of Israel in 1948. Arafat proclaimed the state, with its capital in Jerusalem, on November 15, 1988.

But despite the international dazzle, the PLO had not altered the dilemma that had become evident in September, 1970: Its most basic aim, to create enough autonomy to shape Palestinian society and confront Israel, lay hostage to the whims of embattled Arab states or of their unofficial militias or threatening or opportunistic neighbors. In 1991, for example, when the Lebanese state was taking its first steps towards reestablishing a semblance of effective rule it turned, with the support of its powerful patron Syria, on the PLO in the south, ending its rule after several violent clashes. Arafat's desire to avoid the entanglements of Arab, politics could not protect him from such fury. Indeed, writes Rashid Khalidi, "the fact that Palestinian nationalism has been in nearly constant conflict over the past few decades with both Israel and various Arab regimes is perceived as inevitable by most Palestinians."

Even worse, at such times Arafat and his organization could not protect the Palestinian population. By the last half of the 1980s, this fundamental inadequacy changed the relationship of the PLO to Palestinian society in subtle but substantial ways. One of its first indications came shortly after Syria's intervention, aimed in part directly against the PLO, in the Lebanese civil war in 1976. The intervention offered the PLO's Lebanese opponents an opportunity to launch an attack on the two remaining Palestinian refugee camps in mostly Christian East Beirut. One fell quickly, but the other, Tal al–Zaatar, was besieged for almost two months, with the PLO nearly helpless to relieve the suffering and anguish. Despite substantial concessions to the Syrians, the Christian forces finally razed the camp, killing 3,000 Palestinians and evicting the others.

Another such indication was the notorious sequence of events on September 16, 1982, in the suburban Beirut camps of Sabra and Shatilla: Using Israel's protective presence around Beirut, the Phalangists entered the camps and in less than two days slaughtered anywhere between 460 and 3,000 Palestinians, including women and children—as well as Lebanese, Syrians, Algerians, Pakistanis, and Iranians who happened to be in the camps. The camps thus were added to the list of places marking Palestinian martyrdom, alongside Dayr Yasin, Kafr Qasim, and Tel al–Zaatar.

The PLO's impotence did not seem to affect its popularity, or that of Arafat, among the Palestinians. Polls in 1988, for example, gave the PLO a 90 percent and Arafat a 75 percent approval rating, but there were nonetheless indications of a changed relationship. On the one hand, while remaining popular through its long ordeal in Lebanon, the heroic image of the feday appeared increasingly distant from the immediate needs of the Palestinian population, and another cultural hero was beginning to challenge its dominance— the "RPG kid," named after the anti-tank shoulder rockets he toted to slow the Israeli advance. The stiff price the Israelis paid for the invasion of Lebanon (over 650 dead; 3,500 wounded) catapulted the image of the young martyr, the shahid, into the limelight. The professionally paid feday now had to share the cultural stage with the spontaneous, untrained RPG kids. Later, in the West Bank and Gaza Strip, similar adolescents throwing rocks and taunting Israeli troops would mark the rise of the children of the stones.

On the other hand, many Palestinians were now falling back on their own tenacity for self-protection, a situation reflected in the increasing evocation of the image of the survivor, whose heroism is based on sumud. Perhaps somewhat grandiloquently, Ahmad Dahbur has reflected on such poles of vulnerability and tenacity in Palestinian life:

You hear the news about the Palestinian?
Wherever he is they knife him
famine strikes him and flees
rumor hacks off an arm here, a leg there,

the media joyfully spread the news
the Palestinian rejects
he accepts his days as a sword
a hand that scatters the illusions of others
I testify "endurance is his strength."

Regardless of Lebanese fears, the PLO's power in southern Lebanon remained over an isolated enclave. Once the civil war had ended, the Lebanese state wasted little time in targeting remaining PLO control. Arafat had succeeded in creating a popular leadership among the Palestinians for the first time in their history, and in Lebanon he had even built the semblance of a state. But his attempts to transform that leadership into one that could penetrate and shape Palestinian society beyond the Lebanese arena continued to meet impossible barriers.

PLO leaders had always understood that capturing the imagination of the Palestinians or appealing to them through an attractive ideology would in itself have been insufficient to gain the control they wanted and needed. Moreover, as the dominant faction, Fatah was often at a disadvantage compared to other groups in elaborating an effective ideology. Certainly, none of the others came close to Fatah in garnering outside material support or in sheer size (it probably had 10,000-15,000 men under arms at the end of the 1960s). But, often, their narrower bases allowed them to project more effective ideologies: Fatah seemed a catchall, sending loosely defined, often contradictory messages. It believed in "not engaging in ideological debates about the character of the regime of the liberated state at the present stage as it might split the Palestinians and divert their attention from the struggle against Israel." Sometimes its voice had deep Islamic resonances; at other times, it spoke a language of secularism. Sometimes it seemed to appeal to the downtrodden with the language of social revolution, at others it courted the growing Palestinian middle class. Alain Gresh has rather understated the case in noting that "Fatah is a movement with a variety of tendencies and sensitivities."

Given all its difficulties, the PLO, under the control of Fatah, had managed to establish itself as the recognized leadership of the Palestinians. It had nurtured a national mythology of heroism and sacrifice, the portrait of the downtrodden refugee giving way to that of the feday—which, in turn became the catalyst for the reconstruction of the national movement. In time, armed struggle would give way to more nonviolent activity, both for the sake of international legitimacy and because of the Israeli abilities to deal with armed threats.

But even if violence had failed to reverse al–Nakba, it had succeeded in projecting the Palestinian issue into the center of international concern. The PLCs continuing frustration was that its longstanding enemy, Israel, had also consolidated its power; as it did so, its readiness to make concessions to the Palestinians decreased. Facing this formidable opponent, the PLO, at the end of the 1980s and the beginning of the 1990s, was unable to show tangible gains, despite its political evolution. Along with its other difficulties, the organization's want of definition left its leadership vulnerable to challenges from within and to the rising tide of Islamic movements.

The Iron Wall
Israel and the Arab World

By Avi Shlaim

Ariel Sharon's Big Plan

Two strands in Israeli policy led to the full-scale invasion of Lebanon in June 1982: the alliance with the Lebanese Christians and a desire to destroy the PLO. Menachem Begin strongly supported both strands of this policy. During his years in opposition Begin developed a political-strategic conception that resembled in some respects that of his great rival, David Ben–Gurion. This conception stressed the interests that were common to Israel and the non-Arab or non-Muslim countries and minorities in the Middle East and in its periphery. Within this broad conception the Christians of Lebanon held a special place because they allegedly faced the danger of destruction at the hands of their Arab and Muslim opponents. Begin was determined not to repeat the mistakes of the Munich conference of September 1938, at which Britain and France abandoned Czechoslovakia to Adolf Hitler's tender mercies. Begin likened Israel to the Western powers, the Maronites to the Czechs, and the Syrians and Palestinians to Nazi Germany. He felt that Israel had a moral duty to defend its Maronite allies. At the same time, he was committed to waging war against the PLO because of the attacks it launched across the border from Lebanon. Retaliation was not enough in his view; Israel had to seize the initiative, destroy the guerrilla bases in southern Lebanon, and drive the guerrillas to the north of the country, as far away as possible from Israel's own border. This was the basic conception that determined the goals Begin hoped to achieve by invading Lebanon.

The real driving force behind Israel's invasion of Lebanon, however, was Ariel Sharon, whose aims were much more ambitious and far-reaching. From his first day at the Defense Ministry, Sharon started planning the invasion of Lebanon. He developed what came to be known as the "big plan" for using Israel's military power to establish political hegemony in the Middle East. The first aim of Sharon's plan was to destroy the PLO's military infrastructure in Lebanon and to undermine it as a political organization. The second aim was to establish a new political order in Lebanon by helping Israel's Maronite friends, headed by Bashir Gemayel, to form a government that would proceed to sign a peace treaty with Israel. For this to be possible, it was necessary, third, to expel the Syrian forces from Lebanon or at least to weaken seriously the Syrian presence there. In Sharon's big plan, the war in Lebanon was intended to transform the situation not only in Lebanon but in the whole Middle East. The destruction of the PLO would break the backbone of Palestinian nationalism and facilitate the absorption of the West Bank into Greater Israel. The resulting influx of Palestinians from Lebanon and the West Bank into Jordan would eventually sweep away the Hashemite monarchy and transform the East Bank into a Palestinian state. Sharon reasoned that Jordan's conversion into a Palestinian state would end international pressures on Israel to withdraw from the West Bank. Begin was not privy to all aspects of Sharon's ambitious geopolitical scenario, but the two men were united by their desire to act against the PLO in Lebanon.

Chief of Staff Rafael Eytan was another enthusiastic supporter of military action against the PLO. The IDF had prepared plans for the invasion, code-named Operation Pines, in two versions, a little one and a big one. Operation Little Pines called for the uprooting of the guerrillas from southern Lebanon. Operation Big Pines envisaged a thrust up to the Beirut–Damascus highway, a landing by sea to surround Beirut in a pincer movement, and the possibility of another landing at Jounieh to link up with the Christian forces in the north. Its ultimate target was the destruction of the PLO command centers and infrastructure throughout Lebanon, including Beirut. Operation Big Pines was first brought before the cabinet on 20 December 1981, soon after the annexation of the Golan Heights. This was the meeting at which Begin reported the scathing comments he had just made to the American ambassador following the suspension of the agreement on strategic cooperation. The ministers had hardly recovered from the shock when Begin surprised them a second time by introducing the plan for going to war in Lebanon. Sharon explained that the idea was not to clash with the Syrians in the Golan Heights but to seize the opportunity to achieve their strategic objectives in Lebanon. "If the Syrians start anything," he said, "we'll respond in Lebanon and solve the problem there." Eytan then presented, with the help of a map, the operational plan for reaching Beirut and beyond. The ministers were astonished by the scale of the proposed operation, and several of them spoke against it. Begin abruptly terminated the discussion without

putting the proposal to a vote when it became clear that it would be defeated by a large majority.

Sharon and Eytan, realizing that there was no chance of persuading the cabinet to approve a large-scale operation in Lebanon, adopted a different tactic. They started presenting to the cabinet limited proposals for bombing PLO targets in Lebanon, expecting that the guerrillas would retaliate by firing Katyusha rockets on Israel's northern settlements and that this would force the cabinet to approve more drastic measures. The idea was to implement Operation Big Pines in stages by manipulating enemy provocation and Israel's response. A number of confrontations took place in the cabinet as a result of these tactics. Ministers opposed to a war in Lebanon opposed the more modest proposals for bombing targets in Lebanon because they recognized where these proposals were intended to lead.

Sharon was not deterred from pursuing his preparations for war or his contacts with the Maronites. The Maronites were not a unified group. They were divided into various militias headed by rival warlords; family ties were more significant than religion. Among these militias the Phalange, established in 1936 by Pierre Gemayel on the lines of the Nazi Youth movement, had the closest links with Israel. In January 1982, with the agreement of the prime minister, Sharon paid a secret visit to Beirut to confer with Bashir Gemayel to assess what could be expected from the Phalange in the event of war. At this meeting the capture of Beirut was explicitly mentioned, and the division of labor between Israel and the Phalange was discussed. Begin himself received Bashir Gemayel in Jerusalem on 16 February. At this meeting Begin stated that Israel would enter Lebanon if terrorist activities continued and that, if this happened, its forces would proceed northward as far as possible.

The relationship with Bashir Gemayel and the Phalange was always controversial. Mossad operatives, who developed this relationship and enjoyed the personal contact involved, had a generally positive view of the political reliability and military capability of the Phalange. However, military intelligence had grave doubts on both scores. From the start the IDF experts were cool about the relationship and regularly exposed the shortcomings of the Phalange. In contrast to the Mossad, they did not regard the Phalange as an asset, nor did they trust its leaders. Major General Yehoshua Saguy, the director of military intelligence, was convinced that even if Gemayel were to be elected president of Lebanon, he would turn toward the Arab world. Saguy repeatedly warned his superiors that Gemayel was only trying to use Israel for his own purposes and that, given the close links between Lebanon and the Arab world, he would not be able to make peace with Israel.

Ministers were explicitly warned by the heads of the intelligence community, at a meeting in Begin's home in April 1982, against the idea of trying to secure Bashir Jemayel's election to the presidency. On this occasion the head of the Mossad, General Yitzhak Hofi, sided with Saguy. Both of them cautioned against assuming that it would be possible to engineer Gemayel's election through the good offices of the IDF and then turn around and withdraw from Lebanon a few weeks later. But by this time the personal relationship between Sharon and Gemayel was so intimate and their joint plans were so far advanced that the opinion of the experts was brushed aside and their warning against interference in the Lebanese political process was not heeded. The influence of the experts began to decline as soon as the Phalangists found their way directly to Sharon's ranch in the Negev.

Sharon and Eytan were constantly on the lookout for an excuse to launch an operation in Lebanon. At the beginning of March, Begin convened at his home a meeting of several ministers and the chief of staff. Sharon and Eytan surprised the ministers by suggesting a new reason for an operation in Lebanon: Israel's commitment to Egypt to withdraw from eastern Sinai, including the town of Yamit, on 26 April. Once the withdrawal from Sinai was completed, they said, the Egyptians might cancel the peace treaty; an operation in Lebanon would test their intentions. Yitzhak Shamir, Yosef Burg, and Simha Erlich recoiled from this suggestion. They said that the peace with Egypt stood on its own and should not

be linked to Lebanon. Begin agreed with them, and the suggestion was rejected.

The final phase of the withdrawal from Sinai was carried out in the face of powerful domestic opposition. Professor Yuval Ne'eman, leader of the small ultranationalist Tehiya party, and Moshe Arens, a prominent member of the Likud and chairman of the Knesset's Foreign Affairs and Defense Committee, led the opposition. Ne'eman, Arens, and some of their colleagues wanted to revoke the treaty before it was time for Israel to withdraw its forces and evacuate the civilian settlements between the El Arish–Ras Muhammad line and the international border. They tried to persuade the Israeli public that, with Sadat gone, the Egyptians would wait until all Sinai was in their hands, then renounce the peace treaty with Israel and rejoin the Arab world. Begin resisted this pressure, all the more strongly after President Mubarak wrote to reassure him that Egypt would continue to uphold the peace treaty and the Camp David Accords after the Israeli withdrawal.

As minister of defense, Sharon was responsible for implementing the withdrawal. The most painful and problematic part of the process was the evacuation of the Israeli civilians who had made their homes in Sinai. Generous financial compensation was offered to these settlers, but many of them refused to leave of their own accord. Political extremists from the rest of the country infiltrated into Sinai to demonstrate their solidarity and sabotage the withdrawal. Resistance to the withdrawal lasted several days and was accompanied by heartbreaking scenes on television. But in the end the IDF succeeded in evacuating all the settlers and demonstrators without bloodshed. Sharon ordered the IDF to destroy the town of Yamit to its foundations instead of surrendering it intact to the Egyptians as envisaged in the peace treaty. He claimed that the Egyptians themselves had requested the destruction of Yamit, but this claim later turned out to be untrue. Sharon's real motives for carrying out this barbaric act was a subject for speculation. One suggestion was that Sharon deliberately made the whole process more traumatic than it needed to be so that the Israeli public would balk at the dismantling of any other settlements even for the sake of peace. What the whole episode proved was how ruthless Sharon could be in pursuit of his own designs and how little he cared for the opinion of his ministerial colleagues who had not approved the destruction of Yamit. Begin was well pleased with the energetic and efficient manner in which the evacuation was carried out. He, too, did not regard this as a precedent. Indeed, he proposed a resolution, which found a majority in the Knesset, intended to make it impossible for future governments to sign an agreement that involved withdrawal from the Land of Israel or the removal of Jewish settlements from this land.

The Road to War

Once the Sinai issue was settled, Sharon concentrated even more single-mindedly on his grand design for Lebanon. He knew that the cabinet would not approve a war for the purpose of making Bashir Gemayel president of Lebanon and that it was anxious to avoid a clash with the Syrians, but he was confident of obtaining its consent for an offensive against the PLO. He told the cabinet what it wanted to hear while keeping the pressure on the IDF General Staff to prepare for a major war. Most of the officers on the General Staff accepted Yehoshua Saguy's forecast that a clash with the Syrians would be inevitable, that the Phalangists would remain largely passive, and that the PLO would be defeated but not destroyed. These doubts and reservations, however, were not reported to the cabinet.

One reason for the cabinet's reluctance to go to war in Lebanon was the fear of antagonizing the United States. In July 1981 Philip Habib, a senior American diplomat of Lebanese ancestry, had succeeded in brokering a cease-fire agreement between Israel and the PLO. The two parties, however, interpreted the agreement in different ways. The PLO considered that the agreement applied only to the Lebanese–Israeli front. The Israelis maintained that it required a complete halt to the terrorist attacks on all Israel's fronts, inside Israel, and anywhere in the world. The Americans held

that the agreement meant precisely what it said: "There will be no hostile activities from Lebanon directed at targets in Israel [and vice versa]." In accordance with this interpretation, the Americans repeatedly warned the Israelis not to imperil the cease-fire.

The Americans knew much more about Sharon's plans than he realized. Samuel Lewis was one of the few foreign diplomats who understood that Sharon's ultimate aim was to cause the collapse of the Hashemite regime and its replacement by a Palestinian state on the East Bank of the river Jordan and that this was linked to his plans for Lebanon. Bashir Jemayel made no secret of his wish to expel the Palestinians from Lebanon, and Lewis put two and two together. Lewis also suspected that Sharon hoped that the defeat of the PLO in Lebanon would enable him to dictate his own terms in the negotiations on the future of the occupied territories and give Israel unchallenged control over the West Bank.

Sharon himself displayed the same deviousness in his relations with the Reagan administration as he did in his relations with his cabinet colleagues. He fed the Americans selective information that was intended to prove that the PLO was making a mockery of the cease-fire agreement and to establish Israel's right to retaliate. On 5 December 1981, for example, Sharon told Philip Habib, "If the terrorists continue to violate the ceasefire, we will have no choice but to wipe them out completely in Lebanon, destroy the PLO's infrastructure there. … We will eradicate the PLO in Lebanon." Habib was appalled by the brutality of Sharon's demarche. "General Sharon, this is the twentieth century and times have changed," he blurted out. "You can't go around invading countries just like that, spreading destruction and killing civilians. In the end, your invasion will grow into a war with Syria, and the entire region will be engulfed in flames!"

In late May 1982, after the cabinet had reached a decision in principle to retaliate massively to the next PLO violation of the cease-fire, Sharon invited himself to Washington. His brief was to ascertain the likely response of the Reagan administration to an Israeli offensive in Lebanon.

Sharon met Alexander Haig and his advisers in the State Department on 25 May. According to Haig's subsequent account, General Sharon shocked a roomful of State Department bureaucrats by sketching out two possible military campaigns: one that would pacify southern Lebanon and one that would redraw the political map of Beirut in favor of the Christian Phalange. It was clear to Haig that Sharon was putting the United States on notice: one more provocation by the Palestinians, and Israel would deliver a knockout blow to the PLO. Haig claims that in front of his advisers, and later in private, he repeated to Sharon what he had said many times before: unless there was an internationally recognized provocation, and unless Israeli retaliation was proportionate to any such provocation, an attack by Israel into Lebanon would have a devastating effect in the United States. "No one," retorted Sharon, "has the right to tell Israel what decision it should take in defense of its people."

Sharon professed himself to be well pleased with the result of his mission. On his return to Israel he claimed that the Americans had tacitly agreed to a limited military operation in Lebanon. This is precisely what Haig feared Sharon might say. To avoid any misunderstanding Haig wrote to Begin, on 28 May, to underline his concern about possible Israeli military actions in Lebanon. In his own name and in the name of President Reagan, he urged Israel to continue to exercise complete restraint and to refrain from any action that would further damage the understanding underlying the cease-fire. In reply Begin employed language that demonstrated the depth of his feelings: "You advise us to exercise complete restraint and refrain from any action ... Mr. Secretary, my dear friend, the man has not been born who will ever obtain from me consent to let Jews be killed by a bloodthirsty enemy and allow those who are responsible for the shedding of this blood to enjoy immunity."

Haig and Reagan were in fact Israel's strongest supporters within the administration. Least friendly to Israel was Secretary of Defense Caspar Weinberger, who had purged the memorandum of understanding on strategic cooperation of many of the advantages it could have given Israel and insisted on its suspension and on punitive measures following Israel's annexation of the Golan Heights. Whereas Weinberger regarded Israel as a liability for the United States in its relations with the Arab world, and especially the oil-producing countries of the Persian Gulf, Haig regarded Israel as a strategic asset in the fight against Arab radicalism and international terrorism.

Toward Menachem Begin personally, Haig showed more tolerance and understanding than any of his colleagues. A tough and unsentimental former general, he sensed that Begin's aggressiveness sprang from a feeling of vulnerability. "Begin certainly believes that Israel is besieged," wrote Haig in his memoirs, "but his entire motive is to preserve the lives of Jews. He has no 'complex'— only an inescapable memory of the Holocaust." Begin once wrote to Haig that in his generation millions of Jews perished for two reasons: "(a) because they did not have the instruments with which to defend themselves, and (b) because nobody came to their rescue." Begin was fiercely determined that this must not happen again: "His letters, his conversation, his speeches—and, unquestionably, his thoughts—were dominated, when he was prime minister, by the sense that 'the lives of his people and the survival of Israel had been personally entrusted to him. He once said, when asked what he wanted to be remembered for, that he wished to be known to history as the man who established the borders of the state of Israel for all time." Against this background it is not difficult to see why Haig's letter to Begin, following Sharon's visit, was so gentle or why it conveyed no threat of punishment. The letter certainly did not give Israel the green light to invade Lebanon, but neither did it project an unambiguously red light. Begin concluded that the United States accepted Israel's right to retaliate to an indisputable provocation by the PLO. He did not even bring Haig's letter to the attention of the cabinet.

On 3 June the casus belli that the hard-liners had been waiting for materialized. A group of Palestinian terrorists shot and grievously wounded Shlomo Argov, Israel's ambassador to London, outside the Dorchester Hotel. The gunmen belonged to the breakaway group led by Abu Nidal (Sabri al–Banna), Yasser Arafat's sworn enemy. Abu Nidal was supported by Iraq in his struggle against Arafat's "capitulationist" leadership of the PLO. Abu Nidal customarily referred to Arafat as "the Jewess's son." The PLO had passed a death sentence on Abu Nidal for assassinating some of its moderate members who advocated a dialogue with Israel. Mossad sources had intelligence to suggest that the attempt on Argov's life was intended to provoke an Israeli assault on Arafat's stronghold in Lebanon in order to break his power.

Begin was not interested in the details of who had shot Argov and why. An emergency meeting of the cabinet was summoned for the morning of 4 June. Ariel Sharon was on his way back from a secret trip to Romania. Begin was visibly agitated. "We will not stand for them attacking an Israeli ambassador!" he said. "An assault on an ambassador is tantamount to an attack on the State of Israel and we will respond to it!" Avraham Shalom, the head of the General Security Service, reported that the attack was most probably the work of the faction headed by Abu Nidal and suggested that Gideon Machanaimi, the prime minister's adviser on terrorism, elaborate on the nature of that organization. Machanaimi had hardly opened his mouth when Begin cut him off by saying, "They are all PLO." Rafael Eytan was equally dismissive of this detail. Shortly before entering the conference room, an intelligence aide told him that Abu Nidal's men were evidently responsible for the assassination attempt. "Abu Nidal, Abu Shmidal," he sneered; "we have to strike at the PLO!"

Eytan recommended that the air force be sent to attack nine PLO targets in Beirut and in southern Lebanon. He pointed out that the likely PLO response would be to shell settlements along Israel's northern border. What he did not reveal was the intelligence in his possession that the PLO had issued orders to its frontline artillery units to respond automatically to an IAF attack on the Beirut headquarters with barrages against the Israeli settlements. Some reservations were expressed in the discussion about the scope of the proposed bombing in Beirut, especially because

of the risks of civilian casualties and a hostile American reaction. Eytan assured the cabinet that precautions were being taken to avoid civilian casualties. The ministers approved the operational plan with a heavy heart, for they knew that the air strike would escalate into a full-scale war in Lebanon. Under the circumstances, however, they felt unable to stop the snowball from starting to roll.

In the early afternoon Israeli jets hit the PLO targets in Beirut and in southern Lebanon. They bombed the sports stadium in Beirut, exploding the ammunition dump the PLO had established beneath the grandstand. Two hours later the PLO reacted precisely as it was expected to. It launched an artillery barrage along the entire border, targeting twenty villages in the Galilee and wounding three civilians. President Reagan sent a message to Begin, urging him not to widen the attack after the stadium bombing. Yasser Arafat was in Saudi Arabia, and the Saudis told the Americans that he was willing to suspend cross-border shelling. It was too late. Begin was in no mood to listen. His deepest emotions had been aroused. "Military targets … are completely immune," Begin wrote. "The purpose of the enemy is to kill—kill Jews, men, women, and children."

To the cabinet ministers who convened at Begin's residence in the evening of 5 June, after the end of the Jewish Sabbath, it was clear that the moment of reckoning was at hand. Begin opened the cabinet meeting by saying,

> The hour of decision has arrived. You know what I have done, and what all of us have done, to prevent war and bereavement. But our fate is that in the Land of Israel there is no escape from fighting in the spirit of self-sacrifice. Believe me, the alternative to fighting is Treblinka, and we have resolved that there would be no more Treblinkas. This is the moment in which a courageous choice has to be made. The criminal terrorists and the world must know that the Jewish people have a right to self-defense, just like any other people.

What Begin proposed was a war to remove once and for all the threat hanging over the Galilee, a war along the lines of the plan for Operation Little Pines. In a letter to Reagan the following day, he stated that the IDF would not advance more than forty kilometers into Lebanon. Ariel Sharon, who had returned from Romania in the meantime, was invited by Begin to explain the operational plan to the cabinet. Sharon made no mention of the "big plan." On the contrary, he spoke explicitly of a limit of forty kilometers and stressed that there was no intention of clashing with the Syrian forces in Lebanon. Sharon and Eytan conveyed five principles to the cabinet: (1) the IDF would advance into Lebanon along three main axes; (2) Beirut and its surroundings were not among the targets of the operation; (3) the scope of the operation—up to forty kilometers from the international border; (4) the duration of the operation—twenty-four to forty-eight hours; and (5) there was no plan to have a showdown with the Syrians, and the IDF would accordingly take care to keep a distance of at least four kilometers from the Syrian lines.

However, Sharon did say that a showdown with the Syrians could not be entirely ruled out, but that his intention was to outflank them and threaten them without opening fire so as to force them to retreat from the Bekaa Valley, along with the PLO artillery. He did not say that in his own view, and in that of the IDF experts, a clash with the Syrians was inescapable. This was also the view of Sharon's deputy, Mordechai Zippori, who was present at the meeting. A former brigadier, Zippori was the only member of the cabinet apart from Sharon to have held a senior rank in the IDF. Zippori told the cabinet in plain language that the proposed plan would inevitably lead to a clash with the Syrians. Begin took no notice of Zippori's warning. Simha Erlich asked whether there was any intention of reaching Beirut. He was assured by both Sharon and Begin that Beirut was completely outside the scope of the proposed operation. Begin added that this war, unlike some of their previous wars, would see no deviations from the plan without an explicit decision by the cabinet. Fourteen ministers, including Zippori,

voted for the operation while two abstained. Begin himself drafted the cabinet communique, and it was he who changed the code name from Operation Pines to Operation Peace for Galilee. The cabinet took the following decisions:

1. To instruct the Israel Defense Forces to place all the civilian population of the Galilee beyond the range of the terrorist fire from Lebanon, where they, their bases, and their headquarters are concentrated.
2. The name of the operation is Peace for Galilee.
3. During the operation, the Syrian army will not be attacked unless it attacks our forces.
4. Israel continues to aspire to the signing of a peace treaty with independent Lebanon, its territorial integrity preserved.

Both Eytan and Sharon were later to claim that the cabinet knew in advance that the scope of the operation would not be limited to forty kilometers. Eytan writes in his memoirs that at the meeting of 5 June they presented the "big plan" and that the cabinet approved it. He farther insists that the decision was to destroy the terrorists and that no limit was set to the IDF's advance. The maps he unfolded in front of the cabinet, he claims, had arrows pointing as far north as the Beirut–Damascus highway, and there was no room for misunderstanding what was being proposed. All these claims are contradicted by the record of the cabinet discussions and by the text of the decision that was not made public. This text stated that the cabinet approved the proposal brought by the minister of defense and the chief of staff. The proposal explicitly mentioned a limit of forty or at most forty-two kilometers, extending to the south of Sidon. But in practice the war was conducted in accordance with the "big plan," which was submitted to the cabinet only once, on 20 December 1981, and was decisively rejected by it. Eytan's ploy, as he told some of his colleagues, was to obtain permission for Operation Little Pines and to implement Operation Big Pines.

Sharon conceded, in a lecture he gave five years after the event, that the cabinet decision of 5 June 1982 spoke only in general terms about placing the Galilee outside the range of enemy fire. But he claimed that the political objective of the war required the destruction not only of the PLO infrastructure in southern Lebanon but also of its command posts and bases in Beirut and south of Beirut. According to Sharon, "Everyone involved—in the government, in the public at large, and in the IDF—knew exactly what was meant by the general formulation of the objectives." Yet none of the ministers who took the decision could confirm this understanding. Sharon himself had specifically told them that Beirut was outside the scope of his plan. It was he who chose to interpret the cabinet decision of 5 June as approval of the first stage of Operation Big Pines, and it was on the basis of the questionable interpretation that he ordered the IDF to prepare to capture all of the area up to Beirut, to cut the Beirut–Damascus highway, to link up with the Christian forces, and to destroy the Syrian forces. Sharon knew from his experience in the army and the government that once the IDF hit its stride, it would be difficult to assert political control over its actions.

The Lebanon War

On Sunday, 6 June 1982, four Israeli armored columns crossed the border into Lebanon, and seaborne forces landed south of Sidon. On the first day of the war, they captured Nabatiyeh, surrounded all the Lebanese coastal towns up to Sidon, attacked the PLO forces wherever they could find them, and blocked their route of escape to the north. On the second day of the war, Sharon ordered the IDF to prepare to fight the Syrian forces on their eastern flank and to move toward the Beirut–Damascus highway. On the night of the third day, Bashir Gemayel came by helicopter to the IDF forward command post to meet Rafael Eytan. The leader of the Phalange was told that the IDF would link up with his forces and that he should prepare to capture Beirut and to form a new government in Lebanon. The conversation was not reported to the Israeli cabinet. At this stage there was a broad national consensus, which included the Labor opposition, in support

of Operation Peace for Galilee. On 8 June, Begin assured the Knesset that Israel did not want war with Syria and that all fighting would come to an end as soon as the IDF had cleared a zone of forty kilometers from Israel's northern border. "From this rostrum," declared Begin in dramatic tones, "I appeal to President Assad to direct the Syrian army not to attack Israel's soldiers and then they will come to no harm."

The view from Damascus was very different. Syria and Israel were engaged in a long-term contest for hegemony in the Levant. From Assad's perspective, Begin's appeal must have seemed like a challenge. As Assad's biographer has written,

> Asad and Begin, champions of irreconcilable visions, came to blows, as they were bound sometime to do, over Lebanon in what was to be the goriest engagement in the struggle for the Middle East. Lebanon in the 1980s was the hapless arena for the collision between the dominant and expanded Israel which Begin was determined to build and the rival regional order with which Asad tried to stop him. Each man recognized the other as the principal enemy who could put at risk everything he held dear. In shorthand terms, "Greater Israel" went to war against "Greater Syria," both controversial concepts of uncertain definition but which certainly ruled each other out. The struggle, in a way the climax of their political lives, very nearly destroyed them both.

Even as Begin was speaking, the IDF was engaged in fighting Syrian forces in the central sector near Jezzine. To the cabinet meeting on 8 June, Sharon proposed two alternatives: a frontal attack on the Syrian forces or a flanking maneuver designed to bring about their voluntary retreat. The option of staying away from the Syrian positions was not even mentioned. The cabinet approved the flanking maneuver, which inevitably involved a major clash since the Syrians stood their ground. To signal that they had no intention of retreating, the Syrians also moved surface-to-air missile batteries into Lebanon. This was a defensive move, but Sharon presented it to the cabinet as an offensive move and obtained its permission to attack the SAM batteries. This decision, taken in the morning of 9 June, changed the whole character of the conflict.

No sooner had the politicians given the green light than over a hundred Israeli jets swept over the Bekaa Valley in what was to be one of the biggest air battles in world history. The IAF attacked the SAM-6 sites on both sides of the border, destroying them all. It also shot down twenty-three Syrian MiGs without losing a single Israeli aircraft. At the same time the IDF armored columns continued to pound the Syrian forces on the ground. The Syrians fought tenaciously and brought in reinforcements, and the central sector became the main battleground between the two armies. Israeli forces advanced along the coast to Damur and to Lake Karoun, in the Bekaa Valley. Their aim was to reach the Beirut–Damascus highway and to cut off the Syrian forces from the Lebanese capital, but they failed to achieve this aim before the American-sponsored cease-fire came into effect on 11 June. Some of the IDF commanders blamed the failure on the salami tactics by which Sharon sought to transform a small operation into a big operation. Every time Sharon wanted to go beyond what the cabinet had approved, he had to turn to Begin for permission. By telling Begin each additional change in the war plan was necessary in order to save the lives of Israeli soldiers, Sharon usually obtained Begin's permission, but the process took time. Begin himself later confirmed that Sharon kept him informed of every move made by the IDF—sometimes before it was taken, sometimes afterward.

By the time the cease-fire came into force, the IDF had reached the southern outskirts of Beirut, a distance considerably longer than forty kilometers. Even after the cease-fire went into effect, the IDF continued to creep forward toward Beirut. That night Sharon flew to Jounieh for a meeting with Bashir Gemayel. Different conceptions of the character of the conflict quickly rose to the surface. Sharon wanted the Phalangists to move against the Palestinians who were cooped up in West Beirut and under heavy pressure. Gemayel was content to sit back and let the Israelis do all the fighting. It began to dawn on Sharon that the Lebanese Christians were not going to play an active role in the war against the PLO, yet he had no intention of abandoning this war. On his orders the IDF continued to proceed by stealth until it reached the Beirut–Damascus highway and linked up with the Christian forces. Within the ranks of the IDF there was much resentment of Sharon's methods, of the mounting level of casualties they entailed, and of the false statements made by their official spokesman. But by 13 June the ring around Beirut was closed and Sharon had achieved several of his objectives: the PLO was trapped in Beirut, his forces had linked up with Christian forces, and the Syrian units in Beirut had been isolated from the main body of Syrians in the Bekaa Valley. Operation Peace for Galilee had evolved into an Israeli–Syrian war and then into a siege of an Arab capital.

The next Israeli objective was to eradicate the PLO quasi-government from Beirut. The Christian forces were not prepared to undertake this task despite the offers of support from Israel. Yet for the IDF to capture Beirut in street-to-street fighting would have involved an unacceptable level of casualties. The method chosen was a combination of military pressure and psychological warfare to persuade the PLO that its only alternatives were surrender and annihilation. Air attacks, naval guns, and artillery barrages, as well as loudspeakers and leaflets, were used in a campaign of pressure and intimidation. The campaign was directed against the PLO positions, but it inflicted immense suffering and heavy casualties on the Palestinian population of Beirut.

During the next two months the siege of Beirut was steadily intensified. On 4 July the IDF cut off the water and power supplies to the city but restored them a few days later, following a protest from President Reagan. Four hundred Israeli tanks and a thousand guns kept up the bombardment of Beirut. By the end of the first week in July, five hundred buildings had been destroyed by shells and bombs. On 1 August the Israeli forces stepped up their artillery, aerial, and naval bombardment of Beirut. A paratroop unit occupied Beirut's international airport, while Israeli tanks entered the southern outskirts of the city. The methods used provoked unrest within the army, political protest at home, and mounting international criticism. President Reagan lost patience with Israel and joined in the criticism. He demanded of Begin an immediate halt to the shelling of Beirut and threatened to review U.S.–Israeli relations. Begin replied with a telegram to Reagan that was bizarre in the extreme and suggested that he lived in a different world:

> Now may I tell you, dear Mr President, how I feel these days when I turn to the creator of my soul in deep gratitude. I feel as a Prime Minister empowered to instruct a valiant army facing "Berlin" where amongst innocent civilians, Hitler and his henchmen hide in a bunker deep beneath the surface. My generation, dear Ron, swore on the altar of God that whoever proclaims his intent to destroy the Jewish state or the Jewish people, or both, seals his fate, so that which happened once on instructions from Berlin—with or without inverted commas—will never happen again.

The text of the telegram, which was published in the *Jerusalem Post*, shocked many Israelis, who felt that the memory of the Holocaust should not be invoked to justify the Lebanon War or the siege of Beirut. They were also disturbed by the palpable signs that their prime minister had lost touch with reality and was merely chasing the ghosts of the past. Chaika Grossman, a left-wing member of the Knesset who had actually fought in the Warsaw Ghetto, implored Begin, "Return to reality! We are not in the Warsaw Ghetto, we are in the State of Israel." The writer Amos Oz, who had described Operation Peace" for Galilee as "a typical Jabotinskyian fantasy," conveyed a similar message to the prime minister: "This urge to revive Hitler, only to kill him again and

again, is the result of pain that poets can permit themselves to use, but not statesmen … even at great emotional cost personally, you must remind yourself and the public that elected you its leader that Hitler is dead and burned to ashes."

Alexander Haig, one of the few people who thought that Begin did not suffer from a "Holocaust complex," was himself a victim of Israel's war in Lebanon. During the siege of Beirut he thought that the moment had come to move all foreign forces—Syrian, Palestinian, and Israeli—out of Lebanon and to return the country to the Lebanese under suitable international protection and guarantees. His strategy was to use the shock of the Israeli attack to force the PLO out of Beirut. But toward the end of June he was forced to resign amid allegations that he had placed his country in an untenable position by tacitly approving the Israeli invasion of Lebanon. He was replaced by George Shultz, one of whose first acts as secretary of state was to send Philip Habib to negotiate an end to the fighting around Beirut. Yasser Arafat let it be known that he was prepared to withdraw his men from the city, if appropriate terms and guarantees could be worked out.

The withdrawal of the PLO was now only a matter of time, but one problem was that its members had nowhere to go. Ariel Sharon came up with a suggestion. He asked an Egyptian intermediary to persuade Arafat to lead the PLO back to Jordan and said that, if Arafat accepted, Israel would force King Hussein to make way for the organization. "One speech by me," boasted Sharon, "will make King Hussein realize that the time has come to pack his bags." The message was conveyed to Arafat, who asked the intermediary to give Sharon an immediate reply: "1. Jordan is not the home of the Palestinians. 2. You are trying to exploit the agony of the Palestinian people by turning a Palestinian–Lebanese dispute into a Palestinian–Jordanian contradiction." Arafat also suggested that Sharon wanted to provoke Jordanian–Palestinian conflict to give Israel an excuse for occupying the East Bank of the Jordan. When Sharon heard Arafat's reply, he responded with an obscene curse in Arabic.

Philip Habib's aim was an arrangement whereby the Palestinian and Syrian forces would withdraw from Beirut, Israel would not try to enter the city, and the Lebanese government would regain complete control over its capital. The American and French governments agreed to assign troops to a multinational force whose task would be to supervise the evacuation. Begin and Sharon reacted very differently to the American offer to send Marines to Beirut. Begin wanted a political agreement and was ready to enter into negotiations with the Lebanese government. Sharon wanted to change the regime in Lebanon in accordance with his "big plan" and was fearful that American soldiers would get in his way. On 10 August, Habib submitted a draft agreement to Israel. At this point Sharon, impatient with what he regarded as American meddling, ordered unprecedented saturation bombing of Beirut in which at least three hundred people were killed. Reagan was outraged and made another call to Jerusalem. "Menachem," he said, "I think we've been very patient. Unless the bombing ceases immediately, I'm fearful of grave consequences in the relations between our countries." If Begin's trust in Sharon was being eroded, the cabinet had no trust at all. At its meeting of 12 August, the cabinet stripped the minister of defense of most of his powers, such as the power to order the use of the air force, the armored force, and the artillery, and vested them in the prime minister in the event that the cabinet was unable to meet.

Habib eventually succeeded in arranging for the withdrawal of the PLO to Tunisia. A first contingent of fighters left by sea on 21 August. Arafat left on 30 August aboard a Greek merchant ship with the U.S. Sixth Fleet providing cover. Altogether, 8,500 men were evacuated by sea to Tunisia. Another 2,500 men made the journey by land to Syria, Iraq, and Yemen. Egypt, Saudi Arabia, and the Persian Gulf sheikhdoms refused to accept PLO evacuees. After seventy-five days of heavy fighting, the PLO was banished from its stronghold in Lebanon to the periphery of the Arab world, a good deal more than forty kilometers from Israel's border. Begin was pleased with

the outcome and announced that Operation Peace for Galilee had achieved most of its objectives.

To Sharon it seemed that the stage was now set for implementing phase two of his "big plan": the creation of a new political order in Lebanon. The Lebanese presidential election was scheduled for 23 August, and the weeks of the siege were used for political pressures and manipulations behind the scenes. The Israelis wanted the deputies to the parliament, who elect the president, to feel that national survival depended on choosing a candidate acceptable to Israel. Bashir Gemayel needed Israel's help to obtain the two-thirds majority required by the constitution because a large proportion of the deputies lived in areas under Israeli control. A united front consisting of Muslim as well as rival Maronite deputies decided to boycott the election on the grounds that it was being held in the shadow of Israeli guns. The Israelis had a list of all the deputies, and they did what they could to assist Gemayel's supporters and to impede his opponents from arriving at Beirut to cast their vote. Bashir Gemayel was elected president by 57 out of the 62 deputies who attended the session. When the result of the vote became known, there was ecstatic rejoicing in the Maronite quarters of Beirut. Israelis, too, joined in the jubilation. One group of Mossad men fired a full case of ammunition into the air, convinced that their patience and perseverance had finally paid off.

The telegram from Jerusalem to the victorious candidate read, "Warmest wishes from the heart on the occasion of your election. May God be with you, dear friend, in the fulfilment of your great historic mission, for the liberty of Lebanon and its independence. Your friend. Menachem Begin." Begin, Sharon, and Shamir made no bones of their expectation that, free from Syrian toils, Lebanon would sign a peace treaty with them. Any Syrian obstruction to this program, Shamir declared, would be "a brutal, insolent threat to peace." Bashir Gemayel himself called for the withdrawal of all foreign armies from Lebanon—Syrian, Israeli, and Palestinian. In Syrian eyes he committed the heinous crime of putting Syria on the same footing as Israel. Having received from the Israelis a leg up in mounting the presidential horse, Gemayel was anxious to demonstrate his independence, to widen his domestic political base, and to emphasize the Arab rather than the Israeli orientation of his foreign policy. But the more evasive he appeared, the more insistently the Israelis demanded an early discharge of his political debt. The Israelis wanted nothing short of a peace treaty and full diplomatic relations with Lebanon, as they had previously achieved with Egypt. What the Israelis seemed unable to understand was that, unlike Egypt, Lebanon was too small and too weak to defy the entire Arab world.

On the night of 1 September, Bashir Gemayel was summoned to a secret meeting with Begin in Nahariya, a coastal resort in northern Israel. Begin kept him waiting for two hours. The fragility of the understanding between them did not take long to manifest itself. While Begin demanded open normalization in the relations between Israel and Lebanon and the signing of a peace treaty, Gemayel pleaded for time to consolidate his position and merely mentioned the possibility of a nonaggression pact. Another bone of contention was the future of Major Sa'ad Haddad, the Christian militia leader in southern Lebanon who was financed by the Israelis. Begin remarked that Haddad at least knew which side his bread was buttered on and held him as an example to be emulated. Gemayel countered that he was going to put Haddad on trial for desertion from the Lebanese army. When Begin cut in with the suggestion that Haddad be appointed chief of staff, the meeting disintegrated into a shouting match. The loudest voice in the room was that of Sharon. Sharon reminded Gemayel that Israel had Lebanon in its grasp and told him he would be well advised to do what was expected of him. Gemayel held out both arms to Sharon. "Put the handcuffs on!" he cried. "I am your vassal." The meeting ended abruptly and acrimoniously and without any agreement being reached.

On the day that Begin met Gemayel, President Reagan unveiled a new peace plan for the Middle East. He said that the departure of the Palestinians from Beirut dramatized more than ever the homelessness of the Palestinian people. His plan was for self-government by the Palestinians of the West Bank and Gaza in association with Jordan. He ruled out both a Palestinian state and annexation by Israel. Additional Israeli settlements in the territories would be an obstacle to peace, said Reagan, and the status of Jerusalem had still to be decided. The message was clear: the United States rejected the Israeli claim for permanent control over the West Bank and Gaza. Equally clear was another message: the United States did not think that Israel was entitled to exploit the recent carnage in Lebanon to implement its grand design for Greater Israel. Reagan and his advisers grasped the ultimate territorial purpose of Sharon's big plan, and they firmly rejected it. They acknowledged that Israel was entitled to security along its northern border, but not that it had a right to territorial expansion at the expense of the Palestinians. Small wonder that Begin rejected the Reagan peace plan with all the vehemence he could muster or that he was supported in striking this defiant posture by a large majority of his fellow parliamentarians.

On 14 September, three weeks after his election, Bashir Gemayel was assassinated in his party headquarters, most probably by agents of Syrian intelligence. The assassination knocked out the central prop from underneath Israel's entire policy in Lebanon. With Gemayel's violent removal from the scene, Sharon's plan for a new political order in Lebanon—a plan predicated from the start on Bashir Gemayel personally—collapsed like a house of cards. Sharon feared that the leftist militias and a couple of thousand PLO men allegedly still at large in Beirut would destroy the prospect of a stable, pro-Israeli regime in Lebanon. The assassination was used as the pretext for sending Israeli forces into West Beirut the following day to take up the areas formerly held by the PLO. Sharon ordered the IDF commanders to allow the Phalangists to enter the Palestinian refugee camps Sabra and Mratila, on the south side of Beirut, in order to "clean out" the terrorists who, he claimed, were lurking there.

Inside the camps the revenge-thirsty Christian militiamen perpetrated a terrible massacre, killing hundreds of men, women, and children. Israel estimated the number of dead at seven to eight hundred, while the Palestinian Red Crescent put the number at over two thousand. The carnage went on from the evening of Thursday, 16 September, until Sunday. Already on Thursday evening, not long after dropping their Christian allies outside the camps, Israeli soldiers got wind of the massacre but did nothing to stop it. Begin heard about the massacre when listening to the BBC on Saturday afternoon. He called Sharon, who promised to get a report from the IDF. At first official spokesmen tried to obscure the fact that the Christian militia men entered the refugee camps with the knowledge and help of the IDF commanders. Begin himself said, more than a touch self-righteously, "*Goyim* [non-Jews] are killing *goyim,* and the whole world" is trying to hang Jews for the crime." Nevertheless, as Rabbi Arthur Hertzberg, a liberal American–Jewish leader, prophetically observed, Menachem Begin could not remain in office "if he has squandered Israel's fundamental asset—its respect for itself and the respect of the world." The sense of shock and revulsion in Israel and the international outciy forced the government to appoint a commission of inquiry under Supreme Court Justice Yitzhak Kahan.

In the months after the massacre, Israel continued to sink deeper and deeper into the Lebanese quagmire. The appointment of Amin Gemayel to succeed his younger brother as president did nothing to restore Israel's sagging fortunes in Lebanon. For whereas Bashir had maintained close links with Israel, Amin had always been regarded as Syria's man in Lebanon. Amin Gemayel predictably declined to collaborate with Israel in forging a new political order in Lebanon. The balance sheet of Israel's relationship with the Maronite community was thus singularly disappointing. Within the space of a few months, in the second half of 1982, Israel learned, the hard way, that "Bashir Jumayyil did not fully represent the Phalange, that the Phalange did not represent the whole Maronite community, that the Maronite community did not speak for all Lebanese Christians, and that Lebanon's Christians were no

longer assured of their ascendancy." It was no end of a lesson.

The Kahan Commission presented its report on 7 February 1983. It concluded that Israel bore indirect responsibility for the massacre at Sabra and Shatila, inasmuch as the Phalange entered the refugee camps with the knowledge of the government and with the encouragement of the army. It recommended the removal of the minister of defense and a number of senior officers from their posts. Sharon immediately announced his rejection of the findings and the recommendations of the Kahan Commission. On 14 February the cabinet decided, by a majority of sixteen against Sharon's single vote, to accept the recommendations of the Kahan report. Sharon remained in the cabinet as minister without portfolio. He was replaced as minister of defense by Moshe Arens, the ambassador to the United States.

Arens, a former professor of aeronautical engineering at the Technion, was a Herut hardliner. Yet he understood that neither the public nor the army would put up with a prolonged and purposeless presence in Lebanon or with the daily attrition in casualties. Under his direction, David Kimche, a senior Mossad official and a strong supporter of the Christian conception that had guided Israeli policy in Lebanon, conducted negotiations with representatives of the Lebanese government. The negotiations required over thirty-five sessions and high-level American involvement, including a ten-day shuttle by George Shultz. On 17 May 1983 Israel and Lebanon signed an agreement that formally terminated the state of war and recognized the international border between them as inviolable. The parties undertook to prevent the use of one country's territory for terrorist activity against the other country. Israel was to withdraw its forces to a distance of forty to forty-five kilometers from the international border to an area defined as a "security zone." The area north of the security zone was to be under the control of the United Nations Interim Force in Lebanon. The agreement also affirmed that Major Sa'ad Haddad's militia would be recognized as a Lebanese "auxiliary force" and accorded proper status under Lebanese law. There was one inherent flaw in the agreement: it was conditional on Syria's withdrawing its forces from Lebanon, and Syria did not oblige.

In the summer of 1983 the decision was taken to withdraw Israeli troops from Lebanon in stages without waiting for a concurrent withdrawal by Syria or the implementation of the 17 May agreement by the Lebanese. Once Israel began to withdraw unilaterally and unconditionally, the diplomatic concept underlying the agreement fell away. Moshe Levi, the new chief of staff, was not interested in the political in-fighting that had been part and parcel of the war in Lebanon. He wanted to reduce the size of the army committed to Lebanon, and he wanted his troops redeployed so as to reduce casualties. He and Arens persuaded the cabinet to agree to the withdrawal of Israeli troops from the outskirts of Beirut to the more easily defendable line along the Awali River. The pullback was twice postponed at the request of the Americans, who wanted to give the Christians a chance to consolidate their position. But in August the Israeli forces began their withdrawal from the Shouf mountains. This move did not adversely affect their security. But it had two grave consequences for Lebanon. First, it permitted Syria to regain control over the Beirut–Damascus highway and to reassert its grip over the Lebanese capital. Second, it provoked a fresh round in the age-old struggle for hegemony in the Shouf between the Druze and the Christian militias. The Druze easily gained the upper hand and went on to sack and destroy entire Christian villages, turning thousands of their inhabitants into refugees. The retreating Israelis were caught in the cross fire. Even the Shiites, who had originally welcomed Israel's entry into Lebanon because of the tensions between themselves and the Palestinians, now turned all their fury against the Israeli forces of occupation and against the Christians. Intercommunal fighting was nothing new in Lebanon, but now all the communities had a common enemy—Israel.

Moreover, the war in Lebanon had a very negative effect on Arab perceptions of Israel. By honoring its commitment to withdraw from Sinai, Israel had gained much credit in Egypt and some credit in the rest of the Arab world. Egypt could hold its head high and show the skeptics that the peace with Israel yielded tangible benefits. By invading Lebanon, Israel dissipated all the credit and placed Egypt in a highly uncomfortable position. The massive force that Israel deployed in Lebanon, the scale of the suffering it inflicted, the siege of Beirut, and the massacre in Sabra and Shatila stunned the entire Arab world, and above all the Egyptians. The Egyptians were convinced that Israel's aim was to impose on Lebanon a separate peace by force. While they had an interest in other Arab countries following in their footsteps and making peace with Israel, they utterly rejected the means employed by Israel to this end. The Egyptians did not renounce the peace treaty with Israel, but they recalled their ambassador from Tel Aviv, froze the process of normalization, and took refuge in what Minister of State Boutros Boutros–Ghali was first to term a "cold peace."

The End of the Begin Era

On 28 August 1983 Menachem Begin announced to his cabinet his intention of resigning from the post of prime minister and retiring from political life. The cabinet was completely unprepared for the announcement, and some of his colleagues tried to dissuade him, but to no avail. The only reason Begin gave the cabinet for his decision was a personal one: "I cannot go on." For a number of weeks Begin looked increasingly gaunt, withdrawn, and almost listless. Rumors had been circulating about his poor health and poor performance. But his aides had been doing their best to conceal from, the public the full extent of his physical and psychological exhaustion. That evening hundreds of people gathered outside the prime minister's residence. They included right-wingers who called on him to carry on and supporters of Peace Now who congratulated him on his courageous decision.

After his resignation Begin became a recluse. He retreated to his home a man broken in body and spirit. The reason for his resignation remained something of a puzzle, since he himself never explained why he could no longer carry on. Psychologically, he had always tended to swing from high elation to deep depression, and the death of his wife, Aliza, in September 1982, plunged him into deep depression. On the political plane the war in Lebanon was probably the main cause for his disappointment and despair. The war that Begin said would last two days was now in its second year, with no end in sight. The cost of the war in human lives, to which Begin was particularly sensitive, was mounting all the time. A group of demonstrators outside his house carried a sign on which the number of casualties was constantly updated. At the time of Begin's resignation, over five hundred Israeli soldiers had lost their lives in Lebanon. Bereaved parents blamed Begin for the senseless death of their loved ones. One father sent Begin a harrowing letter that ended with the following words: "And if you have a spark of conscience and humanity within you, may my great pain—the suffering of a father in Israel whose entire world has been destroyed—pursue you forever, during your sleeping hours and when you are awake—may it be a mark of Cain upon you for all time."[51] Begin did have a spark of conscience and humanity in him, at least when it came to Jewish lives, and the burden of guilt finally overcame him.

The Likud's Central Committee elected Yitzhak Shamir to succeed Begin. The contrast of temperament, personality, and style could hardly have been greater. One was volatile and mercurial; the other, solid and reliable. One was charismatic and domineering; the other, dull and dour. One was a spell-binding orator; the other could hardly string two sentences together. Shamir's grayness of character and lack of charisma may actually have helped him get elected. Some Likud members saw him as a sort of Israeli Clement Attlee, as a safe pair of hands, and a welcome antidote to the drama and passions of Begin's Churchillian style of leadership.

In terms of outlook and ideology, however, the difference between Shamir and Begin was not all that great. Both were disciples of Ze'ev Jabotinsky. Both were dedicated to the Land of Israel. Both

subscribed to the lachrymose version of Jewish history, seeing it as a long series of trials and tribulations culminating in the Holocaust. Both were suspicious of outside powers, and both were strong advocates of Israeli self-reliance. In some ways Shamir was more intransigent than Begin. For Shamir there could be no retreat from any territory, not just the territory of the Land of Israel. That was why he opposed withdrawal from Sinai and why he supported the annexation of the Golan Heights. He was generally unreceptive to the idea of bargaining and compromise, his natural instinct being to stand firm in the face of external pressure.

By 10 October, Shamir had formed a coalition that comprised many of the same ministers and parties as before, and the Knesset approved the guidelines of its policy. The new government's main task was to get the IDF out of Lebanon under the best possible conditions and with the least possible risk to Israel. Soon after assuming office, Shamir was handed a paper by the IDF planning division. The planners saw no prospect of Syrian withdrawal from Lebanon and accordingly recommended unilateral Israeli withdrawal. This recommendation ran counter to the trend toward confrontation with Syria that was manifesting itself in Washington under the leadership of George Shultz. Shultz had come to the conclusion that Syria was not amenable to diplomatic pressure and persuasion and that the only language it understood was military force.

The strategic dialogue between the United States and Israel was renewed during Shamir's visit to Washington in November 1983. Shamir agreed not to initiate another unilateral withdrawal as long as U.S. Marines remained in Lebanon and not to initiate a major act of war against Syria without prior consultation with Washington. The allies also agreed to act jointly to exert "constant tactical and strategic pressure on Syria" to force it to enter into negotiations with Amin Gemayel about the withdrawal of its forces from Lebanon. This policy of toughness, however, failed to achieve its objectives. The Syrians had no intention of honoring the 17 May agreement, which completely ignored their interests. The American–Israeli axis was not equal to the task of deterring Syria or keeping President Gemayel's domestic opponents at bay. In March 1984 he was summoned to Damascus and ordered to abrogate the 17 May agreement. Israel's policy shifted as a result from reliance on the Lebanese government and army to seeking security arrangements in southern Lebanon in collaboration with its Christian proxies there. Under Shamir's leadership Israel thus remained involved in the protracted and costly, but inconclusive, conflict in Lebanon.

The political results of the war could hardly have been more disappointing, especially when measured against the expectations of Ariel Sharon, the war's chief architect. Sharon's "big plan" was based on a series of assumptions that collapsed like a row of dominoes when put to the test. The greatest misconception, and the one underlying all the others, lay in thinking that Israel's military superiority could be translated into lasting political achievements. In fact, the exchange rate between military power and political gains has never been favorable in Israel's case, and the Lebanon War was no exception. Sharon misread the Israeli political map by not realizing that national consensus was bound to fracture, given the offensive and expansionist character of this war. In his planning for the destruction of the PLO, Sharon underestimated the organization's resilience and the nonmilitary sources of its strength. Sharon also misread the Lebanese political map and deluded himself in believing that Maronite hegemony could be asserted in the face of all the opposition. Sharon counted on political change inside Lebanon to start a chain reaction that would eclipse all of Israel's enemies and catapult it into a position of unchallengeable regional mastery. The political change that Sharon sought in Lebanon could only be achieved over Syria's dead body. Sharon realized, though he never admitted this to his cabinet colleagues, that the expulsion of the Syrian forces from Lebanon was essential if Israel was to emerge as the dominant regional power. But, once again, he underestimated Syria's tenacity and resilience. Syria suffered serious military setbacks during the Lebanon War, but, like Gamal Abdel Nasser in the Suez War, Hafez

al–Assad snatched a political victory out of the jaws of military defeat.

While Sharon was the main driving force behind the war in Lebanon, Begin bore the ultimate political responsibility for it. Although his expectations were not as grandiose as Sharon's, Begin was also a victim of wishful thinking. By dealing a mortal blow to the PLO in Lebanon, Begin hoped not only to achieve peace for the Galilee but also to defeat the Palestinian claim to statehood in what he and his party regarded as the Land of Israel. Once the PLO had been crushed in its stronghold in Lebanon, so the argument ran, all effective Palestinian resistance to the imposition of permanent Israeli rule in the West Bank and Gaza would come to an end. In short, for Begin no less than for Sharon and Eytan, the war in Lebanon was a war for the Land of Israel. But it was absurd to assume that the Palestinian problem would be solved by military action in Lebanon, since the roots of the problem did not lie in Lebanon. Far from relegating the Palestinian problem to the sidelines, the war in Lebanon, and especially the massacre in Sabra and Shatila, served to focus international attention on the need to find a solution to this problem. Far from reducing international pressure on Israel to withdraw from the occupied territories, the war triggered a shift in American policy from acceptance of autonomy for the Palestinians in accordance with the Camp David Accords to the Reagan plan, which called for Israeli withdrawal from the West Bank and Gaza to make way for a Palestinian homeland in association with Jordan. And far from adding a peace treaty with Lebanon to the one with Egypt, the invasion of Lebanon strained the relations with Egypt almost to the breaking point.

Any pretension to a strategy of working toward comprehensive peace with the Arab world that Begin may have entertained until June 1982 was finally and irrevocably destroyed by the invasion of Lebanon. The war in Lebanon was intended to secure Israel's hold over Judea and Samaria. This was not the war's declared aim, but it was the ideological conception behind it. All Israel's previous wars, with the exception of the Suez War, had been wars of no choice, wars that were imposed on Israel by the Arabs. Even the Suez War enjoyed complete national consensus because it was seen as a legitimate response to Arab provocation, was short, and did not involve high casualties. The war in Lebanon, on the other hand, by Begin's own admission was "a war of choice." War was not imposed on Israel by its Arab enemies. The war path was deliberately chosen by its leaders in pursuit of power and some highly controversial political gains. Much of the credit that Begin received for making peace with Egypt in his first term in office was thus wiped out by the ill-conceived and ill-fated war for which he was responsible during his second term.

Begin's premiership provides an interesting illustration of what students of international relations sometimes call the security dilemma. In the absence of a world government, individual states are driven to acquire more and more power in order to escape the impact of the power of others. But the quest for absolute security is self-defeating because it generates insecurity on the part of one's enemies and prompts them to resort to countermeasures that they see as self-defense. The result is a vicious circle of power accumulation and insecurity. In the case of Begin the trauma of the Holocaust produced a passionate desire to procure absolute safety and security for the Jewish people, but it also blinded him to the fears and anxieties that his own actions generated among Israel's Arab neighbors. By invading Lebanon in 1982, Begin thought he would turn the corner, defeat all Israel's enemies once and for all, and achieve perfect security for his people. But there are no corners in a vicious circle.

The Palestinian War of Independence

The spark that ignited the Palestinian uprising, or *intifada,* was a traffic accident on 9 December 1987, in which an Israeli truck driver killed four residents of Jabaliya, the largest of the eight refugee camps in the Gaza Strip. It was falsely rumored that the driver deliberately caused the accident to avenge the stabbing to death of his brother in Gaza two days earlier. The two men

were unrelated. Nevertheless, the rumor inflamed Palestinian passions and set off disturbances in the Jabaliya camp and in the rest of the Gaza Strip. From Gaza the disturbances spread to the West Bank. Within days the occupied territories were engulfed in a wave of spontaneous, uncoordinated, and popular street demonstrations and commercial strikes on an unprecedented scale. Equally unprecedented was the extent of mass participation in these disturbances: tens of thousands of ordinary civilians, including women and children. Demonstrators burned tires, threw stones and Molotov cocktails at Israeli cars, brandished iron bars, and waved the Palestinian flag. The standard of revolt against Israeli rule had been raised. The Israeli security forces used the full panoply of crowd control measures to quell the disturbances: cudgels, nightsticks, tear gas, water cannons, rubber bullets, and live ammunition. But the disturbances only gathered momentum.

The outbreak of the *intifada* was completely spontaneous. There was no preparation or planning by the local Palestinian elite or the PLO, but the PLO was quick to jump on the bandwagon of popular discontent against Israeli rule and to play a leadership role, alongside a newly formed body, the Unified National Command. In origin the *intifada* was not a nationalist revolt. It had its roots in poverty, in the miserable living conditions of the refugee camps, in hatred of the occupation, and, above all, in the humiliation that the Palestinians had to endure over the preceding twenty years. But it developed into a statement of major political import. The aims of the *intifada* were not stated at the outset; they emerged in the course of the struggle. The ultimate aim was self-determination and the establishment of an independent Palestinian state, which had failed to emerge forty years previously despite the UN partition resolution of 29 November 1947. In this respect the *intifada* may be seen as the Palestinian war of independence. The Israeli–Palestinian conflict had come fall circle.

The *intifada* took Israel by complete surprise. Political leaders and the entire intelligence community were oblivious to processes taking place under their very noses. They were surprised by the outbreak of the *intifada* because they blithely believed in a conception that was out of touch with reality. This conception had a political aspect and a military aspect. The politicians, for the most part, assumed that time was on their side; that the residents of the territories depended on Israel for jobs; that there was tacit acquiescence in Israeli rule; and that, consequently, Israel could continue the process of creeping annexation without running the risk of a large-scale popular revolt. The military experts not only assumed but were confident that their traditional methods would enable them to deal effectively with any disturbances that occurred and that any manifestations of violence by the inhabitants of the occupied territories could be swiftly nipped in the bud.

It took about a month for Israelis to realize that the disturbances were not just a flash in the pan and that they could not go on ignoring the twenty-year-old problem. Israeli society was forced to consider seriously alternatives to the status quo, but the result was bitter divisions and a shift toward extremes at both ends of the political spectrum. On the left there was a growing realization that a political solution had to be found to the Palestinian problem and that this would probably mean negotiations with the PLO and the eventual emergence of an independent Palestinian state alongside Israel. On the right, where ideas of territorial compromise had never been popular, the conviction crystallized that only brute force could bring the trouble to an end. The immediate result of the unrest was a tilt to the right. This was reflected in the growing number of voices calling on the IDF to employ an iron fist in order to smash the *intifada* once and for all.

The *intifada* also accentuated the divisions inside the national unity government. The Likud and the Alignment, the main parties in the government, faced a high level of internal dissent. Neither party was able to devise a clear and consistent policy for dealing with the *intifada*. Within the Alignment, Shimon Peres tilted toward a political initiative and Yitzhak Rabin toward the use of force. Peres resurrected the "Gaza first" idea, originally advanced during the Palestinian autonomy talks with Sadat's Egypt.

He suggested to the Knesset Foreign Affairs and Defense Committee in mid-December that the Gaza Strip be demilitarized but remain under Israeli supervision and that the thirteen Jewish settlements there be dismantled He proposed the dismantling of settlements not as an immediate or unilateral Israeli move but as part of an overall peace settlement. Shamir attacked the suggestion, calling Peres "a defeatist with a scalpel who wants to put Israel on the operating table so he can give away Gaza today, Judea and Samaria tomorrow and the Golan Heights after that." It was Peres and his party, claimed Shamir, who were to blame for the unrest because they encouraged the Arabs to resort to violence. The real problem, according to Shamir, was not a territorial dispute that could be solved through territorial concessions, but a threat to the very existence of the State of Israel.

Yitzhak Rabin, who as minister of defense had the primary responsibility for dealing with the disturbances, was rather closer in his views to Shamir than to Peres. When the disturbances broke out, he greatly underestimated the gravity of the situation and went ahead with a scheduled visit to the United States. On his return he veered to the other extreme, ordering the use of force on a massive scale to defeat the uprising. "Break their bones," he was reported to have said while directing his troops in the field during the early weeks of the *intifada*. These three words gained him international notoriety. He later denied having uttered them. But the image of Rabin the bone breaker stuck. Rabin's aim was to drive home to the residents of the occupied territories the notion that they would not be allowed to make political gains as a result of violence. He also wanted to leave no doubt in their minds as to who was running the territories. To this end he exhorted his troops to use "might, force, and beatings." But it was precisely this kind of arrogant and aggressive attitude that had provoked the uprising in the first place. In the end it was the residents of the territories themselves who demonstrated to Rabin that military force was part of the problem rather than a solution.

On orders from above, the IDF resorted to a whole range of draconian measures in order to crush the uprising. Among its measures were deportation of political activists, political assassination, administrative detention, mass arrests, curfews, punitive economic policies, the closing down of schools and universities, and the breaking up of communal structures. Thousands of Palestinians were arrested on suspicion of conspiring to subvert public order and incitement to violence, and special detention camps had to be hastily constructed to accommodate all the detainees. These extreme measures did not bring the uprising under control. By the end of the first month, it was clear that the IDF's policy was completely bankrupt. Senior army officers began to admit that there was no return to the pre-December 1987 status quo and that the uprising might continue indefinitely.

Academics were quicker than either the politicians or the soldiers to grasp the true nature of the phenomenon that Israel was facing. Yehoshua Porath, a leading expert on Palestinian history, noted, "This is the first time that there has been a popular action, covering all social strata and groups. ... The whole population is rebelling, and this is creating a common national experience." Urban as well as rural areas were participating in the uprising in an exceptional demonstration of national cohesion. In Porath's estimate, the *intifada* accomplished more in its first few months than decades of PLO terrorism had achieved outside the country. Professor Shlomo Avineri, a prominent Labor Party intellectual, observed, "The West Bank and Gaza under Israeli rule are a threat against which the whole might of the Israeli army may not suffice. ... An army can beat an army, but an army cannot beat a people. ... Israel is learning that power has limits. Iron can smash iron, it cannot smash an unarmed fist."

Events in the occupied territories received intense media coverage. The world was assailed by disturbing pictures of Israeli troops firing on stone-throwing demonstrators, or beating with cudgels those they caught, among them women and children. Israel's image suffered serious damage as a result of this media coverage. The Israelis complained the reporting was biased and that it focused deliberately on scenes of brutality in what

was a normal effort to restore order. But no amount of pleading could obscure the message that constantly came across in pictures in the newspapers and on the television screens: a powerful army was being unleashed against a civilian population that was fighting for its basic human rights and for the right to political self-determination. The biblical image of David and Goliath now seemed to be reversed, with Israel looking like an overbearing Goliath and the Palestinians with the stones as a vulnerable David. British visitors naturally took the side of the underdogs. David Mellor, a minister of state at the Foreign Office, gave vent to his abhorrence at the conditions in the Gaza refugee camps: "I defy anyone to come here and not be shocked. Conditions here are an affront to civilized values. It is appalling that a few miles up the coast there is prosperity, and here there is misery on a scale that rivals anything anywhere in the world." Gerald Kaufman, the Labor Party's spokesman on foreign affairs, himself a Jew and a longstanding supporter of Israel, remarked that "friends of Israel as well as foes have been shocked and saddened by the country's response to the disturbances." Within a short time of the outbreak of the uprising, Israel's standing sank to its lowest ebb since the siege of Beirut in 1982.

Israel became the target of outspoken international criticism, from official as well as unofficial sources. The United Nations strongly condemned Israel's violation of human rights in the territories, as it had done many times in the past. To this was now added specific condemnation of the IDF for the "killing and wounding of defenseless Palestinian civilians." The Security Council called for an investigation, and Marrack Goulding, the UN undersecretary-general for special political affairs, visited the occupied territories in January 1988. He met with Foreign Minister Peres, but Prime Minister Shamir refused to see him, because he was "interfering in Israel's internal affairs." Goulding was dismayed by what he saw. He reported that he had witnessed Israel using "unduly harsh" measures in the territories and that, although the IDF had the right to maintain order, it had "over-reacted" to the demonstrations. During the 1988 session of the General

Assembly, nearly a score of resolutions were passed, condemning Israel and calling on it to abide by the Geneva Convention for the protection of civilians in times of war. Israel's delegate to the UN complained that the organization was so biased that "even if we threw rose petals at the Molotov-cocktail throwers, this body would find a way to condemn us."

By far the most serious fallout from the *intifada* was its effect on U.S.–Israeli relations. While the Reagan administration abstained from, or vetoed, many of the UN resolutions condemning Israel, it was privately critical of the Israeli handling of the uprising. The uprising brought about a fundamental change in U.S. policy toward the Arab–Israeli conflict, culminating by.the end of 1988 in recognition of the PLO as a legitimate party in the negotiations. There was a marked shift in American public opinion away from its traditional support for Israel. The uprising sparked sympathy for the Palestinians at all levels of American society. It even prompted some of the leaders of American Jewry to raise questions about the wisdom of Israel's policies and the morality of its methods, for the first time since the war in Lebanon. In government circles there was concern that close American association with Israel despite its defiance of world opinion could have negative repercussions for American interests throughout the Middle East and the Persian Gulf. Earlier attempts to organize an international conference had floundered because no solution could be found to the problem of Palestinian representation and because Likud leaders had opposed the whole idea. America's response to this opposition had been rather mild. With the *intifada* gathering momentum, George Shultz became personally involved again. The result was the first major U.S. effort to solve the Arab–Israeli conflict since the Reagan plan of 1982.

Shultz made two trips to the region in search of fresh ideas and then produced, on 4 March 1988, a package that came to be known as the Shultz initiative. The package followed in the path of the Camp David Accords in calling for Palestinian self-rule but with an accelerated timetable. There was also an important new element: an "interlock,"

a locked-in connection between the talks on the transitional period of self-rule and the talks on final status. This was intended to give assurances to the Palestinians against Israeli foot-dragging. Events were expected to move forward at a rapid pace. First, the secretary-general of the UN would convene all the parties to the Arab–Israeli conflict and the five permanent members of the Security Council to an international conference. This conference would not be able to impose solutions on the participants or to veto any agreements reached by them. Second, negotiations between an Israeli and a Jordanian–Palestinian delegation would start on 1 May and end by 1 November. Third, the transition period would start three months later and last three years. Fourth, negotiations on final status would begin before the start of the transition period and have to be completed within a year. In other words, negotiations on final status would start regardless of the outcome of the first phase of negotiations.

Shimon Peres supported the Shultz initiative and said so publicly. So did President Mubarak. King Hussein, despite some reservations, appealed to the other Arabs not to reject it out of hand. The Palestinian response added up to a chorus repeating the old refrain that the one and only address for any proposals was the PLO in Tunis. And the PLO leaders in Tunis had no intention of letting the "insiders" steal the show by meeting with the American secretary of state.

If Shultz was disappointed with the response of the Palestinians, he was utterly dismayed by the response of Israel's prime minister. Shamir, who had initially given Shultz encouragement, was now singing a different tune. He blasted the idea of an international conference and rejected the interlock concept as contrary to the Camp David Accords. Even more shocking was the discovery that Shamir's interpretation of Resolution 242 did not encompass the principle of "land for peace." He said he was ready to negotiate peace with King Hussein, and with any Palestinians he might bring along with him, but that he was not ready to relinquish any territory for peace. When Shultz brought up the name of Faisal Husseini, a prominent moderate among the local Palestinian leaders, Shamir would say only, "We have a file on him!" Shultz admitted that he did not know the man but suggested that it be kept in mind that he might serve as a partner in future negotiations. "It's a very heavy file," Shamir repeated to stress his point. "Yes," said Shultz, reemphasizing his own point, "but the question is what one *does* with the file." The Shultz initiative was stalled, and its author thought that the main reason for that was Israel's prime minister. He did not say so openly, but he and his aides had a feeling that America's policy in the Middle East had fallen hostage to Israel's intransigence or inability to make decisions.

The *intifada* refocused the attention of the Arab world on the Palestinian problem. At the Arab League summit in Amman in November 1987, the Palestinian problem had been relegated to the sidelines. The *intifada* broke out the following month, and the indifference shown by the Arab world to the fate of the Palestinians was one of the reasons behind it. Now the courage of the Palestinians in resisting Israeli occupation put the rest of the Arab world to shame. In June 1988 an extraordinary summit of the Arab League was convened in Algiers. The summit reaffirmed the role of the PLO as the representative of the Palestinian people in any negotiations and pledged its financial and diplomatic support for the *intifada*.

The two principal losers from the *intifada* were Israel and Jordan. King Hussein was forced to reevaluate Jordan's position. On 31 July 1988 he suddenly announced that Jordan was cutting its legal and administrative ties with the West Bank. Jordan had continued to pay the salary of about a third of the civil servants on the West Bank during the preceding two decades of Israeli occupation. Many East Bankers felt they got nothing but ingratitude for their efforts to help the Palestinians and that the time had come to cut their losses. The king himself felt that Jordan was fighting a losing battle in defending positions that had already fallen to the PLO. After two decades of trying to blur the distinction between the East Bank and the West Bank, he concluded that the time had come to assert that the East Bank was

not Palestine and that it was up to the Palestinians to decide what they wanted to do with the West Bank and to deal with the Israelis directly over its future. As he later put it,

> It was the *intifada* that really caused our decision on disengagement from the West Bank. It was again our lack of ability to get any agreement with our Palestinian brethren. I wish to God they had been frank enough about what they wanted, and they would have got it a long time before. But we were torn apart trying to get all the pieces of the jigsaw together to help them. However, suspicions and doubts got in the way. But, beyond that, we recognized there was a definite trend which started before the Rabat resolution of 1974 and continued all the way through. They could give, they could take, they could do whatever they liked. They could probably give more than we could, but they decided that they wanted to have their say regarding their future, and I simply tried to help them by that decision.

In a press conference on 7 August, the king said that never again would Jordan assume the role of negotiating on behalf of the Palestinians. This statement was probably not meant to be as final as it sounded. But by closing out the idea of a Jordanian–Palestinian delegation and of a West Bank in some manner affiliated with Jordan, the king's decision appeared to the American secretary of state to mark the end of his initiative. A few weeks after the king had announced his decision, he asked the State Department to pass a message to Shimon Peres: the decision to remove Jordan from the peace process was taken in the hope that it would cause the PLO to "see the light and come to terms with reality."

This private message, however, could do no more than soften the blow that the king's latest move was bound to inflict on his partner in the abortive London Agreement. The effect of the public message was to strengthen the position of the PLO and to undermine the Alignment's so-called Jordanian option. The king himself had never liked the term "Jordanian option," for it implied an agreement between Israel and Jordan over the heads of the Palestinians. In his speech and press conference he therefore cleared the air. He said, in effect, that if a Jordanian option for settling the Palestinian problem had ever existed, it was now definitely dead.

From Israel's standpoint the king's speech marked the collapse of a very popular idea. It meant that Jordan was no longer prepared to deliberate the Palestinian problem with Israel; the only issue it would discuss was the question of its own borders. The Israelis were stunned by the speech and initially interpreted it as no more than a tactical move by the king to get the Palestinians to say that they still wanted him to represent them. But when the king asked his supporters on the West Bank not to sponsor petitions urging him to relent, the Israelis were forced to recognize that disengagement was a strategic move, not a tactical one. Even Likud leaders had reason to regret this move, because they realized that the forecasts of all the prophets of doom had come true: Israel now found itself all alone in the arena with the PLO.

Another consequence of the *intifada* was the birth of Hamas. The name is an Arabic word meaning zeal, and also an acronym for the Islamic Resistance Movement. Hamas was founded in Gaza in 1988 by Sheikh Ahmed Yassin, a paralyzed religious teacher, as a wing of the long-established Muslim Brothers in Palestine. To obtain a permit from the Israeli authorities, the movement was obliged to pledge that its fight for Palestinian rights would be conducted within the limits of the law and without the use of arms. Ironically, the Israeli authorities at first encouraged Hamas in the hope of weakening the secular nationalism of the PLO. But the Palestinian uprising had a radicalizing effect on Hamas, and its members began to step outside the bounds of the law. Although the Israelis repeatedly cracked down on the organization, the roots it put down sprouted again, giving rise to more violence each time. In 1989 the Israelis arrested Yassin and kept him in prison

until 1997. Hamas, however, continued to shift from the use of stones to the use of firearms. In 1994 it began, through its military wing, to launch suicide bombs inside Israel. The suicide attacks were undertaken out by individual members of Hamas who carried explosives on their body and detonated them in crowded places such as buses and markets.

While radicalizing Hamas, the *intifada* had a moderating effect on the secular Palestinians. On the one hand, the *intifada* raised the morale and boosted the pride and self-confidence of the Palestinian community. On the other, it did not end Israeli occupation, and living conditions deteriorated in the course of the struggle. Local leaders realized that a Palestinian peace initiative was essential. They were worried that the *intifada* would come to an end without yielding any concrete political gains. Consequently, they started putting pressure on the PLO chiefs in Tunis to meet the conditions that would enable them to enter into negotiations with Israel. Over the years the PLO mainstream had moved toward more moderate positions, but it avoided a clear-cut statement of these positions for fear of alienating the militant factions of the organization. The local leaders now threw all their weight behind the moderate mainstream. They urged the PLO chiefs in Tunis to recognize Israel, to accept a two-state solution, to declare a Palestinian state, and to establish a government-in-exile.

The *intifada* also called for a reevaluation of Israel's policy toward the Palestinians, but this was not an easy task, given the snarled state of the country's political system. Public opinion was divided. Some people thought that the *intifada* was an unwinnable war and that Israel should therefore seek a political solution that would put an end to the occupation. Others urged the use of greater force in order to smash the *intifada*. Both views were represented inside the government of national unity, which consequently tended to cripple itself every time the issue came up. Whenever the government seemed to be making progress, its wheels immediately jammed. Each time it took a step forward, internal forces pulled it two steps back. The government tended to deal with the most pressing operational questions and postpone discussions of the longer-term questions raised by the *intifada.* Thus, in terms of dealing with the Palestinian problem, the government of national unity once again proved to be a government of political paralysis.

Section 4

Hope and Failure, 1993–2010

Introduction

The Oslo peace process, on which enormous hopes had been placed (unjustified, it turns out), collapsed with the outbreak of the second intifada in late 2000. Oslo's failure poisoned intercommunal relations, destroyed any prospect of useful negotiations for several years, and re-opened the door to unilateral initiatives by both Israel and its adversaries. Analyzing why Oslo miscarried, therefore, has value not only for historians, but, potentially at least, for those who would avoid a repetition of that unhappy experience in the future.

Having started in late 1992 with secret contacts, the so-called Oslo negotiations climaxed with well-publicized, high-level meetings in 2000 and early 2001. The most ambitious of these conferences was the summit between the Israeli, Palestinian, and American heads of state at Camp David, Maryland, in July 2000. The final meeting brought Israelis and Palestinians—this time without American participation—to Taba in Egypt in late January 2001. If optimism still attended Camp David, the Taba conference, convening under the shadow of the second intifada, had virtually no chance of success.

The first set of readings, "Camp David and After: An Exchange," provides a contrapuntal, somewhat polemical analysis by Ehud Barak, aided by Benny Morris, on the one hand, and by Hussein Agha and Robert Malley, on the other hand, of the reasons why negotiations failed. According to Barak and Morris, the talks aborted essentially because Yasser Arafat refused to countenance the long-term survival of a Jewish state. Any agreement that would cripple Israel by flooding it with refugees Arafat would have been happy to sign. Short of

that, he was content to see talks run into the sand. Hence, Barak defines Arafat's negotiating posture as a mixture of utter inflexibility and mendacity. What is more, according to Barak, after sabotaging Camp David, Arafat determined to compel Israeli concessions through violence. The second intifada was less a spontaneous Palestinian response to Ariel Sharon's visit to the Temple Mount, than it was part of that long-term strategy.

Malley, who helped organize Camp David, and Agha deny that in 2000 the Palestinian authority was still committed to Israel's destruction. While conceding that Arafat could have been more helpful, Agha and Malley argue that right up through Taba, the Palestinians showed some flexibility on key issues, including territorial exchanges, the division of Jerusalem, even the future of refugees. In their view, the basic problem was, first, that Barak's actions prior to Camp David (especially his toleration of continued Jewish settlements) needlessly antagonized the Palestinians; and second and more basic, that Barak demanded unrealistic concessions. According to Agha and Malley, the second intifada derived from a combination of mounting Palestinian frustration and Israeli overreaction to what began as nonlethal Palestinian protests.

Jonathan Schanzer considers how Oslo's collapse played out in the Palestinian community. During the 1990s, the Islamist resistance group Hamas launched terrorist attacks on Israeli civilians in a concerted effort to destroy intercommunal cooperation—or as they saw it, to prevent the loss of Palestinian rights. The failure of talks, the second intifada, and Fatah's growing incoherence provided a political opening that Hamas quickly filled. Schanzer describes Hamas's upset victory in the Palestinian legislative elections of 2006 and the Hamas military coup in Gaza the next year. He goes on to discuss the effort by Fatah, now led by Arafat's successor, Mahmoud Abbas, and supported by Israel, the United States, and Jordan, to crush Hamas in the West Bank. Thus, in the short term at least, the Palestinian national movement bifurcated territorially as well as politically.

After seizing Gaza, Hamas not only persisted in its refusal to recognize the Jewish state, but sharply increased rocket attacks on southern Israel. At the same time Israel and Western countries pressured Gaza by imposing a financial and economic blockade—and, in the case of Israel, by assassinating Hamas militants and enforcing no-go areas. After a truce brokered by Egypt broke down in December 2008, Israel invaded Gaza in an effort to halt rocket attacks and, if possible, to overthrow Hamas. Lawrence Wright's "Captives" poignantly describes not only the physical damage produced by Israel's three-week incursion, but also the grim hatred still gripping Gazans and their IDF opponents. "Captives" seems to describe at the same time the young Israeli soldier, Gilad Shalit, whose capture in 2006 ratcheted up the conflict; Palestinians in Israeli jails—and much of the population of both Gaza and Israel.

Camp David and After:
An Exchange

Part One

By Benny Morris

An Interview with Ehud Barak

The following interview with Ehud Barak took place in Tel Aviv during late March and early April, 2002. I have supplied explanatory references in brackets with Mr. Barak's approval.

The call from Bill Clinton came hours after the publication in *The New York Times* of Deborah Sontag's "revisionist" article ("Quest for Middle East Peace: How and Why It Failed," July 26, 2001) on the Israeli–Palestinian peace process. Ehud Barak, Israel's former prime minister, on vacation, was swimming in a cove in Sardinia. Clinton said (according to Barak):

> What the hell is this? Why is she turning the mistakes we [i.e., the U.S. and Israel] made into the essence? The true story of Camp David was that for the first time in the history of the conflict the American president put on the table a proposal, based on UN Security Council resolutions 242 and 338, very close to the Palestinian demands, and Arafat refused even to accept it as a basis for negotiations, walked out of the room, and deliberately turned to terrorism. That's the real story—all the rest is gossip.

Clinton was speaking of the two-week-long July 2000 Camp David conference that he had organized and mediated and its failure, and the eruption at the end of September of the Palestinian intifada, or campaign of anti-Israeli violence, which has continued ever since and which currently plagues the Middle East, with no end in sight. Midway in the conference, apparently on July 18, Clinton had "slowly"—to avoid misunderstanding—read out to Arafat a document, endorsed in advance by Barak, outlining the main points of a future settlement. The proposals included the establishment of a demilitarized Palestinian state on some 92 percent of the West Bank and 100 percent of the Gaza Strip, with some territorial compensation for the Palestinians from pre-1967 Israeli territory; the dismantling of most of the settlements and the concentration of the bulk of the settlers inside the 8 percent of the West Bank to be annexed by Israel; the establishment of the Palestinian capital in East Jerusalem, in which some Arab neighborhoods would become sovereign Palestinian territory and others would enjoy "functional autonomy"; Palestinian sovereignty over half the Old City of Jerusalem (the Muslim and Christian quarters) and "custodianship," though not sovereignty, over the Temple Mount; a return of refugees to the prospective Palestinian state though with no "right of return" to Israel proper; and the organization by the international community of a massive aid program to facilitate the refugees' rehabilitation.

Arafat said "No." Clinton, enraged, banged on the table and said: "You are leading your people and the region to a catastrophe." A formal Palestinian rejection of the proposals reached the Americans the next day. The summit sputtered on for a few days more but to all intents and purposes it was over.

Barak today portrays Arafat's behavior at Camp David as a "performance" geared to exacting from the Israelis as many concessions as possible without ever seriously intending to reach a peace settlement or sign an "end to the conflict." "He did not negotiate in good faith, indeed, he did not negotiate at all. He just kept saying 'no' to every offer, never making any counterproposals of his own," he says. Barak continuously shifts between charging Arafat with "lacking the character or will" to make a historic compromise (as did the late Egyptian President Anwar Sadat in 1977–1979, when he made peace with Israel) and accusing him of secretly planning Israel's demise while he strings along a succession of Israeli and Western leaders and, on the way, hoodwinks "naive journalists"—in Barak's phrase—like Sontag and officials such as former US National Security Council expert Robert Malley (who, with Hussein Agha, published another "revisionist" article on Camp David, "Camp David: The Tragedy of Errors"). According to Barak:

What they [Arafat and his colleagues] want is a Palestinian state in all of Palestine. What we see as self-evident, [the need for] two states for two peoples, they reject. Israel is too strong at the moment to defeat, so they formally recognize it. But their game plan is to establish a Palestinian state while always leaving an opening for further "legitimate" demands down the road. For now, they are willing to agree to a temporary truce à la Hudnat Hudaybiyah [a temporary truce that the Prophet

Muhammad concluded with the leaders of Mecca during 628–629, which he subsequently unilaterally violated]. They will exploit the tolerance and democracy of Israel first to turn it into "a state for all its citizens," as demanded by the extreme nationalist wing of Israel's Arabs and extremist left-wing Jewish Israelis. Then they will push for a binational state and then, demography and attrition will lead to a state with a Muslim majority and a Jewish minority. This would not necessarily involve kicking out all the Jews. But it would mean the destruction of Israel as a Jewish state. This, I believe, is their vision. They may not talk about it often, openly, but this is their vision. Arafat sees himself as a reborn Saladin—the Kurdish Muslim general who defeated the Crusaders in the twelfth century—and Israel as just another, ephemeral Crusader state.

Barak believes that Arafat sees the Palestinian refugees of 1948 and their descendants, numbering close to four million, as the main demographic-political tool for subverting the Jewish state.

Arafat, says Barak, believes that Israel "has no right to exist, and he seeks its demise." Barak buttresses this by arguing that Arafat "does not recognize the existence of a Jewish people or nation, only a Jewish religion, because it is mentioned in the Koran and because he remembers seeing, as a kid, Jews praying at the Wailing Wall." This, Barak believes, underlay Arafat's insistence at Camp David (and since) that the Palestinians have sole sovereignty over the Temple Mount compound (Haram al–Sharif—the noble sanctuary) in the southeastern corner of Jerusalem's Old City. Arafat denies that any Jewish temple has ever stood there—and this is a microcosm of his denial of the Jews' historical connection and claim to the Land of Israel/Palestine. Hence, in December 2000, Arafat refused to accept even the vague formulation proposed by Clinton positing Israeli sovereignty over the earth beneath the Temple Mount's surface area.

Barak recalls Clinton telling him that during the Camp David talks he had attended Sunday services and the minister had preached a sermon mentioning Solomon, the king who built the First Temple. Later that evening, he had met Arafat and spoke of the sermon. Arafat had said: "There is nothing there [i.e., no trace of a temple on the Temple Mount]." Clinton responded that "not only the Jews but I, too, believe that under the surface there are remains of Solomon's temple." (At this point one of Clinton's [Jewish] aides whispered to the President that he should tell Arafat that this is his personal opinion, not an official American position.)

Repeatedly during our prolonged interview, conducted in his office in a Tel Aviv skyscraper, Barak shook his head—in bewilderment and sadness—at what he regards as Palestinian, and especially Arafat's, mendacity:

> They are products of a culture in which to tell a lie ... creates no dissonance. They don't suffer from the problem of telling lies that exists in Judeo–Christian culture. Truth is seen as an irrelevant category. There is only that which serves your purpose and that which doesn't. They see themselves as emissaries of a national movement for whom everything is permissible. There is no such thing as "the truth."

Speaking of Arab society, Barak recalls: "The deputy director of the US Federal Bureau of Investigation once told me that there are societies in which lie detector tests don't work, societies in which lies do not create cognitive dissonance [on which the tests are based]." Barak gives an example: back in October 2000, shortly after the start of the current Intifada, he met with then Secretary of State Madeleine Albright and Arafat in the residence of the US ambassador in Paris. Albright was trying to broker a cease-fire. Arafat had agreed to call a number of his police commanders in the West Bank and Gaza, including Tawfik Tirawi, to implement a truce. Barak said:

I interjected: 'But these are not the people organizing the violence. If you are serious [in seeking a cease-fire], then call Marwan Bargouti and Hussein al–Sheikh' [the West Bank heads of the Fatah, Arafat's own political party, who were orchestrating the violence. Bargouti has since been arrested by Israeli troops and is currently awaiting trial for launching dozens of terrorist attacks].

Arafat looked at me, with an expression of blank innocence, as if I had mentioned the names of two polar bears, and said: "Who? Who?" So I repeated the names, this time with a pronounced, clear Arabic inflection—"Mar-wan Bar-gou-ti" and "Hsein a Sheikh"—and Arafat again said, "Who? Who?" At this, some of his aides couldn't stop themselves and burst out laughing. And Arafat, forced to drop the pretense, agreed to call them later. [Of course, nothing happened and the shooting continued.]

But Barak is far from dismissive of Arafat, who appears to many Israelis to be a sick, slightly doddering buffoon and, at the same time, sly and murderous. Barak sees him as "a great actor, very sharp, very elusive, slippery." He cautions that Arafat "uses his broken English" to excellent effect.

Barak was elected prime minister, following three years of Benjamin Netanyahu's premiership, in May 1999 and took office in July. He immediately embarked on his multipronged peace effort—vis-à-vis Syria, Lebanon, and the Palestinians—feeling that Israel and the Middle East were headed for "an iceberg and a certain crash and that it was the leaders' moral and political responsibility to try to avoid a catastrophe." He understood that the year and a half left of Clinton's presidency afforded a small window of opportunity inside a larger, but also limited, regional window of opportunity. That window was opened by the collapse of the Soviet Empire, which had since the 1950s supported the Arabs against Israel, and the defeat of Iraq in Kuwait in 1991, and would close when and if Iran and/

or Iraq obtained nuclear weapons and when and if Islamic fundamentalist movements took over states bordering Israel.

Barak said he wanted to complete what Rabin had begun with the Oslo agreement, which inaugurated mutual Israeli–Palestinian recognition and partial Israeli withdrawals from the West Bank and Gaza Strip back in 1993. A formal peace agreement, he felt, would not necessarily "end the conflict, that will take education over generations, but there is a tremendous value to an [official] framework of peace that places pacific handcuffs on these societies." Formal peace treaties, backed by the international community, will have "a dynamic of their own, reducing the possibility of an existential conflict. But without such movement toward formal peace, we are headed for the iceberg." He seems to mean something far worse than the current low-level Israeli–Palestinian conflagration.

Barak says that, before July 2000, IDF intelligence gave the Camp David talks less than a 50 percent chance of success. The intelligence chiefs were doubtful that Arafat "would take the decisions necessary to reach a peace agreement." His own feeling at the time was that he "hoped Arafat would rise to the occasion and display something of greatness, like Sadat and Hussein, at the moment of truth. They did not wait for a consensus [among their people], they decided to lead. I told Clinton on the first day [of the summit] that I didn't know whether Arafat had come to make a deal or just to extract as many political concessions as possible before he, Clinton, left office."

Barak dismisses the charges leveled by the Camp David "revisionists" as Palestinian propaganda. The visit to the Temple Mount by then Likud leader Ariel Sharon in September 2000 was not what caused the intifada, he says.

Sharon's visit, which was coordinated with [Palestinian Authority West Bank security chief] Jibril Rajoub, was directed against me, not the Palestinians, to show that the Likud cared more about Jerusalem than I did. We know, from hard intelligence, that Arafat [after Camp David] intended to unleash a violent confrontation, terrorism. [Sharon's visit and the riots that followed] fell into his hands like an excellent excuse, a pretext.

As agreed, Sharon had made no statement and had refrained from entering the Islamic shrines in the compound in the course of the visit. But rioting broke out nonetheless. The intifada, says Barak, "was preplanned, pre-prepared. I don't mean that Arafat knew that on a certain day in September [it would be unleashed]. ... It wasn't accurate, like computer engineering. But it was definitely on the level of planning, of a grand plan."

Nor does Barak believe that the IDF's precipitate withdrawal from the Security Zone in Southern Lebanon, in May 2000, set off the intifada. "When I took office [in July 1999] I promised to pull out within a year. And that is what I did." Without doubt, the Palestinians drew inspiration and heart from the Hezbollah's successful guerrilla campaign during 1985–2000, which in the end drove out the IDF, as well as from the spectacle of the sometime slapdash, chaotic pullout at the end of May; they said as much during the first months of the intifada. "But had we not withdrawn when we did, the situation would have been much worse," Barak argues:

> We would have faced a simultaneous struggle on two fronts, in Palestine and in southern Lebanon, and the Hezbollah would have enjoyed international legitimacy in their struggle against a foreign occupier.

The lack of international legitimacy, Barak stresses, following the Israeli pullback to the international frontier, is what has curtailed the Hezbollah's attacks against Israel during the past weeks. "Had we still been in Lebanon we would have had to mobilize 100,000, not 30,000, reserve soldiers [in April, during 'Operation Defensive Wall']," he adds. But he is aware that the sporadic Hezbollah attacks might yet escalate into a full-scale Israeli-Lebanese-Syrian confrontation, something the pullback had been designed—and so touted—to avoid.

As to the charge raised by the Palestinians, and, in their wake, by Deborah Sontag, and Malley and Agha, that the Palestinians had been dragooned into coming to Camp David "unprepared" and prematurely, Barak is dismissive to the point of contempt. He observes that the Palestinians had had eight years, since 1993, to prepare their positions and fall-back positions, demands and red lines, and a full year since he had been elected to office and made clear his intention to go for a final settlement. By 2002, he said, they were eager to establish a state, which is what I and Clinton proposed and offered. And before the summit, there were months of discussions and contacts, in Stockholm, Israel, the Gaza Strip. Would they really have been more "prepared" had the summit been deferred to August, as Arafat later said he had wanted?

One senses that Barak feels on less firm ground when he responds to the "revisionist" charge that it was the continued Israeli settlement in the Occupied Territories, during the year before Camp David and under his premiership, that had so stirred Palestinian passions as to make the intifada inevitable:

Look, during my premiership we established no new settlements and, in fact, dismantled many illegal, unauthorized ones. Immediately after I took office I promised Arafat: No new settlements—but I also told him that we would continue to honor the previous government's commitments, and contracts in the pipeline, concerning the expansion of existing settlements. The courts would force us to honor existing contracts, I said. But I also offered a substantive argument. I want to reach peace during the next sixteen months. What was now being built would either remain within territory that you, the Palestinians, agree should remain ours—and therefore it shouldn't matter to you—or would be in territory that would soon come under Palestinian sovereignty, and therefore would add

to the housing available for returning refugees. So you can't lose.

But Barak concedes that while this sounded logical, there was a psychological dimension here that could not be neutralized by argument: the Palestinians simply saw, on a daily basis, that more and more of "their" land was being plundered and becoming "Israeli." And he agrees that he allowed the expansion of existing settlements in part to mollify the Israeli right, which he needed quiescent as he pushed forward toward peace and, ultimately, a withdrawal from the territories.

Regarding the core of the Israeli–American proposals, the "revisionists" have charged that Israel offered the Palestinians not a continuous state but a collection of "bantustans" or "cantons." "This is one of the most embarrassing lies to have emerged from Camp David," says Barak.

I ask myself why is he [Arafat] lying. To put it simply, any proposal that offers 92 percent of the West Bank cannot, almost by definition, break up the territory into noncontiguous cantons. The West Bank and the Gaza Strip are separate, but that cannot be helped [in a peace agreement, they would be joined by a bridge].

But in the West Bank, Barak says, the Palestinians were promised a continuous piece of sovereign territory except for a razor-thin Israeli wedge running from Jerusalem through from Maale Adumim to the Jordan River. Here, Palestinian territorial continuity would have been assured by a tunnel or bridge:

The Palestinians said that I [and Clinton] presented our proposals as a diktat, take it or leave it. This is a lie. Everything proposed was open to continued negotiations. They could have raised counter-proposals. But they never did.

Barak explains Arafat's "lie" about "bantustans" as stemming from his fear that "when reasonable Palestinian citizens would come to know the real content of Clinton's proposal and map, showing what 92 percent of the West Bank means, they would have said: 'Mr. Chairman, why didn't you take it?'"

In one other important way the "revisionist" articles are misleading: they focused on Camp David (July 2000) while almost completely ignoring the follow-up (and more generous) Clinton proposals (endorsed by Israel) of December 2000 and the Palestinian–Israeli talks at Taba in January 2001. The "revisionists," Barak implies, completely ignored the shift—under the prodding of the intifada—in the Israeli (and American) positions between July and the end of 2000. By December and January, Israel had agreed to Washington's proposal that it withdraw from about 95 percent of the West Bank with substantial territorial compensation for the Palestinians from Israel proper, and that the Arab neighborhoods of Jerusalem would become sovereign Palestinian territory. The Israelis also agreed to an international force at least temporarily controlling the Jordan River line between the West Bank and the Kingdom of Jordan instead of the IDF. (But on the refugee issue, which Barak sees as "existential," Israel had continued to stand firm: "We cannot allow even one refugee back on the basis of the 'right of return,'" says Barak. "And we cannot accept historical responsibility for the creation of the problem.")

Had the Palestinians, even at that late date, agreed, there would have been a peace settlement. But Arafat dragged his feet for a fortnight and then responded to the Clinton proposals with a "Yes, but …" that, with its hundreds of objections, reservations, and qualifications, was tantamount to a resounding "No." Palestinian officials maintain to this day that Arafat said "Yes" to the Clinton proposals of December 23. But Dennis Ross, Clinton's special envoy to the Middle East, in a recent interview (on Fox News, April 21, 2002), who was present at the Arafat–Clinton White House meeting on January 2, says that Arafat rejected "every single one of the ideas"

presented by Clinton, even Israeli sovereignty over the Wailing Wall in Jerusalem's Old City. And the "Palestinians would have [had] in the West Bank an area that was contiguous. Those who say there were cantons, [that is] completely untrue." At Taba, the Palestinians seemed to soften a little—for the first time they even produced a map seemingly conceding 2 percent of the West Bank. But on the refugees they, too, stuck to their guns, insisting on Israeli acceptance of "the right of return" and on Jerusalem, that they have sole sovereignty over the Temple Mount.

Several "revisionists" also took Barak to task for his "Syria first" strategy: soon after assuming office, he tried to make peace with Syria and only later, after Damascus turned him down, did he turn to the Palestinians. This had severely taxed the Palestinians' goodwill and patience; they felt they were being sidelined. Barak concedes the point, but explains:

I always supported Syria first. Because they have a [large] conventional army and nonconventional weaponry, chemical and biological, and missiles to deliver them. This represents, under certain conditions, an existential threat. And after Syria comes Lebanon [meaning that peace with Syria would immediately engender a peace treaty with Lebanon]. Moreover, the Syrian problem, with all its difficulties, is simpler to solve than the Palestinian problem. And reaching peace with Syria would greatly limit the Palestinians' ability to widen the conflict. On the other hand, solving the Palestinian problem will not diminish Syria's ability to existentially threaten Israel.

Barak says that this was also Rabin's thinking. But he points out that when he took office, he immediately informed Arafat that he intended to pursue an agreement with Syria and that this would in no way be at the Palestinians' expense. "I arrived on the scene immediately after [Netanyahu's emissary Ronald] Lauder's intensive [secret] talks, which looked very interesting. It was a Syrian initiative that looked very close to a breakthrough. It would have been very irresponsible not to investigate this because of some traditional, ritual order."

The Netanyahu–Lauder initiative, which posited an Israeli withdrawal from the Golan Heights to a line a few kilometers east of the Jordan River and the Sea of Galilee, came to naught because two of Netanyahu's senior ministers, Sharon and Defense Minister Yitzhak Mordechai, objected to the proposed concessions. Barak offered then President Hafiz Assad more, in effect a return to the de facto border of "4 June 1967" along the Jordan River and almost to the shoreline at the northeastern end of the Sea of Galilee. Assad, by then feeble and close to death, rejected the terms, conveying his rejection to President Clinton at the famous meeting in Geneva on March 26, 2000. Barak explains,

> Assad wanted Israel to capitulate in advance to all his demands. Only then would he agree to enter into substantive negotiations. I couldn't agree to this. We must continue to live [in the Middle East] afterward [and, had we made the required concessions, would have been seen as weak, inviting depredation].

But Barak believes that Assad's effort, involving a major policy switch, to reach a peace settlement with Israel was genuine and sincere.

Barak appears uncomfortable with the "revisionist" charge that his body language toward Arafat had been unfriendly and that he had, almost consistently during Camp David, avoided meeting the Palestinian leader, and that these had contributed to the summit's failure. Barak:

> I am the Israeli leader who met most with Arafat. He visited Rabin's home only after [the assassinated leader] was buried on Mount Herzl [in Jerusalem]. He [Arafat] visited me in my home in Kochav Yair where my wife made food for him. [Arafat's aide] Abu Mazen and [my wife] Nava swapped memories about Safad, her mother was from Safad, and both their parents were traders. I also met Arafat in friends' homes, in Gaza, in Ramallah.

Barak says that they met "almost every day" in Camp David at mealtimes and had one "two-hour meeting" in Arafat's cottage. He admits that the time had been wasted on small talk—but, in the end, he argues, this is all part of the "gossip," not the real reason for the failure. "Did Nixon meet Ho Chi Minh or Giap [before reaching the Vietnam peace deal]? Or did De Gaulle ever speak to [Algerian leader] Ben Bella? The right time for a meeting between us was when things were ready for a decision by the leaders…" Barak implies that the negotiations had never matured or even come close to the point where the final decision-making meeting by the leaders was apt and necessary.

Barak believes that since the start of the intifada Israel has had no choice—"and it doesn't matter who is prime minister" (perhaps a jab at his former rival and colleague in the Labor Party, the dovish-sounding Shimon Peres, currently Israel's foreign minister)—but to combat terrorism with military force. The policy of "targeted killings" of terrorist organizers, bomb-makers, and potential attackers began during his premiership and he still believes it is necessary and effective, "though great care must be taken to limit collateral damage. Say you live in Chevy Chase and you know of someone who is preparing a bomb in Georgetown and intends to launch a suicide bomber against a coffee shop outside your front door. Wouldn't you do something? Wouldn't it be justified to arrest this man and, if you can't, to kill him?" he asks.

Barak supported Sharon's massive incursion in April—"Operation Defensive Wall"—into the Palestinian cities—Nablus, Jenin, Bethlehem, Ramallah, Qalqilya, and Tulkarm—but suggests that he would have done it differently:

> More forcefully and with greater speed, and simultaneously against all the cities, not, as was done, in staggered fashion. And I would argue with the confinement of Arafat to his Ramallah offices. The present situation, with Arafat eyeball to eyeball with [Israeli] tank gun muzzles but with an insurance policy [i.e., Israel's promise to President

Bush not to harm him], is every guerrilla leader's wet dream. But, in general, no responsible government, following the wave of suicide bombings culminating in the Passover massacre [in which twenty-eight Israelis were murdered and about 100 injured in a Netanya hotel while sitting at the seder] could have acted otherwise.

But he believes that the counter-terrorist military effort must be accompanied by a constant reiteration of readiness to renew peace negotiations on the basis of the Camp David formula. He seems to be hinting here that Sharon, while also interested in political dialogue, rejects the Camp David proposals as a basis. Indeed, Sharon said in April that his government will not dismantle any settlements, and will not discuss such a dismantling of settlements, before the scheduled November 2003 general elections. Barak fears that in the absence of political dialogue based on the Camp David–Clinton proposals, the vacuum created will be filled by proposals, from Europe or Saudi Arabia, that are less agreeable to Israel.

Barak seems to hold out no chance of success for Israeli–Palestinian negotiations, should they somehow resume, so long as Arafat and like-minded leaders are at the helm on the Arab side. He seems to think in terms of generations and hesitantly predicts that only "eighty years" after 1948 will the Palestinians be historically ready for a compromise. By then, most of the generation that experienced the catastrophe of 1948 at first hand will have died; there will be "very few 'salmons' around who still want to return to their birthplaces to die." (Barak speaks of a "salmon syndrome" among the Palestinians—and says that Israel, to a degree, was willing to accommodate it, through the family reunion scheme, allowing elderly refugees to return to be with their families before they die.) He points to the model of the Soviet Union, which collapsed roughly after eighty years, after the generation that had lived through the revolution had died. He seems to be saying that revolutionary movements' zealotry and dogmatism die down after the passage of three

generations and, in the case of the Palestinians, the disappearance of the generation of the *nakba*, or catastrophe, of 1948 will facilitate compromise.

I asked, "If this is true, then your peace effort vis-à-vis the Palestinians was historically premature and foredoomed?"

Barak: "No, as a responsible leader I had to give it a try."

In the absence of real negotiations, Barak believes that Israel should begin to unilaterally prepare for a pullout from "some 75 percent" of the West Bank and, he implies, all or almost all of the Gaza Strip, back to defensible borders, while allowing a Palestinian state to emerge there. Meanwhile Israel should begin constructing a solid, impermeable fence around the evacuated parts of the West Bank and new housing and settlements inside Israel proper and in the areas of the West Bank that Israel intends to permanently annex (such as the Etzion Block area, south of Bethlehem) to absorb the settlers who will be moving out of the territories. He says that when the Palestinians will be ready for peace, the fate of the remaining 25 percent of the West Bank can be negotiated.

Barak is extremely troubled by the problem posed by Israel's Arab minority, representing some 20 percent of Israel's total population of some 6.5 million. Their leadership over the past few years has come to identify with Arafat and the PA, and an increasing number of Israeli Arabs, who now commonly refer to themselves as "Palestinian Arabs," oppose Israel's existence and support the Palestinian armed struggle. A growing though still very small number have engaged in terrorism, including one of the past months' suicide bombers. Barak agrees that, in the absence of a peace settlement with the Palestinians, Israel's Arabs constitute an irredentist "time bomb," though he declines to use the phrase. At the start of the intifada Israel's Arabs rioted around the country, blocking major highways with stones and Molotov cocktails. In response, thirteen were killed by Israeli policemen, deepening the chasm between the country's Jewish majority and Arab minority.

The relations between the two have not recovered and the rhetoric of the Israeli Arab leadership has grown steadily more militant. One Israeli Arab Knesset member, Azmi Bishara, is currently on trial for sedition. If the conflict with the Palestinians continues, says Barak, "Israel's Arabs will serve as [the Palestinians'] spearpoint" in the struggle:

> This may necessitate changes in the rules of the democratic game ... in order to assure Israel's Jewish character.

He raises the possibility that in a future deal, some areas with large Arab concentrations, such as the "Little Triangle" and Umm al–Fahm, bordering on the West Bank, could be transferred to the emergent Palestinian Arab state, along with their inhabitants:

> But this could only be done by agreement—and I don't recommend that government spokesmen speak of it [openly]. But such an exchange makes demographic sense and is not inconceivable.

Barak is employed as a senior adviser to an American company, Electronic Data Systems, and is considering a partnership in a private equity company, where he will be responsible for "security-related" ventures. I asked him, "Do you see yourself returning to politics?" Barak answered,

Look, the public [decisively] voted against me a year ago. I feel like a reserve soldier who knows he might be called upon to come back but expects that he won't be unless it is absolutely necessary.

But it's not inconceivable. After all, Rabin returned to the premiership fifteen years after the end of his first term in office.

At one point in the interview, Barak pointed to the settlement campaign in heavily populated Palestinian areas, inaugurated by Menachem Begin's Likud-led government in 1977, as the point at which Israel took a major historical wrong turn. But at other times Barak pointed to 1967 as the crucial mistake, when Israel occupied the West Bank and Gaza (and Sinai and the Golan Heights) and, instead of agreeing to immediate withdrawal from all the territories, save East Jerusalem, in exchange for peace, began to settle them. Barak recalled seeing David Ben-Gurion, Israel's founder and first prime minister (1948–1953 and 1955–1963), on television in June 1967 arguing for the immediate withdrawal from all the territories occupied in the Six–Day War in exchange for peace, save for East Jerusalem.

Many of us—me included—thought that he was suffering from [mental] weakness or perhaps a subconscious jealousy of his successor [Levi Eshkol, who had presided over the unprecedented victory and conquests]. Today one understands that he simply saw more clearly and farther than the leadership at that time.

How does Barak see the Middle East in a hundred years' time? Would it contain a Jewish state? Unlike Arafat, Barak believes it will, "and it will be strong and prosperous. I really think this. Our connection to the Land of Israel is not like the Crusaders' ... Israel fits into the zeitgeist of our era. It is true that there are demographic threats to its existence. That is why a separation from the Palestinians is a compelling imperative. Without such a separation [into two states] there is no future for the Zionist dream."

Camp David and After: An Exchange

Part Two

By Robert Malley and Hussein Agha

A Reply to Ehud Barak

Both sides in the Israeli–Palestinian war have several targets in mind, and public opinion is not the least of them. The Camp David summit ended almost two years ago; the Taba negotiations were abandoned in January 2001; Ariel Sharon has made no secret of his rejection of the Oslo process, not to mention the positions taken by Israel at Camp David or in Taba; and the confrontation between the two sides has had disastrous consequences. Yet in the midst of it all, the various interpretations of what happened at Camp David and its aftermath continue to draw exceptional attention both in Israel and in the United States. Ehud Barak's interview with Benny Morris makes it clear why that is the case: Barak's assessment that the talks failed because Yasser Arafat cannot make peace with Israel and that his answer to Israel's unprecedented offer was to resort to terrorist violence has become central to the argument that Israel is in a fight for its survival against those who deny its very right to exist. So much of what is said and done today derives from and is justified by that crude appraisal. First, Arafat and the rest of the Palestinian leaders must be supplanted before a meaningful peace process can resume, since they are the ones who rejected the offer. Second, the Palestinians'

use of violence has nothing to do with ending the occupation since they walked away from the possibility of reaching that goal at the negotiating table not long ago. And, finally, Israel must crush the Palestinians—"badly beat them" in the words of the current prime minister—if an agreement is ever to be reached.

The one-sided account that was set in motion in the wake of Camp David has had devastating effects—on Israeli public opinion as well as on US foreign policy. That was clear enough a year ago; it has become far clearer since. Rectifying it does not mean, to quote Barak, engaging in "Palestinian propaganda." Rather, it means taking a close look at what actually occurred.

1

Barak's central thesis is that the current Palestinian leadership wants "a Palestinian state in all of Palestine. What we see as self-evident, two states for two peoples, they reject." Arafat, he concludes, seeks Israel's "demise." Barak has made that claim repeatedly, both here and elsewhere, and indeed it forms the crux of his argument. His claim therefore should be taken up, issue by issue.

On the question of the boundaries of the future state, the Palestinian position, formally adopted as early as 1988 and frequently reiterated by Palestinian negotiators throughout the talks, was for a Palestinian state based on the June 4, 1967, borders, living alongside Israel. At Camp David (at which one of the present writers was a member of the US administration's team), Arafat's negotiators accepted the notion of Israeli annexation of West Bank territory to accommodate settlements, though they insisted on a one-for-one swap of land "of equal size and value." The Palestinians argued that the annexed territory should neither affect the contiguity of their own land nor lead to the incorporation of Palestinians into Israel.

The ideas put forward by President Clinton at Camp David fell well short of those demands. In order to accommodate Israeli settlements, he proposed a deal by which Israel would annex 9 percent of the West Bank in exchange for turning over to the Palestinians parts of pre-1967 Israel equivalent to 1 percent of the West Bank. This proposal would have entailed the incorporation of tens of thousands of additional Palestinians into Israeli territory near the annexed settlements; and it would have meant that territory annexed by Israel would encroach deep inside the Palestinian state. In his December 23, 2000, proposals—called "parameters" by all parties—Clinton suggested an Israeli annexation of between 4 and 6 percent of the West Bank in exchange for a land swap of between 1 and 3 percent. The following month in Taba, the Palestinians put their own map on the table which showed roughly 3.1 percent of the West Bank under Israeli sovereignty, with an equivalent land swap in areas abutting the West Bank and Gaza.

On Jerusalem, the Palestinians accepted at Camp David the principle of Israeli sovereignty over the Wailing Wall, the Jewish Quarter of the Old City, and Jewish neighborhoods of East Jerusalem—neighborhoods that were not part of Israel before the 1967 Six-Day War—though the Palestinians clung to the view that all of Arab East Jerusalem should be Palestinian.

In contrast to the issues of territory and Jerusalem, there is no Palestinian position on how the refugee question should be dealt with as a practical matter. Rather, the Palestinians presented a set of principles. First, they insisted on the need to recognize the refugees' right of return, lest the agreement lose all legitimacy with the vast refugee constituency—roughly half the entire Palestinian population. Second, they acknowledged that Israel's demographic interests had to be recognized and taken into account. Barak draws from this the conclusion that the refugees are the "main demographic-political tool for subverting the Jewish state." The Palestinian leadership's insistence on a right of return demonstrates, in his account, that their conception of a two-state solution is one state for the Palestinians in Palestine and another in Israel. But the facts suggest that the Palestinians are trying (to date, unsuccessfully) to reconcile these two competing imperatives—the demographic imperative and the right of return. Indeed, in one of his last pre-Camp David meetings with Clinton, Arafat asked him to "give [him] a reasonable deal [on the refugee question] and then see how to present it as not betraying the right of return."

Some of the Palestinian negotiators proposed annual caps on the number of returnees (though at numbers far higher than their Israeli counterparts could accept); others wanted to create incentives for refugees to settle elsewhere and disincentives for them to return to the 1948 land. But all acknowledged that there could not be an unlimited, "massive" return of Palestinian refugees to Israel. The suggestion made by some that the Camp David summit broke down over the Palestinians' demand for a right of return simply is untrue: the issue was barely discussed between the two sides and President Clinton's ideas mentioned it only in passing. (In an op-ed piece in *The New York Times* this February Arafat called for "creative solutions to the right of return while respecting Israel's demographic concerns.")

The Palestinians did insist that Israel recognize that it bore responsibility for creating the problem of the refugees. But it is ironic that Barak would choose to convey his categorical rejection of any such Israeli historical responsibility to Benny Morris, an Israeli historian called "revisionist" in large part for his account of the origins of the displacement of the Palestinians and for his conclusion that, while there were many reasons why the refugees left, Israeli military attacks and expulsions were the major ones.

The Palestinians can be criticized for not having presented detailed proposals at Camp David; but, as has been shown, it would be inaccurate to say they had no positions. It also is true that Barak broke a number of Israeli taboos and moved considerably from prior positions while the Palestinians believed they had made their historic concessions at Oslo, when they agreed to cede 78 percent of mandatory Palestine to Israel; they did not intend the negotiations to further whittle down what they already regarded as a compromise position. But neither the constancy of the Palestinians' view nor the unprecedented and evolving nature of the Israelis' ought to have any bearing on the question of whether the Palestinian leadership recognized Israel's right to exist as a Jewish state. It is the substance of the Palestinian positions that should count.

Those Palestinian positions may well have been beyond what the Israeli people can accept, particularly on the refugee question. But that is no more the question than it is whether the Israeli position was beyond what the Palestinian people can accept. And it is not the question that Barak purports to address in his interview. The question is whether, as Barak claims, the Palestinian position was tantamount to a denial of Israel's right to exist and to seeking its destruction. The facts do not validate that claim. True, the Palestinians rejected the version of the two-state solution that was put to them. But it could also be said that Israel rejected the unprecedented two-state solution put to them by the Palestinians from Camp David onward, including the following provisions: a state of Israel incorporating some land captured in 1967 and including a very large majority of its settlers; the largest Jewish Jerusalem in the city's history; preservation of Israel's demographic balance between Jews and Arabs; security guaranteed by a US-led international presence.

Barak's remarks about other Arab leaders are, in this regard, misplaced. Arafat did not reach out to the people of Israel in the way President Sadat did. But unlike Sadat, he agreed to cede parts of the territory that was lost in 1967—both in the West Bank and in East Jerusalem. The reference to President Assad—whose peace efforts are characterized as "genuine and sincere"—is particularly odd since Assad turned down precisely what Arafat was requesting: borders based on the lines of June 4, 1967, with one-for-one swaps.

Barak claims that "Israel is too strong at the moment to defeat, so [the Palestinians] formally recognize it. But their game plan is to establish a Palestinian state while always leaving an opening for further 'legitimate' demands down the road." But here Barak contradicts himself. For if that were the case, the logical course of action for Arafat would have been to accept Clinton's proposals at Camp David, and even more so on December 23. He would then have had over 90 percent of the land and much of East Jerusalem, while awaiting, as Barak would have it, the opportunity to violate the agreement and stake out a claim for more. Whatever else one may think of Arafat's behavior throughout the talks, it clearly offers little to substantiate Barak's theory.

2

In his account of why the negotiations failed, Barak focuses only on the Palestinians' deficiencies, and dismisses as trivial sideshows several major political decisions that are crucial to the understanding of that failure. When he took office he chose to renegotiate the agreement on withdrawal of Israeli forces from the West Bank signed by Benjamin Netanyahu rather than implement it. He continued and even intensified construction of settlements. He delayed talks on the Palestinian track while he concentrated on Syria. He did not release Palestinian prisoners detained for acts committed prior to the signing of the Oslo agreement. He failed to carry out his commitments to implement the third territorial redeployment of Israeli troops and the transfer of the three Jerusalem villages.

Barak is equally dismissive of the importance of his holding a substantive meeting with Arafat at Camp David—though here one cannot help but be struck by the contradiction between Barak's justification for that decision (namely that "the right time for a meeting between us was when things were ready for a decision by the leaders") and his conviction that a leaders' summit was necessary. If he felt things were not ready for a decision by the leaders meeting together, why insist on convening a leaders' summit in the first place?

More broadly, from a Palestinian perspective, the issues concerning the timing of the talks were dealt with in ways that were both damaging and exasperating. The Palestinian leaders had called for negotiations on a comprehensive settlement between the two sides as early as the fall of 1999. They had asked for an initial round of secret talks between Israelis and Palestinians who were not officials in order to better prepare the ground. They had argued against holding the Camp David summit at the time proposed, claiming it was premature and would not lead to an agreement in view of the gaps between the two sides. They later asked for a series of summit meetings following Camp David so as to continue the talks. Each of their requests was denied.

In the fall of 1999, Barak was not ready for talks with the Palestinians and chose to focus on Syria. He had no interest in discussions between nonofficials. When, by the summer of 2000, he finally was ready (the negotiations with Syria having failed), he insisted on going to Camp David without delay. And at Camp David he reacted angrily to any suggestion of holding further summit meetings. Barak, today, dismisses those Palestinian requests as mere pretexts and excuses. But it is not clear why they should be taken any less seriously than the ones he made, and on which he prevailed.

All these external political events surrounding the negotiations, in fact, had critical implications for the negotiations themselves. The US administration felt so at the time, seeking on countless occasions before, during, and after the Camp David meetings to convince Barak to change his approach, precisely because the administration feared his tactics would harm the prospects for a deal. As has since become evident, the mood among critical Palestinian constituencies had turned decidedly sour—a result of continued settlement construction, repeated territorial closings that barred Palestinians from working in Israel, and their humiliation and harassment at checkpoints. Confidence in the possibility of a fair negotiated settlement was badly shaken. Israeli actions that strengthened those trends further narrowed the Palestinian leaders' room to maneuver and accentuated the sense of paralysis among them.

Barak's failure to recognize this is peculiar coming from a leader who was so sensitive to the role of Israeli public opinion. As so many examples from both the Syrian and Palestinian tracks illustrate, he was convinced that poor management of domestic public opinion could scuttle the chances for a deal. In his approach to the Israeli–Syrian negotiations, he went so far as to counsel Clinton against moving too quickly toward agreement during the Sheperdstown summit between the US, Israel, and Syria in January 2000, arguing that prolonged talks were required to show the Israeli public that he had put up a tough fight. In December, he had invoked the harsh statement of the Syrian foreign minister on the White House lawn as a reason why he could not show flexibility in their subsequent discussions at Blair House, arguing that the Israeli public would feel he had displayed weakness. He repeatedly insisted on (but rarely obtained) Syrian confidence-building measures in advance of the negotiations to help him sell his proposals back home.

When dealing with the Palestinians, likewise, Barak evidently felt the pressures of Israeli public opinion. He adamantly refused to discuss the issue of Jerusalem prior to the Camp David summit, claiming that to do so would have "torpedoed" the prospects for success. Settlement activity, to which both the Palestinians and the US objected, nonetheless proceeded at an extraordinary pace—faster than during Netanyahu's tenure, with over 22,000 more settlers. This was done, as Barak concedes in his interview, in order to "mollify the Israeli right which he needed quiescent as he pushed forward toward peace."

In short, Barak understood all too well how political developments surrounding the negotiations could affect Israeli public opinion and, therefore, his own ability to make agreements. Yet he showed no such comprehension when it came to the possible effects of his policies on Arafat's own flexibility and capacity to make compromises. That Arafat was unable either to obtain a settlement freeze or to get Israel to carry out its prior commitments Barak views as inconsequential. In reality, the cards Barak was saving to increase his room to maneuver during the negotiations were precisely those the Palestinians needed to expand their own room to maneuver. Ultimately, the Palestinian team that went to Camp David was suspected by many Palestinians and other Arabs of selling out—incapable of standing up to Israeli or American pressure.

Barak's apparent insensitivity to how his statements might affect the other side is revealed in his interview with Benny Morris. He characterizes Palestinian refugees as "salmons" whose yearning to return to their land somehow is supposed to fade away in roughly eighty years in a manner that the Jewish people's never did, even after two thousand years. When he denounces the idea that Israel be a "state for all its citizens" he does not seem to realize he risks alienating its many Arab citizens. Most troubling of all is his description of Arabs as people who "don't suffer from the problem of telling lies that exists in Judeo–Christian culture. Truth is seen as an irrelevant category." It is hard to know what to make of this disparaging judgment of an entire people. In the history of this particular conflict, neither Palestinians nor Israelis have a monopoly on unkept commitments or promises.

3

By now, some of those who said that the Palestinians' rejection of the American proposals at Camp David was definitive proof of their inability to make peace have shifted their argument. Instead, they concentrate on President Clinton's proposals of December 23, 2000, along with the

Israeli–Palestinian talks that took place at Taba, in January 2001, which Barak takes the so-called "revisionists" to task for ignoring.

First, the facts. There is little doubt, as we described in our earlier article for *The New York Review of Books*, that the ideas put forward by President Clinton in December 2000 were a significant step in the direction of the Palestinians' position. It is also beyond dispute that while the Israeli cabinet accepted Clinton's "parameters," Arafat took his time, waiting ten days before offering his response—a costly delay considering the fact that only thirty days remained in Clinton's presidency.

When he finally met with Clinton, on January 2, 2001, Arafat explained that he accepted the President's ideas with reservations and that Clinton could tell Barak that "[I] accepted your parameters and have some views I must express. At the same time, we know Israelis have views we must respect." His attitude, basically, was that the parameters contained interesting elements that should guide but not bind the negotiators. It is clearly an overstatement to claim that Arafat rejected "every one" of the President's ideas, and it certainly is not the message Clinton delivered to Barak.

On a more specific point, Arafat did not reject Israeli sovereignty over the Wailing Wall but over the much larger Western Wall (of which it is a part), which encroaches on the Muslim Quarter of the Old City. A few days later, Barak presented his own reservations about Clinton's proposals in a private communication.

Again, however, it is the conclusion Barak draws from this episode that is questionable. The Palestinians undoubtedly were not satisfied with Clinton's parameters, which they wanted to renegotiate. They were not responding with the same sense of urgency as the Americans or as Barak, who was facing elections and knew the fate of the peace process could decide them. But unlike what had happened at Camp David, there was no Palestinian rejection. On the contrary, the two sides, which had engaged in secret meetings during the autumn, agreed to continue talks at Taba. Indeed, the intensive talks that subsequently took place there ended not for lack of an agreement but for lack of time in view of the impending Israeli elections. In January Prime Minister Barak campaigned seeking a mandate to continue those talks. He went so far as to authorize his delegation at Taba to issue a joint statement with the Palestinians asserting that the two sides declare that they have never been closer to reaching an agreement and it is thus our shared belief that the remaining gaps could be bridged with the resumption of negotiations following the Israeli elections.

If we assume that Barak meant what the Taba statement said, that statement simply cannot be reconciled with his current assertion that the Palestinians are out to achieve the destruction of Israel. That statement also contradicts the constantly made claim that Arafat simply rejected a historic chance to negotiate a settlement.

<hr>

4

The failure at Camp David and the start of the second Palestinian intifada are directly linked in accounts by Barak and others to argue that Arafat's response to the unprecedented offers was to scuttle negotiations and seek to achieve his goals through terror.

Clearly, the Palestinian Authority did not do what it could to stop the uprising, which some of its leaders felt might well serve its interests. It is equally true that Palestinians initiated many acts of violence. Later on, as the conflict continued and intensified, cooperation between the Palestinian Authority and militant groups became much closer, and Palestinians engaged in repeated attacks with the clear and deeply deplorable intent of killing as many Israeli civilians as possible. But the charges against Arafat make another claim as well. He is said to have unleashed a wave of terrorist violence in the aftermath of Camp David as part of a grand scheme to pressure Israel; and Israel, it is said, had no choice but to act precisely as it did in response to a war initiated by others against its will. This assessment cannot be squared with the facts stated in the Mitchell report, which describes an uprising that began as a series of confrontations between largely unarmed Palestinians and armed Israeli security forces that resorted to excessive and deadly use of force.

Barak entirely rejects the notion that Ariel Sharon's visit to the Temple Mount/Haram al-Sharif on September 28, 2000, played any part in setting off the subsequent clashes. To support his case, he asserts that the visit was coordinated with Palestinian security officials. But that is hardly the point. The point is that when we consider the context in which the visit was taking place—the intense focus on the Temple Mount/Haram al-Sharif at Camp David and the general climate among Palestinians—its impact was predictable. As Dennis Ross, Clinton's special Middle East envoy, said: "I can think of a lot of bad ideas, but I can't think of a worse one."

The Mitchell report says:

> On the following day, in the same place, a large number of unarmed Palestinian demonstrators and a large Israeli police contingent confronted each other. According to the US Department of State, "Palestinians held large demonstrations and threw stones in the vicinity of the Western Wall. Police used rubber-coated metal bullets and live ammunition to disperse the demonstrators, killing 4 persons and injuring about 200." According to the Government of Israel, 14 Israeli policemen were injured.

From then on, the numbers of Palestinian deaths rose swiftly: twelve on September 30, twelve again on October 1, seventeen on October 2 (including seven Israeli Arabs), four on October 3, and twelve (including one Israeli Arab) on October 4. By the end of the first week, over sixty Palestinians had been killed (including nine Israeli Arabs). During that same time period, five Israelis were killed by Palestinians.

According to the Mitchell report, for the first three months of the intifada, "most incidents did not involve Palestinian use of firearms and explosives." The report quotes the Israeli human rights organization B'Tselem as finding that "73 percent of the incidents [from September 29 to December 2, 2000] did not include Palestinian gunfire. Despite this, it was in these incidents that most of the Palestinians [were] killed and wounded." Numerous other organizations, including the United Nations High Commissioner for Human Rights, Human Rights Watch, and Physicians for Human Rights, criticized the excessive use of force by the Israel Defense Forces, often against unarmed Palestinians.

Barak suggests that Arafat had planned as his response to the Camp David summit a campaign of violent terror. That is a curious assertion in view of the fact that the Palestinians had argued that the parties were not ready for a summit and that Camp David should be understood as merely the first of a series of meetings. In contrast, as he knows well, Barak conceived of Camp David as a make-it-or-break-it summit. Defining the summit as a test of Arafat's true intentions, he early made clear that he foresaw only two possible outcomes: a full-scale agreement on the "framework" of a settlement, or a full-scale confrontation.

Some things appear beyond dispute. The mood on the Palestinian street had reached the boiling point, as the May 2000 violence had shown and as both American and Israeli official reports had confirmed. Sharon's visit on the Haram was both a pretext and a provocation, a case of the wrong person being at the wrong place at the wrong time. A large number of Palestinians had lost patience with the peace process and felt humiliated by their experience with the settlements and at checkpoints; and many were impressed by the success of Hezbollah in Lebanon, where Israel was believed to have decided to withdraw in the face of armed resistance.

At a tactical level, the Palestinians may have seen some advantage to a short-lived confrontation to show the Israelis they could not be taken for granted. The Israeli security forces, for their part, were still affected by the bloody experiences of September 1996 and of May 2000, during which Palestinian policemen confronted Israelis. They were determined to stop any uprising at the outset, using far greater force to subdue the enemy. Hence the Israeli decision to use lethal weapons, and hence the very heavy (and almost entirely Palestinian) toll of death and grave injury in the early days of the intifada. That, in turn, made it, if not impossible, at least very difficult for the Palestinian leadership to bring things under control; rather, it increased pressure to respond in kind. Some among the Palestinian leaders may have hoped that the uprising would last a few days. The Israelis expected their strong reaction to stop it in its tracks. Instead, in this tragic game, in which both sides were reading from different scripts, the combination of the two may have led to an outcome that neither ever intended.

Again, it is worth recalling the Mitchell report:

> The Sharon visit did not cause the "Al-Aqsa Intifada." But it was poorly timed and the provocative effect should have been foreseen; indeed it was foreseen by those who urged that the visit be prohibited. More significant were the events that followed: the decision of the Israeli police on September 29 to use lethal means against the Palestinian demonstrators; and the subsequent failure … of either party to exercise restraint.

The report concluded: "We have no basis on which to conclude that there was a deliberate plan by the PA to initiate a campaign of violence at the first opportunity."

5

Barak's broad endorsement of Israel's current military campaign is cause for perhaps the greatest dismay. Of course Israel must deal with breaches of its security and look after its people's safety. Israel cannot be expected to sit idly by as Palestinians target civilians and engage in suicide attacks. The question, however, is not whether Israel should respond, but how. One might have hoped for a wise response—one that combined strong security measures with a genuine attempt to end the conflict—and that Ariel Sharon would have imitated his predecessor in continuing the political talks. Short of that, one might have hoped for a response that was driven principally, and understandably, by security concerns. But what has occurred can be deemed neither wise nor understandable. The wanton destruction on the West Bank of basic infrastructure, of civilian ministries, of equipment and documents, including school records, that have no security value—these are acts of revenge having little to do with security and everything to do with humiliating and seeking to break the will of the Palestinian people and undoing its capacity for self-governance.

The recent military action is directly related to the question of what can now be done. Barak appears to have given up on the current Palestinian leadership, placing his hopes in the next generation—a generation that has not lived through the catastrophe, or *nakba*, of 1948. But what of the catastrophe of 2002? Is there any reason to believe that today's children will grow up any less hardened and vengeful after the indiscriminate attacks of the past few months?

Barak also appears to have given up on what was his most important intuition—that the time for incremental or partial moves was over, and that the parties had to move toward a comprehensive and final settlement. While in office, he frequently made the point that Israel could not afford to make tangible concessions until it knew where the process was headed. Yet the unilateral withdrawal he now has in mind would have Israel—in the absence of any agreement or reciprocal concession—withdraw from Gaza and some 75 percent of the West Bank. It would concentrate the struggle on the remaining 25 percent and on prevailing on outstanding issues, such as Jerusalem and the refugees. Worst of all, it would embolden those Palestinians who are ready to subscribe to the Hezbollah precedent and would be quick to conclude that Israel, having twice withdrawn under fire, would continue to do so.

Ehud Barak came into office vowing to leave no possibility unexplored in the quest for peace and departed from office seeking a renewed mandate to complete the talks begun at Taba. Since he left, he has in effect branded the Taba discussions as a sham and hinted broadly that his goal throughout was to "unmask" Arafat and prove him an unworthy partner for peace. As one reads his interview with Benny Morris, it is hard to tell which is the true Barak. Certainly, his wholesale indictment of the Palestinian leaders, his unqualified assertion that they seek the end of Israel, his pejorative reflections on Arab culture, and his support of Sharon's methods are at odds with the goals he once professed.

The interpretation of what happened before, during, and after Camp David—and why—is far too important and has shown itself to have far too many implications to allow it to become subject to political caricature or posturing by either side. The story of Barak is of a man with a judicious insight—the need to aim for a comprehensive settlement—that tragically was not realized. The Camp David process was the victim of failings on the Palestinian side; but it was also, and importantly, the victim of failings on Israel's (and the United States') part as well. By refusing to recognize this, Barak continues to obscure the debate and elude fundamental questions about where the quest for peace ought to go now.

One of those questions is whether there is not, in fact, a deal that would be acceptable to both sides, respectful of their core interests, and achievable through far greater involvement (and pressure) by the international community. Such a deal, we suggest, would include a sovereign, nonmilitarized Palestinian state with borders based on the 1967 lines, with an equal exchange of land to accommodate demographic realities, and with contiguous territory on the West Bank. Jewish neighborhoods of Jerusalem would be the capital of Israel and Arab neighborhoods would be the capital of Palestine. Palestinians would rule over the Haram al–Sharif (Temple Mount), Israeli would rule over the Kotel (Wailing Wall), with strict, internationally backed guarantees regarding excavation. A strong international force could provide security and monitor implementation of the agreement. A solution to the problem of the refugees would recognize their desire to return while preserving Israel's demographic balance—for example by allowing unrestricted return to that part of 1948 land that would then be included in the land swap and fall under Palestinian sovereignty.

Barak closes his interview with the thought that Israel will remain a strong, prosperous, and Jewish state in the next century. In order to achieve that goal, there are far better and more useful things that Barak could do than the self-justifying attempt to blame Arafat and his associates for all that has gone awry.

Mr. Barak and Mr. Morris will reply in the next issue of The New York Review, *and Mr. Malley and Mr. Agha will then reply in turn.*

Camp David and After: An Exchange

Part Three

By Benny Morris and Ehud Barak, reply by Robert Malley and Hussein Agha

Benny Morris and Ehud Barak

Robert Malley and Hussein Agha ["Camp David and After: An Exchange," *NYR*, June 13] still don't get it (or pretend they don't). And it's really very simple—Ehud Barak and Bill Clinton put on the table during July–December 2000 a historic compromise and the Palestinians rejected it. They concede that Barak's offer at Camp David was "unprecedented" and that the upgraded (Clinton) proposals offered the Palestinians 94-96 percent of the West Bank, 100 percent of the Gaza Strip, a sovereign Palestinian state, an end to the occupation, the uprooting of most of the settlements, and sovereignty over Arab East Jerusalem—and Arafat and his aides still rejected the deal and pressed on with their terroristic onslaught.

Yet Malley and Agha continue, in effect, to blame Israel for the descent into war while producing "a smokescreen," in Barak's phrase, of sophistry and misleading nit-picking, that aims to get their man off the hook. Permeating their response is that shopsoiled Palestinian *Weltanschauung*, that someone else, always, is to blame for their misfortunes—Ottoman Turks, British Mandate officials, Zionists, Americans, anyone but themselves.

Malley and Agha, trying to drive home the point of permanent Palestinian innocence and victimhood, speak of "the catastrophe of 2002" in the same breath as "the catastrophe ... of 1948." But how can anyone with a minimal historical perspective compare the 1948 shattering and exile of a whole society, accompanied by thousands of deaths and the wholesale destruction of hundreds of villages, with the two or three hundred deaths, mostly of Palestinian gunmen, and the destruction of several dozen homes in the IDF's April 2002 Operation Defensive Shield, a reprisal for the murder by Palestinian suicide bombers of some one hundred Israeli civilians during the previous weeks?

The answer lies in the realm of fantasy or propaganda—and, unfortunately, much of what Malley and Agha write belongs to one of these categories. They speak of Israel's "indiscriminate attacks of the past few months." Indiscriminate? We hazard to say that no military has ever been more discriminating and gone to such lengths to avoid inflicting civilian casualties. And there were precious few bona fide civilian casualties (despite Palestinian efforts to beef up the numbers with borrowed corpses, double and triple tabulations, the inclusion of dead gunmen in "civilian" rosters, etc., and despite the fact that the gunmen, as in Jenin's refugee camp, were operating from among and behind a civilian "shield"). Human Rights Watch and other groups subsequently concluded that there was no evidence that the IDF had "massacred" anyone in the Jenin camp. Indeed, the only "indiscriminate massacres" that have taken place over the past few months have been of Israeli women, children, and the old by Palestinian suicide bombers, many of them belonging to Arafat's own Fatah organization, in cafés, malls, and buses. But the European media persists in believing the never-ending torrent of Palestinian mendacity; political correctness as well as varied economic interests and anti-Semitism dictate that no third-world people can do wrong and no first-world people, right.

Regarding Camp David and the subsequent negotiations, readers should note that Malley and Agha invariably refer to what "Arafat's negotiators" said or accepted or proposed—never to Arafat's own views and actions. And this is no accident. Arafat himself has never affirmed Israel's right to exist or its legitimacy, and has never waived the Palestinian refugees' "right of return"—and what his underlings "offer" or "accept" can always be denied or repudiated. This is the Arafat method, and Malley/Agha enter the game with gusto, while pretending to their readers that what "Arafat's negotiators" said or did carried the old man's imprimatur. They apparently forget that in their original article ["Camp David: The Tragedy of Errors," NYR, August 9, 2001] they stated: "… The Palestinians' principal failing is that from the beginning of the Camp David summit onward they were unable either to say yes to the American ideas or to present a cogent and specific counter-proposal of their own." So Clinton had "stormed out" and said: "This is a fraud. I won't have the United States covering for negotiations in bad faith." The Palestinians went "through the motions rather than go for a deal," Malley and Agha then concluded.

The new Malley and Agha are busy watering this down. Arafat, they now say, did not reject Clinton's December 23, 2000, proposals; he merely "took his time" in responding. And both Barak and the Palestinians wanted to "renegotiate" the parameters, they say. This smooth, false symmetry is vintage Malley/Agha. They fail to tell their readers that the Israeli cabinet immediately and formally accepted the parameters as a basis for negotiation and that Arafat, on the other hand, according to both Clinton and Ambassador Dennis Ross, flatly rejected the parameters and slammed the door shut.

The question of the "right of return" offers a good example of Palestinian doublespeak. All Palestinian spokesmen, including Arafat (see, for example, his interview in *Al–Ittihad* (United Arab Emirates February 6, 2002) and *Abu Alaa* (at the press conference at the end of the January 2001 Taba negotiations), affirm the unreserved, uncurtailed "right of return" to Israel proper of the 1948 refugees and their descendants, of whom there are today close to four million on UN rolls. When speaking in Arabic, they assure their constituencies—in Lebanon's and Jordan's and Gaza's refugee camps—that they will return once "Jerusalem is conquered" (code for when Israel is destroyed). But when facing westward, they affirm that the "implementation" of that right will "take account of Israel's demographic concerns." Going one better, Malley/Agha state that "there is no Palestinian position on how the refugee question should be dealt with as a practical matter" and that "all" acknowledge that there can be no "massive" return. Really?

"All"—Palestinians and Israelis—understand that concession of the principle will entail a gradual effort at full implementation, in this generation or the next, spelling chaos and the subversion of the Jewish state and its replacement by an Arab-majority "Palestine," a twenty-third Arab state. The demand for the right of return, in the deepest sense, is a demographic mechanism to achieve Israel's destruction, says Barak. This prospect does not greatly trouble Malley and Agha, who (naively? duplicitously?) admonish their readers not to exercise themselves overmuch "on the question of whether the Palestinian leadership recognized Israel's right to exist as a Jewish state." But surely that's the core of the problem—the Palestinian leadership's desire to ultimately undermine the Jewish state.

The origins of the current violence are a further case in point. Malley and Agha, after trotting out some qualifications, leave their readers with the clear impression that the Sharon visit was what caused the intifada. But Israeli intelligence (and the CIA, according to Barak) has strong evidence that the Palestinian Authority had planned the intifada already in July 2000. For example, in March 2001 the PA's communications minister, Imad Faluji, told residents of the Ein al–Hilwe refugee camp outside Sidon: "Whoever thinks that the Intifada broke out because of the despised Sharon's visit to the al–Aqsa Mosque is wrong, even if this visit was the straw that broke the back of the Palestinian people. This intifada was planned in advance, ever since President Arafat's return from the Camp David negotiations, where he turned the table upside down on President Clinton." (*Al–Safir*, Lebanon, March 3, 2001).

Barak characterizes Arafat "and some (not all) of his entourage" as "serial liars." Arafat's credentials as a serial liar are impressive, Malley/Agha's protestations notwithstanding. Take, for example, Arafat's interview with *Al–Ittihad* on February 6, 2002, in which he blamed the Israeli security service, the Shin Bet, for carrying out suicide bombings against Israeli soldiers and civilians; the attack on the Dolphinarium night club in 2001, in which about twenty-five Israeli youngsters died, he blamed on an IDF soldier. Arafat routinely tells anyone who will listen that Israeli troops use "poison gas" and "radioactive materials" against Palestinian civilians (Arafat on Abu Dhabi TV/Palestine TV, March 29, 2002).

To Western audiences Arafat usually affirms his interest in peace or "the peace of the braves" (a Palestinian baseball team?), as he puts it. To Arab audiences, he speaks only of battle and planting the Palestinian flag on Jerusalem's walls (as Saladin planted his flag on Jerusalem's walls, after defeating the Crusaders, back in 1189) and of sacrificing "one million *shuhada* [martyrs, meaning suicide bombers]" in "redeeming Palestine." On May 10, 1994, he told a Muslim audience in Johannesburg that he was engaged in the Oslo peace process much as Mohammed had briefly acquiesced in a truce with the Quraish tribe of Mecca, only to unilaterally revoke it and slaughter them several years later. For good measure, Arafat in that speech said there is no "permanent state of Israel," only a "permanent state of Palestine."

It is worth noting that Malley/Agha conclude by proposing a settlement based on the establishment of "a sovereign, nonmilitarized Palestinian state based on the 1967 lines, with an equal exchange of land to accommodate demographic realities" and the return of refugees to the area that becomes the Palestinian state. But this, almost precisely, is the deal that Clinton and Barak proposed back in 2000—and Arafat violently rejected.

The time has come for the world to judge Arafat by what he does and not by the camouflaging defensive rhetoric tossed out by sophisticated polemicists, Barak says. He refers to Saddam Hussein and Arafat as "the terroristic odd couple" of 1991, who are now back for a second inning, with Saddam helping to fuel the present conflict by inciting the Arab world to join in and, like the Saudis, by paying gratuities to the families of suicide bombers. It is time that the West's leaders, who initially dealt with Saddam and Milosevic as acceptable, responsible interlocutors, now treat Arafat and his ilk in the Palestinian camp as the vicious, untrustworthy, unacceptable reprobates and recidivists that they are.

—Benny Morris and Ehud Barak

Robert Malley and Hussein Agha reply:

One might be tempted to dismiss much of what Benny Morris and Ehud Barak write as hollow demagoguery were it not so pernicious and damaging to the future of both the Israeli and Palestinian people. In the past, and through his words and actions, Barak helped to set in motion the process of delegitimizing the Palestinians and the peace process, thereby enabling Ariel Sharon to deal with them as he saw fit and absolve himself of all responsibility for Israel's diplomatic, security, and economic predicament. Now, the inability to reach a peace deal in the seven months between Camp David and Taba has become, in Barak's and Morris's version, a tale in which Arab cultural deficiency and the Palestinians' inherent desire to destroy Israel are the dominant themes. As Shimon Peres has famously put it, Barak is making an ideology out of his failure. It is time he dealt with the failure, put aside the ideology, and let Israelis and Palestinians return to the far more urgent and serious task of peacemaking.

To begin, a few words about Morris's and Barak's rejoinder, a catalog of misrepresentations that scarcely deserves more. They distort what we wrote about the tragic events of the last few months, the reactions to President Clinton's December 23 ideas, the right of return, the importance of Israel's right to exist as a Jewish state, and the origins of the current intifada. They turn what the world saw as Sharon's dangerously provocative walk on the Haram/Temple Mount into an innocent stroll. They charge the Palestinians with trying to evade all responsibility but then proceed to evade all responsibility on Barak's part, placing the entire burden of failure on the Palestinians while adding for good measure the usual tired accusations about Arab doublespeak, European media bias, "varied economic interests," and even political correctness. They refer to the "Arafat method" by which negotiators, and not Arafat himself, laid out Palestinian positions, without acknowledging that it was precisely the method routinely and quite openly practiced by Barak. Indeed, the desire not to commit himself personally was the reason Barak provided for his refusal to hold substantive discussions with Arafat at Camp David and it is also the reason why he both declined to give his negotiators specific instructions during the Taba talks and asked not to be fully briefed by them.

Then there is the issue of Barak's astonishing remarks about Palestinian and Arab culture that he now seeks to obfuscate. Yet his words in the initial interview were unequivocal. "They are products of a culture in which to tell a lie … creates no dissonance," he pronounced. "They don't suffer from the problem of telling lies that exists in Judeo–Christian culture. Truth is seen as irrelevant." And so on. But, plainly, factual accuracy and logical consistency are not what Morris and Barak are after. What matters is self-justification by someone who has chosen to make a career—and perhaps a comeback—through the vilification of an entire people.

For that, indeed, is the real issue that warrants attention. In Morris's and Barak's crude account, Barak made a most generous offer, the "vicious" Palestinian leadership turned it down because they wanted to get rid of Israel, and all the rest is gossip. But is a man who believes that a whole race or culture is immune to the truth well placed to make such a sweeping assessment or, for that matter, well equipped to strike a historic deal with the people about whom he holds such prejudiced views? Barak deserves credit for understanding the need to end the Israeli–Palestinian conflict and the importance of separation between the two peoples as part of a final peace agreement. But it is worth recalling that Barak opposed the Oslo accords from the outset; before 1996 he was against the inclusion of Palestinian statehood in the Labor Party's platform; he insisted on renegotiating an agreement with the Palestinians signed by his predecessor and then failed to carry it out; and, today, he takes pride in having made fewer tangible concessions to the Palestinians than Benjamin Netanyahu, the right-wing prime minister who preceded him. Are these truly the qualifications one would expect of a man who claims to sit in judgment of the peacemaking capabilities of others?

What is clear from his reply and other recent statements is Barak's utter lack of self–doubt. Yet, by the time he was defeated by Ariel Sharon, less than two years after coming into office, he had antagonized both the religious right and the secular left, not for the sake of high principle but through poor management. His governing coalition had disintegrated. Arab–Israelis had lost all confidence in him. His own Labor Party was adrift and strongly critical of him. He was unable to reach an agreement with Syria. And relations with much of the Arab world were at a lower point than they had been under his hard-line predecessor. The Palestinians, in short, were only one on a lengthy list of people whom he successfully managed to alienate or had failed to deal with successfully. In view of this record, might there not be room to wonder whether Barak's tactics, approach, and cast of mind had at least something to do with the breakdown of the peace process?

Finally there is the question of what, today, Barak stands by and stands for. What, in his opinion, actually happened at Taba in January 2001, and does he accept the positive assessment provided by his official Israeli delegation? It is an assessment he ignores in his reply and that is worth repeating here:

The two sides declare that they have never been closer to reaching an agreement and it is thus our shared belief that the remaining gaps could be bridged with the resumption of negotiations following the Israeli elections.

That statement contradicts the claim made by Barak, and frequently heard from others, that the Palestinians simply turned their backs on a possible agreement. Would Barak be prepared, today, to resume where things were left off and seek to complete the negotiations, as he pledged at the time and as he repeated to the Israeli public throughout his reelection campaign? The question whether a peace agreement can still be reached, in the current situation of appalling daily violence, has become more urgent than ever. We know what President Clinton's ideas were for an Israeli–Palestinian agreement. We know the positions of more than a few Israeli political leaders who in recent weeks have unveiled their own peace formulas. We even know what the official Palestinian proposal is—though it may or may not be something the Israeli people can accept. But can Barak, who likes to tell the left that he went further than everyone else and the right that he gave less than anyone else, let us know what are his specific proposals for a final peace agreement with the Palestinians?

Hamas vs. Fatah: The Struggle for Palestine

By Jonathan Schanzer

Prelude to War

"We have lost the elections; Hamas has won," said Saeb Erakat, a Palestinian official aligned with the Fatah faction. Erakat was visibly shaken. A heavyset, bald man with glasses who often appeared on television during the Palestinian uprising of 2000 to defiantly lambaste Israel's counterterrorism measures in the West Bank and Gaza, Erakat appeared anything but defiant here. His surprising announcement came even before the final election tally had been made.

Fatah members had fired celebratory gunshots into the air in Ramallah the night before. But these celebrations were premature. The Palestinian Central Elections Committee shocked the world on January 26, 2006, when it announced that the Islamist party had won a majority of seats in the Palestinian parliament. There was no refuting the fact that Hamas had earned a legitimate landslide victory; the election was considered by observers to be as free and fair as elections can be in the Arab world. More than one million Palestinians went to the polls to cast their votes. Hamas claimed 76 of the 132 seats (74 under the Hamas banner, plus independents), granting it the right, by Palestinian law, to form a coalition.

Some sympathetic analysts argued that, despite the results, the Palestinians did not truly seek an Islamist government. Rather, their votes for Hamas were an expression of a need for "change and reform," which was the name of the Hamas electoral platform. Others, however, argued that it was "condescending to argue that the Palestinians were somehow unaware that they were casting ballots for the party that advocates violent jihad." Indeed, it was impossible that they were unaware of Hamas's history of brutal violence against Israel dating back to the outbreak of the first intifada in 1987. Moreover, the Palestinian people knew from the Hamas election manifesto dated January 25, 2006, that Hamas sought a shari'a state and all the trappings that came with it. Further, had they merely wished to protest Fatah, they could have voted for other parties. Thus, the Palestinians were fully responsible for the electoral choices they made.

On the day the election results were announced, Hamas leader Ismael Haniyeh flashed a broad smile and held up his forefinger in front of photographers and journalists in Gaza. With cropped salt-and-pepper hair and a neatly trimmed beard, Haniyeh projected a calm confidence, unlike many of his cohorts, whose nerves had been visibly frayed by years of Israeli counterterrorism operations. Haniyeh came of age during the 1987 intifada (he was 24 when it erupted) but had already been active in Islamist politics at the University of Gaza in the early 1980s. His credentials as a Hamas leader were further bolstered by several Israeli arrests and the fact that he was among those deported to South Lebanon in 1992 for his involvement in Hamas. After the wave of assassinations of Hamas leaders that followed the al–Aqsa intifada, Haniyeh emerged as one of the group's top leaders.

Haniyeh's jubilation over the elections results was short-lived, however. After he formed a new coalition on March 29 (he was named "prime minister"), the territories fell into turmoil. Fatah, which took only 45 seats in the election, was unprepared to let go of the power it had enjoyed since the creation of the Palestinian Authority in 1994. Clashes between various Palestinian factions and clans soon erupted in the streets of Gaza.

How did Hamas win? As described in previous chapters, the group's popularity grew steadily over two decades of confrontations with Israel Palestinians of the territories and the diaspora alike came to view Hamas as a source of hope for Palestinian renewal, particularly since the Islamist group had always refused to take part in what was widely viewed as a corrupt Palestinian political system (although it should be noted that Hamas had participated in previous municipal elections). Indeed, the prevailing perception was that Hamas was a pious and ascetic organization that could not be corrupted. Hamas exploited this belief by casting the PLO returnees (*didoun*)—the wealthy Fatah officials who returned from the diaspora to the Gaza Strip and West Bank after the Olso Accords—as corrupt and spoiled by the money they had amassed while in exile. The prevailing Palestinian perception was that Hamas was tenacious and unwavering in its rejection of the Palestinian–Israeli peace process, despite immense international pressure, not to mention coercion by Fatah from within. Hamas also gained popular support from its expansive social networks that provided much-needed services to appreciative Palestinians in ways that the PA never did. Hamas enjoyed a baseline of popularity

simply by buying off a sector of the Palestinian people; the group provided monetary support to the families of suicide bombers and handed out meat to needy families on holidays.

For the Israelis, options were few after the election. The 2006 Hamas legislative victory severely dampened any hopes that Prime Minister Olmert may have harbored for peace. The unilateral withdrawal had backfired. Hamas was now the representative of the Palestinian people through a free and fair election. Above all else, Hamas rejected the very existence of the State of Israel and refused to negotiate that point. If there had been any doubt about Hamas's intentions, its leaders stated immediately after the elections that they had no plans to pursue peace talks or disarm the party's armed wing, the Izz al–Din al–Qassam Brigades.

Washington's options were similarly limited. "I have made it very clear," George W. Bush stated solemnly, "that a political party that articulates the destruction of Israel as part of its platform is a party with which we will not deal." He added, "I don't see how you can be a partner in peace if you advocate the destruction of a country as part of your platform."

America's stance was not a surprise. The Hamas election was an embarrassing black eye to the U.S. democratization efforts in the region. The Palestinian elections that brought Hamas to power had been spawned by the Bush doctrine, which was designed to promote democracy throughout the Arab world. The U.S. president viewed free elections and transparent governance as a means to combat the ideology of radical Islam, which continued to spread unabated and inspire violence against the United States and the West. Obviously, this was not the outcome the administration had been hoping for.

America's decision to back the Palestinian elections was a calculated one. It was due, in no small part, to polling data that all but guaranteed a Fatah victory over Hamas, falsely affirming the popularity of the U.S.-backed government in the West Bank and Gaza Strip. The polls were produced primarily by Khalil Shiqaqi's Palestinian Center for Policy and Research, which conducted three critical studies of Palestinian opinion in June, September, and December 2005. The data indicated that Fatahs support among Palestinians ranged from 44 percent to 50 percent, while Hamas support was said to range from 32 to 33 percent. "With each new Shiqaqi poll," scholar Martin Kramer notes, "U.S. policymakers grew more lax when it came to setting conditions for Hamas participation."

In retrospect, U.S. reliance on these polls was a grave error. Kramer suggests that the polls may have been part of Fatahs election propaganda, in an attempt to project its strength. Alternatively, some analysts quietly wondered whether Shiqaqi, whose brother was the late Fathi Shiqaqi, a founding member of the Palestinian Islamic Jihad, sought to deceive the United States, Fatah, or both. Others, however, defended Shiqaqi, contending that he was a "scapegoat" for America's unexpected and crushing defeat in the Palestinian–Israeli arena.

The elections also constituted a severe blow to Fatah, which captured just 45 seats out of a possible 132. These dismal results were a sign that without Yasir Arafat, the party had little appeal to the Palestinians of the West Bank and Gaza Strip. "This is the choice of the people," admitted 70-year-old Ahmed Qureia, a member of Fatah's old guard. "It should be respected."

While the people had spoken, Qureia's younger colleagues in Fatah wanted the last word. Immediately after the elections, Fatah and Hamas members clashed in front of the Palestinian parliament building in Ramallah. Tensions between the two factions soon spread, continuing regularly in the weeks and months that followed. According to a 104-page report issued by the Palestine Center for Human Rights (PCHR) immediately after the elections, there were reports of "attacks on public institutions; armed personal and clan disputes; attacks on international organizations; abductions of internationals … armed conflicts between security services and armed groups; and attacks on officials." Over 15 months, according to PCHR, 350 Palestinians were killed in the clashes, including 20 children and 18 women, while 1,900

were wounded. The center also estimates that 248 Palestinians were killed "by an escalation in the state of lawlessness." How the center differentiated between casualties from clashes and casualties from lawlessness is unclear.

The first serious clashes, which foretold the real possibility of a civil war, were reported in mid-April, when hundreds of Fatah activists marched to Gaza's parliament compound, throwing stones and shattering windows in a government building. Elsewhere in the territories, tens of thousands of Fatah members marched through the streets, denouncing Hamas, setting tires ablaze, and waving the Fatah party's flag. In Nablus, Fatah-affiliated gunmen stormed a courthouse, ejected dozens of employees, and shut it down.

Tensions worsened on April 22, 2006, when hundreds of students representing the Hamas and Fatah factions at Gaza's al–Azhar University and the Islamic University threw stones and home-made grenades at one another. Fifteen people were wounded, two seriously. Two weeks later, in early May, at least nine Palestinians were wounded in two days of Gaza Strip fighting between the two rival factions. At least four schoolchildren were wounded in the crossfire of predawn gun battles. In another incident, Hamas activists responded to the assassination of one of their members by launching a shoulder-fired missile at a Fatah security services truck, killing two passengers inside.

The violence grew worse after the creation of the "Executive Force" (EF), a new military unit deployed on April 20 by Hamas Interior Minister Said Sayyam, a teacher for 20 years in the Gaza Strip with a long history of Hamas involvement. For weeks, Sayyam had complained that forces loyal to Fatah and the PA were not following Hamas directives. Palestinian President Mahmoud Abbas, as it turned out, had actually ordered Gaza's police officers to stay home in exchange for receiving their salaries as a means to deny Hamas the power that it had earned at the ballot box. It soon became apparent, however, that the EF was not a legitimate police force. Rather than filling the void left by the PA forces and restoring law to the streets of Gaza, the EF became an authoritarian tool that Hamas used to intimidate and exterminate its political foes. The EF adopted many of the extremist views associated with Hamas's military wing, the al–Qassam Brigades. As one new recruit noted, "I'm not Qassam, but I'm in the police force. It's considered jihad."

When Hamas elected to deploy the EF, Fatah correctly viewed the move as a direct challenge to Abbas's PA forces. This again raised the specter of an all-out civil war. Fierce clashes erupted for nearly an hour between the two sides on May 22, as the two factions exchanged fire in front of the Palestinian Legislative Council (PLC) building near the police headquarters in Gaza.

In early June, more brutal fighting was reported between Hamas fighters (including the al–Qassam Brigades) and Fatah fighters (including the al–Aqsa Martyrs Brigade), which led to the death of a pregnant woman and a deaf man, among others. Assaults launched by the two opposing factions against each other continued throughout the month, with reports of abductions, grenades, and rocket fire.

Amid the chaos, Hamas and other terrorist factions did not forget to attack Israel. On June 25, Hamas carried out a daring raid near the Kerem Shalom crossing on the Gaza border. Eight Hamas fighters reportedly utilized an underground tunnel to approach and ambush an Israeli tank, resulting in the deaths of two Israeli soldiers as well as the capture of Corporal Gilad Shalit. Hamas had knowingly crossed an Israeli red line. It was common for the Israelis to endure shelling or other attacks. But when its soldiers were kidnapped, the IDF responded with stronger force. Thus, two days after Shalit's abduction, the IDF launched Operation Summer Rains against several key Hamas targets, adding to the pandemonium that plagued the Gaza Strip.

According to Prime Minister Olmert, the aim of the invasion was "not to mete out punishment, but rather to apply pressure so that the abducted soldier will be freed." Prior to the dawn raid, Israeli fighter planes attacked three bridges and the main power station in Gaza, in order to

limit the mobility of Shalit's captors. If they had not taken out those targets, the Israelis feared that the captured soldier could be removed from Gaza or transferred to another location. In the end, however, Shalit was not recovered. Seeking retribution, Israel continued to target Hamas in the Gaza Strip, even as the Islamist group tangled with Fatah forces.

Surprisingly, the Israeli rage over the Hamas kidnapping of one of its soldiers was almost a side plot during the summer of 2006. While recovering the kidnapped soldier was a high priority for the IDF, the war with Hizbullah on Israel's northern border quickly overshadowed Israel's Gaza operations. That war was provoked when Hizbullah fighters, on July 12, infiltrated Israeli territory from Lebanon and attacked two IDF armored jeeps patrolling the border, killing three soldiers and kidnapping two: Eldad Regev and Ehud Goldwasser. Hizbullah, like Hamas, had knowingly violated an Israeli red line. The result was a 33-day war, marked by thousands of Hizbullah rockets fired on Israel's north and an even greater number of Israeli reprisal strikes against Hizbullah targets mostly in southern Lebanon and Beirut. The conflict raged until the United Nations brokered a cease-fire that took effect on August 14, 2006.

The Lebanon war did not deter the Palestinian factions from warring with one another, however. Armed clashes continued between Hamas and Fatah throughout the summer and fall. By October, the violence had spread throughout the West Bank towns of Ramallah, Nablus, Jericho, and Hebron.

In December 2006, Hamas accused Fatah of attempting to assassinate Palestinian Prime Minister Haniyeh in an attack at the Ralah crossing in Gaza that killed one of his bodyguards. In the war of words that followed, Hamas claimed that Mohammed Dahlan, a senior Fatah strongman in Gaza, was behind the attack. Violence again erupted between the two factions, leading to 20 injuries.

Seeking to regain control, Abbas called for an early election to bring down the Hamas government. Fatah activists in Gaza and the West Bank celebrated this political maneuver, taking to the streets and firing celebratory machine-gun bursts into the air. In response, Hamas accused Abbas of launching a coup against its democratically elected government.

Even before Abbas made this call for early elections, Hamas complained that the Fatah-backed PA had refused to engage with it on issues of governance. There had also been reports of tensions between the Hamas appointees and Fatah functionaries in various ministries as well as fragmentation within the security services. Indeed, each faction retained and developed its own militias. In retrospect, Abbas's call for a new government was probably justifiable. The political tensions that characterized the Hamas–Fatah power struggle had paralyzed the Palestinian legislature.

Meanwhile, violence worsened between the two groups in January and February 2007, leading to a sense that the West Bank and Gaza were more lawless than ever. Specifically, Hamas carried out a string of abductions of Fatah and PA figures. Those who were kidnapped were often beaten; in some cases, "their limbs were fired at to cause permanent physical disabilities." According to PCHR, the Hamas EF stormed private homes and executed their Fatah enemies by shooting them, point blank, in the head. Reportedly Hamas also hijacked a convoy of PA trucks, marking a turning point in the conflict. The EF was not simply trying to kill Fatah members; it was attempting to cut off their supply lines as well.

In an effort to halt the fighting, King Abdullah of Saudi Arabia intervened and invited the leaders of Fatah and Hamas to Mecca to engage in a dialogue designed to end the conflict. Abdullah, a heavyset man often photographed in a headscarf, sunglasses, and a dyed-black goatee and mustache, likely gloated over his high profile diplomatic endeavor with the Palestinians, particularly since it did not include Egypt, his country's political rival. Abdullah was also likely happy to do something positive for the United States; Washington often complained to the Saudis about their role in financing terror and the propagation of radical Wahhabi propaganda.

The top leaders of Hamas and Fatah represented their factions at the Saudi talks, demonstrating a seriousness of purpose and perhaps concerns about the future. Fatah's representatives included Abbas and Dahlan, while Ismael Haniyeh and Khaled Meshal represented Hamas. After three days, the two high-level delegations reportedly reached an understanding, leading to the February 8, 2007, Mecca Agreement. The agreement was based on the so-called Prisoners Document of May 2006. The Prisoners Document was penned by Marwan Barghouti of the Fatah faction and Abdul Khaleq al–Natshe of Hamas, as well as several other prominent Palestinian prisoners in Israeli jails.

According to the text of the Mecca Agreement, both Hamas and Fatah agreed:

First: To ban the shedding of Palestinian blood and to take all measures and arrangements to prevent the shedding of Palestinian blood and to stress the importance of national unity as the basis for national steadfastness and confronting the occupation and to achieve the legitimate national goals of the Palestinian people and adopt the language of dialogue as the sole basis for solving political disagreements in the Palestinian arena.

Second: Final agreement to form a Palestinian national unity government according to a detailed agreement ratified by both sides and to start on an urgent basis to take the constitutional measures to form this government.

Third: To move ahead in measures to activate and reform the Palestine Liberation Organisation and accelerate the work of the preparatory committee based on the Cairo and Damascus Understandings.

Fourth: To stress on the principle of political partnership on the basis of the effective laws in the PNA [Palestinian National Authority] and on the basis of political pluralism according to an agreement ratified between both parties.

A little more than one month later, on March 17, 2007, the two sides agreed to form a national unity government. But, predictably, the brokered calm did not last long. There was virtually no way to sweep aside the pain and animosity that lingered; the bloodshed between Fatah and Hamas had resulted in hundreds of deaths and injuries in 2006 and 2007. In March 2007 alone, the same month that the agreement was signed, there were 46 reported kidnappings of civilians in the Gaza Strip as well as more than 25 killings. The intra-Palestinian violence got to the point that one human rights activist announced that Gaza had "become worse than Somalia." Yasir Abed Rabbo, an executive committee member of the PLO, simply described the situation as "anarchy."

The Palestinian violence had other negative consequences, particularly in the Gaza Strip, where Hamas enjoyed the most control. Foreign aid workers and armed military advisors, who initially sought to provide various forms of aid to the Palestinians, began to flee for their lives. According to one report, several Egyptian military officers stationed in the Gaza Strip were recalled to Cairo due to the raging hostilities. Fearful of violence, the two Egyptian generals who stayed on spent most of their time in Israel, a country for which most Egyptians have little love. The United Nations even considered declaring the Gaza Strip a "dangerous zone," a move that would prompt the evacuation of nearly all foreigners, including the United Nations Relief and Works Agency and other international aid organizations that have provided handouts to the Palestinians for decades.

The violence in Gaza was also directly correlated to a rise in crime. While Hamas and Fatah forces were killing one another, no one was policing the streets. Indeed, the Palestinian media, not known for its candor about negative developments within Palestinian society, reported that crimes, including car theft and abductions, had skyrocketed.

Gazas decrepit infrastructure also paid the price. While the fighting raged, in March 2007, a sewage-treatment pool collapsed in Umm al-Nasser, a North Gaza village. The disaster was ultimately blamed on local residents who were stealing sand from an embankment and selling it to local building contractors. It was later learned that the sewage basins from which they stole were

already stretched well beyond their maximum capacity. The ensuing "sewage tsunami" killed 3 women and 2 toddlers and injured 25. The raw sewage submerged at least 25 homes, flooded the streets, and caused untold damages to the 3,000-person village. Fadel Kawash, head of the Palestinian Water Authority, told the Associated Press that a number of sewage projects, including the one in Umm al-Nasser, had been halted after the Hamas electoral victory in January 2006. In fact, a Japanese project to repair the sewage system had been cancelled. According to one UN official, it was "a tragedy that was predicted and documented."

As Hamas–Fatah violence continued, there were also numerous reports of Islamist groups attacking secular and Christian targets throughout the Gaza Strip. A group calling itself the Islamic Swords of Truth, a self-appointed vice squad, claimed responsibility for bombing the Gaza Bible Society's Christian bookstore and two Internet cafes. In response to these and other attacks, one of Gaza's largest clans gathered to blockade a main road in northern Gaza to protest the targeting of one of their shops by a vice squad. The family demanded that the government bring law and order back to the streets.

Even journalists who covered the Palestinian conflict paid a price. Access to both Hamas and Fatah became more difficult as the fighting raged. Indeed, covering the violence endangered the journalists. In April 2007, Hamas security guards broke up a peaceful protest of journalists who were angered over the Hamas governments inability to secure the release of Alan Johnston, a BBC journalist who had been kidnapped by Gaza's Hamas-linked Dughmush clan in March. The confrontation resulted in three injured journalists.

Thanks to little mainstream media coverage of the turmoil, most of the western world was unaware of the factional violence that continued between Fatah and Hamas through the spring of 2007. Multiple kidnappings took place, as well as machine-gun clashes, peppered with explosions caused by homemade bombs and other projectiles. Both sides suffered many casualties, but Hamas was particularly devastated by the killing of Ibrahim Suleiman Maniya, the 45-year-old leader of the al–Qassam Brigades, who was shot in the chest during a fierce clash between Hamas and Fatah on May 15. Fighting between the two factions during that week resulted in the deaths of 47 Palestinians and wounding of hundreds of others, mostly noncombatants.

Sensing that the violence could get even worse and perhaps threaten regional security, the government of Egypt stepped in to attempt to broker a cease-fire on May 19. As was the case with previous Hamas–Fatah cease-fires, this one lasted only for a few weeks. Soon another round of fighting erupted, which quickly came to be known as the six-day Palestinian civil war.

Hamas Conquers Gaza

On June 7, 2007, Hamas launched a military offensive to conquer the Gaza Strip. By June 13, its forces controlled the streets and Palestinian Authority (PA) buildings, including the presidential compound of Mahmoud Abbas and the massive security compound known as al–Suraya. By June 14, it was clear that all of Gaza was under Hamas control. Abbas had no choice but to dismiss the Hamas-led unity government that the Saudis had helped create in March. He soon appointed outgoing Finance Minister Salaam Fayyad to lead an emergency government in the West Bank. In so doing, Abbas all but conceded that he had lost the Gaza Strip.

The sight of Hamas and Fatah engaging in open battle on the streets of Gaza was certainly not a surprise, given the long history of animosity between the two groups. What was striking, however, was the dismal performance of the Fatah-aligned PA security forces. The battle for Gaza lasted a mere six days, resurrecting memories of another painful six-day war that drastically altered the future of the Palestinian people: the lightning victory of Israel over Egypt, Jordan, and Syria in 1967.

Fatah's forces, trained and armed by the United States and other western nations, had failed miserably in war. According to numerous reports, PA fighters either left the field of battle or even joined the Hamas fighters. Those PA fighters who stood their ground were likely not prepared for their brutal and zealous enemy. According to the Palestinian Center for Human Rights (PCHR), while both factions engaged in countless acts of violence, much of the Hamas violence was indiscriminate, demonstrating a willful disregard for the conventions of war.

According to PCHR, the mid-June violence in Gaza was characterized by "extra-judicial and willful killing," including incidents where Hamas fighters pushed two Fatah faction members from the roofs of tall buildings. Hamas also abducted and executed some political enemies. Reportedly Hamas even killed PA supporters who were already injured, or shot Fatah fighters at point-blank range to ensure permanent wounds. PCHR further reported attacks against private homes and apartment buildings, hospitals, ambulances, and medical crews associated with the Palestinian Authority. All told, the June civil war claimed the lives of at least 161 Palestinians, including 7 children and 11 women. At least 700 Palestinians were wounded. Although history will almost certainly cast Hamas as the aggressor in the battle for Gaza, reports of two authoritative human rights organizations on the June civil war (Amnesty International and PCHR) were careful to blame both Fatah and Hamas. Both reports issued pleas to both sides to end the violence, protect the civilian population, and return to negotiations. The United Nations also sought to be evenhanded. Some states worked to include a clause in a proposed resolution citing "concern about an illegal takeover." The verbiage, however, fell short of assigning blame.

When the guns fell silent, Sami Abu Zuhri, the dark-skinned, bearded Hamas senior spokesman who appeared regularly on Arab television networks, announced that the war had been a defensive one. In what many Fatah leaders viewed as an utterly audacious statement, Zuhri claimed that Hamas had entered into battle to defend itself from a Fatah cadre that was collaborating with the United States and Israel. "There is no political goal behind this but to defend our movement and force these security groups to behave," Zuhri said. He also stated that his organization sought to unify the various armed Palestinian factions under its command, insisting that it still sat atop a unity government. He even stated that the United States should "sit with [Hamas] at the dialogue table on the basis of mutual respect, respecting the elections."

Zuhri did not need to do much to get a rise out of the White House. According to the *Wall Street Journal* U.S. security services were already furious over the loss of the Fatah security complex, which housed the PAs intelligence and military infrastructure—infrastructure the United States had helped to create. After the compound was captured, Hamas claimed to have "acquired thousands of paper files, computer records, videos, photographs, and audio recordings containing valuable and potentially embarrassing intelligence information gathered by Fatah." Washington's fear, reportedly, was that Hamas had gained "access to important spying technology as well as intelligence information that could be helpful to Hamas in countering Israeli and U.S. efforts against the group." Both Washington and Jerusalem also feared that Hamas had stolen the advanced weaponry that had been given to the PA, which Hamas could use on the battlefield, making its fighters harder to defeat.

As Hamas assumed control of the Gaza Strip, it began to govern through a combination of violence, authoritarianism, and Islamism. Ismael Haniyeh, the ascendant ruler of Gaza, officially denied accusations that Hamas intended to establish an Islamic emirate. However, as noted previously, Islamists had launched a string of attacks on Internet cafes and Christian institutions. By November, the British press reported that "only believers feel safe" in Gaza and that "un-Islamic" dress sometimes resulted in beatings.

According to Asma Jahangir, the United Nations Special Rapporteur on Freedom of Religion or Belief: "Women seem to be in a particularly vulnerable situation and bear the brunt of religious zeal. I was informed about cases of honor killings carried out with impunity in the occupied Palestinian territory in the name of religion. Reportedly some women in Gaza have recently felt coerced to cover their heads not out of religious conviction but out of fear."

Hamas proved once again that terrorist groups, much like their Fatah predecessors, were unfit to govern. The Islamist group exhibited an almost criminal indifference to the suffering of Gaza citizens impacted by the violence, lack of services, deepening poverty, collateral damage from the battles, and the predictable Israeli reprisals that resulted from Hamas attacks. Moreover, as PCHR noted in its report, the de facto Hamas government attacked the media and peaceful demonstrations and engaged in the "destruction, seizure, and robbery of governmental and non-governmental institutions." The few, reluctant steps toward liberalization that the PA had taken during its 13-year rule in Gaza—small advances in press and political freedoms, for example—had been wiped out in a matter of days.

Hamas, of course, attempted to highlight the positives. Within a week of the takeover, the Islamists boasted that crime, tribal clashes, and kidnapping had all dropped precipitously in the Gaza Strip, But as former U.S. Envoy to the Middle East Dennis Ross noted, this drop in crime was more than likely the result of fear on the part of Gaza residents rather than a sign of increased or improved law enforcement.

Some reports indicated that Ahmad al-Ja'abari, a senior member of the Izz al-Din al-Qassam Brigades, was behind the dangerous new conditions. Al-Ja'abari, an angry-looking man with an unkempt beard and crooked teeth, spent 13 years in Israeli jails and 2 years in the PA jails. He also survived at least one Israeli assassination attempt. According to the Israeli *Haaretz* newspaper, he was ignoring the moderating advice of Haniyeh and Syria-based Khaled Meshal. Regardless of who was making the decisions, Gaza was suffering.

The first sign of religious violence in the Gaza Strip against non-Muslims—or "Talibanization" as some analysts called it, in reference to the Taliban regime that mistreated non-Muslims and harbored the al-Qaeda terrorist network in the 1990s—was the way in which Hamas mistreated the minority Christian community, mostly Greek Orthodox, which had lived in relative peace for centuries amid Gaza's predominantly Sunni Muslim population. When the June violence first subsided, Hamas announced on Palestinian television that the coup marked the "end of secularism and heresy in the Gaza Strip." On June 14, masked gunmen attacked the Rosary Sisters School and the Latin Church in Gaza City. According to Father Manuel Musalam, the leader of the small Latin community in the Gaza Strip, the Hamas gunmen used rocket-propelled grenades to storm the main entrances of the school and church. Then they destroyed almost everything inside, including the cross, bible, computers, and other equipment. The attack appeared to be entirely religiously motivated, since there were no reports of Fatah fighters in the church or the school "This is more than vandalism," Musalam said. "They forced open the door and entered and destroyed everything. They even put the sisters' beds on fire."

Later that month, according to the *Jerusalem Post*, Hamas kidnapped Professor Sana al-Sayegh, a teacher at Palestine University in Gaza City, and forced her to convert to Islam against her will. Her family's attempts to meet with Hamas leaders to find her repeatedly failed. Requests by community leaders representing Gazas 3,000 Christians to meet with Haniyeh were also turned down. Finally, the Haniyeh government asked Ala Aklouk, a senior Muslim cleric in Gaza City, to look into the case. Aklouk soon told Sayegh's family that the professor had made a personal decision to convert to Islam. "She was too afraid to inform her family that she had converted to Islam," he said.

In September, an attack against an elderly Christian woman triggered fresh fears among Gaza's Christians. A masked man in black clothes knocked on her door late at night, forced his way into her home, beat her on her hands, called her an "infidel," and stole her money and jewelry.

In October, a Palestinian news agency reported that the body of 30-year-old Rami Ayyad, the owner of the Holy Bible Association, was found in an eastern suburb of Gaza City. Ayyad had been missing for a day, and had been receiving death threats from Islamists after they torched his organization's building in late summer. The Holy Bible Association had also been the target of a grenade attack during protests stemming from the cartoons of the Prophet Mohammed that appeared in the Danish newspaper *Jyllands-Posten* in 2005.

According to a Christian news service, Hamas attempted to force all Christians under its rule to become Muslims, submit to Islamic law, or leave the Gaza Strip. By one count, more than 50 attacks had taken place in the first few months following the June coup. Targets included barbershops, music stores, and even a UN school where boys and girls played sports together.

In December 2007, four masked gunmen in the Gaza Strip tried to kidnap a Christian. The man escaped unharmed, but as one Christian leader stated, the incident was "aimed at sending a message to all the Christians here that we must leave. Radical Islamic groups are waging a campaign to get rid of us and no one seems to care."

In February 2008, unidentified gunmen believed to be aligned with Hamas blew up the YMCA library in the Gaza Strip. Two guards were temporarily kidnapped, offices were looted, a vehicle was stolen, and more than 8,000 books were destroyed. That attack came only days after a Hamas "modesty patrol" attacked a Christian youth's car after he was seen driving a female classmate to her home. Both were injured in that attack.

Hamas issued a statement on the Muslim Brotherhood's Web site condemning the YMCA attack, claiming that it sought to preserve the "historic patriotic Islamic-Christian relationship in Palestine," and that the attack served Israel's "agenda." This did little to placate the fears of local Christians, living mainly in the Sheikh Radwan, Zeitun, and al-Daraj neighborhoods of Gaza City.

In May of the same year, unidentified gunmen bombed another Christian institution in Gaza, the Rosary Sister's school. No one was hurt and only minor damagers were reported, but the message was clear. As one Gaza Christian lamented, "the Islamic revival has brought intolerance in its wake."

It was not necessarily easy being a Muslim in the Gaza Strip after the June coup, either. Some 1,000 people, almost all members of Fatah and the PA, were illegally arrested m the first months of Hamas rule by the Executive Force (EF) and the al-Qassam Brigades. They were detained in 23 different locations, according to Amnesty International.

One Palestinian news agency reported that the leader of the EF, Jamal Jarrah, admitted to the use of torture and violence against Hamas's political enemies. Jarrah stated in August that torture occurred in Hamas prisons but that the EF was trying "to minimize violations and avoid them through the training of our members." In response to reports alleging that more than 100 Fatah members were languishing in Hamas jails, Jarrah stated that "if there are, they are there for criminal reasons and not on a political background [sic]."

The allegations of torture continued, however. In September, the EF reportedly abducted five Fatah men who were then transferred for treatment in a Gaza hospital, where evidence of torture was reported. PCHR began to document Hamas torture on its Web site, citing Fatah members who "sustained fractures to the feet" as a result of beatings with sticks. In other instances, Fatah men were "handcuffed and blindfolded" and had pieces of cloth stuffed in their mouths to stifle their screams.

The new rulers of Gaza also abducted and held a number of PA officials without stated cause. In some cases, those victims had held high-profile political positions. In July, for example, Hamas arrested the director of Gaza's electricity company, who was held without charges until December. In August, Hamas also arrested the manager of a bank for no stated reason. In some cases, Fatah leaders were abducted and intimidated in an attempt to persuade the group to cease its challenge to Hamas rule. For example, in January 2008, Hamas abducted one Fatah leader who was later returned to his home without the hair on his head or his mustache. In May, human rights groups noted that Hamas gunmen had illegally detained the governor of Khan Younis in southern Gaza, along with three Fatah activists.

In many cases, the de facto Hamas Interior Ministry in the Gaza Strip justified these arrests as part of its efforts to dismantle networks of "collaborators." As Hamas explained, these were people allegedly hired by Israel to snoop around or even carry out anti-Hamas activities. However, labeling its enemies as "collaborators" was the easiest way for Hamas to detain its Fatah foes, since no proof of their activities was required.

Hamas also took over former government buildings and "nationalized" them. In February 2008, gunmen claiming to be from the Hamas interior ministry forcibly took over the Financial and Administrative Control Bureau offices in Gaza. Two months later, unidentified gunmen set a Fatah building ablaze.

For Gazans who had their rights trampled, there was no redress. According to Amnesty International, Abbas's decision to freeze the salaries of the judiciary in Gaza as punishment for the Hamas coup opened up this legal vacuum. Haniyeh responded by filling the legal void with his own personnel. But by January 2008, only four judges had been appointed.

Shari'a courts became the primary arbiters of disputes in Gaza. These courts, presided over by Hamas-appointed judges, did not adjudicate cases on their legal merit but rather through the prism of Islamic jurisprudence. As Amnesty International noted, the judicial replacements lacked "adequate independence, impartiality, training, oversight, and public accountability." Rights groups were further alarmed when Hamas also created "Palestine Islamic Scholars Association" branches in every district across Gaza. These quasi-legal entities employed up to eight religious scholars per branch but lacked trained legal professionals.

The rulings from these Islamic courts caused further alarm. In one example, two university students reportedly were taken to court in November for "having a romance." The court tried to force them to marry, but the families, which were feuding, refused. In the end, the court "ordered the woman's family to keep her at home and her boyfriend to leave the city for a year."

Those Palestinians who challenged the ad hoc judiciary also paid the price. The al–Qassam Brigades reportedly seized legal papers from a lawyer that attempted to document the confiscation of a car by Hamas. The militiamen ripped the lawyer's affidavit from his hands at gunpoint. According to the *Jerusalem Post,* the Fatah-allied Palestinian chief prosecutor, Ahmed Mughami, was assaulted by Hamas, which alleged that he had "smuggled very important and dangerous information" and had broken the law. Human and legal rights groups documented these and other incidents, but they had no way to resolve them.

Those who held demonstrations against the lack of law in Gaza also suffered. According to the al–Jazeera Web site, two months after the coup the EF beat peaceful Fatah demonstrators who chanted "What is happening in Gaza is not acceptable" and "What has happened to security and human rights?" According to one journalist in Gaza, "Cameramen recording the protest were not allowed to film, or [to] get out of their cars."

In August, Hamas banned unlicensed demonstrations by the Fatah party, citing Islamic law as its basis. According to a Hamas spokesman, the demonstrations were "being used to create chaos and terrorism." In response, Fatah leaders found their own Islamic scholars to issue a ruling against the religious edict so that Fatah could hold open-air prayers on Friday, the Muslim sabbath.

Hamas's apprehension over the prayers was understandable; these gatherings often turned into angry demonstrations against Hamas rule. It was suggested that Fatah even recruited for these gatherings by tempting each attendee with a prepaid phone card worth approximately $50. Once under way, demonstrations often turned violent, particularly when Hamas security forces began forcefully dispersing the crowd, firing in the air, or beating demonstrators and reporters. Associated Press television documented other abuses when it broadcast images of Hamas men beating an unarmed protester with long sticks. In some cases, according to Amnesty International, Hamas forces deliberately shot unarmed demonstrators. In two specific cases, Palestinians were shot and killed while trying to help other demonstrators who were injured.

It is also interesting to note that when Hamas threw rocks at Israelis during the 1987 and 2000 uprisings, the group called this "resistance"; when-Palestinian protestors threw stones at Hamas, the new rulers of Gaza called them "outlaws" and arrested them. Once when Fatah supporters threw stones at police, the Hamas forces opened fire with live rounds rather than rubber bullets or tear gas, as the Israelis usually did. Seven people were killed in those clashes, including a young boy, and dozens were wounded.

In one anti-Hamas rally in November 2007, a group of female Fatah protestors gathered in front of a Gaza police station controlled by Hamas, chanting "Shi'a, Shi'a, Shi'a!" This was a bold and audacious reference to the fact that Hamas was receiving funds from Iran. Unwilling to be insulted, Hamas police attacked the girls and beat some with batons, according to *The Times* of London.

In early January 2008, Hamas violence against Fatah demonstrations reached its zenith. Seven Palestinians were killed and 40 were wounded after a firefight erupted just outside of a mosque in the southern Gaza town of Khan Younis. Hamas alleged that Fatah supporters instigated the clash by firing on worshippers leaving their prayers. The fighting soon spread to other areas around the Gaza Strip. Pro-Fatah rallies were held across Gaza the next day to mark the group's 43rd anniversary. Tensions ran high, marked by blistering verbal attacks, but no violence was reported.

Sadly, there were indications that the Hamas–Fatah rivalry even had made its way to the schoolyard. The *Observer* newspaper in Britain reported that Hamas EF members were intimidating children who wore a Fatah *keffiyeh* and, in some cases, beating them.

According to one Fatah intelligence operative, Fatah welcomed Hamas brutality to some extent. Indeed, it began to view its role in the Gaza Strip as one of provocateur in order to "weaken the Islamists in the eyes of the public." Demonstrations that ultimately ended in violence, the operative explained, helped Fatah in the battle for popular support on the Palestinian street.

Most of the violence, however, went largely unnoticed in the West. One rare but shocking report in the *New York Times* in April 2008 documented Hamas brutality against Fatah activists at al–Azhar University, in which one woman was struck in the leg with an ax.

Hamas understood that attacking its own citizens would not engender goodwill in Gaza or around the world. Therefore, it worked assiduously to cover its own tracks. As journalist Khaled Abu Toameh reported, the EF soon prevented, for a short period, the distribution of three Fatah newspapers, including the *al–Ayyam* and *al–Hayat al–Jadida* dailies, in the Gaza Strip. This is the first time that West Bank newspapers were barred from the Gaza Strip. Hamas even took some of the circulation officials of the papers into custody for a short time. The EF closed a pro-Fatah television station and radio station. In fact, by late summer, Hamas controlled all electronic media in Gaza, except one radio station linked to the Palestinian Islamic Jihad, another Iran–backed terrorist organization.

The Palestinian media were not the only ones subject to Hamas restrictions. According to the al–Jazeera Web site, Hamas attacked two cameramen from the Abu Dhabi satellite television channel in August and stormed the Gaza bureau of the al–Arabiya satellite channel. The EF also detained a German television crew in November after they shot footage in the Gaza town of Khan Younis. In February 2008, Hamas halted the publication of *al–Ayyam* again after it published a cartoon that lampooned Haniyeh.

To control the reporting out of Gaza, Hamas began to issue government press cards to journalists. Predictably, journalists whom Hamas did not like did not receive credentials. The Palestinian Journalists Syndicate protested that the tactic threatened journalists and prevented them from doing their jobs. The syndicate alleged that under the Hamas government's draconian rules, phrases such as "Hamas militias" and "ousted government" were banned. Hamas also announced it would ban stories that did not support "national responsibilities" or those that would "cause harm to national unity."

The more journalists complained, the more difficult Hamas made it for them. The Union of Palestinian Journalists reported that after a series of threats, Hamas forces raided the home of one journalist, Hisham Saqalla. The union further noted that its ranks had been threatened and blackmailed by Hamas on a daily basis. The Foreign Press Association confirmed these reports, claiming Hamas had engaged in "harassment of Palestinian journalists in Gaza." In one example, Hamas prevented journalists from attending a sit-in to protest the fact that the EF was holding two reporters. Hamas warned that anyone who attended the sit-in would be arrested.

Within just months of the June coup, international nongovernmental organizations documented more than 9 assaults on journalists by Hamas and 21 illegal arrests. Reporters Without Borders, an international media watchdog group, noted that Hamas "failed to investigate" these incidents. In May 2008, press reports indicated that Hamas would begin to block websites deemed "unfit according to Islamic rules," raising new concerns over the lack of media freedom under Hamas rule.

By the end of summer 2007, Gaza residents were growing restless. One article in *ash–Sharq al–Awsat,* a London-based newspaper, entitled "Hamas: A Lawless Authority," noted that Gazans openly expressed the fact that they felt "miserable and suffocated" under Hamas rule. The article stated that "law is absent as a result of a paralysis in the legislative tools—all of which have been replaced by Hamas's Executive Force." Gaza was suffering from an "unprecedented paralysis" in nearly every sector of society.

Due to Israel's sanctions against the Hamas government, stores in Gaza were out of many products, and hospitals ran low on crucial supplies, including anesthetics and antibiotics. Seeking to avert a humanitarian crisis, the Israelis eventually allowed certain medical supplies into Gaza but vowed to withhold other nonessentials. Israel's plans for sanctions against Gaza, approved in October 2007, also included the disruption of fuel supplies. Predictably, Hamas dubbed these sanctions a "crime" against the Palestinians. Ban Ki–Moon, the UN's secretary general, also weighed in, saying that cutting off energy from Gaza was unfair punishment. The rationale behind Israel's sanctions, however, stemmed from the realization among Israeli decision makers that if Israel allowed goods to flow through Gaza, it would be providing assistance to its enemy.

Several leftist Israeli organizations attempted to thwart the Israeli measures and appealed to the Israeli Supreme Court to allow fuel, in particular, to flow back into Gaza. The Court denied the motion in January 2008, but the activists vowed to appeal. Israel soon made public its plans for punitive disruptions of electricity in response to Qassam missile attacks out of Gaza, with plans for longer cutoffs, or even permanent cessations, in the future. In an attempt to stave off these punitive measures, Hamas admitted on its Web site that "not every Palestinian who lives in [the Gaza Strip] fires Qassam rockets or even support[s] firing the Qassam rockets."

But Hamas could not blame Israel for all that Gaza was forced to endure. After the coup, numerous newspaper stories documented a repeat of the "sewage tsunami." As a result of Hamas mismanagement, several Gaza sewer pipes burst, which flooded homes and businesses with a foul river of waste that was several yards high. Gazans were infuriated when it was learned that the Israeli-made pipes that were Intended to repair Gaza's decrepit sewage system had been sold to Hamas but used to assemble Qassam missiles and bunkers.

The most anger, however, likely stemmed from the Hamas government's decision to raise taxes on cigarettes. A very large percentage of Palestinians in Gaza smoke (exact numbers are unavailable), and many were said to be "fuming." Lucky Strikes used to cost 10 shekels ($2.50) per pack. After Hamas came to power, the same pack of cigarettes cost 16 or 17 ($4.00 or $4.25) shekels. Reports just a few months later indicated that other American cigarettes could cost Gazans upward of 40 shekels per pack ($10.00). With a faltering economy that was squeezed tighter by sanctions, and most Gazans living below the poverty line, residents could scarcely afford to smoke.

The nicotine withdrawal that many Gazans were experiencing did not help Hamas popularity. Some residents turned to locally grown tobacco and rolling papers but were clearly unhappy about it. As one smoker said, "I roll my cigarettes, and seal them with my mouth, and before I close my lips, I spit on Hamas and Fatah that are squabbling between them for their own interests."

In fact, by December 2007, Gazans were complaining that even the simplest pleasures were hard to find. The goods that Israel barred from entering Gaza included batteries, tobacco, coffee, gasoline, diesel, and even chocolate. Even some locally grown goods were hard to come by. For example, the price of chicken had doubled. Concurrently, there was a surplus in goods such as strawberries, which helped feed the Gaza population. However, whatever was not eaten was left to rot, due to the Israeli blockade on goods coming out of Gaza.

One *Haaretz* story noted that a 15-year-old became an instant celebrity at her Gaza school because her father gave her a can of Coca–Cola that he had purchased abroad. The children in the class all wanted to be photographed with the girl and her can, since carbonated drinks were nearly impossible to purchase inside Gaza.

By January 2008, according to journalist reports and Hamas spokesmen, some 50 to 80 percent of the Gaza population was unemployed, thousands of factories were shut down, and as many as 85 percent of Gazans were living below the poverty line. In less than a year, Hamas had effectively destroyed the small steps the PA had taken in the Gaza Strip, largely with U.S. aid, to make the territory bearable for its people.

Fatah's West Bank

As the Gaza Strip fell into turmoil, Mahmoud Abbas had problems of his own in the West Bank. After the Hamas takeover, the Fatah-backed Palestinian Authority was an emergency government that ruled over the West Bank only, and it had not even been elected. Indeed, the new cabinet, headed by Salaam Fayyad, was a stopgap measure. Moreover, the June Hamas coup in Gaza had thoroughly demoralized the once-dominant Palestinian faction.

Abbas and Fayyad clung to power in Ramallah even as some of their longtime colleagues appeared to have abandoned hope. Senior Fatah leaders such as Nabil Shaath, Mohammed Dahlan, and Hassan Asfour, all formerly powerful ministers in the PA, retreated to Cairo with their families and their wealth. There was even talk that several Fatah leaders had absconded with some $2 billion of Yasir Arafat's hoarded funds after the guerrilla leader's death in November 2004. Analysts questioned whether Fatah would hold a congress in 2008, due to questions about the faction's viability. As one observer quipped, Abbas was "no more than the president of the Muqata compound in Ramallah."

The series of blows that Fatah had endured in 2006 and 2007 prompted Abbas's supporters in Israel and the West to question whether Fatah and the PA could survive in the West Bank. Indeed, as the Hamas Executive Force and the Qassam Brigades built fortified military positions throughout the Gaza Strip in preparation for the next military encounter, questions arose over whether the PA could control West Bank security. Some of the elite PA forces had capitulated immediately to Hamas's more zealous and motivated troops; some, as noted earlier, did not even put up a fight.

It stood to reason, then, that this weakness and lack of will was pervasive throughout the once-formidable PA security apparatus.

Hamas also sensed this vulnerability and sought to exploit it. The Gaza-based Islamists taunted Abbas in late October 2007, saying that "in the autumn, the leaves fall and Abbas will fall." The following month, Mahmoud al-Zahar, the architect of the Hamas military coup, threatened that "what happened in Gaza will also come to the West Bank." He further taunted his Palestinian rivals by saying that his organization "took over Gaza because Fatah is weak and the corrupted ones. They are not trusted. We won twice, once with elections and once again through our Gaza takeover in June."

The West, particularly U.S. president George W. Bush, realized that in order to halt the spread of Hamas rule to the West Bank, Fatah would need an infusion of both funds and weapons. Thus, when it became apparent that Abbas still maintained a modicum of control over the West Bank after the guns in Gaza fell silent, Washington lifted its embargo on direct aid to the Palestinian Authority government (imposed after the Hamas electoral victory). Both Israel and the European Union also joined the United States in an expression of support for a moderate West Bank.

By supporting the decimated Fatah organization when it needed it the most, Israel and America likely realized that they might be able to exact concessions for an Israeli–Palestinian peace deal once Abbas returned to a position of strength. Thus began the flood of aid to the PA in the West Bank.

The West certainly did not believe that Fatah was a party of reformers and democrats. Rather, most world leaders viewed Fatah as the less aggressive of the two warring factions. Since there were no other dominant factions, the West had to back one of them.

On June 18, the U.S. secretary of state, Condoleezza Rice, appeared before a crew of cameras at the State Department and read carefully from a script. Rice announced that up to $86 million in U.S. aid that been previously slated to aid the PA's security forces against Hamas would be redirected to ensure the continued viability of a Fatah-controlled Palestinian government in the West Bank. President Bush followed up in October by announcing a sixfold increase in aid promised to the Palestinians. He allotted $435 million in aid to the PA in addition to the funds earmarked earlier in 2007, The funds were slated for stronger security capabilities but also to avert a possible financial crisis that would send the West Bank into a meltdown.

Abbas appealed to the international community for even more funds. Indeed, international donors promised a total of $7.4 billion through 2010, which amounted to nearly double the traditional combined PA budget for both Gaza and the West Bank. As one analyst noted, the West Bank had not necessarily become stronger. Rather, it had become an "international ward," which did little for its legitimacy.

After a Paris donors' conference in December, the international community continued to promise cash infusions to the PA. Predictably, Hamas spokesman Fawzi Barhum condemned the conference as a "dangerous conspiracy" to divide the Palestinians. He charged that Abbas was "cozying up to the Zionist enemy and the American project in exchange for millions of dollars to strengthen his security forces for his own personal interests."

The most surprising pledges came from Israeli Prime Minister Ehud Olmert, who announced that he would allow Palestinian security forces in the West Bank town of Nablus to receive 25 armored vehicles from the Israeli defense industry along with 1,000 rifles and 2 million rounds of ammunition. The move was shocking in that it was a reversal of Israel Defense Forces policy. Indeed, the Israelis had withheld military materiel from the PA for seven years, after Israel discovered that the copious amounts of rifles and bullets it had provided the PA during the Oslo years for internal Palestinian security purposes were used against it during the al–Aqsa intifada beginning in September 2000.

Olmert's decision was also shocking given Israel's lack of confidence in the long-term viability of Abbas's government. Notably, Likud party politician Benjamin Netanyahu predicted that the new vehicles and weapons Olmert had pledged would also "eventually fall into the hands of Hamas." After all, Hamas inherited a windfall of weaponry after it sacked PA strongholds the Gaza Strip, creating a security crisis for Israel.

The Israelis soon began to question the logic of providing the PA with weapons. In March 2008, Israeli Defense Minister Ehud Barak openly challenged General James Jones, the U.S. Special Envoy, over the need to provide the PA with armored vehicles and weaponry. The fear, he stated, was that Hamas could conquer the West Bank, as it did Gaza, and reap another weapons windfall.

With numerous financial promises in place, Fatah set out to get even with its Hamas rivals in the West Bank. The Fatah-controlled Palestinian security services had rounded up hundreds of known Hamas activists throughout the West Bank as the June fighting raged in Gaza. In one naked act of retribution, masked Fatah gunmen kidnapped Ahmed al–Khaldi, the justice minister of the former Hamas government, as he left a mosque in Nablus. It was not known whether Abbas or any of the PA leadership was involved in that kidnapping or the scores of other reported around the West Bank.

Abbas was, however, directly responsible for dismantling a number of Hamas-controlled city councils (including the one in Nablus) via decree, and he ordered a full review of all charities and businesses tied to Hamas in the West Bank. Some Hamas-run charities, businesses, and political offices were set ablaze before the review even was launched. More than 100 charities were initially closed. In less than one year, some 200 were shut down. Others reportedly have sought to deemphasize their ties to Hamas for fear of being dismantled by PA forces.

In the weeks and months after the coup, numerous media reports confirmed that the Fatah-affiliated Palestinian security forces were working with Israeli security services to arrest or assassinate Hamas members throughout the West Bank. One human rights organization reported that approximately 600 suspected Hamas members had been arrested in the West Bank between June and October 2007. Amnesty International estimated that the figure was closer to 1,000.

Roundups continued into the fall as PA security forces confiscated weapons, set up roadblocks throughout the West Bank, and even fired radical imams (mosque prayer leaders) who supported Hamas. The Saudi *Arab News* also reported in October that Fatah had raided several mosques in the West Bank, confiscating print material produced by Hamas. PA security forces also monitored imams' sermons in West Bank mosques. One rights group alleged that PA security was using "the same practices on Hamas detainees that Hamas is using on Fatah detainees in Gaza." In one example, a Hamas activist was reportedly yanked out of bed in the middle of the night and dragged to a Hebron prison, where he was beaten while hooded and handcuffed. Arrests continued in to the summer of 2008. Palestinians began to wonder whether the Fatah-backed PA was any less brutal than Hamas in Gaza.

Fatah also engaged in heavy-handed press restrictions. PA officials lobbied Egypt to stop airing the Hamas-sponsored al–Aqsa television channel on the state-owned Nilesat satellite system. After Egypt refused, the PA's security services arrested numerous nonviolent members of Hamas, including journalists from the Hamas-sponsored al–Aqsa television channel. PA police also arrested the director of the Amal television channel, which is not affiliated with Hamas but had aired a speech by Hamas's political leader in Gaza, Ismael Haniyeh, which the police said was "illegal." PA police also briefly detained two Hamas officials in November for attempting to hold a press conference in Ramallah.

In December, after the PA shuttered additional West Bank charities in an effort to constrict Hamas's finances, Abbas contemplated a law that would require all political parties to reveal their funding sources and to disclose personal information about their activists. While Hamas was not named specifically, it was clear that this was yet another measure taken to weaken the organizations West Bank apparatus and to cut off funds coming in from Iran and other foreign donors.

By the end of 2007, according to Hamas sources, Abbas's forces had arrested more than 1,000 Hamas members in the West Bank. These roundups and other repressive measures almost certainly helped the Palestinian Authority gain increased control over the West Bank and protect the territory from an attack from within.

For the Israelis, Abbass successes were bittersweet. For years, the PA had claimed that the very presence of Israeli forces in the West Bank made it impossible to detain Palestinians linked to terrorist attacks. Thus, Hamas, Palestinian Islamic Jihad, and the al–Aqsa Martyrs Brigades continued to carry out suicide bombings and other attacks against Israeli civilians. Finally, with a clear interest in neutralizing Hamas, the PA accomplished what it always insisted it could not: an effective clampdown on terrorist operatives within its jurisdiction.

The PA's moderate successes against Hamas notwithstanding, in October 2007, the United States voiced misgivings over the ability of PA security forces to assume the responsibility for securing the West Bank. The PA took crucial steps to improve its military capabilities.

For example, the PA established an officer school to ensure that its senior security personnel learned vital skills. Additionally, the new Palestinian prime minister, Salaam Fayyad, shrank the PA's armed forces by one-third (from 83,000 to 50,000) as a means to save money and produce a better-armed yet more controllable force. Fayyad, a serious and cleanshaven man with glasses, was more of an accountant than a soldier. He made few friends in the security forces when he announced that personnel over the age of 45 were slated for removal, along with thousands of other men and women who were on the payroll but who never served on the force. Some old guard Fatah fighters accused Fayyad, a former official from the International Monetary Fund, of "starving our children." Fayyad responded by promising to remunerate the Fatah security personnel who were cut, but a risk remained that these former Arafat loyalists might switch sides and support Hamas in a bid to take down the Palestinian Authority in the West Bank.

There were additional concerns as well. Fatah and the PA faced an uphill challenge in bringing all of the West Bank under control. The territory is about the size of Delaware, with its estimated 2.5 million residents dispersed among almost a dozen major population centers. For some time, it was believed that the remaining Israeli military presence in the West Bank might help the PA maintain control. Questions remained, however, about security there if the Israelis turned over full control to the PA.

By late October 2007, as 3,500 PA security forces were deployed to the Hamas stronghold of Nablus, the West Bank's second largest town with a population of about 170,000, concern arose that these forces could be outgunned. Specifically, Abdullah Kmeil, the head of PA intelligence in Nablus, admitted that there was only one rifle for every ten officers. U.S. and Israeli military and financial assistance probably fixed this problem, but the crisis of confidence in the PA's military capabilities remained.

With U.S. and Israeli support, Fatah set about addressing other security concerns in the West Bank. In December, Abbas deployed an estimated 500 military personnel to the town of Tulkarem. The men set up checkpoints, searching for weapons and other contraband. In an attempt to restore authority, the PA also began to rebuild its military compounds, which had been destroyed by Israel after the outbreak of the 2000 intifada. The PA also began to pay its soldiers more money as a means to maintain loyalty. Fatah continued to shut down Hamas charities. However, due to international fears that dismantling Hamas services could spark a financial crisis among the Palestinian poor, Prime Minister Fayyad vowed to create 11 new government-approved charities to ensure continuity. In March 2008, the PA announced the creation of a new socioeconomic network—financed by the United States, Israel, the United Nations, the European Union, and Russia—to counter the Hamas *dawa* system by providing aid to some 60,000 persons in the West Bank.

The success of this program, along with continued military assistance, was seen as critical to the survival of the PA's West Bank regime. According to a senior Israeli defense official, the IDF assessed that without a significant Israeli military presence in the West Bank, "Hamas would take over the institutions and apparatuses of the Palestinian Authority within days." The Israeli newspaper *Maariv* also cited concerns that thousands of weapons and millions of bullets—many from Iran—were being smuggled into Hamas hands in the West Bank. Ironically, while Israel was fending off Hamas advances into the West Bank, the PA occasionally tried—and even sentenced to death—West Bank Palestinians for collaborating with Israel. This only contributed to the sense among Israeli and American policymakers that the PA lacked an understanding of its own security predicament.

Washington and Jerusalem, in their bid to save the PA, shared fears about possible Hamas infrastructure lying dormant in the West Bank. Specifically, questions arose over the possibility that Hamas's broad social welfare infrastructure could be used for military advantage. The PA continued to break up Hamas cells; it reportedly arrested some 250 operatives in the West Bank in the first days of January 2008. But finding every fighter was virtually impossible. In early February, one West Bank-based Hamas member made his way into Israel and detonated a suicide belt, killing himself and an Israeli woman while wounding 11 other Israelis. Hamas's cell structure had eluded Israeli forces during both intifadas; it was not hard to imagine that Hamas could continue to survive underground in the West Bank until it could attempt another coup.

Abbas repeatedly expressed public concerns that Hamas already had plans to overtake the Palestinian Authority in the West Bank. He stated that Hamas would try to overthrow him with the help of outside parties, including Iran, Syria, and even Qatar. He continued to order the arrest of Hamas members throughout the West Bank. One arrest led to the controversial death in February 2008 of Hamas member Majed Bargouthi, a West Bank mosque preacher and father of eight, who died in a PA prison. Hamas alleged that Bargouthi had been tortured, sparking an outcry among Hamas members who claimed the PA was engaged in "factional cleansing."

In March, after the February 13 assassination of Hizbullah operations chief Imad Mughniyeh in Damascus, Syria, a senior Palestinian official stated that he believed that Hizbullah was becoming more active in the West Bank, making PA security increasingly complicated. The PA continued to push for more weapons and faster progress with Israel on a final status peace agreement, as a means to solidify power. In April, Palestinian spokesman Saeb Erekat warned that Abbas's government would disappear if peace was not reached.

In early May, the first class of Palestinian security officers trained under a multi-million dollar U.S. program designed to bolster the PA hit the streets of the West Bank. The training had been characterized by numerous difficulties. In fact, one official called the training "a fiasco." With memories of the al–Aqsa intifada lingering, the very sight of trained Fatah men elicited anxiety among Israel's military brass. In mid-May, the IDF rejected U.S. requests to arm the PA forces with personal armor, night vision goggles, and electronic communications.

The PA's need for better equipment became increasingly apparent. Even amid the continued security crackdowns, Hamas occasionally demonstrated its strength. For example, Hamas created chaos in a West Bank refugee camp in May 2008. Fatah claimed that Hamas attacked a Fatah rally, and ransacked the home of a Fatah official.

Fatah's manifold security weaknesses were only part of the problem. Palestinians had simply lost confidence in the long-time leading Palestinian organization. Allegations of corruption continued to haunt Fatah. It was widely believed that Ahmed Qureia, a former PA prime minister, had deposited $3 million in PA funds into his own account. He also battled allegations that his family-owned cement factory was supplying concrete for the construction of the Israeli security barrier, as well as for new homes in Jewish settlements in the West Bank. The PA was further forced to fend off Hamas accusations that it was selling Palestinian land to foreigners.

Given Fatah's struggles, its ability to control the West Bank was far from clear by the summer of 2008. Still, a few factors indicated that the PA might survive, including:

1. Abbas was prepared for a possible coup attempt, and his forces were on guard for a Hamas attack. This had not been the case in June 2007.
2. Abbas enlisted the help of the United States and Israel to protect the PA from a Hamas takeover.
3. It would be considerably more difficult for Hamas to operate in the West Bank if the people there truly did not want Hamas to remain. In light of the turmoil in Gaza, it appeared that West Bankers preferred the status quo.

Captives: Letter from Gaza

from The New Yorker

By Lawrence Wright

In southwest Israel, at the border of Egypt and the Gaza Strip, there is a small crossing station not far from a kibbutz named Kerem Shalom. A guard tower looms over the flat, scrubby buffer zone. Gaza never extends more than seven miles wide, and the guards in the tower can see the Mediterranean Sea, to the north. The main street in Gaza, Salah El–Deen Road, runs along the entire twenty-five-mile span of the territory, and on a clear night the guards can watch a car make the slow journey from the ruins of the Yasir Arafat International Airport, near the Egyptian border, toward the lights of Gaza City, on the Strip's northeastern side. Observation balloons hover just outside Gaza, and pilotless drones freely cross its airspace. Israeli patrols tightly enforce a three-mile limit in the Mediterranean and fire on boats that approach the line. Between the sea and the security fence that surrounds the hundred and forty square miles of Gaza live a million and a half Palestinians.

Every opportunity for peace in the Middle East has been led to slaughter, and at this isolated desert crossing, on June 25, 2006, another moment of promise culminated in bloodshed. The year had begun with tumult. That January, Hamas, which the U.S. government considers a terrorist group, won Palestine's parliamentary elections, defeating the more moderate Fatah

Party. Both parties sent armed partisans into the streets, and Gaza verged on civil war. Then, on June 9th, a tentative truce between Hamas and Israel ended after an explosion on a beach near Gaza City, apparently caused by an Israeli artillery shell, killed seven members of a Palestinian family, who were picnicking. (The Israelis deny responsibility.) Hamas fired fifteen rockets into Israel the next day. The Israelis then launched air strikes into Gaza for several days, killing eight militants and fourteen civilians, including five children.

Amid this strife, Mahmoud Abbas—the head of Fatah, and the President of the Palestinian Authority, the governing body established by the Oslo peace accords of 1993—put forward a bold idea. The people of Palestine, he declared, should be given the chance to vote on a referendum for a two-state solution to its conflict with Israel. Perhaps it was a cynical political maneuver, as the leaders of Hamas believed. The fundamental platform of Hamas was its refusal to accept Israel's right to exist, yet polls showed that Palestinians overwhelmingly supported the concept of two states. A referendum would be not only a rebuke to Hamas; it also would be a signal to Israel—and to the rest of the world—that Palestinians were determined to make peace. Abbas set the referendum for July.

Just before dawn on June 25th, eight Palestinian commandos crawled out of a tunnel into a grove of trees in Kerem Shalom. A new moon was in the sky, making it the darkest night of the month. With mortar fire and anti-tank missiles providing cover, the commandos, some of them disguised in Israeli military uniforms, split into three teams. One team attacked an empty armored personnel carrier, which had been parked at the crossing as a decoy. Another team hit the observation tower. The two Israelis in the tower were injured, but not before they killed two of the attackers.

The third team shot a rocket-propelled grenade into a Merkava tank that was parked on a berm facing the security fence. The explosion shook the tank; then its rear hatch opened and three soldiers tried to flee. Two of them were shot and killed, but a third, lightly wounded, was captured. The attackers raced back into Gaza with their prize: a lanky teenager named Gilad Shalit.

Within days, the Israel Defense Forces, or I.D.F., had bombed the only power station in Gaza, cutting off electricity to tens of thousands of people. The borders were shut down as Israeli troops searched residential areas for Shalit, rounding up males older than sixteen. On June 29th, Israeli officials arrested sixty-four senior Palestinian officials, including a third of the Palestinian cabinet and twenty members of parliament. At least four hundred Gazans were killed over the next several months, including eighty-eight children. The Israelis lost six soldiers and four civilians. Israeli authorities promised not to leave the Strip until they recovered Shalit, but by November he still had not been found, and both sides declared a ceasefire. Nothing had been resolved. Another explosion was sure to come. Certainly, no one was talking about peace initiatives any longer, and that may well have been the goal of those who captured Shalit.

From the Israeli perspective, at least, the Gaza problem was supposed to have been solved in August, 2005, when Ariel Sharon, then the Prime Minister, closed down the Jewish settlements on the Strip and withdrew Israeli forces. The international community and the Israeli left wing applauded the move. But, almost immediately, mortar and rocket attacks from the Strip multiplied. Five months later, Hamas won its parliament victory. Ari Shavit, a prominent columnist for the Israeli newspaper *Haaretz*, told me recently in Jerusalem, "We dismantled the settlements, and then we sat back and said, 'Let's have a new beginning.' What we got was rockets and Gilad Shalit. People became very angry, and Shalit becomes an icon of that frustration."

We were sitting in Restobar, a noisy café in downtown Jerusalem. Nearby, Shalit's parents and supporters maintain a tent; from this makeshift office, they lobby for Israel to release hundreds of Palestinian prisoners and detainees in exchange for Shalit's freedom. Shalit had just graduated from high school when he began his compulsory military service. His father, Noam, has described him as "a shy boy with a nervous smile and a studious disposition," who loved basketball and excelled in physics. Two weeks after Shalit was captured, Hezbollah abducted two other Israeli soldiers, sparking thirty-four days of war in South Lebanon. In that instance, the captured soldiers were already dead; after the war, their remains were returned to Israel, in exchange for five Lebanese prisoners and the remains of hundreds of fighters. But Shalit is presumed to be alive, and his plight has driven Israel slightly mad. There are demonstrations, bumper stickers, and petition drives demanding his freedom. On Web sites and in newspapers, counters chronicle how long Shalit has been in captivity. "Israel is obsessed with Gilad Shalit in a way that no other nation in history has been obsessed with a prisoner of war," Shavit said.

Gaza is a place that Israel wishes it could ignore: the territory has long had the highest concentration of poverty, extremism, and hopelessness in the region. Gaza makes a mess of the idealized two-state solution because it is separated from the West Bank, the much larger Palestinian territory, not just physically but also culturally and politically. In 2005, the RAND Corporation proposed integrating a future Palestinian state with a high-speed rail and highway system that would connect the West Bank and Gaza. Former President Jimmy Carter told me that, in 2005, he and Ariel Sharon had agreed to promote a land swap between the Israelis and the Palestinians that would provide a corridor between the two halves of Palestine.

Such potential solutions have been poisoned by the frustration that both Israelis and West Bankers feel toward Gaza. The political distance between the two Palestinian entities has caused many Israelis to start talking of a three-state solution, rather than two. "Hamas in Gaza is a fact of life until further notice," Yossi Alpher, a political consultant and a former Mossad officer, observed. "All our ideas about dealing with them have failed." Shavit and other Israeli intellectuals have proposed that the Egyptians deed a portion of the Sinai to Gaza, to make the Strip more viable—"a semi-Dubai," as Shavit terms it. The Egyptians have expressed no interest. "Egypt's strategy for Gaza is to make sure it's Israel's problem," Alpher said.

Hamas, which was founded in Gaza during the intifada of 1987, has come to embody the fears that many Israelis hold about the Palestinians. Its charter declares, "There is no solution to the Palestinian problem except by jihad." The document, which is in many respects absurd and reflects the intellectual isolation and conspiracy-fed atmosphere in Gaza at the time, cites the "Protocols of the Elders of Zion," the anti-Semitic forgery, and links Zionism to the Freemasons, the Lions Club, and "other spying groups" that aim "to violate consciences, to defeat virtues, and to annihilate Islam." Part of the paradox of this conflict is that many Palestinians who firmly embrace the two-state solution have voted for Hamas.

In Restobar, Shavit pointed to a spot a few feet away. "In March, 2002, there was a beautiful twenty-five-year-old girl dead on the floor, right there," he said. A suicide bomber had targeted the café, which was then called Moment. That month, eighty-three Israeli civilians were killed by Palestinians. Jerusalem was in a panic. Shavit was living nearby at the time, and on the night of March 9th he heard the bomb explode.

Running to the café, he saw mutilated bodies scattered on the sidewalk. People had been blown across the street. The dead girl was lying near the doorway. Inside, at the bar, three young men were sitting upright on the stools, but they were all dead. "It was as if they were still drinking their beers," Shavit recalled. Eleven Israelis died, and more than fifty were injured. Hamas proclaimed it a "brave attack" intended to "avenge the Israeli massacres against our people."

The Hamas attacks derailed the peace process initiated by the Oslo accords and hardened many Israelis against the Palestinian cause. Photographs of Gazans celebrating the Moment bombing confirmed the dehumanized state of affairs. Gaza became "Hamastan" in the Israeli newspapers. In 2007, after Hamas solidified its control of Gaza, the Israeli government declared Gaza a "hostile entity," and began enforcing a blockade on a population that was already impoverished, isolated, and traumatized by years of occupation.

Hamas was not weakened by the blockade. Instead, the collective punishment strengthened its argument that Israel wanted to eliminate the Palestinians. The only thing that Gaza has that Israel wants is Gilad Shalit, but Hamas says that it will not free him until Israel releases fourteen hundred individuals, four hundred and fifty of whom have been convicted of terrorist killings, including the men who planned the Moment bombing.

On June 25, 2007, several days after Hamas took over in Gaza, the captors of Gilad Shalit released an audio recording to prove that he was still alive. "It has been a year since I was captured and my health is deteriorating," he said. "I am in need of prolonged hospitalization." He urged the Israeli government to accept Hamas's demands for his release: "Just as I have a mother and father, the thousands of Palestinian prisoners also have mothers and fathers—and their children must be returned to them."

Gaza is a sea of children. The average woman there has 5.1 children, one of the highest birth rates in the world. More than half the population is eighteen or younger. "We love to reproduce," Khalil al-Hayya, a senior Hamas official, told me on a searingly hot July day, as hundreds of young boys in green caps shouted slogans at a Hamas summer camp. Hayya, a former professor of

Islamic law, has six children; a seventh was killed by an Israeli bomb.

There is very little for children to do in Gaza. The Israeli blockade includes a ban on toys, so the only playthings available have been smuggled, at a premium, through tunnels from Egypt. Islamists have shut down all the movie theatres. Music is rare, except at weddings. Many of Gaza's sports facilities have been destroyed by Israeli bombings, including the headquarters for the Palestinian Olympic team. Only one television station broadcasts from Gaza, Al Aqsa—a Hamas-backed channel that gained notice last year for a children's show featuring a Mickey Mouse-like figure who was stabbed to death by an Israeli interrogator. The mouse was replaced by a talking bee, who died after being unable to cross into Egypt for medical treatment. The rabbit who followed the bee passed away in January, after being struck by shrapnel from an Israeli attack.

The main diversion for children is the beach, and on Fridays, after noon prayers, the shore is massed with families. Unlike the topaz waters off Tel Aviv, here the sea is murky, a consequence of twenty million gallons of raw and partially treated sewage that is dumped offshore every day. The main water-treatment plant is broken, and because of the blockade the spare parts that would fix it are unavailable. Fishermen with nets wade into the surf as kids romp in the stinking waves.

Israeli authorities maintain a list of about three dozen items that they permit into Gaza, but the list is closely kept and subject to change. Almost no construction materials—such as cement, glass, steel, or plastic pipe—have been allowed in, on the ground that such items could be used for building rockets or bunkers. While Hamas rocket builders and bomb-makers can smuggle everything they need through the secret tunnels, international aid organizations have to account for every brick or sack of flour. Operation Cast Lead—a three-week-long Israeli attack on Gaza, which began in December, 2008—has left Gaza in ruins. "Half a year after the conflict, we don't have a single bag of cement and not a pane of glass," John Ging, the director of the United Nations Relief and Works Agency for Palestinian refugees, told me in July.

(Later that month, Israeli authorities announced that they would allow the U.N.R.W.A. a limited amount of steel and cement. Ging says that that has yet to happen.) Humanitarian supplies that suddenly have been struck from Israel's list of approved items pile up in large storage warehouses outside the Kerem Shalom crossing, and international aid worth billions of dollars awaits delivery. "For the last two school years, Israeli officials have withheld paper for textbooks because, hypothetically, the paper might be hijacked by Hamas to print seditious materials," Ging complained. (Paper was finally delivered this fall.) When John Kerry, the chairman of the Senate Foreign Relations Committee, visited Gaza in February of this year, he asked why pasta wasn't allowed in. Soon, macaroni was passing through the checkpoints, but jam was taken off the list. According to *Haaretz*, the I.D.F. has calculated that a hundred and six truckloads of humanitarian relief are needed every day to sustain life for a million and a half people. But the number of trucks coming into Gaza has fallen as low as thirty-seven. Israeli government officials have told international aid officials that the aim is "no prosperity, no development, no humanitarian crisis."

Visitors enter Gaza at its northeastern end, through the Erez Crossing—a high-security, barnlike building that is rarely congested, because scarcely any Palestinians are allowed to exit, and so few foreigners care to visit. In 2004, the first female suicide bomber for Hamas, Reem Riyashi, a twenty-two-year-old mother of two children, blew herself up there, killing four Israelis. Since then, the Israeli staff has largely been replaced by security cameras and remote-controlled gates.

In Gaza, the rocky hills of Jerusalem have been ironed into a sandy plain sparsely adorned with oleander and cactus, as in South Texas. The area near Erez used to be the region's industrial zone. Until Operation Cast Lead, there were several concrete plants, a flour mill, and an ice-cream factory, but they have all been bombed or bulldozed, and the mixing trucks for the concrete have been knocked over. Houses and mosques and shops lie in rubble; entire neighborhoods have been demolished. Israeli forces concentrated much of their fire, and their wrath, on northeast Gaza. From Erez, one can easily see Sderot, the Israeli town that has suffered the most rocket attacks.

There are eight refugee camps in Gaza, which form a society that is even more isolated that the larger gulag of the Strip. More than seventy per cent of Gazans are descendants of the two hundred thousand people who fled to the Strip in 1948, when the State of Israel was established. "I lived eighteen years of my life in a refugee camp," Ahmed Yousuf, the Deputy Foreign Minister, told me. "It was one square kilometre."

Gaza City is one of the oldest settlements in the world; it is thought to have been established by the Canaanites, around 3000 B.C. The boundaries of the modern Strip were determined after the 1949 armistice between Egypt and Israel. Gaza marked the final redoubt of the Egyptian Army, and the armistice left a ribbon of coastal land, between three and seven miles wide, in Egypt's reluctant control. British authorities, who had once administered Gaza as part of their mandate over Palestine, considered Gaza *res nullius*—nobody's property. The Egyptians administered the territory until the 1967 war, when Israel captured the entire Sinai. Israel and Egypt agreed to try to set up a Palestinian entity that would rule Gaza, but it was clear that neither party wanted responsibility for the Strip, so it remained in limbo, little more than a notional part of a Palestinian entity that might never come into existence.

Gaza's status as a ward of someone else's state changed abruptly with the 2006 elections. Fatah, long the dominant force in the two Palestinian territories, had been expected to win easily, but this underestimated popular resentment against a party that was notoriously corrupt, incompetent, and so careless that it ran several candidates for identical offices. On the ballot, Hamas called itself the List of Change and Reform, although voters knew whom they were voting for. Polls had predicted that Hamas would receive about thirty per cent of the vote; instead, it won a decisive majority in the Palestinian Legislative Council.

International organizations declared that in order for Hamas to be accepted it would have to recognize the State of Israel, renounce violence, and respect extant diplomatic agreements. Hamas rebuffed those conditions, triggering a drastic cutoff of aid. Israel was further shaken when Ariel Sharon, the Prime Minister, suffered a debilitating stroke. (He remains in a coma.) His replacement, Ehud Olmert, declared that the Palestinian government was becoming a "terrorist authority," and that the Israelis would have no contact with it.

Fatah refused to step aside and let Hamas govern. For months, there were large demonstrations by both factions in the West Bank and Gaza, along with kidnappings, gun battles, and assassinations. In March, 2007, King Abdullah of Saudi Arabia arranged a peace accord, but it was merely a prelude to open civil war in Gaza, three months later. During six bloody days in June, Hamas swept aside the American-trained Fatah security force and took over the government that it had been elected to lead the previous year.

These clashes left Palestinians wondering if the differences between their major parties could ever be resolved. The residue is particularly bitter in Gaza. "We are crowded into a very small space," Yehia Rabah, a member of Fatah and a former Ambassador to Yemen, said. "The hate doesn't dissolve very easily. We see each other every day."

Although the new Prime Minister of Gaza, Ismail Haniyeh, emphasized that Hamas had no intention of making Gaza an Islamic state, it took over the judiciary, appointing Islamist judges who impose Sharia on the court system. I was repeatedly assured by Hamas officials, such as Khalil al–Hayya, that they stood for "moderate Islam, the Islam of tolerance and justice and equality," but Gazans who are not in the Party worry. "The whole place is becoming a mosque," a young female reporter, Asma al–Ghoul, complained. She had recently been hassled on the beach by self-appointed morality police, even though she was wearing jeans and a long-sleeved shirt. Jawdat al–Khoudary, a businessman, who is a native Gazan, said that since the Hamas takeover he feels like "a refugee in my own country." An economist, Omar Shaban, said, "The siege has left Hamas with no competition. Secular people are punished. The future is frightening."

One morning, I visited a mosque where about forty teen-age boys were attending a day camp devoted to memorizing the Koran. The Islamic holy book contains more than six thousand verses—it's about the same length as the New Testament—and this summer twenty thousand boys and girls had undertaken the challenge, in camps across the Strip. At the mosque, a small crowd was waiting for the Prime Minister, who was rumored to be coming to talk to the boys. Because Haniyeh is one of the few veteran Hamas leaders in Gaza who have not been assassinated by the Israelis (although they have fired missiles into his office and his home), he's constantly on the move. I was told that his visit to the mosque was my best chance to meet him.

While the boys rocked back and forth on the carpet, reciting in low voices, I was introduced to an elderly refugee and a former member of the Palestinian Legislative Council. Bald and freckled, with a white mustache, he gave his name as Abu Majid. "On 15 May, 1948, I was twenty-two years old," he said. Israel had formally declared itself an independent nation the day before, triggering the invasion by five Arab armies bent on destroying the Zionists. Egypt moved into the Negev Desert, approaching Beersheba, where Majid lived. "The Egyptian Army asked youngsters like me to help with logistics," he said.

After one battle with the Israelis, Majid and a friend dragged several wounded soldiers inside a bunker. A dozen people were already hiding there. That night, Israeli troops discovered the shelter and ordered everyone out. "There were four old men over seventy, one of whom had a wife who was sixty or sixty-five," Majid said. "When she saw the soldiers, she began to tremble." A younger, dark-skinned woman had two boys and a girl. Upon leaving the shelter, with their hands raised, they were shot. "I don't know why I'm alive," Majid said. "The blood came on me. I was one of three who God saved. We were seven days in the desert of Negev before we reached the villages around Hebron." He had family there. His parents, believing him dead, had erected a mourning tent and were receiving condolences when a friend brought news that their son was alive. His

brother slaughtered a sheep in celebration. Majid wept at the memory, the tears streaming into his mustache. According to Benny Morris, the Israeli historian, the fall of Beersheba was marked by many atrocities on the part of the Israeli forces. "A number of civilians were executed after being stripped of valuables," he writes in "1948: A History of the First Arab–Israeli War."

After two hours of waiting for Haniyeh to arrive at the mosque, some members of the audience gave up. Suddenly, a rumor stirred the room. "He's coming after all," a neighbor assured me. Several television reporters appeared, followed by a small convoy, and then Haniyeh strode in, waving at his supporters. He is forty-seven, squarely built, with a round face, and cautious green eyes that float above a trim white beard. He was dressed in a stark white djellabah and a skullcap, which added to his ministerial air. A former dean of the Islamic University, in Gaza City, Haniyeh grew up in the Al Shati refugee camp, in Gaza. In 1989, after the first intifada, he spent three years in an Israeli prison. Then, in a decision that Israel deeply regrets, Haniyeh and four hundred other activists were expelled to South Lebanon, where they formed an enduring alliance with Hezbollah.

By Hamas standards, Haniyeh is a moderate. He has spoken of negotiating a long-term truce with Israel. That places him at odds with many of the Party's top officials. Khaled Meshal, the overall leader of Hamas, lives in exile in Damascus, Syria; a hard-liner, he is more likely to initiate radical, destabilizing actions—such as capturing Gilad Shalit. It is often unclear who sets Hamas policies. A council, dominated by representatives of its underground military wing, governs the Party. Because so many Hamas members have been assassinated, the movement operates as an unsteady collective. Even prominent Party members don't always know who is in control. Haniyeh's authority is further undermined by the fact that Mahmoud Abbas, the Palestinian President, dismissed him as Prime Minister of Gaza, in June, 2007, after the Hamas takeover, and appointed Salam Fayyad, a Fatah loyalist, in his place. Hamas refused to recognize the move, and since then Haniyeh has continued to govern

Gaza while Abbas and Fayyad run the West Bank, under Israeli occupation.

While I was in Gaza, in July, there were talks under way in Cairo to explore the creation of a unity government between Hamas and Fatah, and to make a deal for Gilad Shalit. The Israeli papers were full of expectation about an imminent prisoner swap, but Noam Shalit, Gilad's father, told me that the reports were "ridiculous." He was pessimistic about the prospects for a deal anytime soon. "Hamas ignores every aspect of international conventions," he said. "They would like hard-core killers released. I feel very bad about that." He added that his son's abduction had become "a bottleneck" that had brought all negotiations to a standstill.

At the mosque, Haniyeh addressed the campers on the importance of reciting the Koran. "There are two kinds of people," he advised them. "Those who know the Koran is right and who follow it, and those who turn their backs on the Koran." When he finished speaking, Haniyeh kissed each child who had memorized a third of the Koran, and awarded him fifty Israeli shekels.

Afterward, amid a crush of petitioners, I asked Haniyeh whether the Cairo talks had made any progress. "It's just one step in breaking the siege of Gaza," he said, adding that he hoped the talks would allow reconstruction to begin. I asked if he had had contact with the Obama Administration. Khaled Meshal had responded positively to Obama's June address to the Muslim world, welcoming the "new language toward Hamas" and calling for open dialogue. Haniyeh didn't answer directly. He said that Washington had no veto power over the choice of the Palestinian people but added, "We are ready to deal." He also said that he would step down from his post if he became an obstacle to peace. "The most important thing is the unity of the Palestinian people," he said. "We are willing to do whatever it takes."

I walked outside, among shuttered shops. "The term 'economy' is no longer valid in the Gaza Strip," Omar Shaban, the economist, told me. In 1994, the poverty rate in Gaza was sixteen per cent. (In the U.S., it was 14.5.) But by 1996 the Israelis had virtually shut out Palestinian labor.

And the second intifada, four years later, ended tourism in Gaza; before then, Shaban said, more than ten thousand people a month had visited the territory, many of them Israelis who enjoyed the beaches and the seafood. Most economic activity came to a halt in 2007, with the Israeli blockade of Gaza. Now, according to the U.N., about seventy per cent of Gazans live on less than a dollar a day, and seventy-five per cent rely on international food assistance. In 1994, Shaban said, one wage earner supported six people in Gaza; the dependency rate is now one earner for every eighteen people. Unemployment is practically universal, except for people working for international organizations, or trading in the black market. According to the International Committee of the Red Cross, ninety-six per cent of Gaza's industrial sector collapsed after Operation Cast Lead.

Ever since the Hamas takeover, Egypt, Gaza's nominal ally, has cooperated with the Israelis in enforcing the blockade. The authorities in Cairo have their own reasons for sequestering Gaza. Hamas is a spinoff of the Egyptian Muslim Brotherhood, and the government of Hosni Mubarak worries about contagion. The wall that defines the Gaza Strip along the Israeli border simply turns the corner upon reaching Egypt. Bureaucracy, an Egyptian specialty, forms another kind of barrier. Mohammed Ali Abu Najela, a researcher for Oxfam, was in France when Hamas took over Gaza. "I landed in Cairo, and spent five days in a closed room in the airport with five other Palestinians," he recalls. He and the others were then transported to El–Arish Airport, in the Sinai, where they spent an additional sixty days in the waiting room before they were cleared to go home. Another young man told me that his father had gone to Cairo for emergency medical treatment but was turned away at the hospital, because his travel documents had been signed by the Hamas government in Gaza, not by the Fatah government in the West Bank. The father died shortly afterward.

In January, 2008, Hamas improvised a radical solution to Egypt's restrictions by blowing holes in the security fence surrounding Rafah, the southernmost town in Gaza. Over the next eleven days, hundreds of thousands of Gazans streamed into the Sinai with shopping lists. The Egyptian police formed a cordon that kept Gazans from straying too far into the country. The shops along the border were soon empty. The Gazans went home and the Egyptians sealed up the wall again. (Since then, Egypt has usually opened the border for a couple of days each month.)

Although the West Bank is only twenty-five miles from the Gaza Strip, it feels in many respects even more distant than other parts of the world. The Israelis began requiring special permits for travel between the two halves of Palestine in 1988. Taher al–Nunu is the chief spokesman for Prime Minister Haniyeh. When he was working in the Foreign Ministry, Nunu was allowed to travel around the world, but, like many Gazans, he's never been to the West Bank. "I was in China, Istanbul, and Indonesia, but I didn't go to Nablus, Ramallah, and Qalqilya," he says.

I began to see Gaza as, I suspect, many Gazans do: a floating island, a dystopian Atlantis, drifting farther away from contact with any other society. Omar Shaban told me that, twenty years ago, he could easily drive to Tel Aviv for dinner, and more than a hundred thousand Palestinians travelled into Israel every day for work. "The Palestinian economy was structured to work with the Israeli economy," he said. "Most Palestinians knew Hebrew. There were real friendships." Now, he said, "two-thirds of Gaza youth under thirty have never been outside the Strip. How can they psychologically think of peace? You can fight someone you don't know, but you can't make peace with him."

A nervous-looking young man was pacing on the side of the narrow coastal road outside Gaza City, just past the ruins of the Presidential Palace, which had been destroyed during Operation Cast Lead. My driver stopped for him, and he got into the back seat without a word, indicating that we should continue driving south. It was a Friday afternoon, after prayers, and the beaches were crowded.

Since the Hamas takeover, there have been many warnings that Al Qaeda has infiltrated Gaza. In the summer of 2007, Mahmoud Abbas accused Hamas of "shielding" jihadists. "Through its bloody conduct, Hamas has become very close to Al Qaeda," he said. I had heard about several splinter groups in Gaza that were seen as Al Qaeda affiliates. After extensive negotiations, I was able to arrange a meeting with a representative of one of them. The man in the back seat would guide us there.

We drove past the site of a former Jewish settlement. Across the road were the remains of the greenhouses that the settlers had left behind, intact, with the understanding that Gaza farmers would take them over. The greenhouses were meant to become an important part of the agricultural economy. Gaza's main exports were strawberries, cherry tomatoes, and carnations, destined mainly for Israel and Europe. But then the borders clamped shut and the fruit rotted. The carnations were fed to livestock. Now the greenhouses are nothing more than bare frames, their tattered plastic roofing fluttering in the sea breeze.

Our guide pointed to a rise ahead, where a lookout stood guard over another stretch of public beach. We turned in to a sandy drive and parked behind a row of palm-frond cabanas. The lookout ducked into a Port-a-Potty and emerged with an AK-47 and a 9-mm. pistol. Like the guide, he was quiet and unsmiling. He wore jeans and a plaid shirt. He led me to one of the cabanas, where a heavy man in a blue suit was waiting. The man said that I should call him Abu Mohammed. He politely offered tea.

Abu Mohammed claimed to represent four armed groups that have joined a jihadi coalition. (There is such an alliance, called the Popular Resistance Committees.) "When I speak, I speak for all of them," he told me. "We consider Osama bin Laden our spiritual father." His group follows the same ideology as Al Qaeda, but there is no direct connection. "The siege around Gaza has disconnected us from the outside world," he said. "None of us can travel." In Gaza, he estimated, there were about four hundred armed fighters in cells like his, down from as many as fifteen hundred before the Hamas takeover. When Fatah ran the Strip, it was easier for subversives to operate, he said, but now "Hamas is in full control, and their power is very tight." Hamas, he explained, wanted to dictate when violence occurred in Gaza, and tried to keep the Al Qaeda sympathizers penned in.

As we talked, the lookout with the machine gun dragged in a table, and a tea boy arrived, carrying a tray and glasses. It was sweltering inside the hut. Abu Mohammed took off his jacket; his shirt was soaked through. He had a quiet voice and often stared into space as he spoke. He said that he was a former political-science student who had been jailed first by the Israelis, and later by Hamas officials. He gestured to his suit jacket, now in his lap. During his second internment, "Hamas brought in a moderate sheikh with a suit and a tie and the smell of roses to discuss the way we look," he said, in a wry tone. "If I want to dress like my comrades in Afghanistan and Iraq"—wearing the shalwar kameez, the uniform favored by jihadi veterans—"that's prohibited." Finally, his jailers released him with a warning: "Don't do anything against our ceasefire!" He complained, "We feel we're under a microscope. If an Internet café or a beauty salon is burned, immediately they come round up the people they know. If Hamas suspects I am behind all this troublemaking, they will hang me by both hands and both feet for thirty days—that's the minimum."

I asked what his main complaint was against Hamas.

"We thought Hamas was going to apply Islamic law here, but they are not," he said. He spoke of the "fancy restaurants on the beach" and said that Hamas tolerated uncovered women there. "They have a much more moderate way of life, and we cannot deal with that."

When I mentioned Gilad Shalit, Abu Mohammed smiled and said, "I cannot talk about this, but a member of our group participated." (Three factions claimed responsibility for the abduction: the armed wing of Hamas, the Popular Resistance Committees, and the Army of Islam.) Mohammed said that the participant's name was Muhammad Farwaneh, and that he had been killed during the operation. Hamas now has exclusive control of Shalit. Mohammed said of the arrangement, "We respect this, because of the higher interest of the exchange of prisoners." Recently, his group had tried to carry off another abduction, but had failed.

I asked him what drew young men into his movement. "First, we have a clear ideology," he said. "Some come because they like our style, and they don't want to live by the rules. Those we don't usually put our money on—when they're tortured, we're finished. Some come from Hamas and feel that they were not treated fairly." Others, like him, think that Hamas is not following true Islam. Abu Mohammed said that most of the recruits are fellow refugees, but "many are locals from hard-line families—those who believe there is no middle road."

Joint operations with Hamas, such as the Shalit abduction, had ended. "We have no meetings at all with Hamas," Abu Mohammed said. "It's almost as if they want to finish us." He met my eyes at last. "We know how strong they are and how supported they are on the street, but we can't live underground forever."

Six weeks after this conversation, a group of radical Islamists, calling themselves the Soldiers of the Followers of God, stood on the steps of a mosque near the Egyptian border and declared Gaza to be an Islamic emirate. That afternoon, members of the Hamas military wing and the Gaza police surrounded the mosque, demanding that the radicals give themselves up. A shoot-out erupted, continuing into the night. According to the BBC, at least twenty-four people were killed, including the group's leader, Sheikh Abdul Latif Mousa. A hundred people were wounded. I have not been able to determine if Abu Mohammed was a casualty. One of the Hamas fatalities was Abu Jibril Shimali, a commander of its armed wing. Israelis blame him for orchestrating the capture of Gilad Shalit.

Just outside Rafah, the smuggling capital of Gaza, there is a billboard with a portrait of Shalit, behind bars, juxtaposed with a photograph of a masked Hamas fighter. The Arabic text declares, "Your prisoner will not have safety and security until our prisoners have safety and security." In a place where commercial advertising scarcely exists, the billboard is especially jarring.

Shalit's pale features and meek expression haunt the imagination of Gazans. Though it may seem perverse, a powerful sense of identification has arisen between the shy soldier and the people whose government holds him hostage. Gazans see themselves as like Shalit: confined, mistreated, and despairing.

At the same time, the sense of specialness that surrounds Shalit rankles many Gazans. "Everybody talks about Shalit as if he's a holy man," Ahmed Yousuf, the deputy minister, complained. "The whole world is showing such concern about a soldier who is still young and unmarried." Meanwhile, Israel is holding more than seven thousand Palestinians, nearly nine hundred of them from Gaza, who, like Shalit, are cut off from their families and are sometimes held without charge. "People say, 'What's the difference between their Shalit and our Shalits?' " Yousuf remarked. "We are *all* Shalits."

I spoke to Osama Mozini, a professor of education at the Islamic University, who oversees the Shalit negotiations for the government. A barrel-chested man with a stiff beard, he spent five years in an Israeli prison and was arrested three times by the Palestinian Authority because of Hamas activities. I asked him why he could not be more flexible in his negotiations for Shalit. Israel was plainly eager to make a deal that would involve the release of hundreds of Palestinians, many of them convicted of bloody crimes. Mozini bridled at the implication that the Palestinian prisoners were murderers and Shalit was not. "This one who has been abducted is an Israeli soldier who was on the border throwing shells that were killing Palestinians," he said. "We did not take him from the market or from his family. We took him from a military tank on the Gaza border."

The I.D.F. won't say whether Shalit had been involved in military actions against Gaza, but the tanks that line the border do lob shells into the territory, causing many random casualties. While I was there, a teen-age girl was killed, and her young brother injured, in such an incident. The Israelis maintain a buffer zone along the border about half a mile deep, which places at least thirty per cent of the Strip's arable land off

limits. In practice, the zone is even wider, according to Mohammed Ali Abu Najela, the Oxfam researcher. "Nearly every week, there are reported cases of farmers being shot at," he told me. He said that Gazans understand the rule to be this: "If I can see you, I will shoot you."

Mozini claimed that Gazans whose relatives were being held in Israel were not pressuring him to make a deal for Shalit. "They are backing us up," he said. "Everybody is asking us to stand firm to get our prisoners back, because this is our only chance." According to a recent U.N. fact-finding mission led by the South African jurist Richard Goldstone, there are approximately eighty-one hundred Palestinian political prisoners held in Israel, including sixty women and three hundred and ninety children. (Most of the children have been charged with throwing stones or belonging to an illegal organization.) The Goldstone report, as it has become known, has been decried by the Israeli government, which considers it reliant on biased testimony. In September, President Obama called the report "flawed." Goldstone, the former chief prosecutor of the International Criminal Tribunals for the former Yugoslavia and Rwanda, maintains that the report is fundamentally correct, and has demanded that the Americans specify what the inaccuracies might be.

The treatment of Gazan detainees is harsh; since 2007, they have been barred from any family visits, though they can exchange messages from family members. In March, the Israeli justice department began to consider reducing the privileges of Hamas and Islamic Jihad prisoners to match the likely "incarceration conditions" of Gilad Shalit.

Mozini began reciting the names of Gazan prisoners who had received sentences of more than a thousand years. Hassan Salameh, a Hamas operative, is serving forty-eight consecutive life sentences for recruiting suicide bombers. Walid Anjes helped plan the bombing at Moment and two other devastating attacks. He has twenty-six life sentences. Mozini mentioned a prisoner named Abdel Hadi Suleiman Ghneim: "He was riding in a bus. All he did was grab the steering wheel and take it over a cliff." He laughed. "Sixteen people were dead and many wounded—even Ghneim was wounded!" Ghneim received a life sentence for every person who died on the bus. These punishments struck Mozini as ludicrous. He assured me that Israel had "no choice" but to comply with Hamas's terms.

I had gone to Rafah to examine the tunnels that have created a subterranean economy in Gaza. Everything that goes in or out of the Strip, except the three dozen or so commodities that Israel permits to enter the territory, travels through a hole in the ground, including gas, cows, weapons, money, drugs, cars (which are disassembled for the trip), and people. There are hundreds of such tunnels, and they became a primary target for the Israeli Air Force during Operation Cast Lead. When I got there, tunnel diggers were repairing the damage—practically the only reconstruction work I saw in Gaza. A long, ragged row of tents ran about fifty yards from the Egyptian border amid great mounds of sand, and shirtless men worked their claims. Across the border was a village that had once been a part of greater Rafah before the security fence divided the town. The workers aim the tunnels at different buildings across the border, where collaborators have hollowed out a bathroom floor or a spot under a bed. Most of the smuggling is done at night, honoring the conceit that the excavations are secret, even though an Egyptian police station nearby has a clear view of the tunnellers' tents. Occasionally, the Egyptians crack down, blowing up or flooding the passageways. Tunnels also collapse, especially after bombings, which destabilize the soil. But tunnelling is one of the few functioning industries in Gaza, accounting for some thirty-five thousand jobs before Israel's December attacks.

In the tunnel I visited, three men were on the surface and twenty were underground. A motorized pulley extracted buckets of sand. It can take three months to break through to the other side. The tunnel operator, a young man with a big smile and bright calcium deposits on his teeth, introduced himself as Abu Hussein. The other men laughed: it's a pet name in Gaza for Barack Hussein Obama. The operator charges clients a thousand dollars to ship a ton of raw materials through the tunnel, or fifty dollars for a bag of forty kilos. He said that tunnellers frequently bump into each other underground: "It's like Swiss cheese."

It was through such a tunnel that the captors of Gilad Shalit crossed into Israeli territory. Old Soviet-designed GRAD rockets, now manufactured in North Korea and China, and knockoff missiles from Iran also make their way through the underground highways, which is one reason that Israel felt the urgency to act in December. These weapons have a much greater range than homemade rockets. From the northern end of Gaza, the GRADs can reach Ashkelon, seven miles away, a city of more than a hundred thousand people. A member of the Qassam Brigades, the armed faction of Hamas, had told me that they had upgraded their arsenal of rockets last year, getting "shipments from our own tunnels." The rocketeers use Google Earth to locate a target—the power plant in Sderot, for instance. It didn't bother the brigade member that he was aiming at civilians. "They are not limiting *their* war to military targets," he said.

According to the I.D.F., between 2000 and 2008 some twelve thousand rockets and mortars were fired into Israel; sometimes as many as sixty or eighty rockets a day were launched, but because they are so inaccurate the number of Israeli casualties has been relatively modest: fewer than thirty deaths. Still, the anxiety and fury stirred up by the fusillade placed the government of Ehud Olmert under extreme pressure in the run-up to the Israeli elections of February, 2009. In the police station in Sderot, a "Qassam Museum" displays the exploded carcasses of hundreds of rockets that have landed in the area. Barack Obama visited there as a candidate, in July, 2008. "No country would accept missiles landing on the heads of its citizens," he said. "If missiles were falling where my two daughters sleep, I would do everything in order to stop that." Despite Obama's assurances, the Israeli government decided to get the war over before the Bush Administration left power.

The stated goal for Operation Cast Lead was to "destroy the terrorist infrastructure," but there were larger aims. "We cannot allow Gaza to remain under Hamas control," Tzipi Livni, the

Foreign Minister at the time, said. Six months before the operation began, Israel and Hamas had agreed to a truce. The Deputy Defense Minister, Matan Vilnai, warned that Gazans were "bringing upon themselves a greater Shoah, because we will use all our strength in every way we deem appropriate." Such charged language revealed the degree to which anger permeated the thinking of Israel's military planners.

On December 19th, the six-month truce between Hamas and Israel formally expired. Israel was willing to extend it, but Hamas refused. Haniyeh complained that Israel had failed to ease the blockade, as the agreement had stipulated. Hamas rockets began flying again. By then, Gaza had run out of allies. Yossi Alpher, the Israeli political analyst, who co-edits the online forum bitterlemons.org, was in Europe when the invasion began. "I was having a good stiff drink with a Saudi colleague," he recalled. "He told me, 'This time, do it right.'"

A few weeks before Operation Cast Lead began, Colonel Herzi Halevi, the commander of the 35th paratroop brigade for the I.D.F., was flying over the Strip in a helicopter when he saw three rockets rise out of the Jabalia refugee camp. "I saw the rainbow of smoke, and then fifty to sixty seconds later you see it goes into Sderot," he told me. "It's eleven o'clock in the morning. Children are in school. Whether they live or die is a question of whether they are lucky or not. This is something that no other country can accept."

Halevi, now a brigadier general, is tall and lean, and has a reputation for being an even-tempered, sometimes aloof commander. Like many Israelis, he had come to the conclusion that Gazans deserved what they were going to get. "I had a feeling that on the other side of the fence, in the Gaza Strip, we didn't find a leadership, or even the sound of people in Gaza, saying something different except fighting, shooting rockets, and kidnapping." His long career has taught him that, in dealing with terrorism, "if you are not decisive enough, it is not going to be effective." He had spent much of his career in Sayeret Matkal, an élite hostage-rescue unit. It is likely that rescuing Gilad Shalit was another goal of the operation, although the I.D.F. won't comment on that. "I told my soldiers that was not our mission," Halevi said. "Our mission was to take care that we do not become another Gilad Shalit."

On the morning of December 27, 2008, a training exercise was under way at the police academy in Gaza City. Scores of police officers were in a courtyard. Across the street, children were getting out of school. A pair of Israeli F-16s screamed overhead, part of the first wave of aircraft aimed at police stations, command centers, and Hamas training camps. Explosions engulfed the courtyard. In less than five minutes, dozens of people were killed, and hundreds were wounded.

At the school, many of the students were injured. An Arabic teacher, who asked not to be identified, because he works with international agencies that would not want him to be quoted, carried to Al-Shifa hospital one of his students—a fourteen-year-old boy with shards of glass blown into his back and leg. Parents frantically searched for their children as another wave of aircraft raced over the Strip, targeting the militants who were expected to respond by launching retaliatory rockets. Indeed, one Israeli was killed that day by a Hamas rocket; according to the U.N., the death toll in Gaza reached two hundred and eighty, with nine hundred wounded. It was one of the deadliest days of conflict between Israel and its neighbors since 1967.

That night, the teacher and his family stayed in the house. "The bombing started again—it felt like an earthquake, our home was shaking," he recalls. He was afraid that the windows would shatter, so he removed them. It was freezing weather and the utilities in his home had been shut off. The next day, he went foraging for food and fuel. A mosque near his house had been destroyed. Also nearby was Beit Lehia Elementary School, which the U.N.R.W.A. had turned into an emergency shelter for fifteen hundred people. It was hit by white-phosphorous artillery shells. Such munitions are usually employed to produce smoke screens, but they are also powerful incendiaries. The teacher recalls, "The smoke was very white, and when it comes on the ground it doesn't explode—it just burns." The tentacles of fire that enveloped the school reminded him of a giant octopus. Two children burned to death. An I.D.F. investigation found that white phosphorous was used in accordance with international law. A Human Rights Watch report concluded that "the I.D.F. had deliberately or recklessly used white-phosphorous munitions in violation of the laws of war."

From the beginning, there was a dispute about who among the dead and wounded qualified as a "civilian." Some police officers in Gaza had been recruited from the military wing of Hamas, but the Israelis regarded them all as Hamas apparatchiks. In several instances, armed drones killed children who were on rooftops. Were they "spotters," as the Israelis speculated, or children at play, as human-rights workers in Gaza contended? Such questions demonstrate the difficulty that any urban conflict poses in separating actual combatants from innocent civilians. They also underscore the biases that had taken root in each camp: the Israeli belief that Hamas terrorists and the Gazan people were one and the same; the Gazan tendency to support any act of resistance against the Israelis, no matter how self-defeating it might be.

The air operation lasted for more than a week. Gaza's main prison was struck, even though prisoners were still in their cells. Drones crisscrossed the Strip, using high-resolution cameras for precisely targeted missile strikes. Despite the accuracy of such weapons, Israeli and Palestinian human-rights groups reported that eighty-seven civilians were killed by drone strikes, including twelve people who were waiting for a U.N. bus.

On December 30th, the Air Force began demolishing government buildings and cultural institutions. "The Israeli authorities said they were going to destroy the infrastructure of terror," John Ging, the U.N.R.W.A. director, told me. But they also attacked what he called "the infrastructure of peace," such as the American International School in Gaza, the premier educational institution in the Strip. "It was attacked on two occasions by the extremists," Ging said. "They did not succeed in destroying it. It took an F-16 for that." The caretaker of the school was killed in the attack. The Ministries of Finance and Foreign Affairs, the Presidential Palace, and the parliament were also

struck. "These are the buildings of democracy," Ging said. "We in the international community have been building these for a decade, for a future state of Palestine, and they now lie in ruins." Over a six-hour period, several buildings in the U.N.R.W.A. compound housing the agency's food and fuel supplies were shelled repeatedly, despite numerous calls from U.N. officials protesting the onslaught. Three people were injured.

Meanwhile, Hamas rockets continued flying into Israel. One hit a construction site in Ashkelon, killing a Bedouin construction worker and injuring sixteen colleagues. A mother of four died when a rocket exploded near her car in the center of Ashdod. Another rocket landed in Beersheba, twenty-five miles from the Gaza border, injuring six Israeli citizens, including a seven-year-old boy.

The Israeli military adopted painstaking efforts to spare civilian lives in Gaza. Two and a half million leaflets were dropped into areas that were about to come under attack, urging noncombatants to "move to city centers." But Gaza is essentially a cage, and the city centers also came under attack. Intelligence officers called residents whose houses were going to be targeted, urging them to flee. The Air Force dropped "roof knockers—small, noisemaking shells—on top of some houses to warn the residents to escape before the next, real bomb fell on them.

During the eight days of bombings, the Strip's water and electrical facilities were hit, and many mosques were destroyed. The Israelis assert that mosques served as arms depots for the resistance, and that Hamas placed its own citizens at risk by launching attacks from civilian areas.

All the while, ground troops stood by on the perimeter of Gaza. None of the goals of the operation had been achieved: every day, there were rocket and mortar attacks from the Strip, Hamas remained in control, and Gilad Shalit was still missing. Hamas officials even baited the Israelis, saying, "We are waiting for you to enter Gaza—to kill you or make you into Shalits." That prospect was very much in the minds of some military leaders. The Israeli press reported that soldiers were ordered to kill themselves if they were captured. "No matter what happens, no one will be kidnapped," a company commander told his troops, according to the Tel Aviv newspaper *Yediot Ahronot.* "We will not have Gilad Shalit 2."

A ground invasion began on January 3rd. According to Amnesty International, some Israeli troops were encouraged to fire at "anything that moved." A number of soldiers spoke to a human-rights group called Breaking the Silence about the behavior of Israeli forces during Operation Cast Lead. One said that his orders were "You see a house, a window? Shoot at the window. You don't see a terrorist there? Fire at the window. … In urban warfare, anyone is your enemy. No innocents." Another soldier said, "The goal was to carry out an operation with the least possible casualties for the Army, without its even asking itself what the price would be for the other side." A military rabbi told soldiers, "No pity, God protects you, everything you do is sanctified," and "This is a holy war."

The ground troops attacked Gaza simultaneously from the north and the east. The soldiers expected fierce resistance, but the border areas were spookily empty. Some units spent a week in the Strip without seeing a single Arab. Halevi led the paratroopers into the northeastern zone. The first night, he occupied a small town, El Atatra. "This is what I found," he told me later, in his office, on a military base near Tel Aviv. He unfurled a map, drawn by Hamas fighters, showing where snipers were to be stationed, tunnels had been dug, and improvised explosive devices had been planted. Halevi said of Hamas, "They took a civilian neighborhood and turned it into a military camp." He showed me photographs of arms caches that his soldiers had uncovered in mosques, and of houses that had been booby-trapped. "This is the house of one of the Hamas officers in El Atatra," he said, projecting a photograph of a dummy standing beside a dark staircase. "The dummy is to make us think he is a soldier," Halevi said. "Behind him was an I.E.D. There was also a tunnel. The idea was that our soldiers see the dummy, they run to shoot him, and the I.E.D. explodes. Then the terrorists come out of the tunnel and kidnap our soldiers."

Human Rights Watch has reported eleven instances of Israeli troops shooting civilians carrying white flags, including five women and four children—one of many incidents that human-rights groups say may constitute a war crime. According to Halevi, Hamas fighters had stationed weapons in various houses so that they could fire on the Israelis. When the troops approached, the fighters came outside unarmed, carrying a white flag. Maintaining this guise, they ran over to another arms cache and resumed firing.

The Israeli government has refused to coöperate with investigations by Human Rights Watch and Amnesty International, citing "their biased dispositions." It has also declined to participate in the U.N. inquiry led by Richard Goldstone. The U.N. delegation heard ample testimony about the use of civilians, including children, as human shields. The I.D.F., which is conducting its own investigations into possible misconduct, says that it has the right "to defend its civilians from intentional rocket attacks" and that it "discharged that responsibility in a manner consistent with the rules of international law."

The Goldstone report cites evidence that Hamas also committed war crimes, by targeting the civilian population of Israel with rockets. Halevi said that Hamas also used human shields: "If you launch a rocket and two seconds later hold a child in your hands in order to protect yourself from our helicopters, *you* are committing a war crime." Amnesty International has reported that it found "no evidence that Hamas or other Palestinian fighters directed the movement of civilians to shield military objectives from attacks."

Halevi told me, "The easiest thing would have been to attack from the air with cannons—just erase the town. We didn't even think about that." He believes that his unit took extra risks in order to avoid civilian casualties. One of his officers was killed. "To speak about us like the tribes in Darfur or Bosnia that really exercise war crimes, this is something I can't understand," he said.

Most of Israel's immediate military objectives were achieved within hours of the ground invasion. What followed was the systematic destruction of Gaza's infrastructure. Al Quds hospital, where many of the wounded were being treated, was shelled, under the apparently mistaken belief that a Hamas headquarters was in the building. Meanwhile, tanks fired on houses, mosques, and schools. The Israeli Navy strafed buildings along the coast and the intelligence headquarters in Gaza City, which is rumored to have been built by the C.I.A. when Fatah was still in control. Armored bulldozers took down houses and factories. Israel's Deputy Prime Minister, Eli Yishai, later said, "Even if the rockets fall in open air, or to the sea, we should hit their infrastructure and destroy one hundred homes for every rocket fired." Houses that weren't destroyed were sometimes vandalized. Halevi himself had to send several soldiers back to Israel for ethical violations. "We told them, 'We don't want you, you have a level of morality we don't accept.' " But most of the damage was officially tolerated, if not encouraged. According to various international agencies, fourteen per cent of the buildings in Gaza were partially or completely destroyed, including twenty-one thousand homes, seven hundred factories and businesses, sixteen hospitals, thirty-eight primary health-care centers, and two hundred and eighty schools. Two hundred and fifty wells were destroyed, three hundred thousand trees were uprooted, and large swaths of agricultural land were made no longer arable, in part because of contamination and unexploded ordnance.

Thirteen Israelis died, including nine soldiers—four of them from friendly fire—and four civilians, who were killed by rockets. (Israeli civilian casualties were kept to a minimum because many residents near the border fled the area, and those who remained hid inside fortified bunkers.) Hamas claims that only forty-eight fighters were lost during the entire operation. The toll on Gaza civilians was far higher. According to Amnesty International, fourteen hundred Gazans died, including three hundred children; five thousand were wounded. Israel claims that only eleven hundred and sixty-six Palestinians died, two hundred and ninety-five of them civilians. The Israeli human-rights organization B'tselem has documented seven hundred and seventy-three cases in which Israeli forces killed civilians not involved in hostilities. So far, the group says, Israel has convicted only one soldier of a crime during the operation—for stealing a credit card.

Because the Israeli military forbade international observers and journalists to enter Gaza during the operation, the scale of the destruction was largely hidden from view. One voice in Gaza that became familiar to Israeli television viewers was that of Ezzeldeen Abu al-Aish, a Palestinian gynecologist and peace activist who had trained and practiced in Israel. He often spoke to Israel's Channel 10, giving reports, in Hebrew, about the medical crisis in the Gaza hospitals. On January 16th, the day before the war ended, a tank shell went through a bedroom window of his fourth-floor apartment in Jabalia, killing two of his teenage daughters and a niece, and seriously injuring another daughter and several relatives. His oldest daughter ran into the room to see what had happened, only to be struck dead by a second tank shell.

Moments later, he rang the Channel 10 newsman Shlomi Eldar on his cell phone, in the middle of a broadcast. Eldar answered on air, and the anguished wails of Abu al-Aish on the other end of the line jolted many Israelis. "No one can get to us," the doctor cried, begging for help to get his injured family to a hospital. "My God … Shlomi, can't anyone help us?" Eldar persuaded the Israeli Army to let ambulances through to rescue the survivors.

The I.D.F. initially claimed that Palestinian rockets had struck the building, and then, after that was disproved, that the tank was responding to "suspicious" figures on the third floor. Later still, the I.D.F. concluded that an Israeli tank had fired the two shells that killed the girls.

"We have proven to Hamas that we have changed the equation," Tzipi Livni said on January 12th, five days before Israel declared a unilateral ceasefire and started to pull out of the Strip. "Israel is not a country upon which you fire missiles and it does not respond. It is a country that when you fire on its citizens it responds by going wild."

The morning that the Israelis began their withdrawal, Hamas launched five more missiles at Sderot, then declared its own ceasefire. Khaled

Meshal, who was in Damascus, far from the action, claimed victory for Hamas.

Five months after Operation Cast Lead, Hamas sponsored a workshop in Gaza City on "How to Talk to Israel." Two dozen people attended, most of them academics or journalists. "What Israel knows about Hamas is that Hamas wants to eliminate them," one of the panelists observed. Governing imposes new responsibilities, he said, but since coming to power "Hamas has not changed its speech." A member of the audience said that Hamas had not even decided what to call Israel, pointing out that some speakers had used the term "Israeli entity" and others had called it the "Zionist entity." "You can't say to our own public you are going to throw Israel into the sea and then talk another way to the outside world—you have to have one speech," the audience member said. "We address moderates in Israel with words, and then we also sent rockets to them … We should be responsible but also clear in what we want. The world is not going to wait for us forever."

Many Gazans I spoke to were introspective about Israel's crushing retaliation. A Palestinian aid worker saw the invasion in geopolitical terms. "The war has a double meaning for the whole world, but especially for Iran," he said. "This is how it will be for anyone who would think to play with Israel." Eman Mohammed, a young photographer, told me that she was shocked by the indifference of the Arab world. "Look at the U.S. and Britain, sending convoys of aid," she said. "Maybe we needed this war to look at things in a different way." The sight of buildings being destroyed in Gaza made her more sympathetic to the reaction of America to 9/11. "I thought Osama bin Laden was a hero, but he's not. He's just a corrupted man taking us all to hell."

The teacher in Gaza told me that many children have been reluctant to return to class, because that's where they were when the bombs began to fall. (The Ministry of Education and Higher Education has reported that a hundred and sixty-four pupils and twelve teachers were killed during the operation.) Some of the children have become extremely aggressive, forming gangs. "They don't listen, they don't care what you're saying," the teacher told me. Others are mute, but "as soon as they hear a loud sound they start screaming."

The boy he took to the hospital has become one of the disruptive ones. Before the war, the boy was good at his lessons. "Now he has a dark future," the teacher said. "If he doesn't continue his learning, he is not going to be able to go to the university. He will lose his opportunity to be an effective member of the community. Soon, you will see him on the street."

Ahmed Yousuf warned me, "If there's not a solution in the near future, things will go out of control. At every level, you find people suffering from a siege mentality. They don't know which direction to take. There's no guidance from the world community or from our local leaders. We have lost the wise men among the Palestinians."

Hamas is more firmly entrenched in Gaza than it was before the invasion. It controls the only newspaper and the local television station, and it bans any Palestinian paper that does not reflect the views of the Party. Moreover, according to Israeli intelligence, Hamas is already rearming with high-quality weapons, many of them supplied or paid for by Iran. "They are now smuggling in rockets and rebuilding," General Halevi said. "I tell you, we will come again, in better shape, because we have learned our lessons."

The blockade of Gaza has not been lifted, or even reduced. Soon after the troops returned to Israel, Haim Ramon, then the Vice-Premier, declared that "Israel is facing a serious humanitarian crisis, and it is called Gilad Shalit." He added, "Until he is returned home, not only will we not allow more cargo to reach the residents of Gaza, we will even diminish it." In July, the incoming Prime Minister, Benjamin Netanyahu, echoed this position.

On October 2nd, Hamas released a proof-of-life video of Gilad Shalit, in exchange for the release of twenty female Palestinian prisoners. Shalit appears gaunt but healthy. Three months earlier, Shalit's father, Noam, had travelled to Geneva to testify before Goldstone's fact-finding panel. He made the case that his son's abduction, and the refusal of his captors to allow the International Red Cross to determine if he is alive and well, were war crimes. He used the forum as an opportunity to address the people of Gaza. "Your leaders are fighting to return your sons and daughters from captivity," he said. "This is an understandable desire." But, he added, "the fate of an entire prison population cannot depend on the ransom of one young man ... You know that the injustice done to my son was the trigger for war.

You also know that the release of my son is the key to peace.

"I know that you are short of food," he went on. "Some of your loved ones have been killed—women and children, young and innocent ... As a parent speaking to a multitude of parents, I ask you to understand my family's anguish."

Section 5

Current Perspectives

Introduction

This final section considers some of the larger, recurrent themes running through the history of the last 60 years, starting with the connection between Israel and its patron-cum-ally, the United States.

The excerpts from John Mearsheimer and Stephen Walt's The Israel Lobby set forth their thesis that consistently high post-1967 levels of American support for Israel are best explained, not by democratic affinity or mutual strategic benefit, but by the influence that the Israel lobby wields over America's Mideast policy. As Mearsheimer and Walt use the term, the "Israel lobby" is essentially synonymous with the Jewish lobby. They describe the complex interconnections and activities of various pro-Israel organizations, and the role of politicians, academics, journalists, and public intellectuals affiliated with the lobby. In basic goals and methods of operation, the Israel lobby, they emphasize, differs little from other special interests groups in America. It differs chiefly in terms of its greater political effectiveness.

Critics have charged that the Mearsheimer-Walt thesis minimizes or ignores 1) strategic influences on U.S. Mideast policy; and 2) widespread support for Israel among non-Jewish Americans. Walter Russell Mead addresses both issues, but most particularly he discusses popular attitudes. In his view, Christian America traditionally saw itself as a nation, like ancient Israel, chosen by God for a special destiny. That instinctive identification later blended with a sense that America and Israel faced common enemies, first in Communism and then in Islamic terrorism. The result has been strong sympathy for Israel that extends far beyond the Jewish community. According to Mead, this diffuse and persistent goodwill explains American Mideast policy better than the activities of the Israel lobby, whose membership Mearsheimer and Walt fail to define with any precision, and whose power they vastly exaggerate.

Though diverse in tone and thematic focus, the readings by Azzam Tamimi, Robert L. Bernstein, and Alan Dershowitz express a common theme: an abiding sense of victimization and unfair treatment, shared—ironically and counterintuitively—by both Zionists and Palestinians.

A knowledgeable and highly sympathetic observer of Hamas, Tamimi articulates the outlook and strategy of that organization. In truth, many of Hamas's basic assumptions were shared by the PLO, and indeed by national leaders going back to Hajj Amin al-Husayni. In this view, Palestinians have suffered a grave historic injustice, namely, the systematic theft of virtually their entire homeland by alien invaders. A hostile or indifferent world supported (and continues to support) not the victims, but the perpetrators, of this crime. Given the righteousness of their cause and the determination and ruthlessness of their enemies, Palestinians, Tamimi argues, have no practical choice but to resort to violent resistance, including suicide bombings.

Although penned by Americans rather than by Israelis, the writings of Bernstein and Dershowitz also express a profound sense of isolation and unfair treatment, and as such give voice to sentiments widespread in Israel itself. Both writers argue that the United Nations and human rights organizations, while claiming impartiality, are, in fact, systematically biased against Israel. Such groups, Bernstein and Dershowitz charge, focus obsessively on Israeli wrongs, ignore far more serious Arab offenses, conflate Israeli democracy with Arab dictatorships, and fail to distinguish between accidental and targeted civilian deaths. In their view, most human rights charges against Israel are little more than political weapons designed to delegitimize the Jewish state.

After reviewing Palestinian and Israeli narratives of victimhood, Alan Dowty offers two summary observations reflecting what is probably a consensus among foreign governments and academic observers. First, as a practical matter, a two-state solution, with Israel and Palestine living side by side as separate entities, is far more likely than any sort of binational solution to reduce enmity and violence. Second, to achieve a stable, two-state agreement, Israelis and Palestinians will have to learn to distinguish more clearly between the tactical brilliance and the strategic incoherence of extremist, unilateral forces. Unilateral actions can achieve temporary military or political "victories." But over the long term such strategies seem unlikely to achieve anything more substantial than the indefinite perpetuation of conflict itself.

The Israel Lobby and U.S. Foreign Policy

By John Mearsheimer and Stephen Walt

In the United States, interest groups routinely contend to shape perceptions of the national interest and to convince legislators and presidents to adopt their preferred policies. The interplay of competing factions was famously extolled by James Madison in the *Federalist No. 10,* and the influence of different interest groups has long shaped various aspects of American foreign policy including decisions for war.

When a particular interest group is especially powerful or politically adept, it may influence policy in ways that are not good for the country as a whole. A tariff that shields a particular industry from foreign competition will benefit certain companies but not the many consumers who have to pay more for that industry's goods. The National Rifle Associations success in thwarting gun control legislation undoubtedly benefits gun manufacturers and dealers, but it leaves the rest of society more vulnerable to gun-related violence. When a former lobbyist for the American Petroleum Institute becomes chief of staff at the White House's Council on Environmental Quality and uses this position to water down reports on the connection between greenhouse gas emissions and global warming (before resigning to take a job at ExxonMobil), one may reasonably worry that the oil industry is protecting its interests in ways that may harm all of us.

The influence of the Israel lobby on U.S. foreign policy merits the same scrutiny as the impact of energy interests on environmental regulations or the role of pharmaceutical companies in shaping policy on prescription drugs. We believe the activities of the groups and individuals who make up the lobby are the main reason why the United States pursues policies in the Middle East that make little sense on either strategic or moral grounds.

Were it not for the lobby's efforts, the strategic and moral arguments that are commonly invoked to justify unconditional American support would be called into question more frequently and U.S. policy in the Middle East would be significantly different than it is today. Pro-Israel forces surely believe that they are promoting policies that serve the American as well as the Israeli national interest. We disagree. Most of the policies they advocate are not in America's or Israel's interest, and both countries would be better off if the United States adopted a different approach.

As we have already noted, we are not questioning American support for Israel's right to exist, because that right is clearly justified and is now endorsed by more than 160 countries around the world. What we are questioning—and what needs to be explained—is the magnitude of U.S. support for Israel and its largely unconditional nature, as well as the degree to which U.S. Middle East policy is conducted with Israel's welfare in mind. To begin that task, this chapter identifies the central components of the Israel lobby and describes how it has evolved over time. We also discuss why it has become so influential, especially when compared to potential competitors like the "Arab lobby" and the "oil lobby." The following chapters describe the different strategies that have made it such a powerful interest group and a remarkably effective player in the making of U.S. Middle East policy.

Defining the Lobby

We use "Israel lobby" as a convenient shorthand term for the loose coalition of individuals and organizations that actively work to shape U.S. foreign policy in a pro-Israel direction. The lobby is not a single, unified movement with a central leadership, however, and the individuals and groups that make up this broad coalition sometimes disagree on specific policy issues. Nor is it some sort of cabal or conspiracy. On the contrary, the organizations and individuals who make up the lobby operate out in the open and in the same way that other interest groups do.

Using the term "Israel lobby" is itself somewhat misleading, insofar as many of the individuals and some of the groups in this loose coalition do not engage in formal lobbying activities (direct efforts to persuade elected officials). Rather, the various parts of the lobby work to influence U.S. policy in a variety of ways, much as other interest groups do. One might more accurately dub this the "pro-Israel community" or even the "help Israel movement," because the range of activities that different groups undertake goes beyond simple lobbying. Nonetheless, because many of the key groups do lobby and because the term "Israel lobby" is used in common parlance (along with labels such as the "farm lobby" "insurance lobby" 'gun lobby" or other ethnic lobbies), we have chosen to employ it here.

As with other special interest groups, the boundaries of the Israel lobby cannot be identified precisely, and there will always be some borderline individuals or organizations whose position is hard to classify. It is easy to identify groups that are clearly part of the lobby—such as the Zionist Organization of America (ZOA)—as well as individuals who are key members— such as Malcolm Hoenlein, executive vice chairman of the Conference of Presidents of Major American Jewish Organizations. There are also many groups that are obviously not part of the lobby—such as the National Association of Arab–Americans—and individuals who should clearly be excluded as well—such as Columbia University scholar Rashid Khalidi. Nevertheless, there will always be some groups and individuals whose position is more ambiguous. Like other social and political movements, the Israel lobby's boundaries are somewhat fuzzy.

This situation highlights that the lobby is not a centralized, hierarchical organization with a defined membership. There are no membership cards or initiation rites. It has a core consisting of organizations whose declared purpose is to encourage the U.S. government and the American public to provide material aid to Israel and to support its government's policies, as well as influential individuals for whom these goals are also a top priority. The lobby, however, also draws support from a penumbra of groups and individuals who are committed to Israel and want the United States to continue supporting it, but who are not as energetically or consistently active as the groups and individuals that form the core. Thus, a lobbyist for the American Israel Public Affairs Committee (AIPAC), a research fellow at the Washington Institute for Near East Policy (WINEP), or the leadership of organizations like the Anti–Defamation League (AOL) and Christians United for Israel (CUFI) are part of the core, while individuals who occasionally write letters supporting Israel to their local newspaper or send checks to a pro-Israel political action committee should be seen as part of the broader network of supporters.

This definition does not mean that every American with favorable attitudes toward Israel is a member of the lobby. To offer a personal illustration, the authors of this book are "pro-Israel," in the sense that we support its right to exist, admire its many achievements, want its citizens to enjoy secure and prosperous lives, and believe that the United States should come to Israel's aid if its survival is in danger. But we are obviously not part of the Israel lobby. Nor does it imply that every American official who supports Israel is part of the lobby either. A senator who consistently votes in favor of aid to Israel is not necessarily part of the lobby because he or she may simply be responding to political pressure from pro-Israel interest groups.

To be part of the lobby in other words, one has to actively work to move American foreign policy in a pro-Israel direction. For an organization, this pursuit must be an important part of its mission and consume a substantial percentage of its resources and agenda. For an individual, this means devoting some portion of one's professional or personal life (or in some cases, substantial amounts of money) to influencing U.S. Middle East policy. A journalist or academic who sometimes covers Middle East issues and occasionally reports events that portray Israel favorably—such as the *New York Times* reporter David Sanger or the Duke University professor Bruce Jentleson—should not be seen as part of the lobby. But a journalist or scholar who predictably takes Israel's side and devotes a significant amount of his or her writing to defending steadfast U.S. support for Israel—such as the *Washington Post* columnist Charles Krauthammer or the former Princeton University historian Bernard Lewis—clearly is.

Of course, the level of effort and the specific activities will vary in each case, and these various groups and individuals will not agree on every issue that affects Israel. Some individuals—such as Morton Klein of ZOA, John Hagee of CUFL and Rael Jean Isaac of Americans for a Safe Israel—oppose a two-state solution between Israel and the Palestinians and believe instead that Israel should retain all or most of the Occupied Territories. Others, such as Dennis Ross of WINEP and Martin Indyk of the Brookings Institution, favor a negotiated settlement and have occasionally criticized specific Israeli actions. Despite these differences, however, each of these individuals believes that the United States should give Israel substantial diplomatic, economic, and military support even when Israel takes actions the United States opposes, and each has devoted a significant amount of his or her professional life to encouraging this sort of support. Thus, although it would clearly be wrong to think of the lobby as a single-minded monolith, much less portray it as a cabal or conspiracy, it would be equally mistaken to exclude anyone who works actively to preserve America's special relationship with the Jewish state.

The Role of American Jewry

The bulk of the lobby is comprised of Jewish Americans who are deeply committed to making sure that U.S. foreign policy advances what they believe to be Israel's interests. According to the historian Melvin I. Urofsky "No other ethnic group in American history has so extensive an involvement with a foreign nation." Steven T. Rosenthal agrees, writing that "since 1967 … there has been no other country whose citizens have been as committed to the success of another country as American Jews have been to Israel." In 1981, the political scientist Robert H. Trice described the pro-Israel lobby as "comprised of at least 75 separate organizations—mostly Jewish—that actively support most of the actions and policy positions of the Israeli government." The activities of these groups and individuals go beyond merely voting for pro-Israel candidates to include writing letters to politicians or news organizations, making financial contributions to pro-Israel political candidates, and giving active support to one or more pro-Israel organizations, whose leaders often contact them directly to convey their agenda.

Yet the Israel lobby is not synonymous with American Jewry, and "Jewish lobby" is not an appropriate term for describing the various individuals and groups that work to foster U.S. support for Israel. For one thing, there is significant variation among American Jews in their depth of commitment to Israel. Roughly a third of them, in fact, do not identify Israel as a particularly salient issue. In 2004, for example, a well-regarded survey found that 36 percent of Jewish Americans were either "not very" or "not at all" emotionally attached to Israel. Furthermore, many American Jews who care a lot about Israel do not support the policies endorsed by the dominant organizations in the lobby, just as many gun owners do not support every policy that the NRA advocates and not all retirees favor every position endorsed by the AARP. For example, American Jews were less enthusiastic about going to war in Iraq than the population as a whole, even though key organizations in the lobby supported the war, and they are more opposed to the war today Finally, some of the individuals and groups that are especially vocal on Israel's behalf, such as the Christian Zionists, are not Jewish. So while American Jews are the lobby's predominant constituency, it is more accurate to refer to this loose coalition as the Israel lobby. It is the specific political agenda that defines the lobby, not the religious or ethnic identity of those pushing it.

The attachment that many American Jews feel for Israel is not difficult to understand, and as noted in the Introduction, it resembles the attitudes of other ethnic groups that retain an affinity for other countries or peoples with similar backgrounds in foreign lands. Although many Jews in the United States were ambivalent about Zionism during the movement's early years, support grew significantly after Hitler came to power in 1933 and especially after the horrors inflicted on the Jews during World War II became widely known.

Relatively few Jews chose to leave the United States and move to Israel after its founding in 1948, a pattern that Prime Minister David Ben–Gurion and other Israeli leaders initially criticized. Nevertheless, a strong commitment to Israel soon became an important element of identity for many American Jews. The establishment of a Jewish state in historic Palestine seemed miraculous in itself, especially in the aftermath of the Nazi Holocaust. Israel's achievements in "making the desert bloom" were an obvious source of pride, and a close identification with Israel provided a

new basis for community for a population that was rapidly assimilating into American society and becoming increasingly secular at the same time. As Rosenthal notes:

> To equate Israel with Judaism was a comforting way to avoid the encumbrances of religion by focusing one's Jewishness on a secular state 8,000 miles from home … Synagogues, the new mainstay of American Jewish life in the postwar era, became Israel-centered. A new class of Jewish professionals … arose in the suburbs. They soon discovered that Israel was the most effective means to counter the growing religious indifference of their constituencies. Primarily in response to Israel's overwhelming need for financial and political support, new institutions … arose, and fundraising and lobbying increasingly defined American Jews' relationship to Israel.

American Jews have formed an impressive array of civic organizations whose agendas include working to benefit Israel, in many cases by influencing U.S. foreign policy. Key organizations include AIPAC, the American Jewish Congress, ZOA, the Israel Policy Forum (IPF), the American Jewish Committee, the ADL, the Religious Action Center of Reform Judaism, Americans for a Safe Israel, American Friends of Likud, Mercaz–USA, Hadassah, and many others. Indeed, the sociologist Chaim I. Waxman reported in 1992 that the *American Jewish Yearbook* listed more than eighty national Jewish organizations "specifically devoted to Zionist and pro-Israel activities … and for many others, objectives and activities such as 'promotes Israel's welfare,' 'support for the State of Israel' and 'promotes understanding of Israel' appear with impressive frequency." Fifty-one of the largest and most important organizations come together in the Conference of Presidents of Major American Jewish Organizations, whose self-described mission includes "forging diverse groups into a unified force for Israel's well-being" and working to "strengthen and foster the special U.S.–Israel relationship."

The lobby also includes think tanks such as the Jewish Institute for National Security Affairs (JINSA), the Middle East Forum (MEF), and WINEP, as well as individuals who work in universities and other research organizations. There are also dozens of pro-Israel PACs ready to funnel money to pro-Israel political candidates or to candidates whose opponents are deemed either insufficiently supportive of or hostile to Israel. The Center for Responsive Politics, a nonpartisan research group that tracks campaign contributions, has identified roughly three dozen such "pro-Israel" PACs (many of them "stealth PACs" whose names do not reveal a pro-Israel orientation) and reports that these organizations contributed approximately $3 million to congressional candidates in the 2006 midterm election.

Of the various Jewish organizations that include foreign policy as a central part of their agenda, AIPAC is clearly the most important and best known. In 1997, when *Fortune* magazine asked members of Congress and their staffs to list the most powerful lobbies in Washington, AIPAC came in second behind AARP but ahead of heavyweight lobbies like the AFL–CIO and the NRA. A *National Journal* study in March 2005 reached a similar conclusion, placing AIPAC in second place (tied with AARP) in Washington's "muscle rankings." Former Congressman Mervyn Dymally (D–CA) once called AIPAC "without question the most effective lobby in Congress," and the former chairman of the House Foreign Affairs Committee, Lee Hamilton, who served in Congress for thirty-four years, said in 1991, "There's no lobby group that matches it … They're in a class by themselves."

The influence that groups like AIPAC now enjoy did not emerge overnight. During Zionism's early years, and even after Israel's founding, lobbying on Israel's behalf tended to occur quietly behind the scenes and usually depended on personal contacts between influential government officials, especially the president, and a small number of Jewish leaders, pro-Zionist advisers, or Jewish friends. For example, Woodrow Wilson's support for the Balfour Declaration in 1917 was due in part to the influence of his Jewish friends Supreme Court Justice Louis D. Brandeis and Rabbi Stephen Wise. Similarly, Harry S. Truman's decision to back Israel's creation and to recognize the new state was influenced (though not determined) by intercessions from Jewish friends and advisers.

The tendency for Israel's supporters to keep a low profile reflected concerns about lingering anti-Semitism in the United States, as well as the fear that overt lobbying on Israel's behalf would expose American Jews to the charge of dual loyalty. AIPAC itself had explicitly Zionist roots: its founder, I. L. "Si" Kenen, was head of the American Zionist Council in 1951, which was a registered foreign lobbying group. Kenen reorganized it as a U.S. lobbying organization— the American Zionist Committee for Public Affairs—in 1953–54, and the new organization was renamed AIPAC in 1959. Kenen relied on personal contacts with key legislators rather than public campaigns or mass mobilization, and AIPAC generally followed "Kenen's Rules" to advance Israel's cause. Rule No. 1 was: "Get behind legislation; don't step out in front of it (that is, keep a low profile)."

According to J. J. Goldberg, the editor of the Jewish newspaper *Forward,* Zionist influence "increased exponentially during the Kennedy and Johnson administrations, because the affluence and influence of Jews in American society had increased," and also because Kennedy and Johnson "counted numerous Jews among their close advisers, donors and personal friends." AIPAC was still a small operation with a modest staff and budget, and as Stuart Eizenstat points out, "Not until the mid-1960s did overt organized Jewish political activity on behalf of the state of Israel come into its own." The lobby's size, wealth, and influence grew substantially after the Six-Day War in June 1967. According to Eizenstat, that conflict "galvanized the American Jewish public like no event since Israel's War of Independence … The sense of pride in new Jews,' proud, strong, capable of defending themselves, had an incalculable effect on American Jewry."

The successful campaign against anti-Semitism, aided by the widespread awareness of the horrors of the Holocaust, helped remove lingering discriminatory barriers, and Jewish Americans "lost the sense of fear that had stunted their political will" in earlier years. And because Israel was becoming a central focus of Jewish identity in a world where assimilation was increasingly viable and widespread, there were few reasons not to express that attachment in politics.

The heightened concern with Israel's well-being within Jewish organizations continued during the War of Attrition (1969–70) and the October War (1973). These conflicts reinforced pride in Israel's military prowess, but they also raised fears about Israel's security, thereby reinforcing the Israel-centric focus of many Jewish community relations groups. Albert Chernin, the executive director of the National Jewish Community Relations Advisory Council (NJCRAC, later renamed the Jewish Council for Public Affairs), expressed this perspective in 1978 when he said that our "first priority is Israel, of course, reflecting the complete identity of views of the American Jewish leadership with the concerns of the rank and file." The historian Jack Wertheimer terms this comment a "stunning admission that political efforts to shore up Israel superseded all other concerns of Jewish community relations organizations in the United States."

As American foreign aid to Israel began to exceed private contributions, pro-Israel organizations increasingly focused on political activities intended to preserve or increase U.S. governmental support. According to Wertheimer, "The overall responsibility for lobbying for Israel was assumed by the Conference of Presidents ... and AIPAC. Both had been founded in the 1950s and had played a modest role prior to 1967. The needs of Israel for political support catapulted these two organizations to prominence in the 1970s and 1980s."

This increased effort reflected awareness that backing Israel was costly for the United States and therefore had to be justified and defended in the political sphere. As Morris Amitay, who replaced Kenen as AIPAC's executive director in 1975, put it, "The name of the game, if you want to help Israel, is political action." Under Amitay and his successor, Tom Dine, AIPAC was transformed, from an intimate, low-budget operation into a large, mass-based organization with a staff of more than 150 employees and an annual budget (derived solely from private contributions) that went from some $300,000 in 1973 to an estimated $40-60 million today. Instead of shunning the limelight, as it had done under Kenen, AIPAC increasingly sought to advertise its power. According to one former staffer, "The theory was, no one is scared of you if they don't know about you." In contrast to the earlier patterns of intimate lobbying on behalf of Jews by Jewish advisers and sympathetic gentiles, AIPAC and other groups in the lobby did not define their public agenda as humanitarian support for Jews in Israel. Rather, the evolution of the lobby increasingly involved the formulation and promotion of sophisticated arguments about the alignment of America's and Israel's strategic interests and moral values.

Flush with cash and well positioned in the Cold War political landscape, AIPAC found its political muscle enhanced by new federal rules on campaign financing, which triggered the creation of independent PACs and made it easier to channel money toward pro-Israel candidates. AIPAC may not have been all that formidable in the early 1960s, but by the 1980s, notes Warren Bass, it was a "Washington powerhouse."

Unity in Diversity and The Norm Against Dissent

As noted above, the lobby is not a centralized, hierarchical movement. Even among the Jewish elements of the lobby, there are important differences on specific policy issues. In recent years, AIPAC and the Conference of Presidents have tilted toward Likud and other hard-line parties in Israel and were skeptical about the Oslo peace process (a phenomenon we discuss at greater length below), while a number of other, smaller groups—such as Ameinu, Americans for Peace Now, Brit Tzedek v'Shalom (Jewish Alliance for

Justice and Peace), Israel Policy Forum, Jewish Voice for Peace, Meretz–USA, and the Tikkun Community—strongly favor a two-state solution and believe Israel needs to make significant concessions in order to bring it about.

These differences have occasionally led to rifts within or among these different organizations. In 2006, for example, the Israel Policy Forum, Americans for Peace Now, Jewish Voice for Peace, and Brit Tzedek v'Shalom openly opposed an AIPAC-sponsored congressional resolution (FIR 4681) that would have imposed even more draconian restrictions on aid to the Palestinians than the Israeli government sought. A watered-down version of the resolution passed by a comfortable margin, but the episode reminds us that pro-Israel groups do not form a monolith with a single party line.

These divisions notwithstanding, the majority of organized groups in the American Jewish community—especially the largest and wealthiest among them—continue to favor steadfast U.S. support for Israel no matter what policies the Jewish state pursues. As an AIPAC spokesman explained in June 2000, when concerns about Israel's arms sales to China led to calls for a reduction in U.S. support, "We are opposed to linking Israel's aid under any circumstances because once it starts it never stops." Even the dovish Americans for Peace Now supports "robust U.S. economic and military assistance to Israel," opposes calls to "cut or condition" U.S. aid, and seeks only to prevent U.S. aid from being used to support settlement activities in the Occupied Territories. Similarly, the moderate Israel Policy Forum does not advocate making American aid more conditional but rather focuses its efforts on persuading the U.S. government to work more actively and effectively for a two-state solution. Despite differences on the peace process and related issues, in short, almost every pro-Israel group wants to keep the "special relationship" intact. A notable exception is Jewish Voice for Peace (JVP), which has called for the U.S. government to suspend military aid to Israel until it ends the occupation of the West Bank, Gaza, and East Jerusalem. Indeed, given this position, one might argue that JVP is not part of the lobby at all.

Given their desire to maximize U.S. backing, Israeli officials frequently engage American Jewish leaders and ask them to help mobilize support in the United States for particular Israeli policies. As Rabbi Alexander Schindler, former chair of the Conference of Presidents, told an Israeli magazine in 1976, "The Presidents' Conference and its members have been instruments of official governmental Israeli policy. It was seen as our task to receive directions from government circles and to do our best no matter what to affect the Jewish community." (Schindler thought this situation was "not acceptable," telling the interviewer that "American Jewry is in no mood to be used by anyone.") Yet Albert Chernin of NJCRAC offered a similar appraisal in the 1970s, saying that "in domestic areas we made policy, but in Israel affairs the policy was a given ... In reality [the Conference of Presidents] was the vehicle through which Israel communicated its policy to the community." Ori Nir of the *Forward* quotes an unnamed activist with a major Jewish organization claiming in 2005 that "it is routine for us to say: This is our policy on a certain issue, but we must check what the Israelis think.' We as a community do it all the time." Or as Hyman Bookbinder, a high-ranking official of the American Jewish Committee, once admitted, "Unless something is terribly pressing, really critical or fundamental, you parrot Israel's line in order to retain American support. As American Jews, we don't go around saying Israel is wrong about its policies."

Israel's ability to galvanize support within the United States has been demonstrated on numerous occasions. Zionist (and later, Israeli) officials encouraged American Jewish leaders to campaign for the UN partition plan in 1947 and for U.S. recognition in 1948, and to lobby against the abortive peace plan formulated by the UN mediator Folke Bernadotte in 1948. Coordinated efforts such as these also helped convince the Truman administration to significantly increase economic aid to Israel in 1952 and to abandon a Pentagon and State Department proposal for a $10 million grant of military assistance to Egypt. During the crisis preceding the 1967 Six–Day War, the Israeli government instructed its ambassador in Washington to "create a public atmosphere that will constitute pressure on the [Johnson] administration … without it being explicitly clear that we are behind this public campaign." The effort involved getting sympathetic Americans to write letters, editorials, telegrams, and public statements, etc.—"in a variety of styles"—whose purpose, according to the Israeli Foreign Ministry, was "to create a public atmosphere … that will strengthen our friends within the administration." White House officials eventually asked their Israeli counterparts to shut down the letter-writing campaign, but the Israeli ambassador reported back to Jerusalem that "of course we are continuing it." According to the historian Tom Segev, the White House was "inundated with letters from citizens calling on the president to stand by Israel."

This tendency to support Israel's actions reflexively may be less prevalent today, but major organizations in the lobby still defer to the preferences of Israel's leaders on many occasions. Following the release of the Bush administration's "road map" for Middle East peace in March 2003, for example, Malcolm Hoenlein of the Conference of Presidents reportedly told *Haaretz* that if the Israeli government expressed reservations about the road map, it would have the support of America's Jewish community. And, Hoenlein emphasized, "We will not hesitate to make our voice heard."

Despite the fissures that have emerged between the Israeli government and some groups within American Jewry this community "has generally accepted the principle that in matters of fundamental security there ought to be no public criticism of Israel." According to Steven Rosenthal, "For millions of American Jews, criticism of Israel was a worse sin than marrying out of the faith." Or as Bookbinder once acknowledged, "There is a feeling of guilt as to whether Jews should double-check the Israeli government … They automatically fall into line for that very reason." Recent surveys of American Jewish opinion reveal that roughly two-thirds of

the respondents agree that "regardless of their individual views on the peace negotiations with the Arabs, American Jews should support the policies of the duly-elected government of Israel" Thus, even when both leaders and rank and file of important Jewish–American organizations have serious reservations about Israeli policy, they rarely call for the U.S. government to put significant pressure on the Israeli government.

The norm against public criticism of Israeli policy remains for the most part intact. In October 1996, for example, the president of ZOA, Morton Klein, sent a letter to ADL head Abraham Foxman protesting an invitation to *New York Times* columnist Thomas L. Friedman to speak at an ADL dinner, charging that Friedman "regularly defames Israel and its Prime Minister Benjamin Netanyahu." Klein then circulated the letter to an array of officials at the Conference of Presidents, leading Foxman to denounce him as a "thought policeman." The dispute intensified when David Bar–Ulan, Netanyahu's director of communications, weighed in and declared that Friedman should not be given a platform by "any organization that purports to be Zionist." Though sometimes critical of certain Israeli policies, Friedman is hardly anti-Israel, and Foxman himself is one of Israel's most ardent defenders. But Klein's response shows how deep the opposition to open discussion runs.

A few years later, Edgar Bronfman Sr., then president of the World Jewish Congress, was accused of "perfidy" when he wrote a letter to President Bush urging him to pressure Israel to curb construction of its controversial "security fence." The executive vice president of the congress, Isi Liebler, declared that "it would be obscene at any time for the president of the World Jewish Congress to lobby the president of the United States to resist policies being promoted by the government of Israel." Liebler and others were similarly incensed two years later, when the president of the moderate Israel Policy Forum, Seymour Reich, advised Secretary of State Condoleezza Rice to pressure Israel to reopen a critical border crossing in the Gaza Strip in November 2005. Reich's advice to Rice was reasonable and well intentioned, but Liebler denounced his action as "irresponsible behavior," and the president of the Orthodox Union, Stephen Savitzky, said it was "not only disrespectful to Israel's government but offensive to millions of American Jews who categorically reject such an approach." Liebler also warned, "There is obviously something sick in the state of World Jewry when purportedly mainstream leaders feel that they can lobby freely against the security policies of the democratically elected government of Israel. If this sort of behavior is to be tolerated we may as well write off our one remaining ally— Diaspora Jewry." Recoiling from these attacks, Reich announced that "the word pressure is not in my vocabulary when it comes to Israel."

The reluctance to criticize Israel's policies openly is not difficult to fathom. In addition to the obvious desire not to say anything that might aid Israel's enemies, groups or individuals who criticize Israeli policy or the U.S.–Israel relationship are likely to find it harder to retain support and raise funds within the Jewish community. They also run the risk of being ostracized by the larger mainstream organizations. Although groups like Americans for Peace Now, the Tikkun Community, the Israel Policy Forum, and the New Israel Fund have endured and thrived where Breira [a center-left Jewish organization founded in 1973] did not, other progressive Jewish groups, such as New Jewish Agenda, encountered the same opposition that Breira had faced and lasted little more than a decade. Similarly, although Americans for Peace Now was eventually admitted to the Conference of Presidents in 1993 after a contentious struggle, the progressive Meretz USA and the liberal Reconstructionist Rabbinical Association were denied membership in 2002 despite support from moderate groups within the Conference. On a smaller scale, Jewish Voice for Peace was denied a booth at a major Jewish community event in the San Francisco area on the grounds that it was insufficiently supportive of Israel, and the Hillel chapter at the University of Texas refused to give an organization called Jewish Students for Palestinian Rights space to conduct a study group.

Efforts to marginalize dissenting Jewish voices continue to this day. When the Union of Progressive Zionists (UPZ) sponsored campus appearances in 2006 by Breaking the Silence, an organization of former Israeli soldiers that is critical of IDF operations in the Occupied Territories, ZOA denounced UPZ and demanded that it be expelled from the Israel on Campus Coalition (ICC), a network of pro-Israel groups that includes AIPAC and the ADL. According to ZOA's Klein, sponsoring groups that are critical of Israel "is not the mission of the ICC." UPZ's director emphasized the group's "love for Israel," other groups rallied to its defense, and the ICC steering committee unanimously rejected ZOA's demand. Undeterred, Klein denounced the members of the steering committee and said, "Their mission includes fighting incitement, and yet we are astonished that they would ignore this incitement by Israelis against Israel." ZOA also issued a press release urging member organizations in the ICC to change their votes. The press release quoted an Israeli Foreign Ministry report saying, "The willingness of Jewish communities to host these organizations and even sponsor them is unfortunate … Their negative effect on Israel's image must be stopped." At least one Orthodox group on the ICC steering committee subsequently announced it was now in favor of removing the UPZ.

The Lobby Moves Right

Most American Jews have long supported liberal causes and the Democratic party and a majority of them favor a two-state solution to the Israeli–Palestinian conflict. Nonetheless, some of the most important groups in the lobby—including AIPAC and the Conference of Presidents—have become increasingly conservative over time and are now led by hard-liners who support the positions of their hawkish counterparts in Israel. As J. J. Goldberg chronicles in his important book *Jewish Power,* the Six–Day War and its aftermath brought into prominence a group of "New Jews" drawn disproportionately from hard-line Zionist,

Orthodox, and neoconservative circles. "Their defiance was so strident, and their anger so intense," he writes, "that the rest of the Jewish community respectfully stood back and let the New Jews take the lead. The minority was permitted to speak for the mass and become the dominant voice of Jewish politics."

This trend was reinforced by the campaign on behalf of the 1974 Jackson–Vanik amendment (which linked most-favored-nation trading status for the Soviet Union to Moscow's willingness to permit greater Jewish emigration), by the emergence and growth of the so-called neoconservative movement, and by the Likud party's successful effort to cultivate and strengthen hard-line support in key pro-Israel organizations during the years when Likud was sharing power with Israel's Labor party. According to Goldberg, "The genius of Shamir's strategy ... was to manipulate the central bodies of Jewish representation so that, without taking sides, they became voices for the Likud half of the government." Likud party officials (including Prime Minister Shamir's chief of staff Yossi Ben–Aharon) worked to ensure that the Conference of Presidents was chaired by more conservative officials and also helped engineer the selection of Malcolm Hoenlein as executive vice chairman of the conference in 1986. More hard-line groups were given greater access and attention by Israeli leaders, which reinforced the perception that they were the authoritative voices of the Jewish community. As an adviser to Labor party leader Shimon Peres later admitted, "Ignoring American Jewry was one of the biggest mistakes we made ... We let Shamir's people do whatever they wanted."

This rightward shift also reflects the way decisions are made in some key organizations in the lobby as well as the growing influence of a small number of wealthy conservatives who increasingly dominate organizations like AIPAC. There are more than fifty organizations represented in the Conference of Presidents, for example, and each has a single vote regardless of size. But as Michael Massing points out, "Smaller conservative groups in the conference decisively outnumber the larger liberal ones and so can neutralize their influence.

And that leaves considerable discretion in the hands of [executive vice chairman] Malcolm Hoenlein," who is a longtime supporter of Israel's settler movement and was deeply skeptical about the Oslo peace process.

Similarly, membership on AIPAC's board of directors is based on each directors financial contributions, not, observes Massing, on "how well they represent AIPAC's members." The individuals willing to give the largest amounts to AIPAC (and to sympathetic politicians) tend to be the most zealous defenders of Israel, and AIPAC's top leadership (consisting primarily of former presidents of the organization) is considerably more hawkish on Middle East issues than are most Jewish Americans. Although AIPAC formally endorsed the Oslo peace process in 1993, it did little to make it work and dropped its opposition to a Palestinian state—without endorsing the idea—only after Ehud Barak became prime minister in 1999.

It bears repeating that a number of groups in the American Jewish community are critical of certain Israeli policies, and especially its continued presence in the Occupied Territories. Some of these organizations, such as the Israel Policy Forum or Brit Tzedek v'Shalom, actively promote U.S. engagement in the peace process and have been able to win some minor legislative victories in recent years. Yet such groups lack the financial resources and the influence of AIPAC, the ADL, ZOA, or the Conference of Presidents, whose right-of-center views are unfortunately taken by politicians, policy makers, and the media to be the representative voice of American Jewry. For the moment, therefore, the major organizations in the lobby will continue to advocate policy positions at odds with many of the people in whose name they claim to speak.

The lobby's drift to the right has been reinforced by the emergence of the neoconservatives. The neoconservative movement has been an important part of American intellectual and political life since the 1970s, but it has drawn particular attention since September 11. This group has been prominent in shaping the Bush administration's unilateralist foreign policy, and especially the ill-fated decision to invade Iraq in March 2003.

Neoconservatism is a political ideology with distinct views on both domestic and foreign policy, although only the latter is relevant here. Most neoconservatives extol the virtues of American hegemony—and sometimes even the idea of an American empire—and they believe U.S. power should be used to encourage the spread of democracy and discourage potential rivals from even trying to compete with the United States. In their view, spreading democracy and preserving U.S. dominance is the best route to long-term peace. Neoconservatives also believe that America's democratic system ensures that it will be seen as a benign hegemon by most other countries, and that U.S. leadership will be welcomed provided it is exercised decisively. They tend to be skeptical of international institutions (especially the UN, which they regard as both anti-Israel and as a constraint on Americas freedom of action) and wary of many allies (especially the Europeans, whom they see as idealistic pacifists free-riding on the Pax Americana). Viewing U.S. leadership as "good both for America and for the world," to quote the website of the neoconservative Project for New American Century, neoconservatives generally favor the unilateral exercise of American power instead.

Very importantly, neoconservatives believe that military force is an extremely useful tool for shaping the world in ways that will benefit America. If the United States demonstrates its military prowess and shows that it is willing to use the power at its disposal, then allies will follow our lead and potential adversaries will realize it is futile to resist and will decide to "bandwagon" with the United States. Neoconservatism, in short, is an especially hawkish political ideology

Neoconservatives occupy influential positions at a variety of organizations and institutions. Prominent neoconservatives include former and present policy makers like Elliott Abrams, Kenneth Adelman, William Bennett, John Bolton, Douglas Feith, the late Jeane Kirkpatrick, I. Lewis "Scooter" Libby, Richard Perle, Paul Wolfowitz, James Woolsey and David Wurmser; journalists

like the late Robert Bartley, David Brooks, Charles Krauthammer, William Kristol, Bret Stephens, and Norman Podhoretz; academics like Fouad Ajami, Eliot Cohen, Aaron Friedberg, Bernard Lewis, and Ruth Wedgwood; and think-tank pundits like Max Boot, David Frum, Reuel Marc Gerecht, Robert Kagan, Michael Ledeen, Joshua Muravchik, Daniel Pipes, Danielle Pletka, Michael Rubin, and Meyrav Wurmser. The leading neoconservative magazines and newspapers are *Commentary,* the *New York Sun,* the *Wall Street Journal* op-ed page, and the *Weekly Standard.* The think tanks and advocacy groups most closely associated with these neoconservatives are the American Enterprise Institute (AEI), the Center for Security Policy (CSP), the Hudson Institute, the Foundation for Defense of Democracies (FDD), the Jewish Institute for National Security Affairs (JINSA), the Middle East Forum (MEF), the Project for a New American Century (PNAC), and the Washington Institute for Near East Policy (WINEP).

Virtually all neoconservatives are strongly committed to Israel, a point they emphasize openly and unapologetically. According to Max Boot, a leading neocon servative pundit, supporting Israel is "a key tenet of neoconservatism," a position he attributes to "shared liberal democratic values." Benjamin Ginsberg, a political scientist who has written extensively about American politics as well as anti-Semitism, convincingly argues that one of the main reasons that the neoconservatives moved to the right was "their attachment to Israel and their growing frustration during the 1960s with a Democratic party that was becoming increasingly opposed to American military preparedness and increasingly enamored of Third World causes." In particular, writes Ginsberg, they embraced Ronald Reagan's "hardline anti-communism" because they saw it as a "political movement that would guarantee Israel's security."

Of course, the neoconservatives care about America's security as well as Israel's, and they believe that their policy prescriptions will benefit both countries. In the 1980s, however, some more traditional conservatives—sometimes referred to as "paleoconservatives"—claimed that the neo-conservatives were more concerned about Israel than the United States. For example, Russell Kirk, the well-known conservative political theorist, maintained that "what really animates the neo-conservatives … is the preservation of Israel. That lies in back of everything." The neoconservatives vehemently denied these charges, which led to several bitter exchanges between these contending conservative factions. That conflict eventually subsided, but tension still remains between these two strands of the conservative movement.

A number of commentators have emphasized the Jewish roots of neo-conservatism, even though many of the movement's key tenets run counter to the liberal attitudes that still predominate in the American Jewish community. In *The Neoconservative Revolution: Jewish Intellectuals and the Shaying of Public Policy*, a book that paints a sympathetic portrait of its subject, Murray Friedman goes so far as to describe neoconservatism as "American Jewish conservatism." But not all neoconservatives are Jewish, which reminds us that the lobby is defined not by ethnicity or religion but by a political agenda. There are a number of prominent gentiles who have adopted most if not all of the basic tenets of neoconservatism, to include vigorous support for Israel and a tendency to favor its more hard-line elements. Their ranks include the *Wall Street Journal* editor Robert Bartley, former Secretary of Education William Bennett, former UN Ambassadors John Bolton and Jeane Kirkpatrick, and former CIA director James Woolsey. Although these non-Jews have played an important role in pushing forward the neoconservative agenda, Jews nonetheless comprise the core of the neoconservative movement. In this sense, neoconservativism is a microcosm of the larger pro-Israel movement. Jewish Americans are central to the neoconservative movement, just as they form the bulk of the lobby, but non-Jews are active in both. Neoconservatives are also emblematic insofar as much of their political agenda is at odds with the traditional political views of most American Jews.

The Christian Zionists

The lobby includes another important group of gentiles—the Christian Zionists, a subset of the broader politically oriented Christian Right. Prominent members of this constituency include religious figures such as the late Jerry Falwell, Gary Bauer, Pat Robertson, and John Hagee, as well as politicians like former House Majority Leaders Tom DeLay (R–TX) and Richard Armey (R–TX), and Senator James Inhofe (R–OK). Although support for Israel is not their only concern, a number of Christian evangelicals have become increasingly visible and vocal in their support for the Jewish state, and they have recently formed an array of organizations to advance that commitment within the political system. In a sense, the Christian Zionists can be thought of as an important "junior partner" to the various pro-Israel groups in the American Jewish community

The origins of Christian Zionism lie in the theology of dispensationalism, an approach to biblical interpretation that emerged in nineteenth-century England, largely through the efforts of Anglican ministers Louis Way and John Nelson Darby. Dispensationalism is a form of premillennialism, which asserts that the world will experience a period of worsening tribulations until Christ returns. Like many other Christians, dispensationalists believe that Christ's return is foretold in Old and New Testament prophecy and that the return of the Jews to Palestine is a key event in the preordained process that will lead to the Second Coming. The theology of Darby, Way, and their followers influenced a number of prominent English politicians and may have made British Foreign Secretary Arthur Balfour more receptive to the idea of creating a Jewish national home in Palestine.

The founding of the state of Israel in 1948 gave new life to the dispensationalist movement, but the Six–Day War in 1967, which its leaders saw as a "miracle of God," was even more important for its emergence as a political force. Dispensationalists interpreted Israel's seizure of all of Jerusalem and the West Bank (which, like Israel's Likud party they refer to as Judea and Samaria) as the fulfillment of Old and New Testament prophecy, and these "signs" encouraged them and other Christian evangelicals to begin working to ensure that the United States was on the "right side" as the Bible's blueprint for the end-times unfolded. According to Timothy Weber, former president of the Memphis Theological Seminary, "Before the Six Day War, dispensationalists were content to sit in the bleachers of history, explaining the End-Time game on the field below ... But after [the] expansion of Israel into the West Bank and Gaza, they began to get down on the field and be sure the teams lined up right, becoming involved in political, financial, and religious ways they never had before." Their efforts were part of the broader rise of the so-called Christian Right (not all of whom are strongly committed to Israel) and were clearly aided by the growing political prominence of the evangelical movement.

Yet the influence of the Christian Zionists should not be overstated. Their strong commitment to a "greater Israel" and resulting opposition to a two-state solution did not prevent the Clinton administration from pursuing the latter at Camp David in 2000, did not halt the 1998 Wye Agreement mandating an Israeli redeployment from parts of the West Bank, and, perhaps most revealingly, did not stop President George W. Bush, who has close ties to the Christian Right, from declaring his own support for a Palestinian state in 2001.

There are several reasons why Christian Zionists exert less impact on U.S. Middle East policy than the other parts of the Israel lobby do. Although the Christian Right has been a key part of President Bush's political base (which has to some degree magnified the visibility of the Christian Zionist elements within this broader movement), the alliance goes well beyond the issue of Israel to include a broad array of social issues. Supporting Israel is only one of the many issues that evangelicals like Robertson, Bauer, and Falwell have been concerned with, and it may not even be the most important. Leaders of the Christian Right often claim to speak on behalf of forty million or more professed evangelical Christians, but the number of followers who

care deeply about Israel is undoubtedly smaller. In addition, and in sharp contrast to groups like AIPAC, Christian Zionists lack the organizational capacity to analyze national security topics or to offer specific legislative guidance on concrete foreign policy issues. Surveys of congressional' aides by Ruth Mouly in the 1980s and Irvine Anderson in 1999 found 'little evidence of extensive direct lobbying of Congress by Falwell or other prominent members of the Religious Right on the subject of Israel." Similarly Rabbi Yechiel Eckstein, founder of IFCJ, told the Israeli writer Zev Chafets that a delegation of evangelicals he had taken to visit then National Security Adviser Condoleezza Rice in 2003 "was the only Christian group ever to lobby the White House specifically on behalf of Israel." Even if Eckstein overstated the case somewhat, it is clear that Israel is only one of many items on the evangelicals' list of concerns. By contrast, groups like AIPAC, the Anti-Defamation League, ZOA, and the Conference of Presidents put U.S. support for Israel at the top of their agenda, and their efforts to influence foreign policy are reinforced by think tanks like JINSA and WINEP.

Furthermore, Christianity contains a complex set of moral and religious teachings, and many of its most important precepts neither justify nor encourage unconditional support for Israel. Christian Zionists may believe that biblical prophecy justifies Jewish control of all of Palestine, but other Christian principles—such as Christ's command to "love thy neighbor as thyself"—are sharply at odds with Israel's treatment of its Palestinian subjects. Familiarity with Old Testament stories and other aspects of the Judeo–Christian tradition has not prevented many mainline Christian churches from openly backing a two-state solution and criticizing various aspects of Israeli policy, based on their own commitment to Christian principles of peace and justice. Just as many American Jews do not support everything that Israel is doing, neither do many Christians, including evangelicals.

Christian Zionists also lack the financial power of the major pro-Israel Jewish groups, and they do not have the same media presence when it comes to Middle East issues. Leaders like Robertson or Bauer may get lots of media attention when they speak on moral or religious questions, but media organizations are more likely to turn to the Brookings Institution or WINEP when discussing current events in Israel or the Middle East. For all these reasons, the Christian Zionists are best seen as a significant adjunct to the Jewish elements of the lobby, but not its most important part.

The Lobby's Sources of Power

Why is the Israel lobby so effective? One reason is the wide-open nature of the American political system. The United States has a divided form of government, a well-established tradition of free speech, and a system in which elections are very expensive to run and where campaign contributions are weakly regulated. This environment gives different groups many different ways to gain access or influence policy. Interest groups can direct campaign contributions to favored candidates and try to defeat candidates whose views are suspect. They can also lobby elected representatives and members of the executive branch, and they can try to get their own supporters appointed to key policy-making positions. Moreover, there are numerous ways for interest groups to mold public opinion: by cultivating sympathetic journalists; writing books, articles, and op-eds; and working to discredit or marginalize anyone with different views. For a group that is highly motivated and has sufficient resources, there is no shortage of ways to influence public policy.

The lobby's effectiveness also reflects the basic dynamics of interest group politics in a pluralistic society. In a democracy, even relatively small groups can exercise considerable influence if they are strongly committed to a particular issue and the rest of the population is largely indifferent. Even if the group's absolute numbers are small, policy makers—and especially members of Congress—will tend to accommodate them, because they can be confident that the rest of the population will not penalize them for doing so. As one U.S. senator put it, when asked why he

and his colleagues signed a piece of controversial legislation pushed by the lobby "There is no political advantage in not signing. If you do sign you don't offend anyone. If you don't you might offend some Jews in your state."

The disproportionate influence of small but focused interest groups increases even more when opposing groups are weak or nonexistent, because politicians have to accommodate only one set of interests and the public is likely to hear only one side of the story. Whether the issue is farm subsidies or foreign policy special interest groups often wield political power that far exceeds their absolute numbers in the population.

As will become clear in the next chapter, the Israel lobby enjoys a number of advantages in the competition for influence in the United States. American Jews are relatively prosperous and well educated, and have an admirable philanthropic tradition. They give generously to political parties and have very high rates of political participation. A sizable minority of American Jews is not strongly committed to Israel, but a clear majority is at least somewhat engaged and a significant minority is strongly energized by this issue. When married to the support Israel gets from Christian Zionists, it is a potent base.

Equally important is the impressive level of resources and expertise within the major Jewish organizations in the lobby According to the political scientist Robert Trice, "Most major Jewish groups are characterized by large memberships, well-trained professional staffs, adequately financed social, welfare and political programs, specialized working groups for particular problems and elaborate internal communications networks." Moreover, the existence of numerous organizations at the local and national level explains "the ability of the pro-Israel movement to mobilize rapidly and in a coordinated fashion on a national scale when important foreign policy issues arise."

These efforts are facilitated by Israel's generally favorable image in the United States. As former Senator Warren Rudman (R–NH) once commented, "They have a pretty good product to sell." As we shall see, that favorable image is due in good part to the lobby's own efforts to make sure that Israel is portrayed favorably, as well as the broad sense that the United States and Israel are part of a common Judeo–Christian culture and are linked by various informal connections.

Finally, the lobby benefits from the absence of effective opposition. As one senator explained, "There's no countervailing sentiment … If you vote contrary to the tremendous pressure of AIPAC, nobody says to you, 'That's great.'" Although Arab Americans are a significant minority, they are neither as wealthy, well organized, numerous, or politically active as Jewish Americans. As a group, Arab Americans have not been as successful in reaching prominent positions in academia, business, and the media, and they are also less visible in politics. This is partly because the main waves of Arab immigration to the United States occurred relatively recently and first-generation immigrants are less affluent, less represented in important professions, less familiar with American mores and institutions, less active in politics, and therefore less influential than subsequent generations tend to be.

Pro-Arab organizations are also no match for the major groups that make up the Israel lobby There are a handful of pro-Arab and pro-Palestinian interest groups in the United States, but they are smaller than AIPAC and other pro-Israel organizations, not nearly as well funded, and nowhere near as effective. According to Mitchell Bard, the former editor of AIPAC's *Near East Report,* "From the beginning, the Arab lobby has faced not only a disadvantage in electoral politics but also in organization. There are several politically oriented groups, but many of these are one-man operations with little financial or popular support." U.S. politicians rarely, if ever, complain about pressure from an "Arab–American lobby" and have little reason to adjust their behavior to accommodate it. As Harry Truman famously remarked, "In all of my political experience I don't ever recall the Arab vote swinging a close election."

Moreover, because Arab Americans come from a variety of countries and backgrounds, and include Christians as well as Muslims, they are unlikely to speak with a unified voice on Middle East issues. Indeed, they sometimes hold sharply opposing views. And whereas many Americans sense a degree of cultural proximity between Israel and the United States and believe Israelis are "like us," Arabs are often seen as part of an alien (or even hostile) civilization. As a result, winning hearts and minds in the United States is an uphill battle for its Arab–American citizens in ways that it has not been for American Jews or their Christian allies. Robert Trice's 1981 assessment of Arab-American groups remains true today: "Their impact on most aspects of U.S. Middle East policy remains negligible."

The (Modest) Impact of Oil

Neither Arab governments nor the vaunted "oil lobby" pose a significant counterweight to the Israel lobby. The belief that oil companies and/or wealthy oil sheikhdoms exert a powerful influence on U.S. Middle East policy is widespread and is reflected in the frequent claim that the war in Iraq in 2003 was a "war for oil" and for related corporate interests such as Halliburton. Interestingly, this view is advanced by some of Israel's most persistent critics—such as Noam Chomsky and Stephen Zunes—as well as by fervent defenders like Martin Peretz. More conspiratorial versions of this perspective suggest that personal and financial connections between the Bush family and the House of Saud have shaped U.S. Middle East policy to America's detriment. These various interpretations portray the Israel lobby as just one player among many, and probably not the most important one.

There is no question that the United States has a major strategic interest in the energy resources located in the Persian Gulf. Although the United States currently imports more of its energy from Canada, Mexico, and Venezuela than from states in the Middle East, oil and natural gas are bought and sold in a tightly integrated world market and thus anything that reduces the overall supply is going to push prices up and hurt the American economy. As discussed in Chapter 2, this is why U.S. leaders see the Persian Gulf as a vital interest and why they have taken steps to preserve a local balance of power there and prevent any hostile state from interfering with the flow of oil from that region. This basic fact also explains why the United States has sought to preserve good relations with a number of different countries in the Gulf, despite differing with them on various domestic and foreign policy issues. The importance of Middle East oil led the United States to become a close ally of Saudi Arabia after World War II and is one reason why Washington backed the shah of Iran for many years. After his regime fell in 1979, this same desire to maintain a local balance of power and to keep the oil flowing convinced the Reagan administration to tilt toward Saddam Husseins Iraq during the Iran–Iraq War (1980–88). The United States then intervened to evict Iraq from Kuwait after it seized the sheikhdom in 1990, a policy consistent with the long-standing U.S. policy of preventing any single power from establishing hegemony in the region. A powerful lobby was not needed to encourage these policies, because few questioned the need to keep Persian Gulf oil out of unfriendly hands.

Beyond this obvious interest in preserving access to Middle East oil, however, there is little evidence that either wealthy Arab states or a powerful 'oil lobby' has had much impact on the broad thrust of U.S. Middle East policy. After all, if Arab petrodollars or energy companies were driving American policy, one would expect to see the United States distancing itself from Israel and working overtime to get the Palestinians a state of their own. Countries like Saudi Arabia have repeatedly pressed Washington to adopt a more evenhanded position toward the Israeli–Palestinian conflict, but to little avail, and even wielding the "oil weapon" during the 1973 October War had little effect on U.S. support for Israel or on overall American policy in the region. Similarly, if oil companies were driving U.S. policy, one would also have expected Washington to curry favor with big oil producers like Saddam Hussein's Iraq, Muammar Gaddafi's Libya, or the Islamic Republic of Iran, so that U.S. companies could make money helping them develop their energy resources and bringing them to market.

Instead, the United States imposed sanctions on all three of these countries, in sharp opposition to what the oil industry wanted. Indeed, as we will show in Part II, in some cases the U.S. government deliberately intervened to thwart business deals that would have benefited U.S. companies. If the oil lobby were as powerful as some critics believe, such actions would not have occurred.

Wealthy oil producers such as Saudi Arabia have hired public relations firms and professional lobbyists to enhance their image in the United States and to lobby for specific arms deals, and their efforts have occasionally borne fruit. Their most notable achievement was convincing Congress to approve the sale of AWAGS aircraft to Saudi Arabia in 1982, despite AIPAC's strong opposition. This episode is sometimes invoked to demonstrate the Israel lobby's limited influence and the power of the "Arab lobby," but the latter's victory in this case was mostly due to a set of unusually favorable conditions. The strategic importance of Saudi oil was obvious, the Soviet Union was seen as a serious military threat to the Gulf at that time, Ronald Reagan was a popular president, and his administration pulled out all the stops to win congressional approval. Even so, the sale barely squeaked through (the final Senate vote was 52-48 in favor), and Reagan was forced to withdraw several subsequent arms packages to Saudi Arabia and Jordan in the face of renewed opposition from the lobby and from Congress.

One reason why Arab oil producers have only limited influence is their lack of an indigenous base of support in the United States. Because they are forced to rely on professional lobbyists and public relations firms, it is easier for critics to denigrate their representatives as mere agents of a foreign power. AIPAC's Tom Dine once dismissed Saudi lobbying efforts by saying, "They hire foreign agents like Fred Dutton to do their bidding. Their support is not rooted in American soil." The Israel lobby by contrast, is a manifestation of the political engagement of a subset of American citizens, and so its activities are widely and correctly seen as a legitimate form of political activity.

Furthermore, because most oil-exporting governments depend on large revenues to keep themselves in power, threatening to cut off the supply is not credible and their leverage is thus reduced. Many of these governments also have sizable investments in Western economies and would suffer considerable losses in the event of a sustained economic downturn. Reducing production would drive prices up and make alternative energy sources more attractive, and give the United States and other countries a big incentive to wean themselves from oil dependence once and for all. Because major oil exporters like Saudi Arabia want to keep the industrial powers hooked on oil and gas, they have an obvious disincentive to using what little leverage may be at their disposal. As a result, U.S. dependence on imported energy supplies has not given these countries much influence over U.S. policy.

What about energy companies? These corporations do engage in plenty of lobbying activities, but their efforts in recent decades have focused almost entirely on their commercial interests rather than on broader aspects of foreign policy. Specifically energy companies concentrate on tax policy, government regulation, environmental concerns, access to potential drilling sites, and other practical dimensions of energy policy. For them, foreign policy is normally a secondary concern, and according to Robert Trice, their "primary goal ... is to create a political and economic environment in the Middle East that will allow them to maximize profits. As such, the political interests of corporate actors are generally much narrower than those of the pro-Arab groups."

This relatively narrow focus is apparent when one examines the website of the American Petroleum Institute, the flagship trade association of the oil industry. Five topics appear under the general heading of "policy issues": climate change, exploration/production, fuels, taxes and trade, and homeland security There is no reference to "Israel" or the "Arab–Israeli conflict" anywhere on the site, and few references to foreign policy at all. By contrast, Israel and U.S. foreign policy are front and center on the websites of AIPAC, the ADL, and the Conference of Presidents. As

AIPAC's Morris Amitay noted in the early 1980s, "When oil interests and other corporate interests lobby, 99 percent of the time they are acting in what they perceive to be their own self-interest— they lobby on tax bills ... We very rarely see them lobbying on foreign policy issues ... In a sense, we have the field to ourselves." In addition, American corporations appear to be discouraged from trying to influence U.S. Middle East policy by the fear of retaliation from well-organized pro-Israel groups. In 1975, for example, the revelation that Gulf Oil had underwritten a number of pro-Arab activities in the United States led to public condemnations by the Conference of Presidents and the Anti–Defamation League. In response, Gulf bought a half-page ad in the *New York Times* in which it apologized for its action and told readers, "You may be certain it will not happen again." As Trice notes, "A vigilant, sensitive, and reactive pro-Israel lobby is one reason why U.S. corporations have tended to avoid direct participation in domestic political debates on Middle East questions."

Some commentators believe that oil and gas companies are driving U.S. policy either to gain lucrative concessions in places like Iraq, or to foment instability that will drive up oil prices and enable them to reap windfall profits. Not only is there little direct evidence of such behavior, but it runs counter to the long-term interests of major energy companies. Energy companies do not like wars in oil-rich regions, sanctions, or regime change—the staples of U.S. Middle East policy in recent years—because each of them threatens access to oil and gas reserves and thus their ability to make money, and such events also encourage Americans to think more seriously about reducing demand for the oil companies' main product. Thus, when Vice President Dick Cheney was the president of Halliburton, Inc., a major oil services firm, in the 1990s, he opposed U.S. sanctions on Iran (a policy, as discussed in Chapter 10, driven largely by the lobby) and complained that U.S. firms were being "cut out of the action" by America's "sanctions happy" policy. Cheney's earlier position suggests that if oil companies controlled Middle East policy the United States would have pursued a very different agenda in recent years.

None of this denies that oil companies, good capitalists that they are, will seek to profit from foreign policy initiatives that they did not encourage. It is not surprising that oil companies want to obtain lucrative concessions in post-Saddam Iraq, just as they would have been happy to do business with Saddam himself. On balance, however, wealthy Arab governments and the oil lobby exert much less influence on U.S. foreign policy than the Israel lobby does, because oil interests have less need to skew foreign policy in the directions they favor and they do not have the same leverage. Writing in the early 1970s, the Columbia University professor and former Assistant Secretary of State Roger Hilsman observed, "It is obvious to even the most casual observer … that United States foreign policy in the Middle East, where oil reigns supreme, has been more responsive to the pressures of the American Jewish community and their natural desire to support Israel than it has to American oil interests." In his comparison of the Israel and Arab lobbies, Mitchell Bard acknowledges that although oil companies like Aramco have conducted lobbying campaigns in the past, the effort "has had no observable impact on U.S. policy." Or as AIPAC's former legislative director, Douglas Bloomfield, told *BBC News* in 2003, "AIPAC has one enormous advantage. It really doesn't have any opposition."

The Question of "Dual Loyalty"

This picture of a powerful special interest group, comprised mainly of American Jews and working to move U.S. policy in a pro-Israel direction, is bound to make some people uncomfortable, because it seems to invoke the specter of "dual loyalty," which was once a common anti-Semitic canard in old Europe. The charge, in its original incarnation, was that Jews in the diaspora were perpetual aliens who could not assimilate and become good patriots. According to this now-discredited argument, Jews were thought to be loyal only to each other. The infamous *Protocols of the Elders of Zion,* a tsarist forgery that was exposed and discredited long ago, claimed that Jews operate as a fifth column in the countries where they live, working for a committee of Jewish elders who are secretly plotting to dominate the world.

In this earlier, anti-Semitic incarnation, dual loyalty was in fact a misnomer, as the charge implied that Jews were loyal only to each other and felt no genuine loyalty to their home countries. Today however, both scholars and commentators use the term in a neutral and nonpejorative fashion to describe the widespread circumstance where individuals feel genuine attachments (or loyalties) to more than one country. Thus, in his recent comparison of different ethnic diasporas, the Israeli political scientist Gabriel Sheffer distinguishes among "total," "dual," and "divided" loyalty, and notes that all three responses occur when members of a particular ethnic, national, or religious group are scattered across different states. As discussed below, other thoughtful Jewish Americans have used "dual loyalty" to describe their own attitudes and experiences, but their use of the term is very different from its past employment as an anti-Semitic slander.

Any notion that Jewish Americans are disloyal citizens is wrong. We fully agree with Malcolm Hoenlein, who directs the Conference of Presidents, that "it is safe to say that American Jews are among the most patriotic and loyal of American citizens." As we have made clear, those who lobby on Israel's behalf are acting in ways that are consistent with long-standing political traditions. Indeed, political life in the United States has long proceeded from the assumption that all individuals have a variety of attachments and loyalties—to country religion, family employer, just to name a few—and that American citizens will create formal and informal associations that reflect those loyalties and interests. Consider, for example, a 2006 Pew Global Attitudes survey of Christians in thirteen countries in which 42 percent of the U.S. respondents saw themselves as Christians first and Americans second. These different attachments, which sometimes include an affinity for a foreign country may reflect ancestry, religious affiliation, personal experience (such as overseas study or a Peace Corps assignment), or any number of other sources. It is legitimate for U.S. citizens to express such attachments and affinities in political life; this is in fact what democratic theory implies that they should do. As we have noted, it is even permissible for Americans to hold dual citizenship and to serve in foreign armies—including the IDF—and some have done so.

Americans who work to influence U.S. foreign policy in ways that benefit Israel almost always believe that the policies they favor will benefit the United States as well. As former AIPAC executive director Tom Dine told one interviewer, "I came to this job thinking American foreign policy and how to strengthen America's position in the world. At the same time, I thought a lot about Israel because I am Jewish." More to the point, Theodore Mann, a former head of the Conference of Presidents, said in 2001 that "leading American Jews really feel very deeply that American interests and Israeli interests are one and the same."

While there is no question that this perspective is widely and deeply held, there is a problem with it: no two countries will always have the same interests. It is just not the way international politics works. There have been instances in the past, and there will be more in the future, where U.S. and Israeli interests were at odds. For example, it made good strategic sense for Israel to acquire nuclear weapons in the 1960s, but it was not in America's interest to have Israel go nuclear. Nor is it in the U.S. national interest when Israel kills or wounds innocent Palestinian civilians (even if only unintentionally) and especially not when it uses American-made weapons to do it. One sees a similar divergence of interests in Israel's decision to invade Lebanon in 1982, and in its recent opposition to U.S. plans to sell advanced weaponry to Saudi Arabia and other Persian Gulf states.

There are, however, thoughtful Jewish Americans—including some prominent policy makers—who openly acknowledge that conflicts can and do arise among their Jewish identities,

their understandable interest in Israel's well-being, and their genuine loyalty to the United States. To his credit, Henry Kissinger dealt forthrightly with this issue in his memoirs, writing that "though not practicing my religion, I could never forget that thirteen members of my family had died in Nazi concentration camps ... Most Israeli leaders were personal friends. And yet ... I had to subordinate my emotional preferences to my perception of the national interest ... It was not always easy; occasionally it proved painful."

Kissinger acknowledges what many would deny: tensions are bound to arise whenever Americans have strong affinities for other countries, no matter what the origins of those attachments and no matter how consistently they resolve them on behalf of their homeland. Or as one of Bill Clinton's Middle East advisers admitted anonymously, "We act in America's interest, but through a prism." Another veteran Jewish–American diplomat expressed a similar feeling by saying, "I thank God that I'm not working in Middle East affairs or at the U.N., where you might have to vote to condemn the Israelis."

These statements are in no sense confessions of disloyalty; on the contrary they are admirably honest reflections on the multiple loyalties that all human beings feel and that sometimes come into conflict. The journalist Eric Alterman offered an equally candid acknowledgment in 2003, noting that his own "dual loyalties" were "drilled into me by my parents, my grandparents, my Hebrew school teachers and my rabbis, not to mention Israeli and AIPAC college representatives." But instead of pretending that potential tradeoffs will never arise, Alterman recognizes that "we ought to be honest enough to at least imagine a hypothetical clash between American and Israeli interests. Here, I feel pretty lonely admitting that, every once in a while, I'm going to go with what's best for Israel."

Yet Alterman is not in fact alone. Consider the remarks of Stephen Steinlight, former director of national affairs at the American Jewish Committee. After recounting his own upbringing in America as a "Jewish nationalist, even a quasi-separatist," Steinlight remarks,

The process of my nationalist training was to inculcate the belief that the primary division of the world was between "us" and "them." Of course we saluted the American and Canadian flags and sang those anthems, usually with real feeling, but it was clear where our primary loyalty was meant to reside. I am also familiar with the classic, well-honed answer to this tension anytime this is cited: Israel and America are democracies; they share values; they have common strategic interests; loyalty to one cannot conceivably involve disloyalty to the other, etc., etc. All of which begs huge questions … and while it may be true in practice most of the time, it is by no means an absolute construct, devoid of all sort of potential exceptions … We have no less difficult a balancing act between group loyalty and a wider sense of belonging to America. That America has largely tolerated this dual loyalty—we get a free pass, I suspect, largely over Christian guilt about the Holocaust—makes it no less a reality.

It is important to emphasize that this phenomenon is not confined to Jewish Americans; rather, such tensions are an inevitable feature of a melting pot society that has drawn its citizens from all over the world. It is equally important to note that most American Jews would surely reject any suggestion that they would place Israel's interests ahead of America's if an obvious conflict arose between them.

Jews and non-Jews who believe that the United States should continue to give Israel strong and unconditional support have every right to advocate their positions, and it is wrong to question their loyalty when they do. Yet it is equally legitimate for critics to point out that organizations like AIPAC are not neutral, or that the individuals who run AIPAC, the ADL, the Conference of Presidents, and similar organizations are motivated by an attachment to Israel that is bound to shape their thinking about many foreign policy issues. Why else would Malcolm Hoenlein describe his job as follows: "I devote myself to the security of the Jewish state"? Or why does John Hagee of CUFI address the potential conflict between his support for Israeli settlements and official U.S. opposition to them by saying that "the law of God transcends the laws of the United States government and the U.S. State Department"? If he were not inspired by a strong attachment to Israel, why would Lenny Ben-David, the former director of information and research at AIPAC, agree to serve as Israel's deputy chief of mission in Washington from 1997 to 2000?

It is equally legitimate to question whether the policies advocated by these individuals and the organizations they represent are in the U.S. national interest, just as it is legitimate to question the impact of other special interest lobbies on other elements of U.S. domestic or foreign policy. Their patriotism can be above reproach, but their advice might be fostering policies that are wreaking havoc in a region of considerable strategic importance to the United States and indeed to the rest of the world. To question the soundness of that advice has nothing to do with the older, discredited use of "dual loyalty" to imply that Jews were unpatriotic.

Conclusion

The Israel lobby is the antithesis of a cabal or conspiracy; it operates out in the open and proudly advertises its own clout. In its basic operations, the Israel lobby is no different from interest groups like the farm lobby, steel and textile workers, and a host of ethnic lobbies, although the groups and individuals who comprise the Israel lobby are in an unusually favorable position to influence U.S. foreign policy. What sets it apart, in short, is its extraordinary effectiveness.

Jerusalem Syndrome

Decoding The Israel Lobby

By Walter Russell Mead

John Mearsheimer and Stephen Walt claim that they want *The Israel Lobby and U.S. Foreign Policy* "to foster a more clear-eyed and candid discussion of this subject." Unfortunately, that is not going to happen. *The Israel Lobby* will harden and freeze positions rather than open them up. It will delay rather than hasten the development of new U.S. policies in the Middle East. It will confuse the policy debate not just in the United States but throughout the world as well, while giving aid and comfort to anti-Semites wherever they are found. All of this is deeply contrary to the intentions of the authors; written in haste, the book will be repented at leisure.

That is not to say that *The Israel Lobby* is all bad. Mearsheimer and Walt were previously known as hard-core "realists" who minimized the importance of studying domestic politics and culture to understanding foreign policy. They seem to have abandoned such "structural realism" for what might be called "political realism": the view that the beliefs, values, and interests of various domestic actors shape their perception of the national interest and that the interaction between these domestic forces and international conditions holds the key to understanding policy. This political realism is a significantly richer and more fruitful (if more intellectually demanding and methodologically complex) approach than the

structural realism that Mearsheimer, especially, advocated in the past.

One must also commend the two authors for their decision to focus on an important topic that has not received the attention it merits. The politics of U.S. policy in the Middle East is a subject that is not well understood. Pro-Israel organizations, political action committees (pacs), and individuals do play significant roles in the U.S. political process, and they do influence politicians and journalists. Given the importance of the Middle East in U.S. foreign policy and world affairs, these actors and their influence should be explored. Even if *The Israel Lobby* is in the end not as helpful as they hope, Mearsheimer and Walt have admirably and courageously helped to start a much-needed conversation on a controversial and combustible topic. There should be no taboos among students of U.S. foreign policy—no questions that should not be asked, no issues that should be considered too hot to handle, no relationships or alliances, however deep or enduring, that should not be regularly and searchingly reviewed.

Walt and Mearsheimer's belief that the United States needs to find ways to bridge the gap between its current policies and the national aspirations of Palestinians and other Arabs is correct. But Mearsheimer and Walt have too simplistic

Walter Russell Mead, "Jerusalem Syndrome: Decoding the Israel Lobby," *Foreign Affairs*, vol. 86, no. 6, pp. 160–168. Copyright © 2007 by Council on Foreign Relations, Inc. Reprinted with permission.

and sunny a view of the United States alternatives in the Middle East—a fault they share with the "neoconservatives," who serve as the books betes noires. Overcoming the challenges of U.S. policy in the Middle East will not be nearly as easy as Mearsheimer and Walt think, and the route they propose is unlikely to reach the destination they seek, even if some of their concerns about the United States' current stance in the region are legitimate.

The books problems start very early and run very deep. Mearsheimer and Walt outline the case they plan to make on page 14: "The United States provides Israel with extraordinary material aid and diplomatic support, the lobby is the principal reason for that support, and this uncritical and unconditional support is not in the national interest." Note the slippage. The "extraordinary" support of the first clause quietly mutates into the "uncritical and unconditional" support of the last. "Extraordinary" is hardly the same thing as "uncritical and unconditional," but the authors proceed as if it were. They claim the clarity and authority of rigorous logic, but their methods are loose and rhetorical. This singularly unhappy marriage—between the pretensions of serious political analysis and the standards of the casual op-ed—both undercuts the case they wish to make and gives much of the book a disagreeably disingenuous tone.

Rarely in professional literature does one encounter such a gap between aspiration and performance as there is in *The Israel Lobby*. Mearsheimer and Walt fail to define "the lobby" in a clear way. Their accounts of the ways in which it exercises power, as well as their descriptions of the power it wields, are incoherent. Their use of evidence is uneven. At the level of geopolitics, their handling of the complex realities and crosscurrents of the Middle East fails to establish either the incontestable definition of the national interest that their argument requires or the superiority they claim for the policies they propose.

Beyond these faults, the insensitivity that the authors too frequently display in their handling of difficult topics will leave many readers convinced that, despite their frequent protestations

to the contrary, the authors are sly and malicious anti-Semites. These charges—made inevitable although not accurate by the authors' unwitting and innocent use of certain literary devices that trigger unhappy memories—are generating an ugly, ill-tempered, and thoroughly pointless debate about the authors' character and intentions. In that debate, at least, I can stand behind Mearsheimer and Walt. This may be a book that anti-Semites will love, but it is not necessarily an anti-Semitic book.

In Or Out?

The problems start with the definition. "The Israel lobby," write Mearsheimer and Walt, is "a convenient shorthand term for the loose coalition of individuals and organizations" working "to shape U.S. foreign policy in a pro-Israel direction." The lobby, as they see it, includes both hard-line groups such as AIPAC (the American Israel Public Affairs Committee) and CUFI (Christians United For Israel) and dovish groups such as the Israel Policy Forum, the Tikkun Community, and Americans for Peace Now. All of these groups agree that Israel ought to be defended, and the groups and individuals in the lobby work in various ways to shape U.S. policy toward the Jewish state along what they consider to be favorable lines, but they have occasionally deep divisions over exactly what policies are best for Israel.

Mearsheimer and Walt say clearly that the lobby is neither conspiratorial nor antipatriotic. They concede that the overwhelming majority of those involved sincerely believe that what is best for Israel is best for the United States, and vice versa. Moreover, the tendency to reflexively support the Israeli government has diminished over time. And individual groups that are part of the lobby have broken with Israeli policies at various points, even if the largest groups tend to embrace hard-line views.

Still, questions arise. If everyone from AIPAC to Americans for Peace Now is part of the lobby, what, exactly, is the political agenda the lobby supports? And if a variety of U.S. policies are consonant with the different agendas of different components of the lobby, what criteria should be used to measure the impact of the lobby as a whole? What is the relationship between the internal dynamics of this divided lobby and the politics and policies of both Israel and wider American society?

When it comes down to it, Mearsheimer and Walt do not seem to know who, exactly, belongs to this amoebic, engulfing blob they call the lobby and who does not. Take their own case. They describe themselves as pro-Israel, in that they believe in the state's right to exist. They admire its achievements and wish secure and prosperous lives for its citizens. They state categorically that the United States should aid Israel "if its survival is in danger." They frequently argue that current Israeli policies and U.S. support for them are counterproductive—that is, Washington should make its aid to Israel more conditional not because the two states do not share interests but precisely because they do. Conditional aid, Mearsheimer and Walt believe, will lead Israel to act in ways that ensure its survival while also benefiting the United States. And they care so passionately about this that they have written a long and controversial book on the subject. "We are obviously not part of the Israel lobby," they say. But under their own definition, is that really true?

The argument of *The Israel Lobby* actually seems to boil down to the point that the left wing of the lobby has a better grasp of both the Israeli and the U.S. national interests than the right wing of the lobby does. Mearsheimer and Walt maintain that when U.S. and Israeli national interests come into conflict, the United States should put its own interests first—but this, too, is a view that, as they concede, most members of the lobby share. So what sets the authors apart from the rest of the large mass of Americans, Jewish and non-Jewish, who want Israel to exist and care deeply about its fate but disagree and squabble over what the United States should do in the Middle East? Nothing, as far as I can see. Mearsheimer and Walt have come up with a definition of "the Israel lobby" that covers the waterfront, including

everyone from Jimmy Carter and George Soros to Paul Wolfowitz and Tom DeLay.

Since virtually every possible policy position is supported by some element of this lobby, the lobby never loses no matter what happens in Washington—like the man who always "wins" at roulette because he puts a chip on every square. President Bill Clinton presses Israel to make far-reaching concessions on the West Bank in a proposal that Mearsheimer and Walt agree should still be the point of departure for U.S. diplomacy in the region: obviously, a triumph for the Israel lobby. The Bush administration then shifts direction and stands by Israeli Prime Minister Ariel Sharon as he rejects all talk of territorial concessions: another win for the Israel lobby. Red, black, even, odd: the lobby never fails.

The Wages Of Influence

From a definition like this, no good can come. Unfortunately, Mearsheimer and Walt s account of the U.S. political system is equally vague. Does the lobby use the same techniques or different ones to shape the foreign policy of Democratic and Republican administrations? Does a Labor-based government in Israel have a different relationship with the lobby than a Likud-based one? What mix of political conditions in Israel and the United States makes the lobby's work easier? What political environment poses the greatest challenge? Mearsheimer and Walt have no time for such details.

The book would benefit from a much more rigorous discussion of what the lobby, in its various incarnations and permutations, actually gets. Much of it seems to be straightforward pork-barrel politics: legislation involving foreign aid and arms deals is written so as to benefit Israel, and there is steady pressure on the executive branch to interpret these laws in ways favorable to Israel's interests. But to what real effect? Mearsheimer and Walt provide some estimates about the financial value of these provisions, but it is not clear how important these achievements are, either to Israel's defense strategy or to the politics of the Middle East. They also cite various pro-Israel legislative acts and congressional resolutions that passed by overwhelming margins. A closer analysis of the actual impact of these bills on policy is needed. The U.S. political system is extremely good at providing hollow victories for lobbyists that have little or no real impact on policy—allowing the lobbyists to demonstrate their clout and legislators to score an easy political win. Mearsheimer and Walt never show that the legislative victories represent real control over critical matters of national policy either in the United States or the Middle East.

Also disappointing is their fairly conventional account of the relationship between neoconservatives and hard-line Israeli thinking. Mearsheimer and Walt present neoconservative thought as entirely in sync with—and, indeed, at the service of—Israeli security interests. There are, however, some important differences between neoconservative doctrine and the views of conservative Israelis—in particular about Arabs. The neoconservative belief that the Arab world teems with Lockean democrats ready to build stable and liberal modern states once the dictators are removed could hardly be further from conventional Israeli views about the political culture and developmental possibilities of their neighbors. The Israeli defense establishment was deeply skeptical of neoconservative hopes for a democratic renaissance in the Middle East following the removal of Saddam Hussein. In short, the relationship between neoconservative thought and the worldview of the Israeli right is much more complex than the simplistic picture painted here.

The book's poor analysis of U.S. domestic politics sometimes involves a remarkably slipshod handling of evidence. One rubs ones eyes, frequently, at the spectacle of these two academics earnestly and solemnly presenting fundraising letters and convention speeches and other materials by paid employees of AIPAC and other such groups as conclusive proof of those groups' power and reach. Pro-Israel groups are hardly unique in their need to tout their clout and use the fabled blue smoke and mirrors to magnify their power. That is what every interest group in the United States does, so as to get more resources for its next "vital battle." Mearsheimer and Walt are so fond of this kind of evidence that significant stretches of the book are devoted to the self-serving promotional statements of the lobby. The authors seem to think that such passages provide incontrovertible proof of the lobby's importance: they convict the lobby out of its own mouth, as it were. Unsophisticated readers maybe impressed; those wise in the crooked folkways of Washington will know just how far self-aggrandizing statements by lobbyists can be believed.

The authors' credulity never ceases to inspire. A group of 76 senators signed a pro-Israel open letter to President Gerald Ford. One of the signers, Senator Dick Culver (D–Iowa), later said that he "caved" and signed only because "the pressure was too great." Mearsheimer and Walt are uncritically enthralled and accept the retraction as revealing the true, inner Culver. Perhaps, but all one knows here is that Culver, by his own admission, was willing to say things he did not believe to gain a political advantage. When was he speaking the truth, and when was he seeking approval? Washington is unfortunately well supplied with loose-lipped opportunists who will say anything an audience—any audience—wants them to say. But here and elsewhere, Mearsheimer and Walt seem uncritically and even naïvely willing to take any statement from any source at face value if it will somehow help make their case.

Mearsheimer and Walt argue that financing campaigns is an important source of the Israel lobby's power, but their analysis of this phenomenon leaves much to be desired. Senator Hillary Clinton (D–N.Y.), they breathlessly report, received $30,000 from pro-Israel PACs for her 2006 reelection campaign. In fact, this figure significantly understates the support she received from what the Center for Responsive Politics calls "pro-Israel" money, which amounted to $328,000 toward her 2006 campaign. Still, although that number may look impressive, it was less than one percent of the money Clinton raised for her Senate reelection bid. Against the $328,000 in "pro-Israel" money, she received more than half a million dollars from the printing and publishing industry, $800,000 from healthcare interests, $1 million from groups and individuals interested in women's issues, $2 million from donors based in real estate, and more than $4 million from lawyers and law firms. Had every dime of "pro-Israel" money gone to her opponent, there would have been no significant difference for her campaign.

What was true for Clinton in 2006 was true overall. Pro-Israel PACs contributed slightly more than $3 million to House and Senate candidates in the 2006 election cycle—less than one percent of total PAC spending in that cycle. There were a few individual races in which pro-Israel contributions played a significant role—especially Connecticut Senator Joseph Lieberman's—but in the overall context of U.S. campaign finance, "pro-Israel" money is a drop in the bucket. Moreover, in both 2000 and 2004, much more "pro-Israel" money went to Democratic candidates than went to Republican candidates, and Jewish voters overwhelmingly opposed George W. Bush. If Jewish voters overwhelmingly voted against Bush in both elections, and pro-Israel political groups gave much more money to Democrats than Republicans, how, exactly, did the lobby later control the Republican Congress it so signally opposed? And why should it bear particular blame for the policies of a president whose election it tried and failed to block?

None of this means that the role of pro-Israel groups in campaign finance should not be studied, or that relatively small amounts of money strategically placed and timed cannot have an impact. But Mearsheimer and Walt do not even list, much less take on, the various topics that an examination of the limited role "pro-Israel" money plays in U.S. politics would have to address. This is not serious scholarship.

A Special Relationship

As one might expect from international relations specialists, the book treats the geopolitics of the Middle East more professionally than U.S. domestic politics. Mearsheimer and Walt concede that U.S. and Israeli interests overlapped during the Cold War; for somewhat different reasons, both the United States and Israel wanted to keep the Soviets out of the region. They argue, however, that the strategic link weakened significantly after 1989. They find the close U.S.–Israeli relationship since then increasingly anomalous; the two countries' interests, they believe, are diverging even as U.S. policy remains firmly aligned with Jerusalem. Since this alignment, Mearsheimer and Walt argue, is not driven by common strategic interests or common moral values, it must be driven by the power of the Israel lobby.

Their geopolitical analysis of Israel's position is interesting and in many respects useful. But Mearsheimer and Walt seem not to see how it undercuts the importance of the Israel lobby. According to them, Israel is the dominant regional power, and its enormous advantages in weapons and technology are so great that it has relatively little need for U.S. support at this point. Both the military and the economic aid that the United States offers, Mearsheimer and Walt tell us, can be substantially reduced or even eliminated without undermining Israel's security. But they do not carry this point through to its logical conclusion: if U.S. aid is of relatively limited value to Israel, then threats to trim or withhold that aid will have relatively little impact on Israel's behavior. And if such aid is of relatively little importance in the regional power balance, then the efforts of the Israel lobby to extract more aid from the U.S. Congress are not really that important. In short, U.S. aid does not change the power balance, and withholding that aid would have little impact on Israel's negotiating position—meaning that the Israel lobby, whatever its makeup or power over the U.S. political system, plays no significant role in determining the course of events in the Middle East.

Mearsheimer and Walt also significantly underestimate the importance of the U.S.–Israeli alliance to the United States. If Israel determined that U.S. foreign policy was shifting in a hostile direction, it would have the option of diversifying its great-power base of support. Given Israel's overwhelming military position in the Middle East, and its ability to provide a new partner with advanced U.S. weapons and intelligence information, China, Russia, and India might find an alliance with Israel well worth the cost in popularity points across the Arab world. Israel has changed partners before: it won the 1948–49 war with weapons from the Soviet bloc, partnered with France and the United Kingdom in 1956, and considered France (the source of Israels nuclear technology) its most important ally in 1967. This potential shift is of major concern to the United States. One of the key U.S. objectives in the Middle East since World War II has been to prevent any other outside power from gaining a strategic foothold there. Alliances between other great powers and Israel—the dominant military power in the world's most vital and crisis-ridden region—could create major problems for U.S. foreign policy and significantly reduce the United States' ability to advance the Middle East peace process. Accordingly, maintaining the United States' relationship with Israel while managing its costs is the real challenge for U.S. policy in the Middle East.

Mearsheimer and Walt are correct that returning Israelis and Palestinians to the negotiating table—with proposals based on but in some ways going further than those that President Clinton and Prime Minister Ehud Barak presented at Camp David in 2000—is probably the best way to go. But as Mearsheimer and Walt show, Washington cannot simply impose that agenda on Israel by making threats. Israel cannot be compelled to negotiate on U.S. terms; it must be persuaded. Mearsheimer and Walt's goal of a fresh start in the peace process requires carrots, not sticks. And if and when those carrots are put on the table, will Mearsheimer and Walt denounce the offer as yet another triumph for the Israel lobby, or will they see it as an instance of the United States promoting its interests by coordinating policy with an indispensable local power in one of the world's most explosive regions?

Domestic politics, geopolitics: next is cultural politics—and especially the question of anti-Semitism. There have already been public charges of anti-Semitism, and more will come. Let me be unambiguously clear: those charges go too far. Mearsheimer and Walt state very clearly that they are not anti-Semites, and nothing in this book proves them wrong.

That said, some of the criticism that they will receive on this score is the result of their own easily avoidable lapses in judgment and expression. A little more care on their part could have done wonders in keeping what was bound to be a very heated discussion focused more tightly on the merits of the case.

The authors do what anti-Semites have always done: they overstate the power of Jews. Although Mearsheimer and Walt make an effort to distinguish their work from anti-Semitic tracts, the picture they paint calls up some of the ugliest stereotypes in anti-Semitic discourse. The Zionist octopus they conjure—stirring up the Iraq war, manipulating both U.S. political parties, shaping the media, punishing the courageous minority of professors and politicians who dare to tell the truth—is depressingly familiar. Some readers will be so overpowered by this familiar bugbear that they will conclude that the authors are deliberately invoking it. In fact, Mearsheimer and Walt have come honestly to a mistaken understanding of the relationship between pro-Israel political activity and U.S. policy and strategic interests. It is no crime to be wrong, and being wrong about Jews does not necessarily make someone an anti-Semite. But rhetorical clumsiness and the occasional unfortunate phrase make their case harder to defend.

One problem is that Mearsheimer and Walt decontextualize the activity of Jews and their allies. Attempts by pro-Zionist students and pressure groups to challenge university decisions to grant tenure or otherwise reward professors deemed too pro-Arab are portrayed as yet another sign of the long reach and dangerous power of the octopus. In fact, these efforts are part of a much broader, and deeply deplorable, trend in American education, by which every ethnic, religious, and sexual group seeks to define the bounds of acceptable discourse. African Americans, Native Americans, feminists, lesbian, gay, and transgendered persons—organizations purporting to represent these groups and many others have done their best to drive speakers, professors, and textbooks with the "wrong" views out of the academy. Zionists have actually come relatively late to this particular pander fest, and they are notable chiefly for their relatively weak performance in the perverse drive to block free speech on campus.

The authors also end up adopting a widely used tactic that has a special history in anti-Semitic literature. When anti-Semitic writers and politicians make vicious attacks, Jews are in a double bind: refrain from responding with outrage and the charge becomes accepted as a fact, express utter loathing at the charge and give anti-Semites the opportunity to pose as the victims of a slander campaign by venomous Jews. Nazi propagandists honed this into an effective weapon. Anyone who lived through or has immersed himself in the history of the golden age of European anti-Semitism is keenly aware of this tactic, and when one sees it employed in writing about Israel or the Israel lobby, one naturally assumes the worst: that the use of a tactic long popular among anti-Semites is a sign that a contemporary writer shares their deplorable worldview. The greatest living practitioner of this passive-aggressive form of provocation (and not just against Jews) is former President Jimmy Carter, whose recently published *Palestine: Peace Not Apartheid* set off a firestorm by implying a parallel between the Israel of today and apartheid South Africa. Mearsheimer and Walt wag their fingers at those awful Jews who "smeared" the meek and innocent Lamb of Georgia. How dare the lobby be provoked by Carter's provocation!

To a certain audience, that chain of events signals a powerful and determined anti-Semitism at work. This is wrong, in both the case of Carter and the case of Mearsheimer and Walt. But paying a little more attention to the ways in which modern history has shaped the emotions and responses of participants in Israel policy debates would have helped Mearsheimer and Walt make their case. The relationship between U.S. domestic politics and U.S. policy in the Middle East is far too complex, emotional, and important a topic to be sidelined by red herrings.

The New Israel and the Old

Why Gentile Americans Back the Jewish State

By Walter Russell Mead

On May 12, 1948, Clark Clifford, the White House chief counsel, presented the case for U.S. recognition of the state of Israel to the divided cabinet of President Harry Truman. While a glowering George Marshall, the secretary of state, and a skeptical Robert Lovett, Marshall's undersecretary, looked on, Clifford argued that recognizing the Jewish state would be an act of humanity that comported with traditional American values. To substantiate the Jewish territorial claim, Clifford quoted the Book of Deuteronomy: "Behold, I have set the land before you: go in and possess the land which the Lord sware unto your fathers, Abraham, Isaac, and Jacob, to give unto them and to their seed after them."

Marshall was not convinced and told Truman that he would vote against him in the upcoming election if this was his policy. Eventually, Marshall agreed not to make his opposition public. Two days later, the United States granted the new Jewish state de facto recognition 11 minutes after Israel declared its existence as a state. Many observers, both foreign and domestic, attributed Truman's decision to the power of the Jewish community in the United States. They saw Jewish votes, media influence, and campaign contributions as crucial in the tight 1948 presidential contest.

Since then, this pattern has often been repeated. Respected U.S. foreign policy experts call for Washington to be cautious in the Middle East and warn presidents that too much support for Israel will carry serious international costs. When presidents overrule their expert advisers and take a pro-Israel position, observers attribute the move to the "Israel lobby" and credit (or blame) it for swaying the chief executive. But there is another factor to consider. As the Truman biographer David McCullough has written, Truman's support for the Jewish state was "wildly popular" throughout the United States. A Gallup poll in June 1948 showed that almost three times as many Americans "sympathized with the Jews" as "sympathized with the Arabs." That support was no flash in the pan. Widespread gentile support for Israel is one of the most potent political forces in U.S. foreign policy, and in the last 60 years, there has never been a Gallup poll showing more Americans sympathizing with the Arabs or the Palestinians than with the Israelis.

Over time, moreover, the pro-Israel sentiment in the United States has increased, especially among non-Jews. The years of the George W. Bush administration have seen support for Israel in U.S. public opinion reach the highest level ever, and it has remained there throughout Bush's two terms. The increase has occurred even as the demographic importance of Jews has diminished. In 1948, Jews constituted an estimated 3.8 percent of the U.S. population. Assuming that almost every American Jew favored a pro-Israel foreign policy that year, a little more than ten percent of U.S. supporters of Israel were of Jewish origin. By 2007, Jews were only 1.8 percent of the population of the United States, accounting at most for three percent of Israel's supporters in the United States.

These figures, dramatic as they are, also probably underestimate the true level of public support for Israel. When in a poll in 2006 the Pew Research Center asked whether U.S. policy in the Middle East was fair, favored Israel, or favored the Palestinians, 47 percent of the respondents said they thought the policy was fair, six percent said it favored the Palestinians, and only 27 percent thought it favored the Israelis. The poll was conducted during Israel's attacks against Hezbollah in southern Lebanon, when U.S. support for Israel was even more controversial than usual around the world. One must therefore conclude that many of those who tell pollsters that the United States' policies are fair to both sides actually favor policies that most non-U.S. observers would consider strongly and even irresponsibly pro-Israel. The American public has few foreign policy preferences that are this marked, this deep, this enduring-and this much at odds with public opinion in other countries.

In the United States, a pro-Israel foreign policy does not represent the triumph of a small lobby over the public will. It represents the power of public opinion to shape foreign policy in the face of concerns by foreign policy professionals. Like the war on drugs and the fence along the Mexican border, support for Israel is a U.S. foreign policy that makes some experts and specialists uneasy but commands broad public support. This does not mean that an "Israel lobby" does not exist or does not help shape U.S. policy in the Middle East. Nor does it mean that Americans ought to feel as they do. (It remains my view that everyone, Americans and Israelis included, would benefit if Americans developed a more sympathetic and comprehensive understanding of the wants and needs of the Palestinians.) But it does mean

that the ultimate sources of the United States' Middle East policy lie outside the Beltway and outside the Jewish community. To understand why U.S. policy is pro-Israel rather than neutral or pro-Palestinian, one must study the sources of nonelite, non-Jewish support for the Jewish state.

The Children Of David

The story of U.S. support for a Jewish state in the Middle East begins early. John Adams could not have been more explicit. "I really wish the Jews again in Judea an independent nation," he said, after his presidency. From the early nineteenth century on, gentile Zionists fell into two main camps in the United States. Prophetic Zionists saw the return of the Jews to the Promised Land as the realization of a literal interpretation of biblical prophecy, often connected to the return of Christ and the end of the world. Based on his interpretation of Chapter 18 of the prophecies of Isaiah, for example, the Albany Presbyterian pastor John McDonald predicted in 1814 that Americans would assist the Jews in restoring their ancient state. Mormon voices shared this view; the return of the Jews to the Holy Land was under way, said Elder Orson Hyde in 1841: "The great wheel is unquestionably in motion, and the word of the Almighty has declared that it shall roll."

Other, less literal and less prophetic Christians developed a progressive Zionism that would resonate down through the decades among both religious and secular gentiles. In the nineteenth century, liberal Christians often believed that God was building a better world through human progress. They saw the democratic and (relatively) egalitarian United States as both an example of the new world God was making and a powerful instrument to further his grand design. Some American Protestants believed that God was moving to restore what they considered the degraded and oppressed Jews of the world to the Promised Land, just as God was uplifting and improving the lives of other ignorant and unbelieving people through the advance of Protestant and liberal principles. They wanted the Jews to establish their own state because they believed that this would both shelter the Jews from persecution and, through the redemptive powers of liberty and honest agricultural labor, uplift and improve what they perceived to be the squalid morals and deplorable hygiene of contemporary Ottoman and eastern European Jews. As Adams put it, "Once restored to an independent government and no longer persecuted they would soon wear away some of the asperities and peculiarities of their character and possibly in time become liberal Unitarian Christians." For such Christians, American Zionism was part of a broader program of transforming the world by promoting the ideals of the United States.

Not all progressive Zionists couched their arguments in religious terms. As early as 1816, *Niles' Weekly Register*, the leading American news and opinion periodical through much of the first half of the nineteenth century, predicted and welcomed the impending return of the Jews to an independent state with Jerusalem as its capital. The magazine projected that the restoration of the Jews would further enlightenment and progress—and this, clearly, would be good for the United States as well as for the Jews.

Prophetic Zionists, for their part, became more numerous after the American Civil War, and their views of the role a restored Jewish state might play in the events leading up to the apocalypse became more highly developed. Books and pamphlets highlighting the predicted restoration of the Jews and speculating on the identity and the return of the "lost tribes" of the ancient Hebrews were perennial bestsellers, and the association between Dwight Moody, the country's leading evangelist, and Cyrus Scofield, the important Bible scholar, put the future history of Israel firmly at the center of the imagination of conservative American Protestantism.

These groups of gentile Zionists found new, if sometimes unsavory, allies after 1880, when a mass immigration of Russian Jews to the United States began. Some of them and some assimilated German American Jews hoped that Palestine would replace the United States as the future home of what was an unusually unpopular group of immigrants at the time. For anti-Semites, the establishment of a Jewish state might or might not "cure" Jews of the characteristics many gentiles attributed to them, but in any case the establishment of such a state would reduce Jewish immigration to the United States.

In 1891, these strands of gentile Zionists came together. The Methodist lay leader William Blackstone presented a petition to President Benjamin Harrison calling on the United States to use its good offices to convene a congress of European powers so that they could induce the Ottoman Empire to turn Palestine over to the Jews. The 400 signatories were overwhelmingly non-Jewish and included the chief justice of the Supreme Court; the Speaker of the House of Representatives; the chairs of the House Ways and Means Committee and the House Foreign Affairs Committee; the future president William McKinley; the mayors of Baltimore, Boston, Chicago, New York, Philadelphia, and Washington; the editors or proprietors of the leading East Coast and Chicago newspapers; and an impressive array of Episcopal, Methodist, Presbyterian, and Roman Catholic clergy. Business leaders who signed the petition included Cyrus McCormick, John Rockefeller, and J. P. Morgan. At a time when the American Jewish community was neither large nor powerful, and no such thing as an Israel lobby existed, the pillars of the American gentile establishment went on record supporting a U.S. diplomatic effort to create a Jewish state in the lands of the Bible.

Shared Commandments

Any discussion of U.S. attitudes toward Israel must begin with the Bible. For centuries, the American imagination has been steeped in the Hebrew Scriptures. This influence originated with the rediscovery of the Old Testament during the Reformation, was accentuated by the development of Calvinist theology (which stressed continuities between the old and the new dispensations of divine grace), and was made more vital by the historical similarities between the modern

American and the ancient Hebrew experiences; as a result, the language, heroes, and ideas of the Old Testament permeate the American psyche.

Instruction in biblical Hebrew was mandatory for much of early U.S. history at Columbia, Dartmouth, Harvard, Princeton, and Yale. James Madison completed his studies at Princeton in two years but remained on campus an extra year to study Hebrew. Colonial preachers and pamphleteers over and over again described the United States as a new Canaan, "a land flowing with milk and honey," and reminded their audiences that just as the Hebrews lost their blessings when they offended God, so, too, would the Americans suffer if they disobeyed the God who had led them into their promised land. Today, Old Testament references continue to permeate U.S. political writing, oratory, and even geography—over one thousand cities and towns in the United States have names derived from Scripture.

The most dramatic religious expression of the importance of the Old Testament in American culture today is the rise of premillennial dispensationalism, an interpretation of biblical prophecies that gives particular weight to Old Testament religious concepts such as covenant theology and assigns a decisive role to a restored Jewish state (with Jerusalem as its capital) in future history. An estimated seven percent of Americans seem to hold this theological position (making this group almost four times as large as the American Jewish community), and a considerably larger group is influenced by it to a greater or lesser degree. Proponents of this view often (although not always) share the view of some Orthodox Jews that the Jews must insist on a state that includes all the territory once promised to the Hebrews; they oppose any territorial compromise with the Palestinians and support Jewish settlements in the West Bank. But this is a minority view, even among U.S. supporters of Israel.

Progressive Christian Zionism, on the other hand, is related to Christian ethics rather than prophecy. Much of it is rooted in guilt and a sense that Christians' past poor treatment of the Jews is now preventing Jews from accepting Christianity. For well over a thousand years, the Jews of Europe suffered extraordinary and at times unspeakable cruelties at the hands of Europe's Christians. Although some American Protestants perpetuated this history of intolerance and anti-Semitism, many liberal American Protestants from the nineteenth century forward saw rejecting this past as one of the defining tasks of the reformed and enlightened American church. Such Protestants could (and comfortably did) deplore Catholic anti-Semitism as a consequence of the regrettable corruptions of the church under the papacy, but the anti-Semitic words and deeds of reformers such as Martin Luther could not be dismissed so easily. Many members of the liberal American Protestant churches considered it a sacred duty to complete the work of the Reformation by purging Christianity of its remaining "medieval" features, such as superstition, bigotry, and anti-Semitism. Making amends for past sins by protecting the Jews has long been an important religious test for many (although by no means all) American Protestants.

By contrast, most American Christians have felt little or no guilt about their communities' historical relations with the Muslim world. Many Muslims view Christian-Muslim conflict over the last millennium as a constant and relatively homogenous phenomenon, but American Protestants do not. They generally deplore the cruelties of the Crusades and the concept of a holy war, for example, but they see them as Catholic errors rather than more broadly Christian ones, and in any case, they view the Crusades as long past and as a response to prior Muslim aggression. They also generally deplore the predations of European powers in more recent centuries, but they see them as driven by Old World imperialism rather than Christianity and as such something for which they bear no responsibility. (An important exception deserves to be mentioned: Many U.S. missionaries active in the Middle East forged deep ties with the region's Arab inhabitants and strongly supported Arab nationalism, both from a dislike of European colonialism and out of the hope that a secular nationalist movement would improve the position of Arab Christians. This missionary community contributed both to the development of the Arabist contingent in the State Department and to the backlash in mainstream Protestant churches against Israeli policies in the occupied territories after the 1967 war.)

By 1948, many Christians in the United States felt a heavy burden of historical debt and obligation toward the Jews, but not the Muslims. If anything, they believed that the Islamic world was indebted to American Christian missionaries for many of its leading universities and hospitals and that American Christian support before and after World War II had helped promote the emergence of independent Arab and Muslim states that was then taking place.

Chosen Cousins

The United States' sense of its own identity and mission in the world has been shaped by readings of Hebrew history and thought. The writer Herman Melville expressed this view: "We Americans are the peculiar, chosen people—the Israel of our time; we bear the ark of the liberties of the world." From the time of the Puritans to the present day, preachers, thinkers, and politicians in the United States—secular as well as religious, liberal as well as conservative—have seen the Americans as a chosen people, bound together less by ties of blood than by a set of beliefs and a destiny. Americans have believed that God (or history) has brought them into a new land and made them great and rich and that their continued prosperity depends on their fulfilling their obligations toward God or the principles that have blessed them so far. Ignore these principles—turn toward the golden calf—and the scourge will come.

Both religious and nonreligious Americans have looked to the Hebrew Scriptures for an example of a people set apart by their mission and called to a world-changing destiny. Did the land Americans inhabit once belong to others? Yes, but the Hebrews similarly conquered the land of the Canaanites. Did the tiny U.S. colonies armed only with the justice of their cause defeat the world's greatest empire? So did David, the humble

shepherd boy, fell Goliath. Were Americans in the nineteenth century isolated and mocked for their democratic ideals? So were the Hebrews surrounded by idolaters. Have Americans defeated their enemies at home and abroad? So, according to the Scriptures, did the Hebrews triumph. And when Americans held millions of slaves in violation of their beliefs, were they punished and scourged? Yes, and much like the Hebrews, who suffered the consequences of their sins before God.

This mythic understanding of the United States' nature and destiny is one of the most powerful and enduring elements in American culture and thought. As the ancient Hebrews did, many Americans today believe that they bear a revelation that is ultimately not just for them but also for the whole world; they have often considered themselves God's new Israel. One of the many consequences of this presumed kinship is that many Americans think it is both right and proper for one chosen people to support another. They are not disturbed when the United States' support of Israel, a people and a state often isolated and ostracized, makes the United States unpopular or creates other problems. The United States' adoption of the role of protector of Israel and friend of the Jews is a way of legitimizing its own status as a country called to a unique destiny by God.

More than that, since the nineteenth century, the United States has seen itself as the chosen agent of God in the protection and redemption of the Jews. Americans believed that the Jews would emerge from their degraded condition as they moved from city slums to the countryside-just as American immigrants from all over Europe had built better lives and sturdier characters as Jeffersonian farmers. Liberal Christians such as Adams believed that this would bring the Jews in time to the light of liberal Protestantism as part of the general uplift of humanity. And prophetic Zionists hoped that mass conversions of Jews to revivalist Christianity would trigger the apocalypse and the return of Christ. Either way, the United States' special role in the restoration of the Jews fulfilled gentile Americans' expectations about the movement of history and confirmed their beliefs about the United States' identity and mission.

Settler States

The United States and Israel also have in common their status as "settler states"—countries formed by peoples who came to control their current lands after displacing the original populations. Both states have been powerfully shaped by a history of conflict and confrontation with those they displaced, and both have sought justifications for their behavior from similar sources. Both the Americans and the Israelis have turned primarily to the Old Testament, whose hallowed pages tell the story of the conflict between the ancient Hebrews and the Canaanites, the former inhabitants of what the Hebrews believed was their Promised Land. Americans found the idea that they were God's new Israel so attractive partly because it helped justify their displacement of the Native Americans. As Theodore Roosevelt put it in his best-selling history of the American West, "Many of the best of the backwoodsmen were Bible-readers, but they were brought up in a creed that made much of the Old Testament, and laid slight stress on pity, truth, or mercy. They looked at their foes as the Hebrew prophets looked at the enemies of Israel. What were the abominations because of which the Canaanites were destroyed before Joshua, when compared with the abominations of the red savages whose lands they, another chosen people, should in their turn inherit?" (Roosevelt himself, like his cousins Franklin and Eleanor, was a Christian Zionist. "It seems to me entirely proper to start a Zionist State around Jerusalem," he wrote in 1918.)

Besides a direct divine promise, two other important justifications that the Americans brought forward in their contests with the Native Americans were the concept that they were expanding into "empty lands" and John Locke's related "fair use" doctrine, which argued that unused property is a waste and an offense against nature. U.S. settlers felt that only those who would improve the land, settling it densely with extensive farms and building towns, had a real right to it. John Quincy Adams made the case in 1802: "Shall [the Indians] doom an immense region of the globe to perpetual desolation … ?" And Thomas Jefferson warned that the Native Americans who failed to learn from the whites and engage in productive agriculture faced a grim fate. They would "relapse into barbarism and misery, lose numbers by war and want, and we shall be obliged to drive them, with the beasts of the forest into the Stony mountains."

Through much of U.S. history, such views resonated not just with backwoodsmen but also with liberal and sophisticated citizens. These arguments had a special meaning when it came to the Holy Land. As pious Americans dwelt on the glories of ancient Jerusalem and the Temple of Solomon, they pictured a magnificent and fertile land—"a land flowing with milk and honey," as the Bible describes it. But by the nineteenth century, when first dozens, then hundreds, and ultimately thousands of Americans visited the Holy Land—and millions more thronged to lectures and presentations to hear reports of these travels—there was little milk or honey; Palestine was one of the poorest, most backward, and most ramshackle provinces of the Ottoman Empire. To American eyes, the hillsides and rocky fields of Judea were desolate and empty—God, many believed, had cursed the land when he sent the Jews into their second exile, which they saw as the Jews' punishment for their failure to recognize Christ as the Messiah. And so, Americans believed, the Jews belonged in the Holy Land, and the Holy Land belonged to the Jews. The Jews would never prosper until they were home and free, and the land would never bloom until its rightful owners returned.

The Prophet Isaiah had described the future return of the Jews to their homeland as God's grace bringing water to a desert land. And Americans watched the returning fertility of the land under the cultivation of early Zionist settlers with the astonished sense that biblical prophecy was being fulfilled before their eyes. "The springs of Jewish colonizing vigor, amply fed by the money of world Jewry, flowed on to the desert," wrote

Time magazine in 1946, echoing the language of Isaiah. Two years later, following the Jewish victory in the 1948 war, it described the Arabs in terms that induce flinching today but represented common American perceptions at the time: "The Western world tends to think of the Arab as a falcon-eyed warrior on a white horse. That Arab is still around, but he is far less numerous than the disease-ridden wretches who lie in the hot streets, too weak, sick and purposeless to roll over into the shade." Americans saw a contest between a backward and incapable people and a people able to settle the wilderness and make it bloom, miraculously fulfilling ancient prophecies of a Jewish state.

The Jews had been widely considered eastern Europe's most deplorable population: ignorant, depraved, superstitious, factionalized, quarrelsome, and hopelessly behind the times. That this population, after being subjected to the unprecedented savagery of Nazi persecution, should establish the first stable democracy in the Middle East, build a thriving economy in the desert, and repeatedly defeat enemies with armies many times larger and stronger than their own seemed to many Americans to be striking historical proof of their own most cherished ideals.

The Right Turn

Although gentile support for Israel in the United States has remained strong and even grown since World War II, its character has changed. Until the Six-Day War, support for Israel came mostly from the political left and was generally stronger among Democrats than Republicans. Liberal icons such as Eleanor Roosevelt, Paul Tillich, Reinhold Niebuhr, and Martin Luther King, Jr., were leading public voices calling for the United States to support Israel. But since 1967, liberal support for Israel has gradually waned, and conservative support has grown.

A variety of factors had come together in the 1940s to make progressive gentile Zionism a powerful force in U.S. politics, especially on the left. First, the impact of the Holocaust on American Protestantism was extraordinary. Germany had once provided intellectual leadership for the American Protestant church, and the passive acquiescence with which most German Protestant churches and pastors greeted Nazi rule shocked mainstream American Protestantism to its core. Anti-Nazi German Protestants became moral and theological heroes in the postwar United States, and opposition to anti-Semitism became a key test by which mainline American Protestants judged themselves and their leaders. This profound shock intensified their humanitarian response to revelations about the death camps and the mass murder. The suffering of the displaced, starving, and impoverished Jewish refugees in chaotic postwar Europe made it inevitable that American Protestants, who had for a century campaigned for Jewish rights, would enthusiastically support steps seen as securing the safety of Europe's Jews.

A second factor was the strong support of African Americans for the Jews at a time when blacks were beginning to play a larger role in U.S. electoral politics. During the 1930s, the African American press throughout the United States had closely followed the imposition of Hitler's racial policies. African American leaders lost no opportunity to point out the similarities between Hitler's treatment of the Jews and the Jim Crow laws in the United States' segregated South. For African Americans, the persecution of the Jews was made real to them through their own daily experiences. It also provided them with important talking points to persuade whites that racial discrimination violated American principles, and it thus helped build the strong alliance between American Jews and the civil rights movement that existed from 1945 through the death of King. Even during World War II, the black activists W. E. B. Du Bois, Zora Neale Hurston, Langston Hughes, and Philip Randolph supported the precursor of the Israeli Likud Party in its effort to create a Jewish army. The civil rights leader Adam Clayton Powell, Jr., went further, raising $150,000 for the militant Zionist group the Irgun Zvai Leumi—which he called "an underground terrorist organization in Palestine"—at a New York City rally.

The Soviet Union's support for an independent state of Israel also helped. At Yalta, Joseph Stalin told Franklin Roosevelt that he, too, was a Zionist, and in May of 1947, Soviet Foreign Minister Andrei Gromyko announced before the United Nations that the Soviet Union supported the creation of a Jewish state. This backing, however short-lived, strengthened the view of many American leftists that the establishment of a homeland for the Jews was part of the general struggle for progress around the world. Indeed, in the decades after the war, many American liberals saw their support for Israel as part of their commitment to freedom, anticolonialism (the Jews of Palestine were seeking independence over British opposition), the struggle against racial and religious discrimination, secularism, humanitarianism, and the progressive tradition in U.S. politics. Israel at the time seemed to be an idealistic secular experiment in social democracy; American Jews and American gentiles alike went to Israel to experience the exhilarating life of labor and fellowship of the kibbutz. In 1948, therefore, when Truman decided to support the creation of Israel, he was thinking about not just the Jewish vote. Support for Israel was popular with the blacks in the North, who were attracted to the Democratic Party by the New Deal and Truman's own slow progress toward supporting civil rights. The cause of Israel helped with voters on the left otherwise tempted to support Henry Wallace and the Progressives. And it also helped Truman compete among conservative, churchgoing, Bible-reading southern voters against Strom Thurmond's Dixiecrats. Support for Israel, in fact, was one of the few issues that helped pull the fractious Democratic Party coalition together.

Since the 1967 war, however, the basis of Israel's support in the United States has shifted: backing for Israel has tended to weaken on the left and grow on the right. On the left, a widespread dislike of Israel's policies in the occupied territories and a diminished concern for its security in the wake of its triumph in the war led many African Americans, mainline Protestants, and liberal intellectuals, once among Israel's staunchest U.S. allies, toward growing sympathy with Palestinian

views. Increased identification on the part of blacks with anticolonial movements worldwide, the erosion of the black-Jewish alliance in U.S. domestic politics, and the rising appeal of figures such as Malcolm X and the leaders of the Nation of Islam also gradually reduced support for Israel among African Americans. The liberal Protestant churches, for their part, were newly receptive to the perspectives of those missionaries sympathetic to Arab nationalism, and as the mainstream churches became more critical of traditional American ideas about the United States' national identity and destiny, they distanced themselves ever further from traditional readings of the Old Testament. (On the other hand, relations between American Catholics and the Jews began to improve after the 1967 war, largely due to the Catholic Church's new theological approach toward the Jews since the Second Vatican Council.)

On the right, the most striking change since 1967 has been the dramatic intensification of suppport for Israel among evangelical Christians and, more generally, among what I have called "Jacksonian" voters in the U.S. heartland. Jacksonians are populist-nationalist voters who favor a strong U.S. military and are generally skeptical of international organizations and global humanitarian aid. Not all evangelicals are Jacksonians, and not all Jacksonians are evangelicals, but there is a certain overlap between the two constituencies. Many southern whites are Jacksonians; so are many of the swing voters in the North known as Reagan Democrats.

Many Jacksonians formed negative views of the Arabs during the Cold War. The Palestinians and the Arab states, they noted, tended to side with the Soviet Union and the Nonaligned Movement against the United States. The Egyptians responded to support from the United States in the 1956 Suez crisis by turning to the Soviets for arms and support, and Soviet weapons and Soviet experts helped Arab armies prepare for wars against Israel. Jacksonians tend to view international affairs through their own unique prism, and as events in the Middle East have unfolded since 1967, they have become more sympathetic to Israel even as many non-Jacksonian observers in the United States—and many more people in the rest of the world—have become less so. The Six-Day War reignited the interest of prophetic Zionists in Israel and deepened the perceived connections between Israel and the United States for many Jacksonians. After the Cold War, the Jacksonians found that the United States' opponents in the region, such as Iraq and Iran, were the most vociferous enemies of Israel as well.

Jacksonians admire victory, and total victory is the best kind. The sweeping, overwhelming triumph of Israeli arms in 1967 against numerically superior foes from three different countries caught the imaginations of Jacksonians—especially at a time when the United States' poor performance in Vietnam had made many of them pessimistic about their own country's future. Since then, some of the same actions that have hurt Israel's image in most of the world—such as ostensibly disproportionate responses to Palestinian terrorism—have increased its support among Jacksonians.

When a few rockets launched from Gaza strike Israel, the Israelis sometimes respond with more firepower, more destruction, and more casualties. In much of the world, this is seen as excessive retaliation, an offense equal to or even greater than the original attack. Jacksonians, however, see a Palestinian rocket attack on Israeli targets as an act of terrorism and believe that the Israelis have an unlimited right, perhaps even a duty, to retaliate with all the force at their command. Since the 1950s, when Palestinian raiders started slipping across the cease-fire line to attack Israeli settlements, many Palestinians and Arabs have, with some justification, seen these incursions as acts of great courage in the face of overwhelming power. But such sneak attacks against civilian targets, and especially suicide bombings, violate basic Jacksonian ideas about civilized warfare. Jacksonians believe that only overwhelming and total retaliation against such tactics can deter the attackers from striking again. This is how the American frontiersmen handled the Native Americans, how the Union general William Sherman "educated" the Confederacy, and how General Douglas MacArthur and Truman repaid the Japanese for Pearl Harbor. Jacksonians

genuinely cannot understand why the world criticizes Israel for exercising what they see as its inalienable right of self-defense—for doing exactly what they would do in Israel's place.

In the eyes of the Palestinians and their supporters, the Palestinians—exiled, marginalized, occupied, divided—are heroic underdogs confronting the might of a regional superpower backed by the most powerful nation on earth. But for Jacksonians, Israel, despite all its power and all its victories, remains an endangered David surrounded by enemies. The fact that the Arabs and the larger community of one billion Muslims support, at least verbally, the Palestinian cause deepens the belief among many Jacksonians that Israel is a small and vulnerable country that deserves help. Ironically, some of the greatest military and political successes of the Palestinian movement— developing an active armed resistance, winning (largely rhetorical) support from organizations such as the Arab League and even the General Assembly of the United Nations, shifting the basis of Palestinian resistance from secular nationalism to religion, and winning support from powerful regional states such as Saddam's Iraq and Iran today—have ended up strengthening and deepening American gentile support for the Jewish state.

Christian Brotherhood

Another important factor leading to increased American support for Israel is that since 1967 a series of religious revivals have swept across the United States, with important effects on public attitudes toward the Middle East. One consequence has been that even as the mainline, liberal Protestant churches have become more critical of Israel, they have lost political and social influence. Another consequence has been a significant increase in prophetic Zionism, with evangelical and fundamentalist American Christians more interested now in biblical prophecy and Israel's role in the lead-up to the apocalypse than ever before.

Many evangelical and fundamentalist Christians had shown relatively little interest in

Israel immediately after its war of independence. Biblical prophecy, as they understood it, clearly predicted that the Jews would rebuild the Temple on its original site, and so with the holy sites of Jerusalem in Arab hands, the countdown to the end of time appeared to have slowed. Meanwhile, the secular and quasi-socialist Israel of the 1950s was less attractive to conservative Christians than to liberal ones. With their eyes fixed on the communist menace during the peak years of the Cold War, evangelical and fundamentalist Christians were less actively engaged in U.S. policy in the Middle East than they had been in the nineteenth century.

The Six–Day War changed that; it was a catalyst both for the evangelical revival movement and for the renewal of prophetic Zionism. The speed and decision of the victory of Israel looked miraculous to many Americans, and Israel's conquest of the Old City meant that the Temple site was now in Jewish hands. The sense that the end of time was approaching was a powerful impetus for the American religious revivals that began during this period. Since then, a series of best-selling books, fiction and nonfiction alike, have catered to the interest of millions of Americans in the possibility that the end-time as prophesied in the Old and New Testaments is now unfolding in the Middle East.

Since the end of the Cold War, an additional force has further strengthened the links between the state of Israel and many conservative American Christians. As the religious revival gave new power and energy to evangelical and fundamentalist churches, their attention turned increasingly outward. Past such revivals led to waves of intense missionary interest and activity; the current revival is no different. And as American Christians have taken a greater interest in the well-being of Christians around the world, they have encountered Christianity's most important rival worldwide, Islam, and have begun to learn that the conditions facing Christians in a number of Muslim-majority countries are not good.

Interest in the persecution of Christians around the world is a long-term feature of Christianity,

and not only in the United States. The same church leaders involved in efforts to protect Jews in Europe and the Ottoman Empire were often engaged in campaigns to protect Christians in China, Korea, Japan, and the Ottoman Empire, among other places. The rise of communism as the twentieth century's most brutal enemy of religion ultimately led American Christians to build organizations aimed at supporting believers behind the Iron Curtain. Since 1989, the persecution of Christians by communists has diminished (although not disappeared), and so increasingly the center of concern has been the Muslim world, where many Christians and people of other faiths or of no faith suffer legal and social discrimination—and where, at times, Christians are beaten and murdered for what they believe. Laws in many Islamic countries, moreover, forbid proselytizing and conversion—issues of vital concern for evangelical Christians, who generally believe that those who die without accepting Christ will suffer in hell and that spreading the Christian faith is one of their central moral duties. Mainstream media generally do not make the foreign persecution of Christians a major focus of their news coverage, but that does not prevent this issue from shaping the way many Americans look at Islam and, by extension, at the conflict between Israel and some of its neighbors.

U.S. opinion on the Middle East is not monolithic, nor is it frozen in time. Since 1967, it has undergone significant shifts, with some groups becoming more favorable toward Israel and others less so. Considerably fewer African Americans stand with the Likud Party today than stood with the Jewish army in World War II. More changes may come. A Palestinian and Arab leadership more sensitive to the values and political priorities of the American political culture could develop new and more effective tactics designed to weaken, rather than strengthen, American support for the Jewish state. An end to terrorist attacks, for example, coupled with well-organized and disciplined nonviolent civil resistance, might alter Jacksonian perceptions of the Palestinian struggle. It is entirely possible that over time, evangelical and fundamentalist Americans will retrace Jimmy Carter's steps from a youthful Zionism to what he would call a more balanced position now. But if Israel should face any serious crisis, it seems more likely that opinion will swing the other way. Many of the Americans who today call for a more evenhanded policy toward the Palestinians do so because they believe that Israel is fundamentally secure. Should that assessment change, public opinion polls might well show even higher levels of U.S. support for Israel.

One thing, at least, seems clear. In the future, as in the past, U.S. policy toward the Middle East will, for better or worse, continue to be shaped primarily by the will of the American majority, not the machinations of any minority, however wealthy or engaged in the political process some of its members may be.

Walter Russell Mead is Henry A. Kissinger Senior Fellow for U.S. Foreign Policy at the Council on Foreign Relations and the author, most recently, of God and Gold: Britain, America, and the Making of the Modern World.

Rights Watchdog, Lost in the Mideast

By Robert L. Bernstein

AS the founder of Human Rights Watch, its active chairman for 20 years and now founding chairman emeritus, I must do something that I never anticipated: I must publicly join the group's critics. Human Rights Watch had as its original mission to pry open closed societies, advocate basic freedoms and support dissenters. But recently it has been issuing reports on the Israeli–Arab conflict that are helping those who wish to turn Israel into a pariah state.

At Human Rights Watch, we always recognized that open, democratic societies have faults and commit abuses. But we saw that they have the ability to correct them through vigorous public debate, an adversarial press and many other mechanisms that encourage reform.

That is why we sought to draw a sharp line between the democratic and nondemocratic worlds, in an effort to create clarity in human rights. We wanted to prevent the Soviet Union and its followers from playing a moral equivalence game with the West and to encourage liberalization by drawing attention to dissidents like Andrei Sakharov, Natan Sharansky and those in the Soviet gulag—and the millions in China's *laogai*, or labor camps.

When I stepped aside in 1998, Human Rights Watch was active in 70 countries, most of them closed societies. Now the organization, with increasing frequency, casts aside its important distinction between open and closed societies.

Nowhere is this more evident than in its work in the Middle East. The region is populated by authoritarian regimes with appalling human rights records. Yet in recent years Human Rights Watch has written far more condemnations of Israel for violations of international law than of any other country in the region.

Israel, with a population of 7.4 million, is home to at least 80 human rights organizations, a vibrant free press, a democratically elected government, a judiciary that frequently rules against the government, a politically active academia, multiple political parties and, judging by the amount of news coverage, probably more journalists per capita than any other country in the world—many of whom are there expressly to cover the Israeli–Palestinian conflict.

Meanwhile, the Arab and Iranian regimes rule over some 350 million people, and most remain brutal, closed and autocratic, permitting little or no internal dissent. The plight of their citizens who would most benefit from the kind of attention a large and well-financed international human rights organization can provide is being ignored as Human Rights Watch's Middle East division prepares report after report on Israel.

Human Rights Watch has lost critical perspective on a conflict in which Israel has been repeatedly attacked by Hamas and Hezbollah, organizations that go after Israeli citizens and use their own people as human shields. These groups are supported by the government of Iran, which has openly declared its intention not just to destroy Israel but to murder Jews everywhere. This incitement to genocide is a violation of the Convention on the Prevention and Punishment of the Crime of Genocide.

Leaders of Human Rights Watch know that Hamas and Hezbollah chose to wage war from densely populated areas, deliberately transforming neighborhoods into battlefields. They know that more and better arms are flowing into both Gaza and Lebanon and are poised to strike again. And they know that this militancy continues to deprive Palestinians of any chance for the peaceful and productive life they deserve. Yet Israel, the repeated victim of aggression, faces the brunt of Human Rights Watch's criticism.

The organization is expressly concerned mainly with how wars are fought, not with motivations. To be sure, even victims of aggression are bound by the laws of war and must do their utmost to minimize civilian casualties. Nevertheless, there is a difference between wrongs committed in self-defense and those perpetrated intentionally.

But how does Human Rights Watch know that these laws have been violated? In Gaza and elsewhere where there is no access to the battlefield or to the military and political leaders who make strategic decisions, it is extremely difficult to make definitive judgments about war crimes. Reporting often relies on witnesses whose stories cannot be verified and who may testify for political advantage or because they fear retaliation from their own rulers. Significantly, Col. Richard Kemp, the former commander of British forces in Afghanistan and an expert on warfare, has said that the Israel Defense Forces in Gaza "did more to safeguard the rights of civilians in a combat zone than any other army in the history of warfare."

Only by returning to its founding mission and the spirit of humility that animated it can Human Rights Watch resurrect itself as a moral force in the Middle East and throughout the world. If it fails to do that, its credibility will be seriously undermined and its important role in the world significantly diminished.

The Case for Israel

By Alan Dershowitz

The Accusation

Israel is "the prime example of human rights violators in the world."

The Accusers

"The World Conference Against Racism was preceded by four Regional Conferences whose task it was to draft a composite Declaration against Racism and a Plan of Action. Israel was excluded from the last of the regional conferences in Teheran, which issued the most scurrilous indictment against Israel since the Second World War. There were seven components to the "indictment":

- Occupation is a crime against humanity, a new form of Apartheid, a threat to international peace and security;
- Israel is in essence an Apartheid State;
- Israel is a meta-Human Rights violator (in a world in which human rights constitutes a new secular religion, Israel becomes the new 'Anti-Christ' of our time);
- Israel is the perpetrator of international crimes—war crimes, crimes against humanity, genocide—hence the right to 'armed struggle' and 'resistance' against this 'criminal' state;
- Israel (as a Jewish state) is an 'original sin' established through 'ethnic cleansing' of Mandatory Arab Palestine;
- The reference to 'holocausts' is, in the plural and in lowercase, with Israel an example of a 'holocaust' against Arabs;
- Zionism is declared to be not only a form of Racism, but Zionism itself was declared to be 'antisemitic.'" (Professor Irwin Coder, describing the accusations)

"Every day of the UN Commission on Human Rights' six-week session, which has now finished its second week, begins with a violation of the UN Charter's most basic principle of international relations, 'the equality of all nations large and small.' One UN member is left standing in the halls every morning from 9 to 10 a.m. while all other UN members and observers (including the Palestinian Authority) meet in private strategic and information-sharing sessions in each of the five UN regional groups. That country is Israel. This is apartheid United Nations-style. ... As for the substantive assault on Israel, which this year began Thursday, the Commission record over 30 years speaks for itself:

- Israel has been the only state subject to an entire agenda item every year.
- The Commission on Human Rights has spent more time on Israel than any other country.
- While 11 percent of its total substantive meeting has been on Israel alone, 24 percent of its time has been spent on all other UN states combined.
- 27 percent of its country-specific resolutions critical of a state have been on Israel alone.

"The real double standards? No resolution in the history of the commission has ever been passed on states such as Syria, China, Saudi Arabia or Zimbabwe.

"The fault is not that of the victims, who over the years have complained to the UN by the thousands about gross and systematic human rights abuses in countries such as Bahrain, Chad, Liberia, Malawi, Mali, Pakistan, Saudi Arabia, Syria, United Arab Emirates, Yemen and Zimbabwe. But every year, the commission holds closed-door meetings—the first one held Friday—in which it buries these complaints and refuses to subject such states to the public condemnation of resolutions.

"Commission debates on the Israel agenda item explain a lot. On Thursday, the Palestinian representative, Nabil Ramlawi (whom the Libyan chair calls 'His Excellency, the distinguished Ambassador of Palestine'), said:

"The world condemned the old Nazism in the past ... during the Second World War. ... The world also condemned Zionist Israel for the same criminal crimes it has been perpetrating against the Palestinian people for over 50 years now, starting ... in 1948. ... [T]he world ... has not yet eliminated the New Zionist Nazism and Israel was created through crimes against humanity it perpetrated and which continue today." (Anne Bayefsky, describing the accusations)

The Reality

Israel is the only nation in the Mideast that operates under the rule of law. Its record on human rights compares favorably to that of any country in the world that has faced comparable dangers. Its Supreme Court is among the best in the world, and it has repeatedly overruled the army and the government and made them operate under the rule of law. Israel has among the best records in the world with regard to the rights of women, gays, the physically and mentally challenged, and so on. It also has freedom of speech, press, dissent, association, and religion.

The Palestinian Authority, on the other hand, shows no respect for human rights. It tortures and kills alleged collaborators without even a semblance of due process. It tolerates little dissent and it is intolerant of alternative lifestyles. Palestinian propagandists invoke "human rights" merely as a tactic against Israel.

The Proof

Faced with comparable dangers both internal and external, no nation in history has ever tried so hard to require its military to operate within the rule of law. The Israeli Supreme Court, by all accounts one of the finest in the world, has played a far greater role in controlling the Israeli military than any court in history has ever played in the conduct of military affairs, including in the United States. Although obviously sensitive to the need for security, the Israeli Supreme Court has repeatedly enjoined the Israeli government and its military from undertaking actions in violation of the highest standards of the rule of law.

In virtually every other democracy, including the United States, the courts are extremely limited in their ability to prevent the military from taking whatever action it deems necessary to preserve national security. As the New Tork Times reported: "One of the most unusual aspects of Israeli law is the rapid access that petitioners, including Palestinians, can gain to Israel's highest court. In April 2002, during the fiercest fighting of the current conflict, in the Jenin refugee camp in the West Bank, the high court was receiving and ruling on petitions almost daily,"

Professor Yitzhak Zamir, a former Justice of the Israeli Supreme Court with "a reputation as a strong advocate of civil rights," said that he did not know of "any other country where civilian courts had such broad jurisdiction to review military actions." Even Raji Sourani, the director of the Palestinian Center for Human Rights in Gaza and a strident critic of Israel, says that he remains "constantly amazed by the high standards of the legal systems."

The modern Israeli Supreme Court, under the leadership of its president, Professor Aharon Barak, has taken an activist role in striking the appropriate balance between security and liberty. It has protected the rights of Palestinians, noncombatants, prisoners of war, and others, often at considerable risk to Israeli civilians and soldiers.

The Israeli Supreme Court has been the only high court to directly take on the issue of applying physical pressure (nonlethal torture) to captured terrorists in an effort to secure information necessary to prevent ongoing terrorist attacks. Notwithstanding its recognition that such extreme measures may at such times save lives, it has prohibited their use, thereby acknowledging that Israel must fight the war against terrorism "with one hand tied behind its back," because that is what the rule of law requires. It has prohibited the Israeli military from attacking ambulances, despite its recognition that ambulances are often used to transport explosives and suicide bombers.

> We see fit to emphasize that our combat forces are obliged to abide by the humanitarian rules regarding care for the wounded, the ill, and the bodies of the deceased. The abuse committed by [Palestinian] medical personnel in hospitals and in ambulances obliges the I.D.F. to act in order to avoid such activities, but does not, in and of itself, make sweeping breach of humanitarian rules permissible. And indeed, this is the declared position of the State. This position is appropriate not only as far as international law, on which the Petitioners based their argument,

is concerned, but also in light of the values of the State of Israel as a Jewish and democratic state.

> The I.D.F. shall once again remind the combat forces, down to the level of the single soldier in the field, of this commitment of our forces, based on law and morality—and according to the State, even on utility—through concrete instructions which will prevent, to the extent possible, and even in severe situations, activities which are not in line with the rules of humanitarian aid.

Following that decision, Palestinian terrorists continued to use ambulances. The New York Times, on May 21, 2003, reported a case in which "a would-be bomber hid three times in an ambulance in a bid to get past Israeli troops. ... He then joined forces with a 40-year-old woman, a mother of three, who strapped a bomb to her chest and accompanied him on a taxi ride."

The Israeli Supreme Court has prohibited Israel from holding prisoners as "bargaining chips" for the exchange of prisoners illegally being held by its enemies.

On September 3, 2002, the court decided a case in which the Israeli military ordered the expulsion of the sister and brother of a terrorist who had organized several suicide bombings. They were expelled from the West Bank for a period of two years and moved to the Gaza Strip on the basis of a finding that the sister had sewn explosive belts and the brother served as a "look out when his brother and members of his group moved two explosive charges from one place to another." The court ruled that the expulsion order, which constituted a temporary "assignment of residence" within the occupied territories rather than a transfer out of the territories, was valid only if "the person himself [who is being expelled] presents a real danger":

> One cannot assign the residence of an innocent relative who does not present a danger, even if it is proved

that assigning his residence may deter others from carrying out terrorists acts. One cannot assign the residence of someone who no longer presents a danger. Assigning someone's place of residence may be done only on the basis of clear and convincing administrative evidence. It must be proportionate.

In a companion case, the court reversed the expulsion order:

It was however decided that with regard to the petitioner Abed Alnasser Mustafa Ahmed Asida—the brother of the terrorist Nasser A–Din Asida—the measure of assigned residence could not be adopted. The reason for this was that even though it was proved that this petitioner knew of the deeds of his terrorist brother, his involvement amounted merely to lending his brother a car and giving him clean clothes and food at his home, and no connection had been established between the petitioner's acts and the terrorist activity of the brother. It was therefore held that there was an inadequate basis for determining the petitioner to be sufficiently dangerous for his residence to be assigned.

In its conclusion, the court made the following observation:

The State of Israel is undergoing a difficult period. Terror is hurting its residents. Human life is trampled upon. Hundreds have been killed. Thousands have been injured. The Arab population in Judaea and Samaria and the Gaza Strip is also suffering unbearably. All of this is because of acts of murder, killing and destruction perpetrated by terrorists. ... The State is doing all that it can in order to protect its citizens and ensure the security of the region. These measures are limited. The restrictions are, first and foremost, military-operational ones. It is difficult to fight against persons who are prepared to turn themselves into living bombs. These restrictions are also normative. The State of Israel is a freedom-seeking democracy. It is a defensive democracy acting within the framework of its right to self-defence—a right recognized by the charter of the United Nations. ... [N]ot every effective measure is also a lawful measure. ... Indeed, the position of the State of Israel is a difficult one. Also our role as judges is not easy. We are doing all we can to balance properly between human rights and the security of the area. In this balance, human rights cannot receive complete protection, as if there were no terror, and State security cannot receive complete protection, as if there were no human rights. A delicate and sensitive balance is required. This is the price of democracy. It is expensive, but worthwhile. It strengthens the State. It provides a reason for its struggle.

The entire text of this decision, which is available on the Web, should be required reading for those who claim that Israel does not comply with the rule of law.

It is fair to say that although Israeli actions in combating terrorism have been far from perfect, Israel has been in greater compliance with the rule of law than any other country facing comparable dangers. In contrast to Israel, the Egyptians, the Jordanians, and the Palestinians routinely torture suspects and do not limit their torture to nonlethal applications. In 2002, the Palestinian Authority acknowledged that it tortured a suspected collaborator in order to get him to incriminate his aunt, who was then shot without any semblance of a trial. Jordan has not only tortured suspected terrorists but also their relatives in an effort to loosen the tongues of uncooperative terrorists.

It is interesting to recall that when the Chinese government killed demonstrators at Tiananmen Square in 1989, the first person to congratulate

Jiang Zemin for putting down the demonstration was Yasser Arafat, speaking on behalf of the Palestinian people. This is what he wrote:

> On behalf of the Arab Palestinian people, their leadership and myself, I ... take this opportunity to express extreme gratification that you were able to restore normal order after the recent incidents in People's China. I wish you, close friends, more progress in your endeavour to achieve the hopes, goals, aspirations, stability and security of our friends, the Chinese people.

The same Palestinian propagandists who so loudly and hypocritically complain whenever Israel deviates even one iota from human rights perfection are quick to praise and support every tyrannical destroyer of human rights, ranging from Saddam Hussein to Muammar Khadafi to Fidel Castro.

Like every other nation, Israel has made mistakes in overreacting to terrorism and other threats to its civilian population. It is far from perfect, but a comparative and contextual assessment of its actions demonstrates that it deserves to be singled out for praise, not criticism, for its efforts to combat terrorism within the rule of law and with sensitivity to the rights of innocent noncombatants.

In a 1987 speech, Justice William Brennan, perhaps the most civil libertarian justice in U.S. Supreme Court history, made the following observation of Israel's efforts to balance security and civil liberties:

> It may well be Israel, not the United States, that provides the best hope for building a jurisprudence that can protect civil liberties against the demands of national security. For it is Israel that has been facing real and serious threats to its security for the last forty years and seems destined to continue facing such threats in the foreseeable future. The struggle to establish civil liberties against the backdrop of these security threats, while difficult, promises to build bulwarks of liberty that can endure the fears and frenzy of sudden danger—bulwarks to help guarantee that a nation fighting for its survival does not sacrifice those national values that make the fight worthwhile. ... The nations of the world, faced with sudden threats to their own security, will look to Israel's experience in handling its continuing security crisis, and may well find in that experience that expertise to reject security claims that Israel has exposed as baseless and the courage to preserve the civil liberties that Israel has preserved without detriment to its security....

> I [would not] be surprised if in the future the protections generally afforded civil liberties during times of world danger owed much to the lessons Israel learns in its struggle to preserve simultaneously the liberties of its citizens and the security of its nation. For in this crucible of danger lies the opportunity to forge a worldwide jurisprudence of civil liberties that can withstand the turbulences of war and crisis. In this way, adversity may yet be the handmaiden of liberty.

When a student leader like the one quoted at the beginning of this chapter declares Israel to be the prime human rights violator in the world, he or she is guilty either of abysmal ignorance or malignant bigotry. In either case, he is in very large, although not very good, company. Most reasonable people would rather be lectured about civil liberties and human rights by Justice William Brennan than by Yasser Arafat or the U.N. Commission on Human Rights.

If there is any remaining doubt about the superiority of Israeli democracy and commitment to the rule of law in comparison to Arab and Muslim nations, and even most Western nations, let it be resolved by the Palestinians themselves, who are familiar with Israel's political and judicial institutions. Khalil Shikaki, a Palestinian political scientist who has been polling Palestinians since 1996 about "what governments they admire," found the following:

> Every year Israel has been the top performer, at times receiving more than 80 percent approval. The American system has been the next best, followed by the French and then, distantly trailing, the Jordanian and Egyptian.
>
> In its early days, the Palestinian Authority held fourth place, with about 50 percent approval. Now, it is dead last, under 20 percent. Corruption, mismanagement and the stagnation of the Palestinian predicament have turned the culture of criticism against the Palestinian rulers.

The Palestinians who were polled would also like to see a constitution that would "substantially strengthen and protect the judiciary [which] is now the weakest element of Palestinian governance." This too is modeled on the Israeli judiciary Not surprisingly, Arafat "prefers a weak judiciary." Most dictators do.

Is There Moral Equivalence Between Palestinian Terrorists And Israeli Responses?

The Accusation

There is a moral equivalence between those who deliberately target innocent children, women, the elderly, and other civilians and those who inadvertently kill civilians in the process of trying to prevent further terrorist attacks.

The Accusers

"Suicide bombers are terrorists, and so are the far worse Israeli crimes that we [the United States] carry out." (Noam Chomsky)

"Killing the Future: Children in the Line of Fire, a new report issued today by Amnesty International, details the way in which Palestinian and Israeli children have been targeted in an unprecedented manner since the beginning of the current intifada.

"'Children are increasingly bearing the brunt of this conflict. Both the Israeli Defense Force (IDF) and Palestinian armed groups show an utter disregard for the lives of children and other civilians,' Amnesty International said today.

"Respect for human life must be restored. Only a new mindset among Israelis and Palestinians can prevent the killing of more children.

"The impunity enjoyed by members of the IDF and of Palestinian groups responsible for killing children has no doubt helped create a situation where the right to life of children and civilians on the other side has little or no value.

"Enough of unacceptable reasons and excuses. Both the Israeli government and the Palestinian Authority must act swiftly and firmly to investigate the killing of each and every child and ensure that all those responsible for such crimes are brought to justice,' the organization stated." (Amnesty International Press Release)

"[Pope John Paul II has issued an] unequivocal condemnation of Terrorism, from whatever side it may come."

"We condemn equally ... both the suicide bombings ... and the violence of the Israeli occupation." (National Council of Churches delegation to the Middle East)

"Palestinians will argue that the violence of the Israeli Occupation is far greater, and that the daily combination of torture, house demolitions, humiliating searches, targeted assassinations, and the siege of towns and villages is far worse than anything experienced by the Israeli population. They may be right." (Rabbi Michael Lerner)

The Reality

Every reasonable school of philosophy, theology, jurisprudence, and common sense distinguishes between deliberately targeting civilians and inadvertently killing civilians while targeting terrorists who hide among them.

The Proof

Terrorist attacks against Israelis and Jews have included the following targets:

- A nursery school in which eighteen children and teachers were machine gunned to death
- An elementary school in which twenty-seven children and teachers were killed
- A Jewish community center in which eighty-six civilians were killed
- A Turkish synagogue in which twenty-seven Jews at prayer were killed
- A Swiss airliner headed to Israel in which all forty-seven civilian passengers were killed
- A passenger terminal at Lod Airport in which twenty-seven civilians, mostly Christian pilgrims, were killed
- A Passover seder in which twenty-nine Jews were killed
- A discotheque for teenagers in which twenty-one mostly Russian Jews were killed
- A Hebrew University cafeteria in which nine people were killed
- An airplane filled with Israeli tourists returning from a Chanukah vacation in Kenya

Only the last of these attacks failed. This targeted murder of children, the elderly, and other vulnerable citizens is utterly without any moral justification. Amnesty International has declared such terrorist acts to be "crimes against humanity." Many terrorist acts are not even directed against Israeli civilians—unjustified as that is—but are directed against Jews who live outside of Israel, regardless of their views about Israel. This is anti-Semitic hate violence, pure and simple.

When the Ku Klux Klan perpetrated similar outrageous attacks, although on a far smaller scale, there was universal condemnation. No one condemned equally the deliberate bombings by the Klan and the occasional overreactions by the FBI. Yet there are those who seek to justify the current anti-Jewish outrages as the work of freedom fighters. The reality is that right-wing extremists and Islamic militants are working together in Germany and other European countries to spread "violent anti-Semitism on university campuses." Neo-Nazis have also cooperated with Islamic terrorists in Argentina to perpetrate anti-Jewish violence.

The victims of the Holocaust and other genocides did not take revenge by killing innocent children, even the children of actual perpetrators of the genocides. Yet Israel's enemies—from the Palestinians to the Iranians to the neo-Nazi groups that have worked in collaboration with them—have not hesitated to target children or anyone else, Jew or non-Jew. And many in the international community insist on describing Israel's attempts to prevent these outrages as morally equivalent to the outrages themselves. Among the worst offenders are certain religious leaders who should know better and whose own theologies make a crucial distinction between deliberately intended consequences, such as targeting children, and unintended consequences, even when they cause the accidental death of a child in the process of targeting a dangerous terrorist. The New Catholic Encyclopedia defines the principle of "double effect" as "a rule of conduct frequently used in moral theology to determine when a person may lawfully perform an action from which two effects will follow, one bad, and the other good." It then gives the following example, which perfectly describes Israel's policy of fighting terrorism:

> In modern warfare the principle of the double effect is frequently applicable. Thus, in waging a just war a nation may launch an air attack on an important military objective of the enemy even though a comparatively small number of noncombatants are killed. This evil effect can be compensated for by the great benefit gained through the destruction of the target. This would not be true if the number of noncombatants slain in the attack were out of proportion to the

benefits gained. ... Furthermore, if the direct purpose of the attack were to kill a large number of noncombatants so that the morale of the enemy would be broken down and they would sue for peace, the attack would be sinful. ... It would be a case of the use of a bad means to obtain a good end.

As the philosopher Jean Bethke Elshtain has pointedly observed in reaction to the claim of moral equivalence by some clergymen and theologians:

If we could not distinguish between an accidental death resulting from a car accident and an intentional murder, our criminal justice system would fall apart. And if we cannot distinguish the killing of combatants from the intended targeting of peaceable civilians, we live in a world of moral nihilism. In such a world, everything reduces to the same shade of gray and we cannot make distinctions that help us take our political and moral bearings.

This failure to understand—or worse, to understand but not to acknowledge—the fundamental difference between deliberately targeting civilians and accidentally killing civilians in the course of self-defense reflects moral obtuseness at best and outright bigotry at worst. It also encourages those who deliberately employ the murder of civilians as a means toward achieving "moral equality" with their more humane enemies in the court of public opinion. The cruel irony is that for some bigots Israel is not even regarded as the moral equivalent of its terrorist enemies. Noam Chomsky, for example, regards Israeli and American counterterrorism actions as far worse than the terrorism itself.

The argument I am making is not that two wrongs make a right. It is always possible to find wrongs on all sides. The argument—and it is an argument central to civilization and justice—is that the concept of wrongs is not always a matter of

degree; there are qualitative differences between unintended wrongs and purposeful wrongs. Two dead civilians are not morally equivalent if one was targeted for murder, and the death of the other was the unfortunate consequence of best efforts, including risks to one's own soldiers, to prevent the murder of civilians. Both are wrongs, just as the death of two hospital patients from overdoses of a cancer-treating drug are wrongs. But anyone who cannot, or will not, distinguish between a case where a black patient was deliberately overdosed by a racist, nurse and another case where the patient died after consenting to aggressive cancer therapy that he knew carried a high risk of death is either morally blind or willfully bigoted. Everybody understands this difference, and everyone believes in it in other contexts. But when it comes to Israel, simple intelligence and basic morality are suspended by some who insist on applying a double standard to the Jewish state.

Even if Israel is properly criticized for overreacting in particular cases by placing civilians at risk, there is still no moral equivalence between exploding an antipersonnel bomb made of nails soaked in rat poison whose sole purpose is to maximize civilian deaths and injuries, on the one hand, and targeting terrorists under circumstances in which it is likely that some innocent civilians may die, on the other hand. Both are wrong, but the former is far, far more morally culpable than the latter, because of the differing purposes. No civilized society regards premeditated first-degree murder as morally equivalent to negligent homicide. This is true of the Bible, the Koran, and international law—except apparently when it comes to Israel, where longstanding distinctions and universally accepted rules of morality seem to be forgotten.

It is important for some people to believe that all morality is relative, and there is no absolute evil in the world. This is especially true of people who came of age after the Hitler–Stalin era. Even following the death of those two perfectly evil monsters, there were others who were pure evil, such as Pol Pot and Idi Amin. But they lived in distant lands and were not part of the daily consciousness of most Americans as Hitler and Stalin were. The Vietnam War was seen by many as a clash between morally equivalent aggressors. Fidel Castro was viewed by many on the left as having done some good and some bad.

Yet there is true evil in the world, and the deliberate targeting of children, women, and old people based on their ethnicity or national origin is pure evil, with absolutely no justification. To fail to acknowledge such terrorism as pure evil invites relativism about everything. If it is permissible to target babies and schoolchildren just because they are Jewish, is there anything that is beyond the pale of acceptability? In The Brothers Karamazov, Fyodor Dostoyevsky posed this question in the famous dialogue about relativism between Ivan and Alyosha:

> Ivan: "Imagine that you are creating a fabric of human destiny with the object of making men happy in the end, giving them peace at least, but that it was essential and inevitable to torture to death only one tiny creature—that baby beating its breast with its fist, for instance—and to found that edifice on its unavenged tears, would you consent to be the architect of those conditions? Tell me, and tell the truth."

> Alyosha replied without hesitation: "No, I wouldn't consent."

Remember that Hitler and Stalin both claimed justifications for their policies of mass murder and had large followings that included intellectuals, professionals, and artists. Yet we now understand that nothing could possibly justify the annihilation of tens of millions of innocent civilians, although some Palestinian and Arab leaders still bemoan the fact that Hitler did not complete the job.

Why then are decent people today afraid to call evil by its name? Why do so many insist on finding moral equivalence? And why do so many people describe the worst of evils—the deliberate targeting of children—with positive-sounding terms like "freedom fighting," while describing reasonable efforts to prevent these Nazi-like evils as Nazism itself? Noam Chomsky likes to remind his audiences that Hitler and Stalin both claimed that their genocide was really antiterrorism, as if to suggest that everything labeled antiterrorism—from the building of death camps in which a million children were gassed to the targeted assassination of a single terrorist commander—is morally equivalent.

The day after President Bush brought Israeli prime minister Sharon and Palestinian prime minister Abbas together at Aqaba, Hamas leader Ismail Abu Shanab vowed to continue the suicide bombings, after complaining bitterly that Abbas had acknowledged that Jews had suffered throughout history: "He spoke about Israeli suffering as if Palestinians committed the Holocaust against the Jews, while in truth it is the Palestinians who are being subject to an Israeli holocaust." This historical ignorance or self-deception about the actual role of Palestinian leaders in the Holocaust, coupled with immoral comparisons between Nazi death camps and Israeli self-defense against terrorism, has itself become a barrier to peace.

The political analogue to moral equivalence is even-handedness. It might follow from the false premise that the Palestinians and Israelis are equally at fault for the breakdown of the peace process and the escalating violence, that the international community should be even-handed in dealing with both sides. But it also follows from the undisputed fact that Palestinian leaders are blameworthy for their repeated rejection of the two-state solution and for the resulting escalation of violence, that the two sides should not be treated in an even-handed manner. To reward rejection and violence with even-handedness is to encourage such conduct. There must be a high price paid by those who reject peace in favor of violence, as the Palestinians have since the 1920s. There must be a benefit for those who were willing to accept a peaceful two-state solution in 1937, 1947, and 2000–2001, as Israel was.

Moreover, there must be a price paid by those who start aggressive wars of annihilation and extermination, as the Arab states and Palestinian fighters have repeatedly done. And there should be a benefit for those who successfully defend their civilian population against such aggressive wars. Any other approach will encourage the waging of aggressive wars.

There must also be a price paid by those who have repeatedly allied themselves with, and actively supported, the worst sorts of evil, ranging from Nazism to Saddamism. Similarly, those who support the winning sides of just wars have traditionally been rewarded with favorable treatment.

The concept of even-handedness seems benign, almost moral. As a people committed to equality, Americans generally support even-handedness. We would certainly expect it from an umpire or a referee at a sporting event. We demand it of our government in the treatment of people of different races, religions, genders, and sexual orientations. But even-handedness is not automatically a desirable criterion for dealing with nations and groups that have behaved quite differently—some far better than others—as judged by universally accepted moral criteria. No one expected even-handedness for the Germans and the Japanese following the Second World War, and no one expected even-handedness when the Justice Department confronted the Ku Klux Klan. Most relevantly, no one expects even-handedness between Osama bin Laden's al-Qaeda and those who are seeking to destroy his capacity to inflict further harm on innocent people. We should favor those who seek peace over those who have shown a preference for war. We should favor those who are not seeking to destroy a U.N. member state over those who are.

Shifting from the theoretical to the practical, even-handedness is rarely even. Those who advocate even-handedness between Israel and its enemies generally favor a strong tilt against Israel in favor of the Palestinians. Certainly that has long been true of the United Nations, which talks the talk of even-handedness but votes the vote of a strong bias against Israel and a preference for the

Palestinians, not only over Israel but also over all other occupied and stateless people. The same has been true of most European and Asian countries.

Even Amnesty International has failed the test of even-handedness by falsely claiming that no Palestinian minor has ever been involved in a suicide bombing and that the Israeli Army "targets" innocent Palestinian children. The United States, which has generally been even-handed in fact, as between Israel and the Palestinians, is widely perceived as being unfairly favorable to Israel, whereas those who are in fact unfairly favorable to the Palestinians are widely perceived as even-handed. The United States has voted against Israel at the Security Council on many occasions, sometimes most regrettably, as when it condemned Israel for destroying Iraq's nuclear reactor—an action for which the United States is now quite grateful. Many nations that claim to be even-handed have almost never voted to condemn Palestinian actions.

Even the false argument over why the United States "tilts" toward Israel while the rest of the world is even-handed is often tinged with not-so-subtle anti-Semitism. "The Jews control America," it is claimed and that is why the United States is so pro-Israel. One rarely hears comparable complaints about Muslim or oil influences on French policy. Americans, whether Jewish or non-Jewish, who support Israel because they believe that is the best policy for the United States have a perfect right to try, by democratic means, to influence U.S. policy, especially when so much of the rest of the world is so one-sidedly anti-Israel, as reflected by the one-sided voting results at the U.N. and other international bodies.

If even-handedness is ever to be achieved within the entire international community, it will only happen if the United States does not seek to emulate European conceptions of even-handedness. If the United States were ever to become as even-handed as the international community has been, it would surely encourage continuing aggression against the Jewish state. It would also be morally wrong. Even-handedness toward those whose actions are not morally equivalent is an immoral and dangerous form of artificial symmetry.

Hamas: A History from Within

By Azzam Tamimi

I want to proclaim loudly to the world that we are not fighting Jews because they are Jews! We are fighting them because they assaulted us, they killed us, they took our land and our homes; they attached our children and our women; they scattered us. All we want is our rights. We don't want more.[1]

—SHEIKH AHMAD YASSIN

"This is What We Struggle for"

This is the title of a document written by Hamas's Political Bureau in the late 1990s. It was Hamas's response to a request by a European diplomatic mission in Amman for an explanation of Hamas's objectives, values, and ideals. The document begins with the following statement: "The Islamic Resistance Movement (Hamas) is a Palestinian national liberation movement that struggles for the liberation of the Palestinian occupied lands and for the recognition of Palestinian legitimate rights."

The political language of this document is very different from the highly religious terms in which the Hamas Charter was framed. The Charter, in Arabic *Al–Mithaq* (the covenant), was Hamas's first attempt to produce a written document for others to learn what Hamas stood for. It was published on 18 August 1988, less than nine months after the foundation of the movement. Since then, however, it has hardly ever been quoted or even referred to by the Hamas leadership or its official spokesmen. Their language has become virtually indistinguishable from that of any freedom fighter in Latin America, South Africa, or East Asia. On 7 March 2004, the following statement was placed on the Izzadin al–Qassam internet site by the Hamas leader in Gaza, Dr. Abd al–Aziz al–Rantisi, just ten days before his assassination at the hands of the Israelis:

Hamas's strategy is underpinned by four principles:

1. Our homeland has been usurped in its entirety, but we cannot concede one inch of it.
2. There is an obvious imbalance of power in favor of the Zionist enemy.
3. We do not possess the armaments our enemy possesses, but we have a faith that generates a will that does not recognize defeat or retreat before our goals are accomplished. This is a faith that demands sacrifice for the sake of religion and homeland.
4. The Arab and Islamic umma is weak, feeble, and divided, and is therefore unable to support

the people of Palestine. The international community is hostile to the hopes and aspirations of the Palestinian people and supports Zionist terrorism. Hamas's strategy therefore has two parallel goals:

- to resist occupation and confront Zionist aggression,
- to maintain the unity of the Palestinian people and safeguard the Palestinians from internal strife, which hinder resistance to the occupation.

The Hamas Charter has frequently been invoked by the movement's critics, as proof of either its inflexibility or its anti-Semitism. Until the late 1990s, this did not appear to concern anyone within the movement. Seemingly, the primary concern of the Hamas leadership was to address their own Arab and Muslim constituents inside and outside Palestine, paying little attention to the views of the rest of the world about the movement.

When it was drafted, the Charter was an honest representation of the ideological and political position of Hamas at that moment in time. Hamas had emerged from the Ikhwan (the Muslim Brotherhood), and the Charter was a reflection of how the Ikhwan perceived the conflict in Palestine and how they viewed the world. On the first page of the Hamas Charter, following a quotation from the Qur'an (Sura 3: 110—112), there is a quotation from Hassan al–Banna, who founded the Ikhwan in Egypt in 1928. Banna says: "Israel will be created and will continue to exist until Islam sweeps it away, just as it swept away what came before it." While the Hamas leaders of today would not necessarily wish to revise phraseology of this kind, they are increasingly convinced that the Charter as a whole has been more of a hindrance than a help. Many would admit that insufficient thought went into the drafting and publication of the Charter. Once it had been drafted, Hamas institutions inside and outside Palestine were never adequately consulted over its content. According to Khalid Mish'al, the Charter was rushed out to meet what was perceived at the time as a pressing need to

introduce the newly founded movement to the public. Mish'al does not view it as a true expression of the movement's overall vision, which "has been formulated over the years by inputs from the movement's different institutions." He sees the Charter as a historical document, which gives an insight into Hamas's original philosophy at the time of its establishment. However, it "should not be regarded as the fundamental ideological frame of reference from which the movement derives its positions, or on the basis of which it justifies its actions." Ibrahim Ghosheh takes a similar view. According to him, "it goes without saying that the articles of the charter are not sacred; in other words they are subject to review and revision in a manner that does not contradict the main ideas with which the movement emerged and to which it continues to adhere."

Such clarifications, or reservations, are quite recent. Until the beginning of the second intifada in September 2000, very little debate had taken place within Hamas on this issue, despite the fact that much of the criticism levelled against the movement has involved references to the Charter. It was as if Hamas had totally forgotten that it had issued a Charter, or as if its leaders were completely oblivious to the criticism that had hitherto been directed against it. Only recently have certain Hamas leaders begun to voice their concern that it has perhaps taken them too long to recognize that "the text of the Charter does not reflect the thinking and understanding of the movement." They have only just started to admit that this may constitute "an obstacle, or a source of distortion, or a misunderstanding regarding what the movement stands for."

Hamas has become increasingly visible in the world's media, and a very negative image has often been presented, mostly filtered through the views of Israel and its supporters. This has prompted the senior Political Bureau officials to seek advice on how to counter such negative publicity. Concern over this issue goes back to the mid-1990s, when the Political Bureau was still in Jordan and the movement was beginning to have some contacts with Western diplomats in Amman. However, it was in the aftermath of the events of 11 September

2001 that it took on a degree of urgency. Hamas began to feel that an image-building initiative was needed, in order to counter the efforts by certain hostile media and academic quarters to identify all Islamic movements and organizations with al–Qaeda. Israel in particular sought to capitalize on the American-led war on terror to further its campaign to convince the Western world of its continued strategic value as an ally, despite the end of the Cold War. Israel's contention was that no distinction existed between one strand of political Islam and another, and that Israel stood as a bulwark to protect the West.

A series of consultations conducted in Beirut and Damascus from early 2003 until the end of 200S reinforced the feeling of a number of senior Hamas Political Bureau officials that the time had come for the Charter to be rewritten. A process of consultation culminated in the commissioning of a draft for a new Charter. However, in the aftermath of the Palestinian legislative elections of 25 January 2006, in which Hamas won a majority, the project was put on hold until further notice, lest the new Charter be seen as a measure in response to outside pressure.

What's Wrong with the Hamas Charter?

The current Charter is written in a language that no longer appeals to well-educated Muslims. It may have been a major obstacle in the way of Hamas's efforts to win over pro-Palestinian secular Muslims and non-Muslims to its side. Its language and ideas typify the prevalent discourse of the Ikhwan at the time when the Charter was written, not only in Palestine but elsewhere in the world. The Ikhwan have moved on since then, but the Charter has remained unchanged. Today, the Charter gives the impression that its author wrote it for the benefit of his own immediate circle of devotees, rather than for the public as a whole. The author of the Charter is believed to have been Abd al–Fattah Dukhan, one of the seven founders of Hamas and a long-time leader of the Palestinian Ikhwan. He often acted as second-in-command to Sheikh Ahmad Yassin. At the time of

Hamas's establishment and the publication of the Charter, he was the leader of the Ikhwan in Gaza, at a time when Sheikh Ahmad Yassin had not yet resumed his leadership responsibilities following his release from detention in the exchange of prisoners in May 1985.

The Charter in fact reads more like an internal circular. It has been criticized from within Hamas itself for not having the correct tone for an official document, suitable for the introduction of the ideas of Hamas to the world. Not everyone in the movement at the time felt that the publication of a Charter was necessarily a good idea, though they may not have had any objection to its language or content. With hindsight it seems that the issue of the Hamas Charter formed part of the ongoing process of competition with the PLO. The PLO Charter was utterly secular, and therefore did not reflect the Islamic identity of the Palestinian people or their cause.

Many Hamas leaders now recognize that the fundamental and essential positions expressed in the Charter could be expressed in more universal language that could appeal to both Muslims and non-Muslims alike. Instead of justifying its statements in religious terms, which may mean little to those who do not share the same faith or the same vision, a new Charter should refer to the historical basis of the Palestinian cause. It should give a succinct account of the story of the Palestine conflict as it has unfolded. It should trace the roots of the problem to Europe in the 19th century, showing how the Palestinians have been the victims of the European plan conceived more than a century ago to resolve Europe's own Jewish problem. This was done at the expense of the Palestinians through the creation of a homeland for the "Jewish people" in Palestine. Such an argument would be more universally acceptable than the idea that Palestine is a *waqf* (endowment) "consecrated for future Muslim generations until Judgment Day." As article 11 of the Charter itself explains, the lands conquered by the Muslims from the time of the second Caliph Omar onward were all assigned as *waqf* in order not to be distributed among the conquering troops. The same consideration applies equally to Iraq, Persia,

Egypt, North Africa, and even Spain. The reference to this issue in the Charter was intended to condemn those who were willing to give away any part of Palestine to the Israelis as part of a peace agreement. This is the logic behind the passage: "It is not permissible to concede it or any part of it or to give it up or any part of it; that is not the right of any single Arab state or all the Arab states together nor any king or president or all the kings and presidents together nor any single organization or all the organizations together whether Palestinian or Arab. This is so because the land of Palestine is an Islamic *waqf* (endowment) property consecrated to the generations of Muslims up to the Day of Resurrection; and who can presume to speak for all Muslim generations to the Day of Resurrection?" It is widely accepted today within Hamas that this is strictly a matter of Islamic jurisprudence, and that the Charter is not the best place in which to address it.

However, the biggest problem arising from the Charter lies in its treatment of the Jews. Part of the difficulty here is that of the language employed. The average Palestinian refers to Israelis as *yahud*, which is simply the Arabic word for Jews. Terms such as Zionist or Israeli figure mostly in the writings and conversations of an elite that has received secular education. They are not current in the vocabulary of the common man, and have until recently also been absent from Islamic discourse. When Arabic texts referring to the Israelis as *yahud* are translated into European languages, they may indeed sound anti-Semitic.

In his series of testimonies broadcast on Aljazeera between 17 April and 5 June 1999, Sheikh Yassin refers to the Israelis interchangeably at times as al-isra'iliyun (the Israelis) and at times as al-yahud (the Jews). In the second episode of the testimony, broadcast on 24 April 1999, he spoke as follows: "The Israelis usually deal with the Palestinian people individually and not collectively. Even inside the prisons, they would not agree to deal with the Palestinians except individually. However, we forced our will on them despite themselves and refused to deal with them except through a leadership elected by the Palestinian [prisoners] to face the Jews and resolve the problems with them." Most Palestinians and Arabs unconsciously use similar language. Leah Tsemel, an Israeli lawyer who has been defending Palestinians in Israeli courts for some 30 years, notes that her clients routinely describe soldiers or settlers as *al-yahud*, "the Jews." They complain for instance that "*al-yahud* [the Jews] took my ID card," or "*al-yahud* [the Jews] hit me," or "*al-yahud* [the Jews]" destroyed this or that. She expresses anxiety at the way Israel, in the minds of its Palestinian victims, becomes identified with all the Jews in the world and fears that; consequently all the Jews in the world may be seen as soldiers and settlers.

This problem is not confined to Palestine. The same phenomenon exists across the region, where Jews once lived in large numbers but from which, with a few exceptions, they are long departed. After the creation of the Israel State in Palestine in 1948, Jews living in various Arab countries were exhorted to come to the new Jewish entity, which, having expelled close to a million Palestinians, was in dire need of population. Jews from Iraq, Yemen, and Morocco provided a source of cheap labor, doing work and performing functions the Ashkenazim (European Jews) were unwilling to do for themselves. The Ashkenazim presided over the Zionist colonial project in Palestine and set themselves up as first-class citizens of the newly founded Jewish state, in contrast to the Sephardic or Oriental (Mizrahi) Jews who came from the Arab countries.

Until the beginning of the 20th century, Muslims, Christians, and Jews coexisted peacefully throughout the Muslim world. For many centuries, the Islamic empire, whose terrain extended over three continents, had provided a milieu of tolerance under a system that guaranteed protection for what are today referred to as minorities. Islam, whose values and principles governed the public and private conduct of Muslim individuals and communities, recognized Christians and Jews as legitimate communities within the Islamic State and accorded them inalienable rights. The adherents of both Christianity and Judaism participated on an equal footing with the Muslims in building the Arab–Islamic civilization on whose fruits the European Renaissance philosophers were nourished.

In contrast, in the European lands, the Jews suffered constant persecution. Many sought refuge in the Muslim lands, where they were welcomed and treated as people of the book in accordance with the Covenant of God and His Messenger. This Muslim perception of the Jews remained unchanged until the Zionist movement, which was born in Europe, began to recruit jews in the Muslim lands for a project seen by the Muslims as an attack on their faith and homeland. The change in the Muslim attitude toward the Jews came as a reaction to the claims of the Zionist movement, which purported to represent the Jews and Judaism. Despite the secular origins of the Zionist project and the atheism of many of its founding fathers, the rationale of Zionism sought to justify the creation of the State of Israel in Palestine and the dispossession of the Palestinians in religious terms. The Zionist pioneers invoked scriptural justification for their actions, though few of them truly believed in religion or respected it. Their aim was to bestow religious legitimacy on their project and gain the support of the world's Jews, of whom many had initially opposed political Zionism.

It is for this reason that the Hamas Charter characterizes the problem in Palestine as one of religious strife between the Jews and the Muslims. This idea continues to be dominant in many parts of the Muslim world today. The continued connection of Israel with the Jews, and the Jews with Israel, only reinforces the conviction of many Muslims that the conflict in the Middle East between the Palestinians and the Israelis is of a religious nature. Many Arabs and Muslims find it extremely difficult to believe in the existence of anti-Zionist Jews, who not only criticize Israel but in some instances refuse to recognize its legitimacy.

Articles 17, 22, 28, and 32 of the Hamas Charter embody the accusation that the Jews are engaged in a conspiracy. The last of these articles goes as far as to refer to the Protocols of the Elders of Zion, a false document that purports to represent the plans of a supposed secret society

of Jewish elders to conquer the world. What the author of the Charter wished to suggest was that there was a direct link between a supposed Jewish quest for global domination and the occupation of Palestine. Following a common tendency among Muslim writers of the time, the author of the Charter invoked the Qur'an and the Hadith (the sayings of the Prophet) to substantiate his claims. He seeks to show that there is a continuing Jewish conspiracy against Islam and the Muslims dating from the early days of Islam. Such selective readings and convenient interpretations of Islamic scripture are not uncommon in contemporary Muslim writings. In this case the Qur'an's chastisement of bad conduct and ill manners on the part of some of the Israelites of biblical times, or certain of the Jews during the time of the Prophet Muhammad, are taken out of their historical context. It is remarkable that, though the theory that the Jews are engaged in a conspiracy is in essence un-Islamic, it was widely espoused by Muslim intellectuals across the Arab world at least until the early 1990s. The pervasiveness of such thinking has been a symptom of decline and backwardness, which in turn have been instrumental in precipitating a profound sense of desperation and frustration.

Apart from its limited ability to explain, conspiracy theory tends to ascribe to human beings the powers of the Divine. Thanks to the efforts of thinkers such as Egypt's Abdelwahab Elmessiri, editor of the eight-volume Arabic *Encyclopedia of the Jews, Judaism, and Zionism*, the problem of Palestine is today seen by many Islamists, including leaders and members of Hamas, simply as the outcome of a colonial project. The conflict with Zionism should therefore be explained more in political, social, or economic terms than in terms of religion. There is a growing realization today tnat such explanations have more explanatory power and are more compatible with the Qur'anic paradigm of *tadafu'* (interaction or interplay). Whereas the Qur'anic concept of *tadafu'* favors interpretations of events and situations in the world that offer motivation and hope, the theory that a conspiracy prevails leads to frustration and despair. In the first case, the only transcendental power in the world is that of God who empowers whom He so wishes and disempowers whom He so wishes. One's actions may always be successful, if God wills. In the second case, little can be done to change the course of events, due to the assumption that a certain group of extremely powerful individuals, or community, has conspired to control the world and to seize all its resources. In this case, all contrary action will be in vain.

The only positive reference to the Jews in the Hamas Charter is seen in article 31, which states that "in the shade of Islam it is possible for the followers of the three religions, Islam, Christianity and Judaism to live in peace and security." It is anticipated that, while continuing to underline this historical fact, the new Hamas Charter will be cleansed of the ludicrous claim that there is a Jewish conspiracy. It will instead emphasize the racist nature of the Zionist project, explaining that many Jews are opposed to it. The idea that not every Jew is a Zionist is already widely accepted by the Islamists, who previously believed this was a myth invented by Palestinian secular nationalists. By shedding light on the roots of the conflict, a new Charter should appeal to the world's public opinion, attracting sympathy for the Palestinian victims rather than for their Israeli oppressors. To reach out to peoples and nations across the world, it will also need to adopt the conceptual framework of universal human rights. The new Hamas Charter is also expected to reassure the Jews that Hamas is not opposed to them because of their faith or race, and that it rejects the idea that the Middle East conflict is between Muslims and Jews, defined in terms of their religion. Nor is it between the faiths of Islam and Judaism. Sheikh Ahmad Yassin offered such a reassurance on a number of occasions before his assassination by the Israelis in 2004. The new Charter will stress that Islam recognizes Judaism as a legitimate religion and accords its adherents respect and protection. The Charter must lay down as a basic principle that Jews and Muslims can live together today in peace and harmony, as did earlier Muslims and Jews for many centuries, once the legitimate rights of the Palestinians are recognized and restored. This has been said repeatedly by Hamas leaders since the early 1990s.

Khalid Mish'al told a Canadian TV journalist that the liberation of Palestine "does not mean that either the Palestinian people, or we in Hamas, want to kill the Jews or want to throw them into the sea as Israel claims." He expressed his determination to continue the struggle to liberate Palestine and regain the rights of the Palestinians, but denied categorically that there was a war against the Jews. "No, we do not fight the Jews because they are Jews. We fight them because they stole our land and displaced our people; they carried out an aggression. We resist this Zionist project which is hostile." As for those Jews who do not fight the Palestinians, he said: "I have no problem with them, just as I have no problem with peaceful Christians or peaceful Muslims." He went on to explain that "if a Muslim were to attack me and steal my land, I have every right to fight back. This applies to all others irrespective of their race, identity or religion. This is our philosophy."

The Idea of *Hudna* (Truce)

One thing that will remain unchanged in a new Hamas Charter is the movement's opposition to the State of Israel. If Hamas remains loyal to its founding principles, it will not recognize Israel's right to exist. Born out of the intifada (uprising) of 1987, Hamas declared that it had emerged "in order to liberate the whole of Palestine, all of it." The movement came into existence partly in response to the oppressive treatment suffered by the Palestinians under Israeli occupation in the West Bank and Gaza, and partly because many felt strongly that Fatah, while carrying the banner of the Palestinian national liberation movement, had faltered. Like the membership of Fatah before it, most of Hamas's members and supporters had been refugees or children of refugees whose original homes were not the appalling camps in which they were born or where they grew up. They had previously lived on the other side of the so-called Green Line in the lands now colonized by Jewish immigrants who have come from Europe and elsewhere in the world. Like millions of Palestinians inside Palestine and in the diaspora, the founders of Hamas felt betrayed when the leadership of Fatah, which controlled the PLO, decided to give away the right of return of the Palestinians to their homes.

It is highly unlikely, therefore, that Hamas will ever recognize the legitimacy of the state of Israel or its right to exist. The movement regards Israel as nothing but a colonial enclave planted in the heart of the Muslim world, whose effect is to obstruct the revival of the umma, the global Muslim community, and to perpetuate Western hegemony in the region. Another consideration is that Palestine is an Islamic land that has been invaded and occupied by a foreign power. It would contravene the principles of Hamas's Islamic faith to recognize the legitimacy of the foreign occupation of any Muslim land. This applies all the more to the land that is the site of the first *qibla* of the Muslims (the spot toward which Musliih worshippers face during prayer), and the third most important mosque on earth.

This position is not exclusive to Hamas. Muslim scholars, with a few exceptions, have never ceased to express their absolute opposition to any recognition of the legitimacy of the creation of a Jewish state in Palestine. Over the past century Muslim scholars and jurists have issued numerous fatwas, or religious edicts, declaring null and void any agreement that legitimized the occupation of any part of Palestine. The first collective fatwa on this issue predates the creation of the State of Israel in Palestine. On 26; January 1935, more than 200 Islamic scholars came to Jerusalem from around Palestine to issue a fatwa prohibiting the forfeiture of any part of Palestine to the Zionists. Similar conferences were held and fatwas issued at various junctures in the history of the Middle East conflict. During the Nassirist era (1952–1970) in Egypt, the prestigious al-Azhar Islamic institution in Cairo prohibited any recognition of the State of Israel or any initiative to make peace with it. Sheikh Yusuf al-Qaradawi, one of the most authoritative scholars of contemporary times, frequently reiterated this position, which was unanimously adopted by more than 300 Islamic

scholars from around the Muslim world during a meeting of the Islamic Jurisprudential Council in Kuwait in the mid-1990s. He explained that the fatwa that prohibited the recognition of Israel was based on the consideration that "Palestine is an Islamic land that cannot be forfeited voluntarily." He added that the same fatwa was re-issued at a later Islamic Jurisprudence conference in Bahrain.

However, this doctrinal consideration does not deny the right of the Jews to live in Palestine, provided their presence there is not the outcome of invasion or military occupation. Nor does it prevent Muslims, including the Hamas movement, from negotiating a cease-fire agreement with the Israeli State in order to put an end to the bloodshed and to the suffering on both sides for as long as can be agreed on. The idea of a *hudna* (truce) with Israel originated in the early 1990s. Reference was made to it by the Amman-based head of Hamas Political Bureau, Musa Abu Marzuq, in a statement published by the Amman weekly *Al-Sabeel* the organ of the Jordanian Islamic Movement, in February 1994. At about the same time, the founder of Hamas, Sheikh Ahmad Yassin, speaking from his prison cell, made the first similar reference to the idea of a *hudna*, when he proposed such a truce as an interim solution to the conflict between the Palestinians and the Israelis. Both Abu Marzuq and Sheikh Yassin repeated the offer on several occasions, but failed to interest the Israelis. Recently, Hamas spokesmen have made frequent reference to the idea of *hudna*.

Hudna is recognized in Islamic jurisprudence as a legitimate and binding contract whose objective is to bring about a cessation of fighting with an enemy for an agreed period of time. The truce may be short or long depending on mutual needs or interests. Such a truce would be different from the Oslo peace accords, under which the PLO recognized the State of Israel and its right to exist. The difference is that under the terms of *hudna* the issue of recognition would not arise. This is because Hamas cannot, as a matter of principle, accept that land seized by Israel from the Palestinians has become Israel's. Hamas has no authority to renounce the right of the Palestinians to return to the lands and the homes from which they were forced out in 1948 or at any later time. It can, however, say that under the present circumstances the best it can do is regain some of the land lost, and secure the release of prisoners, in exchange for a cessation of hostilities.

In their justification of *hudna*, Hamas leaders look to the example of what happened between the Muslims and the Crusaders in the last decade of the 12th century. The conflict between the two sides in and around Palestine lasted for nearly 200 years. Of particular interest to Hamas in this regard is the Ramleh treaty concluded by Salah al-Din al-Ayyubi (Saladin) with Richard the Lionheart on 1 September 1192. The truce, which marked the end of the Third Crusade, lasted for a period of three years and three months. During this period, the Crusaders maintained control of the coast from Jaffa to Acre and were allowed to visit Jerusalem and to conduct commerce with the Muslims. In addition, reference is also frequently made to the first *hudna* ever in the history of Islam. Known as al-Hudaybiyah, the name of the location on the outskirts of Mecca where it was concluded, this agreement saw the suspension of hostilities between the Muslim community under the Prophet's leadership and the Meccan tribe of Quraysh. The duration of the *hudna* agreed to by both sides was ten years. However, it came to an end less than two years later when Quraysh breached it with the unlawful killing of some members of the tribe of Khuza'ah, which was allied to the Muslim side. Once *hudna* is concluded, it is considered sacred, and the fulfillment of its obligations becomes a religious duty. As long as the other party observes it, the Muslim side must not breach it; to do so is considered a grave sin. As in the case of other international treaties, a *hudna* is renewable by mutual agreement at the expiration of its term.

The general and long-term *hudna* proposed by Hamas stipulates as a first condition an Israeli withdrawal to the borders of 4 June 1967, which means the return of all the land occupied by the Israelis as a result of the Six-Day War, including East Jerusalem. This would entail the removal of all Jewish settlers from those areas. In addition, Israel would have to release all Palestinians held in its prisons and detention camps. It is highly unlikely that Hamas would settle for anything less in exchange for a long-term truce that could last for a quarter of a century or longer.

The Suicide Bomb

Hudna was Sheikh Ahmad Yassin's solution to the crisis created by Hamas's suicide bomb campaign. In April 1994, Israeli army and intelligence officers visited Sheikh Ahmad Yassin in his prison cell in the hope of obtaining from him a statement that might dissuade Hamas's military wing from carrying out more suicide or "martyrdom" operations. Hamas had launched a series of devastating suicide bomb attacks in April 1994 in retaliation for the massacre perpetrated on 25 February 1994 in al-Haram al-Ibrahimi Mosque in Hebron by an American-born Jewish settler, Baruch Goldstein. Goldstein is believed to have secured the assistance of Israeli troops to gain entry to the mosque, where he fired on the worshippers and threw hand grenades at them as they kneeled during the dawn prayers, killing 29 and wounding scores of others.

The series of revenge acts began at noon on 6 April 1994, when Ra'id Abdullah Zakarnah, an Izzadin al-Qassam Brigades member, drove a booby-trapped vehicle with an Israeli license plate into Afula bus station and blew it up, killing nine Israelis and injuring more than 150. A statement issued soon afterward by Hamas's military wing, the Izzadin al-Qassam Brigades, claimed responsibility for the bombing and warned the Israelis to evacuate their settlements in the West Bank and Gaza. In a clear reference to Goldstein's actions inside the mosque, Hamas vowed to make the Israelis pay for the pain and harassment Jewish settlers inflict on the Palestinians under occupation. On 31 April 1994, Ammar Amarnah, another member of the Izzadin al-Qassam Brigades, carried out the second attack. The target this time was an Israeli Egad bus, at al-Khadirah (Hadera) to the northwest of Tulkarm. Amarnah blew himself up on the bus killing five Israelis and wounding more than thirty. More operations were carried out that year and many more in succeeding years. They were for the most part in response to attacks on Palestinian civilians by Israeli troops or Jewish settlers. Sheikh Ahmad Yassin told his Israeli prison visitors that if they wanted to see an end to these attacks they could make a deal, which could be either limited or comprehensive. In its limited format the *hudna* would at least spare civilians on both sides. In its more comprehensive format it would entail an end to hostilities of all kinds between the two sides. There is no evidence to suggest that the Israelis have ever taken the offer of *hudna* seriously.

Resorted to out of utter desperation, suicide missions—"martyrdom operations"—were controversial when they were first launched. Many Palestinians were initially shocked by the suicide bomb tactic. Some argued against it from a purely pragmatic point of view, arguing that it was so shocking that it would harm the Palestinian cause. The operations were also opposed on the ground that they were, by their very nature, indiscriminate and resulted in killing innocent civilians, something the critics believed could not be justified or legitimized under any circumstance. The Fatah-led Palestinian Authority opposed the operations primarily on the grounds of its commitment to its own version of the peace process and the potential damage such operations could cause to it.

Hamas spokesmen maintained that the suicide bomb was the only means available to the Palestinians to deter those who might emulate Baruch Goldstein from launching further attacks on the defenseless Palestinian population. Over time, an increasing number of Palestinians accepted that the suicide bomb was necessary to offset the balance of power, which evidently favors the Israelis, who have acquired highly advanced military technology from the US and Europe. On the whole, Palestinians have generally approved of and admired the heroism and altruism of the men and women who have volunteered their bodies and souls to go on sacrificial missions on behalf of the cause of Palestine. The more the Palestinians have felt vulnerable, the more

they have supported martyrdom operations and even demanded more. It did not take much to convince those who had qualms that nothing else seemed to be effective as a means of self-defense or deterrence. Nevertheless, Palestinian public support for martyrdom operations has varied. Polls conducted at different times have given different results, but rarely has support for these operations dropped below fifty percent. In a poll conducted in the Gaza Strip by the Norwegian organization Fafo in the first week of September 2005, 61 percent qf those questioned agreed with the statement: "Suicide bombings against Israeli civilians are necessary to get Israel to make political concessions." Fafo also conducted a face-to-face survey with 875 respondents on Palestinian views of the Israeli withdrawal from the occupied Gaza strip. The *Jerusalem Post* reported on 16 October 2003 that a poll showed that 75 percent of Palestinians supported the suicide bombing of the Maxim restaurant in Haifa on 4 October 2003. The opinion poll was conducted by the Palestinian Center for Policy and Survey Research (PSR) in Ramallah. An earlier poll conducted by the Palestinian Authority's State Information Service (SIS) between 11 and 13 June 2002 in both the West Bank and the Gaza Strip revealed that 81 percent of the sample polled objected to the PA's designation of martyrdom operations as terrorist acts. Fifty-two percent of them said the PA resorted to labeling these operations as terrorist actions because of international pressure. The total number of those polled was 1,137, aged 18 years and above, 456 of them from the Gaza Strip and 681 from the West Bank. Incidentally, the poll also revealed that 86 percent of the sample "supported military attacks against Israeli occupation troops and Jewish settlers inside the Palestinian territories." Sixty-nine percent believed that the objective of carrying out martyrdom operations inside Israeli towns was to end the occupation, while 13.4 percent believed the objective was to undermine the peace process. Finally, 11.3 percent said the operations were intended to weaken the Palestinian Authority and embarrass it before the international community.

Until it was employed in Palestine, the notion of the suicide bomb was seen as alien to the Sunni community within Islam, it had been more commonly associated with Shi'ism: the Iranians are believed to have been the first Muslims to employ it. They did so with some success in the war with Iraq throughout the 1980s. Hundreds of Iranian young men were sent on martyrdom missions along the borders between the two countries, to deter the Iraqi troops, who were well-equipped and heavily armed, thanks to Western and Arab support. The tactic served the Iranians well, since their Iraqi counterparts, many of whom had not been convinced of the legitimacy of the war with Iraq's neighbor launched by their government, were not prepared to make similar sacrifices.

The tactic then moved to Lebanon in the aftermath of the Israeli invasion in 1982. The first martyrdom operation within Lebanon took place on 11 November 1982, when a young Shi'a, Ahmad Qasir, identified as a member of the Islamic Resistance, drove his car into the headquarters of the Israeli military governor in Tyre, detonating its 440 pounds of explosives and killing 74 Israelis. From then on, the suicide bomb became a routine tactic employed by the Lebanese resistance against Israeli occupation troops. The most memorable of all suicide bombings in Lebanon were the two simultaneous attacks carried out on 23 October 1983 against the US Battalion Landing Team headquarters and the base occupied by the French Paras, which were situated just 3.7 miles apart in Beirut. The two suicide bombers, both of whom died in the attack, were named as Abu Mazen, 26, and Abu Sij'an, 24. A previously unknown group called the Free Islamic Revolutionary Movement (FIRM) claimed responsibility for the two attacks, which together killed 241 American and 58 French soldiers. FIRM was apparently made up of Lebanese Shi'a Muslims associated with the Amal militia. Hezbollah had not yet emerged, but FIRM may have been its precursor. Lebanon also produced the first female suicide bomber in the Arab world: her name was Sana' Mhaidli. Her car bombing of an Israeli military convoy on 9 April 1985 was claimed by the secular Syrian Nationalist Party.

The Lebanese Hezbollah, founded with Iranian backing as a Shi'ite Muslim response to the Israeli occupation of South Lebanon, inherited the task of resistance and the tactic of the suicide bomb. It continued to employ the technique until Israel withdraw unilaterally from South Lebanon in May 2000, having concluded it could no longer bear the human cost of its military presence in part of Lebanon, in which more than 1,000 Israeli soldiers had died.

Suicide bombing is far from being a uniquely Muslim phenomenon. Elsewhere in the world, the Sri Lankan Tamil Tigers, who struggle for an independent Tamil state, began to carry out suicide bombings in 1987. It is estimated that they have since perpetrated over 200 such attacks. The Tamil suicide bomb attacks were employed primarily to assassinate politicians opposed to their cause. In 1991, they assassinated former Indian Prime Minister Rajiv Gandhi, and in 1993, they assassinated President Ranasinghe Premadasa of Sri Lanka. In 1999, the Tigers attempted to assassinate Sri Lankan President Chandrika Kumaratunga using a female suicide bomber.

Until the outbreak of the second intifada, Islamic groups in Lebanon and Palestine did not deem it appropriate to use female suicide bombers. Hamas was reluctant to recruit female bombers but removed the ban under pressure from its female members, some of whom threatened to act on their own initiative or in association with other factions. The first female bomber in Palestine was Wafa Idris, aged 26, who blew herself up in Yaffa Street in Jerusalem on 28 January 2001. She was the first of ten other female "martyrs." The last of these was Zaynab Ali, who blew herself up on 22 September 2004. The campaign of female suicide bombings was launched by Fatah's al–Aqsa Martyrs' Brigades, which was soon joined by the Palestinian Islamic Jihad and Hamas.

It is very likely that Hamas was persuaded to use suicide bombers when it became clear that the tactic was delivering results in Lebanon. It could not have been a coincidence that the first martyrdom operation was carried out in Palestine in the year after the return of the Hamas and Islamic Jihad deportees from South Lebanon, where for a year they had ample time to listen and learn from their Lebanese hosts. This brought pressure to bear on Hamas's political leaders who, while defending the tactic, were keen not to be directly associated with planning the operations or authorizing them. They delegated this task to the Izzadin al–Qassam Brigades. Hamas spokesmen were at pains to explain the distinction between the military and political wings of the movement. They explained that the latter also ran educational, relief, and media institutions that had to be protected from Israeli reprisals or from punitive measures by the international community. The theory was that the political leadership of Hamas laid down the general policy of the movement, whereas the military wing was an autonomous body that functioned independently of the political leadership, but in accordance with the general lines the political leadership laid down. The Israelis were never convinced by this, and nor were the Americans or the Europeans. By 2003, Hamas and many of the organizations identified as having been associated with it, directly or indirectly, were banned and put on the Western lists of terrorist organizations. The political leaders of Hamas were targeted for assassination by the Israeli army or by Mossad. Some escaped but many died.

Suicide Bombs: Strategy or Desperation?

There has been much debate over whether the tactic of suicide bombing arises from the dire economic conditions suffered by the Palestinians, or if it is simply part of a strategy aimed at the achievement of particular political objectives. It would be wrong to suggest that either explanation necessarily excludes the other. Many visitors to the occupied territories have privately or publicly expressed a degree of understanding as to why the Palestinians resort to these operations. However, the majority of "martyrs" do not come from poor or desperate backgrounds, while many of them are well educated and of good standing in the community. It is true that in general the condition of despair and frustration contributes to the motivation. But it is simply wrong to say that such

operations are a reaction to the grave economic crisis caused by occupation, though they are occasionally presented as such. They have a strategic purpose, and are seen as the only means of pressuring the Israelis, both the government and individuals, to recognize the rights of the Palestinians and eventually to agree to a cease-fire deal that would at least spare the civilians in future.

Hamas is explicit in its objectives. In the document entitled "This is What We Struggle for," cited above, the movement declares that martyrdom operations "are in principle directed against military targets." It explains that "targeting civilians is considered an aberration from Hamas's fundamental position of hitting only military targets. They represent an exception necessitated by the Israeli insistence on targeting Palestinian civilians and by Israel's refusal to agree to an understanding prohibiting the killing of civilians on both sides, comparable to the one reached between Israel and Hezbollah in southern Lebanon." This refers to the agreement concluded between Hezbollah and Israel on 26 April 1996 in the aftermath of the Qana massacre perpetrated by the Israeli army on 18 April 1996. Sheikh Ahmad Yassin has repeatedly offered the Israelis a truce. He is quoted in this same document as saying: "Hamas does not endorse the killing of civilians, but that is sometimes the only option it has if it is to respond to the murdering of Palestinian civilians and the cold-blooded assassination of Palestinian activists."

In an interview recorded for a Canadian TV production company, Khalid Mish'al summed up his view on the martyrdom operations as follows:

> *Martyrdom operations are acts of legitimate self-defense forced on us because the battle between us and Israel is not between equal sides and because the Israeli occupation has not left our land and no one has done us justice. We do know that, as you have said, many sympathizers [with the Palestinians] around the world do not understand the issue of the martyrdom operations which may prompt them to reconsider their*

sympathy. However, we ask, "what is the alternative?" There is no alternative. Had the Palestinian people found the alternative they would have done without the resistance and without the martyrdom operations. They have been forced to resort to them. Nevertheless, we took the initiative more than ten years ago to propose sparing civilians on both sides of the conflict. We said we were prepared to stop the martyrdom operations, provided Israel also stops killing Palestinian civilians including women, children and the elderly and stops destroying homes. Should Israel stop, we would be ready to stop. But Israel refused. Israel wants the Palestinian people to watch the aggression and the occupation but do nothing and refrain from self-defense. In the meantime, it wants to maintain the right to continue aggression, occupation and murder the way it wants. Which law in the world would permit the continuation of this condition whereby Israel is free to commit aggression, occupation and assassination while the Palestinians are denied the right to self-defense? If the world wishes to stop the bloodshed inside occupied Palestine, it should address both sides saying, "Israel must stop the aggression and the Palestinians must stop their military operations." The world should force Israel to withdraw from our occupied land, serve justice to our people and give them back their rights. When they do that then we shall not be compelled to exercise martyrdom operations or resistance operations. Do not demand the Palestinians to give up their right to self-defense while Israeli is continuing its aggression and murder and continuing the occupation of their land and holy shrines."

Tahdi'ah

Hamas only resorted to the suicide bomb in the hope of forcing Israel to agree to spare the civilians on both sides, or, still better, to negotiate a long-term ceasefire agreement. Following his release from detention and his return to Gaza in October 1997, Sheikh Ahmad Yassin offered to suspend Hamas martyrdom operations if the Israelis were ready, as he put it, "to stop their attacks on [Palestinian] civilians, end land confiscation and house demolitions, and release the prisoners and detainees." This is not quite the same as the long-term truce in which he said his movement was ready to engage, provided Israel agree to withdraw from the West Bank and Gaza and dismantled its Jewish settlements. The offer of truce was reiterated in October 1999 by the Izzadin al-Qassam Brigades, who said they were ready to halt their attacks on Israeli civilians "provided Israel stops its settlement activities and land confiscation and provided Israeli troops and Jewish settlers stop attacking Palestinian civilians."

There were at least three occasions on which a "temporary *hudna*" usually referred to as a *tahdi'ah* (calming), was unilaterally declared by Hamas and other Palestinian factions. The most recent *tahdi'ah*, which Hamas continued to abide by at least until 9 June 2006, was agreed upon during the Cairo talks of March 2005; it was supposed to last until the end of 2005 but went well beyond that. The first *tahdi'ah*, however, was in 2002, and was brokered by European Union emissary Alastair Crooke. This *tahdi'ah* was shattered several weeks later, when the Israelis assassinated Hamas leader Salah Shihadah on 22 July 2002. On 29 June 2003, Hamas and Islamic Jihad declared a unilateral truce. The decision to observe this *tahdi'ah* was announced by Hamas leader Abd al–Aziz al–Rantisi, who explained that it was a gesture to give a chance to the newly elected Palestinian Prime Minister Mahmud Abbas to negotiate with the Israelis. This second *tahdi'ah* came to an end seven weeks later, when Israel assassinated the Hamas leader Isma'il Abu Shanab on 21 August 2003. Israel claimed that the assassination was in retaliation for the bombing of a Jerusalem bus that left 21 Israelis dead and more than 100 wounded.

In fact, the Israelis never recognized or accepted the unilateral truces declared by the Islamic factions in Palestine, continuing to pursue their strategy of eliminating whomsoever they considered a potential threat to their security. Throughout the month of July 2003, a number of Palestinians were assassinated in Nablus and Hebron. On 19 August 2003, an attack in Jerusalem was carried out by Ra'id Misk, a native of Hebron, in retaliation for the assassination of some of his fellow Hamas members in Hebron by Israeli army special units after the declaration of the truce.

Israel's refusal to reciprocate led many Palestinians to lose confidence in the usefulness of declaring a unilateral truce. The sense of frustration was heightened when the European Union decided in August 2003 to proscribe Hamas and place it on its list of terrorist organizations. On 6 September 2003, emboldened by the EU decision, Israel made its first attempt to assassinate Sheikh Ahmad Yassin. An Israeli fighter jet dropped a 500-pound bomb on a residential building in Gaza City where Sheikh Yassin was paying a visit, in the company of a number of Hamas figures including Isma'il Haniyah, who in 2006 became prime minister. Fifteen Palestinians were wounded, and Sheikh Yassin was lucky enough to escape with scratches. In a statement given to journalist Graham Usher following this failed assassination attempt, Sheikh Yassin said: "We gave the Israeli enemy a *hudna* for 50 days, but the Israelis did not commit to it. They continued with their aggression, killings and crimes and erected this separation wall that they continue to build. Their settlements are still stealing our land. There are house demolitions and destruction all over the West Bank and Gaza. Just yesterday in Gaza they demolished three towers under the pretext that they were built close to a settlement. Tell me, where are the families living in those towers to go? So it is not a question of what Hamas thinks or what Fatah thinks. It is a question of the Palestinian national interest: does this lie in resistance or in the declaration of a *hudna?*"

The Israelis also attempted to assassinate Dr. Mahmud al-Zahhar with an air strike on his family home that leveled it to the ground. Dr. al-Zahhar escaped with injuries but lost his eldest son in the attack, which left his wife permanently paralyzed and his daughter seriously wounded. At a rally held in November that year, Sheikh Yassin declared that the movement found it futile to observe a cease-fire unilaterally. He said, "We declared a truce in the past, but it failed because Israel did not want peace or security for the Palestinian people." Addressing the same rally, Hamas leader al-Zahhar urged the Palestinians to resume armed resistance.

What Comes After Hudna?

Hamas is silent about what happens when a notional long-term *hudna* signed with the Israelis comes to its appointed end. While Hamas's leaders have left open the length of the term of the proposed *hudna*, regarding this as a subject for negotiation with the Israelis once they have accepted the principle, their general philosophy is that the future should be left for future generations. It is usually assumed that a long-term *hudna* will probably last for a quarter of a century or more. That is viewed as too long a time for anyone now to predict what may happen afterward. There will always be the possibility that the *hudna* will come to a premature end because of a breach. If that were to occur, it would be highly unlikely that the breach would come from the Hamas side. This is for the simple reason that it is a religious obligation on the Islamic side to honor such an agreement to the end, once made, unless it is violated by the other party. Should the *hudna* last until the prescribed date, one scenario is that those in charge then will simply negotiate a renewal.

Another scenario prevalent within the thinking of some Hamas intellectuals is that the world situation will change so much that Israel, as a Zionist entity, may not wish, or may not have the ability, to continue to exist. In principle, there is no reason why Muslims, Christians, and Jews could not live together in the region in future as they lived together before for many centuries. What Islamists usually have in mind here is an Islamic state, a caliphate, which it is envisaged would encompass much of the Middle East. This would reverse the fragmentation that the region underwent as the result of 19th-century colonialism, and of the Sykes—Picot agreement of 1916. The entities thus created became separate territorial states in the aftermath of the collapse of the Ottoman order in the second decade of the 20th century. While the existence of Israel as an exclusive state for the Jews in Palestine is something an Islamic movement such as Hamas could never accept as legitimate, the Jews could easily be accommodated as legitimate citizens of a multifaith and multiracial state governed by Islam. The post-Israel scenario, which has become a subject for debate within Hamas, is one that envisages a Palestine, or a wider united Middle East, with a Jewish population but no political Zionism. This is a vision inspired by the South African model of reconciliation that ended apartheid but allowed all the country's communities to continue to live together. In Hamas's thinking, Zionism is usually equated with apartheid, and its removal is seen as the way forward if Muslims, Christians, and Jews are ever to coexist in peace in the region. It would be impossible for such a scenario to translate into reality without a long-term *hudna*, which for the lifetime of an entire generation would offer communities and peoples in the region the opportunity to restore normality to their lives.

Those who are skeptical about the concept of *hudna* may argue that in reality it signifies nothing but a prelude to the process of destroying Israel entirely. However, without a *hudna*, the Palestinians will continue to struggle for the freedom of Palestine until their right to return to their homes is restored, pursuing that end using whatever means are at their disposal, however violent. The advantage of the *hudna* is that it brings to an end the bloodshed and the suffering because of the commitment to maintain it for a specific time. There will be a breathing space, in which each side can dream its dreams of how the future may look, while keeping the door open to all options. Under normal circumstances, the best option is always that which involves least cost.

Israel/Palestine

By Alan Dowty

During our last visit to the region, we met with the families of Palestinian and Israeli victims. These individual accounts of grief were heart-rending and indescribably sad. Israeli and Palestinian families used virtually the same words to describe their grief.
—Report of the Sharm El–Sheikh Fact-Finding Committee (U.S. Department of State 2001)

Right against Right?

This book began with accounts of the historical perspectives and claims of Jews and Arabs. These perspectives and claims are important to an understanding of the Arab–Israel conflict, since they are the source of many of the concepts and much of the vocabulary with which it is waged. Throughout the text, the conflicting claims have been presented in juxtaposition to each other, challenging the reader to make his or her own judgment. In many if not most places, both sides probably seemed quite reasonable in their own terms, before the juxtaposition. This may help explain why the Arab–Israel conflict, more than most, generates heated partisanship

among outside observers; those who are exposed primarily to one side find that side's arguments utterly compelling—as they are, when taken without reference to the other side's perspective.

Let us take first the Jewish claims. Jews point to a unique historic tie to the Land of Israel, extending over at least 3,200 years, with a continuing (if sometimes small) physical presence throughout that time. Such a bond between a land and a people is unmatched in human history. It has been formally recognized in the modern period by those institutions with the best claim to speak for the international community: the League of Nations, the United Nations, and most national governments. Jews who returned to their ancestral homeland have built a dynamic society that will, within the next generation, be home to over half of the world's Jews—fulfilling Theodor Herzl's vision of a Jewish state as the ultimate answer to anti-Semitism.

To those who argue that ancient history cannot shape modern territorial dispensations, the Jewish answer is that there is no recognized statute of limitations on the restoration of historical rights or the rectification of past injustice for an entire people. Jews were exiled from their homeland and have always prayed for return to it; only in the last century and a quarter did this become possible. Return to a homeland after generations or centuries is not uncommon; there have been numerous cases in the post-World War II and post-colonial world: Greeks, Turks, Germans, European colonists in Asia and Africa. Is the Jewish claim weaker simply because it is *more* ancient than other claims?

All in all, could a fair-minded observer deny any historical connection whatsoever between Jews and the Land of Israel—a connection that is even recognized in the Holy Qur'an? The case is very strong—considered in isolation from other claims.

But now consider the Palestinian case, which rests on one basic incontrovertible fact: Palestinians were the indigenous population of Palestine 125 years ago, and did not invite European Jews to enter their homeland and transform it into an alien state and society. Had the native citizens of Palestine possessed the right of self-determination at the time, they would certainly have acted to block this challenge to their culture, society, and basic identity. Furthermore, this resistance to forced demographic change is in perfect accord with the norms that now prevail in today's world, norms that have stigmatized the displacement (or "ethnic cleansing") of one people by another.

Palestinians are the descendants of all the indigenous peoples who lived in Palestine over the centuries; since the seventh century, they have been predominantly Muslim in religion and almost completely Arab in language and culture. For the last two centuries they have, however, been subjected to an onslaught of Western military, cultural, and economic imperialism, of which Zionist colonialism was an integral part. But the indigenous peoples of the Middle East are no longer in thrall to Western imperialism, and Palestinians are engaged in a national revival for the restoration of their dignity and basic rights.

Could a fair-minded observer ignore the claims of a people who were, after all, in actual possession of Palestine for centuries before Zionism arose? Palestinians also have a very strong case-considered in isolation from other claims.

But of course one cannot consider the two claims in isolation from each other: there is only one Palestine. The most common response, probably, is to pronounce that if one side is right, the other must be wrong; the rights and wrongs must match each other, like the wins and losses in a zero-sum game. But life seldom mimics a zero-sum game. There are clashes of right with right, in which history offers no easy answer about which right is superior to the other. Does the most ancient claim take precedence, or the most recent? Which course best serves justice, or at least creates the least injustice? Tragedy, it has been said, is the clash of right with right. The Arab–Israel conflict certainly fits this definition.

In addition, both Israelis and Palestinians have good reason to think of themselves as victims. Jewish history, as noted in chapter 2, is a chronicle of persecution, culminating in the most horrific genocide in history. Only part of this victimization came at the hands of Muslims or Arabs, but the past left a frame of reference in which Arab attacks today are seen as a continuation of the same unreasoning hatred of Jews. For Palestinians, the image of suffering at the hands of the Jews has been central to their history and very identity; as a people they are defined by victimization. In both cases the suffering was real, creating a deep sense of grievance that complicates any effort to transcend the violence. Victims often do not see the "other" at all, save as a victimizer; nor do they see that how their own acts of righteous anger may be creating new victims. There is a sense that their suffering releases them from constraints and entitles them to act with impunity to secure their rights (Meister 2002). This sense of victimhood on both sides, on top of a strong belief that one is in the right, is what has made this into a "perfect conflict," in the sense of a "perfect storm." It would be difficult to design a conflict with more self-generating power for continued devastation and destruction.

A Practical Solution

It should be clear by now that the Arab–Israel conflict will not be solved by arguments over historical rights or claims of victimhood. This is not to say that such subjects are irrelevant or unimportant. But few if any international or ethnic conflicts are resolved by agreement over rights and wrongs; the issues are too complex, and the actors too self-centered to reach a common conclusion. And in the Arab–Israeli conflict, these issues are particularly complex, and the actors particularly self-absorbed. In the end, rights must be balanced against each other and against reality, and the most relevant yardstick is how to ensure the least *future* suffering.

On both moral and practical grounds, the best and perhaps only path out of this tangle is the two-state solution: partition of historic Palestine between Israel and a Palestinian state. Some Palestinians still cling to the phased solution, relying on the Lebanese model for forcing Israel out of the occupied territories and on demographic submersion for the eventual Arabization of Israel. This represents, however, a complete misjudgment of the strength, determination, and intelligence of Israelis, who will hardly allow themselves to follow this scenario blindly (hence the strong support for separation). Some Israelis also cling to outdated fantasies, believing, for example, that Palestinians will accept less self-governance than other peoples have demanded.

Many features of a final settlement appear more distinct today than they did a few years ago; the Camp David and Taba talks illuminated the basic contours of the landscape, showing what is plausible and what is not. The likely elements of a final agreement were identified in chapter 8; what is much more difficult to predict is how long it will take to get there. How many more ups and downs on the rollercoaster will it take? There is no way to know.

There is another school of thought that needs to be considered, and which was introduced in chapter 7: the idea of a binational state. The vision of Israelis and Palestinians living together cooperatively in a neutralized state, with neither side dominating the other, is undeniably attractive when set against renewed violence. The question of whether such a design is workable in intense ethnic conflicts, however, is seldom examined by the proponents. Binational states have a very poor track record; apart from Belgium, Canada, and Switzerland (a trinational state), stable models are few and far between. More numerous are the cases in which power sharing has broken down, as in Cyprus, Lebanon, Sri Lanka, Pakistan, Yugoslavia, and a number of African states. The "successes," clearly, have been limited to Western liberal democracies in which the ethnic conflict has been muted and largely nonviolent. Conspicuously missing are any examples of power sharing successfully implemented between parties still at war.

Also conspicuously missing is support for the binational alternative from major political groups on either side. Among Jewish Israelis it is limited to the anti-Zionist left and a few idealistic ideologues on the right; some Palestinian citizens of Israel understandably support the idea, since it would remove them from minority status. Palestinians support binationalism in larger numbers, between 20 and 25 percent, but, as noted, this appears to be an expression of frustration with the collapse of the peace process more than adoption of a carefully considered alternative program. Furthermore, the prospect of demographic submersion clearly puts a different spin on the idea among Palestinians; since Palestinians would become the overwhelming majority over time, a binational state would inevitably become more Arab and less Jewish. But Israelis can also count, and the same prospect makes binationalism much less appealing to them—even should they miraculously be coaxed into forgoing the basic Zionist dream of a Jewish state.

The separation of a two-state solution certainly faces many obstacles, such as Jewish settlements in the West Bank and Gaza, shared resources such as water, environmental issues, and economic interdependence. But living together does not make these obstacles easier to overcome. The same problems would remain, but would have to be dealt with daily rather than in one decisive denouement. A binational state would be vastly more complicated, requiring intricate cooperation in every area of public life—and all this from two parties that so far have not been able to forge a common consensus on if and when to talk to each other. It is a gigantic leap of faith to believe that warring enemies who are having trouble agreeing on terms of separation will suddenly be able to cooperate on everything.

In the end, a binational state would give neither side the sense of self-determination and national identity that both have defined as the *sine qua non* of their respective struggles over the last century. This helps to explain the lack of organizational support for the idea; individuals may in sheer frustration turn to binationalism as a slogan, but political parties and movements have to face the explicit conflict with sacrosanct nationalist dogmas. Take just one question that would be raised at a very early stage: What would the immigration policy be? Would the binational state continue to welcome all Jews? Would it be open to all of the more than 4 million registered Palestinian refugees? For both Israelis and Palestinians, the "right of return" is enshrined in basic scripture; without it, the new homeland would have no legitimacy. But if the door were open to all, the resulting demographic war would make previous demographic conflict look idyllic in comparison. In the end, a difficult divorce is better than hostile cohabitation.

Building Foundations: Extremists and Illusions

The road to peace through separation is difficult enough, and there are no magical shortcuts. There are forces that are pushing both sides along this road: realistic recognition of limits, exhaustion of other options, outside pressures, and above all growing fatigue over a stalemate that inflicts constant pain with no promise of ultimate victory. There are also obstacles and illusions along this road that need to be recognized.

One of the major obstacles is extremism, defined as the belief that one's own cause is so righteous that it justifies (or even demands) the use of any means, no matter how violent or how immoral by ordinary standards. Extremists have had a disproportionate influence on the course of the Arab–Israel conflict. The fact that both sides

see themselves as victims has helped to foster extremism, since the absolute conviction in one's own victimhood makes moral restraints seem irrelevant. In addition, it is easier to disrupt the peace process than it is to nurture it; a few activists—even a single person—can in one violent act set in motion a cycle of responses that changes the entire diplomatic and political climate. The assassin of Yitzhak Rabin, for example, could feel with some justification that he had brought about Labor's defeat in the 1996 elections.

Extremists are not "crazy" on the tactical level; their actions are generally calculated to produce an intended effect, which may depend on the reactions of extremists on the other side. Extremists on the two sides are, in a very real sense, allies. Not only are they united in the goal of defeating negotiated or compromise solutions, but they count on each other for the violent actions that, they claim, are the "true face" of the enemy. They serve to validate each other. Moderates in the Arab–Israel conflict, on the other hand, have not yet figured out how to influence the internal dynamics of the other side. Cooperation is still at an early stage, and the idea that the other side is responsive to moderate, as well as violent, actions has not really taken root.

Related to this are illusions that prevail among the wide publics on both sides. Palestinian attitudes toward the violent factions in their own community, for example, are colored by the stubborn notion that the option of "armed struggle" is still a useful and viable option that will push Israeli opinion in a moderate direction. This is of course related to the popular gospel, in all conflicts, that "the only language they [the enemy] understand is force." Despite overwhelming evidence that this was not the case in the second *intifada* (unlike the first, which was much less violent), large majorities of Palestinians favored "military" attacks, including suicide bombings, and believed such tactics would force Israelis to back down.

Palestinians can indeed make Israelis live in fear of terror attacks, but this will not defeat Israel or bring any benefits to Palestinians. In theory, Palestinians surrendered all military options in the Oslo accords; the obligation to refrain from the use of force, and to prevent attacks from Palestinian territory, was written into each agreement, ultimately in the most inclusive language ever devised for such commitments (see the 1998 Wye Accord). For Israelis, the promise of an end to violence was the major incentive in the Oslo process; when violence did not end, the motivation for making further concessions was undermined. The PLO could sell its commitment to end violence for a high price once, or maybe twice, but not repeatedly. By the end of the decade there was no taker; the second *intifada* brought about the election of the most martial Prime Minister in Israeli history, the end of negotiations, and the reoccupation of West Bank cities.

In a sense, Palestinian thinking was not keeping pace with the changes on the ground. Palestinians moved toward becoming a proto-state, as the PA, but clung to the major weapon that had served them as revolutionary movements: low-level violence. The PA was an aspiring state, but it did not take on the basic responsibility of a sovereign state to prevent its citizens from attacking neighbor states, or to prevent the use of its territory for such attacks—a responsibility that Jordan, Egypt, and Syria have generally met. The accession to power of *Hamas* sharpened this dilemma, since *Hamas* refused to surrender "the right of resistance" as a matter of principle. But at some point, if only to preserve its own future bargaining power in negotiations, the PA would have to respect its own commitments to give up violence as a weapon and to move on to the more acceptable weapons of influence among states. One of these weapons, still almost entirely unexploited, is potential Palestinian influence on Israeli opinion. For example, a credible campaign to make it clear that most Palestinians accept, or would accept, a two-state solution as an end to the conflict, and can control those among them who do not, would conceivably revolutionize opinion in Israel. As shown in the impact of Sadat's 1977 trip to Jerusalem, Israeli opinion can be very responsive to dramatic moderate gestures.

But illusions persist on both sides. Israelis also cling to military solutions in situations that call for more than force alone, as seen in the "get tough" responses to Palestinian violence. Though it is commonly stated that "there is no military solution" to the *intifada,* official policy focuses on the military dimension with little or no attention to possible political or diplomatic moves. The major thrust was to convince Palestinians that continued violence would bring no gains, forcing them to return to negotiation with reduced expectations. With Israelis, as with Palestinians, the possibility of influencing the other side's thinking by employing the carrot as well as the stick has not been exploited. If the Israeli government is committed to a two-state solution, there are many ways in which Israel could be acting to make this outcome more appealing to Palestinians and underlining the fact that there is "a way out" of the current impasse. As with the Palestinians, simply making a clear and credible repeated public commitment to a two-state solution would spark some happy confusion on the other side.

Another illusion that needs to be challenged on the Israeli side is the notion that Palestinian self-determination is a bargaining chip that can be held for final negotiations. Self-determination is a universal norm and an almost universal practice; neither the international community nor the Palestinians feel the need to compensate Israel for recognizing what is inevitable. Attempts to rouse international support against Palestinian violations of signed agreements fell flat according to former Israeli Foreign Minister Shlomo Ben–Ami, because even friendly governments considered it normal for people under occupation to resort to violence: "Accusations made by a well-established society about how a people it is oppressing is breaking rules to attain its rights do not have much credence" (Siegman 2001). At this point the remnants of the occupation are a burden, not an asset, for Israel. But as the case for unilateral disengagement is weakened by the "lessons" of the Lebanese and Gaza withdrawals, the difficulties of a negotiated separation between the two parties are again the central reality of the conflict.

Reflections

In its origins, as stated at the outset, the Arab–Israel conflict was a struggle between two peoples fighting over the same land: an objective conflict, as theorists would put it. Yet, in the course of time this core has been enlarged by other dimensions that have developed, some of them also objective (territorial disputes) but many of them belonging to the "subjective" realm: emotions and passions, ideological justifications, religious intolerance, demonization of the enemy, misunderstanding and prejudice, ethnic hatred, etc. It could even be argued, perhaps, that the subjective factors have become, if not the core of the conflict, then at least the major obstacles to its resolution. At Taba, for example, Israelis and Palestinians came close to agreement on the core "objective" issues of the conflict, yet distrust and dislike intervened and led to an explosion that defied all rational justifications. The increased influence of religious dogmatism has only intensified this impasse.

In a sense, I have argued, the conflict is being reduced to its core geographically as Arab states have dropped out of the front line and Palestinians have emerged to speak for themselves. This is, all things considered, a positive development. Perhaps we need to focus on reducing the conflict to its core causally as well, stripping away the layers of accumulated anger and alienation so that a resolution of the basic issues can be achieved. Otherwise, the conflict might outlive the de facto resolution of the issues that triggered it in the first place.